Also by Arlene Croce

AFTERIMAGES (1977)

THE FRED ASTAIRE & GINGER ROGERS BOOK (1972)

Going to the Dance

ARLENE CROCE

Going to the Dance

ALFRED · A · KNOPF
NEW YORK
1982

This Is a Borzoi Book
Published by Alfred A. Knopf, Inc.

Copyright © 1977, 1978, 1979, 1980,
1981, 1982 by Arlene Croce.
All rights reserved under International
and Pan-American Copyright Conventions.
Published in the United States
by Alfred A. Knopf, Inc., New York,
and simultaneously in Canada
by Random House of Canada Limited, Toronto.
Distributed by Random House, Inc., New York.

All of the articles in this book have been
previously published, in slightly
different form, in The New Yorker.

Library of Congress Cataloging in Publication Data
Croce, Arlene.
Going to the dance.
Articles previously published in The New Yorker.
Includes index.
1. Dancing—Addresses, essays, lectures.
2. Ballet—Addresses, essays, lectures. I. Title.
GV1599.C76   1982   793.3   81–44110
ISBN 0–394–52441–1   AACR2
ISBN 0–394–70826–1 (pbk.)

Manufactured in the United States of America
First Edition

Contents

The pieces in this book were all written during a period when going to performances, for me, took on some of the ritual intensity of performance itself. It seemed to me that I was developing a repertory as a critic—isolating and concentrating on certain recurrent themes, much as dancers do when given the same roles season after season. I think, too, that unconsciously I was trying to approach in my writing the conditions of performance, trying not to let the repetitions show too much, trying again and again to view dances that had become an intimate part of my life as fresh experiences. Many of these reviews were written in what was, for me, record time. I found I could write as much in two days as in pre–New Yorker times I could write in two weeks. Speed helped resolve the difficulty of writing "in repertory." But what helped more was the performance of the dancers. Compared with a singer's or an actor's, a dancer's repertory is small. Therefore, the capacity for repetition and renewal must be great. When dancers are able to perform old roles as if they were new, my job is all but done. When a classic is interpreted with new vitality, it constitutes for me a new ballet—a new subject to write about.

Discovering and dealing with the facts of repertory seem an inevitability whether you are a dancer or a critic. One can't just do premières. Yet repeating material with less than ideal spontaneity was a grim enough prospect to some dancers back in the sixties that they tried to do away with repertory entirely. This meant revising the conditions of performance to a point, nearly, of unrecognizability as dance. The rebels of the sixties realized that if they wanted to stay before the public, they would have to bring improvisation under conditions of control, and this meant a tacit acceptance of repertory. The happening, the improv, the unrepeatable "event" (to use the radicals' favorite word for dance) are hardly ever attempted anymore.

The effort to institutionalize other aspects of the rebellion of the sixties, which is what we're witnessing now, has had, to my mind, no results that are interesting, and I haven't written much about it. Luckily, working for The New Yorker, I haven't had to. My assignment there, as I understand it, is to write of things that interest me or that in conscience should interest me; consequently, I cover only about a third of the performances I see. For this freedom, as for many other benefits, I am grateful to William Shawn. To his editorial staff—the proofreaders, the checkers, and the makeup people—go my heartfelt thanks. I am especially indebted to Susan Moritz, my editor, for her patience and unfailing discrimination.

The rounds a dance critic makes in the course of duty are narrow. I go to the same theatres and see the same dancers, the same ballets, and the same people in the audience year in and year out. One member of the audience who always stands out for his fresh response and contagious enthusiasm is Bob Gottlieb, the publisher of this book. It helps to have one's publisher be a dance fan, but when the publisher-fan is Bob Gottlieb, the blessings are incalculable. It was he who planned this book, gave it its title, and discovered the photograph on the cover. And whether he knows it or not, Bob Gottlieb also dictated some of its contents—less by saying to me, as he often does, "You must write about this" (I may or may not follow his orders) than by reacting to what we've both seen in a way that stimulates my thinking. It is fitting that the last word I write in this volume should be one of thanks to him.

Going to the Dance

Baryshnikov's "Nutcracker"

One of the drawbacks to staging *The Nutcracker* without children is that the dancers who take the children's parts look too old to be playing with toys. One of the advantages is that the "children" can then take over the adult roles—growing up into the Sugar Plum Fairy and her Cavalier. Although this gives the ballet a unity it doesn't have when it is cast with children, there is a danger that the dancers, by extending their roles, will stretch the ballet's story beyond its limits. Growing up in *The Nutcracker* means changing a fantasy of childhood into an adolescent romance. And while that change can perhaps be justified in terms of the story's source, it can't be justified in terms of the score. Tchaikovsky's *Nutcracker* is his vision of childhood—of small, orderly, and unstained lives that can be touched by magic. He commonly announced the principal emotions and concerns of his ballets in the overtures: *Swan Lake* begins with a plaintive utterance rising to anguish; *The Sleeping Beauty* brings Carabosse into immediate conflict with the Lilac Fairy; the *ouverture miniature* to *The Nutcracker* is a hovering bubble filled with small scurrying creatures and tingling ice. The lone outburst of passion in *The Nutcracker* occurs in the Sugar Plum adagio. Petipa had asked for "colossal effects," and Tchaikovsky leaves us in no doubt that here, for once, are big people, grand emotions. The young hero and heroine of the ballet may step into these climactic roles, but they have to do so without preparation. Tchaikovsky provides no accompaniment to their growing up.

Tchaikovsky wrote his score to fit a scenario fashioned by Petipa, who ended the narrative portion of the plot with the end of Act I. In Act II, the children enter the Kingdom of Sweets and become spectators at a divertissement. American Ballet Theatre's new *Nutcracker*, which had its première at the Kennedy Center, in Washington, is like most productions that dispense with children—which is to say most productions. The choreography, by Mikhail Baryshnikov, tries to keep the story going in the second act. The sections of the Sugar Plum pas de deux—which is, of course, danced by the two young lovers—are rearranged so that the adagio comes last and is converted into a pas d'action: Drosselmeyer, the impresario of Clara's dream and the architect of all the transformations in Act I, returns to claim her; a struggle of wills ensues, with Clara and her Nutcracker Prince winning out over Drosselmeyer. The victory is celebrated in another transposed dance (Buffoons), and the happy couple lead the company in the final waltz. But at Tchaikovsky's transition to the Apotheosis the scene becomes phantasmagoric, with background figures from both acts appearing and scattering in the dark. The Prince vanishes behind Drosselmeyer's cloak, and Clara is left alone facing the streaming sunlight of dawn.

Since neither the manufactured crises nor the rational "mature" ending is supported by the music, the production leaves an impression of musical insensitivity. But when Baryshnikov isn't forcing his story effects, his choreography is musically sound—simple in construction, sometimes to the point of humility, yet not unconfident. He has less success with ensembles than with solos and duets, but in a first attempt at choreography that is nothing to be ashamed of, and his directing and coaching of the dancers are on the highest level. Several of the duets in the suite section (the Spanish and Shepherds' Dances, and the Russian Dance, which is really a double solo) are good to look at and good for the dancers who perform them, and there are one or two effective solo passages for Clara. Choreographing for himself as the Prince, Baryshnikov shows us nothing about his gifts that he hasn't already revealed (in, say, *La Bayadère*); though his own performance galvanizes the entire production, the choreography is well within the limits of the Soviet "hero" style, and his duets with Marianna Tcherkassky as Clara are models of Stakhanovite vigor in the lift-leap-and-lift-again tradition. (Says the horse Boxer in *Animal Farm*, "I will work harder.") This is the tradition that Baryshnikov has grown up in, and it is the classic Soviet *Nutcracker* that he gives us, with all its sentimental vitality, its tribute to noble youth, and its insistent drawing out and rationalizing of psychological meanings in the libretto—meanings that are better left latent. Baryshnikov occasionally tries to draw out metaphoric meanings. His duet with Tcherkassky in the Fir Forest, to the "journey" music that precedes the snow scene, includes a progression of lifts in which she does fishtail beats and dives—a reminder that in the original story Clara and the Prince travelled to the Kingdom of Sweets in a seashell drawn by dolphins. The only trouble with the image is that Tchaikovsky disagrees with its placing. His "water" music opens the second act.

Like Nureyev's production, which has been performed here by the Royal Ballet, Baryshnikov's appears to have based its story elements on the standard Kirov version, produced by Vassily Vainonen in 1934. Nureyev retained one Vainonen number by way of homage, and Baryshnikov does the same, in a Snowflakes Waltz whose chief charm is the mechanical efficiency with which it uses thirty-two girls to cover the stage and beat time like so many chorines. They do a zoom-on entrance like airplanes, a shuffle-off exit up a ramp, and very little in between. (If this is Baryshnikov's model for ensemble choreography, he's lost.) The original 1892 choreography, by Ivanov, had been abandoned, and it was apparently Vainonen who shoved the most influential wedge between the seams that bonded Petipa's scenario to Tchaikovsky's score. Petipa had drawn upon portions of "Histoire d'un Casse-Noisette," the version of E. T. A. Hoffmann's "Nussnacker und

Mausekönig" which the elder Dumas had written for French schoolchildren. As W. H. Auden noted in his essay on *The Nutcracker*, Hoffmann was "haunted by nostalgic visions of a childhood Eden" and also by "terrors and visions of evil." "Nutcracker and Mouse King" may be understood on one level as a study of sexual hysteria in puberty, and though Hoffmann's principals do grow up, after a fashion, and get married, choreographers looking for material to flesh out a story of tender adolescent love had best look elsewhere. In Dumas, Hoffmann's tale is relieved of much of its cackling horror, but the true author of the *Nutcracker* ballet is neither Hoffmann nor Dumas but Petipa. There is no question that Petipa softens and dilutes the story almost past recognition. Nureyev's has been the most clinical *Nutcracker* to date, and the most horrifying. His mice were rats who tore off the heroine's skirt. Baryshnikov's mice are somewhere between Balanchine's skittering zanies and Nureyev's monsters—they're mice studying to be rats. The Nutcracker doll is broken not by the heroine's naughty brother Fritz but by a tipsy adult guest at the party. Later, this guest returns as the Mouse King, and the other male guests return as the mouse army to be defeated in battle by the Nutcracker, grown to life size and capering about on a wooden horse much as Fritz had capered about at the party. And the Nutcracker's army is composed of soldiers who recall the little-boy guests who had played soldier at the party. During that party, Drosselmeyer had staged in a puppet show a kind of preview of the duel between the Prince and the Mouse King, and Fritz had reacted by leaping up with a toy sabre and looking for someone to fight. But in the transformation scene after the battle the Nutcracker doesn't turn out to be Fritz (Warren Conover); he's a completely new boy, who leads the heroine to the Kingdom of Sweets.

In its doubling of real and dream images, Baryshnikov's staging is very much like Nureyev's, and a puppet show occurs in both productions (as it does also in *Don Quixote*, with the Don reacting much like Baryshnikov's Fritz). Although the standard view of the Nutcracker Prince is that he's a projection of Drosselmeyer, Nureyev may have effected one transformation too many when he had Drosselmeyer actually turn into the Prince, taking both parts himself. Baryshnikov's suggestion that the Prince is a sublimation of Fritz is not quite as queasy. However, it does leave him with the problem of solving just who Drosselmeyer is and what he wants. In the climactic pas d'action, does Drosselmeyer (Alexander Minz) want to return Clara to reality or keep her for himself? Since this production is one that explains the inexplicable, we look up and are not fed. But then the confusing Drosselmeyer doesn't really fit into the picture that Baryshnikov is trying to produce. The keynote to the Vainonen production was struck by one of its mentors, the composer and musicologist Boris Asafiev, when he wrote that the music depicted "the ripening soul of a little girl, at first playing with dolls, and then arriving at the dawn of love through dreams of a brave and manly hero—in other words, the process of the *'éducation sentimen-*

tale.' " Baryshnikov's ballet comes out looking just the way those words sound—sweet, dull, and forced. Vainonen's idea was that Clara should change into a ballerina and dance the Sugar Plum adagio, and Asafiev seems to be looking for a reason to have that happen. Baryshnikov doesn't follow Vainonen's plan (he does refer, elsewhere in his choreography, to Vainonen's adagio, when Tcherkassky is thrown upward by a line of men), but he accepts Asafiev's thesis, possibly because it's the only one that would have allowed him to fit himself into the ballet. And he had to fit himself into it. *The Nutcracker* plus Baryshnikov is the ABT formula for a superhit. Playing superman in a superhit is probably not the best way to start out as a choreographer, but Baryshnikov has managed everything honorably and with a generosity of spirit that carries one along. Of the several Soviet or Soviet-style *Nutcrackers* that we have seen, this one is the best.

The mechanical side of the production is undistinguished. Boris Aronson's Christmas tree is an affair of interlocking parts, and it grows without astonishing us. His second-act set is in sour colors laid on as if by smudged block prints or bubble-gum transfers. Frank Thompson's operetta-ish costumes are relatively sweet, and some of them are as cloying as the Kirov's designs for its Tchaikovsky ballets.

A few days before the *Nutcracker* première came performances of *The Sleeping Beauty*. The production, new last summer, has been touched up by the addition of scenic elements that were missing then, and has been overhauled here and there by Robert Helpmann. In the Prologue, the fairies carried on one by one in shoulder lifts are an improvement on their egg-on-face entrances of last summer, and their variations have been heightened. The Lilac Fairy's variation is now closer to the beautiful version used by the Royal Ballet. Her initial mocking rejoinder to Carabosse—the prim bow in first position—has been restored. Act I: The Garland Waltzers have been given flower baskets as well as garlands. Nothing has been done to improve the choreography. In a prelude to this act, Carabosse appears with her attendants at a spinning wheel, busily preparing the spindle that will prick Aurora's finger. Obviously a counterpart to the witches'-brew scene in *La Sylphide*, and just as foolish, this episode is less unforgivable than what happens at the climax of the act, in the middle of Aurora's coda: a blackout, with Aurora running distractedly offstage followed by the entire court, then dancing down the forestage in front of a scrim, where the spinning wheel has been set up again, with Carabosse evilly beckoning. The court puffs on— too late, of course. When the Lilac Fairy appears, it is *behind* the scrim, and we're back in the garden. Helpmann must have been thinking of the hidden-away room in the castle where in the fairy tale Aurora goes to prick her finger. But there are better ways to stage this bit of action. After she faints into her hundred years' sleep, Aurora is still left lying unattended; then she's carried up the palace stairs high above her bearers' heads, just as if she were dead. The act ends with a new bit of Oliver Messel scenery enclosing the front part of the stage. A vine is lowered and, after the Lilac Fairy mounts it, is raised as she sprinkles glitter dust. Well, all right, but all the poor girl needs is a wand and some space to bourrée around in.

In the second act, the Prince has lost his charming eighteenth-century–style solo and now does an uncharming twentieth-century–style one to the Sarabande. The Panorama is staged with yards of Messel landscape unrolling behind the Lilac Fairy's boat—a simple effect that does not, like most Panoramas, promise more than it can deliver. But the decision to break the act following the Awakening is not a good one for this production. Messel's scenery is designed for a direct transition from the Awakening to the Wedding. This is (or used to be) exciting to see, and, the way Ballet Theatre dances the third-act divertissement, we need all the excitement we can get. As it is now, there's nothing to return to after the intermission but the ballerina, and she had better be a good one. Cynthia Gregory, after a year's retirement, is very good indeed—softer and less chiselled but no less precise. In Aurora she has a role that exactly suits her technique. The role itself is now complete, the Three Ivans having been cut and their music restored to Aurora and the Prince. In another performance, Helpmann made a most gratifying appearance, or set of appearances, as Carabosse (she pops up again in the Awakening)—a role he used to do in the old days, sometimes doubling it with that of the Prince. His Carabosse was feminine, an insulted dowager empress. When ABT's mime, Marcos Paredes, took the role, he played the same ugly hag he plays in *La Sylphide*. Behind that spinning wheel, he looked right at home. —*January 17, 1977*

ℳonkdom

The point of unconventional staging in the theatre is to make unconventional things happen, and the point of making unconventional things happen is to arrive at a form and quality of expression finer than what existed before. The experimental work should say more, do more, let us see more; it should be radical not only in its means but in its objective. But what usually happens in works of this sort is that the means are a substitute for an objective: when we can connect the new and different points of reference along the route—no small feat, as a rule—we may think we've had the whole experience of arriving at a new and different truth. Often, there's a kicker on the way that tells us to be on our guard: things aren't going to turn out differently after all. Meredith Monk's *Quarry* has one of those kickers in the scene called "The Parade of the Dictators." The Dictators are political-fantasy cartoons in the style of *Dr. Strangelove*, but I ignored the lapse. *Quarry* relates a child's impressions of events great and small in the world around her, and because it had been years since I could make even that much sense of what was going on in a Monk work, I held on to the pleasure of comprehension. But I had been warned.

After this bad moment, *Quarry* recovered somewhat. A film was shown as a kind of interlude between two sections. It was an arty film, but it had one great shot: you saw a rock pile and then, as people came out between the crevices, you saw that the rocks were boulders. The switch in scale corresponded to the experience of *Quarry*, with the child's perceptions, inflamed by illness, shifting between domestic minutiae and the outer world of droning airplanes and radio broadcasts. The next event, "Rally," was readily placed: a chorus of gray-clad people shouting in cadence and performing calisthenics could be nothing but the victory of totalitarianism. Singing and marching groups wend their way through the rally; soon they're chasing victims. Someone races madly through the area wiping up yellow X's that have been chalked on the floor. A long silence; everyone lies on the ground, then stands, very still. Suitcases are distributed. Couples enter in coats and hats. A deportation center. Valuables are dropped to the ground. Soon after this scene, *Quarry* ends, with some sort of restorative hymn, but I saw the finale through a blur of disappointment. I had thought that *Quarry* was going to tell a fresh story about a child who is sick while the world is at war, without tightening the classic "Greek" correspondence between the two conditions or asking for reflexive responses to the known facts of the Second World War. I had hoped that Monk would develop the particular rather than the general side of her subject. And, having seen, in the Dictators episode, that she was indeed heading in the direction of general information and secondhand effects, I still didn't expect her to embrace the box office, too. I didn't expect *The Diary of Anne Frank*, but that is what I got.

Quarry, which lasts ninety minutes without an intermission, was a hit when Monk first performed it with her company, last spring, at the La Mama Annex. Recently, it was extended for a two-week run in the Lepercq Space at the Brooklyn Academy. It is Meredith Monk's first big score—the first time she has excited both the critics and the general audience. It is not a dance piece, but it is no other kind of piece, either. The conglomerate idiom of *Quarry* was known as "mixed media" in the sixties, which is when Monk began using it. Like Robert Wilson, she has taken to calling her productions "operas," which may be a reference to the Wagnerian ideal of the *Gesamtkunstwerk*, or total art work. What makes Monk's work distinctive isn't just that she does most of it herself, composing her own music in addition to writing the script, setting the dances, directing the films, and staging the action; she also incorporates into each work a large element of personal mythology. The idea that Monk was creating theatrical vehicles filled with personal meanings for her and for the members of her company, which she calls The House, has kept a segment of the downtown audience riveted from one work to the next. Monk, who takes the central role in all her productions, is the kind of performer who makes a spectacle of herself in every sense. I don't mean that people come to laugh; Monk's personality and her technical skills, particularly as a singer, are much too cowing. But one of the ingratiating things about her is that she invites familiarity. She uses her own life as a text and herself as a hobgoblin heroine; she keens and caws, she dances clumsily, she dresses up funny. In *Quarry* she wears flannel drop-seat pajamas—perhaps the best costume she has ever devised for herself. (The thrift-shop set decoration she permits is not so effective, but let's call this a budgeted *Gesamtkunstwerk*.)

A Monk production is like a crossword puzzle that can be solved by juxtaposing clues. The child whose subconscious dominates the action of *Quarry* lies in the middle of the floor under a coverlet, and we understand that everything we see and hear is as she would see and hear it in her sickroom or follow it in her imagination. Relatives downstairs, distant ancestors, passersby in the street, the sound of bombers overhead, a maid who doesn't speak English but listens to the radio, a mother who is a radio actress—all these characters and incidents are activated on parallel planes, and their semi-intelligibility is the basis for Monk's transition to derangements of a large order: the coming of the Dictators, the persecution of the Jews (who include those same relatives and ancestors). Until that transition takes place, *Quarry* verges on the territory of other works of art that have dealt with children's perceptions. One thinks of Klee's paintings, the opening pages of Joyce's *Portrait of the Artist as a Young Man*, Rimbaud's poem "Les Poètes de Sept Ans," Vigo's film *Zéro de Conduite*. After the transition, *Quarry* becomes showman-surrealistic, One Worldish—an editorial reminding us that no child is an island.

Implicit in the *Gesamtkunstwerk* is a promise of revelation: the arts in combination will yield more than any one of them alone. Implicit in Monk's work is a further promise of self-revelation. She gives us hope that by using and extending herself past decency she'll strike a universal chord. This hasn't happened yet. *Quarry* isn't universal; it's noncommittal.

—*January 24, 1977*

Notes on a Natural Man

As revolutionaries grow older, they are supposed to turn into conservatives. Merce Cunningham, who radicalized an entire generation of American choreographers, is fifty-seven; his company has just given its first solo season in a Broadway theatre (the Minskoff); and he has not begun to change.

He is still a radical, still a classicist, and still a great actor. He has been widely understood as a radical, grotesquely underestimated as a classicist, and barely considered an actor at all. Yet each of these three claims—I base them not only on the Broadway season's repertory but on all I know of Cunningham's work—deserves and supports the others. Cunningham's radicalism at first consisted in divesting dance of all content that did not irreducibly belong to it. As time went on, he manipulated formal propositions, breaking open kernels of academic wisdom and here, too, discarding all but essence. In a way, he saved classical dancing by showing what it could be reduced to and still work. He innovated but he also renovated. *Summerspace*, the oldest work in the Minskoff repertory, was made in 1958 and is a highly conscious reconstitution of several very old ideas about classicism. Its subject moves as far back in time as a Poussin landscape peopled by nymphs and fauns (and even farther, for that was itself a reconstitution) and as far forward as the thousand dells and glades of Denishawn. Cunningham's dancers not only appear and vanish at irregular intervals and move at different speeds but are also seen from multiple viewpoints—not boxed, as in the nineteenth-century theatre. We are comfortable with the continuity of *Summerspace*, with its random pattern and "flow-through" action; we sense its closeness to us and feel its rehabilitating effect. Of course, the lucidity of *Summerspace* is more real to us than the antique subject it contemplates, and so we think of that lucidity as its "real" subject. Cunningham probably does, too. Dances that are their own subject have been his specialty for thirty years.

That a dance be, as he once wrote, "unprompted by references other than to its own life" is the first requirement of classicism. Cunningham has eminently satisfied it. The two other requirements—academic legibility and virtuosity—are also part of his canon. Most of the works in the Minskoff repertory—*Summerspace, Rebus, Signals, Torse, Sounddance*—make nonsense of the statement in a recently published dance reference book that Cunningham "works with isolated movements, far from the academic dance." But, at the same time, he has recognized that dancing is not a pure and finite activity enclosed in its own system of perfection—that it includes drama simply because it reminds us of life. And there is a drama unique to Cunningham, which consists in the play between essential and existential insights—between the sparkling polished gems and the gritty, more or less accidental processes that surround and sometimes disclose them. It is not this drama that I am thinking of when I call Cunningham a great actor, although his extensive development of it throughout his repertory suggests that he is, at the very least, a great actor-manager. During the years when Cunningham was creating and performing the vigorous roles he now allocates to younger dancers in his company, his gifts as an actor were not widely spoken of. He was an actor the way Chaplin was a dancer—no less vivid when asserting this secondary talent, but still asserting it as secondary to his main performance. At this moment, though, Cunningham's acting abilities seem to encompass him. In *Solo*, which he made for himself only four years ago, he comes as close to Stanislavskian realism as the structure of his work can ever have allowed him to come. This is the quiet, hypnotic dance in which he shows us the life of one forest creature after another. Cunningham devotees are not surprised that he has taken his dance from nature or that he isolates, tenses, and relaxes his muscles with animal-like control, but we are startled to find the animals really there. The kind of empirical description that is more characteristic of Cunningham's performance stops on the brink of specificity, summarizing several events in one charged instant or allowing one event to obscure another before we've had a chance to name it—like a cloud cover or a setting sun.

The impression of fleeting phenomena, of mutability, that we get from so much of Cunningham's work is the controlling metaphor of his theatre. It's so easy to understand—there's no way *not* to understand it—that one is baffled by those people who find the Cunningham spectacle baffling. His idea of nature-in-the-theatre rests on the flux that is common to both nature and the theatrical performance; as he says of one of his ballets, "the continuity is change." And in his various impersonations Cunningham has rung changes on the archetypes that in his own person he irresistibly suggests: the faun, the clown, the athlete, and—for those special manmade environments which his theatre sometimes incorporates—the mechanic (in mechanics' overalls). However, Cunningham sometimes *is* baffling. Nothing else in his repertory is as obscure as his own role in *Rebus*. If *Solo* spells out the powers that lie behind the faun archetype, *Rebus* gives us a glimpse of what may lie ahead of the athlete. But that glimpse—who can say what we see there? The manmade environment of *Rebus* reminds one of a studio where the dancers assemble for company class. And, as far as one can see, what takes place *is* a company class or a rehearsal. Only Cunningham seems out of step. *Rebus* is everyday life broken by dream incidents that verge at times on nightmare. And Cunningham, who is isolated from the group but at the center of this dream, acts one of his strangest roles. It may be a direct transcription of life in his Westbeth studio (where it was shown while it was being made), with Cunningham playing the choreographer-teacher marking steps, instructing, guiding, but never really participating. At the end, where his own great solo should be, there are just blurs of activity, as if Cunningham were articulating through a fog. *Rebus* contains the handsomely developed ensemble choreography that Cunningham has been producing lately; there's more of it in *Torse*, a lighter-weight companion piece, in which he does not appear at all. In *Rebus* he manages very nearly to disappear while remaining onstage. I take the title to be a reference to his role, and to be literally descriptive. In *Rebus* he is the key to a puzzle we and perhaps he himself cannot solve.

It may be that the time has come to concentrate less on Cunningham and more on the Cunningham company. At the Minskoff, this was hard to do. The company is no longer a group of soloists but a collective, as the Russians say, and in recent years there has been a high rate of turnover. The stage is a magnifier; on the Minskoff stage there were too many inexperienced dancers. Of the pieces that featured steady, intricate dancing in large groups, *Rebus* and *Torse* suffered from this weakness. *Sounddance*, though, emerged as a triumph, and the season's biggest hit. Why this happened brings up another way in which the company has changed: the matter of Cunningham's collaborators and his modus operandi with or without collaborators. The Minskoff season marked the first time in five years that New York had seen Cunningham works in repertory. Instead of repertory, we have been seeing his Events, which often present new choreography as part of a continuous performance of repertory excerpts. In Events, new and old dances alike are performed to music different from the scores that were commissioned for them, and often without their rightful costumes and without décor. To see *Rebus* or *Torse* as part of an Event is to see substantially all there is to see (although *Torse*, a fifty-two-minute work, has never been given in its entirety). At the Minskoff, the entrances and exits were upstage left, just as they were (and had to be) at the Westbeth studio, and the only décor was a clothes rack for *Rebus*. Events sound, too, is likely to be better than the dreary scores that were provided for both these works. *Sounddance* has lavishly exciting choreography; and, with its décor and lighting by Mark Lancaster and sound by David Tudor, it forms a complete entity. The entrances and exits are made through a center slot in a draped curtain that extends the width of the stage. Each dancer appears, is immediately caught up in the vortex of the dance, and at the end is hurled by centrifugal force back through the slot. The effect cannot be captured in an Event, nor does it seem likely that any other score could do for *Sounddance* what Tudor's *Toneburst* does—raise its energy level to volcanic fury. It is largely because of its sound that *Sounddance* emerged as one of Cunningham's more fearsome works, like *Crises*, *Winterbranch*, and *Place*, though probably what accounts for its popularity is that *Toneburst* has a beat that now and then coincides with the rhythm of the dancing and seems to drive it on. If Cunningham's idea is that any sound can accompany any dance anyplace, I think that events as well as Events prove him wrong.

Squaregame* and *Travelogue*, the newest Cunningham productions, are "game" pieces rather than dance pieces. *Squaregame* has the most beautiful of theatrical-natural sets—the stage bared to the brick wall, with wings exposed and the whole area flooded with white light. A white floor cloth flanked by moss-green borders and stacks of white duffel bags are Mark Lancaster's décor. Buffalo leaps, contractions, backward scuttling runs are the choreography's motifs. There are two outstanding moments in *Squaregame*—one a Cunningham solo with extremely precise movements of the arms and torso (very unlike what goes on in *Rebus*), and the other a duet in which he supports the most talented of his new dancers, Karole Armitage, in some buttery slow falls and then shadows her in an undulant walk on half-toe. In *Travelogue* Robert Rauschenberg returns to Cunningham's stage after a thirteen-year absence and rather overwhelms it: the colors are like candy, but all those chairs, bicycle wheels, color wheels, silk flags, and paint cans are sweets of sin. John Cage's score is in the same overwhimsical vein—a collage of telephone-service tapes, like Weather, Time, Rare Bird Alert, and Dial-A-Joke. *Travelogue* is an escapade in the style of *Antic Meet*, with nothing on its mind. *Antic Meet* (1958) has a little something. Although Cunningham's humor tends to be arch, like Martha Graham's, the best bit in the new piece is his. He enters, furtively snatching up a girl's dropped veil, and in a twinkling becomes both Nijinsky and the kid with the blanket in "Peanuts."

Its musicians' strike settled at last, the New York City Ballet resumed its season with a program consisting of Balanchine's *Symphony in Three Movements*, *Tzigane*, and *Union Jack*—a high-pitched evening ending in a jamboree. *Tzigane* had devouring performances by Suzanne Farrell and Peter Martins; in *Union Jack* Patricia McBride and Jean-Pierre Bonnefous filled out the Costermonger pas de deux with their newest gags, and the "Rule, Britannia!" finale was the patriotic touch that released the audience's spirits. The demonstration surpassed any that has been given to this company at the State Theatre and did not end until Balanchine had peeped through the curtain twice to wave good night.   —*February 7, 1977*

Rudner's Turn

Solo recitals used to be a series of numbers with intermissions, costume changes, and stage waits while the pianist played Scarlatti or Chopin. Now they're more likely to consist of uninterrupted dancing, with the soloist scarcely pausing to take a breath. At her first New York recital, a year ago, Sara Rudner danced for an hour in white sneakers and a black-and-white pants ensemble over red leotard and tights. She didn't unlayer as she went along, though she did stop periodically to towel off. At this year's recital, performed to an overflow crowd at the Cunningham studio, she wore one less garment and was all in black except for the white sneakers. As before, there was no music, and the audience held on to the silence even when she took a refreshment break. Rudner is our champion marathon soloist. She dances the way she dresses—ascetically yet with lots of baggage. When she appears in one of her compound practice kits, it's almost a prefiguration of the program she's going to lay before you: units of closely integrated sequences that develop a rare intricacy of expression and bit by bit make up a picture.

The picture is of Sara Rudner dancing. She does not compose an independent structure, like a choreographer; she refines a procedure or solves a problem, like a soloist. Passionately absorbed in detail, she succeeds in absorbing her audience. Together, we grow ever more fastidious, ever more entranced. Although her technique is not dramatically expressive, it is, I think, innately musical, and I wonder whether these exercise-tasks that she sets for herself, with their unpredictable yet consistently taut rhythm, were not originally organized to music. Each movement—for example, a wonderfully slow backward bend from the knees while holding a high relevé—takes the time it needs to happen in, but she never seems to be moving ad lib or to be relying purely on physical rhythm in moving from one phrase to another. Nor does she limit herself to habitual or idiosyncratic gestures. Two of my favorite Rudnerisms are appearing less and less often. One is the turned-in spraddling jump; the other is that hotfoot dance—three or four lightning shifts of weight in wide plié on dithering toes—which she often accompanies with rapid headshakes. These unique items, as well as a small repertory of spinal shudders and pelvic flips, have found their way into some of Twyla Tharp's ballets. (Rudner, one of the first members of the Tharp company, will rejoin it as a guest artist in May.) The spinal undulations, minutely controlled down to the last vertebra and spaced like waves of the sea, are very special Rudner specialties; she now does them lying prone or supine and sometimes while inching along the floor. Many of the things Rudner does, humorous or sexy in themselves, would be impossible to perform as straight formal exercises without the delicate adjustments that her great dynamic versatility makes possible. She is an acrobat of dynamics. But then she is an unusually gifted dancer in many respects.

Rudner's greatest fascination, for me, lies not in her extremes but in the liveliness and fluency of her middle range. Last year's solo concert was more exciting in its catholicity than this year's, which became at times a little hairsplittingly precious. When I close my eyes and think of Sara Rudner in action, I don't "see" her separating her spine from her stomach, I see that whole area as a continuing focus of interest in her moves through space. Rudner is extraordinarily well placed, with a high center of gravity and sturdy, articulate thighs. One thinks of her as a "seated" dancer. One thinks, too, of her collected weight in transitions, her punctual one-piece arrivals in finishing steps and poses. She has presence in the most physical sense of the term: she's always entirely and unreservedly *there*, a solidly filled silhouette when seen from a distance, a compactly energized figure, palpably primed and brimming, when seen at eye level. Her medium build, fair proportions, rounded limbs, and full head of curly black hair harmonize by nature, and the beauty of her line completes what nature begins. It's an elastic line, with so much inside stretch that it doesn't need to be seconded by outside reach. That kind of line has its counterparts in the ballet world, but only on the highest levels.

A week after last month's solo, Rudner gave one performance of another set of dances at Roundabout Stage One and repeated the set twice at the Cunningham studio. Billed as *November Duets/Molly's Suite*, these dances incorporated some of the material from the solo and added a few new ideas. Music, for one. Peggy Stern, a jazz pianist, played for Rudner and her partner, Wendy Rogers, who wore twin congeries of silk lounging pajamas, sarongs, leotards, shorts, and pullovers—a different combination for every dance. Rogers shadowed Rudner faithfully and well, but the material was arranged for the most part as double solos rather than as duets, and it was Rudner I watched. Apart from her, the piece has no life, yet of the various non-solo attempts at choreography which she has made in recent years I found it the most watchable. The variations in dynamics were remarkable. There was one amusing "anti-dynamics" number that was done sitting in chairs. The dancers shot up an arm or kicked a leg in equalized robotlike accents as Miss Stern played "Darn That Dream." And there was a real duet at the end—a rousing takeoff on the Lindy with Siamese-twin convolutions, danced to "Toot, Toot, Tootsie." At the second repeat performance, Rudner was dancing more wonderfully than I had ever seen her. One step, typical of the sudden contrasts she likes to use, was a flop forward with taffy knees (like Petrushka) which then lifted and transformed itself into a taut attitude balance. That attitude was as flawless as its appearance was sudden. Ideally, I like to see Rudner among her peers and dancing true choreography. Dancing the phone book, as she does when she's on her own or with lesser dancers, she's still a unique object of contemplation, as satisfyingly smooth and perfect of form and color as a brown egg.

Two companies also appeared on the Roundabout program: Rachel Lampert and Dancers, and Senta Driver's group, Harry. Rachel Lampert is a mama-doll–size girl who looks like a young Ruth Gordon and who practices a dying genre—the theatrical anecdote, or revue sketch. *Issue* is a domestic vignette built on two types of old-time adagio act—the one that had an extra person trying to join in and the apache dance, where the partners beat each other up. A bourgeois couple waltzes decorously with violent interjections; Lampert is the child they ignore. Later, as they go into their apache routine, we hear them quarrelling over the still decorous strains of the waltz. Meanwhile, appearing to step out of character, Lampert tells us how when she was five she used to devise stratagems—which she then demonstrates—to exorcise an imaginary household monster. At the fadeout, having tried exorcism one more time, she's humming and waltzing by herself. The association between the parents and the monster is made without being forced, the comedy of the dancing is well done, and though the sentiment isn't fresh, it isn't false. *Home,* a baseball number, starts with some motifs that abstractly resemble bat-swinging and ball-throwing, and develops into a real Moiseyev-style game. There isn't much to see in this piece besides its gimmick, and I found the setting to Haydn disrespectful rather than irreverent. Judging by frequency of performance, *Home* is Lampert's most popular piece. The other things of hers that I have seen have had degrees of brightness and opportunism which are mutually annihilating, but because so few of her contemporaries are even half as good a judge of the audience's ticklability as she is, I think she'll go far.

As for Driver, she has already gone far in a much less anachronistic style. Philosophically balanced on the remains of avant-garde experimentation, she creates out of perplexity. Her satire is very much *en famille,* but she can keep an audience guessing what she's up to and interested in the possibility that she may be up to nothing at all.　　　　　　　　*—March 28, 1977*

Dissidents

In 1969, when he created his *Romeo and Juliet* for the Kirov Ballet, Igor Tchernichov was considered the most talented and original of the younger Soviet choreographers. The ballet, set to orchestral portions of Berlioz's dramatic symphony, is a condensed, abstract rendering of the play's themes, which begins with the two lovers at opposite sides of the stage performing promenades in arabesque and other adagio exercises as mirror images of each other. Mercutio and Tybalt are solitary figures who represent the warring factions, while an anonymous corps de ballet of six couples develops motifs established by the four principals. As an all-dance "symphonic" ballet with little concession to official storytelling modes, *Romeo and Juliet* seems to have been no more subversive than the *Spartacus* that was staged for the Bolshoi at about the same time by the Soviet Union's chief choreographer, Yuri Grigorovich. *Spartacus* also used four principals against a faceless corps de ballet and was more or less abstract in the telling of its story. However, Grigorovich's streamlining didn't eliminate the coarse salesmanship of Socialist Realism, and *Spartacus* was acclaimed. The *Romeo* was rejected at its audition performance by the Kirov repertory committee and banned. Russian audiences saw it only once—when Irina Kolpakova, exercising a prima ballerina's prerogative, elected to dance Juliet at a gala. The original Juliet was Natalia Makarova; a year after the audition performance, she defected in London, and a few years after that Mikhail Baryshnikov, who had been the Mercutio, also defected. The Tybalt, Valery Panov, had in the meantime become the focus of a worldwide crusade against Soviet anti-Semitism; he has since emigrated with his wife to Israel. As for Tchernichov, after five years of staging the standard classics in Odessa, which is nowhere on the ballet map, he moved to Kuibyshev, a town on the shores of the Volga which figured in ballet history once, when it became the home of the Bolshoi during the Second World War. Still under forty, Tchernichov is now a provincial ballet master, unlikely to be heard from again.

Romeo and Juliet has just arrived in this country, a kind of *samizdat* ballet spirited out of Russia by the choreographer's former wife, Elena Tchernichova, who emigrated here last year and joined the Maryland Ballet as a guest instructor. Tchernichova, as a dancer in the Kirov company, had assisted the choreographer in the original production. Quoted in a program note for the Maryland revival, at Baltimore's Lyric Theatre, she advances political as well as artistic reasons for the ballet's suppression: "It [the ballet] was a comment on the Soviet system. Romeo and Juliet are not ordinary people and they die. In Russia everyone is supposed to be alike and think alike. If you have individual ideas, you are killed or sent to prison." And the annotator summarizes, "To Tchernichov, the death of Romeo and Juliet symbolized the repression of ideas in Russia." To Western eyes, this view of Romeo and Juliet as dissidents isn't borne out in the ballet; the lovers are no more "different" than they are in Lavrovsky's ballet to Prokofiev's music, which is still revered in Russia. It may be that in universalizing the tragedy, in stripping it of its *casus belli*, Tchernichov made it uncomfortably applicable to a society that had institutionalized frustration. But American audiences are not likely to perceive the ballet in that way, and they aren't likely to perceive it as artistically defiant, either. Tchernichov's crime was his corruption by Western taste. To Western audiences, ballets like *Romeo and Juliet* are commonplace. If the Tchernichov work were to be taken up by a major company here, it would blend right in with the Crankos and Neumeiers and Butlers, and no one would think it special in any way. Yet the ballet deserves notice. Not only is it much the best modern ballet that we have had from a Soviet choreographer; it is also a more substantial work than many of the Western ballets it resembles.

Like the Berlioz music, the ballet is a meditation on the Romeo and Juliet legend, not a transcription of the drama; and, while nothing is gained by adding choreography to the score's completeness of evocation, the mortal sin of abstract ballet—using the music as a soundtrack for choreographic vagaries—is avoided. If anything, Tchernichov is too schematic in upholding a concept parallel to the music; one wants him to cut loose more often, as he does in the Queen Mab Scherzo—a setting of urgent and blithe solos that strikingly portray the four main characters and the dancers who originated them. Occasionally, he resorts to dance pictograms that spell out meanings. (Paired destinies are indicated by two dancers standing face to face and raising opposite legs à la seconde—not only a pictogram but a cliché.) The long pas de deux, obviously intended to be the showpiece of the ballet, is one of those contraptions that turn dancers upside down and inside out and all but braid their tongues. But these contrivances are outweighed by evidence of a real capacity for design. In this ballet, at least, Tchernichov could put movements together as many choreographers cannot —with a sense of relatedness and consequence. He thought like a choreographer, and specifically like a lyric choreographer. Some of his drama is crude or weak—Mercutio's slow fouetté kicks to express disdain of Tybalt, Juliet's frantic gargouillades following her discovery of Romeo dead—but the weight of the work isn't in its drama; it's in its sensitivity to a pure-dance progression of ideas.

The Baltimore performances had a cast led by Makarova. Juliet gives us more of the ingénue she used to be than of the great dramatic star she has become since leaving Russia. Her performance was steadily lucid, if somewhat uninvolved, and was marred only by her current tendency to hold her head too far forward. In spite—or perhaps because—of Helgi Tomasson's brilliance as Mercutio, one couldn't help seeing through him to Baryshnikov, especially in the feral roll of the head that topped one renversé turn. (There were also a few allusions to Baryshnikov's *Vestris*.) Ivan Nagy in Vadim Gulyayev's role presented his own, poetic version of what seems to have been a standard, rather colorless Soviet Romeo. The Tybalt, done by Sylvester Campbell, of the Maryland Ballet, is a memorial to Panov in his better days as a dancer. The Maryland Ballet, directed since 1974 by Kathleen Crofton, is a well-tuned, capable company that hasn't yet learned the difference between executing steps and dancing them. Balanchine's *Donizetti Variations* was given a conscientious, stiffly accurate performance. The other notable event on the program was Fernand Nault's *Quintessence*, set to Mahler songs—notable because of several passages that bore an extensive resemblance to Eliot Feld's *At Midnight*, also set to Mahler songs.

For Russian émigrés who dance and teach, one checkpoint seems to be Les Ballets Trockadero de Monte Carlo, the all-male ballet company. Alexander Minz, formerly of the Kirov, has staged *Les Sylphides* here, and Mme Tchernichova laid the basis for the rampaging version of *Giselle* Act II which was given its première during the company's recent season at the Palace. Getting choreography straight from Leningrad and then blowing it to smithereens is typical of the Trocks (so called to distinguish them from the Glox, or Trockadero Gloxinia, which is the other, and lesser, travesty company). And contradictions of a similar nature are present in their performances. Many people who watch the Trocks are torn two ways at once— by the similitude and yet the impiety of it all. Ballets like *Swan Lake* and *Giselle* and *Les Sylphides* seem honored in the very act of destruction. The Trocks can often get laughs in these classics by *not* altering the text; if the audience is cued to laugh, it will roar. In *Giselle*, "straight" gags come with frequency, as might have been expected. But then there are other gags, which are extracted from the logic of a situation or a dance phrase: head-on collisions in the sequence of travelling arabesques, Albrecht raising a worshipful face to meet an avalanche of lilies. And then there is simple outrage —the kind that can only be committed by skilled burlesque comedians who are also balletomanes. Hans (Hilarion) and the Wilis follow the prescribed ritual of execution in every detail; then they toss him into the orchestra pit. (A while later, he surfaces and is pounded back.) Then follows the exit of the Wilis in twos and threes, like motorcyclists, which I have always found funny and sinister and beautiful. In the Trockadero production, it is all those things once again. The same qualities are seen in the backcloth that Edward Gorey has designed—a sorrowful vista dominated by weeping willows and dotted with funeral urns—and in the period costumes, by Natch Taylor, who daringly appears as Albrecht, wearing a replica of Nijinsky's bloomers.

I was too late for vaudeville and burlesque, and although the Trocks are undoubtedly more sedate than Minsky's, it pleases me to think they have brought physical comedy back to Broadway. Two and a half years ago, when they began performing, in a Village loft, they were a much less polished troupe of funnymen, and except for the top banana, Antony Bassae, they could scarcely stagger about on point. Bassae, as Tamara Karpova, was inclined to let the comedy come out of the absurd spectacle he presented as a ballerina. He never pulled gags. He went on with his dreamy ballerina fantasy no matter what was happening around him. When he left, the company consolidated its style around the new prima, Olga Tchikaboumskaya (Peter Anastos), and broadened its range to include two or three varieties of giddiness and delirium. The Trocks are a more cohesive, more professional ensemble than they used to be, and they even dance better.

Anastos is a comic in the popular tradition. Subtle and wily, with sudden onsets of dementia, he is the Bea Lillie of ballet. With Taylor (who plays Alexis Ivanovitch Lermontov, a weak-willed danseur noble), Anastos directs the company, and he also does most of its choreography. His latest work, called *Yes, Virginia, Another Piano Ballet*, dismantles Jerome Robbins's *Dances at a Gathering* and its sequels, and sideswipes *Les Sylphides* (guilty by association, I suppose, with Chopin). Parodies of the classics are one thing; because they've been around so long, the *Giselles* and *Swan Lakes* contain the seeds of their own doom—they sometimes fall into self-parody in straight performance. But it takes a sharp eye to spot the peculiar vulnerabilities of contemporary works, and it takes talent to invent parodies of them that other people can recognize and laugh at. I'm not sure but that, for parodies to really work, and get their effects in the same way the object parodied works and gets *its* effects, there has to be a controlling vision commensurate in certain key respects with the original one. Anastos is, in this sense, very close to Robbins; he has the skill to use Robbins against himself. *Another Piano Ballet* is the funniest ballet since *The Concert*, which happens to have been the first Robbins piece to Chopin's music. Anastos doesn't parody *The Concert*, of course, but by providing it with a sequel, twenty-one years later, he brings the Robbins-Chopin cycle to an end.

—*May 2, 1977*

In a Red Tutu

Stravinsky's first ballets for Diaghilev, wreathed in legend, are hard to produce, but of the big three—*Firebird, Petrushka,* and *The Rite of Spring*—the easiest is *Firebird*. Its legend is not as daunting (as a Russian ballet on a Russian subject it was immediately eclipsed by *Petrushka*), its music is relatively tractable, and the vague libretto, pieced together from various Russian fairy tales, yields gracefully to reconstruction. Balanchine has the Firebird come to Ivan's rescue at the end of the Danse Infernale instead of at the beginning, and it makes not a bit of difference dramatically. Many Firebirds have flown since 1910, in dozens of choreographies. Nijinsky was never involved with the ballet, so it isn't cripplingly identified with him. (He did covet the title role and asked to originate it. In response, Diaghilev had Cocteau run up *Le Dieu Bleu.*) Diaghilev wanted Pavlova for the Firebird; if she had danced it, the role might have become unapproachable in the same way. Karsavina, who did dance it, was undoubtedly a great artist, but she was not destined for the kind of exclusive personal réclame that was to turn Pavlova and Nijinsky into symbols of their art.

Yet could anyone then—can anyone now—dance a bird made of fire? Unlike the Swan Queen, the Firebird is never at any time human. The conception is irredeemably fantastic in terms of Western myth and culture —one of those metaphoric constructions available to dancing, but only *just*. In the Karsavina version, created by Fokine, the Firebird is the only character in the ballet who dances on point. It sets her apart from the other females, and it also makes her a different kind of demon—benevolent, we trustingly assume, though her motives are shrouded in mystery. In the Berceuse, she uses those points to drift lullingly over the stage, putting to rest the forces of darkness, and, the last we see of her, she is elatedly poised as the spell of the wizard Kostchei is broken. But she is not a Petipa-style ballerina. Except for the points and the large, flashing jump, Karsavina's Firebird might have been imagined by Ruth St. Denis. Dressed by Bakst in pantaloons and peacock feathers, darting and skimming, she flutters her arms or wraps one arm around her head, the other around her torso, and stares petrified over one shoulder. True to the "Oriental" plastique of the period, the steps are all turned in and there isn't enough variety among them to make up a single Petipa variation. Not that the Firebird is technically an easy role to perform. Opening with a long jumping solo immediately followed by a pas de deux, it is an extremely taxing one. And it is a "character" role.

When Bakst's costume was replaced in 1926, along with Golovine's setting, a new Firebird emerged, who wore a tutu. One of the many things that Fokine, who did not supervise the restaging, found to criticize in it was this appearance of the Firebird "in the form of the stereotyped ballerina." Using the décor that Marc Chagall designed for the 1945 version of the score, Balanchine in 1949 produced *Firebird* as a vehicle for 'Maria Tallchief, who wore a red tutu and a red plume in her hair—a costume that Chagall appears not to have designed. In later years, Balanchine rejected the dancer-in-a-red-tutu idea and sought to bring the Firebird closer to the images in Chagall's paintings. This involved two separate attempts, in 1970 and 1972. In the version we have now, Balanchine has ceased trying to make the Firebird dance. There is even some question whether his version contains the Firebird at all. In spite of the many *Firebirds* that have been produced over the years, the only other version that is well known today is the abbreviated production by Maurice Béjart, in which the role is danced, but not by a woman. The male Firebird, a dancer in red tights, leads a cadre of revolutionaries in denims. In a skirmish (Danse Infernale), he dies but rises phoenixlike, and the others, Clark Kent–like, strip to *their* red tights in time for the finale.

This leaves as the only *Firebird* with a Firebird the Fokine original. Diaghilev's revival of 1926, with the tutu that so distressed Fokine, had sets and costumes by Natalia Gontcharova. The cast was headed by Danilova and Lifar, with Lubov Tchernicheva as the Princess and Balanchine as Kostchei. Colonel de Basil took over the production after Diaghilev's death, and it tottered into the forties. In 1954, Tchernicheva and her husband, Serge Grigoriev, who was Diaghilev's régisseur, restaged it for the Royal Ballet, and Karsavina was on hand to coach Fonteyn. This is the version that American Ballet Theatre has now acquired, with the help of Christopher Newton, a Royal choreologist. The results, as shown in the first week of the ABT season at the Met, are far from good. A choreologist is a reader and writer of dance notation. Newton has given the dancers a set of steps, and steps in 1910 choreography are not to be taken at face value. Steps in 1910 were what you made something out of. If the tutu issue has faded with the years, it's probable that the choreography hasn't—that it always was as thin as it looks to us now. What has faded is the spirit behind it. If Fokine could write the following of a 1937 performance, in the days before choreology was widely used, think what he could write today:

To my absolute amazement, and notwithstanding that there were no members of the original production in the new company, and in spite of the fact that everything was transferred without any written directions from one generation of dancers to another, by word of mouth—or, to be more exact, from feet to feet—I recognized all my steps. Only the groupings had disintegrated, and the climax seemed to be entirely different. I could be amazed, but not overjoyed. Everything seemed to have lost its former force, characteristics and expressiveness, and its former consistency.

In olden times, the dancers performing in the evil kingdom scene went into a frenzy, held together as if by some magic force. Now they were merely performing my steps in a lackadaisical manner.

The historical *Firebird* needs all the help it can get. At the Met première, even Natalia Makarova performed steps in a lackadaisical manner. The lack of turnout in the role is not flattering to her legs, and she doesn't compensate for it by clearly stretching and broadening the plastic tensions in the upper body. It was this upper-body plastique that Fonteyn seized on to fix herself in our minds, proving that she could be a Firebird even without a jump. Makarova has the jump. One wishes that she'd try jumping toward the role instead of away from it. The performances by the Royal corps, as I remember them, had an exuberant, childish energy, if not exactly a frenzy, but the ABT ensembles in the dance of Kostchei's monsters are strangely disconnected as well as lifeless. If in speaking of the disintegrated groupings of 1937 Fokine meant that they'd disintegrated rhythmically, then it has happened again.

Gontcharova's great contribution to the Fokine *Firebird* was her scene change. Previously, the coronation-wedding took place in the garden set. Diaghilev's idea, carried out by the artist, was that the garden should turn into the Holy City, "a countless swarm of churches crowded together." Against this setting, Fokine massed the celebrants in still ranks. The only motion until the curtain falls is the Prince's left arm slowly lifting in the royal salute. A few miscues at the opening kept Ballet Theatre from bringing off the splendor of this scene, but far more damaging was Nananne Porcher's lighting—so poor in the first scene that I could make little more of the scenery and costumes than if they had been what they were for the twenty years after the Royal Ballet's last *Firebird* in New York: pictures in books.

Choreologists of the seventeenth and eighteenth centuries made possible a program called "Baroque Carrousel," which was presented at Alice Tully Hall by the Ensemble for Early Music with the Baroque Dance Ensemble. Shirley Wynne constructed the dances to music by Purcell, Handel, Rameau, and Nicolas Bernier, using dance scores of the period. The results were charming, whether you believed in the authenticity of what you saw or not. Authenticity is so far from the point of our enjoyment in dancing that it wouldn't much matter even if it were possible to be a hundred percent accurate—right down to the leather in people's shoes, the wood under their feet, and the quality of their muscle tone. Such things reflect the environmental pressure of another day and bear on the dancing of another day. And if you could scientifically reproduce these things, you'd still have to guess at the psychology of a dance, on which everything depends. Wynne guessed wrong once. No matter that the title "La Cupis" suggested a portrait of the dancer Marie-Anne de Cupis de Camargo, while a program note invoked her rival Marie Sallé. The real discrepancy was that this "study in mood" for two women with fans was period in technique but modern in temper. If a dance is psychologically in period, it will convince us. In seventeenth- and eighteenth-century dances, the formal academic steps don't need a lot of interpretation, and because of that we can accept a passepied of 1715 more readily than a *Firebird* of 1910. A psychologically in-period *Firebird* would affront our sensibilities. With its Theda Bara leading lady and its chorus-line shenanigans, it's a type of show that dancers of today feel uncomfortable putting on. It's just old enough to be condescended to as old-fashioned but not old enough to be respected as history.

Nicholas Magallanes, who died May 1, of lung cancer, began appearing in Balanchine's ballets and partnering Balanchine's ballerinas in the early forties. He was a model partner, strong and gallant yet unobtrusive; he could set off a ballerina like black velvet under a diamond. His self-effacing manner helped an imperceptive audience to underestimate his importance to the repertory, which was by no means limited to partnering. A recurrent male figure in Balanchine's ballets is the man of destiny. Poet, lover, fortune's fool, he appears in ballets as various as *Serenade, La Sonnambula, Orpheus, La Valse,* and *Episodes.* Magallanes for some twenty-five years was that character. Engulfed by the Sleepwalker, or by several women at once in *Serenade* or in the Concerto section of *Episodes,* Magallanes never seemed to lose his ingenuousness; he had it even as the lovelorn cowboy in the second movement of *Western Symphony.* His beautiful, unemphatic grace was enhanced by these mime roles. As a dancer, he was never imposing. His noted lyricism came from what seemed to be naturally loose and flexible joints; he could look stretchy and unstretched at the same time. No one has ever done the slow backbend to the floor in *La Sonnambula* as well as he, and one remembers him, hung head down and writhing, as Ashton's Rimbaud in *Illuminations.* As a stage figure, Magallanes was unusually easy to be with. That soft-kneed, low-pressure style was ingratiating, he looked good walking, standing, or running, and he lasted. In the seventies, he began retiring his roles, but he never officially retired—a step seldom taken at the

New York City Ballet—and one expected to see him next time round as the Duke in *Don Quixote*. He died at fifty-eight, having left his imprint on dozens of ballets.

I thought of Magallanes during *A Midsummer Night's Dream* at the moment when, as Lysander, he would draw his sword and make an exit in an ambling sort of run. And I thought of a few other dancers who are no longer in this ballet. For its opening week, the company offered several casts in the character roles when it couldn't decently fill out one cast. You were certain to get a good Puck (Jean-Pierre Frohlich, who danced all performances), and there was an alert and tidy corps, but for the most part the first act was either miscast or undercast. Even Frohlich was, in a sense, wrong for his part. With his beauty of style, he could recapture the elegant, mercurial creature that Arthur Mitchell used to dance. But the conception of Puck has been diminished to that of a conventional, goatishly capering "Shakespearean" figure in brown skimpies and a broccoli wig.

Balanchine has condensed the whole story of the play in this one act; it had never seemed longer than it did last week—indeed, it had never seemed *long*. Padding out the incidental music with a few overtures, he succeeds in conveying the impression that Mendelssohn has written a perfect, airtight modern ballet. The illusion cracks only once, when things get a little too tight and, with a flurry uncharacteristic of the ballet's measured pace, the plot threads have to be seized and tied before the sun comes up on "So ends the Dream!" In the second act, a wedding march leads to an eighteenth-century–style diversion (the youthful Symphony No. 9 for strings) with a tender pas de deux. Its subject is the fulfilled dream of love foretold in the first act, and it ends with the most ravishingly protracted dying fall in all ballet. As performed by Suzanne Farrell and Peter Martins, it made up for a lot—and there was a lot to make up for.   —*May 16, 1977*

A Hundred Ways to Make a Dance

Twyla Tharp, in her season at the Brooklyn Academy, included parts of old and new dances in an anthology piece called *The Hodge Podge*. The new dances, which will be seen later this year on national television, are a solo by Tharp to Paul Simon's singing of "Fifty Ways to Leave Your Lover" and a quartet to a Simon medley, and they represent the current Tharp style at its most casually seductive. It would have been interesting to see, along with these dances, something more representative of the early

Tharp than eggs plopping to the floor, a chair being smashed, a hoop turning as someone walks inside it. There were those nondance incidents in Tharp's work of the sixties, and there were antidance incidents—like the relevé in second held during the playing of Petula Clark's "Downtown"— but reviving those antics today in the form of a montage tells us more about the taste of an era than it does about the emergence of Twyla Tharp.

It was in her *dances*—particularly her austere, intricate group dances— that Tharp distinguished herself during the sixties. *The Home Phrase*, from a 1969 piece that was made to be presented in museums, is intricate, all right (the dancers exchange clothing and take turns reading aloud while executing the phrase), but it isn't the kind of thing that made Tharp a supremely different choreographer even then. I can't help feeling that the showy performance of it in *The Hodge Podge*, which would never have been given in 1969, was an attempt, like the selected bits of Dada, to eliminate any suggestion of severity in the works of Tharp's past. But, of course, they were severe. The best of them (*Generation*, *Group Activities*) were inwardly directed, too—entertaining us only as a consequence of entertaining their dancers. In the present repertory, *The Fugue* has that kind of inwardness, and *Cacklin' Hen*, a piece new last year, has it. Such pieces strike a necessary balance with the more extroverted ones, like *Country Dances* and *Sue's Leg*. I don't mean that the dancers enjoy doing the latter works less than the others or that the others are less enjoyable to us; it's a question of aesthetic emphasis. And a work composed with one emphasis doesn't shift easily to the other.

In *The One Hundreds*, a dance of 1970, Tharp began to deal in compressed exposition of movement and in space-time ratios. The work is composed of a hundred phrases performed in silence, one after another. The phrases vary widely. Some involve the whole body in far-flung bursts of activity, others are sparsely constructed—a shoulder, a hip, a turn of the head—and cover only a few feet of ground. All the phrases, no matter what they consist of, take exactly eleven seconds each, with four seconds for recoveries in between. Since there are no transitions from phrase to phrase and no music or aural cues of any sort, the dancers have to keep the whole catalogue in their heads. Performance is a feat of mental memory as much as of muscle memory. *The One Hundreds* was originally performed in three sections designed to expose all the material in decreasing lengths of time. Two dancers did fifty different phrases simultaneously. Then five dancers did twenty. Then all the phrases were represented in one grand eleven-second finale as a hundred persons (who didn't have to be dancers) appeared and did one phrase apiece. Practically speaking, the finale was often impossible to achieve (though it could be faked: thirty people appearing for eleven seconds can look like a hundred). The more manageable, cut-down version, called *Half the One Hundreds*, that was performed in Brooklyn is in two parts: a solo consisting of fifty phrases followed by fifty persons doing one apiece—or at least appearing to be doing one apiece.

Whichever version you see—and there have been other variations in format—*The One Hundreds* is a fascinating exercise in perception. Tharp once described it as "a study in deterioration." In the way that it sums up many of the leading themes of avant-garde dance in the sixties, it is very much a key work. The importance then of eliminating all gaps between how a work is made and how it is to be performed is a theme we can still respond to today. In works like *The One Hundreds* (and like the "task"-oriented movement games devised in that period by Yvonne Rainer and Deborah Hay), performance as a concept apart from execution is ruled out. The works were so constructed that just to perform them correctly was to explain how and why they were made; the choreographers were, in Susan Sontag's phrase, "against interpretation." Tharp's break with that tradition was also a confirmation of it. In 1971, she began working with music, and to *The Bix Pieces*, composed that year, she added a lecture-demonstration explaining "Why They Were Made." But the explanation turned out to be extraneous to the performance. We learned that in order to go against interpretation (of the Bix Beiderbecke–Paul Whiteman music) Tharp had first composed a seventeen-count phrase and elaborated it into movements, which she then set to Haydn quartets. The actual *Bix* dances were Haydn dances transposed and rephrased, and thus (in Tharp's view) safeguarded from the tame interpretative responses that (again in Tharp's view) would have resulted if she'd choreographed directly to the jazz music.

Tharp's *Bix* lecture made public a formal problem that the public had never heard of before, and it proposed a solution that nobody in the profession (except perhaps Merce Cunningham) had ever heard of before. It was a way of explaining to people why Tharp dancing is as good for Haydn as it is for jazz. *Push Comes to Shove*, created five years later, for American Ballet Theatre, explained that correspondence one more time. The explanations in the *Bix* lecture may seem mildly defensive today, but we must remember the fears that avant-gardists of the sixties harbored of repeating anyone else's method of making a dance, and we must remember, too, their explicit fear and defiance of the audience. Tharp sometimes goes overboard in accommodating the audience: she lets her theories be known; she fudges her past; she takes on a few too many "celebrity" collaborators; she ingratiatingly performs the *Half the One Hundreds* solo as if the phrases were dramatizable material. But Tharp has in fact achieved the dream of all the sixties purists by making dances that speak, in new accents, entirely for themselves. Her dances have reconditioned our values and swept away the ideological dividing lines between "classical" and "modern" and "pop." We don't need to be told why they were made—much less how. We can see it happening.

The Bix Pieces, a central work in the Tharp canon, has an introvert-extrovert dual identity that will always be slightly confusing. (Its mixture of subtlety and earnestness confuses the audience these days into laughter at the wrong moments.) But it may be just for that reason that it is especially dear to those who have followed Tharp's career. It was at its best this season when Tharp took over the narrator's role after performing the opening baton solo (and relinquishing the rest of her role to Shelley Washington). The script is in her speech rhythms, terse and flat, and, much as she may try to give it a "platform" quality, it doesn't elevate to false heights, as it can so easily when spoken by others. Other things also helped make this the definitive staging of *Bix*: the dark-gold lighting; the onstage musicians partly concealed by a scrim; their rendition, led by Dick Hyman, of the Whiteman arrangements. Among the dancers, it was good to see Sara Rudner and Kenneth Rinker in their old roles. Rinker returned also to *Sue's Leg*, and Christine Uchida made a fine impression—fluffy, rascally—in Tharp's role.

Country Dances and *Cacklin' Hen*, a quartet and a sextet, were done last year with the Joffrey Ballet under the title *Happily Ever After*. Though they have music in common and are linked by the presence in both of Tom Rawe, they're a lot to take at one sitting; in Brooklyn they were considerately given as separate pieces. *Country Dances* comes from the make-believe-bandstand world of *The Bix Pieces* and *Sue's Leg*. It has Tom Rawe dancing evenhandedly with three women (Washington, Uchida, Jennifer Way), lifting, catching, fishing them out of tight situations. Alone for a moment, he falls repeatedly onto his hands and heaves himself upright. Part of this solo is set to "Cacklin' Hen and Rooster Too," and it's the oddest dance in the piece matched to the oddest musical selection—a steady, wheedling fiddling tune that seesaws in even bar lengths between two notes. The laboring weight of Rawe comes back like an echo in *Cacklin' Hen*, during which the music recurs and is extended for twelve minutes while six dancers shamble and lope and spin in off-center balances pitched low to the ground or cross back and forth in crouching runs. Even the jumps look earthbound. There is a particularly beautiful jump series in the pendulum-like sequence that begins with wheeling arabesques penchées and builds up swing by adding one new step for every man as he joins in. The cast for *Cacklin' Hen* puts Rose Marie Wright with five men, among them the Joffrey's Gary Chryst. Toward the end, they all line up and execute marching formations, with Chryst playing odd man out. (It will be interesting, as we get further acquainted with the piece, to see what this game is all about.) Wright is as noncommittal toward her men as Rawe was toward his women —she brings them on, yanking them one by one out of the wings, like a cook laying out utensils (or a farmer's wife pulling chickens from their roost?), but in the end one of them (Rawe) freezes her in a backbent kiss. If *Coun-*

try Dances is a sleek chromium-plated guitar, *Cacklin' Hen* is a homemade gut-strung banjo; it has the resonance of good folk poetry. So far, it strikes me as the event of the Brooklyn season.   —*May 30, 1977*

White Turning Gray

When a classic is lost—not forgotten but lost, right there on the stage in front of our eyes—we think one of two things must be true: either the performance is totally destructive or the work was not a classic to begin with. I watched Martha Graham's *Primitive Mysteries* (1931) die this season in what seemed, for the most part, to be scrupulous performances. The twelve girls looked carefully rehearsed. Sophie Maslow, who had supervised the previous revival, in the season of 1964–65, was again in charge. Everybody danced with devotion. Yet a piece that I would have ranked as a landmark in American dance was reduced to a tendentious outline; the power I remembered was no longer there. And some new and disturbing element had taken the place of the original content of the piece—a content I have largely to take on faith, because the performances I knew were only partial indications of it. Still, those performances had conviction, and what we see now on the stage of the Lunt-Fontanne Theatre is affectation—a portrait of a rather claustrophobic girls' troupe and its self-martyred leader. Undoubtedly, the piece always had undertones of preciousness. The undertones have become overtones.

We know that Graham's own performances are past recapturing, and we know, too, that the earlier Graham works, which were made on bodies that hadn't been prestretched and refined by ballet technique, are impossible to reconstruct without compromise. When *Primitive Mysteries* was last revived, with Yuriko leading the cast, the same things were said about it that had been said about the revival of 1947—that its performance was weak and inauthentic. But the Yuriko revival was one of the big events of the sixties for the younger members of the audience, whose only contact with the Graham of the thirties was the white-hot intensity of Barbara Morgan's photographs. *Primitive Mysteries* was Graham's first masterpiece of group composition, and it *is* very "white"—a few incisive strokes on a shadowless plain, organized to music by Louis Horst that sounds like a singing bone. It came about after a stay in the Southwest had exposed Graham and Horst to Mexican-Indian Catholic culture and the vestigial paganism of some of its ceremonies. The work, dealing with rites surrounding the Virgin, is divided into three parts—Hymn to the Virgin, Crucifixus, and Hosanna—which correspond to the Joyful, Sorrowful, and Glorious Mysteries of the Rosary.

In 1964, as the dance unfolded on the stage, one could settle into it and begin to understand the "pioneer" vision that the Graham of those days shared with Willa Cather and Georgia O'Keeffe. The formal rigor of the groupings in the Morgan photographs came to life with the force of revelation—no matter that the bodies weren't right. In the sixties, we could be impressed by the power of structure alone; perhaps that isn't enough now. Perhaps there's a statute of limitations on how long a work can be depended upon to force itself through the bodies of those who dance it.

One can pick at flaws in the present revival. The tempo, particularly of the crescendo in the Crucifixus, when the bison leaps turn into runs, seems too fast. The new ending, with the light fading on the final group pose instead of on the group's exit, is too romantic. And Janet Eilber, as the Virgin, floats about in her white capelet like a prom queen. Phyllis Gutelius does it better; with her dour white face tightly concentrating and her stick arms held out in archaic attitudes, she suggests one of those Mexican candy skeletons. But trying to say exactly why *Primitive Mysteries* doesn't work this time is like trying to say why Natalia Makarova isn't right in *Firebird*. She should be precisely that "filmiest and most fairy-like actress-dancer" whom Carl Van Vechten in 1917 demanded in Fokine's ballet, but in spite of a new commitment to the role she just looks dutiful. And that's how the Graham dancers look in *Primitive Mysteries*—dutiful and a little hysterical. Luckily, a film of the Yuriko version was made, which shows something of the vitality the piece had.

The revival of *Plain of Prayer* (1968) was a pleasant surprise. This pseudo–Balinese/Thai/Javanese/Tibetan fable was never a major work, but Graham has overhauled it, and the current version is livelier than the original. The three look-alike goddesses who roam the stage in long white cloaks, the questing hero whom they baffle, the captive princess and her squad of keepers—all are ritualistically involved in some escapade we may dimly imagine we understand. Nothing is quite clear, but then nothing is quite serious. *Phaedra* (1962), which has also been revived, is still being taken more seriously than it deserves to be. It's Graham's X-rated treatment of Euripides; Noguchi provided the peep-show scenery. The Graham of today, who goes on making or remaking ballets for her dancers to perform, seems to me a much more clearheaded thinker than the Graham of the sixties. But it also seems that thinking isn't exactly the same as composing. Though the season's two new pieces are authoritatively fashioned, they are anonymous. *Shadows* is about former lovers who relive their affair in what seems to be a night club—the orchestra plays the Menotti score from an onstage cubicle. As in other ballets of this type, which derive from Graham precedents, there are the dancers who remember and the dancers who dance. Graham here imitates her imitators. And there are moments in *O Thou Desire Who Art About to Sing* (the title is from St.-John Perse)—a piece for a man, a woman, and a length of cloth—that look like a parody of her parodists. Yet she's never as bad as some of her most devoted followers can be at their best.

Westerners who are prepared to romanticize the People's Republic of China had better not look to the Shanghai Ballet. As dancing, it's dull stuff, and only boobies could be moved by the freeze-dried emotions and the formula plots. The creators of *The White-Haired Girl* (who aren't named in the program) have made a systematic selection of steps and gestures from the Soviet repertory and used them to italicize political messages. (The ballet is about a peasant's daughter who escapes bondage and hides in the mountains, where her hair turns white. The seasons pass, and she is liberated by her boyfriend, who has joined Mao's army.) Naturally, there is a lot of righteous standing forth in relevé attitude with clenched hands raised to heaven or brandishing rifles. But the dance effects aren't allowed to carry the show. Arias are sung from the pit, and the propaganda is hammered in by revolutionary slogans projected on the backcloth or emblazoned on banners. I saw the Shanghai Ballet at the Salle Wilfrid-Pelletier, in Montreal, where the company appeared during its tour of Canada; every time a sign went up, applause burst forth, led by the Chinese in the audience. The other presentation on the tour was an even more hortatory program of music and dance highlights. Only half of the acts on the bill consisted of dancing; the songs were mostly of the wall-poster variety, with a few Canadian airs thrown in as encores. But the instrumental interludes were of real distinction—especially those consisting of ancient music performed on ancient instruments. The music for *The White-Haired Girl* was uncredited; presumably, like the choreography, it is a collective effort. It sounded like Puccini or Glazunov, but it was well played. However, when the musicians played folk melodies or music from the Sui or Ching dynasties they gave it a rhythmic force that was very different from the static tension of the ballet.

We heard some traditional music, but we never saw traditional dances. Why has the Cultural Revolution destroyed some of the arts of the "old society" and not others? Although the Peking Opera appears to have been demolished, the visit here in 1973 of Shenyang, the circus troupe, showed that as acrobats and illusionists the Chinese are still supreme. I'd gone to Montreal partly in the hope that some of the marvellous Shenyang acrobatics had crept into the ballet. When the landlord's henchmen attack the father of the White-Haired Girl in the first act, there is about thirty seconds' worth of tumbling, and that's it. I should have known as much from my only previous experience of Red Chinese ballet—a film of the Peking company in *Red Detachment of Women*. But this first Western tour of a Chinese ballet company had been preceded by a publicity barrage that made it sound as if the excommunication of Chiang Ching and her clique (the celebrated Gang of Four) had brought about far-reaching changes of artistic policy in the ballet. No one outside China seems to understand what these changes are, but it is obvious that no effort has been made to use the vigor and brilliance of traditional Chinese theatre—not even in the interests of propaganda. The result is that the propaganda is far less effective than it is in the Moiseyev dances, which do use the traditional skills of Russian folk dancers. Dances on the variety program—such as *Militiawomen of the Grass-land*, which is the Shanghai version of *Partisans*—suggest a paler Moiseyev (and I mean even paler than the Moiseyev is now). *The White-Haired Girl* suggests a Bolshoi that never was. The People's Republic was colonized by Soviet dancers back in the fifties. But the technique has only been adopted, not worked through. And it has been censored. Turnout is prudishly restrained, the women dance in trousers, and the handling of their bodies in supported adagio is kept to a minimum. Male dancing is weak. There is such a thing, of course, as Russian Chinese ballet; it has produced one classic, *The Red Poppy*, which is no longer given, for obvious reasons. Chinese Russsian ballet is ersatz, a paper tiger.   —*June 13, 1977*

Taylor in Excelsis

Paul Taylor is said to turn down offers from the big ballet companies because he prefers to choreograph for his own company of twelve dancers. On a large scale, what might Taylor not do? *Daphnis and Chloe, Le Sacre du Printemps*—one thinks of him for all the impossible jobs.* Or he might astonish us: *The Origin of Species* in three acts, the Berlioz Requiem. But Taylor's largeness of spirit isn't cramped by the scale he does work on. He once made an hour-long ballet to a setting of Beethoven's last quartets, using three fewer dancers than he has now. That was *Orbs*; its subject was the solar system. The music, its celestial spaces undiminished, seemed daringly yet precisely chosen. As a choreographer, Taylor has the largest and clearest rhythm, the fewest shapes and steps and postures, since Michel Fokine. It is a gift that portends popular fame. But Taylor and his company have become popular on their own terms—as an art theatre. Their season at the City Center was turned into a victory festival by the audience—a week of performances celebrating what *most* people are prepared to recognize as dancing, carried to a point of ultimate refinement (what most people are prepared to recognize as art). Newcomers to classical ballet often say afterward, "I liked it, but I don't know enough about it." Taylor, by reason of his gift, is situated halfway between ballet—the superlegitimate art form of the dance—and a phenomenon like Twyla Tharp, whose style may strike

* *Postscript 1982: See page 270.*

people as not legitimate enough. In fact, Taylor's tradition is that of the "modern dance" in the line that descends from Denishawn through Martha Graham. The Taylor company is the last uncomplicatedly modern-dance company to thrive artistically in the post–modern-dance era. However, it's not the modern-dance tradition that has made the company a success with the general public—it's Taylor.

Like Fokine, Taylor looks too simple to be as impressive and hypnotic as he is. Six works were danced at the City Center. From the earliest, a fragment of *American Genesis* called *West of Eden*, to the latest, called *Dust*, the repertory displayed Taylor's achievement since 1975 as essentially one of reconstitution. Nothing is new, but all his formal strengths seem to have become mutually replenishing and indissolubly linked. The gift for pantomime feeds the rhythmic drive/feeds the architectural sweep/feeds the selection of detail. It all falls together in a way that wasn't apparent in *American Genesis* (1973), where the ambitious allegorical plan of the piece kept getting in the way. I think Taylor's dances are becoming more complex in their relation to music. What seems certain is that they have become larger and more lucid to the mind. Most of *Cloven Kingdom* (1976), a satire of contemporary urban manners, appears unrelated to its music—bits of Corelli slashed and offset by modern percussion scores—and the parts that do relate musically would be unintelligible if done in the squarer rhythmic style of *American Genesis*. The satire's savagery is achieved, on or off the music, entirely through devices of rhythm, not through devices of pantomime. The bestiality-of-man theme, one of Taylor's favorites, occurs in both ballets. In the third act of *American Genesis* (not the act seen at City Center), this is stated in feverish "animal" dances of the ragtime era—like the turkey trot and the grizzly bear—which have a pantomime base. In the extraordinary dance of four men in *Cloven Kingdom*, though we get an occasional flash of dangling paw hands, the pantomime is submerged, grunting and thrashing, in the rhythm. *West of Eden*, which tells the story of Cain and Abel in the context of the American frontier, is the best and most excerptible part of *American Genesis*—the suavest piece of choreography. Like the ballet as a whole, it is a big bright comic strip. *Cloven Kingdom*, drawn with a subtler pen, is a cartoon for the society page.

Esplanade, the 1975 piece that brought Taylor a large part of his present-day following, sets walking and running (to Bach) in place of formal dance steps. Most people, comfortable with the dancing that Taylor's company does, are delighted by this switch—especially since the nondancing is so dancey. In the finale, which leaves audiences limp with joy, the dancers throw themselves to the floor in slides like the ones baseball players do. Maybe Taylor's simplicity was always deceptive. Here we see how well he can afford to do without steps—but he never used a lot of steps anyway. His dances seem to spring, instinctive and unmonitored, from primal sources of energy; they engage us at an elementary level. Maybe that's why people who are unwilling to trust their responses at the ballet can relax with Taylor. (On the other hand, he's often the favorite modern-dance choreographer of balletomanes.) *Polaris* (1976) draws from us the same kind of reaction as *Esplanade*; it involves us in areas of perception that are fundamental to our experience of dance. How deeply is that experience influenced by music and by conditions of performance? In *Polaris*, the choreography is kept constant while everything else changes—the dancers, the music, the lighting. It's Taylor's version of Merce Cunningham's practice of taking a dance out of its original context, giving it new accompaniment, new lighting, sometimes a new cast, and calling it an Event. *Polaris* begins with five dancers positioned within Alex Katz's aluminum-framed, open-air cube and wearing Katz's gray-blue bathing suits. The dance that takes place within and around this setting is sportive and airy, like Donald York's music. At the end of the dance, a new cast, wearing identical costumes, replaces the first one, the lighting darkens, the music begins again with a freezing clang and assumes a new, ominous pattern, and we go through a repeat performance, no two steps looking as they looked before. The cube, under Jennifer Tipton's lighting, turns into a place of confinement, and what seemed a pleasant beach party takes on a sinister, orgiastic aspect. Taylor hasn't been corny in his demonstration of variability; using unabashed *Gebrauchsmusik* (York employs a highly serviceable theme-and-variations format), he's kept the two halves of the piece close enough to be interesting to watch. *Polaris* rewards the audience with the fruits of its own curiosity. The only question I have about it concerns the number of times it will continue to fascinate us in its special way. For after several viewings doesn't its variability become invariable?

Taylor may be a self-styled primitive, and he's been guilty of folksiness in the past. But now he's growing bardic, and even his attitudinizing, when occasionally it does crop up, seems merely prosaic—part of the everyday nature of a bard. *Dust*, which was given its world première this season, brings back the blackhearted Taylor of *Big Bertha* and *Churchyard*. All of it is wonderful to look at, but a lot of it is slickly made; it doesn't stick in your throat like *Churchyard*. *Dust* is your basic Taylor totentanz of cripples, lepers, and mutants. The music, Poulenc's *Concert Champêtre*, lends a jangling medieval aura to the pestilence. The dancing is filled with bravura sequences mingling bile and glee; the only moment of pathos—a passage involving a blind chorus—I thought a mistake. The costumes, by Gene Moore, are body tights in neutral colors emblazoned with fanciful multicolored patches that look like suppurating wounds. Moore also did the extraordinary costumes, based on the figures in Minoan frescoes, for *Images*, another new piece, which shows Taylor's talent for mimicry and evocation at its very peak. Set to Debussy piano pieces, the "images" are partially of Denishawn-style antiquity. Mostly, however, they are those ancient frescoes brought alive. A woman's solo, all twinkling gestures for the upper body; a rolling frieze of athletes; a stallion dance with fillies—these are only some of the memorable events with which this piece is crowded. *Images* evokes a buried race of dancers. It is also a picture of today's dancers, all of them bathed and glowing in the kind of innocent sensuality that one thought had also disappeared from this world.   —*June 20, 1977*

Beyond Ballet Theatre

One of the most frequent of the many favorable comments that have been heard about the "Live from Lincoln Center" broadcast of American Ballet Theatre's *Giselle* concerned the conducting of John Lanchbery. For years chief conductor of the Royal Ballet, Lanchbery is now music director of the Australian Ballet. His guest conducting of the televised performance gave viewers the kind of *Giselle* that patrons of Ballet Theatre as a rule don't get. The resident conductors, Akira Endo and Patrick Flynn, do not have Lanchbery's experience; but Flynn, who has been with the company less than a year, seems to be coming along at a faster rate than Endo, who has been music director since 1969. Endo tends to specialize in twentieth-century scores. He does a crackling *Petrushka,* a plangent *Verklärte Nacht* (for *Pillar of Fire*). In the nineteenth-century classics, he conducts absently or inconsistently. At one performance of the Shades scene from *La Bayadère* this season at the Met, his tempo for the opening adagio started slow and got slower. A maundering *Les Sylphides* is a Ballet Theatre tradition; under both Endo and Flynn, the ballet has come to a virtual standstill.

The corps coped valiantly with Endo in *La Bayadère.* (Incidentally, it seems probable that the exaggeratedly slow tempo of the opening has come about through a succession of Endos. Such a tempo would have been highly unlikely in Petipa's day.) But performances of this piece have generally been listless; it hasn't maintained the high place in the repertory it held only three years ago. Strangely, it is the work of the corps, then the big worry point, that has been the most stable element. The dancing of the three Shades, dropping off sharply after those first performances, is now in the competent-to-awkward range. Without Mikhail Baryshnikov or Fernando Bujones, the principal roles lose more than half their lustre. The female lead is not really of ballerina quality; it lacks variety and suspense. A dancer must make it seem to be more than it is. Martine van Hamel, who didn't dance the role in New York this season (she hardly ever does), knows how to do this without altering the choreography. Cynthia Gregory and Gelsey Kirkland add extra pirouettes and balances or substitute their favorite steps.

Natalia Makarova tries to make a dramatic impression. But the secret of expansion in *La Bayadère* lies in perfecting the correspondence of its dance rhythm to the continuity of the score. When a dance phrase is made to flower as if in answer to a musical stress, the effect is automatically one of enlarged scale and vivid projection. But how a dancer is to obtain this effect without support from the pit is a real problem.

Neither Gregory nor Kirkland is receiving the help she needs to become great. Slack musical standards, coaching by committee, artistic direction that is indiscriminately rigid or permissive leave too much of the responsibility up to the dancer herself, and self-teaching can only go so far. Kirkland's début in *Swan Lake* seemed to be a reaction to these conditions; she looked overprepared. The white act was built of polished nuggets edged meticulously into place. The adagio was a matter of extremely soft and gradual extensions into arabesque, with delayed recoveries from that pose to an upright one; of exquisite crestfallen lowerings from point; of full, unhasty, smoothly rounded multiple pirouettes. It was something to savor. The variation, taken at the drastically reduced tempo that has become set practice in this company, was superfine but not interestingly so, and the interjected steps killed time rather than filled it. Some of these interjections were Kirkland's own and some originated with Makarova. That odd retreat to place that twice interrupts the start of the climactic chaîné turns has also become set practice in this company; it can only be explained as Makarova's solution to a space problem at the State Theatre. Why retain it at the Met? In the turns themselves, which Kirkland did brilliantly, one must question the lack of a spot—not for technical reasons (the spot, or direction in which the dancer refocusses her vision as her head turns, is a way of avoiding dizziness) but for the emphasis spotting gives to the head positions that are a part of the poetic imagery of *Swan Lake*. A lot of dancers who, like Kirkland, are more naturally suited to Odette than to Odile imagine that they must soften the profile of the white act in preparation for the black one. Kirkland seems to have felt a need to dispense with all angles in her performance. Her entrance in the coda eliminated the fouetté in the half turn into arabesque, and so another Odette cameo was partially erased. These and other changes caused some outcry, but the only sensible objection to altered text in "the classics" is to wrongness of effect. I'd have preferred some bright substitution for the standard relevé-passé / entrechat sequence, which, with Kirkland's thin thighs and calves, has no dazzle. But even though this Odette abjured dazzle, the overwhelming impression she left of originality and power was not damaged.

The black act took much the same shape at a slightly lower level: confidence and stylishness in the pas de deux, ineffective fancywork in the variation, a conventional and dullish coda. Kirkland prepares for everything but exigencies. If those high, wide attitude spins and triple pirouettes à la seconde had worked out better, she might not have pulled her horns in so far in the turns of the coda. Still, to have attempted steps of overpowering difficulty shows that Kirkland's conception of her role isn't the best she could have. Dazzle certainly belongs in this act, but technical overkill doesn't bring it about. Odile doesn't seduce Siegfried by outpointing him.

Ivan Nagy was the Siegfried, dramatically and pictorially excellent, and the most sympathetic partner any débutante could wish. We saw some fine doublework in the fourth act, and a new ending, in which the joint suicide was accomplished with the two of them going over the brink together. (The swan boat—by design?—did not appear.) Kirkland has recovered her strength after a year of looking and dancing like her own shadow or not dancing at all. The audience that mourned her was entitled to its jubilation at this début. My feeling is somewhat less than jubilant. Kirkland has returned to her Ballet Theatre form, and she can do better. Putting aside errors of conception and execution, which she can correct in future performances, Kirkland is in possession of a clear victory. But there is still room to doubt whether she is back on the road to artistic fulfillment. I've mentioned the lack of guidance at Ballet Theatre. Kirkland aggravates the problem by a tendency, noticeable even in her New York City Ballet days, to aspire to a type of grandeur on the stage which is extraneous to her own true path of development. It's as if she wished to be any other kind of ballerina than the kind she is. When she first took the role of Giselle, looking very *vieille Russie*, her self-confidence and taste made me think she'd soon become more up-tempo and American in it. But today she's as Russian as ever. In the second act of *Swan Lake*, she again looked like some distant Kirov cousin of Makarova's (Semenyaka, perhaps); in the third, she was something between that and Sibley, of the Royal Ballet. With her thin limbs, childlike torso, and long feet, Kirkland may suggest a fledgling, but that's deceptive. She has full articulation and star impact. For dancers, the starring role in *Swan Lake* traditionally signifies the assumption of diva status in the theatre. But Kirkland won't be La Kirkland until we know who she is.

The best performance I saw Cynthia Gregory give this season was of her only new role—*Firebird*. I was a little dubious at first about the arms (they didn't look organic), but this technical weakness turned out to matter not at all. It was a boldly glamorous, intoxicated performance. The ports de bras were persuasive. The sculptural contrasts in the signature poses were clean and tautly stated. The jump was lofty. And Gregory seemed to care enough about the ballet to want to put it over despite the audience's coldness toward it. She was helped by the conductor, Flynn, and by a new partner, John Meehan. Perhaps that combination would also have helped her *Sleeping Beauty*. The bland, musically unresponsive performance I saw this season bore no resemblance to the glowing, firmly molded one six months before in Washington. And a *Bayadère* (the one distorted by Endo) was only capably routined—nothing like the impression Gregory made in the role when she first did it. What is the answer to the puzzle of Cynthia Gregory? When she reappeared last winter, after a year of inactivity, she looked so fresh and strong that it seemed she only needed to build up stamina in order to move on to new heights. Well, the new Gregory, much like the old Gregory, slips in and out of focus. Does she lose interest in her roles once the initial challenge is past? Although Gregory is temperamentally and physically wrong in *La Sylphide* and *Giselle*, she still dances those roles beautifully, possibly because they elude her. Gregory used to lean on the audience for support, and she may miss the fans who used to scream and throw things for her as a matter of course. Gregory is no longer the favorite young American ballerina battling for status against the foreigners —Carla Fracci on one side and Makarova on the other. When Gregory decided to take her year off, several things had already happened to change the way the screamers felt about her. The arrival of Kirkland and the rise of Van Hamel spread the focus of sympathy; Gregory wasn't *it* anymore. Fracci had virtually disappeared, and the foreign wing—indeed, the whole company —was now under the domination of Baryshnikov. He worked with small women—Makarova, Kirkland, Marianna Tcherkassky—and the management seemed to be fixated on supplying him with partners and parts, and to be losing interest in partners and parts for Gregory.

Since Gregory's return, nothing decisive has happened to change her situation, and the partner problem is one she has to share with Van Hamel. Charles Ward and Clark Tippet are soloists who do not belong in the premier-danseur roles they have to assume in order to partner Gregory or Van Hamel. (Meehan hasn't been tried as yet in classical repertory.) But, for the first time since his arrival, Baryshnikov's swath through the company has been slowed. The season brought him no new roles, and he reacted with a blazing-up of wild energy in his customary roles. Sometimes he over-danced or overacted. He lost pathos as Petrushka, making of the character a comic, somewhat brash folk hero. To the solos in *La Bayadère* he applied shattering force. In *La Sylphide*, he anticipated the beat in both dancing and mime.

The day after Kirkland's début in *Swan Lake*, I saw Baryshnikov consume himself in what turned out to be the most appropriate repertory role he has danced since he came to this country—the title role in Balanchine's *Prodigal Son*. The event took place at the Chicago Civic Opera House and was preceded by a string of acts billed as the First North American International Dance Festival. Apart from the dancers of the host company, the Chicago Ballet, no Americans took part in this program. It was a night of exotic wonders. One saw the wondrously twisted line of X from Hungary, the wondrously crabbed feet of Y from La Scala, the magnificent new male ballerina of the Paris Opéra. The friendliest souls in sight were Merle Park and Wayne Eagling, dancing the Balcony pas de deux from *Romeo and Juliet*—and Baryshnikov, who rushed out in *Le Corsaire*, his motor still racing, and turned a triple assemblé so tightly wound that the audience did not realize what had happened. Later on in this first part of the evening, another record was broken by the terrific Elisabetta Terabust, who held a balance in the *Don Quixote* pas de deux longer than anybody has held anything. You can bet the audience realized it.

All the jumps in the Prodigal's role are placed near the beginning. Robert Kotlowitz once described the problem this presents:

> *Its heart lies in [the ballet's] construction, which has two main lines, physical and emotional, that cross like an X. The physical line opens with a huge burst of energy at the top; but from the opening scene on, it descends quietly downhill. Emotionally, on the other hand, it opens superficially and builds steadily upward until the closing scene, when an exhausted Prodigal returns home on his hands and knees and painfully crawls his way across the stage to his waiting father. The problem is to intensify the audience's emotion as the physical movement gets smaller and smaller.*

In addition, Baryshnikov had to do this with a sensation-benumbed audience. But the real challenge was the precedent set by the performance of Edward Villella, the greatest Prodigal of our generation. Baryshnikov, who was taught the role by Patricia Neary, once the Siren to Villella's Prodigal, looked a lot like Villella: he had the same explosive attack, the same devouring passion, the same ability to shrink himself physically in the final scenes. But Baryshnikov's own imprint was stronger than the memory he evoked—not Villella but the Prodigal himself returned.

Ghislaine Thesmar has danced the Siren opposite Nureyev at the Paris Opéra. She must be the most elegant ballerina in continental Europe, and on this bill she was a great relief from the roughnecks. Tall, as coldly enticing as Diana Adams but not as hard as Adams made herself in this role, she is a Siren very much in the classic Balanchine mold, and gave what I shall remember as a classic performance. Members of the Chicago Ballet, unnamed, lent strong support in a staging by Frederic Franklin, and the propulsive conducting for the whole evening was by Patrick Flynn.

—*July 4, 1977*

By Strauss

The New York City Ballet's *Vienna Waltzes* is a major new creation in which nothing new is created. Balanchine has composed a series of genre scenes in fittingly traditional style. Everything in the ballet looks like something we have seen before. Last year's *Union Jack* also paid homage to the genius of a nation, but the charm of *Union Jack* is its outsider's viewpoint—its indefatigable pursuit of the authentic. *Vienna Waltzes* seems to come from within. Balanchine is "Viennese" because he is inside the music. And, because his view of this music and this world has been touched on in other ballets of his, part of the fascination of this latest piece lies in seeing how he converts his old material to a new use, relying on context to change our perception of it. In this, as in so many other ways, he resembles Mozart, whose brilliance consisted as much in his flexibility as in his originality. The ballet invokes both a tradition and Balanchine's service to that tradition. At the end, when the dancers of its separate sections come together in a grand-scale apotheosis of the waltz, we come to know not only what the waltz tradition of old Europe means to Balanchine but what he means to it.

Vienna Waltzes sets three of its scenes to music by the younger Johann Strauss, and one apiece to Franz Lehár and Richard Strauss. In "Tales from the Vienna Woods," the concert waltz and tone poem is staged as a tribute to classic Vienna: young lovers waltz by moonlight among the trees of the Wienerwald, the men elegantly erect in knee breeches and officers' gold braid, the women gracious in long gowns of fondant pink. It is a large, spreading, very soft-focus, but not overly moist affair, and it is filled with a tough-minded baroque etiquette. Even its more intimate images are formal ones, as when the lead couple (Karin von Aroldingen and Sean Lavery) waltzes alone or muses about to the zither melody, or when the men bow themselves off and the women stage a small reception in their private bower for Von Aroldingen's running entrance. The subject of the dances is the lore that we associate with the golden age of the waltz. And since we are gazing upon Old Vienna's greatest legend, Balanchine takes care to keep certain legendary secrets. The choreography unfolds invitingly, heightening the ballroom atmosphere but never sacrificing that atmosphere to demonstratively theatrical effects. Rouben Ter-Arutunian's gauzy trees and foliage canopy create a privileged enclosure for the waltzers. When they dance face to face or in linked groups, their intimacy is insured. Only once, for a few bars at the end, do they turn toward us. The whole spectacle becomes frontal for an instant before it evaporates, the zither is heard again, and the lead couple walks on alone under the trees.

In "Voices of Spring," which follows, Patricia McBride and Helgi Tomasson lead a small ballet of dryads in the same woodland setting. Now we sense that we're seeing waltzing adapted to the theatre, elaborated and amplified in professional style by stars of the ballet. Balanchine amuses us by finding a new way to set the vertiginous opening phrase of the main melody on each repeat. McBride, who looks lusciously round and rosy in this new role, has some turned-in steps reminiscent of her part in *Brahms-Schoenberg Quartet*; they may be Balanchine's salute, by way of her presence, to the Vienna of those two composers. "Voices of Spring" is the only section of the ballet which is danced on point. Heeled shoes are worn in the other sections, and they're hilariously funny in the tricky toe-in, toe-out step that recurs in "Explosion Polka," the number that gives us the coarser side of Viennese high spirits. Some people reacted as if it were emery paper, but to exclude it would be false to Johann Strauss. Sara Leland jumping and landing in a squat and Bart Cook diving between her legs are joyously lewd. The boys are dressed as *incroyables* with stiff collars and puffed hair; the girls, all legs, wear the corset bodices and abbreviated bustles of demimondaines. They all zip around those trees (which ought to have been exchanged for round banquettes), and they mimic a passage in "Tales from the Vienna Woods": the women confer privately, and when the men approach, a sudden whirl (the last explosion) knocks them head over heels.

A change of scenery occurs during the introduction to Lehár's "Gold and Silver Waltz": the forest scenery rises to expose roots which suggest Art Nouveau hangings and fixtures, gilt chairs are brought on, and we are in a plush public salon at the turn of the century. Though the music isn't from *The Merry Widow* (as the program says), the characters are—Kay Mazzo sweeping on in black to have her hand kissed by Peter Martins in Danilo's white-and-red uniform. This is the waltz as a setting for adventure, but Balanchine doesn't dramatize the sexiness of the occasion, and he doesn't seem to have heard the note of decadence in the music. "Gold and Silver" is the weakest and most conventional of the ballet's five sections. When the scenery changes again—this time to a mirrored ballroom in an ice palace—and when women in trailing gowns of white start crossing the stage slowly while the scenery is still in motion, we can feel Balanchine closing his grip. And from here on we stay gripped.

The women in gowns are accompanied by men. When Suzanne Farrell enters, also in trailing white, she is alone, and when she begins to waltz (the music is the first sequence of the *Rosenkavalier* waltzes), she is still alone. From time to time, a man enters, partners her, and drops away after a few measures. She neither acknowledges nor rejects him, and he does not force himself on her. The role was made for Jean-Pierre Bonnefous, who danced it in the preview benefit performance and then had to withdraw because of an injury. Bonnefous had a hovering romantic intensity that added a tragic dimension to his comings and goings—especially in the passage where he shadows the girl as she continues to dance alone, bent in sorrow. Such scenes look based partly on the roles that he and Farrell dance in *La Valse* and partly on the slight but effective Scriabin pas de deux that Balanchine made this spring, in which Bonnefous supports a grief-stricken McBride. Jorge Donn, lately of the Béjart company, assumed the role in the Strauss ballet at a moment's notice for the première and danced it tactfully but impassively. As for Farrell, doing little more than stepping and swaying to the music, she holds us all through its long preparatory section, when the waltz is gasping and sighing itself into being. It breaks out once, and there is an entrance by other couples, a moment when the principals come together in their midst, and another moment, after all have left, when the woman is again alone. But on her exit she flings up her arms, and suddenly lights blaze, the waltz returns in earnest, and the stage is filled—engulfed—by waves of dancers, the men in black tails, the women with their white trains whirling in the air. The surprises have by this time become uncountable, but I'd say there are two main jolts: one is Farrell's exit and the blazing up of the waltz; the other is the continuation of that blaze as we realize that the wave of dancers is not going to subside. For now the stars of the other sections return to music that suggests a widening of Richard Strauss's vision, and the grand finale becomes a swirling, streaming tide of white and black silk. The only flaw in this wonderful "Rosenkavalier" waltz fantasy is the somewhat perfunctory pose on which Balanchine pulls the curtain.

The ballet has been beautifully dressed in different period styles by Karinska, whose seamstresses sewed ruffles inside those Edwardian trains so that they'd flare when lifted. Karinska's materials are always sumptuous. Would that Ter-Arutunian's were, too: his Klimt-like scenery is cleverly conceived and engineered, but there seems to be a bit too much vinyl and Mylar.

Balanchine's treatment of the waltz takes us to the core of its appeal. In waltzing, we lose and recapture our balance more precipitately than in other forms of dancing, and since the momentum keeps pulling us, we want to do it again and again. Every step calls forth another. The waltz is always nostalgic. In the Viennese waltz, the emotion of nostalgia is intense. The second beat of the three-beat phrase is anticipated, so that there is a moment of suspension before the release of the third beat and a feeling of regret when it occurs. The phrase was meant never to end but to repeat its plunge-and-recovery in a dizzying round. Buoyed by its inexhaustible rhythm, dancers of the waltz become seized by visions of the infinite. The lilt of three-quarter time seems to say, "Then, now, and always."

The lilt of the New York City Ballet is impeccably Viennese. Balanchine and his conductor, Robert Irving, have followed the style of Herbert von Karajan, observing the crisp accents, rubato, and sweep of impetus without which Viennese waltzing isn't expressive. And the success of the whole company in this transparent style of dancing is astonishing. Whether subtly graded, as in "Tales from the Vienna Woods," or perilously steep, as in "Der Rosenkavalier," the dynamic transitions are taken in stride. I don't know another company that could do it as well.

Days after a performance, I can still feel its pressure. Effects of contradiction and alteration in scale linger in the mind. The opening dance, large and sprawling, is concisely confiding (and Von Aroldingen gives a performance of great warmth); the small ballabile right afterward makes a consistently grand gesture. These are signature effects of Balanchine's. We have been seeing them for years. On the same all-Balanchine, "all-Viennese" program was the Webern *Episodes*, which used to produce its dainty enormities more absorbingly than it does now, and the Mozart *Divertimento No. 15*, a chamber ballet that has the scale and sweep of five *Sleeping Beautys*. The cast was the strongest in many years. The five ballerina roles were danced by Merrill Ashley, Maria Calegari, Stephanie Saland, Colleen Neary, and Kyra Nichols, with Martins as the male soloist, flanked by Gerard Ebitz and Sean Lavery. —*July 11, 1977*

The Godmother

In *Alicia*, a 1976 documentary made in Cuba and now being shown in New York, Alicia Alonso is asked "What is the hardest part of dancing?" and she answers "Dancing well." She gives a Humpty-Dumpty answer to nearly every other question, too, and her stiffly impassive face yields nothing to the camera. But Alonso's mysteriousness seems to illustrate a powerful truth: that when a dancer's life and art exist fully in the theatre her secrets cannot be called to account in any other medium. Filmed records of performances are, of course, valuable, but their value must be estimated in relation to the actual event. No one who sees a legendary "Black Swan" or *Giselle* in a movie feels he's been given more than a suggestion of what the real thing must have been like. But when the filmed record is of an aging Alonso (as it is in most of the dances in *Alicia*) or an aging Ulanova (as in the 1956 Paul Czinner film *The Bolshoi Ballet*), we can feel pretty certain that the experience isn't a partial one—that there really wasn't much more happening than we see up there on the screen. As a dancer's prowess declines, she becomes more accessible as a camera subject. Alonso is now in her late fifties, and her *Carmen* ballet, which she has been dancing since 1967, looks no different on film from the way it looks on the stage. Margot Fonteyn is actually more vivid in the film version of *Marguerite and Armand* (included in Nureyev's *I Am a Dancer*) than she was on the stage. In *Alicia* we see the young Alonso dance only once—in a performance of the first-act solo of *Giselle*—and it's different from the later Alonso in ways both good and bad. A "Black Swan" filmed in 1967 shows a perfection in multiple pirouettes which is missing in the *Giselle*, yet in the earlier performance Alonso's whole figure dances and has an active humanity that baffles the camera. In the "Black Swan," Alonso has declined to the sum of her specialties, and in *Carmen* (filmed for this movie) the parts seem greater than the whole. We're conscious only of the driving feet and legs; their tireless mechanical force is something the camera can depict clearly. *Alicia* shows the aging process if it shows anything. Most of the dance sequences are too short or too recent to show more than that. A jumble of excitable graphics, cheering audiences, and clips from dances filmed we're never told when, the movie means to celebrate Alonso's still impressive physique and her indomitable spirit. (The camera goes out of focus when she describes her struggle with blindness.) But it exudes pathos. Alonso is seen living for the stage in a way that makes sense only in movies. A personality is caught as if in flight between two media.

Many dancers, when they retire, could take up acting, yet few of them do. Dancers do their "acting" in the classes they teach; their powerful temperaments and techniques of coercion are used on their students. But put them before an audience and they'll blaze again. Alicia Markova and Anton Dolin, presented by Walter Terry at Town Hall last month, reminisced about Diaghilev and their past triumphs, then got up and did mime scenes from *Swan Lake* and *Giselle*. Sitting down and talking, or moving through the patterns they'd traced long ago, Markova and Dolin were casually spellbinding: Markova with that porcelain calm, that concern with "arrangements" which marked her last (late-Victorian) phase as a performer, and Dolin looking as he had never looked—wild of hair and eye, shrewdly dyspeptic of manner, a character out of Beckett. Another highlight was their coaching of two young dancers in the second-act pas de deux of *Swan Lake*. The young Odette was asked to fold herself to the floor in one count. The young Siegfried was urged to lift her without showing effort. These instructions seemed unfollowable, yet on the slow falls backward into the boy's arms, when Markova said "Breeeathe," suddenly there was a difference. One wondered whether, extended and deepened by impromptu contacts and procedures, this "Evening With" could be as absorbing and as instructive to the lay public as the master classes that are given by great singers at Juilliard. Could great dancers, their own legends inadequately fostered by the only recording tools we have—photographs and motion pictures—teach objectively, selflessly, before an audience? At Town Hall, the live appearance was supplemented by a review of the Markova-Dolin years in pictures; it almost seemed a necessity. But no cues were needed either by the moonily nostalgic audience to pamper the stars or by the stars (Dolin especially) and Walter Terry to play upon that nostalgia.

Like Dolin, Alexandra Danilova seems suited by type to certain acting roles, and, like Dolin, she has had some acting experience. (Dolin, a predecessor of Rudolf Nureyev, made movies in the thirties.) In 1948, she had a speaking part in one of her ballets, *Billy Sunday*, and toward the end of her career she appeared in a Broadway show, *Oh Captain!*, with Tony Randall. But in the nearly twenty years since then she has busied herself teaching and staging ballets, leaving us to imagine the Mme Ranevskayas and Arkadinas she might have given us. In the new movie *The Turning Point*, she has a small part, representing the eldest of four generations of dancers. As the coach Dahkarova, she's elegant and charming still, and she suggests the class that the next generation (as played by Anne Bancroft and Shirley MacLaine) doesn't have. Class, apparently, is something you can't hand down the years. But you can't do without it, either. It's the big missing ingredient in this well-stocked but half-baked movie about ballet.

The main issue in *The Turning Point* is age. Looking ahead to a life of coaching like Dahkarova's, the aging Emma (Bancroft) sees herself becoming extinct. Looking back, her friend and former rival Deedee (MacLaine), who has chosen marriage and children, regrets the career she never had. This middle-age crisis stifles the interest we might have taken in the movie's one serious theme—the necessity for continuity in the ballet tradition—and in order to precipitate the crisis the movie concocts an outlandish story. It shows a young dancer, sixteen or seventeen years old, leaving Oklahoma City, coming to New York to join a company described as "the best in the world—well, in this country anyway," getting the lead in an important new ballet, and dancing the *Don Quixote* pas de deux opposite Baryshnikov, all in one summer. Children's books about ballet often indulge in such fantasies, although the most popular of these books, Noel Streatfeild's *Ballet Shoes*, takes a fairly sober approach to its subject. But whereas juvenile fantasies in books don't seem to have caused much mischief, *The Turning Point* may raise temperatures around the country, with countless young aspirants seeing themselves as the Emilia of the film. The goddaughter of the prima ballerina Emma, Emilia doesn't depend on the link to get ahead, and though she sleeps with Yuri, the Baryshnikov character, that doesn't help her career, either. She succeeds on merit. But was merit ever—in real life—so swiftly rewarded? *The Turning Point* doesn't come out and say that in ballet you can sleep your way to the top. Nor does it come out and say that prima status can be won by operators like Emma, who bulldozed her best friend out of a key role. But the movie doesn't gainsay those things, either. And because it seems knowledgeable and hard-nosed, an insider's report on backstage realities, it leaves the impression that the Eve Harringtons and Sammy Glicks can have ballet any time they want it.

The Turning Point is a Beverly Hills view of professional ballet. Trying to use backstage life as material for a realistic, "mature" drama, the script doesn't even develop the aura of truth that clung to melodramas like *The Red Shoes*. In *The Red Shoes*, which starred Moira Shearer, the real-life story that was the basis of the script (that of Diaghilev and Nijinsky) was already so bizarre that we didn't question the absurdities piled on top of it. The movie was made from the viewpoint of infatuated outsiders; it had an appetite for magic. In *The Turning Point*, we can't help wondering why the life decisions of the two self-involved heroines are irrevocable. Dancers have married, borne children, and gone on with their careers. Emma's case is so exaggerated that it appears to have been taken from *Camille*. Looking for a way out of her misfortune, she humiliates herself before her "protector," a dreary businessman played by Marshall Thompson (a former juvenile actor cast so that we can see how he has aged). The movie puts its characters in a mundane setting where we can evaluate cause and effect. When to the question of what she wants out of life Moira Shearer answers "To dahnce!" she has already entered another world, and it isn't Emma's. Hardened pros in the ballet business can't be magnified into legends. Their real-life stories may be touching, but as the stuff of drama they acquire the coarse, unedifying texture of gossip. The real-life story used in *The Turning Point* is partly that of Leslie Browne, who plays Emilia. Leslie Browne, a soloist with American Ballet Theatre, is the daughter of two former ABT dancers, Isabel Mirrow and Kelly Brown, and she's the goddaughter of Nora Kaye, the executive producer of *The Turning Point*—the same Nora Kaye who had her first big success in the Tudor ballet *Pillar of Fire* in 1942 and who became ABT's great dramatic ballerina. In the movie we are told how Deedee's pregnancy (with Emilia) imperilled her chance at the leading role in an epochal Tudorish ballet, and how by encouraging Deedee to have the baby Emma snagged the role and began her career as a great dramatic ballerina. In actual fact, Isabel Mirrow joined Ballet Theatre some years after Nora Kaye had become a star. But it doesn't matter whether the gossip is true or not—what matters is that it's *only* gossip.

Emilia's breathless ascent to stardom, during which Deedee and Emma renew their rivalry by fighting over her, is based on the career of Gelsey Kirkland, who was to have played the part. Even Kirkland had to put in her years of apprentice work, but with her in the role of Emilia the movie might have seemed less preposterous. Leslie Browne is still an unknown, who has done only one big role so far—*The Nutcracker*, with Baryshnikov. Her perfect School of American Ballet body photographs beautifully, and camera illusion helps her dancing withstand Baryshnikov's onslaught. (Classical dancing on film may be unintelligible but it is also sensational. The camera increases a dancer's speed and heightens the physical glamour of stretched limbs. You can imagine what it does for the spectacle of Baryshnikov.) Her best moment as an actress is a little drunk scene in a bar, but then the movie has her come to the theatre drunk and be nursed through her paces as a Wili by Emma, standing in the wings. Typically, the movie invents this highly implausible situation to launch another Deedee-Emma skirmish. It's also typical that, in one of the few scenes that come close to being fun, the fun is secondhand. The drunken-Wili number looks like a resetting (uncredited) of the Mistake Waltz in Jerome Robbins's ballet *The Concert*; no ballet-goer can miss it. Herbert Ross, the director of *The Turning Point* and Nora Kaye's husband, is a former choreographer. He staged the *Swan Lake* parody in *Funny Girl*, but he hasn't used his own ideas in any of the dances in this movie, and he hasn't extended ballet metaphorically to support the story. The little *Romeo and Juliet* passage, cutting from Emilia and Yuri in the MacMillan pas de deux to Emilia and Yuri in bed, is as far as Ross goes. An Ashton solo devised specially for this film is danced by Leslie

Browne under the end titles, when the film is all over, and Emilia's first starring role turns out to be the Vortex solo from *The River*, by Alvin Ailey. This number represents the progressive abstract ballet that an Eliot Feldish choreographer (played by Daniel Levans) has created, much to the annoyance of dancers who would rather feel music than count it. Feldish is not conceivably Aileyish, and neither one is the avant-gardish genius the script wants here. (Isn't it a bit late for the abstract revolution in ballet to be taking place?) There's no equivalent in the film to the *Red Shoes* ballet, and maybe there couldn't be. The story emphasis isn't on how ballerinas are made, it's on how they die. Even though the art of older ballerinas can be expressed more effectively in the movies than the art of young ones, we don't have any active older ballerinas in the movie. (Bancroft, a nondancer, demonstrates Emma's greatest role by collapsing under a cloak.) And even though the movie is full of quotes from well-known ballets, it doesn't view them selectively, with an eye to their dramatic relevance. The most beautiful shot occurs under the opening credits, as dancer after dancer steps into frame in closeup. It's *La Bayadère*—could there be a better symbol in dance of the continuity of the classical tradition? All the fuss about aging dancers could have had at least this much dignity. The film might have said that all dancers are godmothers. But once we've made the transition from the credits to Oklahoma City, where the story begins, we never return to *La Bayadère*. Eve Harrington had her progeny foreshadowed in mirrors at the fadeout of *All About Eve*. *The Turning Point*, a film made by and about dancers—those people who spend their lives before mirrors—cannot reflect its own world.   —*November 21, 1977*

Concentration

Spiral, by Laura Dean, commissioned by the Brooklyn Academy of Music, was given its première last month in the Opera House of the Academy. Dean's concerts of dancing are always interesting—not because they show any great development, but for their unity: their variation on fundamental unchanging textures and patterns. If they could be hung side by side, like paintings in a gallery, we would see that they are all basically the same monochromatic dance, made out of the same irreducible materials. For years—since 1968, in fact (as, for years, the program notes have been telling us)—Laura Dean "has been working with spinning, steady pulse, repetitive movement, and geometric patterning." *Spiral* is the latest of the group works to be done since *Drumming*, in 1975, when the largest development in her work took place—the addition of music in the form of a full-scale concert-hall score. *Drumming* was set to Steve Reich's score of the same title, and although the music and the choreography shared a basic premise, Reich's inventions overpowered the dancing. Since *Song* (1976), Laura Dean has composed her own music—sparse and simple music with vocal sections that can be sung by the dancers themselves as they perform the sparse and simple steps. Her work has grown ever more tightly unified. And, like any work that is austerely planned to keep out idiosyncrasy, it has a high degree of personality. There is now a Laura Dean style of choreography, even a Laura Dean school. And Dean is recognizably part of the New York school of dancers and musicians who appear to be trying to invent folk art.

Spiral, in its play of irregular versus symmetrical rhythm, goes a little further than *Song*—at times it seems to be trying to invent *Les Noces*. (An intervening work, *Dance*, has not yet been seen in New York.) What keeps *Spiral* from growing more complex is the amateurishness of most of the dancing. It is amateurish on purpose; at least, it seems to be part of the methodology of contrived primitivism to solve problems by mental concentration rather than by physical dexterity. The audience has to concentrate as much as the dancers on, say, a port de bras cycle, so as not to get lost in the swim. Because of all the repeats, we have plenty of time to get a grip on the action. Once we get it, we see how, ultimately, the possibility of concentrating in this way leads to the possibility of communing—the dancers with each other, the audience with the dancers. The audience can be turned into a congregation. If Laura Dean were really to force the connection between shared meditation and universal trancedom, she'd be as manipulative as Maurice Béjart. But her tone is light, even frolicsome; she doesn't require unconditional surrender.

However, what you see at a Dean concert you have to be willing to see. Folk art is for the folk—for participants, not spectators. It is concerned with process, not with effect, and unless we let ourselves be drawn into process we aren't going to gain much from effect. (After about the fortieth repeat, a dance step has no effect.) *Spiral* is arranged for eight dancers and four musicians (two pianos, cello, voice). Although, like all the Dean works I've seen, it takes its tribal-rite form from mixed origins (East Indian, Russian, Early American, tap, disco), it is also the least monolithic of those works, and the most watchable. Still, for the most efficient watching one had to get into the sport of it. Counting wasn't necessary; empathy was. For me, blockages occurred, as always, during those extended whirling-dervish spins that Dean dancers love to do. Spinning is their way, during a public ritual, of going on retreat. It gives the viewer nothing to think about and nothing to see. But Dean isn't unaware of her audience's perceptions. Toward the end of the piece, there was a sudden break in the baby-step sequence as the dancers plunged into a unison sauté combination, and as suddenly plunged out of it. This was almost too much to take in. One lost the process and grabbed onto effect. For a few delightful seconds, *Spiral* seemed to be going in reverse.

Andy deGroat started spinning not long after Laura Dean, and, like Dean, he uses relatively untrained dancers. But whereas Dean's group compositions have a quasi-mystical intensity, DeGroat's look like practical organized fun, as if they could be taught to factory workers at lunchtime. DeGroat's dancers galumph around; the pretty salon-type piano music (by Alan Lloyd) that he uses for *Angie's Waltz and Other Dances* is as virtuous as floral chintz. Seen at Westbeth this fall, *Angie's Waltz* was a sprawling dance suite that really did consist of waltzes, polkas, marches, and other classical forms. Their use didn't betray DeGroat into self-consciousness or aggression. The elementary dance steps and the shambling democratic dance manners combined at times to make *Angie's Waltz* look like a rougher, downtown version of Paul Taylor's *Esplanade*. But, despite his links to other choreographers, DeGroat has an interesting dance mind of his own, and an even more interesting music-and-dance mind.

To its *Bournonville Divertissements*, new last winter, the New York City Ballet has now added a grand finale: the Tarantella from *Napoli*, Act III. This brings back the dancers of the first divertissement (the Ballabile from *Napoli*, Act I), recostumed and shaking tambourines; Nichol Hlinka and Daniel Duell return as the lead couple, and Jean-Pierre Frohlich is there to spark the dancing, just as he does in the Ballabile. The big, companionable Tarantella, rounding off the suite of old dances in brilliant style, takes some of the shine off the Pas de Sept (from *A Folk Tale*), which immediately precedes it; and because the Pas de Sept is being danced with less flair than formerly it probably won't be missed if it is deleted. Better than deleting the whole ballet!* *Bournonville* offers some of the best dancing to be seen in current repertory, but audiences haven't taken to it, and it was scheduled for only three performances this season—all before *The Nutcracker*.

Meanwhile, the Pas de Six from Saint-Léon's *La Vivandière* is badly revived by the Joffrey Ballet and audience reception is enthusiastic. Given a string of a half-dozen Saint-Léon excerpts, maybe even the sanguine Joffrey audience would rebel. That time, though, will never come. Except, it is said, for the Paris edition of *Coppélia*, Arthur Saint-Léon's dances weren't preserved in continuous performance, like August Bournonville's. The Pas de Six is a fragment of an 1848 ballet, and it survives because it was published by Saint-Léon as an example of his method of dance notation. Ann Hutchinson Guest reconstructed the steps from Saint-Léon's script and translated

---

* *Postscript* 1982: The Pas de Sept was deleted in 1980.

them into a modern dance script, Labanotation. The dance, which is for a couple backed by four girls, was first staged, from Labanotation, last year for the Joffrey junior company by Guest, and Maria Grandy, co-director of Joffrey II, staged it for the senior company. Of the two casts I saw, only Francesca Corkle had the elasticity and airiness needed for her role, which once belonged to Fanny Cerrito. Everyone else, and sometimes even Corkle, used an attack that was too broad, even, and hard, with no subtlety in plié. The ramrod stiffness this gave to the line of the choreography did indeed suggest pages of notation—it certainly didn't suggest dancing. It was surprising, too, that there was not more nuance in the pointwork—not even as much as there is in the Bournonville excerpts at NYCB, where mid–nineteenth-century practice has been modernized. Women of those days did not dance extensively on point; to raise every possible half-toe to full toe is to falsify the period. The *Vivandière* production illustrates the danger of reviving dances from the past without some means of insuring their safe conduct from the library to the theatre. Whether the Joffrey needed a Stanley Williams (who staged the Bournonville pieces for NYCB) or just simply better dancers, I can't say. But notation, of whatever era, doesn't seem to have been enough.   —*December 5, 1977*

Prose into Poetry

In choreography, if you can't be a genius, then you must be in-genious. Pilobolus Dance Theatre, I would have said a year ago, is simply ingenious. Now I'm not so sure that the gift of ingenuity isn't capable of once in a while surpassing itself, so that we are shaken out of admiration into awe.

Pilobolus is already in several respects a phenomenon. The performers create their own material. What they create is good, it is unique, and it is a big box-office hit. The world of Pilobolus is, in fact, a magical world where fairy-tale success actually can occur. Usually, the price of fame is a move-ment from the complex to the simple. The larger the audience, the greater the need to be understood. But the size of the following that Pilobolus has acquired in recent years seems only to have emboldened it. The company has just finished playing its first Broadway season. Business was excellent. In the repertory at the St. James Theatre were old pieces that have been shaped up and newer ones that have struck out exploratively. Two programs were presented; in both one could trace an impressive growth chart. *Ocellus*, the oldest piece in the repertory, looks back to the early seventies, when the company consisted of four men. Hypnotic but limited, it repeats motifs without expanding its vision. *Ciona*, revised to include two women, has more variety, but, like *Ocellus*, it shows us athletic exuberance undistilled. The great step in the group pieces was taken in 1974 in *Monkshood's Farewell*. Is the title a reference to the addition of the two female members? Alison Chase and Martha Clarke have distinct, and distinctly different, styles both as artists and as performers. I think it was their individual qualities of style, and not just their sex, that changed the troupe and made it complete. *Untitled* (1975) belongs to them; they are gargantuan virgins sailing around a pastoral landscape on men's legs, giving birth, swallowing men whole, even swallowing each other, yet abiding serenely to the end of days.

Pilobolus is, of course, a company of acrobatic mimes rather than dancers. They do not step to a beat but move to a system of cues arranged like a musical soundtrack. Often they move in silence. However, it isn't the lack of an audible measure that makes their "dance" strangely unpredictable. The secret lies in the way the pieces are constructed out of mime continuity rather than dance continuity, and it lies, too, in an increasing urge toward the nonliteral image. *Monkshood's Farewell* is crammed with specific pictorial events that pyramid from the simplest of physical premises—the one that we're familiar with from the kindergarten game of "I'm a little teapot." The company starts with a medieval tournament in which linked limbs and torsos conjure up horses, riders, lances. Gargoyles abruptly appear to herald a sequence of random virtuoso pictures: shoes, bicycles, frogs, monkeys. Then the men all become hunchbacks, lascivious and gentle at the same time. As they look on happily, Martha Clarke is carried away by St. Vitus's dance. This is the funniest headless-chicken act since Imogene Coca's sewing-machine girl went berserk back in the fifties; Clarke, with her large dark eyes and rubber mouth, resembles Coca, too. The fadeout comes on an unexpected note of pathos as three figures are seen bearing on their bent backs three others, who lie upside down and stiff as boards. It's the only nonrepresentational image in *Monkshood's Farewell*, yet—perhaps because it seems strangely related to those dear hunchbacks—it's deeply moving. A lot of the imagery in this brilliant episodic piece suggests Brueghel; in *Untitled* and other dances, it's Edward Lear who comes to mind. *Untitled* has a nonsensical scenario that seems to have been hatched not from literary ideas but from props and acrobatic maneuvers. Making "sense" is a secondary object of the performers; their primary object is to keep going. By the time the piece is over, the women's long skirts, the men's bare or clothed bodies have been used like interlocking parts of a puzzle to build a complete design. *Untitled* never gets explicit in its reference to life, and it doesn't tell us what it means, yet we know wordlessly what it means. The design is there not to dictate our reactions but to set us free.

The St. James repertory included a number of solos and duets. In his solo from *Eve of Samhain*, Robby Barnett, wearing centaurlike shaggy leggings, stalks a steel snake lying on the ground. It whips itself around him; he frees himself, retreats offstage, and reappears in a pouncing leap from a height. The struggle grows intense. The snake dies as it is swung in ever more graceful, ever narrowing arcs. Finally, draped across the hunter's shoulders, it is caressed. In *Alraune*, the illusions are fostered entirely through anatomical manipulation. Moses Pendleton punches his head down into his torso, and later he holds Alison Chase's head so that it appears to float in midair. The Chase-Pendleton duet in which their bodies merge has become a staple of the repertory. It reaches a new peak of refinement in *Shizen*. Here, before the merger takes place, the two remain for a long time apart, holding positions of extreme difficulty. There are bits of mime that suggest (but never specify) a landscape of waving grass, a waterhole, the passage of tall birds. As soon as Chase locks herself around Pendleton's body, the two are one being, and they seem to keep evolving as one being. There is a sequence in which slight separations occur—enough to show the twinship of sexual intimacy. And at the end they are alone again, bent like peasants to the earth. *Shizen* passes as slowly as an Ozu film, to the sound of a bamboo flute. A pure object of contemplation, it marks a decisive advance in Pilobolus style; it's the movement from prose to poetry.

A dance troupe seldom achieves wide success until it is well into its second or third generation and its original brilliance is gone. The Pilobolus company we see today is still in its first generation. As first generations tend to be, it is a mixed band of individuals whose separate talents enrich the common enterprise and add to it the spice of potential dissent. Some of the solo turns look like decompression chambers. Jonathan Wolken's *Pseudopodia* is a wonderful tumbling solo in which his own foot is the hub of the wheel that turns him. It would look right at home in *Monkshood's Farewell*. But his *Renelaugh*, performed in fencing mask with foil, is entirely a private vision. Martha Clarke's solos undersell Martha Clarke. A rigorous form-follows-function comedian, she's constantly trying to build fires from a few carefully selected twigs—a veil and a baggy black dress in *Vagabond*, tin buckets and a floppy Pierrot suit in *Pagliaccio*. Though *Vagabond* isn't as precious as *Pagliaccio*, it's still a bit too choosy in what it reveals of Clarke's range. Yet in her selectivity she can be emotionally precise. The sadness of the moment when she "captures" Chase in *Untitled* could only belong to a very abstemious clown.

All the Piloboli are clowns—even Alison Chase, a statuesque, clear-browed beauty who functions most often as the troupe's indispensable straight woman. The glinting satyr Pendleton and the wolfishly jovial Wolken are just enough alike to set each other off; they could be brothers brought up by different tribes. The remote, poetic Barnett and the handsome

Michael Tracy round off a perfectly balanced set. When a Pilobolus evening is over, one leaves the theatre with a complete experience, refreshed by the company of six of the most extraordinary people now performing.

Is it because so many boring ballets have been set to his music that I have come to dislike Mahler? The Mahler ballet: someone sings lugubriously from the side of the stage while dancers toil up Angst Hill and down Weltschmerz Dale for hours on end. Sexuality, if not repressed, is ambiguous; a Death Figure is bound to turn up somewhere. Mahler is the favorite composer of the deep-think choreographers—the one they all rely on to dye their musings the rich dark brown of significance; not long ago it was Shostakovich who suffered that fate. *Songs of a Wayfarer* is one of the most conspicuous of the Mahler brownies. It is a typical Maurice Béjart pas de deux, with two guys, or one guy and his Doppelgänger, in case we don't believe our eyes. Nureyev, for whom it was created (with Paolo Bortoluzzi), has done it here; Béjart's company has, too, and it is in the repertory of Dancers, where Dennis Wayne performs it with Miguel Campaneria. With only two characters Béjart is able to suggest the whole spectrum: homosexuality is present, and one of the lovers is Death. And Dancers emphasized the consistency of the genre by programming *Songs of a Wayfarer* as a companion piece to another dirgelike duet, this one set to lieder by Lutoslawski. I'd never heard of Lutoslawski, and I'm willing to bet that most people who see *Of Us Two* have as much trouble as I do making out the language the songs are sung in. *Of Us Two*—by Cliff Keuter— carries the brown menace one step further: not only sung accompaniment but sung accompaniment that cannot be understood. Keuter's gloomy ballet is a girl-girl affair. I have no idea whether the text of the songs bears out the folie-à-deux relationship we see on the stage. Does it matter? Does it matter that Mahler's text for *Songs of a Wayfarer* doesn't deal specifically with a homosexual love and doesn't dwell on death? (Béjart seems to have paid less attention to the text than to other Mahler ballets—Tudor's *Dark Elegies*, set to the *Kindertotenlieder*, or MacMillan's *Song of the Earth*, with its depiction of Death as der Ewige, the eternal one.)

Murkiness of this sort has become so routine in ballet repertory that it is practically a convention. Question it, and someone is sure to snap that dancing is a nonverbal art. But Dancers has more than its share of deep-think ballets. (The program note for another piece is a long quotation from Northrop Frye.) Dancers is a new company, formed by Wayne; it arrived last month at the Roundabout Theatre after a year of publicity and many manifestos on the needs, rights, and comforts of dancers. Once it was seen that these requisites didn't include a creative repertory, it was easy for the critics to puncture Dancers' pretensions. The company really is an old-age home for the young. The ballets are banal and technically incompetent, and offer the dancers neither opportunity nor refuge. The first program that I attended opened with—can you believe it, Trockadero de Monte Carlo?—yet another piano ballet. All Chopin, all nocturnes. *Nocturne,* by the company's ballet master, Igal Perry, took thirty minutes that were good for nothing more than the time they gave us to sort out the dancers. The cast of ten included some veterans, but only Helene Roux, who looked to be the youngest, danced responsibly, with shading in her attack and some sense of the difference between the classroom and the theatre. We knew that Dancers wasn't going to be a choreographers' showcase, but it might have been, like the Harkness Ballet of the sixties, an exemplary company of dancers. It isn't, and its costumes, lighting, and musical standards (no live accompaniment) are pretty poor, too.

I won't mention every piece I saw—the temptation to poke easy fun is just too great. But the revival of Todd Bolender's *The Still Point* ought to be mentioned, because the ballet is worth a good deal more than the company just now knows how to give. Parts of the girl's role appear to have been rechoreographed downward and excessively moistened with self-pity. Christine O'Neal needs to be redirected toward the music and away from the drama, and the lyrical line of the first two movements should be tauter. (The third movement was always a loss.) Live playing of Debussy's String Quartet is indispensable here; the ballet is one of the company's few settings of good music which aren't oafish. I must add a good word for *The Entertainers,* by a choreographer new to me, David Anderson. The characters are a bored, vicious girl and her victim; their relationship is described, Ailey fashion, in semi-naturalistic walks, whirls, and kicks—lots of kicks—done to a slow blues. The boy keeps coming back for more, but by the end he's lashing back, and the two have reached a standoff. *The Entertainers* isn't a likable piece, or even a greatly effective one. The title is a mystery. But its languid yet lithe rhythm pulls one along even when the dramatic situation isn't going anywhere. And it was the only piece I saw that gave the dancers parts they could do and look good doing. Even allowing for the extra-sharp presence that this kind of piece can give to performers, I find Nancy Theusen and Michael Tipton sticking in my mind, and it's their *dancing* I remember—far more vivid than in their other roles. Maybe this engagingly loose show-dance style represents the expressive level the company should be seeking, rather than all those portentous and unmusical conservatory pieces.

Dennis Wayne, who was in that Harkness company of the sixties, may be the first artistic director to project a company from his political and professional attitudes rather than from his gifts as an artist. He hasn't attempted to build a display case for himself, and one can only commend his modesty. Most of his ideas have to do with financial goals, not artistic ones. When Wayne says, "There is no such thing as art in America unless there is money," we know what he means. And he has his Rebekah Harkness in Joanne Woodward, the actress, who has poured hundreds of thousands into the Dancers till. But from the looks of Dancers the art is still a

long way off. In a curiously selfless way, Wayne has managed to create a
vanity company.   —*December 19, 1977*

Adagio and Allegro

The Balanchine-Mozart *Divertimento No. 15* is one of those ballets—*Les
Sylphides* and *Jardin aux Lilas* are others—that are famous for never being
done well. Even in the dimmest performances, *Les Sylphides* and *Jardin* are
recognizable masterpieces that never fail to go over with the public, but
Divertimento has remained a succès d'estime for years. Only in the past
year has it begun to win a little public acclaim, in the form of an extra
round or two of applause. It is the ballet that, more than any other, defines
the idealism of the classical style as Balanchine sees it. Of course, we know
that perfection is impossible—that no cast will ever completely realize the
vision Balanchine holds before us—but it is important to feel this as the
tension of idealism, and not as the strain of inadequacy. Balanchine has not
made an intractable or an inhuman piece. Indeed, he has drawn an allegorical irony out of the limitations of classical style, as if to say that
whatever touches both our idealism and our humanity must be ironic. The
ballet has this dual pressure: it voluntarily confesses its limitations even as
it promises us a paradise of beauty and gaiety and sensuality and romance.
We perceive the vanity of attempting so much with so little, and then the
vanity turns to poignance and we know the ballet is going to tear us in
half.

It has five ballerina roles. At the première by the New York City Ballet,
in 1956, the lineup consisted of Diana Adams, Melissa Hayden, Allegra
Kent, Tanaquil LeClercq, and Patricia Wilde. Seldom since then has the
company spread before us a comparable array of talent. In fact, the performance history of this most sublime Balanchine ballet has been fairly
indifferent: in and out of repertory; once in, never lingering long; frequently
announced only to be cancelled; inadequately rehearsed even when adequately cast. There are three cavalier roles, the central one on a par with
those of the ballerinas. Six starring roles must be filled at every performance
by six soloists who are well matched. The answer to why certain dancers
who might be marvellous in *Divertimento* parts haven't appeared in them is
that for one reason or another they don't fit into an ensemble. It's a mark of
the company's current strength that the ballet is at last coming back into its
own. Balanchine is able to cast it two different ways: "tall" and "short."
Though he actually doesn't have two completely different first-rate casts,
that day may not be far off. The "tall" cast is, dancer for dancer, the more

impressive, with Kyra Nichols, Maria Calegari, Stephanie Saland, Susan Hendl or Colleen Neary, Peter Martins, and Merrill Ashley dancing the six variations in outstanding style, and with Sean Lavery and Gerard Ebitz in the two secondary male roles. The five women's roles are more or less equal in size and richness, but two are especially well favored. The climactic whirlwind variation calls for the high-powered allegro technique that at the moment only Ashley possesses—and, in fact, the central role in the ballet belongs to the allegro ballerina. But the plum role may really be the one performed by the third soloist, who has the centerpiece pas de deux in the great supported adagio of the Andante. Nowadays, it is being done by Saland in a broadly conscientious way, which suggests she's trying hard not to rely on her elegant presence. This was the role that first brought Ashley to wide attention, and she may be the only dancer who has done it and the lead, too. But she really wasn't suited to the adagio role. With her bold attack and straitened dynamics, Ashley excels in strongly punctuated, full-throttle adagios like the one in *The Nutcracker*. In legato, and especially in the melting transitions that characterize the Mozart adagio, she's clean but unexpressive. *Theme and Variations* (from *Tchaikovsky Suite No. 3*) has what might be called a supported allegro; Ashley triumphs in it. *Cortège Hongrois* has one, too—a shapeless, evasively constructed pas de deux, which Ashley's aggressive sweep makes remarkably coherent. She hasn't much feeling for the celebrated adagio variation, but adagio is not her first nature. Ashley is allegro through and through; she's uncomplicatedly a specialist and probably the main reason for the success of the *Divertimento* revival.

Divertimento No. 15 is a revision of a 1952 ballet to the same music—the Divertimento No. 15, K. 287, for strings and two horns. Ever since the loss of that earlier version, called *Caracole*, the ballet has seemed to many people better in memory than on the stage. There are aspects of *Divertimento*, too, that live on only in memory. The ballet was made for a smaller stage than the one at the State Theatre. In the adagio, as one pas de deux succeeded another, each seemed to spring in a cantilevered arc from the previous one. Entrances were achieved without the walks to place that are now necessary (the third couple entered with the girl already lifted and beating), and in exits a lift-off would vanish at its crest. The ballet needs a set. David Hays's ivy-hung walls and trellises, which have now been abandoned, didn't succeed in making the stage any smaller, but they did provide some sort of frame, and the arcade at the back of the stage through which the soloists would enter for their variations—a feature of Hays's setting that conformed to James Stewart Morcom's at the City Center—seems indispensable if the variations are to follow upon one another without distraction or pause.

Changes have also taken place in the choreography. Some of the solos have been revised here and there, with no great loss of effect as far as I can see. But a major difference was introduced when Balanchine modified the promenade that climaxes one section of the third pas de deux, making it into the tame, ineffective thing it is now. Originally, as I recall, the girl circled in arabesque, her leg passing over the man's head just as he knelt and stopped her momentum. It was a dangerous move, and, after Allegra Kent and Erik Bruhn fell down trying to execute it, it disappeared. A less explicable change occurred when a new and longer cadenza was inserted at the end of the Andante. To this extended duet for two violins, Balanchine arranged an elaborate set of supported poses and promenades and walks through tunnels for the eight principals which to my mind not only detracts from the heaven-sent image that has just occurred—of the five ballerinas and their three partners interlocked in supported arabesques penchées—but also undermines a similar set of maneuvers which will occur in the finale. What used to happen in the old cadenza was that the eight dancers would simply walk all around the stage in separate paths—an event unlike any other in the ballet—before taking up their positions in two facing lines and executing their révérences. After so much dense, formal dancing, after so many intimate contacts, that aimless walk was exactly the touch of unconscious grace the piece needed, a "fall from the heights" that expressed with daring precision Balanchine's sense of irony in relation to Mozart's. No doubt Balanchine thought the effect too casual.

In *Ballo della Regina*, the new ballet that Balanchine has made for Ashley, she carries bravura allegro dancing to a peak it may never have reached before. The adagio, partnered by Robert Weiss, requires the singing line that Ashley doesn't have and is dispatched with typical efficiency, but her polka variation, whirling to a close with hops in fifth on point, cuts like flying glass. Balanchine seems to have taken Ashley's role in last year's *Bournonville Divertissements* as a sketch for the brilliant new material he has given her, and he has orchestrated the Ashley "theme"—her strangely characteristic ability to move her tall, straight body through rapid and complete changes of shape. Ashley doesn't combine different shapes in the same movement, but she can achieve counterpoint through juxtaposition, and she's so fast she can even appear to be in two places at once. The dances for an all-girl corps (four demisoloists and an ensemble of twelve) are as spontaneous and fresh as the dances for Ashley. Balanchine has designed them for contrast—her fleet footwork against their wide striding and turning, their plasticity against her square-cut, erect style. All this is allegro in range, although as Balanchine allegro it is unfamiliar. Those high, sailing jumps, for example—where did they come from? The ballet makes the audience very happy, especially at the end, when, to slamming final chords, Ashley takes three or four flash poses on the way down from a supported position in écarté to a kneel: it sums up her phenomenal high-speed accuracy.

In spite of the show put on by Ashley, Bonita Borne, Sheryl Ware, Debra Austin, Saland, and the ensemble, *Ballo della Regina* doesn't add up to much. It lacks conviction as a ballet. Weiss's role is trumped up; musically there doesn't seem to be a real place for him, and he gets wedged into corners. (Flat and stiff as he looks, it's still unfair treatment.) The music is the seldom performed ballet from Verdi's *Don Carlos*, written to a libretto that Balanchine has disregarded. Musical echoes of that libretto remain, nevertheless, in passages (*azione mimica*) that don't easily support the straight dancing that Balanchine has choreographed to them. When the orchestra blares out a hymn, the dancers make up a procession to nowhere. In the opera ballet, this was the moment when Princess Eboli, disguised as Elizabeth of Valois, was revealed as "La Peregrina," the pearl beyond price. For Balanchine, Ben Benson has designed filmy costumes and Ronald Bates has lit the stage in soft marine colors, reflecting the undersea grotto where Verdi's pearl fisher sought his treasure. In another ballet to music by an opera composer, *Donizetti Variations*, Balanchine has drawn a sharp, and sharply satirical, picture of Donizetti. But he doesn't appear to have had Verdi's qualities much in mind, perhaps because the music has no particular Verdian savor. (It was one of the composer's attempts to satisfy Parisian taste.) Balanchine's *Ballo della Regina* is a quarter-hour discourse about the qualities of Merrill Ashley.

When Suzanne Farrell dances an allegro role and brings to it an adagio color, as she did this season in *Allegro Brillante*, she creates a complex and interesting event. Farrell wouldn't be interesting in *Ballo della Regina*, since for the most part the role completely blocks out any adagio quality. The prima role in *Divertimento No. 15* doesn't need her, either, as one none too successful fling with it last year showed. For Farrell to captivate in allegro, the role has to be porous. For Ashley, it has to be airtight. *Allegro Brillante* isn't, and she probably wouldn't be terribly exciting in it. It took the enormous range of Farrell to show me that *Allegro Brillante* could be danced, with no loss of allegro values, as an adagio part. (I mean all the way through, not just in sections.) But the big Farrell occasion of the season so far has been her dancing in *Chaconne* the night of the *Ballo* première. To watch Farrell stretching a Farrell part is a front-line experience; dancing just does not go further. On this night, there were quantitative embellishments of all sorts: quadruple pirouettes, sixes instead of quatres in the entrechats, even triple soutenu turns. But quantity is not the end of virtuosity. What Farrell achieved was a heightening of all those fluid transactions between extreme ends of her range—between allegro and adagio—which Balanchine wrote into her role. And though she advanced to the very limit of the ballet's style, she never toppled into distortion. Farrell's choreography in *Chaconne* is already a study in rococo excess. To exceed excess and still not distort: quite a feat.   —*January 30, 1978*

Postscript 1982: I received the following letter from John Colman, a pianist and composer formerly on the staff of the School of American Ballet:

"I am responsible (musically) for the revised cadenza which Balanchine interpolated into the ballet *Divertimento No. 15*. . . . During a rehearsal of the ballet in 1964 or 1965, Robert Irving asked Balanchine if the tempo of the adagio (which your review refers to as the andante) was all right. 'It was all right. Maybe the cadenza is not very pretty,' Balanchine replied. Irving resumed conducting with no comment. Mr. B.'s gaze wandered to where I sat (out front). He beckoned to me to join him onstage. When I had done so, he asked me to compose a new cadenza. The one used heretofore was allegedly by Arturo Toscanini, but Balanchine couldn't believe it. I was to try for something more elaborate—something longer, if necessary; a real cadenza, but in duet form. They would give me a day or two. When it was ready (the next day), Balanchine and Irving heard it, Irving with no comment, Balanchine with warm approval. The cast of dancers was to listen to it, but only to avoid surprises. Choreographically, there was to be no change; they would walk around as usual before the révérence, and then simply wait for the rest of the cadenza. Unfortunately, this simple solution proved to be simplistic. My cadenza had more musical activity than the old one, and what was occurring onstage no longer suggested the aimless, unconscious grace that you admired. Instead, once the walkaround, which ate up only a small fraction of the new music, was over, the dancers seemed to be trying hard to hold on to their equanimity while waiting out, in immobility, an inordinately long pause. Balanchine immediately began to sketch new choreography, which is still being danced after more than fifteen years."

Echo Chamber Music

Is there a greater theatrical adventure than a new Balanchine ballet seen for the first time? Yes: a new Balanchine ballet seen for the second time. At first, swept along at intergalactic speeds, we feel nothing but the novelty and peculiarity of it all—the sensation of being bombarded by clean particles of image and sound. And we are likely to think, as the strokes and details build up to a total impression, Why, how strange—he's never done anything like this before. But the same ballet on another night can suddenly seem entirely plausible. It loses some of its pristine atmospheric dazzle and starts to resemble other Balanchine works—works we've been comfortable with for years. When the new ballet's singular virtues and its categorizable ones are impossible to tell apart, we know that we've assimilated it, and we begin to enjoy the ballet not simply as a new event but as an integrated core expression of the company that produced it. No Balanchine ballet, no matter how enjoyable, is assimilable at first sight—there's too much going on. But the things that usually don't emerge until a second viewing—like structural and categorical resemblances to other ballets—can be upsetting; they can drain away newness before we've had a chance to determine the weight of it, and we know we have to go yet a third time just to see if we can balance things out. Since in New York we have the benefit of leisurely repertory seasons, we do go again, as soon as we can. Sometimes the looked-for progression of thesis-antithesis-synthesis happens right on schedule; sometimes not at all or not for years, and the ballet that is no longer a stranger to us remains at best a distant cousin of the ballets we love. We accept it for their sake, but we don't want to see it often.

For me, the new piece called (after its Hindemith score) *Kammermusik No. 2* may become one of these estimable, avoidable ballets. I've seen it four times and found it each time a fascinating work of craft, undeniably a member of the family, but a fairly unappealing member—the kind that sets out to gain by hard work and good credit what it lacks in bloodlines. Although it belongs among those modern classical ballets danced to modern music, it seems to have married into the Stravinsky-serialism branch, which includes *Agon*, *Violin Concerto*, *Rubies*, *Episodes*, and *Movements for Piano and Orchestra*, rather than to have descended from *The Four Temperaments*, which is the only other Hindemith ballet in the repertory, or from *Metamorphoses*, an early-fifties setting of Hindemith's *Symphonic Metamorphoses*, or from any of the non-Balanchine Hindemith ballets we know about. If, next to the Stravinsky ballets, *Kammermusik No. 2* lacks depth, it certainly has a powerfully thick and busy surface. The care that Balanchine has lavished upon it suggests that he wants no light to come through. He hasn't, as he said of *The Four Temperaments*, made a negative to Hindemith's positive plate; he's made another positive.

Kammermusik No. 2 was composed in 1924, about midway in the series of concertos dubbed "chamber music" by the composer, presumably because of the intimate collaboration of their relatively small ensembles. Scored for solo piano and twelve other instruments, No. 2 is nimble, brusque music, much of it moving at piston pace on irregular, rapidly shifting beats and dealing in complex canonical structures. Balanchine expresses all this and more, and he makes the tight, driving rhythms seem flexible, but the effect of his immaculate response to the music is a ballet that appears oddly closed and, in its superefficient way, defensive. Not that he hasn't a perspective on the score. He has several. One of them is cultural: his summation of the music as part of a particular place and time—Germany in the twenties. It may be pertinent that when Doris Humphrey revived her *Life of the Bee* in 1957, she staged it to the Kammermusik No. 1. This may have been a reaction to the insect pas de deux and winged finale of *Metamorphoses* (although a more noticeable correspondence to *The Life of the Bee* occurs in Jerome Robbins's *The Cage*). But I mention the Humphrey ballet because of the far larger coincidence of its period with the period of the Kammermusik and with a particular climate of design. Balanchine's *Kammermusik* portrays that music as a moment in the history of modernity. He has created a modern antique. It doesn't look anything like the naive expressionism of Humphrey or like what one could imagine of the German modern dances that very likely inspired her. Instead, it looks like Greek folk dance—or, rather, the adaptation of that by German Hellenism. Athletic-aesthetic clubs, robust Dalcrozean youth whose energies gave rise to *Le Sacre du Printemps* before the war and to some part of the environment for "neo-classicism" afterward—these images feed what must be the most schematic music-visualization that Balanchine has done since the Bach-Webern "Ricercata" in *Episodes*.

Indeed, with Bach we start another round of categorical correspondences. *Kammermusik No. 2* relates to the "Ricercata," and both are related to *Concerto Barocco*. Balanchine ratifies the baroque pretensions of the Hindemith score; he capitalizes on its near-deadly pedantry. He seems to relish this involved game of all strategy and no target. Without ever getting mechanical and therefore predictable in his moves, he yet finds a visual rhyme for everything he hears: the double and triple canons cannonading between piano and orchestra are reproduced on the stage between soloists and corps; the two-part inventions for the piano are reflected in two ballerinas dancing the same or similar dances in unison or a few beats apart. *Concerto Barocco* has two ballerinas and a corps de ballet of eight girls; the corps of *Kammermusik* is eight men. Men, perhaps, are more suited than women would be to the figurative atmosphere of the piece and to its blunt, thick strokes, its metronomic austerity. This male Greek chorus is never still but always actively composing and recomposing the perimeters of the action. Spacing is tight; the men move blocklike in and out of place, one move (or so it seems) per beat. The constant shuttling keeps redefining the space. Though the atmosphere of the piece never deepens, it never dies, either; Balanchine keeps us moving inside it. And he has calculated its limited psychological range to perfection. The corps of men enforces the local, historical look (the datedness, if you like) and also a kind of ruthless anonymity that wouldn't be possible with a corps of women. ("Put sixteen girls on a stage," Balanchine has said, "and it's everybody—the world. But put sixteen boys and it's always nobody.") This ballet isn't just faceless, it's also headless. Between the two ballerinas, no one governs. The symmetry is such that one may divide the stage in half at almost any point, watch only one side, and still see all. The split focus recalls parts of the last section of *Stravinsky Violin Concerto*, when we seem to be watching two ballets moving toward each other like sliding mirrored doors. *Kammermusik* carries this doubleness to baffling extremes. Certainly it is motivated by the music, but isn't it unlike Balanchine to be this literal?

Balanchine choreographs his dance in twin sets and never gives us a stereoscope to look through. His ballerinas are Karin von Aroldingen and Colleen Neary, who are physically and temperamentally so dissimilar they're practically opposites. Neary has a small head, a short waist, and very long legs. In Von Aroldingen, these proportions are reversed. Neary is spirited; Von Aroldingen is stolid. Yet these two dancers are never used for contrast. About all they have in common are the roles of Choleric in *The Four Temperaments* and second ballerina in *Rubies*, and their dissimilarities are no more relevant there than they are here. Balanchine seems to have cast them because they are both tall. Isn't it also unlike him to be so inscrutable? In *Kammermusik*, from the material he has given his ballerinas and their partners, Adam Lüders and Sean Lavery, there isn't much we can tell about Balanchine's attitude except that he's been unusually hard on Von Aroldingen, giving her a fat part but, for the first time, letting her limitations show. He's noncommittal toward Lüders and Lavery, seeing to little more than that they function well in the partnering and in some brief solo bits. And he's downright cryptic about Neary. It's true that she hasn't progressed as rapidly as some others have in recent years, but mightn't this role have provided some sort of incentive? Performing for the most part in Von Aroldingen's shadow, she has one witty solo passage of chaînés turned on the heels, then makes a flippant exit. It's almost the only personal moment in the ballet.

But the fact that Balanchine hasn't made the ballet a showcase for anyone in it (except maybe the corps) doesn't mean that he's made an unexpressive or devitalized piece. On the contrary. The ballet boils with precisely directed energies; it's the mirror of an impersonal yet human process, and in that respect it does resemble *The Four Temperaments*. I find the process poetically incomprehensible and I believe it isn't going to become less so, yet the way it's worked out and timed down to the last microsecond is something for other choreographers to study and for all of us to admire. There's an extraordinary image in the last movement of a centrifuge spinning almost out of control before order is restored. I understand there was a lot of switching of costumes before the opening night. The choice settled on football jerseys and tights for the men, with tunics falling to mid-thigh and fillet-bound hair for the women. I can't understand how it could ever have been anything else.

Peter Martins's *Calcium Light Night*, which also entered the New York City Ballet repertory this season, confirmed the good impression I had of it at a preview performance. It begins as modestly as possible, with a young man walking out onto the stage and beginning to dance, as if for himself, to some selections of Charles Ives. He experiments with skids, with kicks through space; he flexes or crosses his feet and walks with a hobbled gait. In one solo, he trails along in bourrées with soft arms, as if imagining, or imagining himself, a girl. In another solo, he leaps with flashing satyr's hooves. He walks off unconcernedly and a woman walks on. As she repeats some of the steps he has just danced, she seems to be the woman he was thinking about. She has a gentle, lyrical solo, but this moment of introspection lasts little more than an arpeggio, and the barbed, militant air she then assumes seems to be more characteristic. She stalks backward on point, turns, and stalks some more. When he returns, to circle her helplessly in high leaps, the monotonous march goes on. Finally, they meet in "arguments" (though the music here is not Ives's "Arguments" but his "Hallowe'en''), a staccato, nonstop seriocomic pas de deux in which limbs become hinges and handles, bodies are clamped together, then slid apart. The choreography makes not one superfluous gesture, everything stands out with bright-edged clarity, and the flatly factual tone communicates an instantaneous emotion. Daniel Duell and Heather Watts are excellent. The stage is undressed except for a square tube of light hung overhead. The uncostumes are perhaps too severe. Watts, in her crimson unitard sheared off at calf and bustline, looks like a thermometer.   —*February 20, 1978*

Visions

Don Quixote is not many people's idea of a Balanchine ballet, yet to anyone interested in what Balanchine ballets are about it is an indispensable work to have seen. And especially to have seen with Suzanne Farrell, for whom its Dulcinea was created. In the course of six performances that closed the New York City Ballet season, Farrell rose to a level of expression that even she may not have hit before in this role. She did all six performances and only got stronger, and by closing night the whole company was rising with her. A story went around that this was the last performance ever of *Don Quixote*. If so, the sick man of the repertory went out with a glorious bang. There was even a new Don, Adam Lüders, who gave the best interpretation of that role since Balanchine himself.

The ballet is a wildly uneven work. Its lows (which include most of Nicolas Nabokov's score) are very low, but its highs can be stratospheric. The weakest sections are in the first act, where, after a prologue showing the wild-eyed Don dreaming of knight-errantry in his study and then beginning to act out his dreams on the plains of La Mancha, we come to the inevitable village-square set. The strain of the establishing scenes is over, the audience relaxes and needs something to applaud. It is always a difficult moment in an evening-long spectacle, and I can't say that any of Balanchine's revisions over the years have solved the problem of appeasing the audience without losing the ballet's focus. The portion of Act I that has always been just right (besides the Prologue, and even that is once-revised) is the Marcela episode, followed by the puppet show in which the Don sees a tiny re-enactment of his own crusade. Curiously, there are precedents for all three of these scenes in the old Petipa-based *Don Quixote* that has figured for so long in Russian repertory. The extent to which Balanchine has repositioned, reworked, and indeed rethought elements of Petipa may become clearer when American Ballet Theatre presents Mikhail Baryshnikov's production of the old ballet this spring. Perhaps the most striking of Balanchine's re-creations, amounting to a whole new invention, is Marcela, one of the many guises of Dulcinea. Marcela is high-caste; from her dress, which is that of a Marie Antoinette shepherdess, we may guess that she is a lady from the Duke's court who affects the simple life. When the Don meets her, she's being dragged through the marketplace by the villagers, who accuse her of having driven a poet to suicide. The Don frees her, and she has a solo that is Farrell's first big moment of the evening. In the old Petipa ballet, the hero— who is not Don Quixote but a poor young barber named Basil—fakes a suicide attempt in order to keep his girlfriend from marrying a rich suitor. This farcical incident comes from Cervantes, and elsewhere in Cervantes Balanchine found the provincial beauty Marcela, for love of whom a young man has died. The lines that apply to the stage character are those in which Marcela explains to the Don that her virginity is her freedom, that she's not responsible for what men may do who love her because she's beautiful but would deprive her of her freedom for the same reason. Marcela's logic and the symbolism of her dress (she flourishes a shepherd's crook as she dances) are enlarged upon in Balanchine's resetting, in Act III, of the Petipa vision scene. In both ballets, the envisioned women are dryads, but Balanchine, a Shakespeare to Petipa's Holinshed, makes sense out of this ancient ballet convention. His text is Marcela's "I was born free, and to live free I chose the solitude of the fields." This season, Esteban Francés's woodland backcloth was missing. The sombre sky that replaced it, together with the prelude recently added to this scene, in which Dulcinea enshrouds the wounded Don in her white veil, seemed to move the atmosphere closer to the Shades scene in *La Bayadère*. The fields of Marcela's solo wanderings have become the Elysian Fields, and we know the Don is very close to death.

Don Quixote amplifies and recapitulates such important Balanchine themes as the Poet and His Muse, His Quest, His Impotence and Vindication. The ballet does not really derive from Cervantes or Petipa; it derives from *Orpheus* and *Le Baiser de la Fée* and *La Sonnambula*, with intimations of *The Prodigal Son* and *Serenade* and *Swan Lake*. Anyone who knows these and other Balanchine ballets will readily see why Balanchine wanted to make a *Don Quixote* for twenty years before he actually did so, in 1965. What might not be so obvious is why the ballet took the form it did—a three-act spectacle with a plot that stops every so often for dance divertissements. The answer is that Balanchine, as in other projects of his, was following, and improving upon, Petipa. And the alternative—an integrated dance drama—does not really exist.

The reason, I believe, is that, unlike Romeo or Othello, the Don is a literary figure whom one cannot imagine dancing. In the old *Don Quixote*, he is entirely marginal, an excuse to get vision scenes going or to provide some low comedy. Balanchine has made the Don a tragic hero—a sainted fool and, at the last, a martyr. Yet after a few adventures in Act I he changes from a man of action into a philosophical presence, someone through whose eyes we see the events of the ballet. The Don, though a poet, is not a lover. Had it been possible to imagine him passionately in love, almost certainly he would have had to be a dancer. But we know that Dulcinea is not real and the Don's longings aren't sexual. He embodies chivalrous attitudes, and Dulcinea is a part of the breadth and constancy of his vision. From legend we know, too, that the Don is tall and spindly and getting on in years, but this alone doesn't make him an unseemly romantic hero for a ballet d'action. Faust—in any serious attempt at a *Faust* ballet—would have to be a lay figure, too, for though Faust's loves are passionate, they are also lyrical and divine. Visionary heroes are more naturally expressed through mime. And Quixote's idealistic fantasies find their perfect theatrical expression in classical dance.

At first, in what he chooses to idealize, Balanchine may seem less than quixotic: he makes the dreams of beautiful and chaste women more important to the Don than the righting of injustices. But this is so because dreams of beauty are more danceable then dreams of justice. Petipa knew it, too. And it is during his short career as a humanitarian that Balanchine's Don comes closest to the buffoon portrayed by Petipa and Petipa's successors. Balanchine shows the oppressed turning on their savior as soon as they have been freed. This would seem unaccountably bitter did he not also show a grandiloquent Don who expects gratitude for his little services. The bleak tone of the comedy is more than a little Chaplinesque, and so is the ultimate sentiment of the ballet, when, at the end, the Don dies mourned by the little peasant girl whom he had idealized as Dulcinea. It is then that we see him through her eyes, a saint; and the idea redawns that he really does expect gratitude for his sacrifices, and more than gratitude. Is *Don Quixote* Balanchine's *Limelight*? Back in 1965, when Balanchine played the Don in the first performance, the emphasis in the death scene was, as it should be, on the way the Don dies. He awoke from his delusions, recognized his friends (including the little peasant), and died "a wise man," as he does in Cervantes. When Balanchine stepped out of the part, he switched the emphasis in the final moments to the girl (Farrell); it is now she who recognizes Quixote and all he has been trying to do. She places on his breast the rude crucifix of twigs and falls to her knees, overcome not only by the presence of a saint but by personal loss. This has always been a bit much; yet it would and did take great acting to convey what Balanchine conveyed in those last few moments, and the change in emphasis probably came about because he had more confidence in Farrell than in whoever was playing the Don. But there's no question that he always meant to make the Don a saint.

The poet a saint? Balanchine's ballet may strike some people as uncomfortably religiose. To others it is uncomfortable simply because it awakens rational considerations that seem beyond the capacities of ballet to express. It is one of the few Balanchine ballets that can be discussed as intellectual rather than purely poetic events, and that is one way we know it is at least in part a failure. The Marcela story is overallusive, and so is the long religious procession at the end. As the Don lies dying, he has visions of the Church Militant, of the Church Penitent, of his books burning. We force our minds a little and decide that this means he has been judged a heretic by the Inquisition. But forcing our minds is precisely what we don't want to do at the end of a long, complex, image-studded ballet; we want the images to continue inseparable from their meaning. When they don't, ambiguities cloud the scene. The religious procession is just a procession. Every kind of ecclesiastical costume turns up, and finally it's the Church Ambivalent parading through the Don's chambers. Burning books are easy to show on the stage, but "Inquisition" is not a concept that a ballet can express, and *why* the books are burning cannot be made clear.

Farrell's return in 1975 to a role she had largely outgrown pointed up the ballet's deficiencies; it seemed to lie in ruins around her. But though we may well have seen the last of *Don Quixote*, as of this season Balanchine hadn't lost interest in it. There was a new jota for the villagers to perform at the opening of the marketplace scene. Hyperinventive, like the folk dances in *Coppélia*, it was all the dancing I wanted at this point in the story. (The Don and Sancho have just embarked on their adventures.) But it turned out to be the prelude to the Pas Classique Espagnol that was added to the ballet a few years ago. This extended and rather contrived number for twelve dancers in pimento, black, and white creates the break for applause for which Balanchine had searched so long (and a dancer like Merrill Ashley can whip up a real stir), but to me it is Balanchine conceding his failure to meet the special demands of Act I. When we pick up the Don again, he's already a famous madman. And the Marcela episode, previously the high point of the act, is undercut, because Marcela is no longer the first ballerina the audience sees.

The Pas Classique corresponds to the wedding divertissement that is danced in the Petipa ballet by Kitri and Basil. Up to its insertion, Balanchine had avoided the idiom of ballet Spanish—I assumed because he thought it a cliché. Of course, there is still that non-cliché suite of exotic dances in the second act—dances so heavy with perfumes of Ethiopia, Morocco, and Bali that an innocent little Courante Sicilienne looks out of place. Unlike the Pas Classique, the court divertissement is a contribution to the ballet's atmosphere. Probably the dancers are the Duke's slaves (and the counterpart to Petipa's gypsies), but their pagan sensuality is no affront to the Christian knight. He suffers instead a ritual hazing at the hands of decadent courtiers, is beaten, mocked, and scourged. It's in this act that the ballet's beauties start to mount up and the drama of Don Quixote truly begins. For the courtiers' sarabande, the Pas de Deux Mauresque, the ghastly masquerade of the hazing, and the spectacle of a pathetic staggering old man braced by the young girl of his dream, Nabokov has provided good, even memorable music, and there is more of it in the pas d'action of the last act—a frenzied solo for Dulcinea, a racing coda. But, music or no music, Balanchine is now in complete command of the action and his invention soars.

The ballet has always been a soloists' display case. More débuts took place in these six performances than in the whole winter season. Foremost among them was Lüders as the Don. Where Balanchine suggested a vigorous grandee, Lüders—like Richard Rapp, who was the first to take the role over from Balanchine—looks mild and frail. But Lüders is different from all the other young men who have played this role. He doesn't have to cover up so much of himself. His small head might be the shrunken skull of an old man. With his pale coloring and deep-set eyes, he suggests a fanatic whose brain has been burned dry by obsession, but he has the strength of that obsession, too. His long legs are stiff with bravado. And he pursues Dulcinea as an ideal, not as a woman. In the dancing roles, new and compelling images were created by Kyra Nichols in the Rigaudon Flamenco, Peter Naumann (in a good makeup) in the Danza de la Caccia, and Nichol Hlinka in the Pas de Deux Mauresque. Nichols made an event of size and power out of the presto variation in Act II but, like everyone else who has danced it since Marnee Morris, missed the amazing full stop in attitude fondue. Stephanie Saland's dancing in the companion variation and in the Ritornel was lovely to see, impossible to feel; Susan Hendl in the same roles was smaller but stronger in contour and attack. Act III is, of course, Farrell's act. It is the young, hungrily and almost heedlessly expansive Farrell who is on view here, and the Farrell of today dances her former self with no loss of rapacity. On opening night, I thought she looked underpowered except in the heavenly lifts guided by Sean Lavery. But by the closing performance she was delivering miracles: performing further out on the periphery of her balance than I had ever seen her—all but falling—and with absolute confidence in that gyroscopic center of hers. Did Balanchine ever really say "Ballet is woman"? He did say, in a *Life* article at about the time of the première of *Don Quixote*: "Ballet is one place where art flourishes because of a woman: woman is the goddess, the poetess, the muse. That is why I have a company with beautiful girl dancers. I believe the same is true of life, that everything man does he does for his ideal woman. You live only one life and you believe in something and I believe in a little thing like that."

—*March 6, 1978*

The Mercists

Spring thaw in New York always brings us the modern dance. Would that it brought us another name for it. The species of theatrical performance which developed largely outside the spectacular opera-house ballet tradition and which we call Modern Dance is, like Romantic Ballet, a part of history. Labels are prejudicial and confining, but we need some other way to refer to dancing that is more than one generation removed from Martha Graham, who is going on eighty-four years old. I have heard "post-modern," and its very weakness and temporariness recommend it. For the recycling age we live in, post-anything sounds right. Actually, in dance there's a fairly explicit tradition that for years has cried out to be called—after its preceptor—mercism. If Ruth St. Denis and Ted Shawn could become a noun (Denishawn), why not Merce Cunningham? We have had mercist companies for quite a while now. Even as Cunningham himself goes on dancing and choreographing, companies headed by his descendants and disciples pop up everywhere. They've been especially ubiquitous in the past few weeks, appearing at Dance Umbrella, at the American Theatre Laboratory, and at Cunningham's studio in Westbeth. The climax of the series was a two-week stand by the Cunningham company itself at the Roundabout Theatre.

Mercism isn't the only kind of downtown dance activity, and its manifestations are diverse. But generally one identifies it by a commitment to dancing exclusive of music or décor. This commitment to the dancer moving in silence and creating his own space reflects one of Cunningham's paramount concerns—the one that he has held on to longest. Passing concerns of his (happenings, improvisation, nondance experimentation) recur ghostily in the work of a permanent radical fringe that borders both dance and the spoken theatre. At the moment, we can see one of those periodic inflations of a Cunningham idea taking hold in this sector. Just as the younger generation in the sixties inflated Cunningham's proposition that any movement can become *part of* a dance into "Any movement can be a dance," there are those who are now expanding his insight about the ambiguity of movement into a fascination with ambiguity in all things. Often surface appearances aren't merely allowed to contradict each other, they're directed to. Applied ambiguity blankets many post-modern evenings. One is apt to find more props than dancing; sound runs to verbal texts. Dance reviews, with their endless speculative remarks about roses that could be noses or whatever the mind supposes, are beginning to mirror the lifeless quandaries posed by these students of the mystique of ambiguity. When faced with one of their impenetrable puzzles, I think of John Cage's advice to Richard Kostelanetz: "Use your experience no matter where you are." It is good advice. Taking the responsibility for the effect of a piece—following what Cage called (in Kostelanetz's book about him) the "nonintentional" aspect—can sometimes be the only way to watch it. And there's always the possibility that what is not intended may be more effective, and even more productive of "meaning," than what is. In Mel Wong's *Harbor*, at ATL, the dancing became involved with a display of conceptual art. After about twenty minutes of total inscrutability, I knew I was going to have to get *Harbor* unjammed from an unworkable intention. Wong happens to be a skilled choreographer in the mercist vein, and I found I could enjoy the dancing even though I couldn't tell what it was meant to be about. *Harbor*, though, is far too long to experience just on this level. I couldn't play with pure dance and accidental ambience for the nearly two hours that Wong had chosen to press his intention. As he became more abstruse, with the dancers declaiming numbers or speaking fragmentary sentences or pouring colored water from various plastic containers, I had to become less so—less privately and more professionally interested in what I was seeing. It's not my favorite way of watching, but one can't make mystery out of ready-made mystique. One can't and still hold on to one's respect for the dance craftsman that Wong so truly is.

At mercist lecture-demonstrations, audiences will sometimes ask how much they should know of the creative methods used in a dance in order to appreciate it. The question, not at all a dismissible one, means that they've detected the presence of a process that doesn't disappear into a result. It may also mean that the process looks as if it would be more interesting to watch or to know about than the actual dance it has produced. Process is often deliberately on view in mercist pieces; it's right up there in Viola Farber works, inseparable from production. My difficulty with Farber is that the process is too obvious: the sectional construction, for instance, that tells me where one day's composing ends and the next day's begins. And one day is as good as another—the process isn't selective. Farber may be the purest mercist around, although I'm told she has no intention of imitating Cunningham's approach to composition. Her work is like Abstract Expressionist painting. You follow it (as you follow all dancing) for the *act* of creation, not for the sake of some disembodied product that creation leaves behind; but you also get the record of what creation involves—you get interruptions and distractions and second thoughts and wipeouts. If Farber were capable of virtuoso brushwork, a long, chuntering piece like *Dinosaur Parts*, seen at Dance Umbrella, might be wonderful. In a new work, *Turf*, she seems to have narrowed and concentrated her means. I watched it with absorption and wondered how much the use of Poulenc's organ concerto alongside the dancing had to do with the relatively flexible and tidy effect. (The David Tudor score used for *Dinosaur Parts* affected me like a dentist's drill.)

Cunningham has initiated more new ideas for theatrical performance than any other choreographer. It's no wonder he has so many followers. Because the material he has brought into being is so richly suggestive, any number can play. When a Cunningham-inspired idea fails, one is still glad it has been tried. Yet ideas by themselves don't make art; they do tend to disappear the moment they're realized. In Cunningham's own best work, as in all works of art, a negotiable idea becomes transparent expression; nothing is left of it but the talent that produced it in the first place. No one who has been influenced by him is working anywhere near Cunningham's level, and one sees—and hears—lots of ideas. Many choreographers, mercist and nonmercist, have tried to get spoken words to work as an accompaniment to dance. The mercist method is to have no direct correspondence between the words and the movement. However, not even Cunningham himself has managed to make them equal partners. Words always dominate; arranged in nonsensical patterns, they still steal the attention away from dance. (The relationship is like that of words to music. Most people identify a song's meaning through its lyric, not through its music. Irving Berlin's "Blue Skies," for example, is a "happy" song, even though its music is a dirge.) Margaret Jenkins, a San Francisco–based choreographer who taught for many years at Cunningham's New York school, collaborates frequently with a poet, Michael Palmer. A voice-over, speaking words in several of the Jenkins pieces that were done recently at Westbeth, forced me to consider meanings that didn't seem to belong to the dances. *About the Space In Between* had a text dealing with Ludwig Wittgenstein, but for me it was really "about" what the title declared it to be about. Jenkins has a keenly sculptural sense of negative space, which she often exploits choreographically both in her own dancing and in that of the group. A void may appear, speaking volumes, only to be retracted, altered, or recharged by a solid shape. Jenkins dancers are firmly centered (centering to dancers and potters means the same thing), and though not especially wide in turnout, they have a powerful thrust from the inside of the thigh. The strong legs and strong, flexible feet are legacies from Cunningham, emphasized by Jenkins. Such emphases give these dancers a uniform noneclectic technique. The foremost mercist company on the West Coast, they appear to be specialists in a very special, insular sense. Not that they're provincial; at least one piece, the epigrammatic *Videosongs*, would have made the reputation of any New York company. But both in the excessively brainy pieces and in the straitened technique there's a little too much hothouse conditioning. More New York appearances would be good for them and us.

A very impressive sound accompaniment to a couple of Cunningham's Events in his Roundabout series was devised by John Cage from his *Mesostics re Merce Cunningham*. The *Mesostics* (a variation on acrostics) are made of words, but they impinge on the ear as pure sound consisting of discrete syllables. Cage published his puzzle poems a few years ago, using within each one many different Letraset typefaces and sizes. He then used the typefaces and sizes as musical notation, letting them dictate pitch, timbre, loudness, and duration. At the Events, the *Mesostic* songs didn't reverse the usual effect of verbal texts on dance, and this was because their performance by the Greek tenor Demetrio Stratos was overwhelming in its virtuosity. Stratos has a voice like no other I've heard; he can switch registers so that they seem to overlap, he can produce drones and ululations with uncanny bell-like overtones, and from a lesser artist than Merce Cunningham he would have stolen the show. I saw the second of two performances with Stratos. Cunningham performed more than he had the week before, when the sound was electronically produced by David Tudor. He was obviously responding to a challenge, and he drew from himself an extraordinary variety of movement, some of it unmistakably and unerringly timed to coincide with Stratos's singing. He is just now in excellent diabolical form, and the occasion brought out his weirdest strokes of wit and drama. He twice held a difficult pose on a bench a very long time while the company danced. He did a slow, foppish solo, full of sly, curlicuing wrists and implied flashes of lace handkerchief. After an appalling minute of complete silence on an empty stage, he entered wearing white coveralls and lay face down, without moving, for another minute. Perhaps his best dance moment was a kind of fractured conga in those same coveralls. Cunningham, now in his late fifties, avoids extremes of movement; he holds to his middle range and makes it seem like a full diapason. All his effects are concentrated, delicate, precise, yet never small. As for the company, the constant addition of new members keeps it looking on the green side, although much individual progress is being made. At the two Events I saw, the choreography was drawn in full or in part from *Torse, Winterbranch, Changing Steps, Canfield*, the wonderful and seldom performed trio called *Crosscurrents*, and *Westbeth*, a made-for-TV work. Cunningham's personal repertory consisted of an apparently endless supply of solos that he keeps in his sleeve.

No one who saw Gus Solomons, Jr., performing with the Cunningham company in the sixties can forget the impact of his tall body and fantastically long legs—as long and thin above the knee as they are below. Solomons could easily have been a male Judith Jamison; instead, he has become a serious choreographer. The company he brought to the Dance Umbrella was the second one of his I've seen; it's young and sunny. Solomons still looks all line, with relatively little muscle—a man who has grown stilts. He did a solo called *Signals* while his music director, Mio Morales, attempted a bit of Demetrio Stratos. *PsychoMotorWorks*, an ongoing company project, had a lot of classical ballet in it, in the form of syllabus positions. Two excerpts were performed; both ended with lively sets of allegro in which Solomons tried for speedy, agile footwork—the only one of Cunningham's adherents, as far as I know, to do so. But outside ballet no one except Cunningham has the secret of allegro. *Bone Jam* was about life experience.

It bounced along in episodes broken by blackouts. The dancers, wearing half-masks, appeared in everything from underwear to overcoats, and the movement, which included a good many jokes, ranged from rag-doll limpness to long, clear sweeps and hard, directional changes on a big scale. It was one of what might be called Solomons's junk dances, but there weren't so many bottle caps this time. A good, entertaining piece.

Speaking of life experience, the remarkable thing about the mercists is their aesthetic unity. Their backgrounds are widely dissimilar (Mel Wong is of Chinese descent; Gus Solomons, Jr., is black), and their dancing has been a melting pot. Mercism is really about dancing as experience; it has a built-in dryness and objectivity, and from both dancer and spectator it demands a certain taste for the leaner virtues, for moral disinterestedness. Many people, especially Europeans, find that antitheatrical. Privileged deprivation may be an exclusively American trait—Wasp American, at that. Théâtre du Silence, a French company with a modern repertory, opened its New York season (at the Beacon) with a highly unreticent version of Cunningham's greatest lyrical piece, *Summerspace*. The Rauschenberg stippled backcloth was bathed in an orange glow, the sparse piano score, by Morton Feldman, was overamplified, and the dancing was heavy and coarse. It's a company of lusty athletes; one gets the impression that for the French, avant-garde dance is a form of *le sport* or *le sexe*. Whether they know it or not, the French are temperamentally non-mercist (*non, merci*).

I heard people say that, before they knew better, they took the Théâtre du Silence to be a deaf-and-dumb theatre. That made me think of Remy Charlip and how much I wish I'd seen his work for the National Theatre of the Deaf and the dances that were derived from it. Charlip was once a member of the Cunningham company, creating roles in *Summerspace*, *Rune*, and *Antic Meet*, among other pieces. He's a noted designer, an illustrator and author of children's books, as well as a dancer and choreographer, and his gift for visualization and animation stops, apparently, at nothing. There never has been anything like his collaborations, a decade ago, with Al Carmines, the most amazing of which actually wrung a dance oratorio from *The Sayings of Mao Tse-tung*. These days, he is working in theatre mostly as a soloist, but in any one of his appearances all his talents manage to be on view. At his Dance Umbrella concert, he began by having his silhouette traced head to toe on brown paper with the arms showing different positions. Then he painted the silhouette blue and flew it as an ensign for the rest of the program. Everything about Charlip suggests consistency, smoothness, and wholeness. His cookie-cutter silhouette, his drawings, and his dances all resemble each other. His art is mime-based, but he is able to draw more abstract inferences from mime than many choreographers can from dance. In *Glow Worm*, he moved about the stage telling stories of his boyhood aloud and using the sign language of the deaf as a counterpoint to both movement and speech. The words, the mime language, and the mime movement supported each other gracefully, but the clear separation between them suggested melancholy dissociation. It's an effect Charlip gets by means of pure mimicry in *Meditation*. As Massenet's insulting, silky music plays on, Charlip slowly contorts his face in a series of agonized or grotesque expressions divorced from emotional contexts. He works on a very small scale with exquisite balance and discretion. Charlip is someone who might look at home in Japanese ceremonial dress. A lightweight, yes, but also a master.

—*April 3, 1978*

Broadway Downbeat

Book musicals are dying, revues are dead. One-man shows and chorus lines survive, with nothing in between. No-star ensembles are in, along with "theme" collages instead of plots, and the choreographer is still king of Broadway. I go to musicals hoping for a renaissance of musical comedy, but most of the shows around are apologetic tributes to bygone eras that didn't question, as our era seems to, the very idea of light, upbeat, lyrical entertainment. *Annie* and *On the Twentieth Century* are set in the thirties, as if by evoking an extraordinary musical-comedy era they could awaken the genre. Then there are the actual revivals, like *The King and I* and *Hello, Dolly!*, both of them choreographer-directed shows, and *Timbuktu!*, which is a restaging of *Kismet* by the choreographer Geoffrey Holder. *Timbuktu!* shows Holder at top strength not as a director or choreographer but as a costume designer. He uses color and line in fabric with a sense of scale and fantasy that isn't in his staging. The whole production is static but gorgeous: more baubles, bangles, and beads than ever before, with no armature to hang them from. The musical *Kismet* was an Arabian Nights spectacle; most of the songs, based on melodies by wise old Borodin, have been kept in the current version, which takes place in Moslem Africa and has an all-black cast. The lyrics about drifting and sifting and ascending out of the commonplace into the rare have the same wax-fruity beauty they had in Baghdad. Holder's boom-lay-boom African dances are as unserious as the original "Orientale" choreography, by Jack Cole. But instead of the bulging edifice of operetta the show keeps on building sumptuous friezes made of costumes. The first-act finale to "Night of My Nights" is a procession very like the one in Holder's ballet *Dougla*. When it leaves the stage for the aisles of the Mark Hellinger, we don't feel it has spilled over because of excess. With so many cubic feet of unused stage space, Holder hasn't earned the right to that kind of gesture.

Timbuktu! reduces the spectacle of *Kismet* to one decorative element. In

On the Twentieth Century, the show is Robin Wagner's train set. Bob Fosse's *Dancin'* actually congratulates itself, in a spoken prologue, for ascending into the rare by dispensing with plot and characters, just as if every other musical in town were stuffed with boys meeting girls. The trend toward the reductive, the skeletal, the downright monomaniacal has been in motion a long time. It's a natural consequence of expecting one omnipotent soul—generally a choreographer—to be responsible for not only how a show looks but what it is about. Fosse himself provided the content—such as it was—of *Chicago*, a few seasons ago. The book, of which he was co-author, was only an excuse for the irrationally obscene conceits he piled on in the staging. For a book show, *Chicago* was as near to decadent abstraction as it could possibly get, and by eliminating the book altogether *Dancin'* takes the logical next step. Supposedly, in showcasing Fosse's talent as a choreographer rather than as a choreographer-*auteur*, *Dancin'* frees him from the taint of decadence, because if decadence is style trying to do the work of substance, surely whatever substance there can be in an all-dance show is more than accounted for in the style. The position of most reviewers of *Dancin'* has been that it's perfectly good as a dance show if dance is what you want, but not if you want a real musical. I agree that it's no substitute for a musical, but I don't agree with the implication that Fosse's kind of dance show is the best you can get. Is it because Fosse's style has dominated show dancing for so long that we've come to accept them as synonyms? Fosse *always* puts style in place of substance, even when the substance is dance. In *Dancin'*, as in *Chicago* and other shows, he doesn't work in dance terms—he works in images. In its own way, *Dancin'* is as static as *Timbuktu!* Fosse's images don't arise spontaneously out of links and contrasts between dance shapes, they're locked into those convulsive, writhing movement-chunks he habitually makes his dances out of. His choreography is without wings—literally and imaginatively grounded. But it always makes instantaneous contact with an audience.

Few choreographers have succeeded without a sense of the kinetic. Massine, the most successful choreographer of his day, was one. Fosse, with Broadway and Hollywood at his feet, has been successful beyond anything Massine could have approached, and now, as if demonstrating his freedom from the compromises and restrictions that go to make a commercial success, he stages on Broadway the kind of event that belongs more properly to the world that was once Massine's. But even in that world the choreographers who can sustain a whole evening by themselves are few. *Dancin'* is sustained on Fosse's nerve. He's not just a Broadway choreographer doing ballet's thing; he's trying to use the medium of choreography to stretch unkinetic images into dances. Brendan Gill, in reviewing the show a couple of weeks ago, spoke of it as "unabashedly self-celebrating." For all its brashness, the show is remarkably self-aware, too. Fosse knows his limitations, and he knows how to make them look like powerful artistic choices marked by daring and style. He even throws us off the scent by claiming to have chosen the only course open to him. More breathtaking than his claim to have got rid of plot lines is his inclusion of a "tour de force" in which the dancers nail their clogs to the floor and perform a whole number without moving their feet. Footwork has about as much to do with Fosse style as lariat-twirling: gyrating body shapes are the essence of that style. Shoulders roll, pelvises grind, and knees boggle; the feet aren't in it. "A Manic Depressive's Lament" is about someone who's glad to be unhappy. The song ("I've Got Them Feelin' Too Good Today Blues," by Jerry Leiber and Mike Stoller) and the dance that goes with it *seem* to go against tradition, but Fosse's movement, which is nothing if not a tradition, is naturally manic-depressive. It suits the ambivalent mood of show business today, and it turns perennial "up" numbers like the strutting top-hat-and-tails routine into downers. (The latest example of the up-downer occurs in *The Act,* a show starring Liza Minnelli, with dances by Ron Lewis.) Buoyancy, gaiety, optimism are beyond the limits of this strenuous low-down technique. When Fosse wants to get happy, he's still strenuous. Squeezing out happy juice, he gets syrupy. The most wistful number in the show is "Dancin' Man," a tribute to Fred Astaire. The dancers, instead of tapping, slap their thighs numb. We know it's the best they can do.

Fosse's dancers often seem to be winding themselves around a core of wistfulness. Inside his dance is a better one trying to get out. Some of his coolest images are impressions of the effect that truly elegant show dancing has upon us: they're externalizations of a feeling about dance. The feeling is openly presented. The dancers look out at us; they trust us to know what they mean. A number such as "Recollections of an Old Dancer" is disarming and boring at the same time. Boring because it doesn't move like a dance, disarming because it speaks right up and says it never meant to. "Recollections," a quasi soft-shoe, is relatively gentle. Fosse's dancers strike attitudes as representative as public statues, and in the hard-punching numbers they can seem to grow to frighteningly huge, pythonesque proportions. They're like big photo-realist paintings come to life. At their cheapest, they're editorial cartoons. The would-be satirical closer, "America," is wearily efficient rather than scathing. Although it's one of the show's two big mistakes, a moment in it has conviction—American women pictured as infantile sluts. It's as appalling as anything in *Chicago.* "The Dream Barre," in which Charles Ward as a timid ballet student fantasizes his seduction of the girl next to him in class, is the other big mistake—not just because it's slobberingly offensive but because it's off base as satire. Nobody except Ward looks like a ballet dancer. Show dancers with unstretched thighs should do their barres backstage.

Jerking from one stance to the next like flip pictures, Fosse's dancers are best when they are backed up by a pounding beat. "Percussion," a fast, slick suite of dances to drums, cymbals, and other noisemakers, is a demonstration of your classic Fosse twitch-and-slink. The suite includes a solo to Varèse's *Ionisation*: not good. Neither Charles Ward nor the pit traps player has the virtuosity Fosse needs here. The big killer in the show is "Benny's Number," staged to an arrangement of "Sing, Sing, Sing" as recorded at Benny Goodman's 1938 Carnegie Hall concert and played live by stand-ins for Goodman, Gene Krupa, Harry James, Jess Stacy, and the others. The music is a powerhouse that shakes Fosse loose from some of his mannerisms, but he really responds only to "Krupa." In the musical passages, he is dismayingly literal. When "Goodman" slides to his famous high C above A, what do we see but the boys sliding their hands up the girls' thighs, and for the (equally famous) odd and delicate "Stacy" interlude he uses a curious sidling tap duet that mimics the music. "Benny's Number" looks like something Fosse has meant to do for a long time, and you can't watch it without wanting with your whole soul to see it work. Fosse succeeds in putting it over—but as a conventional show-stopper, with ladders and trapezes in the finale. This is, after all, jazz, and Fosse's experience is with show music. He hasn't developed the range for the jazz epic that "Sing, Sing, Sing" is. With the relatively modest big-band forces of "Big Noise from Winnetka" he's on safer ground, and he turns out another Fosse classic— one that resembles his memorable trio "Steam Heat." The "Winnetka" number doesn't sink in—it's little more than a crossover during a stage wait. But the throwaway may be a deliberate reminder of the stage wait in *The Pajama Game* that made "Steam Heat" possible.

Fosse's involvement in the material he uses for *Dancin'* is inescapable. The show discloses and focusses his personality and his abilities as no other show yet has; it's practically confessional theatre. It confirms and defines his talent, while aiding our suspicion that he is a driven and cynical man, but it also reveals a degree of self-knowledge that isn't given to many in the entertainment field, and here I include Fosse's peers in the "artistic" branch of the profession. Only two doors down the street from *Dancin'*, Rudolf Nureyev is appearing, for the first part of his stand at the Minskoff, in dances by Murray Louis. Of course, there's no one in the cast of *Dancin'* like Nureyev or with any real star wattage to speak of, and Murray Louis has credentials as an artist which Fosse doesn't have. Yet when a Broadway engagement in the glare of Nureyev's publicity holds those credentials up to the light, Louis comes off as knowing a lot less about his craft and his capabilities than Fosse does about his. Louis is a twitcher, too, and the quality of the movement he gives his dancers—rigid above the hips, spongy below, as if they were so many beanbag ashtrays—may be no worse in its way than Fosse's patented slither. But the follow-the-bouncing-ball choreography is, I think, a good deal worse, because it's habitually set to Ravel or Bach or Schubert. When it's set to Cole Porter songs (arranged by William Bolcom), it tells obvious jokes; we can laugh, because we know it isn't art anymore.

The name of Louis's Cole Porter ballet is *The Canarsie Venus*, and the action, which is reminiscent of the 1943 musical *One Touch of Venus*, fits right in with Broadway nostalgia. It has a Walter Mitty type (Nureyev, if you please) being seduced by the goddess (Anne McLeod), who has been washed up on a beach crowded with litterbugs. Fosse, in *Dancin'*, may be aspiring to the crown of choreography, but he hasn't given up being a showman. Showmanship in Louis's case means that his usual crudity turns into fatuous sleaze. The simple little story of Nureyev changing from mouse into lion under the goddess's touch isn't made clear. As a comedian under Louis's direction, Nureyev is vacant and heavy. It doesn't hurt his popularity with the audience. Like Liza Minnelli, he's impervious to flops. Nevertheless, it's sad to see him, too, hitting Broadway in a down show.

—*April 24, 1978*

Studying the Masters

The Shuberts, who booked the Eliot Feld Ballet this winter in Los Angeles, have just presented the company here, at the Plymouth. If the trend continues, this time next year Broadway houses will be filled with dance attractions. The big draw at the Plymouth was the guest artist, Mikhail Baryshnikov, in a new solo devised by Feld. The last time Feld and Baryshnikov worked together, they produced a messy, bad-boy parody of a superstar turn. Parts of *Santa Fe Saga*, the new number, look like a sobered-up version of that earlier piece, but the juvenile swagger has, if anything, become more pronounced. And what Feld means by it is a question. *Santa Fe Saga* seems to deal simultaneously with a boy's dream of Wild West virility and an adult's scorn of stereotypes. It isn't very clear-minded, and Baryshnikov, in a set of campy buckskins, danced the role more honorably than Feld may have intended.

Fortunately, Feld's other new ballet, *La Vida*, is one of his good ones. Set to Aaron Copland's brief orchestral rhapsody *El Salón México*, it doesn't make the mistake of trying to develop more action than the music can hold; it develops just enough. Indeed, the choreography is practically toe-to-toe with this flamboyant yet tightly controlled score, and when the music is over, there isn't a drop left of the ballet. Feld has understood the deceptive latitude of the score. He responds to it by taking two or three visual motifs and turning them obsessively this way and that, until their clustering facets produce a compacted vista we can identify with Copland's. *La Vida* looks like a Mexican mural exploding inside a Lucite cube. The *salón* becomes a visible boxed space. To say that little happens within the space may be perfectly true; little that looks like dancing is allowed by the structure of the score. *El Salón México* is not one of Copland's ballet scores, and although some of the movement adapts Mexican folk dances, most of it is a hermetic reconstitution of the art works that other people have made on Mexican themes. *La Vida* is Feld's name for what we recognize as "El Arte." An anthology of impressions of impressions, the ballet is always one or two removes from its ostensible subject. Feld's purely conceptual approach doesn't suggest the processions in *Billy the Kid* as much as it does George Platt Lynes's photographs of *Billy* or of another "Mexican" ballet of the same period, Paul Bowles's *Pastorela*. A poncho handled with stiffly hieratic implications and a dance with a snake headdress are very reminiscent of Martha Graham's terminology in such a piece as *El Penitente*. But my guess is that Feld mainly has in mind the murals of artists like José Orozco. When he slings girls head downward on men's backs, he gets a toiling-peasant/ beast-of-burden theme to merge with decorative chevron patterns, just as Orozco did. And his surrealistic jokes—female legs sprouting from male backs, a phallic sombrero turned flowerlike to the sun—supply the same touch of comic distortion to the landscape which one hears in the music.

Feld's designer, Willa Kim, whom I usually find incapable of seriousness, here restricts herself to the few iconographic shapes that are essential to Feld's idea. Her hot, earth-toned colors, her bands and striations are forceful, clear, and true to the subject, and Feld skillfully integrates them with his choreography. The only dubious note is the overstylized snake headdress. It's largely because of Kim's frivolity that *Santa Fe Saga* doesn't look like the companion piece to *La Vida* that it was evidently meant to be. Whereas in *La Vida* Feld collaborated with Kim, here he permits her to set the tone. She sets it low, with tarty leather peekaboo chaps that turn Baryshnikov into a midnight cowboy, an image so dumb that Feld's attitudinizing and woolgathering become openly pompous. He's like some infatuated but hopelessly distant European discoursing on the Far West (*la psychologie du centaurisme*, perhaps). The Morton Gould music is strident rather than flamboyant, and the choreography confuses consistency with repetition. Baryshnikov's joyous baroque spirit as well as his Russianness gives the whole thing language difficulties. Feld's method as a choreographer is a frank attempt to make art out of art by copying existing models in other people's ballets. Sometimes he succeeds in converting a model to his own purposes; often he achieves only a reduction. *La Vida* seems to have worked because it synthesizes many models in many art forms; it gave Feld room to make an original statement. But *Santa Fe Saga* picks apart and rehashes antinomies that were perfectly intertwined in the singular poetic statement made by Eugene Loring long ago in his portrait of Billy the Kid. Feld once danced the role of Billy at American Ballet Theatre. He adds nothing to our idea of it now but his willingness to keep us up half the night talking about it.

The first thought that occurs to most people who are struck by the absence of craft in new choreography is that the new choreographers aren't watching the right models. The assumption is that they know what to watch for. Many young choreographers are blind to the presence of craftsmanship and many more prefer to work exclusively from their own habits and proclivities as dancers, spinning choreography out of their bodies like silkworms. A lot of the choreography that we see is studio work passing for performance. It's rare to find a choreographer who watches and learns as well as Daniel Levans does. One of the directors of the youthful company that calls itself U.S. Terpsichore, Levans has been making ballets only since 1974. Each one seems to have taught him something new. In this, he's like the young Eliot Feld, who set out to learn his craft by doing what the masters had done before him. Levans doesn't work as close to the originals as Feld did and still does. The first two pieces of his that I saw were a Bach ballet that was much more than "one of those" and a captivating version of Stravinsky's Duo Concertant that in no way resembled the familiar version by Balanchine. This season, during the company's stand at the Brandeis High School auditorium, I managed to see two more Levanses, and again both of them struck me as enterprising works that had obviously been aimed at extending his skill into new areas of expression. But they were also talented, secure, and satisfying on a level well beyond apprenticeship. The more daring of the two, a première, was a large group piece in the Russian grand manner arranged to Glazunov waltzes. Almost no one but Balanchine and Ashton composes in this tradition anymore, and one would not have expected a twenty-four-year-old American choreographer, working without live music or experienced dancers, to produce the glistening bubbleweight ballet that Levans produced and to sustain, moreover, a sense of period style. Levans went back even further than Balanchine and Ashton, using only steps that would have been known to Petipa.

But the key to Levans's success wasn't in the steps; he doesn't in any of his pieces strive for steps that are in themselves striking. (It is a mistake to identify invention with the appearance of a vivid step.) Levans seems able to look beyond components to the entire wide, variable range of connections between dance phrases and musical ones out of which a ballet is built. He sees the sweep of that kind of continuity, both its immediate gratification and its long-run effect. That is, I *felt* much of the time during *Concert Waltzes* that he saw those things or soon would see them; although the ballet was lively and buoyant, it wasn't consistently clear in its design. The other amazing thing about the piece, besides this grasp of a key principle, was that, for something so traditional, it didn't look derivative—didn't look like Balanchine, or even like Petipa. Maybe it looked like Levans, though he's still experimenting in too many styles for us to tell. Oddly enough, the only work of his I know that does recall someone else's is another piece on the same program—*Canciones Amatorias*, to the Granados songs—and it recalls Feld. Levans was (as Levins) a soloist in Feld's first company; he played Arnold, the choreographer in the film *The Turning Point* who seems to have been based on Feld. But I don't think the relation needs to be stressed. Levans has already declared his independence and his promise.

Although Levans has obviously picked up a lot from established choreographers, he may have gained his most crucial perceptions by instinct, before he began to study choreography formally. Access to great ballets is certainly good for the aspiring choreographer, but it doesn't seem to make the difference it should make. Oscar Araiz is an Argentine who works in Canada as resident choreographer for the Royal Winnipeg Ballet. I've no idea how many masterpieces Araiz has seen; from the look of his work, which has been shown here recently both by the Winnipeg and by the Joffrey, I'd say very few. Yet Araiz seems to have grasped the same essential principle that Levans has. In quality of expression, there's no comparing the two. Levans has elegant taste, and Araiz's is naive and indiscriminate. He has absorbed, too, a lot of the poisonous, phony rhetoric of American modern dance. Apparently, he believes himself to be a dramatist concerned with character and conflict, but his gift is for absolute dance drama, with no connection to psychology. All the pieces of his I've seen are disappointing even when they're not outright failures, because Araiz never makes a move that isn't captioned, and many of the captions are unintelligible. Yet, seen sheerly as dance events timed to musical scores, the same ballets can have unusual scope and power.

Actually, you don't need to adjust your way of looking; the unwaveringly acute rhythm pours right through the text it was designed to support. I'm thinking now of the piece called *Heptagon*, which just entered the Joffrey repertory—not the *Romeo and Juliet* that has been there awhile. This *Romeo* doesn't work on any level. Araiz scraps the known story and starts with a troupe of dancers who divide themselves into factions. Hostilities break out, they start putting on costumes, and soon they're identifying themselves with Shakespeare's characters. But the Prokofiev score, which sticks pretty closely to the play's scenario, still isn't given its due. Araiz drops parts of the musical narrative, uses other parts for protracted dance arias, and undermines emotional logic by casting three ballerinas, one after another, in the role of Juliet. (Doesn't this also undermine sanity? Have alter egos ever worked in dance?) What marvellous new sense it is all supposed to make is likely to elude us as the fights and killings pile up in the music, leaving Araiz no choice but to follow the plot just as closely as Lavrovsky and MacMillan and Cranko did in their productions. Araiz can't tell us a better story than Shakespeare and Prokofiev do. Neither can he make us forget that story; it's too much for him, as it would be for anyone else who tried to reduce it to skeletal fragments in the interests of a higher and purer expression.

In his version of *The Rite of Spring*, performed here by the Winnipeg,

Araiz again did variations on the story that is written into the music, and again the meanings were stuck onto the movements instead of being discharged by them. Not that Araiz should have told Stravinsky's story straight —he's no storyteller at all. I was impatient with the ballet, and yet I couldn't look away from the stage. The finale was something I won't forget, though I can't remember what in the scenario called it forth: a girl climbs halfway up a pyramid of bodies, falls back down, tries again, and is still trying with a desperate hunger to reach the top when the lights go out. Though he is not yet forty, Araiz seems set in his ways, and will probably never abandon his chosen idiom. And why should he, when truly dismal failures like *Family Scenes* win him praise? Done for his Argentine company, the ballet misuses Poulenc's Concerto for Two Pianos as a setting for a strained drama about prim people in starched collars. Araiz hears none of the wit and irony in the music. Strangely, it's another Poulenc score, the Organ Concerto, that gives him his best ballet. Everybody's using that concerto these days; Araiz's use of it in *Heptagon* shows more persuasively than anything else of his I could mention the raw dance power that even a sanctimonious thesis—disciples will turn on their master—can't conceal.

Sometimes coincidences occur in the use of a plot or a score that are like unannounced contests. The palm for the worst extant setting of *The Rite* undoubtedly goes to Glen Tetley for his production at Ballet Theatre; it's weak in every way that it can be, save—sometimes—performance. *Heptagon* is superior to José Limón's *The Traitor*, with which it shares a plot, and it is far superior to Tetley's *Voluntaries*, with which it shares a score. I guess people think Tetley makes dancers look sexy. Dancers in his ballets, wearing their inevitable luxe unitards, always seem to be writhing and stretching in a steam bath. Tetley emphasizes turns and extensions and lifts as exposés of the body beautiful. There's never any dance meaning in his sequences; the continuity seems designed to keep dancers narcissistically happy with their reflections in the studio mirror. If ever there was a repertory composed in the isolation of the studio, Tetley's is it; he's the ultimate silkworm. Dancers love the workout his ballets give them, and audiences love to see them working out. But shouldn't there be a little more to a ballet than dancercise? Tetley has no rhythm, either plot-related or music-related; he has no ideas; he hasn't even a sense of the kitsch he's perpetrating in the guise of art. His latest ballet for ABT, *Sphinx*, enters the repertory with straight-faced program notes on Greek mythology and Cocteau, whose *La Machine Infernale* gives the ballet its semblance of a structure. Well, Cocteau would have known that you'd have to do more with the big stainless-steel playground slide that Rouben Ter-Arutunian provides for the Sphinx's throne than just lie on it. Can't it move? Can't those four-story-high wings be portals for entrances and exits? Can't Martine van Hamel as the Sphinx be a glamorous creature instead of a dull and stuffy dancer working on her routines? And can't Clark Tippet and Kirk Peterson, who play Oedipus and Anubis (the jackal-headed god of the dead, the program explains), be more than two other dancers using the same studio? The music going on in the background is unbelievably the same Martinů concerto that Paul Taylor used for one of the most exciting sections of *American Genesis*. And Willa Kim's unitards, decorated with wispy reminders of Noguchi's Greek bones-and-entrails period, hold whatever theatrical style the piece can claim.

Van Hamel is too large a woman to lift easily or she might have been treated like the women in *Voluntaries,* who get hauled around like dead weights. And the movement—not just the lifts—is peculiarly crotch-happy. The women who spread themselves in midair or on the ground, their part-ners who can't seem to put their hands anyplace else. . .   After a quarter hour of this has passed and no other sound has arisen besides the music's reverent groan, one starts to think that Tetley may be having us all on. *Voluntaries* is his tribute to John Cranko and is said to be Tetley's best bal-let. Let those who see in him a vigorous creator decide which is his worst, and let Heaven defend Cranko from his friends. The Joffrey has acquired Cranko's *Brouillards*, which has been recognized as a signature piece, though only about 40 percent of it is good. Of the nine dances, to Debussy preludes, I like "Bruyère," "Les Fées," and "Des Pas sur la Neige," and I sort of like the title number. The rest I don't care for, but I won't fight about it. Choreographers of tomorrow could safely train themselves on anything in this ballet. But what if they go to *Voluntaries* instead?   —*May 8, 1978*

Arts and Sciences
and David Gordon

Performance art, a newish category, consists of the making and exhibiting of visual events, which may or may not be dances, but which have their existence in time as well as in space. Most performance art originates in painting, sculpture, or music, and it ends in theatre—usually a kind of wordless theatre that resembles dance. Excitement comes from impurity—from the impingement of various art forms on each other or from the attempt to extend the scope of one art form beyond its normal boundaries. In the dances of the painter Sylvia Whitman—or perhaps one should say in the paintings of the dancer Sylvia Whitman—human performers and décor merge on the same figurative plane. Her most recent concert (or exhibit), held at the Truck and Warehouse Theatre, was filled with images that began as paintings or assemblages and extended themselves through manipulations in performance. Sometimes a line was crossed which turned an art object into live theatre, but that didn't happen often.

Performance art aims at transformation, and the process whereby two or more art forms (or communications systems, such as video) are reciprocally reconditioned by the exchange of ideas is a complex one. Where there is complexity, there is likely to be confusion. In a recent presentation at the Brooklyn Academy, Kenneth King used dance, spoken commentary, visual aids, and some highly inventive props to transmit a number of thoughts about science and culture, none of which emerged with clarity. King is one of our most cerebral gagmen, and not one of our most cogent. His various means kept diverting attention from each other, and the evening disintegrated into a bewildering display of resources and strategies. Among his most powerful resources is the one he uses least—his fascinating refinement as a dancer. King would rather think, write, and speak; he is obsessed with linguistics. Even in this attempt at a protean (or, as he might say, protein) media spectacular, there were too many words.

One of the most controlled and sophisticated performance artists is David Gordon, who also happens to like words, although he classifies himself as a dancer, not a writer. (I don't know of many writers who have been attracted to the form; those who have been have generally seen it as an occasion to lay their verbal gifts aside.) Gordon, too, can be a wordsmith, but his current work is characterized by brilliantly elliptical dialogue or parodies of real conversations. Whether it's delivered by the performers or by taped voices, this verbal material is balanced and coordinated with choreographed movements that reveal the same flair for selection and for lifelike imitation. Gordon's type of dance movement is the simple, technically ungroomed movement that was promoted in the post-Cunningham rebellion of the sixties by Yvonne Rainer and others. Gordon, who worked with Rainer, is the first to use this movement nonideologically. He seems to see it paradoxically —as being interesting in itself but also somewhat absurd in its presumptive amateurism. Valda Setterfield, his wife and partner, is a former member of the Cunningham company. A trained dancer, she's particularly good at projecting the double edges in the material. Because he is by nature a satirist and a critic, Gordon has instinctively developed into an avant-garde comedian. The subject of his new evening-length piece, *Not Necessarily Recognizable Objectives*, is performance. By the end of the evening, the inference that he is criticizing his own performance—as dancer, choreographer, scriptwriter, and host (the event was held in his loft on lower Broadway)—as well as the conventions of performance has grown into a certainty.

The piece begins as Gordon and Setterfield circle the space slowly in a jog-walk. They wear satin gym pants, white shirts, jogging shoes. An atmosphere of trial, of self-tempering, begins to gather. Meanwhile, a voice catalogues, casebook-style, the perils of performance. Another voice (Agnes

Moorehead's in *Sorry, Wrong Number*) pleads with an operator to dial a wrong number on purpose. Soon we find ourselves unable to distinguish the planned accidents from the real ones. The action pauses momentarily and an ingenious floundering conversation takes place—ingenious because we can plainly see that it's being read from posters on the wall. But, in spite of the cue cards, there's a place where the talk takes off on its own. We grasp this when the entire conversation, which deals with the course the performance is to take, is repeated with the roles reversed, and we come back to the improvised section. Whether we recognize it or not, Gordon has made a point about perception and about conventional ways of listening and reacting in the theatre. He can be quite ruthless in pressing this point. Later in the action, a similar incident occurs after three other members of the troupe have joined the principals and become confused about the next step to take in a walking pattern. Somebody says, "Oh, now I know what to do," and instantly the line and the gesture (hand clapped to head) are incorporated by all five dancers into the pattern. Was the confusion real? Of course not. Gordon now springs his trap. On the next repeat, "Oh, now I know what to do" is said not with dancers smiting their brows but with them holding their noses, and even as we begin to laugh Gordon takes the laugh out of our mouths and puts it in the mouths of his dancers. The line then becomes " 'Oh, now I know what to do' [laugh]." And to this demonstration of indifference to our reaction we *really* don't know how to react.

Gordon creates a triple-distilled mixture of dance, drama, and words. The text develops an almost insidious relevance to the movement, and the movement keeps commenting on itself. Specific sequences take on new aspects when they're done faster or more slowly, by different people, in different directions, or with as little as one element in the sequence varied. A bewitching women's trio, which follows a simple loop pattern of slowly descending to the floor, rolling over, and getting back up, is complicated by the tightest unison possible: the women are pressed one inside another the whole time. Gordon adds a final variation to the roll on the floor and accompanies it with the sunrise music from *La Fille Mal Gardée*—a touch that mingles humor and erotic mystery. Another movement sequence is a series of dashes broken by abrupt directional shifts and off-balance skedaddling whirls. It runs like a spine through the piece, alternating with its companion motif, the slow jog in a circle. Gordon keeps this material so clearly focussed that we easily see it turning over on itself, its effects as differentiated as the words in the dialogues. Gradually, within its limits, the piece develops a disarming openness. We know that if anything can happen, it surely will.

David Gordon does not look like a dancer. He has an actor's weight and presence, fierce black hair and whiskers that set off a sleepy expression, and a resonant voice. He is soft and shaggy in texture and sensuous in movement, with an overall look of ovals slipping within larger ovals. Sometimes in motion he looks as if he had popped out of Max Fleischer's inkwell. His personal peak in *Not Necessarily Recognizable Objectives* is reached when he does a solo, first having told us on a tape how aware he is of the egocentric temptations of soloing, how he has arranged to undercut these by having his group comment as he performs, and how we mustn't be fooled into thinking *he* thinks this will do anything but force us to pay all the more attention to "his person" (Gordon talks of himself Mailerishly). He does the solo, which appears to be made up of all the movement material in the piece so far, to the accompaniment of remarks that send up crowd psychology, cultural fetishes, dance criticism—everything that performers have nightmares about. And dreams of revenge, too. How to end? The four remaining dancers are given the same solo to do in the form of a round, ending as Gordon ended, by slipping behind a sliding door. Thus we conclude with another recapitulation in a different form, which makes it a fresh statement.

It is very hard to break the spell of a satirist. I find among the many pleasures of Gordon's work that it places the work of other performance artists in perspective. He seems to stand midway between those who are moving from a fine-arts base and those who are moving toward it. In the work of painters, sculptors, and other nondancers, performance art is an impulsive movement toward theatre. The impulse of dancers like Lucinda Childs and Trisha Brown is to imitate nondancers in a kind of backward progression out of the theatre and into the gallery. Childs and Brown reduce dance to its basic elements, and even delete some of those basics. As a gallery art, dance doesn't withstand scrutiny the way its neighboring arts do—it's had to give up too much to get there. In thinking about this kind of rarefied, conceptualized dance, I've tried to resist the idea that the move away from theatre which it represents is for a dancer a move against nature. But in the nontheatrical arts "theatre" is abstractly present. So for a painter's or a sculptor's image to take on the dimensions of live performance reifies something in its nature. Separating dance from theatre doesn't make dance more lively—doesn't make it strong in its own right, the way a self-sustaining art like painting is strong. The mistake here is to confuse theatre explicit in dance with theatre implicit in painting. Rudimentary dance as its devotees see it is really subrudimentary. The result is not the transmogrification of an art form but its reduction to a scientific exercise. "Performance science" might be the correct term for what Childs does when she walks backward as swiftly as she walks forward and without breaking rhythm. It's a parody of the refined technique we see in ballet dancers, a bit as if technical standards in dance could be adjudicated by the Bureau of Weights and Measures.

·   ·   ·

On the new wood floor of the Opera House stage at the Brooklyn Academy, Douglas Dunn and a company of thirteen dancers performed, on different evenings, *Lazy Madge*, with the audience seated onstage, and *Rille*, with the audience in its accustomed place. *Lazy Madge*, Dunn's name for an ongoing group project, was looser in format than *Rille*, a première. There was otherwise not a great deal of difference. At the time, I enjoyed *Lazy Madge* more, because Dunn's dancers, who work at varying levels of proficiency and imagination, are more watchable at close range, and also because the lack of any musical or sound accompaniment wasn't as deadening as it was when they were seen at normal theatrical distances. Long-distance viewing isolates and enhances Dunn's own sophisticated performing style at the expense of the group. In memory, *Lazy Madge* decomposes to a pile of shtick, and *Rille* is all but lost; besides Dunn's role in it, I can recall very little. (The experiment of switching the audience's viewpoint might have been more gripping if Dunn had cast both pieces with the same dancers.)

I last saw Dunn on this stage five years ago, when he was dancing with Merce Cunningham's company. A tall, thin, straw-colored man, with a slack, impalpable style, Dunn in those days often looked semi-collapsed. Now his slackness has a flyweight elegance. He keeps a thread of tension loosely wound, ready to tug at; the phrases are tossed lightly but observably together or are strung in casual juxtapositions. He still has his airiness, his butterfly skitter, but he has acquired edge. This is something that hadn't been apparent, to my eye, in the studio performances I'd been seeing him give. And somehow, there on the big stage, the sensitive touch of his feet on the floor was extraordinarily affecting.

Dunn has taken Cunningham as one of his obvious models, with mixed results. Like Cunningham, he's a naturally lyrical dancer, with a long line and fast feet, but sometimes he seems to be giving us pallid imitations of the way Cunningham looks now. As a choreographer, Dunn hasn't yet reached the point where his work can stand alone and absorb us for seventy minutes, like a Cunningham Event. His dancers don't appear to be coerced in any particular stylistic direction, and they don't push themselves technically. There is a company look based partly on Dunn's personal style and partly on the free play of individual initiative. Dunn, who with David Gordon used to belong to the improvisatory group called the Grand Union, seems to have put together his own Grand Union ideal. *Lazy Madge* followed a kind of continuity that suggested a game plan. Favored shtick included the single air turn with arms outspread, the jump (arms same) with a hip wiggle in midair, hopping in circles, striding in fourth position, hopping with small ballonnés. Lying on the floor, two dancers would hold hands and squirm intently without letting go. I don't know where the company is going, but Dunn's arrival is good news.

.   .   .

The James Waring retrospective held at the Judson Church on two week-ends in April commemorated a gifted man. In his time—he died in 1975, at fifty-three—Waring was an original thinker, an astute critic, a man of astoundingly wide-ranging tastes with an astounding way of demonstrating them. High art and low, he was among the first to prove, were not neces-sarily mutually exclusive, and they often lay side by side in his work. Luck-ily, he was also a dedicated teacher. There was no knowing Waring without learning from him. As a choreographer, he was not invariably skilled, and the dances of his that were showcased at the Judson, together with the revival at the Riverside Theatre a few months ago of his ballet based on *The Phantom of the Opera,* are far less impressive than his costumes, which he designed and in most cases made himself. Waring's true talents lay in the decorative arts and in staging and direction. Then, too, many of his dances were made for students and semi-professionals, and, while even these lim-ited pieces contain exciting theatrical ideas, they are not especially provoca-tive to see today.

Waring was one of those men who can accurately be described as forces. He inspired the devotion of a generation of dancers and choreographers, several of whom are named above. Some of his best teaching was done indirectly, as a gentle confidence between friends, for Waring was, despite his enormous influence, a gentle and diffident man. His delicacy can be sensed in his dances, along with the range of his fancy, but this is really an oblique way of appreciating Waring the man, and it is a way that can open itself only to those who remember.   —*May 15, 1978*

From a Far Country

Theme and Variations, the only Balanchine ballet performed by the American Ballet Theatre, returned to the repertory this season reportedly at the request of Mikhail Baryshnikov, who danced it twice before announcing that he would be leaving soon to join Balanchine's company. The announce-ment came a few days before the local première of Baryshnikov's produc-tion for ABT of the Petipa-Gorsky-Minkus *Don Quixote,* and the odd timing seemed to suspend the dancer between two phases—the one that, as a member of the New York City Ballet (which also does *Theme and Varia-tions*), he is about to enter, and the one to which, as a Ballet Theatre star, he increasingly found himself returning when no more good new roles were to be had. *Don Quixote,* as produced in Leningrad by the Kirov Ballet, gave Baryshnikov his first starring role in a full-length ballet. Like the version of *The Nutcracker* which he also made for Ballet Theatre, *Don Quixote* represents Baryshnikov's career in Russia, and it gives us a farewell glimpse of his dancing in the style that nurtured him but has ceased to challenge him. At thirty, in exile, Baryshnikov has brought Russian demi-caractère style to a peak of perfection. If he had remained in Russia, he would have been, after Vladimir Vasiliev, the one who carried it on. But Baryshnikov four years ago elected a different destiny. In his last few weeks at Ballet Theatre, he not only looked ahead to his new career and back to his abandoned one but also summarized his Ballet Theatre years, dancing some of the best roles he has had since coming to the West. It may be symbolic that his farewell ABT performances in New York were scheduled to be in Jerome Robbins's *Other Dances*, a piece that he can also perform at the New York City Ballet, and Twyla Tharp's *Push Comes to Shove*, the most original as well as the most popular choreography anyone has made for him so far.

While at ABT, Baryshnikov worked with nearly every choreographer who could have offered him a chance to do something new and different (the new and different being defined more often by Baryshnikov's experience than by ours). When the novelties seemed to have run their course, there were the revivals. We saw him dance Bournonville for the first time and Fokine's *Spectre de la Rose* and *Petrushka*. Not the least that can be said of the two works that he himself revived from models in the Soviet repertory is that they give American dancers and audiences something new and different. The second-act mime speech of the Nutcracker Prince begins with a formal gesture (which Baryshnikov, in approved contemporary Russian style, deletes) that means "I come from a far country," and then goes on to relate what happened there. Baryshnikov's revivals relate what goes on in another ballet tradition, in a far country. Whatever we may think of their merits as ballets, *The Nutcracker* and *Don Quixote* are authoritatively and discriminatingly staged, and all the dancers are conspicuously well coached; it is not Baryshnikov alone who benefits from the experience—if, indeed, it can be said that dancing his old vehicles benefits him at all. Although the central role of Basil, the barber, in *Don Quixote* doesn't extend Baryshnikov's range, he packs it full of his accustomed specialties—it's the *most* of Baryshnikov in a certain style. By his brilliant dancing, we can see that he wishes to speak well of his training and to commemorate it. But more important than this sentiment is the special understanding that lies behind it—Baryshnikov's understanding of recovery and commemoration as vital elements in the creative process.

One loss caused by Baryshnikov's early departure from the ABT season at the Met is his Prince Florimund, a piercing note of authenticity in a generally hapless production of *The Sleeping Beauty*. (And he may never now double Carabosse and the Bluebird, as we were once promised he would.) The principal male role in *Theme and Variations* is to some extent fashioned after the Prince in *The Sleeping Beauty*; Baryshnikov dances it with the eighteenth-century grace of deportment that is characteristic of his

Florimund. He understands and projects a connection. In fact, the closer one looks at it, the more the style of the ballet as a whole recalls the Petipa classic. Balanchine may have arranged the resemblance at the suggestion of the Ballet Theatre management. In the impressively documented new book *American Ballet Theatre* (Knopf), Charles Payne says that the idea of using the last movement of Tchaikovsky's third orchestral suite for a ballet first occurred to Max Goberman, who in 1947 was the company's musical director. He proposed a work in the Petipa style—"one," Payne writes, "that would fill the same function in the repertory as did *Princess Aurora*."

> *He passed on the suggestion to [Lucia] Chase and [Oliver] Smith, who approached Balanchine with the question, "Could you do an opening ballet for Youskevitch to this music?" Balanchine took the score and returned shortly with the answer, "But of course."*

Princess Aurora was a suite of excerpts from *The Sleeping Beauty*: the fairies' adagio and variations from the Prologue, selected divertissements from the last act, and the Rose Adagio. Toumanova added the grand pas de deux. Tchaikovsky's Tema con Variazioni, the climax of his Suite No. 3 in G, consists of a brief aria plus twelve variations, the last of which is a handsome polonaise that arrives three times on the crest of an enormous crescendo. The music's dance character is irresistible; it's the kind of music that habitually played through Tchaikovsky's "theatre of the mind," and it contains aspects of fomal rigor that anticipate the creation, five years later, of *The Sleeping Beauty*. For his ballet, Balanchine decided on a hierarchical cast: a ballerina, a danseur noble, four female demi-soloists (who possibly correspond to the fairies), eight corps de ballet girls (who may be their attendants), and a male partner for every girl. Apart from the principal dancer, however, the men do not enter until the finale, where their appearance creates a wave of excitement that rolls right to the end of the piece. Although *Theme* is often linked with other, more grandiose Balanchine-Tchaikovsky ballets, like *Concerto No. 2* (formerly *Ballet Imperial*) and *Diamonds*, and although one identifies by a few recurrent steps and figures the watermark it shares with *Symphony in C* (made the same year), it is very different in effect. *Theme* achieves its sensations through modest means. The variations develop organic permutations of basic ballet gesture; out of this process—so similar to that of *The Sleeping Beauty*—the imagery of the piece materializes.

The enchanted feminine microcosm of Petipa's Prologue and Vision Scene reappears in the form of concentrated dance études. In one of the first, twelve women become a chain, or garland, winding and rewinding like the maze of a formal garden. The image expands and deepens in the most nostalgic of the women's dances, set to a trembling reverie in the music; the eight attendants form another chain of support for the ballerina as her body in an extended balance describes an array of transformations. Merrill Ashley, in the New York City Ballet production, spreads before us the complete fanlike gamut of ballet logic, folding her long body first into croisé front, then into effacé front, écarté, attitude effacé, and at last lengthening into penchée arabesque. The développé transitions between the poses are like the pleats of the fan. There is a brisk fugue for the corps, flanked by two solos for the male star. In the first, we recognize an elaboration and mobilization of the simple preparatory stretch-and-point exercise with port de bras that had occurred at the outset of the theme. The dancer swings from side to side and then from front to back in low vaults through space. A flurry of pirouettes decelerates in a seamless return to the "theme" gesture. The second male variation begins with eight ronds de jambe sautés pitched high off the ground, alternating with piqué-attitude balances, as the orchestra fires its first volley of chords. At the second volley, the step sequence is eight daunting double air turns separated by pirouettes. Baryshnikov sometimes lands from his air turns with one leg held in passé and pirouettes from that position. This time, he took the passé on the ground as part of a quick relevé preparation, for an effect of unstraining evenness throughout the sequence. (In another optional complication, which I'm told Youskevitch introduced —I've actually seen only Villella do it—the turns may be done alternately to the left and to the right.*) The ballerina's solo variations are no less taxing: whirring through her allegro paces, she's Aurora rewritten in lightning. Evocations of the great Petipa role flash before us—pas de chat/pirouette, a rhythmic lunge striking tendue positions in fourth while the arms sweep through directional changes, and, in the finale, a pas couru ending in the dainty, girlish tendue-front pose that Margot Fonteyn had her picture taken in a thousand times. But the Aurora of *Theme* was Alicia Alonso, and the role still demands a technician of power. For Gelsey Kirkland in the New York City Ballet revival of 1970, Balanchine added gargouillades; it became the role in which, through gradual conquest of its difficulties, she rose to principal status.

Kirkland and Baryshnikov have performed *Theme* together before, but until this season they had given only one performance in New York. Fittingly, their third and final performance at the Met is a live telecast. The ballet is to Kirkland what *Don Quixote* is to Baryshnikov, a cradle, although it still obviously excites and challenges her. Her original partner, Villella, is reincarnated in Baryshnikov's combination of quick attack, compact delivery, and delicacy. With partners like this (or like Helgi Tomasson, another leading exponent of the male role), Kirkland has sustained the quality of refinement and transparency in the ballet which Balanchine emphasized in the 1970 revival (when he supplemented it with dances to the other sections of the suite). Ashley, with her technique of pure crystal, sustains it, too. Her new partner this season, Adam Lüders, is well launched

---

* *Postscript 1982:* This has become standard at New York City Ballet.

toward success. (His steppingstone to *Theme* was his triumph last season in *Cortège Hongrois*.) At Ballet Theatre, there have been some fine *Theme* ballerinas—notably, Martine van Hamel and Cynthia Gregory—but they've had to fight a distorted tradition built up by years of hard-hitting performances. Now in the new production it is possible to glimpse a far-off vision of court and castle as exquisitely fashioned as the inside of a Fabergé egg. This is not Petipa's world but a distanced memory of it. The new scale turns the pas de deux into a fantasy of active mutual consideration and delight, a conversation in whispers and sighs; one seems to hear the voices of children, not those of the suave sophisticates who possessed the ballet for so long. (When Balanchine refers to Petipa here, he chooses to quote not only the grand pas de deux but also Puss in Boots and the White Cat.)

For the first time in my experience, an ABT *Theme* looks Balanchinian. Its tempos are faster even than those at the New York City, which after a period of unreasonable high speed have recently been relaxed. (Speaking of "a thirty-two-minute ballet," Charles Payne surely intends twenty-two minutes; ABT's official running time is twenty-one minutes.) And it includes wonderful details that Balanchine in his inscrutable wisdom has deleted from the version done by his own company. One such detail is the double line of battements front done by the corps girls as they fall backward into their partners' arms; it's like two rows of swords flashing a salute to the demis as they enter with the second group of men. Desmond Heeley has recostumed the piece none too flatteringly, using the hard-to-wear kind of tutu that sticks stiffly out over the hips, like a Japanese parasol. The other costume details are an improvement on the hard corsets of André Levasseur which the company used to wear, although the colors are not as much of an improvement on the Nicolas Benois designs for NYCB as one might have hoped. There is no décor; instead, a cold gray wall surmounts the scene. And Jennifer Tipton's lighting is, for her, uncreatively dim both here and in *Don Quixote*. The blackout at the end of *Theme* seems unwarranted.

Don Quixote is a ballet not only from another country but from another age—one that hasn't passed its secrets on to us. Loosely constructed as one more or less continuous dance suite broken by interludes of pantomime, slapstick, and exotic or fantastic spectacle, it needs space to sprawl in. But its various elements—particularly the comedy, in which the Don figures mainly as a straight man—aren't all equally alive to a modern audience. The trouble is, cutting only makes the piece more shapeless, because then its discursiveness has no chance to develop depth. Trying to retune this lumbering contraption, Baryshnikov has allowed only as much filler as will throw the dancing into relief, and the trouble with *that* is the monolithic expression of the dancing. The idiom throughout the piece is Russian Spanish, with one classical divertissement (the Vision) in the second act and another (the Wedding) in the third. Between the larky lovers, who carry the main action, and the secondary characters there is no difference in style. One sees angled torsos and backbends everywhere, especially in Act I. Within the Russian school, there used to be categories—character, character-grotesque, and so on—for dancers and mimes alike; *Don Quixote* in the old days must have been a festival of categories. But beyond a slightly stylized classicism (demi-caractère) contemporary dancers don't much care to go. Baryshnikov cuts as many gypsies as he can out of the second act. His deletions make the show flat, but they also make it taut, smooth, and needless to say fast. There are only two bumps: an awkward transition to the Vision Scene and, later, a stage wait. The Don, incidentally, doesn't take Basil's girlfriend, Kitri, for Dulcinea, as he does in the Nureyev production that was filmed a few years ago. But, though Baryshnikov probably means to give dignity to the Don's vision by embodying it, the Dulcinea that has been imagined by the designer, Santo Loquasto, is a large woman who looks like an over-dressed infanta: a staid conception for a ballet, to say the least.

Having heard negative reports about Loquasto's contribution—indeed, about the production as a whole—I was surprised, once past that repetitious first act, to find so much that was so pleasant. Unlike Nureyev, Baryshnikov seems able to see what the audience sees. What neither Baryshnikov nor Nureyev can do anything about is the disappointingly thin choreography for the corps de ballet in the Vision Scene. Was it ransacked long ago to furnish other Petipa-Minkus revivals? The variations are sound enough, but they have been passed around. The first is often done as part of the *Corsaire* pas de deux, the next is an interpolation from *Paquita*, and the last has a slightly used *Bayadère* look. Other numbers might be questioned in this way. The Petipa inheritance is a puzzle; somehow, the more we see of it, the less there is.

Opposite Baryshnikov's Basil, Kirkland's Kitri presented a remarkably accurate picture of a high-flying, heels-up Russian soubrette. Kirkland is a marvellous mimic as well as a marvellous dancer. I was mesmerized by her diminutive Plisetskaya—she even gets the rocking-horse lurch going into the high jetés passés of the opening waltz—until at some point in the second act I grew sick of it. Kirkland in this role dances from facility; high leaps, high kicks front and back, backbends, quantities of turns—all are comfortably within her range. Her effort goes into stylization and characterization—into vixenism and fan-snapping and other tempestuous effects, and into the achieving of a hard and glossy "closed" performance. Although it is never less than talented, it is never more than impersonation. Does Kirkland really think we'd rather see a Kitri stereotype than the Kitri that she uniquely could be? Cynthia Gregory's robust, witty, but softly radiant performance on the following evening proved that Kitri doesn't have to be a toughie. There was evident delight in her response to her partner, John Meehan, and to her new conductor, John Lanchbery. Meehan, who had given a colorful performance the night before as Espada, the bullfighter, showed both courage and style as Basil. His dancing is not star caliber, but it is solid and vigorous in the Russian tradition. This is the tradition that he has been trained in, by the way, and it belongs to him; it's not a guise. —*May 22, 1978*

The Children of Sixty-sixth Street

Overcast skies, dankness, gloom. A spiritless tribute to the French nation, *Tricolore* is a ballet to forget as quickly as possible. The New York City Ballet, which introduced it this season out of some misbegotten loyalty to the virtue of finishing what you've started—in this case, a trilogy of nationalist extravaganzas which already included *Stars and Stripes* and *Union Jack* —seems to forget it in performance. The dancers look as if they hated it quite as much as the audience does; their dour little faces and dutiful movements tell us that they won't help the least bit, even with a turkey that they know will fold. I understand the feeling, although I don't think it is the place of professional performers to let such feelings show. Whether on the stage or off, we are all miserable at *Tricolore*, and there's a certain comfort in the universality of the experience. The ballet, a failure in every department, turns out to have no partisans—none. In the audience, an élan of dejection starts to take hold. The ballet's makers hear the evil quips, laugh, and pass them on. *Tricolore*: this is what it's like to be totalled at the New York City Ballet.

Four days later, the scene changes. The School of American Ballet gives its annual workshop performances. The sun is actually shining, and on a vintage crop of new dancers, too. The school, which was founded by George Balanchine and Lincoln Kirstein, feeds graduates into the New York City Ballet and other companies around the world, and has been holding annual recitals for the past thirteen years. In the nearly ten years that I have been attending, I can't recall a bigger concentration of talent or a higher level of achievement. I see by comparing programs that many of the dancers who impress me this year also appeared at last year's recital. I can remember two or three of them well enough to notice the improvement in their work; the others didn't register at all. A year in the life of a fifteen- or sixteen-year-old can make a big difference. What seems to have happened during the past year is that all at once a generation of great promise has burst into its first flowering.

The performances—two, on the same day—take place in an atmosphere of serene excitement. The comfortable little Juilliard Theatre is packed out with relatives, friends, students, professional dancers, dance professionals. Lynn Stanford, a school pianist, plays the opener, the pas de trois from *The Guards of Amager*. (For the rest of the program, Stephen Colvin, a second-year Juilliard student, leads the Juilliard Conductors Orchestra.) This Bournonville selection, which was the dance highlight of the remarkable 1871 ballet that was performed here for the first time by the Royal Danes only two years ago, scarcely looks the same dance. Long-lined American bodies stretch it into new but no less congenial shapes. SAB-style Bournonville was invented by the distinguished Danish teacher Stanley Williams for his American pupils. With male pupils, it's almost as wonderful as the real thing. With females, it's getting to be an independent form of expression—a unique and spectacular outgrowth of the old Danish tradition. The New York City Ballet has already mastered that tradition in its *Bournonville Divertissements*. Now, with strong replacements in casting such as Sandra Jennings in Merrill Ashley's difficult role and Peter Schetter in the Pas de Sept, it is showing the process of assimilation which mastery rests upon. The deeper in the ranks those replacements come from, the more clearly the fact of assimilation emerges. Jennings graduated from the school in 1974, Schetter in 1976. The way this year's graduates Victoria Hall and Jerri Kumery float through the *Amager* trio with Cornell Crabtree makes the transition from Copenhagen to New York complete. American dancers everywhere are taking Bournonville more seriously than they used to, if only as a fortifier of technique. I saw a very presentable *Napoli* suite, staged by Toni Lander, with the *Flower Festival* pas de deux as the centerpiece, done by young dancers at the Riverside Dance Festival, in March. They were members of the Ballet Repertory Company—the junior wing of American Ballet Theatre—and only a few years older than the dancers of the SAB workshop performances.

The workshop program is carefully designed to display versatility. The main choreographers besides Bournonville are Balanchine and Robbins. A contribution by Alexandra Danilova is a workshop tradition. This year, she produced an engaging suite of dances to Glazunov's *Scènes du Ballet*. Danilova sets different challenges for boys, for little girls and big ones, for aspiring soloists, for partners in an adagio. Each challenge methodically incites a different kind of dance "scene." In the finale, everyone comes together in a lightly sociable polonaise; as this last picture forms, one suddenly understands what the *"scènes du ballet"* are all about. Throughout the ballet, the pace is moderate, the spacing of the dance figures is nice and wide; there is plenty of time to concentrate, to fill out one's place and plan the next move. Danilova teaches old Russian virtues; she inculcates an understanding of genre. And it is in Danilova's grand adagio for five couples that we get our first extended view of this new generation's nuclear group of girls—all with small heads and waists, full thighs, and astonishing long legs that sweep the sky like the beams of searchlights. The model is obviously

Suzanne Farrell, but Farrell as she really is—not the perilous exaggeration of her type which was popular a few years ago. The new girls have strength and precision; though they're soft, they're never bland. The technical sophistication doesn't seem fanatical or premature. These are Balanchine women, and they're right where they should be—poised for entry into the next phase, which will turn them into Balanchine dancers.

Intermission. A general reckoning that the girls this year, as so often before, are better than the boys, but the boys are better on the average than usual. A few boys and many of the outstanding girls have already been taken into the company. The star of last year's workshop, Patrick Bissell, was far above the male average. He has since joined American Ballet Theatre and in the current New York season has successfully partnered Martine van Hamel in *La Bayadère* and Cynthia Gregory in *Theme and Variations*. Bissell is over six feet tall, and a genuinely gifted dancer. In ABT he is the counterpart of Peter Martins in New York City Ballet, but the dancer he most reminds me of is the Bolshoi's premier of the fifties and sixties, Nicolai Fadeyechev. Bissell has the same sunken chest, wide hips, and long feather-light legs, the same soft landings, the same accommodating manner toward a ballerina. He is also handsome, with a mane of curly dark hair, bright dark eyes, and dimples. In the classical adagio of *Graduation Ball*, he partners Leslie Browne (SAB, 1975), who has been gaining strength this year and is now the best of Ballet Theatre's second-rank soloists.

The Robbins ballet, *Interplay*, is so well danced that Robbins has asked the cast to repeat the performance on an NYCB program. The manners in *Interplay* are dated and the jazz is sedate, but it is a soundly constructed ballet on a classical base, and its progression is a joy to watch. Each time I see it, I love it more and dancing more. A perfect vehicle for young dancers, it demands athletic drive and strictly correct style. Not every cast can satisfy both demands while holding them in balance (and, in fact, the boys in this production aren't uniformly great at it). As long as this remains true, *Interplay* will remain in repertory. Timothy Fox, the most advanced of the boys in the workshop, manages five double tours without preparations (the maximum everywhere has been four) at the matinee. In the evening, he takes the leading male role in Balanchine's *Divertimento No. 15*; Roma Sosenko, the lead girl in *Interplay*, is the principal ballerina.

Divertimento done by kids! The week before, the Pennsylvania Ballet showed its new production of this supremely delicate and difficult Balanchine-Mozart ballet at the Brooklyn Academy, and I admired the company's verve and, as always, its savvy. The Pennsylvania doesn't dance Balanchine in Balanchine's style, but it knows how to convert Balanchine ballets to its own idea of classicism. This idea involves an emphatic attack, a clipped phrase, a rhythm more or less squarely timed to the music. Above all, it stresses poses as climactic elements in a phrase—the arrival, not the journey, matters. I think the style conceals most of what is appealing in

Balanchine, but other values come through—solid, comfortably rooted burgher values. The Pennsylvania's *Divertimento* is "Viennese," while Balanchine's is "Italian." Although a few of the Pennsylvanians—William DeGregory (Theme), Tamara Hadley (Fourth Variation)—look as if they'd be very fine in the lighter, more fluid Balanchine style, the others look happy just as they are. It is a serious, enthusiastic production, very successful on its own terms. The SAB students, on the other hand, dance *Divertimento* in Balanchine's way, or at least in the way it was set for them by Suki Schorer, a former company soloist who is now an instructor at the school. If it is not the airy invention we sometimes get in company performances, that's because the dancers are young, not because their technique is; their wildcat energy—so different from the relaxed power they will have five years from now—pours unmodulated from the stage. Separate and all but equal sets of soloists are provided for each performance, with only the excellent and beautifully formed Barbara Seibert (Third Variation) and the Theme boys (Robert Weigel, Christopher Fleming) repeating their assignments. Roma Sosenko isn't one of the tall beauties—she's small, with a large head, like Tenniel's Alice (I hope nobody makes a ballet), shapely limbs, and intimations of personality. To many, her precocity recalls Gelsey Kirkland's at the same age.

Precocity of a near-shocking order is seen in the set of ballroom dances that Jean-Pierre Bonnefous has fashioned for eight children who cannot be more than eleven or twelve years old. Bonnefous doesn't condescend to the children; *Quadrille* consists of tiny versions of nineteenth-century adult party dances, with themes of courtship and etiquette taken straight. The girls cast intriguing over-the-shoulder glances; the boys do grands jetés and pirouettes, a little numbly. The whole ritual, in *Nutcracker* dress, is elaborately varied and rhymed to *Fledermaus* excerpts—a very skillful piece of choreography. If I had the workshop on videotape—and I wish I had, because two performances are, as a rule, all we ever get—I suspect that this is the part I would run over and over, for all that it reveals of instinct and artifice in dancing, of sexual character, of the beginning of wisdom and the end of innocence. And I would run the whole tape years from now, when whatever is in store for these young dancers has come to pass. Why don't they make a movie about the children of Sixty-sixth Street? The tradition is rich enough; the dedication is as sterling, the accomplishment as exhilarating as in any of the great ballet centers of the world. And the possibilities for sequels are practically endless.

In the Pennsylvania production of *Symphony in C*, phrases are meticulously cut into steps, and this overclarified way of moving seems to be the subject of Benjamin Harkarvy's new ballet for the company, *Signatures*, which seeks to isolate the dancers' personal characteristics for choreographic comment and development. I suppose that this objective and the overclarification of the movement supply a programmatic focus for audiences unused to modern choreography, and I don't underestimate the need for such a focus, but *Signatures* is really like any other expository piece designed to present a company (*Fanfare* comes to mind several times)—and one that would have been twice as good at half the length and without the tendentious score, by the company's music director, Maurice Kaplow. The version of *Symphony in C* is the shorter, and to me sweeter, version that we used to see at NYCB before Balanchine inserted all the musical repeats. But Francia Russell's staging of *Divertimento*, like Schorer's, is the up-to-date Lincoln Center one, which modifies the many beautiful entrances and exits conceived by Balanchine for the smaller stage of the City Center. On the stage of the Juilliard or the Brooklyn Academy, those effects would have been lovely to see again, had they been restored.

As for *Tricolore*, let the record show that the choreographers of its various sections were Peter Martins, Jean-Pierre Bonnefous, and Jerome Robbins, who were substituting for Balanchine after he fell ill earlier this spring. No one could have made more sense than they did of the sour, vaporish score, by Georges Auric—not even Balanchine himself, who commissioned it. And if the music hadn't defeated them the scenery and costumes would have—miles of starched lace and tat from Rouben Ter-Arutunian's workbasket. Unfortunately, the company had already announced a program called *Entente Cordiale*. As things are now, plan to spend Part II in the bar, drinking vast amounts of New York State champagne.   —*June 5, 1978*

Love Story

In 1889, Crown Prince Rudolf of Austria-Hungary went to the royal hunting lodge at Mayerling, where he joined his seventeen-year-old mistress, killed her, and then killed himself. Heart failure was given as the reason for Rudolf's death; his mistress, Mary Vetsera, was buried secretly. The facts got into the papers in little more than a week, but the cause of the tragedy remains the object of speculation. Mayerling has become a famous love story and Rudolf a famous dissolute prince. The standard Rudolf of historical fiction carouses until a beautiful, innocent girl enters his life. Because he cannot free himself from an unhappy marriage, he and the girl commit suicide. In fact, court protocol did demand that Rudolf stay married, but it did not prevent him from taking mistresses. His father, the Emperor Franz Josef, kept a mistress and was encouraged to do so by the Empress, whose special friend was an English colonel, Bay Middleton. Vetsera was not an innocent, and Rudolf was not redeemed by her love. Just the opposite seems to have been the case.

I get this information from, of all places, a new ballet. In *Mayerling*, produced by the Royal Ballet, Kenneth MacMillan takes on the job of historian in addition to that of choreographer. Having pursued a mixed objective, he comes away with mixed results. MacMillan has perceived that the fictitious Mayerling is an inadequate dramatic subject but not that the real Mayerling is too much for him—or any choreographer—to handle. If he had taken the same romantic approach to the two doomed lovers as the movies that were made about them, he might have a better ballet; certainly he'd have a more popular one. MacMillan tries to tell the truth about the double suicide, he gets involved in matters that can't be expressed in dance, and the ballet is relentlessly gloomy. The Arie Crown Theatre, in Chicago, where I saw it, enhanced the gloom. A brick auditorium in a convention-site complex, the Arie Crown feels twice the size of New York's Felt Forum and just as dead. The enormous proscenium has no focus; a pit orchestra can barely be heard. *Mayerling*, which demands pinpoint concentration from the audience, was lost. What was the Royal Ballet doing in such a place anyway? Ironically, because the Metropolitan Opera House was unavailable, it chose to bypass New York completely.

Mayerling follows a MacMillan pattern. From the beginning, he has adapted literary or historical material, and often material that had previously been used for plays, operas, or movies. *Romeo and Juliet*, of course, was already cast in ballet form when MacMillan staged it, but before that there was *The Burrow*, based on the Anne Frank story; *The Invitation*, from two novels that had inspired movies; and *Las Hermanas*, from Lorca's play *The House of Bernarda Alba*. Then came *Anastasia* and *Manon*. In all these, MacMillan worked to provide roles of stature for women, and those roles may be the best part of the MacMillan pattern. *Mayerling* has not only the Mary Vetsera figure but the Countess Larisch, Rudolf's procuress and former lover; Empress Elisabeth, his mother; Princess Stephanie, his wife; and Mitzi Caspar, a prostitute who was his mistress. The ballet traces the events that led to Mayerling in a series of encounters between Rudolf and these women. The encounters—except for the one with Mitzi, who has many men—are staged, in mime or dance, as duets. And here MacMillan remedies the chief flaw of *Manon*, which also depended on duets between the principals: he has made each duet emerge from and crystallize a different dramatic situation. What is more striking, however, is that each duet is a variation or a comment on the theme of venery, which MacMillan places at the heart of poor Rudolf's misery.

Apart from MacMillan's remarkable sex scenes—they're as far beyond the sex scenes in Tudor's ballets as contemporary movies are beyond movies of the forties, yet they're never inhuman or exploitative—the major reason to see *Mayerling* is the brilliant performing by the women of the Royal Ballet. The secondary male roles are on the flat side, and MacMillan never succeeds in making much more of Rudolf than he appears to have been in life—a titled creep forever Hamletizing around the house with a skull in one hand and a gun in the other. Rudolf's debauchery and decline are clearly, if somewhat mechanically, staged, and they seem to have been the chief facts of the young prince's life. Of the various explanations for his suicide which have been advanced, MacMillan's researcher and scenarist, Gillian Freeman, offers several in her program notes on the ballet: "Rudolf—fraught by disease and despair; dependent on morphine . . . trapped by his loveless marriage with no hope, now, of a male heir; implicated in the Hungarian Cause; accused of attempting to murder the Emperor at a Shoot—had reached an impasse from which extrication seemed impossible."

None of this explains why Vetsera, too, had to go. Sentimental movie biographies made the affair end in a death pact between star-crossed lovers, and in a ballet we could accept that superficiality not only because it's conventional (or "classical") but because frustrated love is danceable. What MacMillan gives us—and he really piles it on—is satiated love, and he has made it danceable, too. Because we have to accept what we see happening as the true cause of the double suicide, we come to believe that Rudolf killed out of some fearful equation he had reached between sexual excess and death. The only stageable motive in Gillian Freeman's list is the first—"fraught by disease." All the rest of her scholarship never gets onto the stage, though MacMillan certainly tries. ("The Hungarian Cause" is four men in uniforms who shove Rudolf around a bit. "Dependent on morphine" is the ugly verismo of a real needle in a bare arm—no stylization at all.) Even the disease—syphilis—can't be clarified. MacMillan can only show us *a* disease. But because he has been able to do that much he has been able to make a complete story unfold—one that may or may not be the story of Mayerling. As always, a ballet can tell us what a ballet is equipped to tell us—nothing more.

MacMillan pushes so insistently against the nature of his art and what it is equipped to express that now and then he achieves breakthroughs and returns a kind of strength to it which has been long absent. The strength of mime, for example. The several intense mime passages include a Hamlet-and-Gertrude–like scene between Rudolf and his mother, his proposing a suicide pact to Mitzi Caspar, and the Countess Larisch's visit to the Baroness Vetsera and her obsessed, love-struck daughter. The first and third of these scenes work, because words would add nothing to them. Rudolf visits his mother on his wedding night: the point of the scene is to show the Oedipal repression that each suffers from, and I don't know how any modern audience can miss the point. And as soon as you see what the scene is about you see that it is being purely expressed—that it's not an attempt to get across a message that only words can convey. MacMillan has been able to do it because even in a spoken play the characters would be inarticulate. When Rudolf proposes suicide to Mitzi, we need rather more than his rubbing of a revolver against his neck and then hers—we do need words. But in the scene of the three women planning Mary's romance with Rudolf, words are irrelevant; their "chatter" is delightfully clear. This passage is staged with the rhythm and tension of a scene in a D. W. Griffith movie. Played by Merle Park, as the Countess, Lynn Seymour, as Vetsera, and Gerd Larsen, as her mother, it struck me as one of the most wonderful things MacMillan has done, comparable in security of outline and detail to the extended mime scenes in Bournonville played by the Royal Danes. Yet "silent movie" is still one of the most opprobrious terms that the public can find to throw at a mime ballet, and to this insult I can only say that there are silent movies and then there are silent movies. In Griffith's, one often doesn't need or want titles. The meanings are already clear without them— indeed, the meanings would only be reduced by verbalization. The fact that the medium couldn't speak was not a hindrance when a Griffith or a Sjöström made us see that it needn't. Part of the battle for legitimacy that dance has had to fight has been over its dumbness, and the wholesale prejudice against mime may have something to do with the assumption that, since talking pictures dropped mime, it must be obsolete everywhere. But saying that all the action in a ballet should be danced (rather than mimed) is like saying that a movie should be all talk. There are story ballets that need mime; and, as the two passages that I've cited show, it is by no means an impure or inferior form of expression.

The trouble with *Mayerling* is that, despite its moments of unorthodox success, it really can't decide what medium it wants to be unorthodox in— stage or screen. The several movie analogies I've drawn are forced by Mac-Millan's indecision. He appears to have wanted a stage spectacle with movielike flow, and, with the help of Gillian Freeman, who has also written movie scenarios, he partly obtains it. Nicholas Georgiadis has cooperated to the extent of providing a neutral backdrop—brown curtains suspended from brass rods—against which one or two pieces of furniture or stylized racks of dressmaker dummies may be placed to indicate settings and "extras." (The tavern where we meet Mitzi is a little dressier.) Yet the action doesn't move smoothly from set to set, as it might in a movie; there have to be forecurtain scenes to cover the changes, and all those scenes are superfluous or ir-relevant. One of them even spoils, by anticipating, the scene in which the Countess primes Mary to seduce the Prince. Although the whole Mayerling story eludes translation into ballet terms, some of the worst devices in the ballet are those not of a choreographic mind but of an academic mind trying to "visualize." I was puzzled until I read one of Freeman's ingenuous ex-planations: "An atheist, he [Rudolf] seems always to have had an obsession with guns and with death, which is why there is a recurring motif of explo-sions—fireworks as well as firearms—throughout the ballet."

The score—miscellaneous Liszt—has been effectively arranged by John Lanchbery. Three different *Transcendental Etudes* accompany the climactic pas de deux of the three acts; in all three, one reacts over and over to the brutal or ecstatic contortions, the headlong rushes and daring handholds— not to their excitement as stunts but to their sense as drama. Several of Rudolf's most tormented solos are set to soft, silken music, as if to under- line his impotence. An effect I don't recall seeing before in a ballet by a Western choreographer is MacMillan's extensive use of female character dancing—especially in the choreography for Elisabeth's ladies-in-waiting, who are characterized entirely in dance as sedate, heavy ladies, although in actuality they are young and slim. (It's time, though, that MacMillan changed his prostitute type; it's become as much a cliché as Agnes de Mille's or Bob Fosse's.) Like a playwright's, MacMillan's characterizations are open to interpretation by the performers. I saw two casts, each lending a different emphasis to the drama. Rudolf is the longest and, with all the acrobatic part- nering, undoubtedly the most arduous role, yet it's also the most pallid. David Wall, who originated it, could not have been at his best in Chicago. Overweight from weeks of inactivity forced on him by an injury, and made up like an impassive, droopy-lidded Olivier, he also appeared emotionally stagnant. Stephen Jefferies, more introspective than Wall, forced some color into the role; his Rudolf seems to cringe from himself, and he kills out of self-disgust, shooting down his mistress and then himself like wild dogs. Vetsera in Lynn Seymour's performance was a sensual glutton; in Alfreda Thorogood's, a morbid gnome. Georgina Parkinson as the Empress ap- peared tired the night I saw her, but she did suggest the weakness and vanity that Elisabeth has in common with Rudolf. Monica Mason stressed the glacial narcissism that made Elisabeth insensitive to her son's needs. Wendy Ellis was the better of two Stephanies. Between Jennifer Penney and Ros- alyn Whitten—both of them sweet, daisylike girls—I could not find the Mitzi who betrays Rudolf. David Drew as the English colonel, Leslie Ed- wards as the prime minister, and Michael Somes, unrecognizable in bald- domed walrus makeup as Franz Josef, lent their presence to the court scenes. The traditional "jester" role was danced by Graham Fletcher as a cab-driver. The towering performance was Merle Park's as the go-between Countess. With her twisted motives, her meddling, and her inscrutable satis- factions, Park's Larisch is more an eighteenth- than a nineteenth-century figure, and she's also enviably lively—a life force, in fact. It is with Lar- isch's downfall and the extinguishing of her light that MacMillan sets the scene for the deaths at Mayerling.

It's easy to be scornful of a ballet over which Synopsis presides to such an extent, a ballet that has explosions in it, a syphilitic, drug-addicted hero, and a protracted grope in every pas de deux. It is easiest of all to deny that *Mayerling*, which seems to be made up completely of acrobatics and mime, is even a ballet. But those for whom the Royal Ballet holds any fascination will want to see it in this curious, crippled, provocative work by its master choreographer. The genius of the English in mime, so closely allied to their literary genius, is amply eloquent. And in a single stream of dance metaphor growing ever more narrow and deep MacMillan succeeds in telling a story that may never appear on any printed page.   —*July 3, 1978*

Hello Posterity,
Goodbye Now

Dance, the ephemeral art, is rebelling against its condition. Like mayflies who want to be cast in bronze, dancers are putting their dances into retrieval systems. Films and videotapes preserve choreography that might otherwise have been entrusted to disputable notation or partial memory. Preservation has become a cry, a right, a guarantee. Ballerinas we read about in childhood linger onstage through their fifties. Pioneer days are revived so that audiences who came along two and three generations too late can "catch up." Of Martha Graham at eighty-four it is written in ads that "her legend dances on." Even Broadway-show choreography, which is more responsive to passing trends than ballet or concert dancing, is being institutionalized—snatched from the oblivion that by its very nature it courts and "reconstructed" for today's audience. If dance does develop a visible past, like other visual arts, it will take a great step forward in legitimization—perhaps the greatest since the Royal Academy of Dance, founded under Louis XIV, codified and named the various positions and movements. But in developments of this size there are always unplanned consequences to look out for.

It's too early to tell what effects on our dance culture the Mighty Betamax may have. But without the help of electronics we are evolving a method of going backward in time: we have the commemorative performance, in which dancers appear not as themselves but as ghosts of former dancers, dancing ghost ballets. Whole repertories—Fokine's, Graham's—consist of commemorative performances. And wherever, in general, you find dances being given out of a need to prolong rather than to create a theatrical moment, there you find commemorative performance. This doesn't mean we must do only dances of our own time. A ballet created the day before yesterday can have a retardative spirit, while one made thirty or fifty years ago can seem filled with fresh inspiration—a true classic. It is folly to look at commemorative performances the same way we look at contemporary ones. Since the past is the past, since performing technique is cumulative and irreversible and will inevitably alter even the hardiest of "texts," since we're only going to get our contemporaries anyway, and not the great legends we've heard about, it's best to go with the thought of taking instruction from what we see. Art is the great teacher, as Shaw remarked, and even dead art has something to say.

What happens when we try to resuscitate dance that isn't high art? I was skeptical of the American Dance Machine before I saw it. I didn't think it would be entertaining, and I didn't think I could learn anything from it. I was wrong on the second count. The American Dance Machine is a new company organized by Lee Theodore, a former Broadway dancer (she was Anybodys in the original *West Side Story*), with the aim of keeping good show dances from vanishing along with shows they were part of. So far, most of the dances that the ADM does are from shows that are still on the straw-hat circuit. Nothing earlier than *Carousel* is represented; the latest excerpt is from *Bubbling Brown Sugar*. And the majority of these dances come from shows that were directed by their choreographers or heavily influenced by them. As a result, the dances are embedded in their original contexts and can't easily be excerpted. (Wasn't "integration" the great technical triumph of those shows?) The dances that get into the ADM repertory appear to be chosen without regard to their excerptability, and they have to be introduced by a bit of patter about where they originally fit in the shows. Most of them are chorus dances. Not Michael Kidd's choreography for Gwen Verdon is selected from *Can-Can* but his "Quadrille," a relatively ordinary group number. The star turns—the reason we might have gone to see a show in the first place—are not only unexcerptable, they're unreproducible. On the ADM program at the Century Theatre is "Satin Doll," a routine choreographed and performed on television by Carol Haney in 1962. I had not seen it before—few had, and that's the point of the reconstruction. But watching the company's Haney substitute doesn't make it possible to see at long last whatever it was Haney had; we can only see what Haney worked with and take instruction from that.

If the law of irreversible technique applies in ballet and concert dancing, it applies with double force here. Most of the time, you can't tell when a dance was made; the technique is echoless. And of those choreographers whom we think of as having made the strongest imprint on show dancing in their time—Robert Alton, George Balanchine, Jack Cole, Jerome Robbins —there is no sampling. There is nothing from any of the Katherine Dunham revues. One can sympathize: the rights-and-permissions problem must be a perpetual headache. And physical recovery must in many instances be impossible. The dances that Doris Humphrey and Charles Weidman did on Broadway might be very interesting to see today, but they are probably forgotten. Specialty numbers are by definition lost. It may be that the decline of specialty and star performing in shows—a decline that began as long ago as the forties but steepened in recent years—makes the advent of something like the ADM feasible. One reviewer called the company a sequel to A *Chorus Line*. Like *Dancin'*, it's part of a trend. It also makes a lot of pre–*Chorus Line* shows look like prologues. Because so many of the ensemble routines were arranged as killers by their choreographers, the audience takes quite a battering before the night is over. Although it's very noisy and its idiom isn't one I admire, the Kidd "Quadrille" struck me as strong evidence of his talent. Onna White's resourceful "If the Rain's Gotta Fall," from *Half a Sixpence*, and Danny Daniels's "Clog Dance," from *Walking Happy*, were also events that I'm glad to have found out about. What keeps these numbers from being magical is not the high pressure so much as the lack of rhythmic and dynamic variety. Agnes de Mille's folk ballets of the forties were in an elevated idiom I like even less, yet nothing else on the program was as refreshing as her "Come to Me, Bend to Me," from *Brigadoon*. The dancing was clear without being forced; it had some complexity, even a touch of unpredictability; and it opened up space. It was interesting to see how all that conspired with a pleasant tune (here very badly sung by an offstage voice) to create a setting for the emotion that was part of the original show.

Perhaps it's just a question of temperament, but I find the pitiless verve of contemporary Broadway nightmarish. To others it may be careless fun—"energizing," as somebody says in *Saturday Night Fever*. But I often wonder why an audience needs to be in the theatre at all. Theatrical illusion isn't given a chance to develop. Nobody seems to believe in the kind of cordial rapport that can exist between a performer and his audience. Singers and dancers have given up trying for it; they project themselves so mechanically that they get a return whether the audience responds or not. Sitting there watching these numb rituals, a viewer can gradually go numb himself—it's like being the wall in a squash court. For live performance to have entered this state, it must have passed through a long process of devaluation. Miking, which is obtrusive in so many shows (not in the ADM's), can sever the performer from the sound he's making. Then, too, performers who regularly tape television shows may soon get the habit of treating every audience like a studio audience and giving sealed-off performances. Magnetic tape is making us indifferent to the actual moment of an event; it's destroying "the art of the moment." Dance archivists are turning the loss to advantage, but how long will it be before the frozen moment acquires that pre-frozen look? Commemorative performances are all around us. We who hand on our moment to posterity have become posterity ourselves.

The New York City Ballet is the only one of the world's great companies which produces all its own choreography. Even a *Coppélia* or a *Bournonville Divertissements* qualifies as a house production, germinated in School of American Ballet classes and workshops. For its second première of the season, the company did something unusual: it put on a collection of works in progress, mostly by Jerome Robbins, under the title A *Sketch Book*. By the end of the season, one of these works, headed *Verdi Variations*, was on its way to a place in the repertory. The cast consisted of Kyra Nichols, Peter Martins (in a role later taken advantageously by Daniel Duell), and four of the youngest men in the corps. Robbins is said to be adding women. When completed, the piece should make a ballet that will be pleasant to see often. Robbins has taken the sweetest and bounciest dance music from *I Vespri Siciliani* and *I Lombardi*. Thoughts of Balanchine's recent *Ballo della Regina*, which is also set to Verdi, are fruitless; the ballets are not really comparable. The one thing they have in common is bright roles that set off their ballerinas, and here Robbins has inevitably been less effective than Balanchine—anyone would be. Nichols's role contains some fascinating twists—the directional switches in the chaînés at the end of the solo, for example—but it doesn't supply her with the kind of technical challenge which is also an idealized definition of her potential. And although the ballet is sunnier and more relaxed than Robbins has been in some time, it's also a little cautious, a little too laid back. In Duell's dancing of the principal male role (which was made for him), the ballet acquired some edge. Perhaps with expansion it will acquire more.

Other parts of A *Sketch Book* gave us the more ceremonious Robbins in a suite of the dances for men that he has been working on for some time. The first, for a company of sixteen in eighteenth-century dress, took the form of a fencing class, with a mass drill followed by separate exercises (dances) for three, then six, then two—sort of a *Konservatoriet* with foils. The music was by Handel; in the duet, it changed to an eccentric, scrapy composition for double bass by Heinrich von Biber, and the two dancers (the brothers Daniel and Joseph Duell) did turning leaps around the stage, slicing the air with their foils. *Solo* looked like one of the *Goldberg Variations* set to Telemann's Fantasies for Unaccompanied Violin. A long dance in three parts, it contained some very inventive material for D. Duell, whom Robbins seems to have selected as his chief interpreter these days. Robbins appears to be working at giving the NYCB male corps a much-needed look of weight. Duell's combination of elasticity and gravity may be exactly what he wants. The non-Robbins contribution was a gentle, mock-romantic pas de deux for Heather Watts and Sean Lavery: music by Rossini, choreography by Peter Martins. Wandery, repetitious, and over-long at its first performance, it was tightened and smartened up by its last. Martins uses a lot of small connecting steps for an effect of wary logic; the final sweep-off comes as a prepared-for joke. His ballet of a season ago to Ives music, *Calcium Light Night*, has been inserted by Balanchine in his own *Ivesiana*, where its presence is disruptive. Apart from looking trivial next to Balanchine's choreography, Martins's ballet is a ballet of the seventies, whereas Balanchine's evokes images that are of Ives's period as well as our own.

For the sake of our local pride, it may be just as well that the Royal Ballet didn't play New York this year. Its new *Sleeping Beauty* would have put American Ballet Theatre's production, now two years old, to further shame, and that at a time when it had undergone yet another batch of feckless revisions. I should say partly feckless. Carabosse's passages in the Prologue are beginning to tie in with the music and with her sister fairies, and there are changes for the better in the choreography of several of the variations. Other changes in this act are fussy rearrangements of standard effects; more niggling revisions occur in the following acts, and jolting tucks are taken in the score. The few improvements are minor; the big change that needs to be made is in emphasis and tone. The dancers give each moment the same weight, as if uncertain which moments are the ones that make the ballet a masterpiece. The season saw many different casts, as usual. An occasional Aurora had an occasional success, but there's no point in discussing this or that dancer as long as the production itself is unrealized.

Watching Ballet Theatre do *Beauty*, one begins to doubt the status of the old ballet. The dances seem thin, the story hopelessly artificial, the roles insufficiently demanding. Watching the Royal, one doesn't know where to look, there is so much to see. Style attaches to every move: a unison port de bras can become an event of magnitude. When the fairy flock arranges itself along the footlights in one of its perfect tableaux (which aren't in the ABT version at all), we see a picture of eternal youth and beauty, and we see motion in its stillness like the pieces of a reflection which float together on the trembling surface of a pool. Not a static or separate image but a materialization, the picture emerges as the grand resolution of countless small strokes, gestures quick and slow, that had been going on since the rise of the curtain. The cohesion of these strokes and the perspective they create for the major happenings and climaxes of the ballet are part of what *The Sleeping Beauty* is about. It's the grand manner, and it's no more of an unreachable fantasy than was Versailles, which is the implied setting of the ballet. To get perfection of detail, harmony of proportion, motion in stillness (and stillness in motion), you need a finely tuned ensemble, and you also need a good director. The new Royal *Beauty*, supervised by Ninette de Valois, has everything it needs.

It is a lavish but not an opulent production. The sets were cramped on the stage of Houston's Jones Hall, but the hall is acoustically a warm place; under Ashley Lawrence, and especially under Anthony Twiner, the Houston Symphony was a sensitive accomplice of the dancers. Several dances from the epochal 1946 production have been restored—Ashton's Garland Waltz, Florestan and His Sisters—along with some from subsequent productions.

The best of these is Ashton's Sapphire variation, now given by one of the Sisters. I would like to see it where Ashton originally put it, in the Prologue, as the variation of a seventh fairy. Without an uneven number of fairies, the Lilac Fairy can't be central, and she should be. I believe Petipa contrived this by making dance roles for the six fairies and a mime role for Lilac. He never did choreograph a Lilac Fairy variation.

David Walker's designs, of an exceptional delicacy, put the time of the story back where it belongs, in the seventeenth and eighteenth centuries, and echo some of the features of the Oliver Messel version, which ABT has acquired. But the scale is more modest—more history-book than storybook. Carabosse is played by a young woman. Her mime speeches in the Prologue have been extended through the musical passages that used to be given to the other fairies; the soft music feminizes her. Lynn Seymour plays the part in a passionate fury; Monica Mason glares magnificently, like Glenda Jackson. What we lose in grotesquerie we gain in glamour. In the Panorama, we see the boat moving across the mouth of an ocean cave, a lovely effect that is over too soon. So, too, with the moment of the Awakening when, on a chord Tchaikovsky did not write, the curtain is dropped until it can rise on the polonaise in the third act. This clumsy transition is the production's only serious flaw. The onstage transformation in the first (1946) version of the Messel production kept the action climbing. Without such an effect or a reasonable substitute there is really no point in linking Acts II and III. (At Ballet Theatre, there is now an intermission between the acts.) But the main objective of this newest Royal Ballet production, its third in ten years, has been achieved. *Beauty* has been reborn.   —*July 10, 1978*

News from the Muses

When Diaghilev asked me about the "argument" of my Apollo, *I answered that none exists, and that this is the key to the mystery of Terpsichore.*

IGOR STRAVINSKY

Of the sixty-eight "Russian Ballets" produced by Serge Diaghilev in the years between 1909 and 1929, not more than a handful survive in living performance as masterpieces with the heat of inspiration still in them. I would name only four: Fokine's *Les Sylphides,* Nijinsky's *L'Après-midi d'un Faune,* Nijinska's *Les Noces,* and Balanchine's *Apollo.* It is difficult for a New Yorker to speak thus of these four ballets—or, indeed, to speak of them at all. The first has not been given a worthy performance in this city since the last visit of the Kirov Ballet, in 1964; *Faune* can be seen in London and Paris but not in New York; by *Les Noces* I mean the Royal Ballet revival shown here in 1967 and never again, so poor was its reception; *Apollo* has been out of New York City Ballet's repertory since 1973.* (A respectful but blurry production was mounted by American Ballet Theatre in 1974–75 without Balanchine's supervision.) The Diaghilev ballets that we have been seeing in the past few seasons—*Schéhérazade, Le Spectre de la Rose, Firebird, Petrushka, Parade,* and *Pulcinella*—may have been masterpieces in their day, but they have no chance in ours. Although the music retains its appeal, the impact of its realization onstage is unrecapturable. A clue to the loss is the value that was assigned to dancing in those days—fairly low compared with music, scenery, costumes, story, and mime. A dance virtuoso like Nijinsky was expected to work as much with the last three elements as with dance and bring everything to a focus in his performance. To dancers and audiences trained in the aesthetic of modern classicism, the color, the drama, the "mimetic body" of Fokine are likely to seem extraneous to the lyric impulse of dance. Part of our trouble with *Les Sylphides,* the most purely lyrical of Fokine's works, is that purity to us is sterility to Fokine. When Nijinsky's roles are danced, our usual impression is that something has been left out of the choreography. The great exception is the ballet he created for himself. *L'Après-midi d'un Faune* is totally a dance conception, to which nothing in the way of color or drama need be added by the performer. Simple as that conception is, it suits our modern faith in the efficacy of dance as art; we can see that every move is an eventful stroke of choreography valued for its own sake.

Les Sylphides suits this faith of ours, too, although audiences of the time undoubtedly saw it nostalgically as recapitulating a host of nineteenth-century ballets blancs, with their aura of woodsy melancholy. The stages through which the early drafts of *Chopiniana* passed to become the ballet that Diaghilev titled *Les Sylphides* represented Fokine's accommodation of the new principle of poetic distillation. *Chopiniana* was Romanticism; *Les Sylphides* was about it. In the four surviving masterpieces of the Diaghilev era, the emphasis on dance as absolute expression grew ever more ritualistic in its intensity. The dances themselves took on the nature of archaic naive ritual. Nijinsky the choreographer cultivated atavisms; the revolution begun in *Faune* culminated in *Le Sacre du Printemps—The* Rite *of Spring.* Lost after seven performances, it is the missing link between the two sibling ballets. If we had it to revive today, might not the choreography of *Sacre* stand equal to that of Nijinsky's *Faune* and Nijinska's *Noces?* When we remember the relative infrequency of absolute-dance ballets in the Diaghilev repertory, when we note the links among their authors (Nijinsky, Nijinska,

---

* *Postscript 1982:* See page 180. *L'Après-midi d'un Faune* was produced by the Joffrey Ballet in 1979 and by American Ballet Theatre in 1980.

Stravinsky account by themselves or with others for nearly all of them), then we must presuppose a consistency at least of purpose. The subject of *Les Noces* was another ritual—a Russian peasant wedding, celebrated in such a way as to remove all traces of anthropological realism. Nijinska restored the pointwork that her brother had banned (the two girls in his *Jeux* were restricted to high half-point), but anyone who has seen the ballet knows that this was not done out of academic piety. The academy had been effectively smashed. By 1928, the next-to-last year in the life of the Ballets Russes, Balanchine could use academic technique in *Apollo* as Nijinsky had used anti-academicisms in *Faune*—for the purpose of asserting cardinal priorities of substance over decoration, invention over representation. The danse d'école was reinstated with the full force of the conviction that this, too, was the dance absolute, as pure as any ceremony of the race, not to be confined by the merely ornamental usages of dull ballet masters. Stravinsky, presiding over the trio *Sacre*, *Noces*, and *Apollo*, had much to say both in precipitating and in resolving this crisis in the poetics of dance. A balletomane even before his adoption by Diaghilev, Stravinsky perceived the highest expression in dance to be purity in whatever mode—dancing with no meaning apart from itself. Nijinsky showed that the aim of dance technique was essentially clarification; its first concerns were with balance, gravity, rhythm, proportion—not with turnout, toe shoes, and the eight directions of the body. This was bedrock definition, and because of the power of its demonstration theatrical dancing, which was growing pretty, grew beautiful once more.

Stravinsky became a classicist. ("Neoclassicist" was the term.) The occasion of *Apollo* called forth much self-definition. "I feel myself to be far from the aesthetic of Fokine," he wrote in explanation of the change in the temper of his work. (Fokine, of course, had staged Stravinsky's first ballets.) "We were saturated with Classicism at the time, and today it has returned with a new and doubly powerful fervor. . . . I consider Petipa to be the greatest artist of all, the founder of a choreographic canon without rival." It is possible that Diaghilev's production of *The Sleeping Beauty* in 1921, for which Stravinsky arranged portions of the score, brought about this estimate of Petipa. It certainly was the gateway for many a neoclassicist of that generation. In *An Autobiography*, published here in 1936, Stravinsky devotes several paragraphs of commendation to the production. There is no hint of his ever having held a different allegiance, as there is in the set of remarks I have just quoted from, which are included in *Stravinsky in Pictures and Documents*, by Vera Stravinsky and Robert Craft, to be published this fall by Simon & Schuster. Here Stravinsky says, after dissociating himself from Fokine, "One evolves, and I have the luck to have very little memory, which is what enables me to begin each new step of my life forgetting the past." In the autobiography, mention of Diaghilev's *Sleeping Beauty* inspires the much-cited credo in which Stravinsky speaks of his "profound admiration for classical ballet, which in its very essence, by the beauty of its *ordonnance* and the aristocratic austerity of its forms, so closely corresponds with my conception of art." He continues:

> *For here, in classical dancing, I see the triumph of studied conception over vagueness, of the rule over the arbitrary, of order over the haphazard. I am thus brought face to face with the eternal conflict in art between the Apollonian and the Dionysian principles. The latter assumes ecstasy to be the final goal—that is to say, the losing of oneself—whereas art demands above all the full consciousness of the artist. There can, therefore, be no doubt as to my choice between the two. And if I appreciate so highly the value of classical ballet, it is not simply a matter of taste on my part, but because I see exactly in it the perfect expression of the Apollonian principle.*

There is providence in the history of the creation of the ballet *Apollo*. Although obviously intending it for Diaghilev, Stravinsky was fulfilling an American commission, and the world première, with choreography by Adolph Bolm, took place in the auditorium of the Library of Congress, in Washington, D.C., on April 27, 1928. The production did not outlast the festival of modern music it was commissioned for; Stravinsky did not take part (he apparently thought there was going to be more attention from the White House), preferring to concentrate his energies on the impending European première. This had choreography by Balanchine, whom Diaghilev thought of as his "American" choreographer. Exactly nine years from the day of the première of the "false" *Apollo*, Stravinsky would conduct the New York première of Balanchine's version, and eventually the two of them would become American citizens. *Apollo* is both a native and an adopted son of America. Yet in its fiftieth-anniversary year the only commemorative production in the country took place in Chicago, as part of that city's annual International Dance Festival of Stars. As it happened, the troupe that provided choreography for the Washington première was Chicago-based. Adolph Bolm had opened a school in Chicago, and the dancers were his students. Ruth Page, Bolm's Terpsichore and later the founder of her own company in Chicago, remembers little about the ballet today. Elise Reiman, the Calliope (and the Terpsichore in the Balanchine version of 1937, at the Metropolitan), recalls only that the hardest choreography she was given was an attitude promenade with one arm around Bolm's neck, "so the dancing was probably on a very elementary level." It is widely supposed that Balanchine cannot be drawn into any plan to honor the masterpiece of his youth. When I asked Geraldine Freund, the organizer of the Chicago festival, how she managed to get his permission to stage it, she said, "I went to him and asked." Mikhail Baryshnikov starred as Apollo, the sequel to his appearance last year at the festival as the Prodigal Son. We've had many interesting Apollos (though few as interesting as Baryshnikov), but not many good Prodigals. The reason may be that the role of the Prodigal requires an acting as much as a dancing gift. In a recent interview with the New York *Times,* Balanchine stressed, as he so often has, the paramountcy of pure-dance expression, saying, "You're not supposed to act in my ballets. I don't like it. Acting is so banal. You have to be a great actor not to be banal." The modern aesthetic he helped shape does not altogether smother *The Prodigal Son.* It is a durable, beautiful work—the only other Balanchine ballet that remains from the Diaghilev years. But it is not on the summit with *Apollo.*

For the Library of Congress, the patron Elizabeth Sprague Coolidge had commissioned a half-hour ballet from Stravinsky on a subject of his choice. Stravinsky says that *Apollo* was "the first attempt to revive academic danc-ing in a work actually composed for the purpose." *Les Sylphides,* of course, was set to orchestrated Chopin, and it was a classical ballet on a romantic subject. *Apollo* was a classical ballet on a classical subject, from Greek mythology—the kind of ballet that had been out of fashion for a hundred years. The subject was the Apollo *musagète*—Apollo as leader of the Muses, an aspect in which the god appears often in the history of art. There were in mythology nine Muses, and the terms of the Coolidge commission called for not more than four dancers. It may have been with *Les Sylphides* in mind—he specifically envisioned a white ballet—that Stravinsky nar-rowed his choice to one male and three female soloists: Fokine's cast minus the corps de ballet. Stravinsky's Muses, he explained, are the ones who to-gether inspire ballets:

> *Calliope, receiving the stylus and tablets from Apollo, personifies poetry and its rhythm; Polyhymnia, finger on lips, represents mime. . . . Finally, Terpsichore, combining in herself both the rhythm of poetry and the eloquence of gesture, reveals dancing to the world, and thus among the Muses takes the place of honor beside the Musagète.*

(Just as in *Les Sylphides* one sylph is singled out to dance a pas de deux with the Poet.)

As befits a ballet conceived on the Apollonian principle, there is no story in the usual sense of a drama. Stravinsky in his program note referred to "a play without a plot." Dancing that is free to express only itself may alone penetrate the mystery of Terpsichore. However, there is a narrative of sorts. In the Prologue, Apollo is born to Leto, laboring on a mountaintop on the island of Delos. The program's language is biblical: ". . . and the earth smiled beneath her, and the child sprang forth to the light." The props specified include swaddling clothes in the form of "a white veil of fine tissue . . . bound . . . with a golden girdle." Leto's handmaidens bring the godling nectar and ambrosia, which are not in Balanchine's ballet, instead of a lute, which is. After a blackout, the youth Apollo is shown alone, testing his powers. The Muses enter, and he chooses his favorite in a competition that recalls the Judgment of Paris. The action is all formal dancing, consisting of five solo variations (two for Apollo), a pas d'action, pas de deux, coda, and apotheosis. In the last, the god has reached his maturity, all arts commingle in his indivisible glory, and the four divinities wend their way back up the mountain, where they await the chariot that will fly them to Parnassus.

A sign that Stravinsky may not have planned the (mimed) use of a lute is his failure to include its sound in his orchestration. Later, Orpheus will have a lyre, which we hear. The orchestra for *Apollo* is all strings, by which the composer hoped to revive a taste in Western music for melody. *Apollo* is, in fact, one of his most melodious scores. The wonderful "polyphonic web" of the pas de deux was not spun, according to Robert Craft's documentation, until the end of composition. The changing tempos in the coda may have given the clue to the form of the pas de deux which Stravinsky had been seeking, for he writes the word *"zakluchainiye"* ("solution") in the manuscript at that point and goes on to complete what Diaghilev described as "a dance adagio in which the first musical part plays at a speed twice as fast as the second, three times as fast as the third, and four times as fast as the fourth. Thus the same melody has four different aspects." Stravinsky also writes, at the head of the score, "*Voici cet 'Apollon' dit 'Musagète,' c. à d., qui amène la Musa Ver'igor.*" ("Here we have that Apollo called Leader of the Muses, that is to say, the one who leads the Muse to Igor.") The Muse Ver'igor is Vera Sudeikina, who was to become Stravinsky's wife. Stravinsky has called the true subject of *Apollo* versification, but the only scansion that the lay ear may be aware of is in the variation of Calliope, which is cast in the iambic hexameter of the classical French alexandrine. This is a twelve-syllable line divided by a caesura into two equal parts. An epigraph taken by the composer from Boileau's *L'Art Poétique* serves as an example of the form and a piece of advice to the poet:

> *Que toujours dans vos vers le sens coupant les mots*
> *Suspende l'hémistiche et marque le repos.*

(Richard Howard's translation is "Let meaning in your verse that shapes each word / Always halve the line so that a rest is heard.") Stravinsky had the year before finished the opera-oratorio *Oedipus Rex*, to a libretto by Jean Cocteau, and problems of prosody evidently stayed with him. *Oedipus* was also the first of his theatrical works to deal with a Greek mythological theme. But *Apollo* reflects classical French culture, not classical Greek. Bolm as Apollo wore a "Grecian" tunic of chain-mail mesh, a helmet with a plumed crest, and long Louis XIV curls. He also equipped himself with a lyre. A former member of the Ballets Russes, Bolm was a projection of *le Roi Soleil*, like the hero of *Le Pavillon d'Armide*, who ventures into the legendary past of ancient Greece (and like Florestan XXIV, the monarch of *The Sleeping Beauty*). Apollo as the Sun King may not have been precisely Stravinsky's idea, but the classicism of Versailles—in music and dance as well as poetry—was certainly on his mind. As was the contemporary Paris of *le jazz hot*. Reinterpreting the Greeks was then and for some years to come a preoccupation of French arts and letters. In the same year as *Oedipus Rex*, Diaghilev produced *La Chatte*, with Serge Lifar as the hero of an Aesop fable dancing Balanchine's choreography in a geometrical setting of clear plastic.

Diaghilev's *Apollon Musagète* followed Bolm's by six weeks. On June 12, 1928, the curtains of the Théâtre Sarah-Bernhardt opened on the birth scene, which had been omitted in Washington. It is night. A pavane, played largo di molto at first, accelerates to a panting climax. At the conclusion of Leto's labor, a small crevice in the mountain comes to light, and a wrapped bundle rolls out. Two nymphs, Leto's handmaidens, pull the bundle erect. Running in widening circles, they unwind Apollo's wrappings as he stands motionless. When they reach the last layer, he takes a preparation and spins himself free. The Christ Child was wrapped in swaddling clothes. Russian peasants customarily swaddled their babies. But Serge Lifar's entrance was also reminiscent of Ida Rubinstein's in *Cléopâtre*: she emerged from a sarcophagus as a bandaged mummy; attendants solemnly unwound veil after veil until, with a gesture of triumph, she flung off the last. It is interesting to compare this variation on Plutarch's Cleopatra, who rolled herself in a rug, with a scene related by Balanchine in that same *Times* interview. Talking about his revival, in Copenhagen in 1931, of *La Légende de Joseph*, a ballet by Richard Strauss that he can never have seen, he says that he rearranged the libretto so that when Joseph was sold by his brothers "they put him in a Persian carpet and he rolled out, naked. It was very good." After Apollo is born, the choreographer introduces the first of his ceremonial images—the "wheelbarrow," in which one handmaiden supports the other as she carries Apollo's lute. Balanchine's choreographic style at this time was distinguished by imaginative, sometimes outlandish acrobatic constructions. Observers of *Apollo* in its first season were especially struck by a grouping that occurred at the end of the Prologue. Eric Walter White, the Stravinsky scholar, describes an Apollo "left swimming in the air, balanced about his navel upon a pillar formed by the four erect legs of the recumbent goddesses, one of the most curious of the succession of static poses which make up Balanchine's choreography to this 'ballet.'" The scene was soon replaced by the simpler and more expressive one of Apollo, helped by the nymphs, learning how to play his lute and beginning to come alive to the power of music. One can only assume that by "static poses" White, who in later years came to write enthusiastically about the choreography, is referring to those constructions of Balanchine's which are really visual metaphors. Instead of the nymphs' bringing Apollo his lute in a wheelbarrow, which would have been a homely enough image, entirely true to the pastoral setting, the nymphs *are* a wheelbarrow. This is magic, and yet it's still homely. The "swimming lesson" that everyone now notices is the one that Apollo gives Terpsichore at the end of their pas de deux, where, balanced prone on his bowed shoulders, she seems to become the crest of the wave he dives through. The "troika," or "chariot," with its harnessing of the three Muses in a lively chase, and the "boat," where a girl's upright body lifted ahead of a travelling group suggests a ship's prow parting the waves, are fantasies that we seem to see through the spume of Apollo's fountain at Versailles. Most beautiful of all: the "peacock," which is made of legs in arabesque lifting high, higher, and higher still in a fanlike spread behind the body of the god as he stands braced for his ascent to Parnassus. Glenway Wescott once suggested that the ballet should be re-titled "Apollo's Games with the Muses." He meant, of course, children's party games—the kind that used to be called "tableaux." The "Sistine ceil-ing" occurs at the start of the pas de deux, with Apollo touching his finger-tip to Terpsichore's. Its tinge of self-consciousness is the only thing in the ballet that reminds us of Balanchine's actual—as opposed to his spiritual—youth at the time. He was twenty-four. Only geniuses are really young at twenty-four; the rest of us are just childish.

Although *Apollo* is an allegory, its meaning does not collect inside these separate graphic metaphors but spreads beyond them, where it is sustained by the larger seriousness of dance images and dance continuity. That such a spreading out should be possible is not only necessary to the story *Apollo* tells—it is the story. In Apollo's lute solo, his dance with the Muses, and Calliope's solo, we follow a dance for its implications as human behavior, perhaps getting a bit pleasurably lost along the way but still grasping a clear thought. By the time of Terpsichore's solo, which so endears her to Apollo, we have unconsciously switched to another, more dazzling context for watching, which feels like thought itself. *Apollo* has been a classic of our theatre for so long that no one stops to think anymore how difficult it must have been to create Terpsichore and make her special *in a ballet*. And on Stravinsky's terms! Balanchine had to invent a mistress of classical dancing —one whose natural ease of expression was beyond question. He had to convey that dancing is the finest of the Muses' arts, because it is the closest to Apollo's art, music; yet the sister variations could not be unmusical. To make matters worse, Diaghilev had decreed that Balanchine give the role to Alice Nikitina instead of Alexandra Danilova. The men compromised, and the two ballerinas alternated in the role. There appear to have been differ-ences between Nikitina's and Danilova's versions of the solo, and periodi-cally since then Balanchine has made slight changes in the choreography to suit different interpreters. Nikitina, the first Terpsichore, was a long-legged, cat-eyed woman with an elegantly boyish body. Danilova, an en-chantress even then, recalls that Balanchine put more airwork into her version, including some large sissonnes that have since disappeared. The ballerinas of the New York City Ballet have always danced the same cho-reography, although Suzanne Farrell's grand-scale reproportioning of it in

1963 was in itself a new feature. (Farrell danced some anniversary performances with Peter Martins in Monte Carlo this spring, and Nikitina, who was to die a short time afterward, came to see them.) One of Balanchine's great achievements in Terpsichore's solo is the startling sense of an onward flow of motion that continues through four sudden stops in a casual turned-in pose, each stop corresponding to a musical rest in which the sense of a musical design also continues. Terpsichore toys calmly with contradictions, as if trying to catch herself unawares. The sinuous plastique of the poses she stops in keeps presenting the same image, but is it the same? Is it moving sculpture that we see or static dance? And she applies other tests: regulation school steps are crisscrossed with countless small novelties—foot flexions, stabbing toes, heelwork. Contrariness is one of the characteristics of the dances in *Apollo*. We see driving leaps that do not advance, leaps that go *down*, back-front reversals that seem to maintain the mysterious constancy of a shape even as it changes. We see, in other words, an examination and also an expression, in rawer terms, of the complex logic of classicism as Petipa had developed it. The whole Ballets Russes circle knew what Balanchine was about, and Diaghilev is said by his régisseur Serge Grigoriev to have considered *Apollo* Stravinsky's greatest ballet.

Lubov Tchernicheva, Grigoriev's wife, danced the original Calliope. She was a beautiful woman who customarily did character roles—Thamar, Zobeide in *Schéhérazade*, the Wife in *Le Tricorne*, the Princess in *Firebird*. Calliope's solo has a mime base; it mirrors the pangs of literary creation and is comical and touching. A "pang" is heard as a thudding D-minor chord at the end of every hexametrical phrase; here Balanchine, a world away from Martha Graham, set a contraction. Calliope's poetry is inscribed in the air with sweeping grands ronds de jambe; a secret message scrawled in the hand is shown to the mighty Apollo, who turns his head away in distress. Now it is Polyhymnia's turn. It seems typical of Balanchine's wit to give the Muse of heroic mime an all-dance variation and one of exceptional difficulty. Polyhymnia requires a technique strong enough in turns and jumps to be sustained without the aid of the arms, for throughout the solo one arm holds a finger pressed to the lips and the other beats time. Unlike Calliope, who groans and falters, Polyhymnia scampers through her paces, hardly able to contain herself. The ground seems to skid out from under her feet. But her exuberance betrays her in the end—she opens her mouth and blabs, and is disqualified by Apollo. The choreography contains a sequence of double en dedans pirouettes into a stop in high arabesque. Recovering, the dancer now steps ahead, kicks high, and crosses the front foot over the other at the ankle—an *Apollo* motif. The combination is often simplified by separating the pirouette from the arabesque. The role was created for one of the most extraordinarily endowed dancers of the day—Felia Doubrovska. Polyhymnia's characteristic backward-tilting stance, its legginess emphasized by point tendue, seems, in one version or another, to have stamped itself in the annals of ballet. Felia Doubrovska says that Balanchine originated it for her in *La Pastorale*, in 1926. In écarté, straddling a recumbent Prodigal, it is viciously and famously triumphant. But is there not some relation here to the Hostess in Nijinska's *Les Biches*, of a few years before? In Apollo's role, notably in his stealthy sidewise approach to the Muses at the end of the pas d'action, there are traces of the Faun.

Apollo's solos are danced to a pavane and a sarabande, two forms well known to the Sun King, who once performed the role of Apollo in one of his own court ballets. The moderate tempos and terre-à-terre steps were suited to Serge Lifar, a gifted performer but no virtuoso. Lifar was Diaghilev's pet and the star of the company. He really did look like a Greek boy-god, according to Danilova, with his small, perfect head, olive skin, eyes like dark-green pools, and a pug nose that had been straightened by injections of paraffin. "We used to tease him about that," Danilova remembers. " 'Lifar! Don't sit in the sun, your nose will melt!' But he was unbelievably built when he was a young man. His waist was twenty-three and a half inches, one centimeter thinner than mine. And he had beautiful hands." Worshipping Aphrodite in *La Chatte*, Lifar had lifted his beautiful hands, and the same palms-up gesture of invocation appears in Apollo's second variation. As the arms curve up and down, crossing and recrossing the body in preparation for flight, they become the pinions of the eagle, who now leaves the nest. Apollo was the son of Zeus, whose symbol was the eagle, and of the mortal Leto. Balanchine has characterized Apollo as "a wild, half-human youth who acquires nobility through art," but this conception has been confused over the years by dancers who picture instead some Hellenic ideal of manhood. Balanchine's is not the Golden Age Apollo. A contemporary review called Lifar "Etruscan" and "archaic." His lack of refinement as a classical dancer was emphasized by "rough" or "wrong" passages in the choreography like the downward flow of energy in the legs when they swing at full pendulous force and unexpectedly levitate the body. There is a difficult corkscrew pirouette, and a few leaps which derive from the decathlon. It was a sports-conscious age, like our own. Balanchine's first American Apollo, Lew Christensen, seems to have incarnated the image of an Olympic all-rounder. In the revival of 1957, Jacques d'Amboise was a model of rangy athletic grace, and, for many, D'Amboise remains the great Apollo. Neither Edward Villella nor Rudolf Nureyev has quite lived up to expectations in the role, although both might have if they had performed it earlier in their careers. As for Peter Martins, it must be the only role in which his looks and his magnificent noble style work against him. He is unswervingly accurate in every step, yet he can't really show the god growing up; the radiant calm of the apotheosis is in the same key as everything else. Baryshnikov is a radical Apollo. At the beginning of the second scene, when the air resounds with music of his own making, his intensity is almost Dionysian. His senses gape; his energy is raw. Although Apollo is commonly thought of as an "adagio" role, Baryshnikov, alone of the Apollos I have seen, understands how the dancing might supply the percussive dimension that is absent in the score. He is an Apollo who could play a drum as well as a lute. Even when Apollo learns majesty and control, Baryshnikov does not present himself as a polished dancer. He is still a primitive who recognizes in the discipline of classical art a sensuous complicity with his own genius. Later in the season, joining the New York City Ballet at Saratoga, Baryshnikov made a blazing début in another Stravinsky ballet, *Rubies*. A sophisticated version of his Apollo, the performance was an unconscious demonstration of Balanchine's belief in the persistence of archetypes, in changeless change.

For Balanchine himself, this first collaboration with Stravinsky was, as he later declared, a decisive experience. From what he called "white music, in places white-on-white," he learned to concentrate his means, to seek a controlling image. "It seemed to tell me that I could dare not to use everything, that I, too, could eliminate." The wide croisé pose in fourth fondu in which Terpsichore seems to frame her own portrait at the start of her variation and the consistency of the frame as she steps out, turning under the overhead arm (to music that recalls Calliope's iambic feet), reappear like an echo in the pas de deux, when out of a supported pirouette she suddenly flies onto Apollo's thigh and sits there as he strides and pivots, only changing her arms in fourth position to complete the echo. Later in the pas de deux, another echo, this time of a passage in one of Apollo's variations, occurs as the two advance toward each other all but kneeling, one foot dragging behind. When they do kneel, she offers him her upturned palms and he drops his head on them, a gesture that will be repeated in the coda with all three Muses. In the coda, too, there's an electric moment when Terpsichore runs on, bringing her sisters news of her exciting dance with Apollo, and her side-to-side lunging sissonnes recapitulate in jazz rhythm the syncopated lunges in the "dance lesson" of the pas de deux. Partly because of its Stravinskian-jazz element, the ballet will always remind us of its period. However, the first few times I saw *Apollo*, in 1957, it looked more "twenties" to me than it ever has since. The effect of the years stretching between it and us has been to soften the impact of its period and its precocity. Or perhaps it was the effect of the style that NYCB dancers evolved for it—a plushier, more amply defined, and, by the end of the sixties, rather too solemn style. Yet even in the fifties the ballet's links to *The Prodigal Son* (which followed it by one year) seemed more tenuous than those to *Concerto Barocco* or *Agon*. Next to their fluent articulation, its classicism is experimental—but boldly so, not warily. One can still feel the sensation of so many bright discoveries—of Balanchine finding new idiomatic uses for the language of Petipa, turning it this way and that, as Apollo turns his lute, with eager curiosity. It is unimaginable that anyone watching this work fifty years ago would not have recognized its choreographer as the man to carry theatrical dancing into its next great phase. But most of the applause was for Lifar, and a few years later, after Diaghilev's death, it was Lifar—without whom, Sacheverell Sitwell wrote, *Apollo* and *Prodigal* could never again be achieved—who was expected to assume control.

The choreography of *Apollo* did not attract much critical acclaim until Balanchine revived it for Ballet Theatre in the forties (when the epithet "Musagète" was dropped from the title). The 1957 NYCB revival coincided with the première of *Agon* and was produced in budget décor: a wooden staircase going up the side of a booth out of which the birthed Apollo sprang, a kitchen stool on which he sat while the Muses danced. The women wore short white tunics. Apollo was in black tights with white shoes and socks; for the second scene he added a shirt made of two white triangles knotted at the corners. The production was hailed as a revelation, and more or less faithful replicas were seen wherever *Apollo* was given. In very few of these productions has Balanchine participated directly, but he has his trusted régisseurs. Patricia Neary, one of the great Polyhymnias of the sixties, produces the authorized version these days. In Chicago, the stage was set with a black drape over the booth; Balanchine had requested that the birth scene be omitted. He is now said to feel that the ballet cannot be done without proper scenery and costumes, and that, as long as it must exist in concert form, only excerpts should be presented. The Terpsichore was Allegra Kent at her unpredictable best; with Baryshnikov she came astonishingly close to the luminous, definitive performances she used to give with D'Amboise. As Calliope, Georgina Parkinson was a gallant last-minute substitute for Dominique Khalfouni. Nanette Glushak was an inadequate Polyhymnia. One wonders why an appropriately dressed *Apollo* cannot be produced today. The Diaghilev décor was adapted from two paintings by the quaintly "primitive" stylist André Bauchant. Stravinsky had wanted De Chirico. Although he deplored the Bauchant décor in print, Mme Stravinsky said recently that he really liked it—especially the giant floral still-life that was used as a frontcloth: "It was so unexpected that it pleased him in some mystical way." Of the various settings of *Apollo*, Balanchine is said to prefer Tchelitchev's landscape for a 1942 production in Buenos Aires. In the apotheosis, the hills and trees turned into human faces. This was an uncanny transcription not only of Tchelitchev's easel work at that time but of the action of the ballet—the god emerging from the hillside. Noteworthy costumes for the Muses were devised by Chanel in 1928 to take the place of the original tutus. These were off-white tunics of wool jersey cut in uneven lengths and cinched with Charvet neckties, a touch borrowed from the playing fields of Eton. Lifar kept his original, somewhat characterless rose-colored tunic and gold sandals.

Apollo is the first of Balanchine's ballets to reach the age of fifty. His attitude toward the anniversary may be likened to Diaghilev's when celebrations were proposed for his twentieth Paris season. Grigoriev records that Diaghilev begged off:

> "I am afraid I abhor jubilees in general and my own in particular. A jubilee is the beginning of an end: something that rounds off a career. But I am not ready to give up. I wish to continue working. . . ." He paused a moment. "I wish to remain always young."

—September 11, 1978

Just Another Rumba

The hardest years in the life of a dance company are toward the end of its first decade. By then, if the company isn't weathering the strain of success—if it doesn't know how, in the face of inevitable physical deterioration, to maintain the standards that brought it success in the first place—it is in real trouble. There may even come a point where the standards themselves are drawn into question; we begin to wonder if they were ever really there or if we still want them around. Eliot Feld and Arthur Mitchell both started their companies nearly ten years ago, and both have been through hard times. There's no hard time, though, like the present. In a year-old interview by Clive Barnes which is reprinted in the program for the Feld Ballet's fall season at the Public Theatre, Feld talks about how difficult it is to build a company. "It is easy to get it started, but when you get to the nitty-gritty, it is hard to endure—talent is only one-tenth of what it takes to go on. And you have to suffer lean times, artistically as well as financially." There is no reason to suppose that Feld's views would be any less sober today. When he disbanded and then, five years ago, re-formed his company, many people, and perhaps Feld himself, believed that the crisis was behind him. A director of a dance company learns to endure perpetual crisis.

Just last year, Mitchell, too, faced extinction when he lost most of the top dancers in his company—Dance Theatre of Harlem—to Broadway and Hollywood. Without disbanding, Mitchell quietly reconstituted his company, and it was this almost all-new Dance Theatre of Harlem that closed a two-week engagement at Columbia University's Wollman Auditorium last week. Virginia Johnson and Melva Murray-White are still there; the exemplary Ronald Perry now leads the men's division. Mitchell has restocked the repertory with unfamiliar pieces by new choreographers from all over; no brand names here. In some ways, notably in male dancing, the company is stronger than it was before. But having to retool at just the time when it should have been coming into its own has cost it something. No second-phase effort, no matter how resourceful, can ever have the momentum of the first phase, which comes from the excitement of novelty. Dance Theatre of Harlem, made up of black dancers performing in classical style, is doubtless still a new idea to some people. But the evangelical surge that lay behind the impetus of its first years is over, the dancers who personified it are gone, and the company is having to generate a more subtle interest. It has the power to do that, partly because ideology was never what DTH was about anyway. Black classicism as an italicizing and enriching extension of American classicism is no insular dream; it has solid prospects, which can be glimpsed in everything that DTH does. But as long as it remains a goal, and not a reality, it gives rise to theories of the false premise, and some will call it an illusion.

Coincidentally, DTH and the Feld company are just now fighting to keep from becoming a part of show business. From the look of their recent New York seasons, Feld is fighting less hard than DTH. The trifling nature of the two works that were given premières at the Public Theatre, together with their easy mass appeal, showed Feld on the verge of becoming Joseph Papp's Bob Fosse. There was nothing in either *Danzon Cubano* or *Half Time* that would not pass as an interlude in a show; the ensemble portions of *Half Time* even worked the same territory as the weakly satirical patriotic revue that closes Fosse's show *Dancin'*. This material was so unoriginal by the time Fosse put it on Broadway that it is a shock to see Feld toying with it. But Feld probably didn't have Fosse's ballet in mind as much as his own star-spangled mess of a pas de deux for Baryshnikov and Christine Sarry a few seasons ago, called *Variations on "America."* Feld is not a lazy worker, but talk about insular! He seemed not to realize how stale the image of the strutting majorette and the macho athlete already was—he was too buried in his own devices to look up. In *Half Time*, there are some passages that work despite their banality—a slightly myopic baton twirler isn't bad as comedy, and a pas de trois has respectable choreography—but they aren't enough to offset the numbing obviousness of the rest. At the performance I saw, which won the dutiful applause of the Papp audience (none more dutiful), Feld staged an encore consisting of the finale repeated in its entirety. It was dispiriting to think that Feld probably meant to parody Broadway-type excess.

Feld likes to work in series, and *Half Time*, to band music by Morton Gould, is another panel in his series of "American" variations. *Danzon Cubano* is an appendage to last season's *La Vida*, which also used an Aaron Copland score. Willa Kim, Feld's current designer, is another link in the series, and in *Half Time* her flag-emblem costumes (they made me think of sixties cocktail glasses) help to link Feld not only to Feld but to Fosse—she's his current designer, too. Feld performances are beginning to resemble those coordinated interior-design craft shops that let you stylize your home by buying the whole store. And Feld's own craftsmanship, compulsively economical, is getting that modular look. It can easily look pinched, too. *Danzon Cubano* barrenly repeats a few rumba motifs. Where in *La Vida* Feld was able to build dimension into a comparably small movement core, in *Danzon Cubano* he can only exhaust the "Latin" torsions and rocking pelvises; no juice comes from this played-out papaya. *La Vida*, too, drew some of its volume from allusions to other art works, and this tendency can also work against Feld. Since the rumba piece doesn't develop, instead of watching attentively to see what the references mean to Feld we sigh "Jack Cole" or "Katherine Dunham" and let it go at that.

The dance style of the company is the same as the style of the choreography that Feld produces—tight, even-textured, clearly shaped steps, smoothly interlocked. The dances are assembled like stackable units; visually and musically, they have no inner mechanism for expansion or contrast. Measured against a classical standard, they show little variety in the body's contour; they are insufficiently flexible as to the position or base the body moves from. Feld doesn't have the demagogical instinct that makes coarse appeals to an audience—that's why his occasional coarseness is so grating—and one of the surprising things about him is that, for all the loyalty he commands from the Papp public, he still has no audience rapport. (The gratuitous encores and "character" bows he now goes in for are possibly attempts at ingratiation. The curtain call for *Danzon Cubano* is the oddest—utterly out of keeping with the ballet.) He does have, technically speaking, a simple and rather rigid, easy-to-read choreographic style. He also has a company to match it—the girls so indistinguishably blond and bland, the boys so individually grotty. People have been told that this is art, and they ask less of it than they might of a Broadway show. The trap for Feld, who can hardly afford to reduce his equipment, is to start giving them less.

I haven't seen *Doin' It*, the evening-length Broadway-style show that Dance Theatre of Harlem has been touring, but I sense a wavering between what that must represent and the classical ballets the company presented at Wollman Auditorium. I think there's a fake antithesis here. True, the repertory holes are being filled with square plugs—not because that's the "classical" alternative but because so few choreographers can be found (few can even be named) who understand the company's special distinction. The possibilities of black classicism were crystallized a few years back when DTH first appeared in Balanchine's *Agon*; the dancers revitalized the ballet and were released by it as well. But, of course, with the exception of Arthur Mitchell himself, *Agon* was composed for white dancers (of the New York City Ballet), and, even if that were not the case, its horizon is that of another era. In the current DTH repertory, the piece that comes closest to setting off the same kind of spark in the dancers is one choreographed,

Balanchine-style, to Stravinskian jazz. Like all derivative things, it makes much of surface manner, but suddenly, in the third and fourth movements, something erupts out of the music (the *Ebony Concerto*), the choreography takes off on its own, and for at least one excitingly long period it almost soars. There's a limp acrobatic adagio for Melva Murray-White (a specialty of hers), and, later, three gallants maneuver between two trios of girls. Here the company dances with a powerful elegance, although it must still hold too much power in reserve; the rhythms of the choreography aren't as consistently importunate as they might be. The ballet is called *Introducing* . . . (presumably because of some scene-setting preliminaries that start the action), and it is the work of the Singapore-born choreographer Choo San Goh, who composed it originally on the Washington Ballet, where he is now based. It's easy to see why Mitchell acquired it. But another ballet by Goh, also borrowed from Washington, doesn't suit DTH nearly as well. *Variations Sérieuses*, named for Mendelssohn's piano variations, Opus 54, is a lyrical study in linear pictorial arrangements and oddities of pose. DTH dancers are distressingly confined by such a piece; they like to move and use their jump, collectively the finest in American ballet. One saw that jump intermittently in *Troy Game*, choreographed for the men of the company by Robert North. The style of this piece is jocular-jock; the defensiveness is even part of the choreography, which keeps nearing flash points of real dance power and then diving for cover under another hearty "masculine" joke. It's to the credit of the cast, headed by the wonderfully elongated yet compact Ronald Perry, that one remembers the high dance moments as well as the funny business. *Doina*, by the British choreographer Royston Maldoom, looks as though the dancers got it through the mail, step by agonizing step. The costumes for the all-female corps are head-to-foot shrouds, which give the dancers a webbed, unhatched look. One of them attaches herself to a full-grown male who has wandered into the incubator, and the two come sadly to know their doom as the others hobble on and off. The other new pieces were about dancing, and I'm sorry I didn't care for them more. One was a swirling, romantic pas de deux by Arthur Mitchell, which, unlike the things he did for the company in its formative years, seemed aimed more at pleasing an audience than at challenging the dancers. Set to a popular song, *The Greatest* was a bit like commercial-spot choreography. Perhaps it was Mitchell speaking about the company through the words of the song: "I believe that children are our future / Teach them well and let them lead the way."

Unlike the Feld company and many, many other companies, the members of DTH have a thorough dance education; they are trained to dance, not just drilled in repertory. That is why they usually look better than their choreography. Mitchell and his co-director, Karel Shook, have developed a school along with a company, and the one feeds the other. The only other American ballet company seen regularly in New York of which that happens to be true (apart from the New York City Ballet) is the Pennsylvania Ballet, and it is also the only other company with a firm sense of style. Compared to these two smaller ensembles, American Ballet Theatre and the Joffrey might as well not have their schools at all. (Although Feld has just opened a lavishly equipped new school, it isn't clear yet how far he intends it to serve the company.) Because they produce superior dancers, the Pennsylvania and the Harlem companies have trouble finding new ballets that are good enough. One hears much of the choreographer shortage, and it certainly exists, but from what I've seen of established companies both in this country and abroad the crying need is for good dance instruction; given the condition that most companies are in, good choreography would be wasted. Yet the competition for choreographers is such that an Arthur Mitchell has to shop as hard as any other company director and settle, in most cases, for hand-me-downs that—again, in most cases—are imitations, not original works. The Harlem dancers have to punch through too ·many clichés to get at the smoky night-club rumbas of the *Ebony Concerto;* you can see how if they got any closer they might be really dangerous. Is there no bright young choreographer willing to feast with these panthers?

—*October 9, 1978*

Quintessence

As the curtain rises on *Fractions,* the dancers are posed facing in different directions, and their stillness is charged with the kind of tension peculiar to Merce Cunningham. It is a memorable, emblematic opening, and *Fractions,* as it unfolds, has the concentrated energy of a great signature work. When it is over, it seems to have summed up everything important in the Cunningham canon and yet to have weighed not an ounce. *Fractions* is one of the new works that were presented in the Cunningham company's repertory season at the City Center. It was conceived as choreography for television and was taped a year ago in the Cunningham studio. I have seen the tape; it is the finest piece of video choreography anyone has yet made. (A longer version, extended by the use of different takes of identical material, .was· seen in the New York area on cable TV just ahead of the City· Center season.) The dance is divided by four cameras; in the image that we see, quotient and remainder appear side by side and change constantly. In the past, Cunningham has experimented with split screens and chroma-key arrangements. Here he simply sets up TV monitors in the studio to catch the overflow from the main image. Along with solid-color panels, by Mark Lancaster, which are positioned around the space in a different relation to the dancing from what we see in the stage production, the monitors are part of the set. They may show closeups of the dancers being photographed or they may register background action or action not within the range of the main camera. The multiple viewpoints may suddenly contract to a partial viewpoint and the entire frame may be filled with, say, Karole Armitage seen only from the hips up as she goes through the maze of an elaborate pas de deux. Her partner, Robert Kovich, becomes a mysterious erotic presence. Cunningham, alone of the choreographers who have worked with television, has assumed that defining TV space is necessary to the projection of a dance in TV terms. (Twyla Tharp's brilliant *Making Television Dance*, for PBS, was about television more than it was about dance; it was electronics commenting on itself.) And Cunningham's acute sense of how to use television is related to his theatre choreography. The diffused focus, the interchangeable perspectives, the simultaneous play of discrete elements are readily translated to fill the TV void. The same factors that make Cunningham choreography as interesting to watch close up as from a distance make it televisable; as in figure skating, which is also a good show on television, space is fluid. To watch the videodance *Fractions* is to watch the medium find its dancing master. Is it just a coincidence that Lancaster's scenery for Cunningham's latest solo, *Tango*, is a tuned-in (but silent—John Cage provides the sound) television set?

The stage version of *Fractions*, which was first given last winter in Boston, is so reorganized and replotted that only in the content of the choreography can we recognize it as the same dance; even the dancers seem transformed. No monitors are to be seen. (Occasionally, someone will appear over to one side, taking up a position on invisible chalk marks and then walking off. It is typical of Cunningham to take away the cameras and leave their subjects.) *Fractions* may be the most successful of Cunningham's videodances because it's really about dancing, and "television" is metaphorically present in its conception—a part of the real world of change which Cunningham believes in and makes dances about. Unlike *Westbeth*, a former video experiment, *Fractions* isn't fancy and self-conscious, with one eye on the lens; it's a natural happening, whether you see it on the tube or on the stage, and it may be the closest any choreographer has yet come to working with absolute integrity in two media at once. If I prefer the theatrical version, that's because I prefer the theatre. Even Cunningham hasn't shown me where the poetry is in television, although he has shown me its wit. The closing minutes of *Fractions* build to an ensemble section in which the dispersals and regroupings are punctuated by the repetition of a single phrase: three pliés in rhythm followed by plié-hold. On television, credits were flashed over the holds as if they were frozen frames. But there can be no TV equivalent of the moment when, onstage, a group freezes to isolate a solitary leap. There doesn't seem to be any such thing as "solitary" on television—not even when Karole Armitage is alone in her pas de deux.

People are either on camera or off. In the theatre, Kovich's supporting role in the pas de deux is, of course, fully seen, and it is still almost entirely "below frame," but the beautiful poses he takes as he leans away from Armitage's hovering body or embraces it from underneath place the action clearly on two planes. Armitage, with her amazing high extension, is as secure in her upper realm as she would be on point; no ballerina was ever more gracefully or daringly cantilevered. And the drama of it is Kovich's also.

It is impossible to discuss Cunningham's choreography these days without discussing his dancers, many of them newcomers. There was another influx this year, and some former members—Louise Burns, Catherine Kerr —have returned. But for the first time since the turning-over process began, about two years ago, the company has lost its raw-recruit look, and among the girls especially there is a new, sharp sense of style. Armitage exemplifies it; Lisa Fox, Kerr, and the others reveal it, too. It's based on the high, free-swinging leg extensions they all seem to have under admirable control from the inner thigh. What thunderous grands battements these women produce, and what floating footwork! Armitage's développé is impeccably skewed as it swings into one of Cunningham's favorite positions—neither à la seconde nor quatrième devant. Cunningham loves to skew classical standards, to be oblique where ballet is direct and direct where it's oblique. Seeing legs whip straight back from a zigzag fouetté into penchée arabesque is like crossing a divide when the bridge is gone; you feel the full impact of what hasn't happened in between. There are many such moments in Armitage's solo in *Fractions*. (Fox does a slightly different version.) As she kicks, turns, and strides in huge seconds and fourths, she seems in a very real sense to be breaking ground. Old structures crumble; air rushes up. A lot of the material in *Fractions* is not really new; it's canonical. Perhaps working with television and with so many new dancers made Cunningham want to recover and restate his foundations. In any event, *Fractions* enters the repertory at precisely the right moment. It's a stabilizer. Wonderful as Cunningham's recent work has been, a concise, limpid experience like *Fractions* hasn't happened in some time. The piece doesn't fall into sections; neither does it become monomaniacally urgent, like *Torse*. In its organic development, its suspenseful configurations, *Fractions* reminds me of the older works, which are represented in the current repertory by *Summerspace* and *Rune*. In those pieces, the dancers are as sensuously alert and free as forest creatures in a clearing. *Fractions* brings to mind St. John of the Cross's "lions, harts, leaping does." It is quintessential Merce.

Inlets also has some of this characteristic nature poetry, with unusually small, elegant transitions. Beautiful Giacometti distances, too (there are only six dancers), and a few curiosities: a recurrent "Greek" pose, a broken-footed walk in relevé, a group tableau that looks like a climax. But I'm not sure it's the dark, enigmatic piece that the décor, by Morris Graves, makes it out to be. The big shiny "sun" that travels slowly across the backcloth, the scrim that makes everything misty, even the very handsome sulphur-by-day, cobalt-by-night lighting, by Charles Atlas, press far too hard. The choreography is Cunningham at his most gently uninsistent. Another curiosity is the Graves poster that was offered for sale during the season. It links a big solar semicircle to two coiled serpents. The colors are the same as those we see on the stage, but the pronged, writhing shapes are far from the earnest romanticism of the set. Animal imagery appears in the costumes—unitards dyed in patches of dark gray and worn with rhinestone dog collars. Cunningham, in addition, has one white and one black foot, which throws his famous parallel position into high relief. Jasper Johns has also made a striking set of costumes for *Exchange*. Together with his lighting, the gray-over-pastel coloring suggests a theme of shadows and smoke. The choreography, though, comes in a thick flow of exuberant invention. *Exchange* is a cornucopia: some of the dances look like points of origin for things in *Fractions* or *Inlets*, and the piece as a whole looks as if it could furnish an entire repertory. I wish I had been able to watch it more closely, but my concentration broke about halfway through under the battering of David Tudor's score. Cage's water and fire music for *Inlets* didn't get in the way of my enjoyment, and Jon Gibson's flute solo for *Fractions* enhanced it. If the tenebrous décors for *Inlets* and *Exchange* were discordant, they were not destructive. But how can you watch a dance with V-2 rockets whistling overhead? Of all the aspects of the Cunningham revolution, music remains the most problematical. Some of the dissociated-sound scores that Cunningham uses are more interfering and dictatorial than planned settings would be.

Quite a few young women are clacketing around in tap shoes these days, showing off techniques learned from the jazz dancers of a former generation —men like Stanley Brown and Charles Cook and Honi Coles. The new tappers are all white, and almost all are displaced modern dancers; a disconcerting number of them have performed with Meredith Monk or had their interest whetted by Twyla Tharp's use of tap. They want not so much to revive a bygone era as to develop tap into a contemporary art form. But at their concerts one tends to hear pre-rock jazz and see the dancing that went with it. Jazz dance was largely the province of black male hoofers, and it was primarily acoustic; it seldom got off the ground and into the air. There were also spectacular "flash" acts, like the Nicholas Brothers, but women did not often venture into virtuoso hoofer territory, because, whether in the air or on the ground, the technique was physically unflattering. It still is; in tap-dancing, a woman has to work hard to avoid looking like she's working hard, and those who study with aging hoofers have to beware of absorbing their heaviness. A young woman doesn't need a low plié; she needs height in the upper back, loose hips, more flexibility in the ankle than in the knee. And she needs to develop something in the way of a body line for her audience to look at. I'm aware that these sexual distinctions probably don't interest the new breed of female tap-dancers, but who could be interested in the low-primate stuff they're turning out now? Some of these girls are very articulate students of jazz-tap history; they're trying to rescue a dying art. But almost none of them have seen how to re-create the art in respect to their own needs and gifts.

Gail Conrad is an exception to all this; she may be the only woman choreographer in the currently expanding tap field whose objective isn't laying down irons like a man. It was through watching Conrad perform with her group last month at the Theatre for the New City that I began to see what the others were missing. Conrad's carriage is consistently buoyant, her line is attractive, her sound is delicate and full. A small, active redhead, she casts herself slightly tomboy, but this is plainly her adaptation of a musical-comedy convention—she has none of that neutered look the other tappers seem to think is appropriate. Conrad's personality is clear, sweet, and strong, and the four members of her company are just as vivid as she is. In this single fact may lie her greatest accomplishment as a choreographer, for as the evening passes it becomes evident that only Seth Tomasini, the gangling leading man, and Conrad herself have a high-grade technique. Bob Duncan, though a practiced performer, is not yet in their league as a tap-dancer. Anny DeGange and Muriel Favaro can best be described as enlightened amateurs. Conrad's choreography presents her performers at their various levels of strength without revealing inequalities that might hamper the show. With all of them dancing up to capacity in their tailor-made roles, the show becomes transparently and engagingly a set of full-length "character" portraits. The two unfledged women dancers (who are also Conrad's pupils) are especially charming. DeGange is round and bouncy, a sturdy New Yorker; the tall and glamorous Favaro, with only three months of study, looks like Rita Hayworth doing the Shorty George.

One way to vary a tap step is to travel it. Conrad calls her hour-long show *Travellers: A Tap Dance/Epic*, and the dances are strung on a thread of a story about a mixed bunch of travellers in South America. So fine is this thread that the show was half over before I saw where it was going. No other tap choreographer I know has attempted a whole show on a single theme. Conrad has done it, but how much scope dancing of this sort can impart to a theme is a question. At times, Conrad seemed to evoke the curious unmoored sensation of foreign travel, and the evening took on an avant-gardish hallucinatory tinge; at other times the atmospheric bits about tourists reading maps and going to the beach and taking pictures seemed intended as nothing more than rests between dances. I wouldn't be surprised to learn that *Travellers* took the form of a Latin American travelogue because of the music. Not only are the sambas and rumbas and cha-chas good for tap-dancing, they also avoid the dilemma of having to choose between a jazz stereotype and a rock experiment. A swinging five-man ensemble played the music (when it was not on tape) and entered good-naturedly into the show. *Travellers* was that rare success—an intelligently staged home-made fantasy. It kept you off balance—no tricks, no hit material—yet happily absorbed. *—October 23, 1978*

The Spoken Word

Robert Joffrey keeps adding laurels to the crown he wears as uncontested master of revivals. *A Wedding Bouquet* is the prettiest thing he has done since *Les Patineurs*. Both of these ballets, by Frederick Ashton, revived from the original Vic-Wells productions of 1937, are decorated in a fresh-water palette that seems to have slipped away with the war. William Chappell's lantern-lit forest in *Les Patineurs* has a honey-toned glow; its intricately laced branches have been marvellously reproduced in cutouts, which give a burrowing depth to the forest. Some of Lord Berners's pastels in *A Wedding Bouquet*—a "spring" counterpart of Chappell's "winter"—appear to have gone slightly acid, but his mild, floral-scented country air is still delicious to breathe. Although *A Wedding Bouquet* is not as well per-formed as it is well produced (like most Joffrey revivals), something of the past is alive in it; in its way, the ballet is as evocative of its time and place as *The Green Table, Parade, Rodeo,* and *New York Export: Opus Jazz* are of theirs. All these pieces are in repertory this fall, being as faithfully kept up as if each and every one were a classic. The Joffrey restorations are uncom-fortably jostled by the Now ballets of Gerald Arpino, which have a way of becoming Then almost before their first season is out. Last season's *Suite Saint-Saëns* is unconscious self-parody; I don't want to dwell on it except to suggest that the time may have come to divide the dancers into two wings—one to do Joffrey's revivals and the other to do Arpino's ballets. No com-pany can serve two ballet masters. Dancers whose style has been coarsened by Arpino cannot be expected to perform Joffrey's Ashton. *Monotones II* (to Satie's *Gymnopédies*), which used to be given a respectable perform-ance, has now faded; *The Dream* has yet to be mastered. Even *Les Patineurs,* which doesn't present nearly as many difficulties, is roughly handled by nearly everyone in it. The dancers are most at ease with the calculated vulgarity of *Jazz Calendar*—their high is Ashton's low.

In *A Wedding Bouquet*, the problem is more elusive. Its dance style is not as critical to its expression as are the manners and customs that the style elaborates. One might describe the ballet, which concerns the cast of char-acters at a large, frilly provincial wedding at the turn of the century, as a set of Anglo-Saxon attitudes, even though its locale is a French village and one of its authors is Gertrude Stein. A *Wedding Bouquet* is as preciously English as the English ever get. Whatever it was understood to be in 1937—some saw it as a satire of *Les Noces* or *Jardin aux Lilas*; others called it the ripest comedy of manners that English ballet had produced—it is no more than a brittle period toy today. What we get from this revival is a picture of the fashionable and precocious minds that created it—Berners's and Ashton's and Constant Lambert's, mostly. Gertrude Stein's seems to have been conscripted. Berners, who wrote the music and designed the scenery and costumes, was the senior member of the trio. Ashton and Lambert, who both helped with the scenario, were the bright young things. Since the ballet has no reality now apart from the particular atmosphere of creativity which it evokes (in which even the dancers shared: the young Margot Fonteyn as Julia comes back to us; Julia the character does not), it was a happy stroke on Joffrey's part to arrange Anthony Dowell's guest appearance as the Narrator. The Narrator is outside and inside the ballet at once, and he seems to be imagining it as it goes along. Besides standing for its creators, Dowell stands for the whole Royal Ballet. As he talked, my mind went back—not to that wedding but through the years from the Royal to the Sadler's Wells to the Vic-Wells Ballet and its talented young men, down for a weekend at Berners's country house, throwing themselves about the library in transports of inspiration while their sly host sat at the piano, swooping now into a tango, now into a waltz. Dowell, taking the part that Lambert created, contrives the faint suggestion that he's playing Lambert's puppet, sitting on a gargantuan institutional knee, with his voice piped in from afar. Normally radiantly handsome, he slicks back his hair for this role, makes up his face like a wooden doll's whose eyes and teeth flash as if hinged together at the back. Dowell makes no attempt to force connections between the words and the action; the voice, as warm and flat as (one suspects) the champagne he sips, is engaged but noncommittal. Getting delicately plotzed as the ballet rolls on and letting his head loll slightly, like a dummy's, is a good idea, too.

The Joffrey is the only company other than the Royal and its affiliates to revive this ballet in recent years, and I don't think that even the Royal would try it today without Ashton there to coach the dancers. The characters are all his inventions; though the cues come from Gertrude Stein's text, they are Stein cues. (What must a dancer make of "Thérèse. I am older. Than a boat"?) The Royal choreologist Christopher Newton does a good job, but he misses important details, like the joke about Julia's dog coming and hogging the foreground in the group portrait. The dancer should strike the kneeling arabesque pose from the opening tableau of *Les Sylphides*— not just fling her leg in the air. Besides Dowell's, there are two outstanding performances—by the endlessly resourceful Gary Chryst as the Groom, and by Lynn Glauber, a new member of the company, as the Bride. The others are not bad; they're just not there. And neither is the ballet.

When the Narrator says, "Webster was a name that was spoken," we understand him to mean Webster the officious maid—the role that was modelled on Ninette de Valois and danced by her in the first production. In the Stein play from which the line was taken, "Webster" refers to Daniel Webster. How Daniel Webster came to be a name that was spoken at a French country wedding is a mystery that must lie coiled within the greater mystery that was the art of Gertrude Stein. She had her house in the French countryside, and when Ashton came to visit her after the ballet was produced she took him on a tour of the village, pointing out the originals of the characters she had in mind when she wrote the play. (I have this information and most of the foregoing facts from David Vaughan's admirable study *Frederick Ashton and His Ballets*, published by Knopf.) To these characters she gave equivocal or non-French names, like Josephine, Julia, Ernest, and Guy. Was Stein really writing about her French neighbors "in English" or was she writing, as so often seems the case in her other work, in English for English's sake, taking in this instance her neighbors as a pretext? Stein claimed that her native language had become more precious and meaningful to her in France. It had become in fact a dream language—a secret garden that she cultivated by digging up roots. In "They Must. Be Wedded. To Their Wife"—the main source for *A Wedding Bouquet*—the language is all porous description and cryptic epigrammatic observation that could be applied to any fluster-prone social occasion anywhere; even the fact that it is a wedding must be largely inferred. Language so majestically impartial has power in the theatre—maybe only in the theatre. Especially when allied with music, it can produce an effect of queerly formal continuity, of harmony on top of chaos. This chemical reaction of words and notes was Virgil Thomson's discovery. Not until her collaboration with Thomson, in the opera *Four Saints in Three Acts* ("Pigeons on the grass, alas"), was it Gertrude Stein's intention to compose another kind of music, much as Edith Sitwell had done in *Façade* ("Daisy and Lily, lazy and silly"). According to David Vaughan, Berners originally composed *A Wedding Bouquet* for a singing chorus, and that was the way it was performed at first. I've never heard the sung version, but the change to a spoken narration must have altered the relation of words and music from something like Thomson's setting of *Four Saints* to something more like William Walton's setting of *Façade*. (Ashton, of course, had made the choreography for both those works.) The speech that rattles along in rhythm to the music in *A Wedding Bouquet* has an inescapably English, Sitwellian ring. The frivolity is all wrong for Gertrude Stein. In spite of Anthony Dowell's untheatrical voice and deadpan delivery, the effect is incongruous, like tying ribbons on an elephant.

David Gordon's latest piece, a polyphonic construction for dancers and dancers' voices, is called *What Happened*. I've no idea whether Gordon intends homage to Gertrude Stein, but Stein certainly was a patron saint of the theatre and dance people who, like Gordon, performed at the Judson Memorial Church in the early sixties. One of the great events of those years was a production, featuring a cast of dancers, of the Stein play *What Happened.* (Al Carmines wrote the music, sounding neither like Lord Berners nor like Virgil Thomson.) In that period, it seemed that words could be used with dancing only if they were by Gertrude Stein, and I must admit that, ever since, whenever they weren't they haven't sounded right to me. Either the dancing reports what the words are already saying or it strays so far from the verbal meaning that I can't guess what connects the two. Stein's sentences have the virtue of specifying nothing while keeping the attention focussed; they make a good landscape for dance. Remy Charlip, the choreographer-mime, was one of the first to realize that words, whether they are spoken or sung, lucid or nonsensical, had somehow to occur on the same plane as the action. When Merce Cunningham and John Cage combined forces in *How to Pass, Kick, Fall and Run,* with Cage assuming a role based on the Narrator in *A Wedding Bouquet,* they kept the words and the dancing on separate planes, and the result was that Cage distracted us every time he opened his mouth.

David Gordon's recent work goes beyond Remy Charlip's gestural orations; he has found a way to equalize speech and gesture so that neither becomes completely an illustration of the other and both are submerged in complex and unpredictable patterns. The distinctive Gordon touch is commentary. He is not, or not often, an abstractionist. He means to make a point about perception and he means us to notice it. Yet as a reflexive parodist he is capable of subverting his own intention. When is there a point to having no point? We go around in Stein-like circles. His *What Happened* begins with the sound of some fearful street accident and its aftermath. This lasts a little over a minute, and then seven women, dressed in white sports clothes, start talking at once. As they talk, they move, making signs that are sometimes connected to what they say and sometimes not. The individual stories are all eyewitness accounts of the accident. Everyone uses the same words but not at the same time, and not everyone seems to be giving the same account. The movements follow suit. Gordon's mime language is an elaborate rebus made out of parlor games and Delsarte; words like "baby," "son" (sun), "avail" (a veil), and "hope" are acted out with a lunatic precision. "Which" is a swoop, a grimace, and a cackle, on one count. When two or more stories coincide, they stop momentarily, like cars at an intersection, or one may ricochet unexpectedly off another. You never get the full story, or even one clear version of it, but then you don't want things to be clear; you want the hubbub and the echolalia and the mazelike counterpoint to last as long as they can. Eventually, the narrative slips bit by bit into a fugal "To be or not to be" recited in full, with dissociated gestures.

And this is only Part One. Variations follow, and the piece ends in a triple canon.

What Happened was given with some earlier work on a program that opened the fall season of the American Theatre Laboratory. The retrospective showed Gordon's progress distinctly. As his work is becoming more concentrated in its lifelike analogies and descriptions, it is growing in formal beauty. —*November 6, 1978*

The San Francisco Version

Is ballet the last outpost of provincialism? In the cities of the Middle West, one sees businessmen in bright-green polyester suits and eyebrow glasses, and one understands how style is only a matter of emphasis: the man in the green suit could be a millionaire, and in New York he's probably disconcerted by the run-down streets in the neighborhoods where the rich live and by the unprepossessing if not actually grimy façades of the town houses. Provincialism in the sense of doing clumsily what the big city does well may no longer exist except in ballet, where standards of comparison are tugged apart not by regional taste but by regionalism itself. Far-flung centers of activity have to cope with vacuumatic conditions. The absolute standard cannot spread itself farther than the eye can see, and in classical dancing, which is marketed live and live only, quality is provably affected by what there is of it to see. In the San Francisco Ballet, which recently paid New York a visit, I felt I was seeing a genuine provincial company, whose ways would never be my ways, and while I was pondering what geography had to do with it I realized: Not so damn much after all. New York is not San Francisco, but for part of the ballet season it might as well be—indeed, we can only wish it were. The stuff at Lincoln Center in the summertime is worse than anything the San Franciscans showed, Nureyev is constantly fronting for foreign companies of questionable value, and New York sighs over it all. The San Francisco Ballet has better dancers, more finely schooled, than the Ballet Nacional de Cuba, the Berlin Opera Ballet, and the Dutch National Ballet, all of which have been through here in the past year, trailing press notices of glory. Technically, the San Francisco is about on a par with the London Festival Ballet or the National Ballet of Canada, which also stop at Lincoln Center, and though it isn't as financially well off as those ensembles, it has more spirit. It is provincial in the accepted sense: the repertory, for the most part, is a pastiche of things done in a bigger way back East or by foreign companies of pedigree such as the Royal Ballet.

And, as pastiche goes, it is very good. Compare this so-to-speak first-rate provincialism with the vulgar neo-provincialism of the Stuttgart Ballet. The San Francisco follows trends, while the Stuttgart is said to set them. But at least the San Francisco follows trends in ballet. The Stuttgart isn't about ballet at all; it's a kind of ballet entertainment built around dramatics and stunts, and a powerful impression it makes wherever it goes. Each company has reacted to its vacuum in a different way. And how New York reacts is a test of our provincialism. Perhaps it is enough to say that, as things stand now, next summer the Stuttgart will return on schedule to the Metropolitan but the Royal Ballet won't.

The San Francisco was playing New York for the first time in thirteen years, bringing to the Brooklyn Academy its version of Prokofiev's *Romeo and Juliet* and ten shorter works. It was a proud showing. All the ballets had choreography either by Michael Smuin or Lew Christensen, the company's directors, or by their protégés John McFall, Robert Gladstein, and Tomm Ruud. Although the at-home repertory in the souvenir program listed Balanchine, Robbins, and the first American production of Ashton's *La Fille Mal Gardée*, the company obviously wanted to impress New York with its self-sufficiency. It relies as little on guest stars as on outside choreographers, and it has begun to commission its own music. Next year, five world premières are projected, four with original scores. All this autonomy speaks well of local support: after forty-five years of somewhat tenuous existence, this oldest of American ballet companies is flourishing. Of course, the company isn't as self-sufficient as it may think, as long as everything it does is more or less déjà vu. But its imitations of standard ballets can be instructive. Some of the imitations are so remarkable that I wondered why they aren't exciting: why the Gladstein-Stravinsky ballet, set to the same music and using some of the same devices as *Rubies*, still couldn't do what *Rubies* does—pull you into its world. But maybe the very fact that Gladstein's choreography put the question in my head in spite of my conscious resolve not to compare it to Balanchine's is a measure of how far he had succeeded in making his piece work. If there is one quality that separates master choreographers from good choreographers, it is the ability to sustain long sequences of coherent rhythm. It is this that creates figurative interest in a dance. Steps, no matter how inventive or ingeniously combined, have in themselves no power of poetic suggestion. The manipulation of steps is a game that fascinates professionals. But above gamesmanship there is another level, on which we are all—professionals, amateurs, veterans, newcomers—one audience. That is the level on which dancing, by the alchemy of its rhythm, transfigures life. Technically speaking, this means that the choreography has elastic scale and tension—it keeps moving and changing in ways you feel but don't see. To be able to recognize a technical feat makes no great difference to one's pleasure; it just prolongs the pleasure by providing a semblance of an explanation. Many people spoil their pleasure by asking for explanations in advance. They don't believe that at the ballet we are all connoisseurs—that, in fact, it is the poetic objective of ballet to awaken a kind of natural connoisseurship in us. (Some of us just haven't got it. People who ask "What should I look for in ballet?" are really asking about technique, and there's nothing wrong in that—although there's no short answer, either. But no amount of technical knowledge will enlighten people who have looked on ballet with innocent eyes and seen nothing.) The San Francisco doesn't get us up to this level, but it does put us within striking distance. It easily persuades an audience of its seriousness and the seriousness of ballet. I should like to see it put its persuasive charms more intensively to work on itself. When the company learns to project itself with the continuous and coherent force that it lacks now, it will have learned the beginnings of style, and that could make it a company of national importance.

As the flagship production, *Romeo and Juliet* is a shrewd choice. Michael Smuin's staging—simple, broad, nailing down the meaning of every scene—gets at the reasons for the ballet's popularity and capitalizes on them. Prokofiev's *Romeo* is the mass-audience version of Shakespeare, without the poetry (which is usually so ill-spoken that it can't be understood anyway), and with the emphasis on spectacle, violence, and pathos. Contemporary twists are latent in any production of the play. The ballet hardly needs to sell the frustrated-youth angle: its young lovers are kids because most dancers are kids. Without the balm of poetry, the lovers' story becomes one long, piteous scourge; it's almost as if Romeo and Juliet were being punished for the sin of passionate love. The ballet has lots of appeal for homosexuals—not only in the youth-passion-frustration theme but in the many large roles for male dancers. Until the last act, the ballet belongs mainly to Romeo and his friends (and enemies). Juliet flits palely through, usually wearing a nightgown, while the boys are in tights and codpieces. But the heart of the mass audience beats in sympathy with the display. Audiences applaud the young men who carry the show—applaud them sentimentally for being dancers and outcasts from normal society. Their presence affects us psychologically as part of the morbid romanticism of the ballet. *Romeo and Juliet* may be the only ballet in standard repertory that homosexuals can identify with emotionally without distortion.

Prokofiev's scenario was constructed from Shakespeare without, as far as we know, the collaboration of a choreographer. Its awkwardness is irremediable; there is no recourse open to the choreographer but to follow it as closely as the composer did. Efforts to interject more dancing are doomed. The ballet is inescapably ambulatory, and its pantomime is naturalistic. Prokofiev did not anticipate José Limón. Choreography that goes with Prokofiev may be tedious as well as awkward, but choreography that goes against Prokofiev in order to press its own ideas is unintelligible. Michael Smuin takes the scuffed but straight road of Lavrovsky, Ashton,

Cranko, and MacMillan, and avoids the isolated byways of Neumeier, Araiz, and Nureyev. He proceeds with caution but not without flair. He maneuvers the scenario now in the direction of family entertainment, now toward a sophisticated, "modern" interpretation. He doesn't minimize the fact that there are more boy-boy than boy-girl scenes (on the contrary), but he makes the boys' prankishness seem callow rather than epicene. Lady Capulet carries on a full-scale affair with Tybalt (so the lamentations that Prokofiev wrote for her over Tybalt's corpse have some justification), and Lord Capulet is a philanderer. The lovers are cuddly, the duels are boisterous, with lots of horseplay and clanging steel, and the comedy is in the four-square squat tradition of operatic mime. The Nurse, though played by a woman, is conceived in the masculine terms of the English-pantomime "dame." The MacMillan production for the Royal Ballet is more tasteful. Smuin, who has the impresario touch of a Belasco, occasionally stages gratuitous bits of action: a confrontation scene with too many star-crossed lovers, a protracted struggle between Romeo and Paris in the tomb. And the heaving about of Juliet's inert body by her bereaved father does not sit well with the stunned grief of the music. Smuin's greatest theatrical stroke comes in the funeral, when, after a hooded procession has crossed the stage, a scrim rises to the drumroll that unleashes the full orchestra in the wail of the dead march, and we behold the appalling blackness of the crypt.

Smuin's showmanship has so much energy it's a pity the performing can't be more full-blooded. The scene in the ballroom, when Juliet's attention should gradually shift from Paris to Romeo, is perfunctorily done, although we can see that opportunities to develop it exist in the staging. The balcony pas de deux is disappointing: small-scale "correct" dancing that projects no feeling for the drama. More disappointments are in store: more insipid lyrical pas de deux and amateurish bouts of mime. However, the bold masculine street dances, particularly the Queen Mab trio, and the duels are on a high level. Smuin can't pull rounded performances from his dancers, and his Juliets (I saw Diana Weber and Susan Magno) are maidenly and dull, but he gets full value from the men's dancing. And what would *Romeo* be without that?

Shinjū, also by Smuin, is a sort of Japanese *Romeo and Juliet*, in which the lovers commit ritual suicide and bleed red streamers. His *Songs of Mahler* is in yet another overfamiliar genre—the lieder ballet. Smuin's choreography always has a sunny vigor; it is cleanly modelled and spacious in design. With all his skill in the use of acrobatics, he doesn't torture the rhetoric—he dares to be simple. I don't enjoy the genres he's working in at the moment (happily for me, he left his Mozart Mass ballet at home), but I do enjoy his talent. *Quattro a Verdi* may also qualify as generic in this year of Verdi ballets. A formal pas de quatre for two couples, it was fine in its separate parts—which included several variations and two sweet adagios—

but it went compositionally astray. Curiously, Lew Christensen's work has the same flaw, although with Christensen I often feel that it's his mind rather than his technical control that's wandering. *Il Distratto* starts as subtle satire and ends as bumptious burlesque. *Divertissement d'Auber*, a pas de trois, is finely wrought in a technically close-knit style, but its tone is uneven. The total impression is inexplicably eccentric. Even *Stravinsky Pas de Deux* (set to *Four Norwegian Moods*), choreographically the most distinguished work of the season, was somewhat inconclusive. The comedy classic *Con Amore* I recalled from happy days at New York City Ballet, and I was chagrined at the hard and forced manner of its performance by the San Franciscans. All these pieces except the first need more stylish performing than the company is able to supply. David McNaughton in *Divertissement* and as the Thief in *Con Amore* showed remarkable natural elevation and ballon but not much in the way of form. Dennis Marshall, in a number of roles, still has the individual elegance he had at American Ballet Theatre and that same technical fault in the carriage of the head. In general, the dancing of the San Francisco men is apt to be ragged but bright. The women are stylistically neater but unimpressive, and they're weaker on point than one would guess from their strength in relevé. In John McFall's *Beethoven Quartets* (the music is an assortment of movements from various quartets—a numbing idea), the choreography is mostly unisex, and it's the men who perform the adagios. Why should McFall be doing a kinky Hans van Manen ballet? There is a strong and honorable tradition of male dance at the San Francisco Ballet which began even before Lew Christensen followed his brothers Harold and Willam there. And from Lew Christensen, now entering his seventies, comes the precedent for the aggressive young group of choreographers led by Smuin. Oddly enough, their work—on this showing, at least—derives from everywhere but the Christensen repertory. Maybe he's just too eccentric, and maybe his mind does wander, but it is a choreographic mind of no small distinction. The Christensen ballets hold a provocative secret. They ought to be much better known than they are.

One of the ways that Agnes de Mille's choreography enhanced Broadway musicals was by capturing some image that turned out to be organic to their expression but that no one else could have foreseen. And it is her images, bearing her personal stamp, that prevail in the mind when the show is gone. Think of *Oklahoma!* or *Carousel* and at once a genie in ruffles leaps in the air and claps its heels. De Mille's dances, coming in the midst of a show, vividly stylized it. When her choreography is the whole show, as in the pieces she has made for ballet companies, the dancing frequently isn't strong enough in its own right, and the behavioristic character movement she specializes in can seem arbitrary. *Rodeo* is a success because it's arranged as if it were a segment of a show, and it fixes its own context for the dances. The dance style is small and close to the body, like an extension of acting, but we read it easily, because the characterizations of the Cowgirl and the Head Wrangler and the Champion Roper are large and clear.

The Joffrey is giving De Mille's latest ballet, *A Bridegroom Called Death*, and it is a curious event in many respects. It tells a story, from Germanic folk legend, about a young woman drawn to a stranger on her wedding day, but De Mille seems reluctant to press a story interest as firmly as she would have in the old days, and instead devotes much of the time to lyrical-folk dances. They're not very interesting. The folk dances are too straight to hold any drama, and the ballet technique is powerless, like a pastel derivative of Fokine. The dances were probably meant to set a context for the story, but things don't turn out that way, perhaps because the process is against the De Mille grain. In *Rodeo*, after all, the story set the context for the dances. In the new piece, De Mille instinctively avoids a heavy expressionistic style, and, even though she has not found the right alternative and the dances don't work, the restrained emotional atmosphere does. In spite of its theme, it's a benign ballet, with some of the equivocal charm of folk tales. I could have done with a less folksy heroine, and I guess I understand, though I can't quite accept, the casting of red-haired Russell Sultzbach as Death. But the emotion of the piece is not a frivolous one. Unfortunately, the Schubert songs De Mille uses for a score (this is another lieder ballet, alas, and badly sung) expose the wispiness of the material. The ballet needs more protection—lighter music, perhaps, with a heavier sound.

—*November 20, 1978*

Fashions at the Ballet

At benefits and matinees, audiences tend to be indiscriminate and unfocussed; sometimes they're uncomfortable, sometimes they only act that way. The matinee audience is a peaceful one once it gets settled, but that always takes a while. Handbags must be dug through, compartments unzipped and then zipped up again, candy bars unwrapped, watches wound and set. The matinee audience used to wear large hats, which it gladly removed on request. Now it wears bangle bracelets. If you ask it to stop jangling, it doesn't know what you mean. This audience loves everything it sees. The benefit audience does not even love itself. It is touchy and sleepy; at peak moments in a performance it will begin perusing its program in a belated attempt to discover why it came. Small children used to appear only at matinees. Now they are turning up at benefits, too—the price of a ticket apparently being less than that of a babysitter. Small children love ballet, and they are not a nuisance except when they ask a lot of questions out loud. The questions are usually perceptive; it's the answers they get that can kill a performance for you.

Opening night at New York City Ballet was a gala benefit. The ballet was *Jewels*, and it was the occasion of Mikhail Baryshnikov's début with the company in New York, dancing Edward Villella's part in *Rubies*. He next appeared in *Coppélia*, another benefit. In neither case did the audience do what forecasts had said it would do—go crazy for Baryshnikov and ignore everything else. Both performances got a warm, appreciative response; the applause was in just proportion to the provocation. Baryshnikov both times won an ovation, but so did Suzanne Farrell and Peter Martins in *Diamonds*, and so did Patricia McBride and Shaun O'Brien in *Coppélia*. The reactions tallied with the reactions to the same ballets performed with the same casts last summer before non-benefit audiences in Saratoga. Baryshnikov fever is not a media hype: the NYCB season is a sellout because of him. Is it he who inspires this new dignity and attentiveness in benefit audiences or is it just the shock we all feel at seeing him in the midst of Balanchine's company? The opening took place in a celebrative atmosphere. Between *Rubies* and *Diamonds*, wine and canapés were served on all levels of the house, and the audience went around saying, "I think the audience is behaving very well tonight, don't you?"

Baryshnikov dances *Rubies* with a feral intensity; he's not as cockily urbane as Villella, and he's less a competitor for McBride than an accomplice, who mirrors her every mood, and sometimes wittily travesties her movement. The accents in the "tango" are sharper than they have been in some time. Baryshnikov has, by muscular nature, the measure of "Villella" attack—the short jabs, the feints, the sudden gear-shifting spurts. But his timing is becoming more assertively his own. Some of the choreography is changed in minor ways; it has not been embellished as the two solos in *Coppélia* have been. Here Baryshnikov dances more in his customary style, and he adds his customary steps. There aren't enough additions to the first solo; it begins excitingly but then reverts to the version done by Peter Martins and Helgi Tomasson, which isn't spectacular enough for them, either. The second solo, though, is a beautiful waltz variation that Balanchine choreographed originally for André Eglevsky. It opens with the high suspended cabrioles that Eglevsky was famous for and ends in a spiralling burst of air turns and pirouettes. Baryshnikov somehow found room for his double assemblé turning in both directions and ending in low arabesque; he converted the final pirouette into multiple spins in attitude and the final air turn into an amazing pop-up split jump. As at American Ballet Theatre, he made a delightful Frantz. But roles that confine him to his specialties are not what he came to NYCB to do. And *Coppélia*, even in this superior version, is not an NYCB specialty. Baryshnikov might easily have overwhelmed its first act; the years at Ballet Theatre pumping up insolid material would have taught him how. Instead, he appeared, performed succinctly, and withdrew. And the audience did not riot.

Baryshnikov has become the No. 1 glamour boy of the arts, and he does seem to be attracting to the State Theatre the glittering crowd that normally goes to the Met to see the foreign companies or Ballet Theatre, with its foreign stars. The New York City Ballet has never courted fashion, though it has courted popularity—a very different thing. *Jewels* is a consciously designed popular hit—an introduction to Balanchine and a showcase for his stars. It is also gaudy, with a brutally opulent décor by Peter Harvey, and Karinska costumes that look expensive. Usually when the curtain goes up on *Emeralds*, there's a gasp. On opening night, when the "in" crowd gasped, was it in horror? The costumes, designed in 1967 and slightly remodelled since then, have the look of the fifties about them: blocklike ankle-length tulle skirts, which make the girls look hippy; wired bras and headdresses. A wire lavallière hangs from the flies; the wings are covered with drapes that look dipped in cement. From their fringes cut-glass teardrops dangle, catching the light, which is green, of course, with violet undertones. (On a clear evening at the outdoor theatre in Saratoga, there's always a moment when the lighting in *Emeralds* exactly matches the sky.) The basic décor reappears in *Rubies* and *Diamonds* with appropriate color changes and variations in costuming. The scheme is hardest on *Emeralds*. In *Rubies*, the dancers wear short red tunics; in *Diamonds*, conventional white tutus. These aren't so bad, and anyway both ballets, which still have their original ballerinas, are so sturdily well performed that one can forget the way they look. Also, in the perspective of Balanchine's output over the years, they're not as compellingly different in conception as *Emeralds* is. *Rubies* gives us the lighter-weight Stravinsky, in the tradition of *Jeu de Cartes* and *Danses Concertantes*. *Diamonds*, to my mind, was better done before as *Ballet Imperial* (*Tchaikovsky Concerto No. 2*). As a Farrell show, it is still entrancing, but the ultimate great Farrell performance of the moment is more likely to occur in *Chaconne*, which also provides a big role, with commensurate possibilities, for Martins. *Emeralds*, however, is like nothing else in the repertory. It is all andante in effect, and stands virtually motionless in memory, shimmering through a veil of mist. Gentle Fauré wrote the two suites of incidental music from which the score is drawn. *Shylock* accompanied the adaptation by Edmond Haraucourt of *The Merchant of Venice*, and *Pelléas et Mélisande* was written for a production of the Maeterlinck play. The music reflects the period of French infatuation with Wagnerian medievalism; it's *Tristan* transmuted into mellow romance. In the ballet, there is a little heraldic pageantry and a lot of courtly love. Two women—one regal, one virginal—dominate it. (Merrill Ashley and Karin von Aroldingen are miscast; they're not only in the wrong roles but in the wrong ballet.) Each has a solo, and the fantasy of the steps and gestures is peculiarly intimate: what a man imagines an elegant woman does when she's alone. The first, set to "La Fileuse" from *Pelléas*, recalls the extravagant elation of a Petipa jewel fairy. The second, to the "Sicilienne," is more introverted, more girlishly whimsical. This, perhaps, is Mélisande. A "Mélisande" pas de deux, in which a knight tracks his lady as she walks a winding path on point, is echoed in the grave processionals of the epilogue. Balanchine added this walking ending recently; the literal gravity of it makes the frothy stiff costumes all the more inappropriate.

Emeralds—all of *Jewels*—ought to be redecorated. A new chic audience, provided one really attaches itself, might stimulate more tasteful designing. The Karinska shop's costumes for recent productions, such as *Chaconne*, *Vienna Waltzes*, and *Kammermusik No. 2*, are a lot better than they used to be. But does New York possess a chic audience? A couple of months ago, *W*, the biweekly digest of *Women's Wear Daily*, published its lists of "in"s and "out"s in various categories and included among the Dance People who were "in" Mikhail Baryshnikov, George Balanchine, Suzanne Farrell, and New York City Ballet. "In"s and "out"s are a good game when the choices are guided by some underlying principle that we can guess at, but the lists that *W* puts together appear to be packs of names selected at random, as if it would be more amusing to have no underlying principle. The abdication of taste in our time is sometimes celebrated as morally regenerative, but at *W*, one feels, hollow rationales like that don't apply. Non-taste is just part of the fatigued atmosphere—fallout from the self-scandalization of the sixties—in which today's fashion flourishes. In this atmosphere, the process of inclusion/exclusion by which fashion has long set itself standards falls apart. There are no standards; it's just as outrageous—and as meaningless—to be on a list as off it. Even the fact that most of the designers that *W* designates as "in" turn out to be leading advertisers and most of the "in" people are their clients doesn't taint the bland equanimity of the choices with the clarity of commercialism: the choices would be the same whether commerce intervened or not. I suspect that life and art at the ballet will go on much as before. (American Ballet Theatre without Baryshnikov, *W* threatens, is "out." I doubt it.) A new costume show at the Metropolitan Museum reminds us that the world of fashionable society and the ballet have traditionally exercised a mutual fascination. In the first years of the Ballets Russes, Parisian dressmakers of high style took their cues from Diaghilev's designers. Later, Chanel, a patron of the ballet, became the first of the celebrated couturiers to design costumes. But the tradition seems to have confined itself to Paris, where Roland Petit was able to revive it after the Second World War. That period, lasting only a few years, now seems as remote as the Diaghilev era. The one vestige we have of it in New York is the categories in W, which rates Theatre, Film, and Dance People (along with just People) but not Opera or Concert People. Dress designers still care about ballet. Is Zubin Mehta "in" or "out"?

—*December 4, 1978*

Glissade

I know nothing about figure skating and have no excuse for my ignorance other than to say, with R. P. Blackmur, that "all knowledge is a fall from the paradise of undifferentiated sensation." Skating seems to me sublimely undifferentiated in its effects. Everything is borne along on a lulling current. At high moments, a sense of exhilarating speed is broken by the body's twisting through the air, like a fish caught on a line, and then the lull resumes until the next paroxysm, which may be one of those insane blurred turns on one spot called a "scratch spin." Yes, it's "like" dancing—dancing in outer space. These very wide sudden contrasts are not enough if you think exhibition skating should be more than a set of thrills—if you're looking for a parallel to real dancing. The different shapes that the body takes in the air are almost indistinguishable, and, as far as erudition is concerned, it isn't as important to know the difference between a double axel and a double toe loop as to *see* it. Skating doesn't make as great a drama of visual and rhythmic distinctions as dancing does. It makes a spectacle of hypnotic evenness—delightful as trivial fantasy but death as the serious fantasy that art is. That it can be looked at seriously at all is largely owing to the talent and vision of John Curry. There are skaters who are dancers, and there are skaters who are dancers who are artists. Curry is one of the latter. "IceDancing," his show that opened a few weeks ago at the Felt Forum and moves soon to the Minskoff, is a logical extension of the championship form he displayed at Innsbruck in 1976, but Curry has left the Olympics far behind.

"IceDancing" is not to be confused with that boringly literal Olympic category ice dancing, which in its rigid exclusion of the spectacular is practically anti-skating. Nor is it a traditional ice show, with squads of skaters scuffing down the ice dressed as Dutch windmills. Curry's aim, as I understand it, is to legitimize skating as an art without losing the seductive appeal of motion on ice. The first show he put together, called "Theatre of Skating," was a commercial success. I saw it in a long run at the Palladium in London last year; in England Curry is a national hero. But the show was aesthetically confusing. Curry seemed to have done nothing more than put a dance company on ice. The result, for the most part, was an uninteresting compromise: neither skating nor dancing. The Palladium stage could accommodate none of the effects of momentum that are possible in the arena; giving up too much of the arena for the stage was, I felt at the time, Curry's biggest mistake. The Felt Forum can hardly be said to have a stage at all. It has a wide, shallow platform that becomes a wide, shallow rink. Several of the group ballets, such as Donald Saddler's *Palais de Glace* and Jean-Pierre Bonnefous's *Icemoves,* lose focus as a result of lateral spread. But the show worked, possibly because since "Theatre of Skating" Curry has managed to get a company of skaters to keep the constant performance tension of dancing without looking marooned. No one, of course, does it as well as he; the others use concentration and projection, while Curry's method is in his dance-trained muscles—you can see the difference in his bearing. Curry's greatest distinction, to me—greater even than his long, perfectly balanced line—is that he always looks lifted out of his ·skates, as if he were riding a stream of air. His contact with the ice is resilient: he's able to go up or down, to stretch or contract, at will. And the freedom of his style is what the ice dancers of the future should be training for. In Keith Money's book about him (published here by Knopf), Curry tells how he learned to jump from the coach Gus Lussi, who put him in a confined space and forced him to use muscular coordination rather than the momentum that most skaters rely on. At the Palladium, I was struck by the fact that, although the show was cramped and inexpressive, Curry himself seemed to have plenty of room. Skating needs space, but perhaps not as much as custom dictates. (The Minskoff stage is smaller than the Felt Forum's but more regular in shape.)

Curry never learned to jump really high, but then his skating isn't spectacular in that way. In his Olympic year, Twyla Tharp made him an arena solo in which all the elements of the competition skater's art were dismantled and reassembled in a new form. It's likely that no skater had ever jumped the way Curry jumps in *After All*—not just a few times with long preparatory glides in between but five times in a row in one circuit of the ice. Tharp understood the coherence and subtlety that Curry was working for. After the explosive jump section of the solo (which is set to a portion of Albinoni's Trumpet Concerto in B Flat), she staged a daringly long diminuendo ending, which Curry sustained, riding his momentum until it died. In the original version, composed for the vast rink at Madison Square Garden, the delicacy and duration of this was effective, but the abbreviated version given at the Felt Forum had no comparable power. And it was anticlimactic: the audience wanted to applaud after the fast section and didn't get the chance. After the slow, ambiguous finale, it didn't get the ballet. Curry, though, came back to this very quiet mood later in the show and did something amazing. Travelling slowly forward in arabesque, he suddenly halted, lifted the blade onto "point," lowered it, and began travelling backward. It's the tiniest as well as the most magical effect I've ever seen a skater produce, and it drew the biggest gasp of the evening. The ballet was *Afternoon of a Faun*, to the Debussy music, staged for Curry by Norman Maen. There's something very right about the piece. The long, slow, gliding phrases fit the music; the Faun suits Curry's air of reserve and his elfin face. And Cathy Foulkes, whose reticence matches Curry's, is a beautiful, fresh-limbed Nymph. But the production is too literally modelled on the Nijinsky ballet. Mottled tights and dappled-glade lighting are incongruous on ice; tights with skates aren't the most pleasing combination. (Curry has worn flared trousers in this role, or else ankle cuffs, which somehow contrived to give the skate boots the suggestion of hooves.) Except for that one relevé, most of Curry's movement is stretching and bending as he glides, like a moving hinge. The *Faun* crouch, with the torso angled and one foot tucked behind the other knee, is overused. There is a place for *Faun* in Curry's repertory, but a version as old-fashioned as this contradicts the innovative spirit of the show.

I don't want to give the impression that everything Curry does is dear and delicate. In Peter Martins's *Tango-Tango*, which is conceived partly as a serious composition based on traction and momentum and partly as a parody, he turns into a hipster and then—as Jo Jo Starbuck, in her new Farrah hairdo, slinks across the ice to meet him—into a lounge lizard. His classical cool is not on the same wavelength as her flaming wanton, but that only makes the number more effective. Jo Jo Starbuck, the heroine of Ice Capades, is a superb skater who in her performances with Curry is obviously entering a new dimension. To her technical precision she's adding a sexy wit and a depth of commitment that one can only call passion. She deserves to do more than the current repertory allows, and she ought not to be stuck with the murky "modern-dance" number *Myth*, by Robert Cohan. This is the one out-and-out fizzle in the show. Most of the show's choreography isn't as inventive for skating as it might be, but Cohan hardly seems to realize that he's on ice. The Kenneth MacMillan number, a whirlwind solo for Curry to Study No. 5 of Liszt's *Feux Follets*, is a clear success but not a very revealing one. There is a manège of turns that, except for the extraordinary stamina it would take to get through it on dry land, might have been choreographed for Anthony Dowell. Although Curry has enlisted a wide range of ballet and modern-dance choreographers, he himself may prove to be the best of the ice choreographers. He already knows about skating and dancing, so what occupies him, while the others are trying to uncover technical affinities, is skating and music. Skaters' music has never been very well done. Unseemly, jaggedly edited tapes are the rule in competition and exhibition skating, and the bland soundtracks at the professional ice shows should set no standards, either. At "IceDancing," the audience heard good music, possibly for the first time in a show of this type, and Curry's two ballets—*Moon Dances*, to Saint-Saëns's *Carnaval des*

Animaux, and *Anything Goes,* to Leonard Bernstein's *Candide* Overture—had an expressive sweep in relation to their scores. The crescendo in the overture was the night's most invigorating moment, and Starbuck was wonderful in it.

One of the problems that Curry hasn't tackled yet is that of the ensemble: not only training dancers to be skaters or—more difficult—skaters to be dancers but devising choreography for an ensemble which registers as a mass rather than a gathering of individuals. "IceDancing" has no corps, not even a small one. It has no wizard soloists beneath star rank. This throws the program out of balance. Curry should at least be able to alternate his exhausting solos from night to night. There is every reason to suppose that the ranks will be filled. "IceDancing" comes at a time when audiences are ready to look at skating as a performing art and to demand more taste and sensitivity in its presentation than they customarily get from the big arena shows. Turning professional, as many Olympic medallists do, need not mean the death of inspiration. Curry's influence has reached the whole skating field, not just the professionals. "Superskates," the annual gala benefit for the U.S. Olympic Fund, which brings together past and present Olympic champions and contenders (and which gave *After All* its première), is beginning to reflect Curry standards in the quality of music and the structure of individual programs: there's less filler now, and more action. This year, Robin Cousins, the young British champion who has absorbed so much of Curry's example, showed himself a stylist of individuality and power. The American David Santee made the transition into the major ranks. Of the newcomers, Lisa Marie Allen, with her big, cushy style, and the very lyrical Simone Grigorescu, formerly of Rumania, looked best to me. "Superskates" is where we also see Toller Cranston, who for a while was Curry's most publicized rival as premier danseur of the ice. Cranston, introduced as "author, painter, and superskater," is a camp performer and an uneven one. At his best, there's not a chink in his style, which is based less on his skating proficiency than on his baroque line. The Cranston curl, the Cranston swastika (other skaters make T's and X's—he makes swastikas), the Cranston ginch, the tight attitude-glide with one hand gripping the raised heel or knee, and, not least of all, the large, raped-Medusa head around which he sometimes throws a serpentine arm make him a subversive figure in this world of sweetie-pies. But this world is changing now, and Cranston's act, which he customarily ends sliding down the ice in a kneel, is getting a bit Liberace. This year, he even did a Sonja Henie tippy run. Toller Cranston, too, can take piqué arabesque on ice. Somehow, though, it isn't the same.   —*December 18, 1978*

Balanchine's Petipa

Harlequinade is a two-act Petipa ballet of 1900, remade as inconspicuously as possible by Balanchine. To illustrate what I mean by "inconspicuously," take the last of the episodes that make up the action. Harlequin sets a trap for Columbine in the Enchanted Park, where, having just signed a marriage contract, they will spend the rest of their lives. The trap is a portable birdbath; it spins like a top—three little harlequins keep it turning. Birds flutter around the small silver cascade, and Harlequin shoos them away. Then Columbine comes to take a long drink, bending low in flat-footed arabesque penchée. He captures her, and their pas de deux explores that deep penchée as, reperched at his arm's length, she dips and swoops close to the ground. A moment later, Harlequin is himself spinning like a top, one leg extended like the point of a compass, the spangles on his diamond-patterned costume throwing off light. For an instant, this whirl of light and the other whirl it reminds us of—the fountain—plus the corps of birds and the long-throated birdlike image of the girl are made to contain each other loosely in a structure of mutual celebration. It's Balanchine springing *his* trap, creating one of those crystal moments of pure captivation out of the oddly assorted events he has set before us. Harlequin's spin isn't just one more event, it's a catalytic explosion, and Mikhail Baryshnikov's cyclonic grande pirouette has never had a more appropriate setting.

Yet the structure of correspondences, all but subliminal, does nothing more than captivate. Like Harlequin's capturing Columbine only to set her free, it dissolves as soon as we see it, without celebrating itself. The nascent imagery of the scene, which another choreographer—Ashton, for instance —would have developed, is left undisturbed. Balanchine, like Petipa, is content with its suggestive drift—more than a tender conceit yet less than a metaphor. He gives us a kind of parable of forms—naive, with rough edges. He doesn't coach us for a response. As the sequence builds up, it accumulates elements of harmony and elements of contrast and relief (those birds have one of the dizziest entrées right in the middle of it), and all we're conscious of as we watch it is the pressure of concentration. Nothing so official as a "meaning" is ever delivered—here or anywhere else in the ballet. *Harlequinade* is one of Balanchine's most innocent and vulnerably affectionate works, and one of his least popular.

The Harlequin of the ballet is the eternal Harlequin of mischief and protean tricks. Contemporary audiences may see him as unsympathetic, and the harlequinade as coy fantasy or rootless frivolity—which it very often is.

In any case, there are people who have never seen the ballet and don't want to go, because they're pretty sure they won't be amused. Balanchine's way of seducing these people over the years (the piece was first done in 1965 and was revised in 1973) has been to give them more of what they don't want: more children, more merrymaking (which really *is* rootless), gaudier costumes. But even the hard-core ballet public resists *Harlequinade*—I suspect because it isn't "Balanchine." That is, the traditional material isn't sufficiently filtered and doesn't express a "contemporary point of view." What's deceptive about *Harlequinade* is that Balanchine's re-evaluations occur within the material, not outside it in the form of a commentary. The steps may not be Petipa's but their quality of expression is. And is Balanchine's at the same time. For a comparison, see his *Swan Lake*, in which both the surface and the depths of an old ballet have been organically reconceived. The expressive mode of *Harlequinade* would be recognizable to Petipa; a modern-day "reinterpretation" probably would not; one that searched out pithier characterizations and metaphors certainly would not. Perhaps it's a question less of craftsmanly connection than of spiritual identification. When Balanchine is dealing directly in the Petipa tradition, as in *Harlequinade* and *The Nutcracker* and *Raymonda Variations* (and in his other variations on *Raymonda*), he works in a nonaggrandizing way. He converts the material to a new purpose, makes it serve new dancers, without stamping it with a new personality. This leads to accusations that he doesn't revise as well as he copies. There's nothing in *Harlequinade* like the Waltz of the Flowers, but then we love the Waltz for the way it appears to spring directly from its music and its period. Although it originates in the same period, nothing in *Harlequinade* was destined to be as wonderful as that. Petipa, too, knew the difference between Tchaikovsky and Riccardo Drigo, and valued them both. As far as metaphors go, it is enough for Columbine to be a bird—when she isn't being a doll—as it is for Harlequin to be a cat. Harlequin's feline dance character seems to have been set long before the ballet. Whether Petipa invented specific connotations for Mathilde Kschessinskaya, the first Columbine, I have no idea. It does seem to have been Columbine's ballet, though Kschessinskaya disdained it, passing her role on to such successors as Olga Preobrajenskaya and Anna Pavlova. Georgi Kyaksht, the first Harlequin, was succeeded by Nicholas Legat and Mikhail Fokine, the latter of whom would compose *Carnaval*, with a Harlequin made famous by Nijinsky. (Baryshnikov's first performance in *Harlequinade* drew some of its plastique from portraits of Nijinsky.)

The ballet's stylistic precedents are somewhat hazy. Russians saw harlequinades at the *balagani*—the covered stages at the Russian fairs. Alexandre Benois, who commemorated the *balagani* in his décors for *Petrushka*, writes, in *Reminiscences of the Russian Ballet*, about the harlequinades he saw there as a boy, and he describes the same Harlequin figure who, in some of the same episodes, found his way into Petipa's ballet. If, as Benois writes,

"Harlequin was given exactly the part that he played in our old *balagani*," either the ballet must have reflected the people's theatre to a degree unsuspected by historians of the Petipa years, who always picture the Imperial Ballet enclosed in a bubble of sanctity, or the people's Harlequin represented the francophiliac culture of St. Petersburg, which also seems unlikely. The Imperial Theatres were under the direction of I. A. Vsevolojsky, a typical product of that culture, and it was Vsevolojsky, as Benois also informs us, who conceived the Harlequin ballet, drawing on his memories of the féeries he had seen in Paris. Petipa, a Frenchman, would have known all about that; both men had, in fact, turned to the féeries a decade before, for *The Sleeping Beauty*. The style of the ballet *Arlekinada*, or *Les Millions d'Arlequin*, as it was also known, conformed to the sophisticated taste of the capital. It was romantic, pretty, "French." The Pierrot was (and is) the lazy, woebegone mooncalf popularized by French mimes. But as the servant of Cassandre, Columbine's father, he's a fink, ratting on the lovers and creeping into the audience's affections only by bungling most of his servile assignment. He doesn't have a great deal in common with that other hero of the *balagani*, Petrushka, who was a Russian Pierrot so well assimilated that he is still universally accepted as a symbol of the Russian soul. Drigo was of course, Italian. His music for the ballet is contemporary with *Cavalleria Rusticana* and *Pagliacci*, and sounds that way. For an Arlecchino who is youthful and elegant, both poet and lover, he composes a lace-doily Serenade, the hit of the score. Balanchine stages it with a minimum of dancing, as if to draw our attention to the mandolins in the pit. But when a nuptial anthem is wanted at the end of the ballet, the orchestra bursts into the French drinking song "Malbrouck s'en Va t'en Guerre," which is known in this country as "For He's a Jolly Good Fellow."

With all this for a background, it's not surprising that the style of Balanchine's production is polyglot, a merry jumble of Russian, French, and Italian influences. Rouben Ter-Arutunian's scenery, modelled on the Pollock's toy theatres of Victorian England, adds a fourth influence and reminds us of the long and rich tradition of the English harlequinade. Ter-Arutunian's lighting has always seemed unatmospherically dim in Act I, and in Act II the stage is blatantly sidelit, so that leaping shadows are thrown on the wings by the dancers' entrances and exits. The shadows can be excused as magic-lantern effects suitable to a toy theatre, but, although there must be moonlight in Act I if there is to be a Serenade, the moon ought not to be clouded over. Ter-Arutunian does not provide a Pierrot moon, perhaps because the bulk of his scenery was designed not for this production but for a New York City Opera *Cenerentola* in 1953. The part of it that belongs to *Harlequinade* is the house of Cassandre, with its twin turntables, which allow the statue of La Bonne Fée, Harlequin's protectress, to come to life and Harlequin himself to be miraculously restored after he's been dismembered in a rout. There's also a balcony that lowers itself to the ground. (I thought I'd seen all the scenery's magic tricks when suddenly, this season, Baryshnikov made an exit through the wall of the toy theatre.) The choreography in Act I is concerned mostly with getting the cast into and out of the house and Harlequin together with Columbine, who has been pledged by her father to a wealthy fop. It's all business, a farcical ballet d'action, but it isn't busy, and the perfection of its shape cracks only once, when Balanchine abruptly introduces a stageful of revellers from a nearby carnival, which is never alluded to again. The variations for the principals—Columbine, Harlequin, Pierrette, and La Bonne Fée—and the smoochy Columbine-Harlequin pas de deux are seamlessly joined to the action. The only "divertissement" number (apart from the tarantella-fugue of the revellers) is the pas de quatre done by the four ladies of Harlequin's entourage, a picturesque bunch of couples dressed in espresso-black seventeenth-century outfits whom the program calls Les Scaramouches. This pas de quatre, currently undersold in performance, is one of the gems of the repertory. Stylistically, it embraces both the art and the life of Petipa's period, it comes from deep inside the ballet, and it smiles. If there is a Waltz of the Flowers in *Harlequinade*, this is it. But the pas de quatre is unique in Balanchine in being designed for larger, seemingly older, and slightly fatuous women, who do needlepoint steps that insist on propriety. Balancing it is the march of the drunken foot patrol which used to arouse a steady ripple of laughter and applause. Now the *carabinieri* are too obviously drunk, and they don't seem to know of any propriety to insist on.

The plot of the ballet is a series of happenings stitched together by Petipa, probably from evenings at the *balagani*. Harlequin Serenades Columbine; Harlequin Meets les Sbires (minions, that is, of Cassandre, visually recalling the devils of the *balagani*); Harlequin Wins His Baton (precursor of the slapstick?), His Money, His Columbine. The story ends early in Act II and is followed by one more set piece: Harlequin and the Birds. After that, it's all dancing. According to Russian historians, Petipa's Act II went on too long and dragged. The same could be said of Balanchine's, which has two extensive divertissements—one performed by squads of children, the other by principals. Children, revellers, Scaramouches, and a flock of birds make four separate corps de ballets; the little stage becomes overstuffed. And Drigo's charming, voluble score grows garrulous. (He could write bird music by the yard.) The events in Act I and the start of Act II are continuous in time, but Patricia McBride is no longer deterred by that fact from changing her costume. (To clinch the joke, the wrap that Pierrette follows her with should also change. And what prevents the trickle of gold coins from the Fairy's cornucopia from becoming a real flow? The ushers might take up a collection.) One of McBride's finest moments is in this ballet— the second-act solo, with its long, long, and slow series of déboulés on point ending in a curtsy and three blown kisses. Her partnership with Baryshnikov has yet to rival the vitality of her partnership with Edward Villella, who created this Harlequin, but her Columbine, made of ovenproof porcelain, endures. Deni Lamont as Pierrot and Shaun O'Brien as Léandre, the foppish suitor, after all these years give undiminished performances. This season, there were two new Cassandres. Frank Ohman's was only moderately effective; he betrayed the primary failing of the amateur mime—going dead when he didn't have a "line." But Andrei Kramarevsky's—bluff, violent, yet humane—was the best Cassandre we have had. Elyse Borne was the perkier of two new Pierrettes; Stephanie Saland acted extremely well, but her dancing lacked flair and her dusky glamour looked wrong in the role. The glamour role in the ballet is La Bonne Fée, though occasionally it is good to see it well danced, as by Colleen Neary. (This role is full of flatfooted penchées, but, unlike Columbine's, they don't speak bird language. Balanchine's steps take their color from situations and contexts; that's why he can change historic choreography—which he says was always changing anyway —and stay within a historic style.) Sheryl Ware currently leads, or misleads, the Alouettes—a vibrant, springy dancer in a part that calls for a brittle, flighty, almost edgy quality. At a matinee, Daniel Duell made a début substituting for Baryshnikov. Duell as Harlequin was a bit like Saland as Pierrette, only he was plainly much happier dancing than acting. Harlequin, who doesn't really dance much, needs mercury in his blood. Baryshnikov and Villella have it. Jean-Pierre Bonnefous, a great character dancer, made Harlequin live almost entirely through plastique—he was as stealthy as a cat burglar. When Duell turned away from the audience, launching his Serenade toward Columbine's balcony, his back didn't sing.

The season has been thick with débuts, and, as the company passed its thirtieth year, anniversaries began to pile up. *The Nutcracker* has now been with us a quarter of a century. Astonishing to think it is half as old as *The Prodigal Son*. Not many people are heard to call the ballet *Nutcracker Suite* now. That shows how far it has risen in the public consciousness, not only in New York but in dozens of cities around the country where it is performed annually. Another mark of its popularity and of the popularity of ballet generally is that this year the New York City Ballet's five little boys in Act I actually were little boys, not little girls in tams. In the alternate cast, four of the five roles were taken by boys. Kramarevsky, who teaches a most influential and difficult men's class at the School of American Ballet, made another good début as an anarchic, remote, eighteenth-century Drosselmeyer, and O'Brien's sterling performance, in a more avuncular vein, acquired further lustre. The business of the clock's hands had been adjusted: we heard eight chimes and it was eight o'clock. Drosselmeyer hardly ever failed to reset the clock at midnight, when the wild, dark fantasy begins. Watching Balanchine's production, particularly this part of it and the rest of Act I, could leave one in no doubt about why the ballet has been such a great success. It's a pyramid of theatrical marvels, each one outdazzling the last. But I think we aren't as much impressed by the dazzle as we are moved by the emotion it represents; a kind of mounting ecstatic melancholy holds us in its grip. And the most transfixing moment of all is the tableau in the forest, in the falling snow. Here, in the immense, waiting silence, the little Nutcracker is changed into a prince, and no one sees it but the audience. Ter-Arutunian's Act II backcloth was removed two seasons ago and replaced by his decorative arrangement of pendant fruits in a pink void. This is more tasteful than Rumpelmayer's Mountain and far lower in calories, too. But it's an evasion. The Kingdom of Sweets is a *place*. None of the many débuts in this act were really notable—not even Baryshnikov's as cavalier to Elyse Borne's Sugar Plum (it was an appearance, predictably powerful, for the record)—just as none were unacceptable. Lourdes Lopez restored rhythmic tension and credible exoticism to the Arabian dance, and Heather Watts's easy high jump and flexible impetus made her the most vivid of the Dew Drops even though the upper body had an unintegrated, careless look.

Aren't the mice in *The Nutcracker* a parody of the Drinking Companions in *The Prodigal Son*? And though the two ballets are worlds apart, isn't there something in the mixture of spookiness and outlandish distortion and comedy that makes the dream in *The Nutcracker* resemble the orgy scene in *Prodigal*? The Son might almost be entering an E. T. A. Hoffmann landscape. In its fiftieth year, the ballet has been given new costumes, based on the original Diaghilev production. For his first performance of the season, Baryshnikov wore a modified version of the Serge Lifar outfit that was inflicted on him in the recent television production. Baryshnikov is physically and in almost every other way as unlike Lifar as he can be, and by the second performance he'd reverted to the simple leather harness and brief chiton worn by previous NYCB Prodigals. Although the costumes are always attributed to Rouault, they have in fact been by various artists over the years, starting with Vera Sudeikina in 1929 and including Esteban Francés in the fifties. The two backcloths, which represent Rouault's own work, look shabby. Repainting would make the current restoration complete.   —*January 22, 1979*

Other Verdi Variations

Last summer, the New York City Ballet gave us a cluster of works in progress among which was a setting by Jerome Robbins of ballet music from Verdi operas, notably Spring from *The Seasons*, the dance divertissement in *Sicilian Vespers*. Now Robbins is presenting all four seasons, and instead of the second première that the company would ordinarily be putting on we get an alternate cast in Fall. Does it make that big a difference whether you see McBride-Baryshnikov or Farrell-Martins? Yes, it does. Robbins, who likes to work in series (*Dances at a Gathering, In the Night, Other Dances*), has arranged different solos to different music for Baryshnikov and Martins. The choreography for McBride and Farrell is substantially the same, but their very dissimilar styles transform it. Seeing the two versions of *The Four Seasons* may be difficult just now, when tickets are scarce. You get no help from the company, which, as a matter of policy, never announces casting more than a week in advance. But cancellations are often available at curtain time, and, partly because of its double star cast, the ballet is a hit. It will have to be around a long time if it is going to be seen twice as often as most hits.

Will the other parts of the ballet stand up under repeated viewings? Robbins has taken a calculated risk, and his calculations are so nice that two times is just about all most people will need or want to see the ballet. One could, of course, watch the Baryshnikov or the Farrell section forever, but fanaticism must expect to pay a price. It isn't as great a price as Balanchine exacts in *Tchaikovsky Suite No. 3* from those who only want to watch the *Theme and Variations* forever; still, Winter, Spring, and especially Summer are not in the same eye- and nerve-popping class as Fall. That may be in the nature of things: Fall is arranged, after Verdi's scenario, as a bacchic revel. But even allowing for camp appeal, vulgarity, shameless exhibitionism, and all the other necessary attributes of bacchic revels, Fall has the edge over Spring, the next-best section of the ballet, in being more explicitly Verdian in expression. I mean that Robbins has here caught something quintessentially innocent in Verdi's music, has joined his own enthusiasm to it, and has given it full value in his choreography. Spring, by comparison, is a little guardedly neutral, unwilling to surrender respect for Verdi's genius to a recognition of its quality. Or it may be that Spring, which we first saw under the title *Verdi Variations*, is Robbins's homage to the eternally undivided, objective, and harmonious art that is Verdi's—and that is not Robbins's. If so, the outcome of a sentimental, dissenting artist's celebrating a peacefully attuned one is mere blandness or pleasant efficiency. In characterizing Verdi and Robbins, I am using terms that Isaiah Berlin borrowed from Schiller for his essay "The Naiveté of Verdi." Robbins, I think, sees Verdi in Berlin-Schiller terms as "in music at least . . . the last 'naive' artist of genius," but he's unable to encompass this aspect of Verdi steadily. It's as if in Spring he were able to encompass only a list of must-nots. The material for Kyra Nichols and Daniel Duell is so restrained, so limpidly organized, that it looks inhibited; its classicism is negative, like "corrected" character dancing. And since their débuts in these roles last summer Nichols and Duell have become even more measured and methodical. Duell is given choreography that is far from easy, yet he makes it look *too* easy—overanalyzed, drained of excitement. Nichols is so controlled that the audience applauds her for a beauty and a lady, too. Verdi's zephyrs are really breezy; they're not in this ballet. (A male corps of four bounding *haricots verts* isn't quite enough.)

In Verdi's ballet, originally produced during the third act of *Sicilian Vespers* at the Paris Opéra in 1855, the leading dancers of the four divertissements emerged from a basket at the behest of Janus, god of the new year. In the New York City production, which was designed in period style by Santo Loquasto, Janus hails four allegorical figures in drapes (Father Winter, Primavera, etc.), who then leave the stage to return one by one with their (dancing) entourages. It's obvious—at least to Loquasto, who has used every cliché in the book—that what will now take place is a ballet about ballet. But Robbins has made no consistent attempt to reproduce the style of a mid-century opera divertissement. He follows the elaborate scenario, but not with blind faith. (Or with strict logic. Having frozen his dancers to shivering tremolos, he does not unfreeze them when the music melts into droplets of pizzicati.) His instinct is to follow instead the dance impulse of the music, and in this he is right. Isaiah Berlin wrote of the Verdi operas that we need no outside information, no orientation, to understand them, and the same is true of the Verdi ballets. However, there's one instance when Robbins's instinct plays him false. Summer is the shortest of the Seasons, little more than an interlude between Spring and Fall. Verdi composed a languorous oboe solo over a drone bass followed by a sprightly waltz that dies away at the first sign of Autumn panic. The passage, amusing and evocative in itself, is one of those with a direct influence on later ballet music—the bacchante's dance in the second act of *Sylvia* and the Arabian dance in *The Nutcracker* both recall it. Robbins's choreography, an understated cooch dance, lets the associations stand, but it neither draws them out nor adds anything. Bart Cook's role is vague; Stephanie Saland's is decorative; six girls make their bends adornings. This disconcertingly blank *scène dansante* suggests thinning resources, and not, as Robbins may have intended, a prelude to the afternoon of many fauns, nymphs, and satyrs.

In the final section, the allusions to ballets past are so ripe that to an audience with a decent awareness of dance history they'd be almost past mentioning. But culturally we're so deprived that all we can think of as we watch Robbins's bacchanal is the last time we saw one like it, which was in the repertory of the Bolshoi Ballet. Robbins's corps de ballet enters en masse in a split leap to a crouch, just as I recall Lavrovsky's doing in *Walpurgis Night*. Loquasto's tunics and shifts—grape for the corps, scarlet for the principals—are something like the Bolshoi's. Jean-Pierre Frohlich's Pan suggests the Yagudins and Vasilievs of the Bolshoi as well as the Puck danced by Frohlich in Balanchine's *A Midsummer Night's Dream*. Robbins's ballet, like Lavrovsky's, belongs to a conventional genre that probably had its origins early in the last century. Certainly it was a genre by Verdi's day, and it lasted into Ravel's (*Daphnis and Chloë*). Still, for most of us, the Lavrovsky precedent exists. I believe that it exists for Robbins and that he has invoked it deliberately to clarify certain points of divergence and connection between Mikhail Baryshnikov's background and that of the American dancers he is seen among now. Point of divergence: When can the Bolshoi—or the Kirov, which knows *Walpurgis Night* well—have seen dancing (as opposed to running, leaping, and posing) like this? Point of divergence: Could any Russian bacchant ever look so lightweight, so collegiate? Baryshnikov seems almost unnaturally vivid in the midst of American dancers. They surround him in a crouching run, going nowhere in particular, while he is on a headlong debauch. And his singularity is heightened in his variation, in which he throws himself forward in plunging stag leaps, then backward into high jetés passés. Images of sensual abandon arise purely from fertility of technique. Robbins's choreography asks Baryshnikov for everything he knows about jumps and turns. You can almost see the entries under "grande pirouette" expanding as Baryshnikov does it: with knee bends, with sautés, in every variety of attitude, and sometimes without turning to a finish but simply stopping dead, impeccably à la seconde. Point of connection. Baryshnikov's technique is a one-man revolution waged on the same principles as the most advanced Western choreography. He embodies the drive to "do more" and do it bigger and faster than ever before.

Temperamentally and technically, the role of the ballerina suits Suzanne Farrell better than it does Patricia McBride. One might know that without seeing McBride do it. Seeing her, one might not know it. Robbins always composes felicitously for McBride; she has difficulty only with a few of the uncentered pirouettes that are a Farrell specialty, and she does chaînés instead of the string of double soutenu turns that Farrell knocks off. And she doesn't in Baryshnikov have the superbly sensitive partner that Farrell has in Martins. But Martins is a slightly uneasy Bacchus, and he needs his own costume as much as his own variation. (Perhaps, like McBride, he should wear a wig.) The variation, like Baryshnikov's, is set to a selection from *Il Trovatore*. Fittingly for a stylist of the Danish school, it's all turns and beats; he performs page after page of batterie. Then Martins goes Russian, with his magnificent double assemblé en tournant performed as he runs ahead of a snake line in the galop. Farrell's great voluptuary is a projection of her virtuoso technical capacities. Her precision, like Baryshnikov's, is epicurean. At her first performance, her variation was so astonishing in its speed, in its extreme and subtle wit, that most people in the audience didn't realize what had happened. Farrell, whose health for the past year has been unreliable, hasn't been consistently at her best this season. If only as the occasion for the reassuring return of a great dancer, Robbins's ballet has served its purpose.

Of course, it has accomplished more than that. Once again, Robbins has come to the aid of the company when it could not count on another major première. He has provided it with a ballet-of-the-moment, focussing the excitement we feel right now about New York City Ballet. His casting of tandem star teams may seem a bit American Ballet Theatre, but Robbins doesn't flaunt his stars without accommodating them as artists.

Since ballets have no existence apart from performance, it's inevitable that they change over the years, just as the performers do. Deterioration is also to some extent a part of the natural process of repertory, and in a repertory the size of Balanchine's it can sometimes spread past tolerable limits. *Who Cares?* has largely fallen apart; recent performances of *Theme and Variations* have been scarcely worth the long sit through *Suite No. 3*. A change that is very hard to take is the one that has come over *Agon*. This is the result not of decomposition but of recomposition; the whole ballet has been systematically overhauled, studded with quirks and affectations, and generally made to look like Modernism Made Easy. The loose, equivocal, hip style of the early years can never, perhaps, be restored—it left too wide a margin for error. But this new, overaccented, overpunctuated *Agon* is an impostor. Even Farrell and Martins, scooping through the pas de deux, broadcast their effects. Oddly, this development coincides with the continued veracity of *The Four Temperaments*, which, despite a few arbitrary revisions near the end, still looks like *The Four Temperaments*. Baryshnikov's growing accuracy of style as he works his way into the Melancholic variation is something we can measure; it's progress toward a legible goal. And *Serenade* still looks like *Serenade*, especially when it is danced as it was a week ago. Kyra Nichols gave the cleanest and most expressive Tema Russo I have seen in many years. With Colleen Neary, Joseph Duell, and Adam Lüders, it was a cast that made me happy even with the mite-size heroics of Kay Mazzo as the ballet's tragic heroine.

—*February 5, 1979*

Repertory Dead and Alive

The final weeks of a long, exhausting, and exciting season such as the one the New York City Ballet is now having take their toll in injuries and illness. Scheduled dancers drop out, replacements must be prepared, sometimes at short notice, and pretty soon there aren't enough rehearsal hours left for next week's programs. The ballets that do not appear on the bills until late in the season—particularly if they're unusually complex or delicate ballets —may have to be sacrificed as the emergencies pile up: either cancelled or put on in an underrehearsed state. So far this winter, only two ballets and several pas de deux have had to be pulled—a not bad record for a company that maintains a year-round active repertory of more than fifty ballets.

Not bad, that is, until we consider that the cancelled ballets were *Tchaikovsky Piano Concerto No. 2* and *Divertimento No. 15*—two of Balanchine's greatest. The loss then is far greater than the numerical facts can express.

Sheer numbers, though, tell a tale. This repertory, the world's largest, plays its home city twice a year in nine-week seasons (along with five weeks of *The Nutcracker* every winter). A decade ago, when the average number of repertory weeks per season was eight, the average number of ballets was just under fifty. This means that the ratio of ballets to performance weeks—the ratio on which the company has been operating for some time now—is six to one, and it's unmanageable. The company has never been able to keep six ballets in top-quality motion for every week that it performs—no company ever has—yet it drives itself on, and the standard explanation is that it must, because of the subscription system. Subscribers are said to have an obsessive thirst for variety and novelty. Yet in the years before subscriptions were instituted the company was flogging itself along at an incredibly steep five to one. That might be a more reasonable ratio for today. The demands of subscribers account for only a small amount of the seasonal pressure; the rest is brought about by habit of aspiration. (In the old days at the City Center, programs often consisted of four ballets every night, and a principal dancer would appear in two or three of them.) The audience can see when the company is pushing itself and when it isn't, but pressure that goes beyond the logical expectation of a reward may not be so easy to appreciate. The New York City Ballet acts as if it had got sidetracked in the first phase of proving Blake's theory that you can't know what is enough until you know what is more than enough. Its audience these days is benign. But if audiences in general are more willing than ever before to accept the kind of grand and serious folly that ballet is—and it seems that they are—does that mean they'll accept everything about the way ballet is presented to them? When you talk about the ways ballet companies are run, you're talking about ways to rationalize the irrational, and a great deal of superstition enters the talk. At NYCB, one good argument for keeping an inflated repertory is that disrepair tends to strike hardest at ballets that are not performed every season. Yet staples like *Symphony in C* and *Serenade* can be performed year in and year out and still go through drastic fluctuations in quality of performance. Ballet is intrinsically inefficient. Just when you've got optimal accuracy costed out in man-hours, something magicks it away.

Another problem is that until the sixties the company's repertory was formed for smaller stages than the one at the State Theatre. Some of the Balanchine classics have been expanded since the move to Lincoln Center; others look troublingly small in their current productions. Perhaps the time has come to set up a second company, to perform the older, smaller works that have resisted the transition to the larger stage. What would we not give to see *Liebeslieder Walzer* again, danced in its full original décor on the stage of the Juilliard Theatre? There, too, ballets like *Divertimento No. 15*,

Agon, and *Donizetti Variations* could regain their proper dimensions. And new ballets might be born that could never be conceived at the State Theatre.

Orpheus came back into the repertory this season—its first revival since the Stravinsky Festival, in 1972. For the occasion, which marks the thirtieth anniversary of the founding of New York City Ballet, Mikhail Baryshnikov made his début as Orpheus, and Francisco Moncion appeared in his original role of the Dark Angel. Kay Mazzo was Eurydice, and there were two other débuts: Heather Watts as the leader of the Bacchantes, and Adam Lüders as Apollo. Baryshnikov gave a strong, thoughtful, deeply committed performance, wrong in every move. It wasn't his fault; he had cancelled two performances in order to rehearse a role to which he is ill suited. Orpheus is passive, turned-in—a mime rather than a dancer. The role, like the ballet as a whole, is cast in the hieratic mime of the forties. Baryshnikov's mime was in the modern Russian tradition of dance-acting; he sniffed out the dance implication in every gesture and gave that full play. For the first time since he joined the company, he looked a stranger. His Orpheus is a romantic hero, a protagonist. Balanchine's is a disinterested artist, submissive in the grip of fate. The role was drawn on the loose line and introverted stance of Nicholas Magallanes—hardly a prototype for Baryshnikov. The production itself came on looking like a scrappy dress rehearsal. The second performance was smoother, but again there were accidents and mistakes. The projections that mirror the rocky landscape in the first scene rose on the horizon as we began the descent to Hades; they reappeared, as they should have, on the return trip; but as Orpheus regained Earth they rose again, instead of sinking. The great white silk curtain that drops like a veil of mist to envelop the principals on their journeys is a notorious hazard. In the first performance, the dancers had to fight clear of it; in the second, Moncion was cut off from his downstage exit. But these things have gone wrong before without affecting the tragic mystery of the ballet. This time, there was no mystery and no intimation of one—just a sketchy recital of events that were once part of a treasured ballet. *Orpheus* in its present form is a token reminder of the past, not a serious revival. Composed in an unemphatic narrative style, the ballet is an ashen meditation permeated by the sweetish odor of death. The veil dropping between earth and the Underworld is the shroud of the dead. The effect is derived from Tchelitchev's décor for an earlier ballet, *Errante*; it is related to the veils in *Giselle* and *La Bayadère*. Orpheus at Eurydice's grave begins the ballet; Apollo ends it by conjuring from blood-soaked ground a flowering branch that bears the immortal lyre heavenward. But this production seems to have been pervaded by a death wish. Perhaps we should read as its reigning symbol the fact that the twist of ivy that should hang from the branch is missing.

There are many people who hold *Orpheus* in beloved memory, not least because its première, in 1948, was a turning point in the fortunes of American ballet. After the première, which Stravinsky conducted, Balanchine and

Lincoln Kirstein were invited by the City Center to form New York City Ballet. Kirstein includes the sequence *Apollo, Orpheus,* and *Agon* among the fifty historic masterpieces in his book *Movement and Metaphor.* And there are countless personal testimonials to the ballet's impact. I never shared in the apocalypse that was *Orpheus.* By the end of the fifties, when I saw it for the first time, it was embedded in a triumphant New York City Ballet repertory. It looked unique (and still does)—a distant relative of a Martha Graham piece—and the pas de deux was impressive then and for many years to come. But one could be critical. What about the Furies scene, where some people moved rocks while others did vehement high kicks and wagged their elbows? Later, I found my objection, and much more, in a laudatory review by Edwin Denby ("A pity the Furies' dance in Hell is of no value"), and Denby was at the theatre on the first night of the current revival. He remembered vividly being overcome by his first impression of the ballet; during intermission he'd sat slumped in his seat, attracting the concern of ushers. He described Maria Tallchief as Eurydice—her large, handsome head and shoulders, her dramatic weight and torsion in the pas de deux in which, climbing Orpheus' back, winding her legs about him, she seemed to drag him heavily downward. The erotic urgency of this passage I had witnessed myself. ("Eurydice writhes at her husband's feet like a mountain lioness in heat," Denby had written.) By contrast, Kay Mazzo was as light as a stick of balsa. Dramatically and sculpturally, Baryshnikov's chunky contours were unrelated to her skeletal ones. Denby also spoke nostalgically of the Epilogue. Apollo appears bearing the severed head of Orpheus and drawing from it eternal song—a rite I have never seen performed with anything like the evocative power that seems to have been intended for it. But in a more intimate house you could begin to guess what it meant. The idea of performing the small works of the repertory on a small stage like the Juilliard's is Denby's; I pass it on eagerly. It might be the way to a restoration of *Orpheus.* In 1972, the company went to some trouble to present Noguchi's famous décor in a revised and rescaled version, and the look of the whole production dropped a notch in meaning—from barren to desolate, from provocative to eccentric. Now the scuba-diving helmets and hoses, the bodies decorated with ropes and pancakes just seem a curious anticipation of High Tech. The Bacchantes still have their 1972 wigs, which look like Orlon sea grass, and unfortunately they dance not wildly but flamboyantly, like the corps in *The Cage.* But the moment when Orpheus and Eurydice join hands for the journey home and a pale ribbon slashes the wall with a glimpse of sky is still magical.

Sometimes, as with *Orpheus,* we see performances that are really dress rehearsals. Other times, we see a very different thing: a performance in which experimentation and danger are present to a degree that no rehearsal could have anticipated, and the ballet is, in effect, created before our eyes. In a penetrating interview in the current *Ballet Review,* Suzanne Farrell says that performances can't really be rehearsed—that "a performance is a process, an enactment that must be done in accordance with the speed and dynamics of the music on a given night." Three performances in one week of *Vienna Waltzes* were stations on the road to that kind of spontaneous perfection. Because of the "process" that its performances have been revealing, this ballet seems to me the current pinnacle experience to be had at New York City Ballet. It's the great ballet of the repertory right now, and I say that with full appreciation for the resurgence of established classics like *Symphony in C* and *Serenade* and *The Four Temperaments* and for the canny estimate of current company strength that Robbins offers in *The Four Seasons*. *Vienna Waltzes* is what it is partly because it is a still new portrait of the company. The novelty may be wearing off, but not the validity of the characterization. And it is designed as a full-company vehicle. It's a big statement, munificently set on the big stage, using all the company's resources: its wonderful orchestra, its roster of principals (pre-Baryshnikov). But it has stature as well as scope and panoply. *Vienna Waltzes* was, from the first, taken much too lightly as box-office bait, a kind of Viennese counterpart to *Union Jack*, which had been a great hit the year before. The suspicion that a multitudinous non–ballet-going public was waiting outside the gates of Lincoln Center for Balanchine to make an hour of Strauss waltzes was enough for people who should have known better to dismiss the ballet in advance as unserious. But then the dancing itself was condemned: not complex enough, not inviting choreographically, not *dancing*. It is always strange to see the example of one kind of Balanchine ballet set against another, as if there were a "good" (progressive) Balanchine who needed to be defended against a "bad" (commercial) Balanchine. There are bad commercial ballets by Balanchine; it is more challenging to try to distinguish them from the good ones, like *Vienna Waltzes*.

However, *Vienna Waltzes* is only in part a good commercial ballet. The opening, "Tales from the Vienna Woods," may properly be described as a commercial masterpiece, and when the dancers learn how to perform it better it could become something more than that. The men in this section wear their mustaches and uniforms a little bit as if they were embarrassed by them. Their courtship of the women is lacking in ceremony, spirit, dash. Hussars used to be fixtures on the ballet stage; our boys have never seen Hussars. (Couldn't the Film Society of Lincoln Center arrange to screen Max Ophuls's *Liebelei* for them?) "Voices of Spring" had to be done this season without Patricia McBride, who has in it her ripest role. Merrill Ashley is too tall for Helgi Tomasson to partner comfortably; by the end of the week the disparity was barely noticeable. Ashley had caught on to the carefree, heady Romantic style, and Tomasson, whose grasp of style has about it an almost moral tenacity, seemed to tower. The role is Oberon as King of the May. Despite an inappropriate costume (it's that same Fauntleroy suit he wears in other ballets), Tomasson understands the artificiality of the conception. He sweeps sedately through his glen, and we know that he rules a gaslit-and-muslin forest. "Voices of Spring," more delightful and enriching each time I see it, is not the great composition that the last section, "Der Rosenkavalier," is, but it can lay claim to a status just below the first rank. It's *Valse Fantaisie* lifted to the level of, say, *Allegro Brillante*. The exuberantly coarse little polka and the "Merry Widow" scene may be chocolate-boxy, but I find no fault in this. (The wigs that have been added are something else.) Mazzo's entrance as the Widow seems to have finally settled on a definitive staging, and as the central couple waltzes (to Lehár's "Gold and Silver") the small corps spreads and retracts itself like a fan. Peter Martins has the gift of magnifying his partner. His complete absorption as he turns her across the floor, his way of leaning back slightly, as if dazzled, are indispensable to the illusion that Balanchine wants to create. Sean Lavery in the "Vienna Woods" section has adopted Martins's manner toward his partner; it's less striking in Lavery only because his torso is shorter. Lavery's gallantry is in his long greyhound legs and precise foot positions.

The period style of *Vienna Waltzes* is deliberately fantastic. Lavery and the rest of the Hussars waltz to music written in 1868, but their costumes suggest a much earlier period. The "Merry Widow" women's dresses are turn-of-the-century, while their escorts wear the frock coats of fifty years before. But if the men, too, were matched with the date of the music, they'd look like bankers. Karinska has produced visionary costumes that enhance the spirit of the time, and not the letter. Balanchine's survey of various waltz eras extends from the Congress of Vienna, in 1814—the congress that waltzed with such mighty reverberations—to an elegant ballroom in the heart of Europe a hundred years later. This is the night the waltz breaks down. Tomorrow the guns of August will open fire. The history of three-quarter time up to that point is summarized by what Lehár and the younger Strauss could invent at their most inspired. (Would we really have preferred Balanchine to make a documentary survey to possibly less sumptuous sound?) It is music written for dancers. The disintegration of waltz time, as imagined by Richard Strauss, has never before been danced, as far as I know. To get through the piece, with its steep rubatos, its dizzying fadings and revivals of impetus, the entire company must be alert to "the speed and dynamics of the music on a given night." And so, this season, they have been. Much depends on the conductor. My performances were led first by Robert Irving and then by Hugo Fiorato. The flickering changes of step and momentum in Farrell's own great performance were different every night. So was the moment of "immolation," when her exit becomes the signal for the flooding of the stage with light and with waltzers.

In this finale, the music was so transparently alive, the dancers so restively responsive, that a mood of anxiety arose in the audience which did not entirely evaporate when the curtain went down. Balanchine does not soothe us—he shakes us and threatens us with catastrophe. The atmosphere of the "Rosenkavalier" waltz goes way beyond *La Valse*; in fact, there's a breathtaking moment when the men whirl and rush forward in a diagonal line that reminds us of *La Valse* and its boundary of virtuosity. The men cross that boundary. From then on, as the ballet repeatedly slides and skitters over thinnest ice, the tension starts to mount, and there's no relief from it. The big swirling stage is a spectacle of controlled hysteria. *Vienna Waltzes* is no longer getting the ovations of its first months. Whether that's because the audience has changed or because the ballet's intentions are more exposed, I cannot say. But those who see in it nothing but a big simple hit are as estranged from it as those who want nothing but a big simple hit. —*February 19, 1979*

Popular Song

Twyla Tharp's season at the Brooklyn Academy, her first local engagement in two years, had her customary brilliance, her customary showmanship, and a few surprises. Three of the four premières were set to contemporary popular music. This isn't surprising in itself; ever since *Deuce Coupe*, Tharp has been the mistress of a theatrical pop style based on the music that young people all across the country have danced to for recreation. Some of these pop pieces of hers have lasted, some haven't, but all of them have striven for contact with the genuine. Few people have an ear for the vernacular as discriminating as Twyla Tharp's. *Deuce Coupe* (done for the Joffrey Ballet) made me hear the Beach Boys as musicians, not just as pop phenomena; some lesser experiments have used music by Chuck Berry, Keith Jarrett, and Frank Sinatra. When it comes to popular music, Tharp will invariably strike the richest vein, and though she's not a folk-culture vulture, she believes in mining the mother lode whenever she can. The beautiful collection of old-time fiddling tunes in *Country Dances* and *Cacklin' Hen* may or may not be an implicit condemnation of the Nashville sound. What Tharp's choice suggests to me is not so much aesthetic purification as respect for a tradition that survives at some cost to those who keep it. In the script that is read at each performance of *The Bix Pieces*—a script in which Tharp outlines her creative process and gives us something of a credo—she wrote, "It seems to me that aesthetics and ethics are the same." There's an austerity in her vision that carries over to her material like a stamp of approval. Even Sinatra sounded austere—noble and bardic—when she used him. But, much as she may enliven the musical *Hair*, she cannot ennoble it. *Hair* (the forthcoming film version, for which she has done the choreography) uses Tharp's craftsmanship without her vision. Its songs have their own vision, bathetic and self-important, and Tharp's technique can only provide appropriate stylistic filters and blot up excess moisture. Along with samples of her choreography for *Hair*, the Brooklyn season included excerpts from a projected large work that also looks like a Broadway show—one that promises to start where *Hair* and *Grease* left off. From this, we get a picture of Tharp untrammelled and at large in the world of the commercial theatre, and the surprise is that it's not a more entertaining picture.

This projected show-style work was shown in five discontinuous fragments billed as *Chapters and Verses*. The music was a miscellany: an Edwin Franko Goldman march; some fifties-style rock; an explosive and protracted disco sequence. One section, called "Calisthenics," had a lot of shouted dialogue. Another was accompanied, to predictable effect, by the "Mickey Mouse Club" theme music. The dancers, who wore Santo Loquasto rehearsal togs throughout, appeared three-fifths of the time to be playing kids; all the noisy references to kidvid and phys. ed. and rock and transistors and hot rods (a car is driven onto the stage) were fifties-generation references, and they had a packaged look and feel. The performing, too, was in a glib, super-Broadway style that I have never before associated with Twyla Tharp's company. An exception was William Whitener's solo to the Mickey Mouse anthem. In spite of its determination to amuse, it did amuse. The choreography is all in-place. With its floppy spine and arms, its wide épaulés braced against turned-in legs, it looks like a satire of Paul Taylor, and it may be a personal memento of the year that Twyla Tharp spent in Taylor's company before forming her own group—a memento of her artistic adolescence. Why this one real reminiscence should occur among so many prefabricated ones is not clear, and it isn't clear, either, how directly autobiographical any of the material is meant to be. We can only tell that some of it looks familiar in the wrong way. I don't believe that Twyla Tharp ever was one of these gassy teen-agers or that she wants me to think she was. I believe she must have some salvific intention; who else could we rely on for the authentic corrective to popular stereotypes? But I can't see from the fragments she has given us what she means by reproducing the fictitious fifties. Until the finished work is produced, I'll be confused about how the parts of it fit together and what its point of view is.

Just now, the only sections that are unambiguously, if not undisconcertingly, brilliant are the opening and closing sections: the march scene ("The Hard Circus") and the disco scene ("Street from the Night Before"). The march is one of those exhilarating numbers that turn the stage into a kind of trampoline—the dancers bound to center, execute a stunt solo or in combination, and bound off. Only, of course, they're Tharpian stunts, filled with switches on standard feats. A girl does a daring flip, is caught in midair, and is thrown to another catcher. You follow her trajectory only to see that you've missed a second girl being caught in the same way. The disco scene is also organized bedlam; it's Inferno's Dante. It goes on, like *Cacklin' Hen*, until it touches infinity, and then it goes on some more. The tempo of the dancing, which is dazed and druggy, is half that of the beat of the music; the dancers aren't driven, they float. Although John Simon's music is unmodified disco, there are no references in the choreography to recreational disco dancing. Groups pour onto the stage, slowly riot, fall in clumps to the ground, scatter, and fade into the fiery dark of Jennifer Tipton's lighting. Each dancer does his own dance, but no one seems independent of the group save Sara Rudner, who is very much a focal point. The others writhe around her, leave her, and come back; she herself may vanish for periods, but she always returns. The sensation of this recurrent return to center is curiously like watching a movie. The choreography implies closeups, tracking, fades; it has the kind of fluid, invisible continuity that we associate with the dreamiest effects in movies. The group dances for *Hair*, though arranged for the camera, don't have this continuity. What they do have is consistency of image. We can see what good camera meat they will make. "Street from the Night Before" has consistency of image, too—it's an unbroken stream, and it never leaves its single level of pressure. But, unlike the *Hair* dances, it selects and differentiates its effects. Toward the end, the dancing begins to speed up, but it never joins the beat; it stays ungripped and keeps its wholeness, and even when the music stops it still goes on. What relation this curious musical asymmetry could have to the hypnotic movielike continuity of the dancing is a question to ponder. Has Twyla Tharp found a new way of eliding the effects of stage and film? Has mixed media—a great cry of the sixties—become transmedia?

But we were talking about pop. During 1903, a new solo arranged by Tharp for herself, I again got that sinking feeling. Not from Tharp, who was dancing extremely well and looking her smartest, in her frizzed hairdo and silk pants ensemble by Loquasto. She has a personal chic that has misled many people into thinking that chic is all she has. In fact, Tharp can't function as an artist on the silk-pants level, and her passing-fad pieces are becoming increasingly transparent. There was that Paul Simon suite a couple of years ago; the new solo, to three songs by Randy Newman, is even less significant. Newman, whose songs I'm not conscious of having heard before, was represented here by "Sail Away," "Suzanne," and "Dayton, Ohio—1903," and from these selections I got the impression of a fake-naive artist: one of those croaking balladeers of our time who reverse the priorities of corruption. Newman's art is horsehair on the outside, cretonne on the inside. Since the music (on tape) seemed not to have influenced the choreography unduly, we could glide right over it, just as Tharp did. In the last song, which lends the solo its title, she was especially fine, lengthening and contracting the kinetic arc of an impulse as if she held it on a rubber band. But as a "collaboration" the piece is dubious. Can Tharp believe that

Newman is close to the mother lode? Maybe she feels that this music is the best of the contemporary stuff—better than *Hair*, different from the pop that she consciously employs in *Chapters and Verses*. Something in Tharp has need of a contemporary statement. Her problem is that contemporary popular and theatre music isn't being written for dance. Dance music is first of all a conception in time, and in its temporal division, or rhythm, pop music these days is perfectly square. The smashing beat of disco is, as Tharp demonstrates, self-annihilating—equivalent to no beat at all. What with disco and the balladeers and the arrangers who pass for composers on the theatrical scene, a choreographer has pretty much to invent time. Pop used to be made for dancing. Since it became a troubadour's art form, even melody has languished. Harmony has become more important. Dancers are looking for a releasing rhythm or a good tune, and the music just keeps on changing chords.

In another and very different wing of her repertory, Tharp burrows happily in the annals of jazz. She could concentrate on jazz exclusively, but there's no sign that she will. Even for a choreographer of her range and daring, there is too much wealth here. Besides, jazz has no presence in popular music today; you can't get it on the car radio. One of the secrets of Twyla Tharp's rapport with her audience is that she's believably an in-touch person—someone who can make sense of the babel on the car radio. We've seldom had fine artists who were also figures in popular mythology. Twyla Tharp may not have made it into the league of Buster Keaton, Fred Astaire, and Louis Armstrong, but their aura is congenial to hers. So far, we've felt her connection with them mainly in her great jazz dances, which are essentially dances of commemoration. This series, which began in 1971 with a now classic work to Jelly Roll Morton (*Eight Jelly Rolls*), appears to have been consciously shaped around maestro pianists. Besides Jelly Roll, Tharp has given us Scott Joplin, Fats Waller, Art Tatum, and, as the latest entry in the series, Willie the Lion Smith. She even gave us, in the prelude to *The Bix Pieces*, Beiderbecke as a pianist ("In a Mist"). I don't know what this emphasis on piano means; perhaps it's nothing more than an orderly way of cutting through different jazz styles and periods. The Smith piece, called *Baker's Dozen*, is arranged for the largest company Tharp has had, and it's the most physically powerful of the jazz ballets. With six women and six men, Tharp has made an extended essay in partnering, and the duets are full of astonishing events—not just acrobatically astonishing, like the lifts that the specialty dance teams at the Savoy used to do, but poetically astonishing, with a wild sexual kind of comedy and perverse spirit. In the choreography for "Tango à la Caprice," the dude suavity of the dance becomes a subject of comment, but without ever ceasing to interest us as dance. *Baker's Dozen* (the title may come from the fact that one of the twelve roles is written for two dancers—Twyla Tharp or Sara Rudner) is a series of dance vignettes that pass laterally across the stage; much of the action takes place just at wingside. The device acts like a spotlight (or like old-fashioned movie-musical cutting), picking up one couple or group, then another. In "Relaxin'," a girl falls head-first out of the wings into a boy's arms. He has to throw her back twice and then dodge as another girl runs at him full tilt. Alone at last, the boy (Richard Colton) does an engaging shimmy kneeling on the floor.

Willie the Lion Smith straddled the eras of ragtime and swing. A contemporary of James P. Johnson and Eubie Blake, he died in 1973. Dick Hyman played the four compositions used in the ballet, which date from the thirties. Loquasto's off-white costumes, with their drape shape, suggest Harlem sharpies of the thirties and early forties. Under their sarongs the women wear velvet trousers that look like leg warmers, and the choreography is nutty enough to take it. There's a flushed, excited self-awareness in this piece. It recalls a period in social dancing when people, as now, lost control of themselves. But then a dance floor was packed with incident, with virtuoso turns, intimate jokes, hectic little gallantries. And all of it alive and bouncing in the plenitude of rhythm. Palmy days at the Palm Gardens, with women falling out of the sky.   —*March 5, 1979*

Nureyev as Nijinsky,
Babilée as Babilée

In the Ken Russell film **Valentino**, Nijinsky kept popping up, almost as if the casting of Rudolf Nureyev as Valentino had thrown Russell into a dreamy quandary over which legendary male star he really wanted to make a film about. In the first reel, Valentino teaches Nijinsky to tango, and in another scene Valentino is posing as the Faun for what it is hinted are lascivious photographs taken with his wife, Natacha Rambova, at the instigation of her friend Alla Nazimova. With a few changes in character and circumstance, Russell's fantasy could have centered on Nijinsky; poor Nazimova appears to be playing Russell's conception of Diaghilev. On the face of it, Nureyev as Nijinsky would seem to be good casting (Anthony Dowell played Nijinsky in **Valentino**); in his Faun costume, he looked more at ease than he did in Valentino's sheik or gaucho gear, and the glimpses we got of him in Faun plastique were tantalizing. Surprisingly, when Nureyev made the film he still hadn't danced the role; he is dancing it for the first time in his current season at the Mark Hellinger, where, with the Joffrey Ballet, he is performing a program of Diaghilev revivals. His Faun is as pictorially attractive as it was in the movie. With his wide shoulders, tapering waist, and low-slung hips, he is able to make the planar oppositions in the role clear without strain. But the performance is too heavily anchored in static oppositions, and their delicate, fluid force is retracted as soon as the Faun changes his pose. Nureyev moves from pose to pose as if from one living picture to another; the sense of the choreography as one long unbroken gesture is imperfectly sustained. And the sense, too, of the Faun as the depiction of adolescent sexuality. Nureyev doesn't luxuriate in the movement; when he lies on the rock or tenses his prone body in the air, he doesn't give us a feeling of blood-heat steeping his vitals. To judge from the photographs, Nijinsky had a thickness and grossness in this role which the elegant Nureyev doesn't have. But critics have often compared the two dancers, and there is a creaturely warmth that exists like a bond between them. Nureyev's power in slow motion, which he displayed so lavishly in his younger days, was his strongest link to the Faun. It was this extraordinary power—Nureyev could even jump slowly—that made people use Nijinskyesque language about him ("animal magnetism," "elemental force," "pantherine"). The Faun is cast in slow motion but not broadly cast in space. Nureyev's dancing years ago lost its broad arc and separated into dozens of small peaks. But that doesn't explain why it still cannot recover its span when circumference is not a problem. What does explain that, I think, is Nureyev's deficiencies as an actor.

A generation ago, the Faun was danced perhaps too much as a mime role, but when a dancer as gifted as Nureyev fails to make obvious connections between continuity of phrase and dramatic motive we can see how large a part pantomimic skill played in Nijinsky's conception. Because Nureyev doesn't grasp the "why" of the Faun's movements, he turns the plastique into something arbitrary, to be dropped or caught up as a token reference to another age. Nureyev's dance instinct tells him that Nijinsky didn't hold himself perpetually twisted between profile and en face—he's free enough with that overprized aspect of the role. But the Faun's responses (to the Nymphs, to the veil) and the graphic sense they gradually make within the total ritual of self-absorption which those famous flat poses enclose—these aspects slip through the cracks that are literally breaks in a regimen of poses.

Nureyev stays on the surface in his two other Nijinsky roles, too. In *Le Spectre de la Rose*, he dances with something like his old power but without the poetic perception that would have enriched the meaning of the dance. And he is a truly terrible Petrushka—waggling, flapping, hunching like a small boy in need of a bathroom, and turning up a piteous little face. It takes something for Rudolf Nureyev to become as a little child, and his effortful bad acting is inflamed by pathos—he's a sob-sister Petrushka. Perhaps because he's so lamentably miscast, you want to see him bring something original to the role, something no one else would have thought of. And he does: he thumbs his nose at the Old Showman at the end of the ballet. This only confirmed that Nureyev hadn't understood Petrushka's "speech" of protest earlier in the ballet, hadn't been able to project it with the requisite force, and hadn't seen how Fokine drew upon it for the gestures at the end. Not all Russian dancers of Nureyev's generation are as far from Nijinsky and Fokine as Nureyev is. It happens that the finest Petrushkas I've seen— Gary Chryst, Michael Smuin, George de la Pena—were not only Americans but good actors. They also *danced* the part of a spineless rag doll with bobbling head and sightless eyes; acting and dancing were not for them separable phases of the role. Although American ballet hardly bothers with such distinctions, these dancers are character dancers. Nureyev appears to have been categorized early in his career as a danseur noble, and the Russians, with their insistence on categories, would never have expected him to act any role but that of the Prince. Nijinsky did do Prince roles, but, as his biographer Richard Buckle tells us, "the straight-forward princely role, romantic or heroic, was not really in his line":

> *Whereas most male dancers spent their lives being just that and nothing more—cavaliers always at hand to lift the ballerina and take a secondary place—he had begun to specialize in roles that were more fantastic.*

Born into an age of resurgent male dancing, Nureyev, the cavalier, demands Nijinsky roles as his rightful legacy. But Nureyev is as out of place in Nijinsky's repertory as Nijinsky would have been in his—not because of their differing relation to the ballerina but because their talents projected them into different spheres. Nureyev's career may be understood in part as an attempt to gain and hold center stage without a repertory that places him there. So he has become the usurper, encroaching on the ballerina's territory with extensions of the Prince's role or taking over "roles that were more fantastic." In *Le Spectre de la Rose*, he dances a part that Nijinsky himself came to loathe as "too pretty." Apart from its exotic aspect, *Spectre* is a danseur-noble role carried to an extreme of virtuosity and endurance— virtually a nonstop allegro solo, offset but hardly interrupted by passages of doublework. The Specter guides and shadows the ballerina; it's too much to say that he partners her. Yet from the moment he enters through the window until he jumps out again, it is implicitly a partnering role. The evening I saw him, Nureyev did his most vigorous and sustained dancing in this. His energy was higher than it had been for some time; he connected his phrases; he didn't sag in a landing or reprop himself after a finish. In an effective costume by Toer van Schayk—a modified petalled cap à la Nijinsky and a unitard of dark rose red tapering to flame points of greens and grays—he looked slim and handsome. Yet his port de bras was sketchy, and he danced almost totally without reference to the girl. The lack of arms— those enveloping Art Nouveau arms which it is hardly possible to exaggerate—is less crippling to the role than the notion that the Specter, supplicant, imploring, seductive in every move, could be dancing by and for himself. Nureyev's insularity reached its peak when, while Denise Jackson waltzed around the stage, he held a high relevé in fifth with his gaze fixed on her empty chair. But that was no worse than the moments in the other ballets—Petrushka's nose-thumb, or the Faun's stopping to adjust the veil with a shatteringly brusque practical gesture seconds before the climax of the ballet—which showed a Nureyev fundamentally out of sympathy with the artist and the era he celebrates.

The evening's credentials are otherwise in order. *Petrushka* is the Joffrey's well-staged production, with Gary Chryst appearing this time as the Old Showman. I saw Jackson as the Ballerina and Christian Holder as the Moor. *Spectre*, staged by Nicholas Beriozoff and designed after Bakst by Geoffrey Guy, is on loan from the London Festival Ballet, and *L'Après-midi d'un Faune* is reconstructed from the production by Ballet Rambert. Rouben Ter-Arutunian supervised the washy version of Bakst's original backcloth. *Parade* was also on the program—another noteworthy Joffrey revival, lethargically conducted by Allan Lewis. The rest of the performance was in the capable hands of Seymour Lipkin.

In dance encyclopedias, the "B"s begin with Babilée, Jean, b. Paris, 1923. Never having seen Babilée dance and never expecting to know first-hand how he looked at the height of his fame, which was in the late forties and early fifties, I went to see what, on the opening night of the Maurice Béjart company's run at the Minskoff, had been unveiled as *"une surprise"* —a new ballet starring Babilée. A personal appearance made by an aging dancer was all I hoped for; with any luck, it would be no more damaging to Babilée's reputation than the silly Isadora vehicle fashioned by Béjart for Maya Plisetskaya a few years ago. Well, the curtain went up on a semi-darkened stage, and there, behind a box-shaped jungle gym, stood Babilée, a shortish, compactly muscled man in a sweatshirt and baggy jeans. Stepping inside the box and grasping its supports, he began a few elementary exercises in which one saw the speed and economy of motion of a perfectly conditioned athlete. Then, quite suddenly, with no handhold to speak of and no sign of exertion, he rose up the side of the box and hung in space, and one saw Babilée. And went on seeing him—not only the Babilée of the complex acrobatic feats in *Le Jeune Homme et la Mort* (one of which simulated death by hanging) but also the galvanic Babilée who could flash from stillness to violence in *Till Eulenspiegel*, and even the classical Babilée who danced a fabled Bluebird. And (the lights having brightened) one saw the commanding head, with its noble aquiline face so like that of an American Indian, and the silky shock of hair—a slightly creased Cocteau drawing come to life. It was, of course, a Babilée whose spectacular powers are operating now on a diminished scale. Yet they are no less vivid for that. Babilée makes not one false move, nor one that is hasty or incomplete. His aura is tragic but equanimous—not intense, like a young man's. Most miraculously, among all his qualities the one he was loved for—his reposeful violence—is still there; we can see it. In the midst of a spasm, his center is always calm. And in the midst of calm he appears ready to explode.

Béjart calls the ballet *Life*. It seems to be about an isolated man of middle years who may not want to end his isolation. Babilée is partnered by a young beauty, Catherine Dethy. Her comings and goings are keyed to his moods, and with her last entrance, from far upstage and behind him, comes the moment of decision. Babilée makes their sudden exit together inevitable yet impulsive. I saw two performances: he took her hand two different ways; both ways were engimatic. But Babilée is an enigmatic artist, and he performs as if the heart of his mystery were at stake. Because of him, one could watch the whole ballet attentively and have something to ponder when the curtain went down. What is a star for, if not to shed light? I imagine that many in Béjart's audience had never heard of Babilée. But whether you watched the ballet to see Babilée or Babilée to see the ballet, you had a real experience.

The rest of the Béjart programs were polyester. People speak of Béjart as if he were a choreographer. He is, rather, a purveyor of sensation, like the movie directors Russell and Fellini, and ballet is just one of the glutting effects he uses. And yes, he *uses* dancers—hollows them out and consumes them. Every time I see the Béjart dancers, they've lost more muscle tone and added more makeup. The company these days is more openly a drag show than it used to be. As W. C. Fields says of the city (in *The Fatal Glass of Beer*), "It ain't no place for women, but pretty boys go there." Béjart's other guest artist this season is Judith Jamison, who goes right along with the bitchy-cute leering and wiggling. Béjart has put her to work in his version of *Le Spectre de la Rose*, one of a number of pieces (others are *Gaîté Parisienne* and *Petrushka*) that take famous ballet scores and substitute phantasmagorical effusions for the original choreography. Another formula has the phantasmagoria set to "shocking" collage scores—Schumann lieder, say, alternating with bits of Nino Rota, or Bach alternating with tangos. Those who can't defend Béjart's choreography will still praise his theatricality. But what Béjart's sense of theatre comes down to is an addiction to greasepaint, flashy costumes, masks, boys cast as girls, dual and triple identities, and silences broken by hideous bursts of laughter. The same chunks of leaden diablerie churn senselessly through one ballet after another, usually with some young man at the center pressing his fists to his temples. True, the continuity is always jarring, but it's so deliberately, preeningly inconsequential that after five minutes it has no punch. Béjart shapes his ballets with a channel selector, and he's learned to be derisive toward seriousness. The solemnity of the hippie-ritual ballets of the sixties has been displaced by the cynicism of the seventies. When a genuine event happens on his stage, it's almost as if he weren't responsible. *Life* has the silences, the jagged discontinuities (Bach and bongos), and Babilée gets a migraine at one point. But it also has a performer in whom grandeur of style is so much a personal attribute that it shows itself helplessly. In such surroundings, after so many years, *c'est vraiment une surprise.*   —*March 26,* 1979

Postscript 1982: Nigel Gosling, who with his wife, Maude Lloyd, reviews dance in the London *Observer* under the name Alexander Bland, objected to my review of Nureyev, citing specifically the nose-thumb at the end of *Petrushka.* Apparently, this gesture is customary in European productions of the ballet. To Gosling, it is "typically Stravinskian . . . the equivalent of Charlie Chaplin's last defiant twirl of his cane at the end of the reel." And Gosling quoted what Stravinsky had written to him in 1958 in response to an inquiry on this point: "The 'ghost' at the end is the *real* Petrushka making the character in the play before only a doll. The ghost's gesture is certainly not so much one of triumph as a nose-thumbing to the magician." Stravinsky's letter to Gosling appears in *Stravinsky in Pictures and Documents,* by Vera Stravinsky and Robert Craft—a book that sits on my shelf. I could have and should have quoted Stravinsky's remark in my review. It came as a surprise, though, to hear that Fokine would have inserted a *literal* nose-thumb. As I wrote to Gosling, the absence of that gesture from American productions suggests that Fokine omitted it when he staged the ballet in this country. I think he was right the second time.

Soundtracks

Although many modern choreographers have worked closely with composers, this hasn't been an age of notable dance music. The choreographer-composer collaborations that we've known outside the ballet seem to have sprung up on the understanding that the music would be secondary to or entirely separate from the dance. It was easy to see the sense of this arrangement in the days when, as Merce Cunningham noticed, so much choreography was nothing but journalism—reporting on what the music was already saying. But to get music to accept a secondary or independent position in a dance work, something had first to be done to it to stop our hearing it as dance music, and this is where John Cage came in. Music, or what most of us recognize as music, quickly became nonexistent. In the work of Cunningham and of the generation that followed him, dances have been more often accompanied by noise, by silence, or by speech. The motive for this wasn't entirely aesthetic; electronic scores succeeded for the most part in replacing orchestral ones because for hard-pressed dance companies in the sixties there was no choice. The choreographers who, like Paul Taylor, continued to draw on the existing orchestral repertory often could not afford to have the music played live. Nothing is as deadening to a dancer's musical instincts as having to perform constantly to tapes. (I mean, of course, recordings of scores, not scores originally composed on tape.) Taylor's company was among the few that were aware of the hazard. In fact, it was Taylor who sought and maintained a standard for musical choreography when all about him were losing theirs in the welter of sonics. Now that music is coming back, it's principally Taylor we have to thank.

The big turn was executed early in this decade by Twyla Tharp, with *The Fugue*—a musically structured work danced in silence. Actually, this was the first of two half-turns. Almost immediately afterward came the dances that were set to music—*Torelli* and *Eight Jelly Rolls*—and the counter-revolution was made. Tharp's audiences were prepared for *The Fugue* not only by earlier experiments of hers but also by the sense of a musical order in many of Cunningham's works, which, as his Events show, does not often concur with the sense of his musical (or nonmusical) accompaniment. It has taken the rest of the seventies for other choreographers to find their own way back to music, but again they may not have been entirely aesthetically guided. Choreography as a serious vocation is not economically the rough road it used to be—though it is still far from safely paved—and one can almost account for aesthetic developments by the growth of an audience and the increased availability of government and foundation grants. It's significant that although no directives were issued along with the grants, many of the recipients have chosen not only to work with music—in some cases for the first time—but to deal with original scores. It does seem evident that for choreographers to flourish they have to become rich enough to pay composers as well as musicians.

Viola Farber was one of the first of Merce Cunningham's dancers to go out on her own and choreograph. Although she has used traditional, non-Cagean music before, she has usually been ironic about it. Not until the past year have I noticed a lyrical purpose in her work. As far as I can tell, Farber doesn't really choreograph to music—she sidles up to it, ponders some momentary correspondence in it that reaches her ears only, and gallops off. The next correspondence will be one we'll hear; then it's her turn again. *Local* had a cheerful *bal-musette* sort of score, by Alan Evans; every now and then it sounded stuck in a crack. The dancers, wearing blue jeans, walked in wide strides, jumped hugely, and seemed famished for space. Their customary big-scale attack made the Dance Gallery, where the première took place, look even more confining than it is. But the remarkable thing about the piece was how unaggressive it was. Without reducing the scale of her work, Farber had purged it of violence. *Local* is a holiday for the dancers. In *Private Relations*, a New York première, the mood is again unusually gentle and subdued, but bit by bit, as the work moves on, its intensity accumulates some of the old oppressiveness. This time, there were many more direct correspondences between the dancing and the music—a tape of the Tapiola Children's Choir of Finland. Those high, sweet, keening voices, breaking from time to time into distressed outcries, were singing what sounded like a folk Mass. I have a perhaps irrational bias against dances with sacred implications—dances by Western choreographers, that is. They make me feel like a Druid. *Private Relations* made me feel like a Druid in arrears at collection-plate time. Somehow, even the thought that this was Farber's most coherent, most beautifully developed, let alone most temperate choreography in years seemed irreverent. The piece sustains a slow, even, legato pace against flurries of quick movement, twitches of panic. In the first ten minutes, the dancers feeding one by one out of the dark and into a path of moonlight were like disturbed children tossing in their sleep. After that, the atmosphere became more claustral. Partners struggled in attempts at mutual aid; a messenger from the outside brought no relief; fights broke out. These are "incidents" that can be read rather easily, I think, in the choreography—or, rather, in between the choreography and the music—but I don't want to suggest that there's some drama being played out. Farber's style is allusive rather than descriptive. After about thirty minutes, there's an epilogue that wants to spread hope, but it doesn't quite work. *Private Relations* may be Farber's *Kindertotenlieder*; its emotion, however, is untransferable. Perhaps such emotion always is. As a formal composition, though, it is an admirable piece of work.

In its steady legato flow and use of music as an atmospheric soundtrack, *Private Relations* reminded me of a Merle Marsicano work. But, seeing a Marsicano concert last weekend at the American Theatre Laboratory, I realized again that nothing is like a Marsicano work. She uses music not really as atmosphere but as parallel suggestion, the way Cunningham seems to at his best, and it is always very low in volume. In *Fragment for a Greek Tragedy*, a solo performed on this program by Julie Fraad, the Morton Feldman score sounds like someone playing slow organ chords at night in a basement two houses away. With *The Garden*, a new work, we overheard some pieces by Webern of the same delicacy and precision as the choreography. But there's a uniquely volatile, almost ectoplasmic relationship between Marsicano's dances and her chosen music. You never can tell what each is going to discover in the other. The Webern underlined the movement's fineness of detail, yet against that tiny figured ground the five women dancers looked as enormous and weighty as Picasso's classical nudes with the sea air hard as porcelain around them. It's an effect I'd noticed in Marsicano's work before—the simultaneous delicacy and deliberation that create a poignant contradiction in appearances—but never had I seen it so systematically exposed as in *The Garden*. Another constant wonder is the way the dancers can weave an emotional spell even though they're presented with the clarity and neutrality of figures in a landscape. In *The Garden*, as the spell deepens melodramatically, the modelling becomes vaguer, lightly brushed in, as if following the outline of memory. The ending, a very beautiful mannerist figment, depicted the various poetic selves hoarded from the private theatre of childhood. Marsicano's work leaves the paradoxical sensation of a ponderous smoke bubble. It may be the most economical yet the most luxurious dance theatre we have.

Kenneth Rinker's concert at the ATL consisted of a dexterous and witty full-evening piece—the first group piece of his I'd seen and the first to be done in New York. Rinker, who used to dance with Twyla Tharp, has been running workshops for young dancers, and his newest piece reflects something of workshop practice, beginning with Rinker himself arriving early, changing his clothes, setting his stopwatch, and running through some preliminary material. The other dancers, who have arrived in their hats and coats, execute the phrases they already know. Then they, too, go to the coat rack, and talk while changing their clothes. What we then see looks like a rehearsal, complete with rest and lunch breaks, and it culminates in a section called *Footlight Suite*, in which everyone wears black and all the movement we've seen is laid out in performance format. Rinker, like Tharp, is interested in the exposition of a process. We don't have to understand the process to enjoy it, but then we feel the reality and the seriousness of it very differently from the way the dancers feel it. Rinker charms us by being very intent on process and good-naturedly refusing to care that we're finding him and not it the whole point.

The highly inventive setting for the dances, composed by Sergio Cervetti, is a set of variations on "Forty-second Street," the old tap-dancer's song. Cervetti's process, involving various keyboard instruments and synthesizers, is as complicated as Rinker's, and I won't attempt to describe it, either, but it is not at all complicated to listen to, and, like the dances, it is a great pleasure. It strikes me that Cervetti does the opposite of Rinker, in that he magnifies a pop song into an evening-length score whereas Rinker condenses the personalities and styles of thirteen dancers into a single organism. But both artists are craftsmen of the baroque. A good subtitle for the piece—which is called *40 Second/42nd Variations*—might be "Busby Berkeley Meets the Baroque."

One of the recent converts to music is Judy Padow, a minimalist choreographer. In a concert at the Brooklyn Academy's Lepercq Space, Padow and her group performed dances in silence and dances set to music of various kinds—classical, folk, jazz, and country. The demonstration showed that music of any kind makes Padow's simplified movement—walking, skipping, rolling—look elementary in a way she may not intend. A solo in which she did some minimal stepping and swinging of her arms to a Chopin waltz (Opus 34, No. 2) could scarcely be different, as a dance experience, done without the music. The choreography certainly answers no need of the music, and why minimize Chopin? Like progressive exercises in composition, other dances added more devices—canons, retrogrades, and the like. The suites done to Bartók folk dances were choreographically the most developed of all. But as the technique brightened, a strange thing: the whole motivic pattern of the dances tended to disappear. We were back to basic

Bennington movement, and I'd thought it was against that ROTC of dance that the minimalists were rebelling. Judy Padow, it turns out, hasn't rebelled against the basic Bennington idea that rhythm is meter. Her dances are rhythmically lifeless, silent or not.

For me, the best thing about a Goodspeed revival of an old musical is the choreography of Dan Siretta. If *Very Good Eddie* was a double scoop of homemade peach ice cream, Siretta's dances were the crystal dish it was served in. His staging of "The Tickle Toe" was certainly the bright spot in the deplorably campy *Going Up*. Siretta's work never gives way to condescension, and when everyone else is working on the same level of serious enthusiasm—as in the current *Tip-Toes*—we have a bonny show. *Tip-Toes*, now at the Brooklyn Academy, gives us the most expansive view of Siretta's talent to date. He uses every opportunity to set the small stage (of the Helen Carey Playhouse) flowing with rhythms and cross-rhythms, and he always keeps the show's period in focus. The production is an especially faithful one: many of the original musical arrangements are used; there is only one interpolated number ("Why Do I Love You?"); and the chorus reappears for the "Sweet and Low-Down" encore carrying kazoo trombones, as in the original production. But not only can Siretta reproduce known effects; he can project himself into the fantasy life of the past. I was expecting a lot from him in "When Do We Dance?," and I got it. Siretta accounts both for the still active influence of Vernon and Irene Castle and for the eruptive impact of a wild new dance, the Charleston, without ever confusing our sense of period style or making a muchness of the transition. The year of *Tip-Toes* was 1925, the country was in a ferment of change, as it always is, and the ferment is what Siretta captures; he doesn't foist on us the specious drama of "eras," with the tango standing for one thing and the Charleston for another—it's all one revel, but it's not an undifferentiated revel. This is history precisely understood. By the end of the twenties, show dancing had a leaner, harder look, and Siretta mirrors this in his don't-mean-maybe tap dances for *Whoopee!* (at the ANTA Theatre). I accept without question the darkening implication here—that show dancing, which had all along been evolving into a tributary of the mainstream of social dancing and growing ever more specialized, had at last cut itself off. At the same time, of course, it was producing stars whose specialties were truly spectacular. The new *Whoopee!* has in Eddie Cantor's role a young comedian, Charles Repole, who is Cantorishly monotonous and beguiling in the way that Cantor became only after he'd been in movies awhile, and who has no specialty of his own to weight his presence. (It might be nice if he were a better dancer.) This *Whoopee!* falls by default to the supporting cast, which, luckily, is very strong and very funny.

The comics in *Tip-Toes* are only about as funny as their material, and the starring role was written for a dancer—no getting out of it. (Queenie Smith, the first Tip-Toes, evidently danced the closing production numbers on point.) Georgia Engel's tap-dancing lessons began with this show. She's far less professional than Repole, but she triumphs, because she reminds us of nobody but herself. We are persuaded that if Georgia Engel had been around in 1925 this would have been her role and she would have been trained to it. As it is, she fits into that tiny select category of star-amateurs which includes Audrey Hepburn in *Funny Face*. Her dancing is only intermittently impressive (as in some smooth spot-turns); Siretta's staging and a typically lively Goodspeed chorus do the rest. Russ Thacker, who looks like his name, is Engel's partner—experienced, tactful, an able performer in his own right. He has a more iconographic identification with the twenties; we don't quite believe he's real. In his big romantic duet with Engel to "That Certain Feeling," the two of them swoop about with their knees bagging in the approved manner of present-day ballroom-dance champions. It's Siretta's one unconscious anachronism. The quotation from Astaire and Rogers with which he ends the number is quite conscious; if Engel had learned something of Ginger Rogers's buoyant carriage (it began in her instep), we'd have been spirited right through to the thirties. The Goodspeed time machine breaks down now and then. But it still gives us moments of clear vision—many more than, in our deprivation, we have any right to expect.

—*April 9, 1979*

Bourgeois and Blank

Richard Strauss's *Le Bourgeois Gentilhomme*, billed with Purcell's *Dido and Aeneas* by the New York City Opera at the State Theatre, is not an opera, although in its first version, in 1912, it prefaced an opera—Strauss's *Ariadne auf Naxos*. Neither was *Le Bourgeois Gentilhomme* conceived by Strauss as a ballet, although there are dances in the score. Strauss had collaborated with Hugo von Hofmannsthal and Max Reinhardt on a German production of Molière's play, with incidental music. Strauss's model was Lully, Molière's composer and one of the first great architects of dance music. However, neither by intention nor by adoption is Strauss's score great dance music; even the dance episodes are only serviceable. These were incorporated into an orchestral suite drawn from the score, and out of that George Balanchine, no less, has tried three times to make a ballet. The present occasion is perhaps the least successful of all.

It's difficult to believe that so musical a choreographer as Balanchine has really remained attached to this music over the years; what seems far more plausible is that his association with *Le Bourgeois Gentilhomme* is one of those developments in his career which lie outside his creative life. He has never produced the ballet for any of his own companies.* His first version of it was made for René Blum, who had reconstituted the Ballets Russes after Diaghilev's death. The production took place in Monte Carlo in 1932. Boris Kochno's book concentrated on the banquet scene of the play, with its ballet divertissement and its mock-Turkish ceremony of initiation, which could be rendered as straight vaudeville. The would-be gentleman appeared with his tailor, dancing master, and fencing master in a kind of prologue to the banquet, and in the end he yielded his daughter Lucile to her lower-caste lover, Cléonte, who had presided in disguise as the Son of the Great Turk. Balanchine's ballet was two-thirds pantomime. Though its lead dancers were Tamara Toumanova as Lucile and David Lichine as Cléonte, its main attraction appears to have been Alexandre Benois's scenery and costumes. The 1944 New York revival, which Balanchine supervised for Sergei Denham's Ballet Russe de Monte Carlo, maintained this pattern. The stars were first Nathalie Krassovska and Nicholas Magallanes and then Alexandra Danilova and Frederic Franklin, but again the décor, by Eugene Berman, stole the show. Probably it was the whole point of the show to begin with. The ballet, described by 1944 reviewers as a spectacular trifle, depends inordinately on a designer of exceptional invention and style. Both Benois and Berman were at their ease in French baroque design. Both had the wit to exercise the full range of options that are open to the designer of *Le Bourgeois Gentilhomme*—the chance to evoke not only the magnificence of a royal entertainment but also the pretensions of M. Jourdain. In a *Dance Index* monograph for 1945, Allison Delarue comments on Berman's production, "It is a lavish piece with a drop-curtain that at once creates the ambitious world of M. Jourdain's *nouveau riche* household. The main backdrop of the throne-room is dry and dark and slightly sinister. The costumes, a *carrousel de Louis XIV*, are effectively displayed against it, and the divertissements, one after another, create fountains and pyrotechnics of color."

Rouben Ter-Arutunian, who is responsible for the current production, has in the past produced formidable pastiches of baroque design. But his throne room exercises none of the options. Instead, it suggests that some Jourdain *de nos jours*, heaping on the glitz, has designed it. (For a drop curtain, there's a plain looped gauze that goes up and down to separate the scenes of the prologue.) In the perspective of its distinguished antecedents, Ter-Arutunian's work could not fail to seem paltry. But we don't have to look at it that way to see how bad, how vacant of expression, it is. By the standards of his own *Vienna Waltzes*, Ter-Arutunian is self-condemned. This hit ballet, done two years ago with Balanchine, is the real precedent for

---

* The City Opera production entered the City Ballet repertory in 1980, where it was danced mainly by Suzanne Farrell and Peter Martins.

the City Opera's mounting of *Le Bourgeois Gentilhomme*. People no longer remember Benois, or even Berman; there is no way for patrons of the New York City Opera or the New York City Ballet to know and compare visual designing on such a scale of opulence. Although the City Ballet revived and commissioned sets from Berman just before his death, the choices (*Danses Concertantes, Pulcinella*) weren't lucky. In any case, the tradition of opulence at both the City Opera and the City Ballet is the tradition of opulent costs, not of opulent imaginations. *Vienna Waltzes* is much too shiny, yet it can lay claim to being the most distinguished production ever attempted at the State Theatre. The climactic "Rosenkavalier" scene, with its mirrored walls and acres of streaming silk, is just this side of glitz; it's literally dazzling, and it seems to represent all that passes for visual glamour in this house at a conscious peak of inspiration. I include the architecture and décor of the theatre's public spaces. The State Theatre, like all of Lincoln Center, is a monument to grandiose ambitions, with enough glitter to satisfy a million Jourdains a night. Ter-Arutunian in *Le Bourgeois Gentilhomme* gives us a dribble of baubles in a gray-and-white setting; some candelabra flank a huge wall hanging that looks like a rhinestone blanket. The costumes, as is usual with this designer, are a good deal better; the blue for Patricia McBride turns her ceramic looks into a Della Robbia madonna. The strange thing about this provincial production, though, is that it's unresonant—not the conscious glossy affair that one might have expected after *Vienna Waltzes*. As a *pasticheur*, Ter-Arutunian can be most effective. In *Le Bourgeois Gentilhomme*, he has no viewpoint; in *Vienna Waltzes* he had in mind Klimt and Viennese Art Nouveau. For the last waltz, he produced a fantastic space and at the same time a realistic description of the State Theatre drop-dead look. He and Balanchine have come together again in this place. Richard Strauss has once more provided the occasion. Molière's great parvenu is the subject. And nothing has happened; the mirror that could have shown us ourselves is blank.

This production also brings on Rudolf Nureyev as Cléonte, which has become a superstar role. He appears right away and starts putting on disguises. He's the tailor who measures Jourdain; then, with a tricorne, a small mustache, and a pocket-violin, he gives him a dancing lesson; next, he's the fencing master; and, finally, in turban and pantaloons, he's the Son of the Great Turk. In all these changes, the staging observes Hofmannsthal's original direction to the entertainers at the feast, which was that they make up in full view of the audience. The idea seems to relate, too, to the quick-change artist that Nureyev has become, hopping from company to company, from role to role. Actually, of course, Nureyev doesn't change; he's always Nureyev, and it seems doubly impossible that when Cléonte dances with Lucile she doesn't recognize him and has to wait for him to unmask. McBride's role is that of a melting Niobe perpetually in croisé. It is gratefully conceived and gratefully danced; as always with McBride, the angles and the emotion are one. But we've seen it all before. Jean-Pierre Bonnefous as Jourdain we've not seen before. Mountainously padded and with a bald pate under his Louis Quatorze wig, Bonnefous is never less than a vivid presence but unfortunately never more. A mime Jourdain who is, moreover, Cléonte's patsy doesn't give any interpreter much to go for. Bonnefous spends so much of his time reacting and being befuddled that we're surprised by the ending, when he's alone and preening before his mirror and a bit of character flashes out. Even within its limitations, the role is unshaped, and in the scenes between him and Nureyev at the banquet—scenes that suggest a kind of prototypical Victor Moore and William Gaxton skit—there's a general absence of shtick. The audience laughs with relief when some flunkies climb under a carpet and carry Jourdain for a lumpy "elephant" ride, but the event isn't built up to, and attention isn't fixed on any sort of exchange between the patsy and his tormentor.

Except for the dances, one has the sense of watching the ballet's action as background that has suddenly, and to its great embarrassment, become foreground. Of those dances, the most inviting is the classical pas de sept danced by young women, with one young man, from the School of American Ballet. The choreography of the ballet, credited to George Balanchine and Jerome Robbins, is another of those *Pulcinella* puzzles. To my eye, the pas de sept is identifiably Balanchine except perhaps for the end. It's simplified choreography, a flick of the maestro's sleeve, yet its cleanliness and cohesion distinguish it. Is it a memory of the thirites or of the forties, or a whole new dance? The opening pas d'action sets Nureyev a challenge that he meets not so much in the accuracy of his various disguises as in his swift timing when he assumes and doffs them. He's leisurely and deft enough to let us see to our complete satisfaction how he looks in each costume. He doesn't act; he models a vest or a cloak, and that's his characterization. There are few performers who can handle clothes and props with Nureyev's skill. Here he works up a Chaplin-like speed and agility, his beautiful hands fly to their tasks, his spirits run high. Although this is not the kind of ballet that a dancer can carry by himself, Nureyev makes you feel he'd do it if he could. And it's not the kind of ballet that can bear out evidence of a "collaboration" between Nureyev and Balanchine or Nureyev and Robbins. Cléonte's dance solo is of a more advanced design than Nureyev's solos have been of late, and it keeps him in the air longer. But the pas de deux and coda are of slight interest. The ballet brings us no great news. It was a coup for the New York City Opera to put together its list of great names, and it must have been painful indeed when in the midst of preparations Balanchine's doctors ordered him back to rest. But the expectations were surely unreal to begin with. A game of touch football can never look like an NFL championship playoff. As the chosen project, *Le Bourgeois Gentilhomme* was a virtual guarantee that the contacts between Nureyev and Balanchine's world could never be more than minimal.

The dances in the Purcell opera were originally to have been by Balanchine, who is credited in the program with having collaborated in the direction of the pantomime scenes. Peter Martins did the dances, on a raked and very glossy platform—a surface that defied the very idea of dance. (The designer was again Ter-Arutunian.) As attendants of Dido and Aeneas, young SAB students struck desperately decorative poses; the more active passages were handled mostly by the dancers of the Opera. The choreography, on the dim side, seemed unintegrated with Frank Corsaro's direction.

Paul Taylor's two new works, given during his company's season at the City Center, are pure off-the-wall Taylor. The more accessible of the two, *Diggity*, has the dancers moving freely to the eclectic rhythms of a commissioned score by Donald York—extraordinarily freely, considering that they are everywhere hedged in by the scenery, which consists of dozens of standup life-size silhouettes of dogs, painted on metal by Alex Katz. The dogs are all over the stage, looking cheerfully noncommittal, and the dancers have to negotiate choreography that simultaneously acknowledges and ignores the dogs' presence. Not one dog gets knocked over; not one shin gets barked. The dance—insofar as we can rise above its setting to notice it as a dance— is one of Taylor's most lyrically expressive. But the whole experience of *Diggity* has a surrealistic tension, and surrealism—a word I never thought of using in connection with Taylor before—pretty much defines the quality of the other new work, *Nightshade*.

Diggity is quite obviously related to *Private Domain*, another of Taylor's collaborations with Alex Katz which was shown this season. In *Private Domain*, the proscenium is masked so that our view of the dancing is always a partial view; the effect is like peering through the slats at the activities of some highly tumescent bathers under a boardwalk. But I wonder whether Taylor has ever done anything like *Nightshade* before. Possibly parts of *Scudorama* qualify—the parts that, like *Nightshade*, are composed of images rather than of dances. In *Scudorama* (1963), the images were of a broadly discontented society, easy to identify. In *Nightshade*, we don't know where we are. An ancestral American landscape is suggested by the late– nineteenth-century costumes, but we never do put our feet down on dry land. Most of the time, we're adrift on a roiling sea of obsessions both sexual and racial. The choreography, obscurely propelled by these obsessions, never develops or resolves them; the sea turns into a backwater impossibly brackish, and the implication, for anyone who tries to follow the piece as the story of the "emergence" of our civilization, is that we end up nowhere, too encumbered by our beginnings to move. Technically, *Nightshade* is an admirable paradox for a choreographer to have achieved—an immobile current. Poetically, it may be something altogether different from what its technique suggests to me now. Taylor's darker pieces always take a while to settle into shape. But, puzzling though it is, *Nightshade* is something to have seen in its first season. It may never exercise quite this fascination again.

For a score, Taylor has used excerpts from the wateriest and most odious Scriabin, and he uses them advisedly; the music tastes sweetish, like water from a nightstand. Gene Moore has done the costumes, which seem to be adaptations from Max Ernst, and Jennifer Tipton has lit the piece. There is some bravura bronze cross-lighting as the choreography reaches a climax which ranks among the most ghastly-beautiful effects I've ever seen lighting accomplish, but at the beginning the stage is so dark that the action can't be seen clearly.

David Gordon, like Paul Taylor in his pieces with Alex Katz, challenges the balance of our perceptions, but with Gordon visual challenges are invariably complicated by aural ones. It's the correlation between what we see and what we hear that Gordon emphasizes in these tantalizing data-processing workouts of his, which generally last an entire evening. The latest Gordon evening, held at his loft on lower Broadway, began with Valda Setterfield, in an old-fashioned woollen tank suit, taking up a great many poses on the floor. As she did this, we overheard on tape a conversation that she'd had with Gordon while he rehearsed her in these same poses. The tape wasn't coordinated with the poses we were watching; the correspondences were, or seemed to be, entirely random. But the experience of watching Setterfield run without hesitation through her awesome repertory—some of the poses were only fractional variations of others—and listening to her detailed discussion of every move with Gordon worked like a sharpening tool on our faculties: we were ready to see and hear what lay ahead.

An Audience with the Pope (or This Is Where I Came In) began, almost as an extension of the Setterfield piece, with projections of photographs of poses. Not Setterfield but the Pope (David Vaughan) was pictured in the act of slowly sitting down, folding his hands, and composing himself for what was undoubtedly going to be an ordeal. Meanwhile, we heard a taped pseudo-historical lecture on the origin of the papal audience, and Gordon entered and danced a long, evenly phrased solo, which in its methodical non sequiturs recalled Setterfield's sequence of poses. When visual/aural meanings began to gather in our minds, they had to do not so much with the pseudo-facts we were being told about the Pope and the effect of papal custom on language—such as that "poppycock" comes from "*Papa*" (Pope) and "*cacare*" (to defecate)—as with the nature of fact itself. The papacy became a provisional factual construction, a nominal principle around which to organize the evening's data. Popes could have been newscasters, sailors, or Boy Scouts; what mattered was that the evening rise and float on its own terms. It did when Setterfield returned and, with Gordon, went through a repeat of his solo while muttering to herself (about popes, popes, popes). By this time, the steady layering of movement facts had reached the same level of reality as the verbal ones, and we were enclosed in a system of absolute communication.

Such finespun constructions have to break down, and though the evening went on for another hour or so respelling the material in a succession of group dances, for me it broke down soon after the duet. It's Gordon's great gift that even at the end of an overextended program like this, one leaves feeling refreshed and not stymied. —*May 7, 1979*

Enigma Variations

Antony Tudor's new ballet *The Tiller in the Fields* has all the earmarks of a sequel to his last piece, *The Leaves Are Fading*, which was also produced by American Ballet Theatre: the music is by Dvořák, the scenery is by Ming Cho Lee, and the ballerina is Gelsey Kirkland. But except for its authoritative shaping of dance sequences and dance images and its inimitable musical elegance, *The Tiller in the Fields* turns out to have nothing in common with the earlier work. *The Leaves Are Fading*—it was done in 1975 and is still in repertory—is a romantic pastorale, a shade too extended and exquisite for its own good. *Tiller* is a folk ballet that seems to run itself deliberately into a wall. Tudor may feel that he has dropped a bombshell in the way he ends the ballet—with the heroine sidling out onto the stage and opening a huge sweater to reveal that she's pregnant. In the last few seconds, the hero reconciles himself to the situation, and the two run off happily together. But if that's what the ballet is about, why didn't it tell us sooner?

Like the oranges that spill onto the stage at the end of *Undertow*, Kirkland's pregnancy arouses our curiosity at the last minute and leaves it unsatisfied. In *Undertow*, though, Tudor has provided an experience full enough that the oranges don't matter. Once past the seduction scene, *Tiller* doesn't crest again until we get to that rounded belly, and then it's over. The ballet might almost be a danced preamble to an opera; instead of running off, its characters might usefully burst into song and start analyzing their condition in the manner of *Jenůfa*.* The choreography has its beauties; the accents are always fresh and challenging, the phrase shapes unpredictable. The leading male role, danced at the première by Patrick Bissell, is technically meaty and full of forthright vigor. There's a male sextet that improves

* *Postscript 1982:* In fact, the ballet's libretto resembles not Janáček's *Jenůfa* but his song cycle about a peasant who is seduced by a gypsy girl, *The Diary of One Who Vanished.*

on a similar number in *The Leaves Are Fading*. The new ballet has Tudor's eye and ear, but what on earth can be on his mind? It's not as if he forewarned us by striking a particular tone. The seduction is not a comic seduction; it isn't even erotic—nothing about the ballet is. The painted scenery evokes a Slavic Happy Valley where peasants cavort in an endless round of grape harvests and village fêtes. Kirkland's allure appears at first to be entirely in keeping with this sugary setting—it's oddly pubescent. But Tudor sees her as the strange wild girl of the village who drives the hero mad with delight. Bissell, of course, is twice as tall and heavy as Kirkland, and she bobs like a paper doll at the end of his arm. (The disparity recalls Kirkland's duets with Jacques d'Amboise in Balanchine's *Firebird* of 1970.) She wears a head scarf and a shapeless chemise that hangs down in points. When she's racing around in this getup (by Dunya Ramicova, who costumes the rest of the cast in straight ballet-peasant dress), Kirkland looks like a crazy baby.

Tudor isn't in control of the effect he creates with Kirkland in this role. Yet he appears to have more decided ideas about her than about anything else in the ballet—decided but not developed. We never learn whether the strangeness is the girl's real nature or only the boy's view of her. We never see the other villagers react to her, although Tudor uses these other dancers in pairs as a suggestive counterpoint to the love duets. A spark flickers through those duets—a sense of the erotic fear and excitement that a young man might feel on falling in love for the first time with someone who's really original and different. But this idea burns bright only for a moment or two; it isn't worked out in the ballet. Tudor, it turns out, is more interested in creating an aura of sprightly mysticism around the Kirkland character. He projects into the role (traditionally the gypsy seductress) the dated charm of those dear little Central European sparrows who enchanted the English theatre forty or more years ago. Kirkland becomes Elisabeth Bergner or Luise Rainer; she's a mystical waif. We have no one in our theatre at the moment who's like this. The sensibility to project such an image is long gone. Tudor pushes a half century of evolving feminine archetypes aside. Crucial to waifhood is a lack of sexual vitality. My first thought when Kirkland pulled open her sweater was: Can a baby become pregnant? Kirkland isn't Lolita; she's Tudor's constant nymph.

When the curtain goes up on *Apollo* at New York City Ballet, Mikhail Baryshnikov is standing in the middle of the stage in a relaxed tendue-front pose, one arm raised, the other holding a lute against his hip. He swings the free arm in circles, as if drawing music from the lute. This gesture signals the start and the end of Apollo's first solo, but it occurs in the current, "revised" production only once, and it's at the end: the whole solo has been cut. After the arm-circles, Apollo pivots slowly in attitude, holding the lute before him, and the three Muses enter. From there on, the choreography is much as it was six years ago, the last time the complete ballet was performed by New York City Ballet. Except that, with the prologue also missing, the setting has been reduced to a kitchen stool on a bare stage, and the way the apotheosis is done now, the dancers walk single file into a path of light which shines from the wings and there take up the famous "peacock" pose: Apollo braces three arabesques raised in an arc or halo behind him. This luminous incident has been moved from its place earlier in the apotheosis. Repositioning it not only leaves a blank in the progression of the dance; it forces our admiration in a way that seems alien to the spirit of *Apollo*. The pose, one of the casual wonders of the ballet, used to float into view and dissolve, leaving its light to irradiate the events that followed: the Muses' act of self-dedication, when they throw themselves in mighty lunges to the floor, and the abrupt decline into humility with which the ballet ends. Swift pain followed by the enduring sweetness of a pain that can cut no more—that was *Apollo* in its final moments, and all the dancers did was draw themselves erect and walk to the back of the stage, then up some steps to a promontory. There, posing in profile, they faced the future as the curtain descended. It's very difficult to gauge the effect of novel arrangement of a classic, but my feeling is that this new look of climactic exaltation is more impressive to those who have never seen the ballet before than to those who have.

Baryshnikov dances an incomplete role, yet his performance is not incomplete. I first saw him in the part a year ago, in Chicago. His dancing combined primitive force and elegance; it was about as clear an expression of Balanchine's intention as I could have hoped to see. That same force and elegance are to be seen in Baryshnikov's current performance but as qualities less lavishly and carelessly exposed. The scope of the role has been compressed into fifteen tight minutes. All the dance values have been refocussed, and the dynamics have been heightened so as to bring out even more of their radical intensity. The choreography of *Apollo* is about dancing inventing itself at Creation's first dawn, and the growth of the god is traced in the maturation of his art. Baryshnikov preserves those meanings. Much as we need to see him in the full ballet, we're bound to admire the gifts of concision and integration that this edited version brings out. The performance is a synoptic miracle; it's as if everything that we don't see had been taken into account in everything that we do see. Well, almost everything. The extended pirouette by which Apollo frees himself of his swaddling clothes in the prologue has no counterpart in later portions of the ballet, and extended pirouettes are a Baryshnikov specialty. Yet the performance is so organically composed that we don't miss a thing. This Apollo would be Apollo if he were forced to dance the role in a phone booth. Heather Watts, Bonita Borne, and Elyse Borne are stiffly conscientious as Terpsichore, Calliope, and Polyhymnia. This is not a cast that can rise to the challenge of a Baryshnikov. The look-alike Borne sisters lend a pictorial symmetry to the ensembles which the casting of Patricia McBride as Terpsichore might have enhanced. The Bornes are McBride "types," whereas Watts is more in the Suzanne Farrell line. Her frame is the right size and heft for Baryshnikov, but her wiry line and rigid upper back were not made for Terpsichore.

Balanchine's attitude toward *Apollo* has long puzzled admirers of the ballet. It has survived inadequate casting in the past, but the new "concert" version may not be so lucky. State Theatre audiences were comparatively cool toward *Apollo* when it was moved there from the City Center, and they never really warmed to it. It is a chamber ballet, and its proportions as well as its delicacy and restraint are not helped by the big stage. Cutting it down and depriving it of a set aggravate the problem. And, whatever his reasons for suppressing sections of his choreography, it is certainly odd of Balanchine to cut the Stravinsky score. *Apollo* is the first of those masterpieces by which the world came to know the name of Balanchine. It is the fountainhead of his repertory and of that moral elation with which he was the first, after Petipa, to invest classical dancing. The allegorical text of the ballet shows how poetry, mime, and dance fuse with music to create classicism. The peacock shows that fusion taking place. The image of harmony breaks, and now the pact of harmony is sealed: that's the meaning, as I read it, of those long legs extending in lunges—forward, ever forward—and those reaching hands gathered and gripped like reins in Apollo's single hand. From there, all four principals turn and walk to the end of the ballet. The apotheosis shows us the martyrdom of the artist, but though its mood is solemn, it isn't oppressive or gloomy. Maybe the most profound of the ballet's numberless revelations is in the freezing simplicity of this ending, as if it contained the voice of God saying to the artist, "Thou art the most mortal of men."   —*May 21, 1979*

"Swan Lake" and
Its Alternatives

Why is it that the record companies do not keep up with developments in ballet? Three years ago, when *Chaconne* was first done by New York City Ballet, I could not buy a complete recording of the dance music from Gluck's *Orpheus and Eurydice* which Balanchine uses (the Monteux recording had been deleted from the catalogue), and I still can't buy one. Nor can I find all the selections from the *Pelléas* and *Shylock* of Fauré which Balanchine uses in *Emeralds*. Nicolas Nabokov's *Don Quixote*, a full-evening ballet, was, like it or not, a distinguished commission, but it ran its thirteen-year course in repertory without ever being recorded—not even in the form of a suite. In England, the work not just of composers but also of choreographers is honored: there are discs for Frederick Ashton's *La Fille Mal Gardée, Monotones,* and *A Month in the Country.* When was the last time an American label honored a Balanchine ballet besides *Stars and Stripes?* These omissions reveal, all too openly, an indifference to our dance culture. One can't help being disappointed by the record companies' attitude; still, one doesn't expect them to care as much for culture as for commerce. The strange thing is that they're indifferent even to the popularity of ballet. It comes as a shock to discover that there are still no complete recordings of the charming scores for *La Sylphide,* the Shades scene in *La Bayadère,* and *Harlequinade,* or of Prokofiev's finest ballet, *The Prodigal Son.* These ballets, after all, have been around a long time, and current box-office idols perform them. When it comes to hits in the making, the record manufacturers don't seem to know what's going on. Sheer greed should have led them to contrive tie-ins with *Dances at a Gathering* and *Vienna Waltzes.* The commercial appeal of the Stuttgart Ballet (*Eugene Onegin, The Taming of the Shrew*) and the Alvin Ailey company (*Revelations*) is virtually untapped. Many of the ballet records in the stores have been there from the days, twenty or thirty years ago, when records were more responsive to events. If Hershy Kay's arrangements for *Stars and Stripes* and *Cakewalk* are steadily available, why not also his *Who Cares?* and *Union Jack?*

Where the record companies have been good in recent years is in issuing the most popular nineteenth-century ballets. Until 1974, there was not a single stereo recording of *The Sleeping Beauty* in its entirety. Now one can buy scrupulously complete and sumptuously engineered recordings of all the Tchaikovsky classics, and even a record of the ballet music from his operas. In spite of a few dubious spinoffs (such as "Baryshnikov's *Nutcracker"*), the records keep to a high level of authenticity. I believe *The Sleeping Beauty* plays better in the theatre when it is cut—specifically, when Acts II and III are merged. A complete *Swan Lake* would last over three hours. But theatrical practice should not govern recordings.

Contemporary ballet records may be getting too scrupulous. Even the best of them force us to listen to repeats that can make sense only in the theatre. And in the case of *Swan Lake* authenticity can lead to confusion for listeners who have seen the ballet. The *Swan Lakes* that are being marketed are all versions of the complete edition of the score that was issued in Moscow in 1957. Every note that was ever written by Tchaikovsky for the ballet is here. Yet the Moscow score, like every previous published score, is based on the original edition of 1877—the Ur-*Swan Lake,* which has never made its appearance in a theatre. Nearly all of the *Swan Lakes* we see derive from the St. Petersburg production of 1895. Notes for the current recordings invariably cite the changes that were made in 1895, but they also recount the ballet's 1895 plot in relation to its unchanged musical structure, as if this were the way the ballet was actually given at its world première. What little information we have on that 1877 Moscow production suggests that although the choreographer, Wenzel Reisinger, followed Tchaikovsky's scenario as it then stood (this was also revised for St. Petersburg), he had no compunction about ignoring the composer's musical divisions. A performance score from this production has not survived, so we don't know how much of the published score was actually heard by Moscow audiences. What seems certain is that as the ballet piled up performances and went through new productions they heard less and less. In spite of this rough handling, and in spite of choreography that was universally condemned, all the Moscow productions appear to have been very favorably received. Roland John Wiley, in an unpublished doctoral dissertation on *Swan Lake*, from which I have drawn much of the historical information in this article, notes that the Moscow *Swan Lakes* have been thought of as failures because the St. Petersburg version enjoyed such a lasting success. Produced by Marius Petipa and Lev Ivanov, with the music revised by Riccardo Drigo, the world-famous 1895 version is comparatively well documented. We have Petipa's sketchbooks, and the choreography exists in Stepanov notation, so we can make pre- and post-production comparisons. (Petipa planned but apparently did not use a maypole in Act I, perhaps because a late-summer, early-autumn setting was specified.) But the important comparison is with the *Swan Lake* of 1877—Tchaikovsky's score not as it was produced but as it was published. While our record companies give us this *Swan Lake*, our ballet companies give us the "definitive" one, which means a modified Act I, an Act III revised almost beyond recognition of Tchaikovsky's original premise, and an Act IV pieced out by substantial interpolations. These, and Odile's variation, are Drigo's orchestrations of piano pieces by Tchaikovsky. Later hands that dealt with the score also left their mark on it, and they were not as subtle as Drigo's. In Act II, which the composer considered the best part of his ballet, the editing was relatively light, but here, too, as Wiley explains, Drigo interfered with the symbology of Tchaikovsky's harmonic scheme.

The more we learn about the first production of Tchaikovsky's first ballet, the more we realize how much depended on the composer and his instinct for the theatre. Although he sought advice from his choreographer—the kind of detailed advice which he was later to obtain from Petipa for *The Sleeping Beauty* and *The Nutcracker*—he appears to have been on his own much of the time. The score, unlike the two later ones, is badly organized in terms of theatre logic and stagecraft. When, occasionally, we hear something going on—when the trumpet fanfares constantly interrupt the waltz in the ballroom scene—it sounds like an awkward attempt at a stage direction. Tchaikovsky was the first great composer in a hundred years to write a full-scale ballet. He loved *Giselle*, and probably used it as a guide, but his leitmotivs are closer to Wagner's than to Adam's. (Wiley also builds the case for a "*Lohengrin* connection" to *Swan Lake,* citing thematic and melodic similarities.) There is no question of Tchaikovsky's instinct for dance; this, combined with his sense of theatrical fantasy, operates freely in *Swan Lake,* but it does not operate practically. Even in the most famous scenes—the swan scenes, staged by Ivanov—we feel that the music is suggesting more than is really happening on the stage. In the standard Act IV, the gulf between the music and the action is a painful fact that convention forces us to ignore. *Swan Lake* is the greatest unstageable ballet ever written, and it is at its greatest, perhaps, in passages—usually left out of productions—where we cannot guess what is happening or what Tchaikovsky meant by them. Yet their visionary allure is so strong that we make a place for them anyway in our minds. *Swan Lake* may be unstageable, but it is never unreal. When Tchaikovsky, having finished the score, heard *Sylvia,* he remarked with characteristic overstatement that his own work was "trash by comparison." He meant that *Sylvia* was a ballet.

Can the Ur-*Swan Lake* ever be wrested from its composer's imagination and brought to the stage? There have been sporadic attempts. The best known, by Vladimir Burmeister, took place in Moscow in 1953 and in Paris in 1960, but Burmeister used a new scenario. The production is still danced at the Paris Opéra, complete with its egregious happy ending. Jack Carter's versions for the Teatro Colón in Buenos Aires (1963) and London Festival Ballet (1966) rearranged the 1877 score in an attempt to follow the original scenario. Neither of these productions succeeded in keeping Petipa-Ivanov off the boards for long. During the sixties, *Swan Lake* was put through a wave of experimentation in many lands; this was a response both to the 1957 edition of the score and to the impact of Soviet performance traditions as revealed by Western tours of the Bolshoi and the Kirov. The only innovation that has been roundly accepted is the deletion of Benno, the Prince's friend, from the Act II adagio. The presence of the extra man in the pas de deux had a historical justification, which was universally judged to be inadequate. But Benno's participation, besides making the pas de deux unlike any other in the world, was a poignant reminder of the Prince's youth. If only for those now lost moments when Odette entered and poised herself on his outstretched arm instead of on Siegfried's ("The falcon cannot hear the falconer") or alighted on his thigh to be retrieved by Siegfried, I would wish to see Benno again. The best contributions to the innovative *Swan Lakes* of the sixties were Ashton's—especially his pas de quatre, which was retained when the Royal Ballet reverted to Petipa-Ivanov, and his Act IV, which will be restored this winter. Ashton used to great effect in this act the curious pounding dead march that Tchaikovsky placed in the pas de six of Act III—a passage as inscrutable as his inclusion in Act I of what we know as the Black Swan pas de deux.

The wave of experimentation was succeeded by a wave of reaction, and on the crest of this second wave American Ballet Theatre brought us its

version of Petipa-Ivanov, staged by David Blair. This production spells
Swan Lake to a good many people, even though its Act III wades right into
the depths of the problem that confronts any producer of Swan Lake—the
Odile problem (she was not designated the Black Swan until recent times),
which is only partially solved by transferring the pas de deux from Act I.
Blair forced a solution by perpetrating a key change in the start of the pas
de deux worse than any wrought by Drigo. I don't suppose it matters. Like
every Swan Lake I have ever seen, even the most misbegotten, this version
invariably holds the audience under a spell. The corps choreography in
the white acts, never strongly danced, has paled away, and in Acts I and III
the aristocratic style needed for the dances and for what Alexandra Danilova calls "deportment" is caricatured. Nevertheless, because the action
follows a credible outline laid down by men of sympathy and genius, one
can sit and dream. Recently, I was asked how many times I had seen Swan
Lake. Incredulity usually lurks in this question—an implied "How can you
stand it?" Yet the answer is not "Because I love it." Like so many others, I
go to Swan Lake not to re-see a ballet but hoping to see the ballet beyond
the ballet. The performance is only the occasion for meditating on what
might have been. Tchaikovsky's unrealizable vision is large enough to have
made what one can see of it the most fascinating ballet in the world. At
ABT, the ballet has become a star vehicle, and no Tchaikovsky ballet was
meant to be that. One's meditations are necessarily provoked by this or that
star performance. This season, I saw and enjoyed the performing of Natalia
Makarova and Anthony Dowell, Martine van Hamel and Patrick Bissell,
and Cynthia Gregory and Peter Breuer. The ballerinas are all at fault in
taking the second act too slowly. Slow is a dancer's idea of serious, but the
danger is that her accent will smear, her line turn ropy. Perhaps the ponderous second acts were what made Act IV look so bright in every case. And
who created that pas de deux to the interpolation "Un Poco di Chopin"?
Not Ivanov, surely, or he would have had to use Benno again, which would
seem intolerable in this musical and emotional context. Since Roland John
Wiley tells us that Nicolai Legat's Siegfried tried, early in the ballet's
career, to dispense with Benno (but was overruled by balletomanes), it is
probable that we are seeing Legat's emended pas de deux in Acts III and
IV. For a popular masterpiece, too little is known of the lore of Swan Lake.
There are many, many reasons to await further researches by Wiley and by
other Tchaikovsky scholars, such as David Brown, whose newly published
Tchaikovsky: The Early Years, 1840–1874 (Norton) stops just short of
Swan Lake.

This season, Suzanne Farrell made one of her infrequent appearances in
the Balanchine one-act Swan Lake, and I meditated on what the Swan
Queen might become if Farrell were given new choreography to perform.
Everything she did stretched the old steps beyond their conventional limits;

her port de bras was congenitally incapable of accepting the conventional poses. In Farrell, adagio dancing moves decisively away from the contained pose-to-pose evolutions that, even in Balanchine's advanced version, characterize Odette. Farrell is a great white northern bird who lifts the swan's pathetic whisper to a tragic cry. Balanchine's condensation does the same thing to the ballet. It is not just the second act that he gives us but a medley of the second and fourth acts, and no fourth-act finale has ever been so spectacular as the wheeling and diving of Balanchine's flock and the terrible isolation of his lovers as they withstand the fury of cosmic winds. Balanchine's ballet is a *Swan Lake* rhapsody; I am caught up in it as in no other version of the ballet, because, although it isn't the traditional *Swan Lake*, it's the essence of what attracts me in *Swan Lake*. To mention just one moment: during the adagio (which is a jeweller's appraisal and resetting of Ivanov), the hunters come out and stand with a swan on each arm, and at once all the bewildering beauty of the ballet's fantasy about hunters and swans and sorcerers crystallizes in a single heraldic image. The choreographer has done my dreaming for me.

In the course of thirty-five minutes, Balanchine manages to use both of the Act IV musical interpolations. To me, this indicates his acceptance of these inventions of St. Petersburg as fragments of the true cross—there was no other *Swan Lake* and there never can be. Neither of these fragments is as well danced as in former days; in "Valse Bluette" the accents that were created for Marnee Morris's timing have been regularized, and "Un Poco di Chopin" (Odette's variation) is less a dance than a dramatic cameo with trills on point, perfect for the dancer it was choreographed for, Melissa Hayden, but for very few others. This season, however, the lovely pas de neuf (Tchaikovsky's "Dance of the Little Swans") took on life and warmth when its leader was Stephanie Saland or Lourdes Lopez, though some details in the choreography have disappeared. Rouben Ter-Arutunian's décor is still appropriate; his backcloth has the chill of Chesley Bonestell's lunar landscapes. But audiences may no longer feel so romantically remote from *Swan Lake*. Since Balanchine mounted this production (1951, revised 1964), the four-act ballet has become familiar, and a version that was once an audience favorite now seems to generate moderate disdain. Weak casting of the ballerina role in the past few seasons hasn't helped. But audiences who have outgrown a one-act *Swan Lake* and whose curiosity has been aroused by the complete score on records will not find what they're looking for in the full staging. Luckily, Balanchine has produced several other essays on *Swan Lake*. There is the great adagio in *Symphony in C*, which is an indirect descendant of Ivanov's adagio, and there is the second movement of *Diamonds*, which descends from *Symphony in C*. Tchaikovsky Piano Concerto No. 2 stands in relation to *Swan Lake* much as *Theme and Variations* stands to *The Sleeping Beauty*. The resemblance is to be found more in moods than in steps. The closest *Concerto No. 2* comes to a quotation is in the second scene, when the ballerina approaches the kneeling "prince," takes a farewell arabesque, and backs away from him down a tunnel of arms that lift to let her pass. The choreography ranges over the whole of the old ballet, evoking a spectrum of genre scenes. The pas de trois of Act I has its reflection in a beautifully elegiac trio for a woman and two men, and much of Act I's nervous pomposity and glee is in this first movement of Balanchine's. The second movement is like a white act, and the folk dances of the last movement flashingly recapitulate the third act's suite of nationalist dances. But nothing in *Concerto No. 2* is outside Balanchine's personal world; he makes us feel that this poetic realm is his by inheritance. *Concerto No. 2* is one of those all-in-all ballets of his, like *The Four Temperaments* and *Prodigal* and *The Nutcracker*—ballets that sweep through every variety of emotion, tearing us this way and that. The grand perspectives of the piano concerto are dramatized in dancing that is spacious, clear, and, in human terms, temperate. The ballet's countenance is placid. Yet we are gripped by an underlying tension—the tension of scale and sweep and the more intimate tension of mood. It's a secret-cabinet, stifled-melodrama ballet. Somewhere deep inside the ballerina-danseur relationship we sense the dagger, the tea rose, the chain-mail glove: all the fun, in short, that *Swan Lake* should be. The ballet, a choral showpiece, is being luminously danced this season in new costumes, easier on the eye; the leads I saw were Merrill Ashley, Sean Lavery, and Kyra Nichols. It's the one, of course, that used to be called *Ballet Imperial*: a beautiful title, no more confining than *Concerto Barocco*.   —*June 11, 1979*

Ballet Alert

I talked last week to Carmel Capehart, the founder and chief operator of Ballet Alert, a new telephone service that supplies up-to-the-minute information on the local performance schedules of all the major companies. "It's a real godsend during the peak of the dance season, when it's hard to keep up with who's doing what," said Miss Capehart, a vigorous-looking gray-haired woman in a dirndl and a National Dance Week T-shirt. "Before Ballet Alert got going, last winter, those of us who attend lots of performances would have to depend on the grapevine for last-minute cancellations and cast changes. We'd spread the word like a chain letter—only, of course, by phone. Once, I remember, three ballet companies were playing side by side and a festival of major moderns had just opened in Brooklyn when an epidemic of Asian flu hit. Trying to monitor that situation took seventeen of us, between Staten Island and New Rochelle, and we'd be on the horn all day long. Add that to the cost of tickets, taxis, and drinks après-ski and you're getting into some heavy expenses." Miss Capehart and some of her friends found themselves cutting back on their floral tributes to ballerinas. They even sold the program-shredder they'd used to make confetti for Cynthia Gregory ovations. But it was not economy that drove them to start Ballet Alert so much as sheer frustration. "There was the time Kyra Nichols was out of *The Four Seasons,* then in, then out again, all in one day," said Miss Capehart, with a sigh. "Sometimes who'll dance isn't decided until the performance is about to begin. Of course, we can't even now keep up with things like that, so we're always careful to give the time along with our information, just like the weather report."

Miss Capehart, who received this year's Adidas Award in public relations for her down-to-the-wire bulletins, maintains her contacts with balletomane inner circles. "Without their input," she told me, "I couldn't keep up. There are people who knew when Mikhail Baryshnikov was going to do *Tarantella* even before he knew himself. On the other hand, everybody thought Stephanie Saland would do *Swan Lake* this season, and that didn't pan out. Of course, I release nothing without the confirmation of company managements, even though it's sometimes hard to get it in time. When there are cast substitutions, the management people are often the last to know. The waiters in O'Neals' and Dazzels have known for hours. I try not to make a habit of calling up the dancers themselves—especially the ones who've been taken sick or who've been injured. I did call Patricia McBride to see if she was dancing *La Source* with Helgi Tomasson and was told that she'd gone to the theatre to rehearse. Well, in the meantime Merrill Ashley and Peter Martins were announced, and we put that on our tape. In the event, Ashley did it, but with Adam Lüders, not Peter Martins, so we were half right. We did catch Kevin McKenzie, though, going in for Patrick Bissell in the third act of *The Sleeping Beauty.* Bissell had pulled a leg muscle the night before and suspected he might not get through the whole performance—which was a pity, because it was his New York début in the role. But we didn't call him, he called *us.* And when Gelsey cancelled the rest of her season at American Ballet Theatre recently, she put a message for us on her answering machine before she left town."

I asked Miss Capehart what her biggest scoop had been.

"No doubt about that," she said. "Baryshnikov's début in the Costermonger pas de deux in *Union Jack.* He did it twice in one day without telling anybody. If we hadn't caught wind of it, nobody would have been there but the audience."

We settled down over steaming glasses of Russian tea, and Miss Capehart talked a bit about Ballet Alert's early days. "We had to overcome a credibility gap," she said. "Ballet Alert retains, I think, the pizzazz of good old word-of-mouth, but in the beginning that was a liability. Some people weren't sure our information could be trusted. The breakthrough came this spring when we found out Jolinda Menendez was going to do the lead in *La Bayadère* instead of Martine van Hamel. Nobody believed us. They went anyway. Menendez did do it, and they believe us now, all right. Most of our reports have to do with cast changes. So far, we haven't had too many changes of program this season. New York City Ballet actually got *Tchaikovsky Piano Concerto No. 2* and *Divertimento No. 15* on, I'm glad to say, though not always with the scheduled casts. And there were only two major program disruptions at Ballet Theatre, both because of an injury to the same dancer. God knows, a ballet dancer's life is fraught with hazard. But few people realize the hazards that ballet-*goers* have to face. For example, there're those one-shot performances that sometimes crop up out of emergencies; balletomanes learn to look for them. One man, a fan of Yoko Morishita, dialled us from his office in Boston, learned that Morishita was substituting for Kirkland in *La Bayadère* that night, and flew in on the shuttle. Just as his cab reached Columbus Circle, there was one of those cloudbursts we've been having a lot of recently, and the motor stalled. When he got to the Met, it was one minute past eight, the performance had started, and the ushers wouldn't let him take his seat. He had to watch *La Bayadère* on television in the viewing room, and the reception was so poor he couldn't tell Yoko Morishita from Janet Shibata. That's not as bad, though, as the story I heard about the lady who came to the New York première of *Désir*, John Neumeier's pas de deux for Natalia Makarova and Anthony Dowell, and got Peter Gennaro's soft-shoe duet for Dowell and John Curry instead. Of course, the change was announced, but it somehow failed to register. She thought she was seeing Makarova in a top hat. Well, we exist to forestall that sort of confusion. And I may say that, with the current season as chaotic as it is, we're rapidly becoming indispensable to the city's ballet life."

—*June 25, 1979*

Out of Denmark

August Bournonville's *My Theatre Life*, translated into English by Patricia McAndrew and published last month by Wesleyan University Press, was originally issued in Danish in three installments—the first in 1848, just as Bournonville's career as a dancer was ending, and the last in 1877–78, just before he died, having served fifty years as director of the Royal Ballet in Copenhagen. The life was long and filled with events; as Bournonville writes about them, they touch not only on ballet but on theatrical, operatic, and concert life from London to Moscow, and they play against a backdrop of political affairs, in which he took a special interest. Bournonville was one of the age's great spectators, though not in the prodigious class of a Goethe, a Stendhal, or a Berlioz. What he lacks in depth he makes up in range: he seems to have been everywhere, known everyone, and written it all down. Personal memoirs, travel diaries, ballet synopses, poems, portraits of con-temporaries are arranged as they were in the original edition, with no regard for continuity or for entries of greater or lesser consequence. It is disconcert-ing to come across pages of theatre statistics that would have been better relegated to an appendix. The reader must separate Bournonville the observer from Bournonville the recorder. In doing so, he may discover Bournonville the writer, who consciously set out to reveal himself and his times. He is a man of culture with a reflective turn of mind. His nature is kindly, open, and dispassionate; his eye, as might be expected in a choreographer and mime, is expert in registering the color and detail of human behavior; and as he grows older he gains rather than loses tolerance. It is in the later pages that McAndrew's translation becomes especially sensitive, reflecting the for-mation of a mature literary style. Resigned to change, to the transience of fame, the author in his last years is glowingly benign. He seems to have reached the goal he prescribed thirty years before for the retired ballet master: "Write about the art in which you once shone, and be glad that your genius has changed into *espirit* just as love can change into friend-ship."

Bournonville enchaînements strike us today as modern in their speed, complexity, and economical wit. Bournonville's critical sensibility is also modern, in that many of his pronouncements are valid today. He himself, however, was not a progressive, either spiritually or politically. Speculating on the reason for the lack of outstanding actors, he writes:

> *I dare to offer the hypothesis that it is the equalizing process, which runs through all of modern life and manifests itself in so many other situations, that is causing coryphées to disappear, while over-all skill is becoming more and more common. People do not make such amusing blunders as they did in the old days, but then, striking flashes of genius are no longer the order of the day. In short, the great "types" are disappearing from the boards of the theatre as well as from the stage of the world, and even the distinguishing features of the various social classes are being wiped out by the leveling influence of education and upbringing.*

If there is anything that stands between Bournonville and us, it's his puritanism in matters of public taste. Time and again, he reproves some stage spectacle for falling into "the mud of sensuality." He dislikes dancing that is "lascivious." (Spanish dance and, more surprisingly, the Russian classical ballet fit into this category.) These strictures may very well have originated in the unkempt conditions that were coming to dominate the theatre he was raised in. Dancing had ceased to command respect as a profession. In every country, there were ballet girls who were indistinguishable from prostitutes. Bournonville, born into a cosmopolitan but dignified theatrical family, was determined to elevate the status of his art. By the end of his first term as head of the Danish ballet, he is able to compare Copenhagen favorably with dissolute Paris or London. Although his word "decorum" covers freedom from other kinds of institutionalized corruption as well, such as censorship and claques, and although Copenhagen's liberalism may have come about through its isolation from main currents on the Continent, one comes to believe that Bournonville by choice stood apart from the prevailing sexual aesthetic of his day. His most famous ballet, *La Sylphide,* is an adaptation of Taglioni's *La Sylphide,* and is not truly representative of his art, which was rooted in what the Danish scholar Erik Aschengreen has called the Biedermeier tendency in the Danish audience. In the course of *My Theatre Life,* Bournonville becomes the genius of the Danish ballet and one of the most honored men in the theatre of his time. He could have taken up posts of enormous influence in any of half a dozen European capitals, including the then paramount ballet capitals, Paris and Milan, but because he valued "freedom" he chose Copenhagen. It is one of the ironies of our repertory that the only extant pure products of the Romantic era are the work of a man who rejected, in large measure, the erotic substance of the Romantic ballet.

It is easy to find the personality of this large-spirited, gregarious family man in his ballets. It is more difficult to link what seem to us prejudices of a moral nature with an aesthetic result. Since dancing moves in time and changes with the years, we cannot even be sure what Bournonville's aesthetic intentions were. *My Theatre Life* doesn't tell us; for all its pertinence, it must join the long shelf of books by dancers which don't discuss dancing. *Etudes Chorégraphiques,* Bournonville's as yet untranslated technical handbook, is no more enlightening, since it deals in dance's vocabulary of steps, and not in its poetic language. (Extracts from *Etudes Chorégraphiques* appeared in *Bournonville and Ballet Technique,* by Erik Bruhn and Lillian Moore. The exposition was technical rather than aesthetic. *The Bournonville School,* a four-volume collection of exercises with notation scores and musical accompaniment, edited by Kirsten Ralov and published last year by Marcel Dekker, is another, more comprehensive classroom aid.) Our most faithful Bournonville text remains the dances themselves, however suspect they may be. The choreographer himself did not expect his ballets to outlive him by more than twenty years; that a full dozen of them have come down to us is testament to the rehabilitative powers—and needs—of successive generations of Danish dancers and régisseurs. Only Danes claim to know what has changed and what has remained the same. Yet even Danes may experience the trouble that the rest of us have whenever an artifact of the nineteenth century is placed before us. The passage of time has caused convention to become content. Because we can see the things that were invisible, or else taken for granted, in an earlier age, we assume just

those things—convention, fashion—to have been at the center of consciousness, and it is those external features we look to for meaning. Meanwhile,
the real meaning is escaping us. Dancing revived from another period, despite all the precautions of the revivers, is perceived in modern terms. Just
as musical instruments after Mozart's time changed the sound of Mozart,
contemporary dancers unknowingly change the stress and attack of old
choreography. Often, the attempt to be correct and faithful to the "text"
robs the dance of its core of vitality; the steps are invested with a literalism
they may never have had before—the result of an insistence on pointillistic
clarity which its proponents have mistaken for purity. In the choreography
of our own age, this kind of clarity may have the effect of purity, because we
have come to believe in dancing as its own subject. But was Bournonville an
"abstract" artist?

Hoping for an answer from the most authoritative source, I went several
times to see the small group of soloists from the Royal Danish Ballet who
were performing all-Bournonville programs at the City Center. These dancers
in a way had set themselves up for the question. Except for the one-act
dancing-school ballet *Konservatoriet*, which was given complete, another set
of Bournonville exercises arranged in the form of a ballet, and a few special
turns, all the numbers on the programs were excerpts from ballets with
plots. Like New York City Ballet's anthology *Bournonville Divertissements*, the Danish assortment gave no hint of plot connections—it was a
series of straight dances. (An exception might be made of the *La Ventana*
excerpts, which included a few mime passages.) But in the New York City
Ballet rendition of Bournonville, part—if not most—of the fascination
comes from the unusual sight of Balanchine dancers using their own style as
a kind of heightened definition of the old dances and striking sympathetic
parallels between Balanchine and Bournonville all along the way. The Danish dancers have no modern tradition of their own; with them, I fear, the
"modern" Bournonville is more of a pretense than a reality. When they try
to present repertory nuggets in a showcase format, they have no backing to
make the nuggets expressively distinct. What sparkles out at you are the
components—the tinily faceted steps. Unless they are performed in a way
that puts them into perspective, all steps will eventually become the
same step. One way to get perspective is through character implication. The
Flower Festival in Genzano pas de deux and the *Napoli* excerpts are traditionally done with character touches, and the Danes, who are the liveliest of
mimes, made these dances excitingly real. In most of the other dances, they
had left their character kits at home. Bournonville, if I understand him
correctly, did not compartmentalize dancing and mime. Even if he did, in a
program of excerpts these compartments should not be watertight. Only
Niels Kehlet, the senior member of the troupe, remembered to mime
through the dancing, and he tried so hard and got so little response from the
others that at times he looked quite mad.

If perspective cannot be extrapolated from plot or character, it has to come from the dancing itself. And here is the fatal weakness. The dances just don't stand up all by themselves. To begin with, the technique separates the upper from the lower body. Above the waist all is steady and calm while below there may be paroxysms of footwork. The two halves of the body come together in those great sailing jumps, and from time to time one sees a turn that isn't a pivot and comes from that same clearly located center. The modern ballet dancer is faced with the challenge of pulling coherence out of the Bournonville phrase, which is typically a long and twisted affair, and of not going rigid from the effort to coordinate two centers of energy. After that, he can start thinking about becoming a virtuoso. Like the very young, well-drilled modern technicians they are, most of the Danish dancers in the City Center engagement were content to propose conditions under which virtuosity might occur. They gave us neat feet, lots of stretch and turnout, punctilious arm and head positions; but they often didn't meet the main challenge. They looked incompletely active—even flat. When Peter Martins appeared (as a guest artist), he made a continually engaging little theme out of back-to-front and side-to-side changes, and the inconsistencies in the bifocal style just melted away. Martins's dancing has a plastic energy, deep and full and round; that's not all it has, but it's enough to make him an intelligible and lively figure on the stage. It, and not his pointed feet and his turnout, is the base of his virtuosity. Martins, of course, has spent the last ten years learning about intelligibility from Balanchine. I'm not suggesting that his countrymen should also go to Balanchine's school—only that they need to show a more modern energy range if they're going to give us strictly classical dance.

Danish dancers are so likable, such devoted executants, it's a pity their technique can't do more for them. Kehlet, still in possession of his power-fully individual, blunt-soft style, was especially fine in *La Ventana*. Most of the younger people, though, seemed stranded between centuries. Of the women, Eva Kloborg had the most expressive phrasing and the sharpest ear. It was while watching her in the *William Tell* pas de deux that I realized how important Bournonville's carefully calibrated musical scores were to him. (*My Theatre Life* closes with a tribute to the composer Hans Christian Lumbye.) When a passage in the choreography appeared stylistically not quite credible, it was usually the music that called it to my attention. Dinna Bjørn was always comfortably inside her music and deliciously inside the Old World look of the dances. Linda Hindberg was the opposite type—expansive, severe, "Russian." Then, there was robust, articulate Anne-marie Dybdal, delicate Lise Stripp, and the winsome soubrette Anne Marie Vessel. But Bournonville ballet is a man's world. Why post-Bournonville choreographers never developed a female-adagio complement to the male-allegro principle is a mystery that Danish dance historians have yet to explain. Those in charge of preserving this repertory seem to have overprotected it (from lascivious and wanton women?). A few interpolations in the style of *Giselle*—the latter-day Russian *Giselle*—would have done no harm and possibly would have helped the women achieve parity with the men.

The guest artists who were added for the City Center engagement were all men—Peter Martins, Adam Lüders, and Peter Schaufuss. Interest centered, however, on two very gifted younger men, Ib Andersen and Arne Villumsen. Andersen is the more immediately impressive, but after a while I found less of him there to be looked at than of Villumsen, even though Villumsen is an uneven and at times devastatingly unready performer. When he is at his best, though, his rhythm is as expressively coherent as Kloborg's, and his long, loose-limbed body coils around a visibly active full-length core. Andersen's gifts are still unintegrated. He does step after step with ease; in the *Amager* pas de trois, the combinations are unrelenting, and exist only to prove how beautifully he can execute them. But this is pointillism, after all, and it's a very peculiar condition for dancing of any age to have fallen into. If we see anything in dancing, the first thing we see is its vitality, yet because of "educated" responses—in dancers as well as in audiences—it's the last thing we miss. Seeing clearly at the ballet is sometimes such an effort that we no longer know when we're not attracted to what we see. Vitality in dancing, though, depends on a more than optical brilliance—it has to do with rhythm. It's a dynamic process for the spectator as well as for the dancer, and I think we're helplessly attracted—magnetized—by it. We are not magnetized by steps. At the City Center, I saw circles within circles of the leg. I saw long and difficult step sequences rendered with a diagrammatic perfection that must be the envy of every other company in the world. But I'd just spent some hours with their author, a man whose favorite adjectives were "natural" and "harmonious." It's disappointing to get stainless steel when you've been expecting old gold.

Virgil Thomson was on the Dick Cavett show recently, and, speaking about Orson Welles, he said something like "You can't lose your talent, but you can lose your inspiration." It's easier to understand this general truth in connection with Welles, who sins through excess, than in connection with an artist like Jerome Robbins, whose failures seems to have no drive left in them. Robbins can be curiously self-nullifying. We know that *Opus 19* is his only because he puts so many of his mannerisms into it; there are a good many of those rhythmic bounces in plié, and the quotations—from his own ballets, from Balanchine's—are thicker than usual. Otherwise, *Opus 19* might be by Kenneth MacMillan. (The two men have been choreographing the same pieces of music lately. Are they acquiring a craftsmanly resemblance as well?) In Robbins, loss of inspiration *looks* like loss of talent. Although he's had a long career, with many peaks of productivity, when he's in the shallows it's as if he'd never been on the heights—never shown any individuality or had much creative energy to draw on. *Requiem Canticles*, produced in 1972 for the New York City Ballet's Stravinsky Festival, may have been the last confidently bad Robbins ballet, and it didn't have drive, precisely—only aggression. Since then, he's gone up and down, but the downers have looked persistently listless.

So it is with this latest piece, which Robbins has titled after his score, Prokofiev's first violin concerto. *Opus 19* is not as weak as *Dybbuk Variations* or *Chansons Madécasses*; it's one of Robbins's more disappointing works because it was made for Mikhail Baryshnikov, who was involved in two of Robbins's recent successes, *Other Dances* and *The Four Seasons*. Baryshnikov's presence doesn't seem to have caught Robbins's imagination this time. Out of an apparent desire to fashion something new and different for his star, Robbins has concocted a set of eccentric "signature" moves connected by equally eccentric travelling passages, such as rolling chaîné turns in a crouch. Baryshnikov has the task of imposing consistency and variety on this material, and he almost does it. At each performance, he became more securely suggestive—more exact in rhythm and inventive in range, more vivid and reasonable in his motivations and transitions, and more lucidly insistent on the soft edges and legato phrasing that characterize most of the choreography. The ballet is texturally different from anything he has done before, but texture isn't the most exciting thing in the world for a male dancer to work with. Indeed, a fair portion of the Baryshnikov role looks as though it could be done by a woman, on point. When the music calls for a show of bravura, the choreography doesn't come through. The choreography for Patricia McBride is more jagged and more bracing, and she performs it with that happy authority she always shows immediately in a Robbins part. (In Balanchine, she may take several performances to hit her stride.) Role reversal, which was a theme in *Dybbuk Variations*, is almost but not quite a theme here. Instead, Robbins works out a hero-destiny motif, with a pattern of mysterious comings and goings. McBride several times enters and leaves, concealed by the ensemble. The ensemble several times enters and leaves without her. Besides that, its chief function is to echo the principals; it's a Mortimer Snerd corps, sidling on, going "Uh-huh, yup, yup," and sidling off. The concerto is strange and beautiful music, and Robbins handles his otherworldly hocus-pocus very effectively. But "handle effectively" is just about all he does. It's a drearily efficient piece.

In none of her many theatrical manifestations—sung, spoken, or danced —is the masochistic, degraded heroine of *La Dame aux Camélias* more resistible than she is in a new, full-evening ballet presented at the Met by the Stuttgart company. Verdi's *La Traviata* is a special case: it lavishes great music on a story that should have waited for Puccini. In *Camille*, Garbo was photographed—symbolically?—like part of a woman, her head and her broad shoulders swelling out of her décolletage like a bust on a pedestal. As the celebrated cougher, Bernhardt is also to be seen in film fragments, writing letter after letter and then, felled at last, toppling into bed. Fonteyn spent the major portion of *Marguerite and Armand* snivelling at men's feet or gasping her lungs out in staggering bourrées. Now we have *Lady of the Camellias*—choreography by John Neumeier, music by Chopin (a miscellany that refuses to meld into a score), and, as Marguerite Gautier, woeful Marcia Haydée, who seems to have drawn her characterization from Edward Gorey's *The Hapless Child*.

With Neumeier, the talent-or-inspiration question fades into the larger question of why he chose to be a choreographer in the first place. Nearly every piece of his I've seen has saddled itself with affected literary conceits that can't be worked out in the theatre. This one goes back to Dumas's novel for its fatalistic comparison of Marguerite with Manon, and the parallel is staged at unbelievable length. Since Marguerite's legend supplanted Manon's for the nineteenth century (and I believe for us as well), we don't need a fate symbol for her—she's one herself. But the Manon business helps pad out the evening. Jürgen Rose has designed about eleven costume changes for Haydée in a determined effort to make her look chic. I'll say no more about that. Nothing about this event is discussable. I've hated every ballet I've ever seen done by the Stuttgart. This time, let's call it antipathy to the material.   —*July 9, 1979*

Ᏸlue and White

In a poem he once wrote about New York City Ballet, Kenneth Koch referred to ballets like "the blue-white sea / Outside the port-hole: Agon, or Symphony in C." The image came back to me in the closing weeks of the spring–summer season as, one by one, *Chaconne* and *Square Dance* and *Tchaikovsky Piano Concerto No. 2* appeared, all part of that same blue-white vista, all island realms, cloud-capped Illyrias. The nacreous grotto of *Ballo della Regina* is part of it, too. With its sparkling aquatic imagery, this ballet is as real and complete a metaphor as nature in Verdi. Balanchine's *Ballo*, in fact, is an abstraction of the underwater ballet in *Don Carlos*. It seemed a slight, irregular piece when it was first done, eighteen months ago. This past season, it emerged as one of his freshest visions—transparently a mid–nineteenth-century neoclassical seascape, with bravura waves and naiads surging through the foam or glowing like pearls in the deep. A streaking cataract named Merrill Ashley holds the whole thing together. It isn't unusual for Balanchine ballets to hit their peak a year or more after the première; the miracle is that they don't take longer. *Vienna Waltzes* has a huge ensemble and a long, rhythmically complicated finale. Yet the ballet arrived last winter, having taken no longer to find its form than the compact little *Ballo*. Perhaps it can be said of repertory companies that all things created in the same moment are equal to that moment. Although *Ballo della Regina* and *Vienna Waltzes* and *Kammermusik No. 2* and *Union Jack* seem to break down into different categories of Balanchiniana, it may be that in twenty years they'll look alike as products of the late seventies, just as *Square Dance* and *Agon* look alike as products of the late fifties. One might wonder, too, about dancers. Is there a late-seventies breed, difficult for us to distinguish now, which may leave its stamp on the repertory in the same way that Marie Jeanne and Mary Ellen Moylan stamped the forties, Maria Tallchief and Tanaquil LeClercq the fifties, Diana Adams, Allegra Kent, and Suzanne Farrell the sixties? There's already a seventies-model corps de ballet, which we *can* distinguish, because its nucleus is that exceptionally talented group of girls who a year ago graduated into the company from the School of American Ballet. This influx has given the company not only the youngest but perhaps also the strongest corps in its history, and very likely it's what has made possible within the same six-month period the fully developed *Ballo* and *Vienna Waltzes*—ballets that fill very different expressive purposes. (Study the choreography for similarities and you'll see that not even the waltz phrase is the same.) For these revelations and for restoring *Agon* and the *Tchaikovsky Concerto* to form after several disquieting performances last year, one must also thank the supervision of the assistant ballet mistress, Rosemary Dunleavy. The contributions of a fine corps and régisseur wouldn't mean much, though, if it weren't for the italicized achievements of individual dancers—those who lead all the rest. The ones I'm about to name aren't part of any breed or class; they're just the dancers whose progress or prominence has impressed me most in the past two months.

The characteristic look of Merrill Ashley in the midst of one of her exciting and highly specialized dances is a look of angular intensity. She dances with even force yet with a naturally oblique expression; even en face she seems half turned away from you. Or, about to turn away, she'll square off with a suddenness as disconcerting as a full-in-the-face glance from a passerby. Her allegro is filled with rapid-fire monosyllabic interjections; through the brilliance of it audiences sense an understated, all-business style that is specifically and flatly American. This year, Ashley began to open out and show us a more than cordial warmth; she has freed her head so that it floats graciously; she's beginning to get a real ballerina glow. It is a thoroughly happy development. Her phrasing is just as clipped, her angles just as severe, but something about the way she presents herself makes us happy to see her. We can tell she's aware of her sharp edge and ready to use it provocatively. The technician who demanded the audience's respect has become a performer who commands it. In *Ballo della Regina, Square Dance,* and the last movement of the *Tchaikovsky Concerto,* there's even a whiff of comic self-enjoyment.

But though Ashley has developed her performing style, her dance style hasn't changed. Last winter, there were moments when she'd suddenly expand in a slow movement—prolong the start of a phrase or the length of its connection with the next phrase—and she'd look unguardedly beautiful. I haven't seen any of those moments recently. In adagio passages she still shows a too-crisp attack, a tendency toward overswift completion of a phrase, and an unwillingness to depend on her partner for support. It's a little as if Ashley thought that her punctuality and surgically clean execution were all that keep her from being a dull dancer—as if speed and more speed could make of her angularity an object of wit. (Actually, she's narrow only from the hips up; her fullest torsion is a one-quarter twist of the knife. Her legs are lovely, even voluptuous.) And she's in danger of settling for some technical strengths at the expense of others because they make her a "personality." Ashley may always be too hearty for *La Source* and *Donizetti Variations,* but there's more, technically speaking, to these roles—not to mention *Emeralds* and the *Symphony in C* adagio—than she's interested in exploring right now. There's more to Merrill Ashley, too.

Apollo, Tarantella, the revival of *Orpheus,* and the Costermonger pas de deux in *Union Jack* called forth from Mikhail Baryshnikov what certainly must be the widest range ever demonstrated by a male dancer in a single season. Baryshnikov's feat was all the more impressive in that it included the mastery of a role in which he'd been miscast last season. Orpheus is all but invisibly a dance role, and the mime is so low-key that for a Soviet-trained dancer it, too, may as well not exist. I still don't think Baryshnikov is the right choice for the part; it's against-the-grain casting of the kind that isn't productive, even for the audience. Nevertheless, after his overemphatic performances of last winter Baryshnikov returned to the ballet with a style so changed and subdued that it looked like a conversion. But then his assimilation of new and radically different styles has been amazing from the start of his career in America. As the Costermonger, he instinctively improvised his way through a role that, again, did not need him and that already has two very able interpreters. Baryshnikov wasn't like Jean-Pierre Bonnefous, who is handsome and fatuous, or like Bart Cook, who plays a wizened Cockney. Baryshnikov's personal style is really more Cagney than Cockney. But not even *Push Comes to Shove* prepared me for how funny he was. I expected diabolical glee; I didn't expect such a showering of gags or such a spirit behind it—the wriggling, ecstatic, outrageous, pandering spirit of vaudeville itself. He not only got the gags going, he got Patricia McBride to respond delightfully, and the two worked together better than they have in anything else. In *La Sonnambula,* McBride was the Sleepwalker and Baryshnikov was the Poet—another mime role, but one that I believe he is mistaken to perform as passively as Orpheus. Perhaps he appeared passive only because the role, with its links to the tragic heroes of *La Sylphide* and *Swan Lake,* doesn't cut across our expectations of what he's like onstage, the way Orpheus does. In any case, as nondancing roles go, the Poet seemed to me the lesser achievement.

Suzanne Farrell went back to the principal allegro role in *Divertimento No. 15* and, for the first time, captured it. She did it by scaling down her attack on the variation and rephrasing it musically. The adagio portion of the role, which is all short lines, small jumps, and supported figures, she lengthened by dancing it as connected events in a single phrase. In the Sanguinic variation of *The Four Temperaments*, another unaccustomed role, there was smooth performing and a fertile array of ideas, which will undoubtedly be developed in further performances. Farrell also returned to the *Tchaikovsky Concerto*, a ballet she used to dance in the sixties, and by the end of her first solo, with its heart-stopping unsupported pirouettes into penchée, had repossessed it. After this, the ballerina goes off, and she keeps coming and going all through the ballet. Perhaps because we're used to seeing her hold the stage for long periods and build extended structures, the *Concerto* doesn't seem to give us enough Farrell. But it could become another of her azure kingdoms, somewhere near the polar regions of *Diamonds* and *Vienna Waltzes*. If it doesn't—if there were no other ballets for her but those two and *Chaconne*—Farrell would still have a repertory. Her performances are occasions for unique and unrepeatable happenings and have to be spoken of as one-time events: "The *Diamonds* of Saturday Night Closing Weekend," "The Great Saratoga *Chaconne*." Recently, I watched her give the minuet in *Chaconne* with a sly sforzando attack I'd never seen before, brightening each step like sunlight behind a cloud. At the next performance, I don't think I saw any sforzando, but the light was still there. And the delicacy of this effect of illumination came from a dancer who can, when she wants to, lift a leg and hurl it like a bolt of lightning. Her great capacity for extreme contrasts and invisible transitions led Robbins to fashion a Farrell supervariation in *The Four Seasons*, which is strangely ineffective. Not that it isn't ingeniously made and brilliantly danced. But it's such a barrage of daredevil effects that we can't get the sense of it as a dance. Farrell has to run off to a spattering of applause in a stupefied silence. (Peter Martins's "Russian" variation, which he now does instead of his "Danish" one, is similarly loaded, and it doesn't get all the applause it calls for, either.)

One of the most commented-upon aspects of Farrell's technique is her aplomb—for example, in the big battements that send her off balance while she hurls those bolts, or in the supported adagios where she doesn't seem to need the man's support. What one notices upon further study is that Farrell doesn't place herself, or her partner, or her audience, at the mercy of her facility in these matters. The battements are an element of syntax, not a separate event thrown in for its own sake, and Farrell often does rely on her partner. Even when she doesn't—when she's thrilling us by not needing his assistance—she never suggests that she doesn't need *him*. The illusion of the ballerina's independence—or of any feat in dancing—will always count for more than the mechanical proof of it.

Sean Lavery. Tall, strong, angelically correct, he is perhaps the finest example of the pure danseur-noble type to have been produced by American schooling in a generation. (Not the School of American Ballet this time but the independently run New York School of Ballet.) It's true that at times he dances as if he had all that and more to uphold. Lavery is still very young— only twenty-two—but his propriety makes him look younger and greener than twenty-one-year-old Patrick Bissell, at American Ballet Theatre. This season, in the double bill of Stravinsky miniatures *Monumentum/Movements,* a light seemed to go on inside Lavery. Partnering Farrell, he began to use his upper-body weight like a man's instead of a boy's. He continued to do it as the cavalier in *Ballo della Regina,* and it only increased the fantasy of the role: he seemed to belong to the same order of mythical creatures as the women—he was a Triton, not a mortal interloper. My other picture of the new Lavery comes from *Dances at a Gathering*—the role that is usually done these days by Peter Martins—and there was a premonitory flash earlier in the season in the *Tchaikovsky Concerto,* his most becoming role to date. Maybe this is the role he will grow up in.

A blond daddy longlegs of a dancer with Danish classical technique, Adam Lüders seemed an eccentric blend of Bournonville and Hans Christian Andersen when he joined New York City Ballet a few years ago. He was tall and a good partner—assets never to be discounted in Balanchine's company—but it seemed that he would never work out as a dancer in Balanchine's repertory. In addition to his recalcitrant physical proportions, there were serious infirmities of placement and coordination. His looks and a noticeable flair for acting seemed to stamp him a character dancer, of limited usefulness to Balanchine. If Lüders ever does play Coppélius or Drosselmeyer, it won't be because he has to. He's unquestionably a dancer, and this has been his year. Oddly enough for a dancer with character sense, his two biggest achievements have been in classical roles. (He was miscast as the lover in *La Valse*; his predatory, fey quality doesn't look right there or in *The Four Temperaments.*) Replacing Peter Martins in *Divertimento No. 15,* he was wholly admirable. There's a dizzying manège of swinging half-turns in the air that alternate direction (it makes *me* dizzy just to think of it); Lüders rolled through it with no loss of focus. He is one of the lanky young men of ballet who seem to be popping up everywhere, and like the others—ABT's Bissell and Kevin McKenzie, the Royal Ballet's Mark Silver, the Bolshoi's Alexander Bogatyrev—he seems in need of special guidance to complete himself technically as a dancer. But Lüders has already come incredibly far. Who ever thought four years ago that one day he'd take Martins's place in *Divertimento*? Or in *Chaconne*? That it would be he and Farrell meeting in that silence and dancing like two snow leopards?

Stephanie Saland is physically a larger Gelsey Kirkland, and though she's not as gifted a dancer she is sometimes presented as if she were. She did *Square Dance* with Helgi Tomasson, a charming performance overcast by the lengthening shadow of G. (for gargouillade) Kirkland. (Although Kirkland never actually performed *Square Dance*, it would obviously have been her part if she'd stayed with NYCB.) Saland, though, had by the time of *Square Dance* established her individuality in a dozen varied repertory roles, and except for Lüders she's the most improved dancer in the company this year. Long before this phase of progress began, Saland was compulsively watchable because of the elegant carriage of her head and arms and her warm, glamorous presence. She's still very much an upper-body dancer. The port de bras in the Violette Verdy solo in *Emeralds* looks second nature to her. Maybe a few more *Square Dances* are needed to sharpen her footwork. Saland is an instinctive actress, and her sense of theatre makes me think of Jillana, a dancer of the fifties and sixties whom she also physically resembles. As the Coquette in *La Sonnambula* (a Jillana role), Saland was all soft malice, and she was also astonishingly precise last winter as a last-minute substitute for McBride in Costermongers.

Judith Fugate, who did the other ballerina role in *Emeralds* (you couldn't miss her pear-shaped points), is always pleasant to see: accurate, musically sensitive, daring. In *Dances at a Gathering*, she took the most acrobatic of the women's roles. She was one of a host of débutantes in the ballerina roles of *Divertimento*, and she may have been the best. Fugate doesn't project the way she dances; if she did, we might appreciate her even more. Her Beauty in the Beauty and the Beast episode of *Ma Mère l'Oye* is only a bit, because Fugate's miming before the mirror is vague and unconcentrated. Heather Watts, who certainly does project, has been getting a number of ballerina roles lately. She looked happiest, to me, in the McBride part in *Dances at a Gathering*—really relaxed and happy, as if it were dancing she loved, and not competing with other dancers. But the competition is part of the fun of watching New York City Ballet—fun for the audience, at least. I like to see dancers like Lourdes Lopez, Sandra Jennings, Carole Divet, and Nichol Hlinka get parts. I'm dashed when a potential soloist like Peter Schetter leaves the company and quits dancing, buoyed when he suddenly returns. He's had no brilliant opportunities yet, but wait until next season. Repertory is destiny.   —*July 23, 1979*

Kylián's Way

It's not often that a choreographer can make audiences sit up and forward in their seats and watch the stage with shining eyes. I didn't find as much to watch in the ballets of Jiří Kylián as I did in his demonstrative audiences. It was a spectacle of enjoyment that had something self-conscious about it, as if people were watching themselves watch Kylián and being doubly tickled: not only was Kylián wonderful but they were, too, for responding to him. Kylián, the thirty-two-year-old artistic director of the Netherlands Dance Theatre, was making his New York début with eight ballets. A ninth, *Return to the Strange Land,* as slickly confident but not as ambitious as some of those in the Netherlands repertory, had been given a few weeks before by the Stuttgart Ballet at the Met, and its reception had been ecstatic. The press had already turned Kylián into a conqueror, but the audiences who attended his company's two-week season at the City Center weren't just bowing down on cue. I think they were genuinely stimulated by what they saw and relieved not to be reacting to a critical hype. One might interpret the reception of the company as the return of feeling, yet the feeling was not without a disturbing element. The people who adored Kylián didn't seem to want just to applaud good work; they wanted to celebrate their sense of personal gratification. The applause was peppered with those falsetto woofs that seem to be taking the place of bravos. Why should the sound of people going into a tizzy be changing in this way? Is it another mark of the Me generation? Bravos, olés—all the traditional audience vocables—say, "*You* were wonderful"; they're directed to the performer. These wordless woofs say, "*I'm* wiped out."

Kylián, born in Czechoslovakia, studied Graham-style modern dance in Prague and ballet in London. He joined the Stuttgart Ballet and worked under John Cranko. Four years ago, he became resident choreographer of the Netherlands company, which had an eclectic modern repertory of European and American choreography. As I recall that company from its previous American tours, it moved on an identifiable classical-ballet base and had ranking soloists. Kylián has transformed it into a welded ensemble, an instrument as responsive to his idiomatic personal style as Eliot Feld's and Paul Taylor's companies are to the personal styles of Feld and Taylor. There are no soloists—indeed, there are no solos. Kylián's smallest unit of expression is the duet, and he prefers his duets doubled. A duet that is not doubled is as likely to be a double solo as a standard pas de deux. These devices widen the magnetic field of the action at the same time that they insure anonymity. You watch nothing for its singularity, everything for its duplicable speed, shape, and finish. Though the company is not large, it seems to be a marvel of universal conditioning, every dancer formed inside the same bubble and impelled by the same breath. And the other things one notices are in line with this impression—the tiny vocabulary of steps, the repetitious patterning, the men's and women's roles evened by unisex choreography. The Netherlands makes a fetish of impersonality, but so do many American modern-dance companies. What interested me was the extent to which the company's blank, impersonal, controlled look became expressive in Kylián's hands and affecting to his audiences. I'm speaking now of his all-dance ballets, the most potent of which—*Sinfonietta, Symphony of Psalms,* and *Glagolitic Mass*—accounted for the success of the whole season. The nondance ballets were parables of modern life in which impersonality is simply a reflection of moral and social chaos. Everyone must have seen at least one of these bric-a-brackish happening-ballets by now, done by other choreographers. *Children's Games,* a Kylián version of that white asylum where people move slowly and portentously, crawl around in cages, try to build something, fight, make love, and are all the while pursued by death figures, seemed to take in every influence, from Anna Sokolow and Alwin Nikolais to Robert Wilson and Kei Takei. It even threw a few of Mahler's *Kindertotenlieder* into the noise-band soundtrack. Against this vision of clutter and noise and rebuke, the clean, smooth dance shapes of *Glagolitic Mass* were like a balm, wiping away the sins of the world with a few incantatory passes through space. The faceless crowd reappeared in redeemed form. I don't think I'm making too much of the juxtaposition.

Kylián's art, modelled on the trim, organic shapes of so much American dance, is very differently motivated. Where most American dance is non-tendentious in its aesthetic choices, American-derived European dance is not only tendentious but specific. The few steps he uses are "strong," "gutsy" steps, chosen for their impulsive, urgent look. A Grahamish rond de jambe cross step that keeps pulling the body off its center is invariably the takeoff for the careering flight of the Kylián dancer. A typical sequence will go cross step, jump, cross step, jump-jump. And there are signature dances as well. A favorite form of pas de trois is the woman pulled and dragged on a steeplechase course between two men. It stands for rape, for exaltation, for fun; presumably, it's the music that determines the mood. Kylián likes liturgical music; it's easy to see why the most common adjective his admirers use is "exultant." The word attaches itself to all the runs and rushes and bucking leaps and up-and-away lifts.

But not all of Kylián's movement is captioned. Like that other choreographer-prophet Maurice Béjart, Kylián likes occasionally to preach sermons of ambivalence. Although he reintroduces the easy emotional correlatives that most advanced American choreographers have sought to avoid for the last thirty years, he doesn't make quite the suggestive references one might expect to the texts of Stravinsky's psalms or Janáček's vernacular folk Mass. I don't mean that there aren't penitential postures in the Stravinsky and pietàs in the Janáček and cruciform lifts in both; Kylián deals freely in the nondenominational religiosity of expressionistic modern dance. But one sees these gestures primarily as token allusions to the nature of the experience that is taking place in the music, not as part of any parallel to that experience which is taking place in the dance. Forget that we really don't need to see a dance parallel; would it be worse than the cheerful tastelessness that uses psalms—*these* psalms, especially—or Masses as neutral soundtracks for dance fantasies? Which is worse—clunky José Limón–style piety (see his setting of Kodály's Missa Brevis) or Kylián's ambivalent theatrics? One of Kylián's most forceful passages of choreography comes at the end of his staging of *Symphony of Psalms* where Stravinsky has set words of praise and jubilation glowing to contemplative, slow-moving harmonies. Kylián's response is a protracted view of his dancers inching their way upstage into a gulf of blackness, with their backs to the audience. Is it distractingly effective or effectively distracting? If any words fill our minds, they're more likely to be Eliot's despairing parody of Milton—"O dark dark dark. They all go into the dark"—than the words we are actually hearing: "*Omnis spiritus laudat Dominum*" ("Every spirit praises the Lord"). Is it that Kylián doesn't understand any kind of exultation but the leaping-up kind? More likely, it's that he understands how to flavor the juicy feeling we long for with a little of the modern skepticism we can respect.

The décor of the Stravinsky ballet is a wall of Oriental carpets hanging in layers, as in a showroom. The wall dissolves into darkness at the end. We understand that the carpets are "unrelated," as in a Merce Cunningham décor, yet when they dissolve at the same moment the choreography is giving us its "wrong" response to the music, we may feel that we're getting a statement about Kylián's uncertainty as an artist. Ambivalence, skepticism, uncertainty: they're practically a summation of the situational aesthetics that have guided the Netherlands Dance Theatre. Although the carpet décor is by an American, William Katz, it has the same enigmatic menace as all those coolly disengaged backdrops by the Dutch master of the form, Jean-Paul Vroom, and by other Dutch artists. The sensibility of the Dutch loads Cunningham's simple idea of disassociation with intimations of anxiety and estrangement. Vroom's art is familiar to us from the ballets of Hans van Manen, one of the original members of the Netherlands company. Kylián's choreography echoes or extends many of Van Manen's devices, and he also shares with Van Manen an attachment to heavy concert-hall scores—music of profundity and of questionable suitability for dance. In the thirties and forties, Massine made vaguely programmatic ballets about Man and Fate to music by Brahms, Shostakovich, and Beethoven. The dominant school of European choreography, which was fomented by the Dutch and by the

German-based Cranko and maintained by such practitioners as Jiří Kylián and John Neumeier, has tried for twenty years to match big-scale, Massine-style significance to choreography that is as musically responsible and co-herent as Balanchine's—a case of wanting to eat your cake and cut your calories, too, and a task made insuperably difficult if, like Cranko and Neumeier, you were unmusical to begin with. I don't think Kylián has succeeded where the others have failed, but I think he has succeeded in finding a point of kinetic union between music and dance and building something that looks like a ballet upon that point. Van Manen belongs to the old school of music visualization, and his visualizing has always struck me as static. The sole Van Manen ballet in the Netherlands repertory this season, *Songs Without Words*, has the kind of anecdotal relation to the music which in Kylián becomes a series of polished kinetic links. It's as if Kylián had found a paraphrase in movement which distills anecdotal mean-ing and makes the music move. While I wouldn't have chosen the untypi-cally modest *Songs Without Words* to illustrate Van Manen's connection to Kylián, no ballet could better illustrate Kylián's connection to the man I have been wanting to mention all through this article—Jerome Robbins.

Set to selections from Mendelssohn's piano suite, and with a larky cast of eight, *Songs Without Words* appears closely modelled on *Dances at a Gathering*. But Van Manen can't make up his mind how much anecdote the music will bear; the choreography is uneasy and musically arbitrary. Rob-bins, as we know, whips right through the dilemma; he establishes at the outset something that might be called anecdotal rhythm. Its impetus comes from feelings, situations, and moods that Robbins has heard in the music, and you can follow it whether you hear what Robbins has heard or not. The motive may be an anecdote, but the impetus is free. This is Robbins's main resource as a choreographer. It is not, compared with Balanchine's main re-source, a pure instinct for rhythm; it's a narrative instinct. Compared with Van Manen's main resource, though, it's very pure. And Kylián has under-stood it. I wouldn't call his kinetic paraphrases of musical sounds and of emotions "under" the sounds *rhythm*, precisely, but whatever sort of rhythmic parody Kylián has devised seems to have come into being in between *Transfigured Night* (1975), a heavy, four-square treatment of Schoenberg's *Verklärte Nacht*, and *Sinfonietta*, to Janáček (1978), and to have been developed in *Symphony of Psalms* (1978), which contains a few passages of homage to the Robbins of *New York Export: Opus Jazz*. Whether is can be developed further, Kylián has not yet shown. Is it Robbins or Stravinsky whom he salutes in his opening tableau straight out of *Les Noces*? Stravinsky's rhythm seems to have dictated a subtlety one doesn't find elsewhere in Kylián's work. For the most part, Kylián's rhythm is cadential, and that may be why I can't feel it as dance rhythm. Dance rhythm implies momentum, an elastic continuity. Kylián uses a sharp cadence that keeps falling back on itself and repeating. The sensation of force is additive rather than cumulative. *Glagolitic Mass* is a series of dances; one or two of them start out on irregular counts, but before long they've become caught in strings of reflexive ongoing cadences. And it makes no difference whether two or twelve dancers are onstage; there is no change in pressure or scale. Each dance starts at zero and gallops right up to the level of the previous one. Kylián, like so many choreographers, thinks to hold our interest by keeping the shapes as large and open as possible. But he doesn't set "large" and "open" against anything that might make us appreciate those choices as dance values. If one were to arrange dynamic options in terms of contrasting pairs—say, big/small, heavy/light, hard/soft—Kylián would most of the time choose Column A, seldom Column B, never a little of both. Big/light and heavy/soft are beyond him. But then they're beyond most choreographers, American or European.

Kylián reminds me of many people. He uses a tiny assortment of steps, like Paul Taylor, though without Taylor's variety of effect. (His idea of dynamic contrast is to use women as lighteners, doing the same steps as men.) He is as much a cultist of music visualization as Van Manen, though not as depressingly bent on step-for-note literalism. He turns music into emotion, sort of like Jerome Robbins, by means of punchy rhythmic devices. And one would have to go all the way back to Kurt Jooss to find another Central European choreographer who has attained the same level of success. The choreographer whom Kylián most resembles, though, is Doris Humphrey. Humphrey was a structuralist who could reduce a Bach concerto to a nest of mixing bowls; the bowls were brown. Kylián, also by simplification and reduction, pretends to lay bare the intent of music; he doesn't care about structure, he cares about sensation. Just as Humphrey could always squeeze out one more mixing bowl, Kylián can keep his motorized ballets charging ahead as long as the music holds out, on and on into the dark.

The Royal Ballet's production of *The Sleeping Beauty*, which I saw last summer in Houston and again a few weeks ago in Montreal, has still to rid itself of imperfections in the Panorama-Awakening scenes. These are the scenes on which the ballet traditionally founders, and the Royal's failure is the more to be regretted for scuttling what up to then has been a superb production. It cannot be said too often how transparent Tchaikovsky's intentions are in this ballet, how they shine infallibly through misstaging. Yet when the person in charge of the misstaging is as determined and skillful as Ninette de Valois has been in the present instance, license is welcome and transgression can seem like invention—up to a point. Tchaikovsky did not write Carabosse to be performed by a woman; that much seems certain from the livid grotesquerie of the music. To force femininity on the characterization, De Valois has had to blanket certain of Tchaikovsky's effects with her own. It works. Monica Mason gives the performance that justifies the idea. As her carriage is drawn offstage and she makes the gesture that says, "Remember [what I have foretold]!," her huge eyes open wide with fright; she has already been forgotten once.

But De Valois has given us more of Carabosse than we need to see. When Tchaikovsky "remembers" her, it is only glancingly; after Act I, he doesn't bring her on. The memory comes in the Sleep music, but there onstage is the creature, at the heart of a giant spiderweb, and she confronts the Lilac Fairy—another event that Tchaikovsky didn't arrange. She'd even been present earlier, with her minions, as Lilac and the Prince disembarked, well before the orchestra completed their journey by water and the musical cue for Carabosse was heard. What seems to happen at this point is that the Royal, having started the boat ride, is loath to stage it in full. So we fade out on a forest drop while the Water music continues and those incongruous land events with Carabosse occur. Still, nothing seems to be drastically wrong, and a moment later, when we have penetrated to Aurora's bedroom and Lilac, drifting in extended bourrées, is clearing it of malign spirits much as the Firebird banishes the monsters, the production is once again invincible. From here it rises with the Prince's entrance and his awakening kiss. Then: calamity. I do not miss the interpolated Awakening pas de deux that I am told used to be staged at this moment. But, after all the time it has spent breaking in the new production, shouldn't the company have arrived at a more feasible and musically more honorable transition to Act III than a jolting tutti chord, a blackout, and a pause during which the orchestra looks for its parts and people scramble to their places behind the curtain?

The company did not give of its best in the Act III divertissement in either of the performances I saw at the Place des Arts. The orchestra, under Emanuel Young, performed unsteadily both times. And in all the fairy roles the ballet was weaker or else no stronger than it had been last year. One had the sense of young dancers arrested in an eternal state of promise. A Lilac Fairy ought to be giving us secure double en-dedans pirouettes. At Lilac level and above, though, style falls off. There is no Bluebird. Lethargy and small-scaled execution robbed both the Auroras I saw of distinction. There is nothing wrong with being small. Jennifer Penney has the same snowflake delicacy as Makarova and Semenyaka, Gelsey Kirkland and Judith Fugate. But Penney has been taught to use her long, sweetly turned, raylike limbs in short or end-stopped phrases of limited impact. After a while, her small-featured perfection comes to seem minor. The larger and more solidly built Lesley Collier succeeds in imposing herself; her Rose Adagio was as accomplished as Penney's but more forceful. In the Vision scene, though, her legato was sluggish. Like the production as a whole, the Auroras tended to slacken in interest. Their Florimunds, David Wall and Mark Silver, gave unmemorable performances except for the adagio variation, which, if we must have one, now ranks as one of the better interpolations. The worst: Kenneth MacMillan's Hop o' My Thumb, if only because it violates the over-all sense of Petipa style. It is, of course, the Royal's complete conviction in this style that carries us through. Though one may fault the production, nothing in it is garbled or vulgarized. The Royal can make the rational and humane spirit of the ballet more real than any other company, and what it understands by Petipa tradition is worthily upheld. (One can hardly see Leslie Edwards in his thirty-fourth, and possibly liveliest, year as Cattala-butte without thinking about tradition.)

La Fin du Jour, a new MacMillan ballet, is a satire on the Jazz Age set to Ravel's Piano Concerto in G. Heartless and artificial, like the music, it's concerned less with what fashionable people did for recreation than with how they looked doing it in terms of the iconography of the period. The choreography and Ian Spurling's costumes and scenery draw on the syn-thetic and the decorative as if there were some archeological deposit to be found in the modish visual jargon of the late twenties and early thirties. And there is. Although the piece discloses nothing beneath its glittering surface, as it goes on it turns out to be about something real—style as an object of human passion. The first section, not terribly interesting, is a social frenzy, with dancers chugging about like mechanical dolls in marcelled hairdos of powdery pink, purple, and blue. In the next part, two of the jazz dolls (Penney, Merle Park) pull goggles over their eyes and, as teams of men manipulate their bodies in passes over the ground or through the air, be-come fliers. Another moment, and they are flying machines. The choreogra-phy recalls the "Bunraku" episode of *Rituals*, where MacMillan was unable to sustain and intensify his vision as he does here. The movements of the two women are sometimes in counterpoint, more often in unison, but Mac-Millan's doubling has a meaning that the doubling of Kylián or Van Manen doesn't have: it carries the implication of persons becoming involved in and identified with machines. (Kylián's and Van Manen's ballets just *are* ma-chines.) At the end of this section, the two robot aviatrixes are alone, and they totter on their points all over the stage, bumping into each other again and again until they bump each other out of sight. This absurdist *ballet mécanique* ends with a party scene quite different from the first—a scene with men in evening dress doing tumbling tricks and huge, porpoiselike leaps that reminded me of Paul Taylor's *Cloven Kingdom*.

At the climax, everyone falls to the floor, and Merle Park slams shut a door that gives onto a twilit garden vista. The end of the day is the end of an era; but MacMillan's inventions have carried us beyond thoughts about a period.   —*August 6, 1979*

Theory and Practice
in the Russian Ballet

The first season of the Bolshoi Ballet in America, twenty years ago at the Metropolitan Opera House, consisted of *Giselle, Swan Lake, Romeo and Juliet, The Stone Flower,* and a batch of excerpts and short ballets which made up two "Highlights" programs. *The Stone Flower* was the sole modern work; at least, that is the way it was presented and, in large part, received. It was also the sole work with choreography by Yuri Grigorovich, who is now the company's artistic director, and that must have been the reason it was chosen to open the current Bolshoi engagement at the State Theatre, which is not only an anniversary season but also a Grigorovich retrospective. The choice is otherwise inexplicable. If *The Stone Flower* is remembered here at all, it is for the performances of Vladimir Vasiliev and Ekaterina Maximova in the two leading roles. Maya Plisetskaya, a heroine of that first season, was from all reports (I saw Nina Timofeyeva) an engaging Mistress of the Copper Mountain. None of these dancers from the original Bolshoi cast are with the company in New York; in fact, they're part of an anti-Grigorovich faction that has been touring independently. Reviving *The Stone Flower* under these conditions draws attention to the existence of controversy and the hollowness of the ballet's importance.

One of the subjects of the controversy is the new Grigorovich production of *Romeo and Juliet,* which starts its run here this week. The separatists are saying that Grigorovich intends to replace the standard version, by Leonid Lavrovsky; Grigorovich says that both versions will be retained. It's unlikely, though, that the Lavrovsky *Romeo* will ever again be toured. Turn back to 1959, which was the last time it was seen here, and New York opinion is overwhelmingly negative. Ulanova's performance was praised, but the production was judged to be old-fashioned, because it contained long stretches of the kind of melodramatic pantomime that hadn't been seen on a New York stage since the days of David Belasco. This is not a point on which local opinion is likely to have changed. *The Stone Flower,* coming at the end of that riotously successful début season, was given what might be called an indulgent reception. It, too, had a Prokofiev score, but a much inferior one. And it had a thin and unreal story about a stonecutter who has to choose between making art for the people and pursuing ivory- (or, in his case, malachite-) tower perfectionism. The story is unreal not just because you know how it will come out but because it is, in dance terms, incomprehensible. Grigorovich used three kinds of dance: lyrical-adagio, character-folk, and, for the scenes in the glowing green underground kingdom of precious stones, a spiky type of *ballet moderne* the like of which hadn't been seen here since Adolph Bolm was staging his city-symphony/iron-foundry ballets in the early thirties. In none of his chosen modes could Grigorovich express the dramatic point of the libretto that was outlined in the printed program or work up the least bit of suggestive atmosphere. Yet because he *didn't* use pantomime the Russians claimed the ballet was an artistic advance, and some American critics fell in with the claim. After all, what did we know in 1959?

When Grigorovich succeeded Lavrovsky as artistic director, he continued to make no-pantomime the signpost of progress. But in the whole course of Russian dance history, as recorded by Russian dance historians, it is hard to find a native choreographer who is *not* progressive in this way—even Lavrovsky is extolled for his promotion of all-dance expression. Only, of course, what looks all dance in one era looks a lot less pure later on, and in the pages of history the same choreographer turns into a reactionary the minute the next promoter gets ready to "reform the ballet." In a country where the story ballet is the only type of ballet tolerated, the use or non-use of mime is kept dangerously alive as an issue. Grigorovich really does choreograph everything as dance action. His trouble is that he must go on doing it for three hours, and after about twenty minutes the glad-sad-mad-bad slots tend to get all stuffed up. Twenty years later, *The Stone Flower* is still rigidly inarticulate, although, compared to the samples of Grigorovich's work we have seen since, it comes off as inoffensively naive. The second-act suite of folk dances includes some entertaining gypsy night-club antics and ends with the scene that in 1959 had audiences at the old Met yelling: the evil bailiff, lured by the Mistress of the Copper Mountain, is swallowed by the earth. The yells were for Vladimir Levashev, the great character dancer of that period, whose thrashings as the trap took him down and down ran up and up an emotional scale from bewilderment to panic to insane terror—an effect that the perfunctory heaves of Yuri Vetrov on opening night this season didn't begin to suggest. Anatoli Simachev was a more imaginative villain on the next night, but emotionally he embraced about half an octave. Along with Simachev, Andrei Kondratov as the stonecutter and Svetlana Adirkhayova as the Mistress of the Copper Mountain performed with more authority than the first-night cast, Leonid Koslov and Valentina Koslova, though they were no better as dancers. Koslova, stylistically gauche, has Ann Marie De Angelo–type power; Adirkhayova has layers of polish over technical weaknesses. Neither has the acrobatic precision or the spirited charm the part needs if it is to be rescued from the comic strips. The Mistress of the Copper Mountain is a slit-eyed slitherer. (In the original tale that the libretto comes from, she's a metamorphosed lizard.) She does all her chaînés with angled elbows, and at the end of the ballet she tries several times to persuade the hero to stay by leaping on him from a crouch. This young man is also a stereotype—the bluff, honest folk hero in a tunic

—and his chaste girlfriend, who wears an ankle-length nightie through the whole ballet, is an active bore. I don't ask to see the original cast at this late date. It is hard, though, to believe that Vasiliev and Maximova could have made an impression in roles like these. Because of the steps, one can still see Vasiliev's shadow, but Maximova disappears into Ulanova—the aging Ulanova who had originated the role of Katerina in *The Stone Flower* a few years before, in another version of the ballet, choreographed by Lavrovsky. If you look at pictures of Ulanova in her prime, you see a commanding beauty, but by the fifties she'd become a vestal virgin, a pure and simple soul—the soul, in fact, of the people. When Maximova entered the company, she was Ulanova's protégée, and Maximova's role in *The Stone Flower* was the Ulanova stereotype, just as the Mistress of the Copper Mountain was the Plisetskaya stereotype; the two women had been played off against each other before, as Maria and Zarema in *The Fountain of Bakhchisarai*. Dramatically and symbolically, the role of Katerina is absurd —at one point she defends her virtue against the villain with an upraised sickle—and choreographically it is feeble. Grigorovich relies on his favorite step, renversé in attitude, and a few other things that can be done in a nightgown: low arabesques, hobbling on point, or, in a lighter vein, hobbling on point backward. Mysteriously, the flashing Ludmila Semenyaka was the dancer scheduled for Katerina on opening night, but because of an injury she withdrew and the role was danced in the first three performances by Irina Prokofieva—a large, weighty woman, who is probably not as dim a dancer as the role made her look.

The sacred/profane polarity in feminine type-casting seems to be standard Russian practice. Grigorovich used it again in *The Legend of Love* (Shirin/Queen Mekhmene-Banu) and *Spartacus* (Phrygia/Aegina), Lavrovsky used it, and both men could probably claim antecedents in *Giselle* (Giselle/Myrtha) and *Swan Lake* (Odette/Odile). In his production of *Swan Lake*, though, it isn't the ballerina roles that interest Grigorovich; he turns his good/evil polarization formula onto Siegfried and Von Rothbart, the sorcerer, and tries to suggest, through many a renversé in attitude performed à *deux*, that the two are alter egos living inside the same character. The suggestion has no expressive purpose; it's just there to be fooled with, like a new tassel or drape. This *Swan Lake*, I understand, is a modified, censored version of the radical production Grigorovich wished to put on. Nevertheless, it contains its share of experimental follies; it's about the most senseless of the novelty *Swan Lakes* that are still around, and, with its bleary unit set and swamp-gas lighting, the ugliest. The production, which dates from 1969 and was seen here in 1975, is another point of friction in intracompany politics. The dancer Maris Liepa characterized as "barren" and "monotonous" the new choreography; he might have added "insensitive." There is novelty, and then there is unfeeling novelty. Grigorovich has the many trumpet fanfares in the score "played" onstage by heralds of the court—six trumpeters where Tchaikovsky has two. But this is a minor annoyance compared with the moment at the end of the ballroom act when he has those six blaring away lustily while the rest of the court falls about in lamentation. It's then that you want the earth to open and swallow the whole thing up.

However, the Bolshoi is the Bolshoi, and a maladroit *Swan Lake* is preferable to a *Stone Flower* for showing off the company, its style and its school. About two minutes into Act I, the impression of dull and absent performing left by *The Stone Flower* was dispelled by the big ensemble waltz. Here were young men and women happily absorbed, effectively deployed, visibly connected to a tradition. I have faint but stirring memories of Act I as it was in the former Bolshoi version—of an elegantly framed vision of haughty young aristocrats disporting themselves in a Botticelli autumn garden. And that vision comes back to me in the present production even though the garden is gone, along with its frame of animated onlookers. The dancing shows such sensibility—so many details of step and accent which the eye picks out like metallic threads through a great tapestry—that one begins to grow a little afraid, as if in the presence of numbers of strangers all with finer instincts than one's own. What one is seeing is style—style as a system of preferences that has to be bred into a company. That's why the sight of it is scary. But isn't part of the reason we go to the ballet the tragic thrill of seeing so many accomplish what for one would be remarkable? Particularity of behavior elevated to group expression is what draws us to the great companies with the great corps, like the Bolshoi, especially when they do *Swan Lake*. It's the expectation of seeing in the tragic action of the ballet a logical parallel to what has already been fulfilled in the creation of a corps de ballet and the creation of a ballerina. The ballerina is the principle of the particular within the general, and the corps is the principle of the general within the particular, and each is achieved tragically, out of the depths of human pride.

One can't have cheap artistic direction and still have tragedy on the grand scale appropriate to ballet. From the way the Bolshoi dances *Swan Lake*, I'd say that its artistic direction is mainly benevolent—negligent or partial at worst. The great waltz in Act I is an adaptation of what I can recall seeing in the sixties; Grigorovich's fussing has mostly to do with pointwork. I think the women used to wear heeled shoes in this number— the men, too—and the effect of that is still there. The tiny chassés in the basic waltz step have been converted into small amounts of taqueté; the oddness of inflection is the same, and so is the delicate balance of the whole figure as it waltzes. The women show becoming oppositions in neck, waist, thigh, and ankle; they're moderately vivacious, while the men are moderately aggressive. But the medium temperature is calculated against the extreme rigor of the lakeside acts. When the transition to the lakeside begins (the two acts are played consecutively), Grigorovich destroys the mood right away with his "conception," and he undermines the entrance of the swans by rushing them out of nowhere into a formation at the start of the act. But when they make their traditional entrance, in flying sautées arabesques, the show resumes its proper perspective. The Bolshoi is still the greatest turned-in ballet company in the world, and its swans, as usual, draw their bigness of scale from the instep and lower leg rather than, as Western swans do, from an open hip and mobile thigh. But then there is the wonderfully alive Russian back. Those backs and those strong and pliant feet somehow collaborate in and cultivate a look of strain and confinement which has nothing to do with technical inadequacy. This is swan deportment in Bolshoi terms. And the suspense of Bolshoi phrasing—behind the beat, with linking steps inordinately inflated, climaxes unpredictably tossed away —adds its baffling fanciness to the total worked-over, slightly sweated weight of Bolshoi style. When these swans are in their human form, they're sitting in clammy castles making lace.

Natalia Bessmertnova is the Swan Queen who bears out the corps in its most ponderous aspects, but she's really not released in the role. With her beautiful turned-in plastique, Bessmertnova makes rapturous broken-winged pictures in this ballet; when she flies, though, she flies right out of it into another world. Her second-act adagio is so evenly accented and molded, and every bit of it is so heavy, that it seems twice as long as it is. In Odile's variation, which appears to have been made on her, she had a bright moment, and in the last act she had another, riding around the stage in huge jetés. Bessmertnova danced two performances, with two different Siegfrieds, both of them talented and accomplished young dancers. Alexander Godunov, whom we last saw here in 1974, may be the more accomplished. From a rawly energetic performer he has developed into a classical dancer of distinction, and his personality has opened and sweetened. Although Alexander Bogatyrev has, as they say, filled out, his listless attack and casual demeanor make him a pipe-and-slippers Prince. In the finale to Act I, he violated Grigorovich's idea of a Siegfried who does nothing but dance by actually appearing to sight swans overhead. Both of these performances of *Swan Lake* were graced by Irina Kholina's light and speedy solo in the first-act pas de trois—except for this plum an unexcitingly arranged piece of choreography. From its low point on opening night, the company has slowly, very slowly, begun to come alive. We are still waiting for Semenyaka in something other than *The Stone Flower*, and so far Nadezhda Pavlova and Vyacheslav Gordeyev have danced only in *Spartacus*. For many of us, these two dancers have been among the world's legendary performers ever since we saw them and Semenyaka and Godunov make their startling New York débuts six years ago. *Spartacus*, in which Gordeyev must be tigerishly heroic and Pavlova kittenishly consoling, doesn't allow much more than a glimpse of what artists like this can do. But that glimpse was enough to touch off pandemonium in the audience. Yes, the beauty and power are still there, brighter and steadier than before, and holding out every promise of dazzling us apocalyptically in the weeks ahead.

—*August 20, 1979*

The Bolshoi's Pathetic Fallacy

In the Bolshoi's new *Romeo and Juliet*, there are no pillows in the pillow dance, no swords in the duel scenes, no *duels* in the duel scenes, and Juliet does not rush madly along the apron and back with the potion. There is no bed or balcony. The designer, Simon Virsaladze, shrouds a bare stage in blood-dimmed gauze, through which we catch vague glimpses of tiled roofs or coffered ceilings or the well-known coastline of Verona. There is no funeral, and no tomb scene in which Romeo lifts high the limp body of Juliet. Instead, it is Romeo who flops lifelessly in a terminal pas de deux (the scenario has been rearranged to allow Juliet to awaken before he dies), and both lovers in death are lifted high above the heads of the mourners as the curtain falls. Bodies lifted high, supine or upright, above the crowd constitute a favorite tableau of Yuri Grigorovich, the choreographer of this *Romeo and Juliet*; he manages to work it into most of his ballets, and he literally excels himself when he has Tybalt lifted up in triumph by a mob of brawling Capulets and then the Duke of Verona rise right behind him even higher.

These scenes and others, more dimly insistent, suggest an attempt to dislodge the touchstones of the old Bolshoi *Romeo* and replace them with new ones. But the production as a whole has a more overweening aim, which is to tell the entire three-act story in dance terms—with dancing going on not just whenever it is appropriate but consistently and inevitably, whether it is appropriate or not. It is as if a schoolboy had undertaken to rewrite the play *Romeo and Juliet* in sonnets from beginning to end. The compulsive stylization leads to inflexibility and sameness in all those technical areas—plasticity, rhythm, proportion—that must be exploited to the full in order to sustain a full-evening composition. Out of continually changing tensions in these areas a choreographer builds interest in a drama. It isn't enough to have "story sense"—you have to have the sense, too, of the way stories move in space and time. John Cranko had story sense; so do a lot of scriptwriters who could have done as good a job as he of licking *Eugene Onegin* for the ballet stage. Grigorovich lacks even this elementary what-happens-next acuity. What happens next in one of his ballets is generally what happened a minute ago. In *Romeo and Juliet*, scene with Nurse leads to scene with Nurse. The storytelling burden falls on Prokofiev, but as the evening wears on, the music is more and more disinclined to support the action in its blind, monolithic course. By the third act, Grigorovich and Prokofiev are so far apart that only mystique connects them—the mystique of *Romeo and Juliet* as a great popular hit and as the only classic that Soviet ballet has contributed to the international repertory.

Perhaps this is the reason—the familar, beloved music—that Grigorovich hasn't tightened the score in the interest of creating a comprehensive dance drama. If mime is prosaic, dance is compressed and metaphorical; it naturally takes a lot less time to make its points. Grigorovich, though, goes in the opposite direction, reorganizing and stretching the score to include sections that have customarily been deleted. In the third act, this brings on a case of what Russian critics once diagnosed in Petipa as "divertissementitis." There is some evidence that Prokofiev's first thoughts about his *Romeo and Juliet* were of a Petipa/Tchaikovsky–style ballet. That is how Frederick Ashton perceived it when he staged his 1955 production for the Royal Danish Ballet. The marketplace scenes were formal corps dances; the ballroom scene was a suite of ensembles. But Ashton's conception was unified. Grigorovich's is merely omnivorous: Everybody dance! He even tries to convert the lovers' intimate scenes into visions of the Romantic ballet by filling the background with a drifting group of damsels in pink tulle. To complement this suggestion, Romeo and Juliet, relentlessly lyrical, appear to have memorized long passages of *Giselle*. Paris, by contrast, is a classical dancer who, with Juliet's entourage, dances the Classical Symphony in Act I. (Get it? Romantic equals soft, classical equals hard.) Such normally lay figures as the Duke of Verona, the Nurse, and Tybalt are given dance assignments; even Friar Laurence is pressed into partnering service and lays unpriestly hands on Juliet's person. Lady Capulet, she of the sundered bodice and wailing backbends, needs no augmentation, but she gets it anyway—a train of ladies-in-waiting acts as a wailing chorus when Tybalt dies. Tybalt's choreography appears to be based mainly on the bullfighter pirouettes and postures in *Don Quixote*; in fact, all the Capulets, including the Nurse, are Spanish. The marketplace merrymaking may be derived from the Italian-opera–style festivities in the earlier version of the ballet; it also looks like the folk dancing in *Don Quixote* or the carmagnole in *The Flames of Paris*.

The merrymakers bang noiseless tambourines, which are in wide use at the Bolshoi—perfect props for all the pseudo-serious choreography, tokens of its pretensions to style when it's incapable of elementary differentiation. Grigorovich's stylistic borrowings in *Romeo* aren't reshaped to the purposes of *Romeo*; they're ready-mades plunked down in new contexts and expected to deliver new effects. Actually, the only new effect that Grigorovich achieves is the villainy of Tybalt, an extension of the clenched arrogance of the ballet matador. Most of the time, he isn't even trying for effects of characterization; he's trying to choreograph by decree, with results that look for all the world as if what used to be vilified as "formalism" had now taken hold as official artistic policy in the USSR. If that word can be applied to anything, surely it's to the meaningless surface conformity we see here. I was astonished to notice that the Veronese guard marches in the goosestep of the Roman legions in *Spartacus*: Grigorovich had even borrowed from himself—not because he wanted to portray the Veronese as fascistic, like the Romans, but because if they marched in ordinary fashion someone might accuse him of naturalistic movement. Goosestepping is dance marching. The Russians who write the articles in the official souvenir program for the Bolshoi are careful to refer to Grigorovich's vocabulary as "classical dance as an expression of human emotion," as if all that were one word. And from watching Grigorovich's ballets you do get the impression that he thinks emotions are contained in the steps. Romeo's reaction on sighting Juliet on her bier is a string of double sauts de basque—a step he'd already performed so often that it doesn't even qualify as a unique reaction. And you sit there wondering who could believe this. Does everybody in Russian dance circles have this automatic trust in dancers as characters, steps as feelings? Are they going around in long hair and miniskirts spouting some Soviet version of "The medium is the message"? A saut de basque, nakedly propounded, is not a cry of pain. The ballet *Etudes* should have proved once and for all that classical *forms* have a structural coherence but are no more intrinsically dramatic than the harmonic series in music. The choreographer, Harald Lander, justly equates classroom combinations with Czerny keyboard exercises; the result is a smashing non-ballet.

When Grigorovich has got everything the way he wants it—an overlong, unsortably profuse three-act score blanketed in dance steps that no one can deny are dance steps (haven't we seen them in our favorite ballets?)—to whom does he present it? He has responded to the challenge of a new *Romeo* not as an artist but as a politician. Whatever looks like dance is in, whatever looks like mime is out. Meaning, expression, interpretation of life—the things the politicians used to want explained as clearly as in an editorial cartoon—have been reconstrued by this new dialectic, I wish I knew how. The success of Grigorovich's mindless abstractions could only come about in a social atmosphere that is itself abstract. Although Grigorovich's rule is now under protest by some of the Bolshoi's outstanding established dancers, his choreographic method isn't one man's aberration. The tendency of Russian ballet in the twenty years since its reintroduction to the West has been toward a simulation of pure expression —not dance as metaphor but dance as not-mime, a definition arrived at by negation and without further qualification. This, of course, creates a literalism that can be subjected to simple empirical tests and an emptiness that can be filled by intellectual apologetics.

The only Western choreographer who seems to have a place in the derivative patchwork that makes up Grigorovich's *Romeo* is John Cranko. One can see the ancestry of Grigorovich's Mercutio not only in Cranko's Mercutio but in the Joker of his *Jeu de Cartes*. It may be that Grigorovich intended these affinities to pay tribute to the man whom he is known to respect as the choreographer who had done the most to revitalize dance drama. Cranko's method—which caught on, interestingly enough, at just about the time of the vogue for Marshall McLuhan and "nonverbal communication"—consisted largely of dancing his way through the action of a libretto, although in his *Romeo* (which was modelled on the same verismo Bolshoi production Grigorovich now seeks to replace) he didn't totally dispense with mime. He came closer to doing that in *Eugene Onegin*, which many consider to be his best work. Grigorovich, of course, eliminates every vestige of naturalism. In Grigorovich's *Romeo*, the duels between the Montagues and the Capulets are like those noiseless tambourines: they've become rhythmic swipes through the air, with no contact and none of the sound of clashing steel that is traditionally a part of these dances. (It's like hearing the "Anvil Chorus" without the anvil.) The long knives the men carry instead of swords are slung behind their backs, out of harm's way when they do air turns and leaps. And when Mercutio suffers his death throes and makes light of them, he can't strum his sword, as he used to in the old production, so he's given Grigorovich's idea of a dance equivalent—a shoulder stand with his legs sticking up in the air. In fact, he dies in this position. There have been plenty of variations on this famous death scene; only in Grigorovich's is Mercutio's ridicule lost sight of and Mercutio himself made ridiculous.

I don't believe Grigorovich means to make Mercutio ridiculous; the ridiculousness is a logical consequence of making Mercutio a capital-D dancer. The role is really a trap for the choreographer. Mercutio, of all Shakespeare's characters, is most plausibly realized as a dancer. Yet in this all-dance ballet he is not more vivid than he is in productions that mix dance and mime. And it's not so much that Grigorovich lacks the talent to make Mercutio brilliant as that he lacks control. Mercutio appears to be acting without motive and from sheer high spirits; the audience sees this and decides that, of all the characters whom Grigorovich has deprived of motive in this storyless story ballet, only Mercutio has a right to that much freedom. We turn to him with grateful applause: "Why, he's just a dumb dancer!" But the character must die. Here's where Grigorovich should have called out motive, for Mercutio is pathetic in death only insofar as his gaiety in life was a reaction to danger; the clan wars have got him in spite of his bravado. But Grigorovich is able to refer us only to Mercutio's superficial existence. Even though "He dies as he has lived" is the way he means us to understand this death, if Mercutio hasn't lived except as a performing seal among other seals, there's no strength of meaning in his death—it's just the exit of a clown. The coarse choreography only makes matters worse. When Nijinsky died upside down in *Schéhérazade* ("But a blade flashed and he fell headlong, to spin on the back of his neck with his legs thrust rigid in the air," as Cyril Beaumont has written), the violence and ecstasy of the image expressed the rampant sexuality of the Golden Slave, truly dying as he had lived. Mercutio's pose doesn't have the resonance of metaphor. Grigorovich's practice as a choreographer has all along and with increasing aggressiveness been that of a man gripped by the pathetic fallacy of the emotive power of dance steps and poses. His quotations in *Romeo* are talismanic. Yet it doesn't matter whether he draws on Nijinsky or Cranko or creates some utterly unbeheld "dance" variation on the death of Mercutio. A character who hasn't lived cannot die.

I think one can see where Grigorovich's confusion connects with Western precedent. One can see, too, without knowing what pressures lie behind it, that excess flows from this confusion as surely as he who says A must say B. Cranko's ballets are, for me, hysterical and trivializing, but Grigorovich's are nihilistic. The *Onegin*, which I saw again this summer during the Stuttgart Ballet's season at the Met, could not be redeemed even by our greatest dancer-actress. Natalia Makarova, who by reason of her beauty, temperament, skill, emotional refinement, and style could have created an ideal Tatiana, was nullified by a role where her qualities mattered less than a flashy kind of acrobatic talent and a feverish pulse. These, taken together, constitute the Cranko hieroglyph for "dance." Makarova reproduced it well enough, and the audience reacted as if jabbed by hot pokers. The point about Cranko's choreography is that it makes audiences believe they're seeing modern, in-tune-with-the-times ballet without giving them a single dance moment. Grigorovich gets the message, only his ballets are not for audiences, they're for commissars.

The role of Juliet was created on Natalia Bessmertnova and performed by her at the New York première. Apart from some ugly modern attitude-lifts, Juliet is an exhaustive recapitulation of Giselle, which happens to be Bessmertnova's greatest role and the role that ballerinas typically choose to grow contentedly old in. If the ballet stays in repertory, Bessmertnova's Juliet will be an additional lease on the life of her Giselle—a handsome present indeed from her husband, Grigorovich. As for Nadezhda Pavlova, who danced on the second night, neither the tame choreography nor the big, stiff, all-concealing Romantic tutu is appropriate. Pavlova, with *her* husband, Vyacheslav Gordeyev, as Romeo, performed more urgently and appealingly than Bessmertnova with Alexander Bogatyrev, but, like Makarova in *Onegin*, they didn't make as much of a difference as one had hoped. Mikhail Tsivin, looking like a powerful Deni Lamont, was all this Mercutio could be, and Alexander Godunov had a personal triumph as an almost mystically brutal Tybalt.

Little more than a week later, Godunov defected. The detention of his wife, Ludmila Vlasova, at Kennedy Airport shifted the terms of the drama from artistic to political and legal ones. But the question all season had been whether and how Grigorovich has responded to the new talent in the company represented by Godunov and Pavlova and Gordeyev and Ludmila Semenyaka. Godunov's act—the first of its kind by a Bolshoi dancer—spoke for him. Ironically, Godunov had shown the most impressive development under Grigorovich's direction. He is, at twenty-nine, a fine example of a modern-day Bolshoi premier. Gordeyev, although he is also Bolshoi-trained, looks more like a Western classical dancer. Perhaps as a concession to their large New York audience, he and Pavlova were given starring roles in three of the five ballets the company did here. They had exposure, and they danced like dynamos, but they looked out of key with their roles and with the rest of the company. Gordeyev was shown in the three phases of Bolshoi masculine style—Heroic (Spartacus), Romantic (Romeo), and Exotic (Ferkhad in *The Legend of Love*). One of the world's most sophisticated dancers, he was buffeted by idiomatic corruption in the first (Godunov was a better, more Herculean, Spartacus), callously drained in the second, and just plain miscast in the third, where he was called upon for *Corsaire*-style gesticulations and hurtling squat-spins en l'air. As a performer, Gordeyev overrode all these abuses, but we never saw him at full technical capacity or in the mood of quiet elegance with which he sustains technical feats. In *The Legend of Love*, a revival being seen here for the first time, he did display again and again that well-remembered catapulting grand jeté of his, and frequently Pavlova was there leaping at his side, as loftily, as hungrily, as tirelessly as he. This was her best appearance of the season. The ballet is conventional Soviet kitsch with a Turkish setting that one is invited to take not too seriously (Grigorovich had a lighter touch in his earlier days); even so, the story is treated with unreasoning contempt. The score, by Arif Melikov, is serviceable dance music in elevated folk style with a Max Steinerish love theme. A recurrent *misterioso* passage, scored for strings, was for some reason heard on tape. There are plenty of costume changes—trousers, tunics, veils, the lot—for the two principal ballerinas, who play sisters (Pavlova and Nina Timofeyeva); Gordeyev, as the man they rivalize over, wears turbans. The enormous corps, too enormous for the State Theatre stage, does Radio City Music Hall routines, one of them remarkably like *Ravel's "Bolero."* Nothing happens until the second act, when, after weeks of fitting herself into one Bolshoi norm or another, Pavlova suddenly bursts out in an adagio with Gordeyev that is a sweeping reassertion of her gifts. There is something both casual and electric in her attack that is uniquely Bolshoi, but in the way she spirals and plummets and cuts the air she's unlike any other Russian dancer. She has matured physically into an astounding beauty; the prodigious legs are now part of her; and her incomparable flair is without disproportion or exaggeration. Yet though she still has it in her to revolutionize Bolshoi ballerina style, Grigorovich's idea of her seems to be that she's Bessmertnova all over again. Although Pavlova is turned out, she doesn't always use her turnout. You can see the power driving down the inside of her leg, clotting the thigh, loading the foot. The lovely infinite expansiveness of the grand style is denied her. Much the same thing seems to be happening to Ludmila Semenyaka, although with her the symptoms take the form not of impacted power but of laxity. Her *Swan Lake* had the fantasy one remembered from her performances of four years ago but not the perfection of form and scrupulous detail.

I can imagine how the gruelling ballets of Grigorovich might satisfy the work ethic of young dancers who are prevented by crowded schedules from performing often enough in their megalopolitan home theatre. Still, Godunov took off. One could wish for those who remain more than the glory of work. It may be significant that in two of Grigorovich's ballets, *The Stone Flower* and *The Legend of Love*, the hero is an artist who rejects his private destiny and chooses a life of work among the people; it's *Le Baiser de la Fée* in reverse. The Bolshoi turns more than the dying Mercutio upside down. *—September 3, 1979*

Trooping the Colors at Covent Garden

From my hotel in London, which was on the Strand, I could walk two ways to the ballet at Covent Garden. One was straight up Bow Street to the front of the Royal Opera House; the other was around the back, across the large square next to the site of the famous evicted market, now under restoration. Both routes had their rewards. The marketplace, temporarily void and silent, flanked by Inigo Jones's church and what remains of his colonnade, presented a classical perspective that cleared the mind for the performance to come. As one neared the stage door, the narrow streets filled with people and small cars inching their way, providing a delightful agitato overture. The great thrill of approaching the theatre from the front was the sudden sight of its pediment and white columns jutting from the ramble of streets and shops—as surprising as finding a four-poster in an upper berth. The Covent Garden district is still a dream landscape, though no longer so inhospitable after dark. New galleries, boutiques, and late-hours restaurants add their sparkle to the jumble of vistas. The Opera House, placed on a height, faces nowhere in particular and is impossible to approach head-on. Unlike the Paris Opéra, it is not a magnet; one comes upon it and its counterpart the Theatre Royal, Drury Lane, amid the swarm. These great structures reassert the idea of a theatre embedded in life, not artificially remote from it. The Opera House, especially, appears extended and involved in the affairs of the city yet with just enough of a break in logic to command authority. Our old Met was a bit like this; the new one could have been more so if it had been built on the same spot. (And a "cultural complex" on an already animate site might have prevented Bryant Park and the area south of Forty-second Street from falling into oblivion.)

On a violet evening in September, Covent Garden was a pleasant place to be, with the façade rising above the tootling traffic and letting in quietly chattering crowds. Close to curtain time on opening night of New York City Ballet's season, Balanchine was seen sauntering alone and serene among the crowds. I imagine the pleasures of the place have spoken to him many times; contrasts in scale, leaps in logic are to be found in his ballets, and the style of New York City Ballet—serious, self-challenging—implies a seamless connection between the practice of classical dancing and our common human fate. Locally, the company brings out aesthetic connections as well; we know it speaks of and for New York—the best of New York—and we are eager for that to be understood abroad. But the sense in which ballet is important to us in New York is not understood abroad. Old World opera houses are built to human scale; they're designed for the kind of experience our own expensive, overscaled, ice-cold theatres can only contradict. The New World cannot afford these theatres intended for an élite; we have to build for the acquisitive audience. Yet in imperilled cities like New York the dream of middle-class affluence has clouded over. New York City gives me sustenance in the form of New York City Ballet, yet I can't afford to live there—live, that is, in one of the enclaves that keep the frightening realities of city life at bay. Lincoln Center is an enclave within an enclave. When it was built, it seemed to reflect the philistine notion that art is outside life—an excrescence. Now it reflects the sense that art is outside life—a refuge. It has never stopped being a monument to middle-class values, but only if you're a beleaguered middle-class New Yorker can you know what it truly stands for.

It may be because we were driven to create these monster theatres out of economic need and greed that we prize what goes on inside them so highly —it's all we've got. Art in America comes very dear; art anywhere does these days. The new theatres are almost always as ugly as they are unserviceable. One has only to cross the Thames to see what a horror of a modern cultural complex can be constructed in London, a city of theatres. Covent Garden may be old-fashioned, but few other theatres are as perfectly focussed. The audience, upstairs and down, sits collected, stretching its two arms toward a brimming stage. There are slightly over two thousand seats. At the New York State Theatre, there are slightly under three thousand. One might suppose that in that difference lies the sacrifice of intimacy to grandeur, but the Opera House at Kennedy Center in Washington, where the company is playing now, is closer in size to Covent Garden and somehow it misses both intimacy and grandeur. The State Theatre, which was supposed to have been a gift to Balanchine, has instead been a problem—one that he has worked tirelessly to surmount—and the staging of his repertory at Covent Garden revealed further aspects of his resourcefulness in dealing with the State Theatre's recalcitrant proportions. There were, of course, ballets that simply looked better on a smaller stage because they were made for one—ballets like *The Four Temperaments* and *Square Dance*, which were created before the move to Lincoln Center. *Stravinsky Violin Concerto*, a State Theatre ballet (but a remake of a 1941 work), assumed a more concise power in its new setting. To my surprise, such recent "small" works as *Ballo della Regina* and *Kammermusik No. 2* came over much as they do at home, and *Chaconne*, which I had expected to change quite a lot, looked absolutely itself. The biggest difference came in *Jewels*, of all pieces, which suggests that when he made it, early in his State Theatre career, Balanchine hadn't quite attained mastery of the new space. A smaller stage enhances it. At Covent Garden, *Diamonds* was majestically ample, less effusive; *Emeralds* took on a hothouse glow; and *Rubies* was positively scandalous. *Vienna Waltzes* and *Union Jack*, the two blockbusters, appeared cramped. The blah reaction to them of the British public was less predictable. At Covent Garden, the audience sits close enough to see its own face in the mirror in *Vienna Waltzes*. But the intensity of that experience had to be exchanged for a more confined surge of massed waltzers in the finale. The quintessential State Theatre ballet, *Vienna Waltzes* had other problems, too—the same ones it has in New York. An hour of waltzes was thought frivolous and boring, and the spectacular scale of the work was scarcely more appreciated than the reduced one of *Liebeslieder Walzer*, also an hour long but with a cast of only eight dancers. The ballet, long out of repertory in New York, had failed when the Royal Ballet produced it earlier this year. *Liebeslieder* in New York was never a hit; it is not, as *Vienna Waltzes* is, made of hit material. But in London it wasn't a critical success, either. The British critics, who differ in their views of Balanchine, are virtually united in the opinion that he and his dancers are not "romantic," not "lyrical." For some of the older and more insensitive reviewers, when a Balanchine dancer is really "in," he or she is said to be fit for the Royal Ballet—it's the ultimate accolade. Fortunately, there are now critics who avoid evaluating one company stylistically to the detriment of the other. The American accent of the Jerome Robbins ballets was readily appreciated; spotting the American Balanchine behind some of his disguises proved more difficult.

Although *Union Jack* was also made for the big stage of the State Theatre, it seemed destined for Covent Garden from the start. Opening with a sustained flourish of Scottish pageantry, it next brings on the Pearly King and Queen in a highly idiosyncratic music-hall turn, and concludes with an extended hornpipe festival danced by the entire company. The use of British popular and folk material involves no pretense on Balanchine's part; he sees it all from the outside, and the humor of impertinence is as much a part of *Union Jack* as the tribute of parody. The Colonel Blimps of the London press who chose to get huffy over such solecisms as "The British Grenadiers" and "Colonel Bogey" serving as hornpipe tunes ("We must bear firmly in mind," wrote one of these wattles-shakers, "that they *mean* well") were in the minority. Most of the negative reaction had to do with Balanchine's apparent willingness to waste a company of splendid dancers on trivialities. In New York, the curiosity of seeing seemingly authentic folk dances performed by *those* dancers makes *Union Jack* a double-barrelled exotic attraction. To Britons, the Scottish suite may be long-drawn-out and lacking in consequence. To Americans, it has a ritualistic simplicity not unlike some of our more austere avant-garde dance. And what could be simpler than the chorus of signal flags wigwagging "God save the Queen" while the band thunders out "Rule Britannia"? This must surely be the greatest nondance apotheosis that Balanchine has ever arranged, to the greatest of Britain's ceremonial hymns. (Only "Pomp and Circumstance" seems to me as nearly great.) There are two points I should like to make about the supposed shallowness or inferiority or irrelevance of *Union Jack*. One is that emotional experience in the theatre is indivisible and is not necessarily finer for having come about through pure dance than through pure mime. The ending of *Union Jack* is palpably an expression of the same mind that conceived the endings of *Symphony in C* and *The Four Temperaments*; if Balanchine does not discriminate among his poetic resources, why should we? The other point is that here, at last, we have a keenly characterized folk-style ballet that asks of its dancers something besides dancing. Could not critics who for years have categorized, and castigated, the New York City dancers as anonymous instruments of choreography sense the moment that signifies a change? (The Blimp I quoted a moment ago realized that there was something different going on, but concluded that Balanchine failed whenever he stepped outside his pigeonhole.)

In *Union Jack*, the dancers are asked to be Scottish or English, with an American accent, of course. It is assumed that the imposture will be funny. I suppose it's possible to miss the point if you yourself are Scottish or English; and humor is less often a bond than a wedge between nations. Another divider is classical style in dancing. Although *Union Jack* doesn't contain any classical dances, it is danced by classicists, and it gathers its impact almost entirely from that fact. There's a whole series of Balanchine ballets that might be labelled "A Classical Choreographer Looks at——." The series includes not only *Union Jack* but such ballets as *Stars and Stripes*, *Who Cares?*, *Square Dance*, *Tzigane*, *Western Symphony*, and *Scotch Symphony*. Sometimes the titles reveal the material that Balanchine is looking at, or "classicizing," sometimes not, but the ballets are all part of a process of analysis that ends in the annexation of new territory for classical dancers. *Union Jack*, the most radical of the series, goes another route.

It anatomizes classical values in its subject without making a classical ballet out of it. It seems to stand alone, yet if it were to be presented at Covent Garden all by itself or by another company, it would not make nearly as much sense as it does in repertory. It is as vivid a portrait of New York City Ballet as any of the other pieces I have named. It is not, and was not meant to be, a portrait of Britain.

Very wisely, Balanchine did not present *Union Jack* until the third, and closing, week of the Covent Garden season, when it was part of a gala attended by Princess Margaret. Patricia McBride and Bart Cook danced the Pearlies; in the hornpipe section, Suzanne Farrell and Peter Martins were sharper and funnier than they had ever been before; all the dancers were warmly applauded. But the piece was accepted at face value as a deliberate counterfeit or an engaging trifle, or else not accepted at all. I was reminded of New York's initial reaction, in 1958, to *Stars and Stripes*. Once again, Balanchine's innocence was being equated with the naiveté of his material. That innocence of his does not hesitate to probe the mundane. In routine it finds variety, in well-worn clichés it finds a seductive secret. The material is transformed. British parade-ground performance is in actuality more exhilarating to me than Balanchine's use of it in *Union Jack*. It's the principle of it that he has caught—the mesmerizing power of mass locomotion. The drag step of the brigadiers in the Mountbatten funeral procession, merely by slowing down and stressing the toe with a delicate battement tendu, indicated the gravity and sensitivity of the occasion. Balanchine's regiments do not imitate this or the regular British-soldier march step—hard on the heel with the feet apart and the belly out. That just seems to go with the bump-toed shoes of soldiers, not the slippers of dancers. Strictly regulation protocol for slow tempos calls for marchers to hold their arms stiffly at their sides. Again, Balanchine has chosen a style more appropriate to dancers. And we should look at his regiments against the background of their dance style in the repertory at large. When we do, *Union Jack* gets sweeter and funnier (and shorter), and Balanchine's face comes out from behind his ostensible subject, be it Highland flings, reels, or military marches. What the British call his "personal classicism" is the quality of emphasis he gives to enduring elements of dance that are, like configurations in a picture puzzle, hidden in the real world of movement. He has taught us to see these elements—us, the American people. And I would have hoped that by this time the term "personal classicism" could have given way to "American classicism" or even "classicism." It happens that at the moment no one else is practicing in that shop on such a scale of consequence or such a level of responsibility.

Something in the pattern of Balanchine's work tells us that he is a man who does not believe in coincidences. *Union Jack*, made in the year of the American bicentenary, salutes Great Britain. It also commemorates and capitalizes on *The Triumph of Neptune*, a ballet about Great Britain that Balanchine had arranged for Diaghilev fifty years before. Then twenty-two years old, he had also danced a featured role. His collaborators were two Englishmen, the composer Lord Berners and the writer Sacheverell Sitwell, but we assume that what the ballet mainly expressed was Diaghilev's idea of a Victorian pantomime. *The Triumph of Neptune* opened at the Lyceum Theatre (where last month the American Friends of Covent Garden gave an opening-night party for New York City Ballet), and was a success. The scenery was based on the traditional toy theatres of Pollock and Webb, and the costumes adapted national dress with what one recent writer has called "Diaghilevian whimsey." *Union Jack*, presented in London in the fiftieth-anniversary year of Diaghilev's death, uses as part of its décor a drop curtain modelled on the red swags of the British toy theatres. When it was lowered at Covent Garden, it touched a chord of association that it could never sound in New York. Balanchine, the last of Diaghilev's choreographers and the only one who is alive today, is seldom sentimental, but I believe he has always had a soft spot for England. Repeatedly, during his visit, he praised English manners and customs to interviewers. If he hoped to be praised in return, he didn't let on. To the veteran dance critic Alexander Bland he admitted that his not settling in London many years ago was probably a good thing because he isn't dignified enough for England, where "if you are awake it is already vulgar." A small enough joke, to which Alexander Bland returns the comment "Though technically fastidious, he certainly lacks the regulator of good taste, which is one of Britain's hallmarks." And he doesn't smile when he says it.

Sniffy good taste—chauvinism, in other words—has certainly regulated relations between Balanchine and British ballet in the past. On this visit, New York City Ballet's first in fourteen years, most commentators held their tongues on the subject of costume and décor. The New York City Ballet is badly underdressed, and the Royal Ballet is badly overdressed; but the subject of discussion this time was dancing. Every country recognizes two classical traditions—its own and Russia's. Where British observers warmed to New York City Ballet, they tended to see resemblances to the Kirov, if not to the Royal. Mikhail Baryshnikov's presence helped strengthen that connection. But to an American the existence of a Russo-American New York City Ballet is as incredible as that of an Italo-English Royal Ballet. Roots and blossoms should not be confused. It takes time to be able to make those distinctions in a foreign company. If British audiences are given a chance once every fourteen years or so (the last London seasons of New York City Ballet were in 1952 and 1965), they'll never do it. I would hate to have had to wait that long between visits of the Royal Ballet. And then to have to deal with a repertory of twenty-eight ballets in three weeks! Programs were preposterously overloaded, no ballet was given more than three times, and tickets were priced at a top of thirty dollars. Yet the Opera House was full each night; audiences took a battering and staggered away dazed. "Stimulating" was what they called it. Mary Clarke, summarizing in the *Guardian*, kindly referred to "a big repertory so carefully paced that even as late as last Thursday important new works were being added." Those included some of Balanchine's knottiest Stravinsky pieces.

For reasons that are not entirely clear to me but have mostly to do with money, it has not been possible for New York City Ballet to have regular London seasons. As a result, Americans know far more about British ballet than the British know about ours. There used to be a feeling around the country that, owing to its many U.S. tours, the Royal belonged partly to us. If the Royal's influence here is on the wane, it may be because American companies are at last making their way in cities outside New York and establishing a tradition of their own. In return for elevating our standard of judgment, the American audience gave the Royal Ballet dimension; it's what the company lacks now even more than it lacks ballerinas. The Royal is sinking into a cozy provincialism. I hate to see it happen—it offends my proprietary instincts. Yet those instincts tell me that there may be some clue to salvation for the Royal in the example of New York City Ballet. Not, certainly, a stylistic example, but a functional one. There is, for example, no tradition at the Royal Ballet of choreographers who also teach. That sets it apart not only from NYCB but from nearly every other dance institution in its period of greatest growth. There is also—and here more sensitive areas must be approached—no record anywhere in the history of ballet of ballerinas being formed by a matriarchy. The English ballet world is rife with its Mims and Madams—blessed, brilliant ladies of iron convictions and awesome accomplishments. But perhaps not the right kind of vision just now. Sir Frederick Ashton, who, like Balanchine, is seventy-five this year, takes curtain calls with regularity and always with emotion. The British are lavish with their celebrations. Of Sir Frederick they ask nothing but that he bask in their applause while they remember him when. Yet too much of the Ashton repertory has been lost, owing to the public's indifference down through the years. At Sadler's Wells Royal Ballet, I saw revivals of *Les Rendezvous* and *The Two Pigeons*—ballets that in successive eras have defined British classical style. It's another world; just compare Ashton's gypsies in *The Two Pigeons* with *Tzigane*. But it is still the world that used to be American by adoption. Watching these ballets, I was impressed all over again with Ashton's long and patient effort to get dancers and audiences used to metaphoric rather than literal associations in dance gesture. He goes at times against the grain, for British dancers are almost all by nature good mimes and British dance critics are by custom devotees of acting and susceptible to coquetry—what one of Balanchine's ballerinas calls "eyebrow dancing." I also saw two new ballets made for the hard-working Sadler's Wells company. Kenneth MacMillan used the native gift for histrionics in a consciously overwrought and not very fresh mime drama called *Playground*. David Bintley, a talented young choreographer, made an old-fashioned pantomime-style piece called *Punch and the Street Party*. His music was the Berners score for *The Triumph of Neptune*; his story was new. I liked the piece a lot, but it did appeal to the tourist in me. A company must guard against doing too often what it does best. For American dancers whose capacities as actors are small, *Union Jack* is a character ballet. It shows that going against the natural tendency of an expressive gift can sometimes bring out an intimate truth. The colors it flies are our own. —*October 15, 1979*

The Romantic Ballet in Copenhagen

Some years after he produced it, August Bournonville called A *Folk Tale* "my most perfect and finest choreographic work, especially as regards its Danish character." Bournonville habitually drew on the folklore of many nations for his atmospheres—Scotland for *La Sylphide*, Italy for *Napoli*. A *Folk Tale*, with its trolls and elf-maidens, its glimpses of craggy metaphysical depths, does have a Nordic gleam of inspiration which we may well believe he never surpassed. Still, his high estimate of the piece can be endorsed by a non-Danish audience. So it proved at the week-long Bournonville Festival in Copenhagen that was held last month to mark the centenary of Bournonville's death. Each night, the Royal Theatre was packed by foreigners, many of whom had come especially to see the ballets that are never toured—A *Folk Tale*, *Kermesse in Bruges*, *Far from Denmark*, *Napoli* in three acts. The Danes, who normally emphasize the Danishness of these ballets or their remoteness from modern taste, had taken special pains with the preparation of A *Folk Tale*. Kirsten Ralov mounted a new production. EMI issued a record of the complete score. Preview performances in Tivoli in September featured Peter Martins as guest artist. Before the festival performance, visiting critics were invited to two days of dress rehearsals with both the festival and the alternate casts. Ralov gave a lecture-demonstration on the bedchamber scene in the third act. The ballet even had its own poster, on sale in the theatre lobby. And it was not until the next-to-last program that it was given, with Lis Jeppesen in the ballerina role. Jeppesen is the newest and youngest ballerina in the Royal Danish Ballet, its candidate for international stardom. On the festival's first night, she was Poul, a cadet in *Far from Denmark*; the role traditionally heralds great things. On closing night, she danced the title role in *La Sylphide*, coached by the most celebrated Sylph of modern times, Margrethe Schanne.

On the applause meter, A *Folk Tale* did not rank as high as the third act of *Napoli* or *Kermesse in Bruges*, which, despite its familiar fragile pas de deux in Act I, comes down to us as a low-grade farce. But it is probably the production by which the festival will be remembered.

In the week's three Romantic ballets—*La Sylphide* (1836), *Napoli* (1842), and A *Folk Tale* (1854)—we see the progression of the Bournonville strain of Romanticism. All three plots deal with a human being in thrall to creatures from another world. James, enchanted by the amoral Sylph, is lured into destroying her and is himself destroyed. Teresina in *Napoli* and Hilda in A *Folk Tale* are more ambivalent characters. In the third act, they are happy to be restored to their original condition, but the second act finds them happy in their captivity—happy in another way. The suggestion of Romanticism is that young women may move between the two worlds, while of young men who engage supernatural forces a terrible price is demanded. In Bournonville's plots, it is Christianity that pulls the errant girl back to life; demons recoil at the sign of the cross. When Albrecht tempts death in *Giselle*, the crucifix protects him, but for the not notably God-fearing Frenchmen who wrote the ballet it was to be Giselle's love rather than her piety that saved him in the end. In Bournonville, happy endings are contrived through the use of miraculous medals and sacred springs. Act III of *Napoli* begins with pilgrims gathering at a shrine of the Virgin and ends with the populace resoundingly celebrating the miracle of Teresina's return. Here is that famous suite of dances, the definitive expression of Bournonville's ideal of wholesome, joyous youth. In A *Folk Tale*, the idealism never finds a climactic image. The pious folk are theatrically dull; but for the timely arrival of a troupe of gypsies in a pas de sept, the trolls would carry the day.

It is impossible to see Bournonville's Romantic ballets without being struck by their mythological resonance and their links to other nineteenth-century works—links that are stronger than the international sisterhood of sylphs, wilis, naiads, and swans. The "Danishness" of A *Folk Tale* lies in its unparalleled troll scenes; nothing else in nineteenth-century ballet matches the second act, when Muri the troll queen and her two awful sons Viderik and Diderik preside at a reception for trolls of all ages. (In these scathing caricatures of human behavior, the comedy is the indirect kind at which the Danes excel. In *Kermesse in Bruges*, they're no better than the cast of some old Bob Hope or Danny Kaye movie.) But while the second act is like nothing else, the first act is virtually a model for the Hunt scene in *The Sleeping Beauty*. Birthe, the vicious young heiress of the manor, who enters with a riding crop and sets the peasants hopping, corresponds to Petipa's countess. Birthe is engaged to Junker Ove, a pale loiterer (Désiré), whose lack of interest in the fun enrages her. She flirts with Mogens (Gallison the tutor) and plays a trick on him in a game of blindman's buff. When the hunting horns call, she appeals once more to Ove, is rebuffed, and leaves without him. The Hunt was a standard scene—there is one in *Giselle*—yet the details (the whip, the humiliation of Mogens/Gallison) are too close to be coincidental. Petipa's valued Swedish colleague Christian Johansson had been a pupil of Bournonville's. When the Danish master visited St. Petersburg in 1874, he was received by Petipa and Johansson together. Another connection to the Imperial Ballet at this time was that between the courts of Denmark and Russia. The Danish princess Dagmar married a tsar, becoming the Empress Marie Feodorovna. In his memoirs, *My Theatre Life*, Bournonville mentions "my position as dancing master to several Russian diplomats." He also taught royal children. There were many routes by which reports of *A Folk Tale* could have reached ballet circles in St. Petersburg.

The Sleeping Beauty was created in 1890, and its fame started a new train of influences. The possibility exists that Act I of *A Folk Tale* was remade after the Petipa ballet became known, but that it could be in so many comparable details an echo rather than a precursor is denied by the music and the smoothness of its fit to the choreography. And it is remarkably advanced music for its time. Tchaikovsky was not the first symphonist of the ballet; even before Delibes there appears to have been a precedent for the artful blend of motives, for the seamless construction that we associate with serious ballet music. Again, the possibility of backward formation exists, but Danish dance historians who admit excisions and interpolations in other ballets do not tell of any alteration in the score of *A Folk Tale* over the years, either by its original composers or by other hands. It was the work of J. P. E. Hartmann (Act II) and Niels W. Gade (Acts I and III), who were father- and son-in-law and who composed here with no break in substance or style. The music sounds somewhat like Mendelssohn, which is right for its period but not for its *ballet* period. The only outstanding ballet score to have been composed around the same time was the Paris Opéra's *Le Papillon*, in 1860, with music by Offenbach. Then came the Delibes-Minkus *La Source*, in 1866. Hartmann wrote other ballets for Bournonville, for which the choreography is lost. Gade is the composer of the second act (The Blue Grotto) of *Napoli*; the music is heavier than that of the rest of the ballet (which was by house composers) yet more trifling than the music of *A Folk Tale*. Perhaps meddlers are to blame for this curious sound—a bit like Wagner writing *Giselle*.

If the major surprise of the festival was the second act of *A Folk Tale*, the major disappointment was the second act of *Napoli*. A ballet that ends so wonderfully must surely be wonderful all through, but alas. The historian Allan Fridericia has some interesting things to say about this:

> None of Bournonville's own dances to the second act are preserved. They are all the work of later productions. Drastic and frequent cutting of the score during the period from 1900 to 1971 has resulted in so gaping a

monotony that audiences began to call "The Blue Grotto" the "Brønnum Act" because ballet lovers preferred a refreshment pause at the nearby and well-known Copenhagen restaurant. Just as the music has been cut, so has the act lost its underlying conflict, that which according to Victorian morality is a twisted view of fidelity. Instead the power of the Madonna picture has grown to an absurd degree. Bournonville, who was both deeply religious and a great man of the theatre, would never have depicted belief in the power of Christianity by using such primitive theatre effects.

All the festival lacked was the opportunity for further intellectual investigation of this kind. Bournonville devotees from all over the place, and especially from the United States, came to Copenhagen, and undoubtedly were stimulated by what they saw. But no papers were read, there was no formal exchange of ideas, and program notes were printed only in Danish. The week's revelations in any case were too primary for much sophisticated discussion. We need detailed performance histories, starting with all the surviving works. Meanwhile, the current reconstructions of the ballets can be disputed with confidence only by those whose research or whose acquaintance with the repertory has been long and deep. Outsiders may only point to what has not been convincing. In the sketchily choreographed second act of *Napoli*, Ralov's steps come from Bournonville, but they do not add up to a facsimile of a Bournonville ballet d'action. In *A Folk Tale*, Hilda's homecoming lacks drama. And the plot falls right down through a hole that opens up in this scene. It has been shown that Hilda, a human child raised by trolls, was switched in her cradle for Birthe, the troll child, who was raised in her place. In the homecoming scene, though, Hilda is readily recognized as the long-lost daughter. Whom, then, was Birthe taken for, and why was she raised an heiress? To follow Fridericia's reasoning from Bournonville's intentions, would not "a great man of the theatre" wish to have this scene rethought for plot logic and restaged for suspense? (The music is quite exciting at this point.) The wild chorus of elf-girls who whirl wili-like around Ove in Act I never make a reappearance. Would Bournonville have thrown them away so quickly? Ove, traditionally a mime role with no dancing, was changed in 1969 to accommodate a brief duet with Hilda; when Peter Martins took the part, a solo to a musical repeat was added. These are minor concessions to modern taste. But Ove's detached classical solo is out of harmony with the dance design of the ballet. In the very next scene, Birthe dances a decorous solo that is disturbed by eruptions of her troll nature. *A Folk Tale* is a character ballet; mime and dance are swept along on the same current of action.

Birthe, a difficult role, needs comedy and pathos. The solo, in which these elements must be held in balance, is a more tightly integrated version of Giselle's Mad Scene. Linda Hindberg, of the festival cast, was a ravening beauty, Annemarie Dybdal a hot-blooded termagant. Both were charming, but old photographs of Margot Lander and Ralov showed what the young dancers had missed—a Birthe who twinkled with sexual mischief. It should also be clearer than it was in this production how much damage the troll girl has already done to her fiancé when we meet him. Ove is under a spell not just of romantic melancholy but of morbid desire—he's in love with death. After his pact with Hilda (like Siegfried's pact with Odette), he clings for dear life to the goblet she has given him. Just as the goblet of life symbolizes Hilda's origins, it is Ove's destiny—he will drink healing waters from it and be freed—and Ove himself is a symbol of the wasteful passions of the age. He isn't really a hero; he's James or Albrecht reduced to a single attitude, one that we feel Bournonville detested. Arne Villumsen was the perfect icono-graphic Ove—pale, dark, obsessed, a man of few gestures. Villumsen's face recalls the actor Henry Daniell: the same hooded, withdrawn gaze, the same ability to glower without changing expression. Unsurprisingly, he is a great James. Yet it was his galvanic Gennaro in *Napoli* that persuaded me of Villumsen's major stature as a performer; until then he'd seemed too diffi-dent for star roles. His Hilda was Jeppesen, as attractive here as in every-thing else she did. This is an extraordinary dancer, gifted with ballon, with aplomb, with a lively sense of shape and continuity in phrasing, and with an ability—irresistible in a Romantic ballerina—to look even younger than she is. Like Lynn Seymour and Gelsey Kirkland, whose slightly wayward qual-ity she shares, she can make an audience rejoice in her presence. As the Sylph, with a hairdo and manner à la Schanne, she looked faintly old-fashioned; and she must guard against pertness. She was a bolder, though not a sweeter, Hilda than Mette-Ida Kirk, whose mime scenes I preferred for their stillness and variety. Hilda's life among the trolls took on an infinity of suggestion in Kirk's performance. Jeppesen had Hilda's leaping spirit, but Kirk had her tenderness; I would go back to Copenhagen just to see her reject Diderik's marriage proposal.

To Niels Kehlet, Fredbjørn Bjørnsson, and Lillian Jensen I think I pre-ferred the marginally more serious Johnny Eliasen, Hans Jakob Kølgård, and Mona Jensen as Diderik, Viderik, and Muri, but it was a hard choice. In gen-eral, festival casting wasn't always as considerate as it was here or in *Napoli*, where Eva Kloborg was a lovely Teresina, and Bjørnsson, Henning Kron-stam, and Niels Bjørn Larsen appeared in supporting roles. I must also mention the striking performance of Sorella Englund as an unusually young Madge in *La Sylphide*, amply bearing out the theory of the critic Svend Kragh-Jacobsen that Madge and the Sylph are sisters. There was always impeccable ensemble performing to be seen, especially in the thickly cast "vaudeville ballets." *Far from Denmark*, though, really is inscrutable to the non-Danish eye. Not only are cadets played en travestie but numbers of gentlemen in a party scene romp around dressed as women, which gives us travesty of quite another sort. Then the "boy" cadets do a dance dressed as women. Can there be sociological roots to those sex-change operations? I wrote about *The King's Volunteers on Amager* when it was done in New York three years ago. It's a more penetrable ballet by far, and the festival performance was a buoyant one, yet here, too, are oddities of casting; the way the roles are allocated in the second scene doesn't square with the first. The short all-dance ballets were *Konservatoriet, La Ventana,* and *Flower Festival Pas de Deux,* in the last of which Heidi Ryom, another of the strong young women the company is breeding nowadays, was partnered by the brilliant Ib Andersen, who is to join New York City Ballet. The way the Danes dance Bournonville is not the way it is done in New York. But whether the style is "historic" or "anachronistic" it is lucid on its home ground. The age of a theatre, the tempo of a city, the scale of its architecture prepare an ambience. To see the Royal Danish Ballet at home is to see it plain. One can still dissent from its style, but the pleasure of clear and consistent vision is such that one doesn't. It just feels better not to.

—December 24, 1979

Shuffling Cards of Identity

The talk turns to current entertainment, and you say, "Have you seen Bette Midler's show?" or "Have you seen *The Black Stallion*? It's wonderful," and people smile understandingly and start edging away. Praise Dance Theatre of Harlem and you get the same reaction. There are some things people would rather not enjoy. They don't exactly disbelieve your good news, but unfashionable good news is a burden. Bette Midler may be wonderful, but she isn't "in" wonderful, the way she was a few years ago, and she seems to have slipped out of the place prepared for her by the popular-culture experts. The same thing has happened on another level to Dance Theatre of Harlem. As in Midler's case, there was an initial experimental, somewhat precious phase, and then a period of expansion and consolidation, toward which people may feel less protective. Or maybe they feel they've taken one reading and would rather not have to go back for another. DTH was once pigeonholed as the black company that did classical ballet. It still is, of course, although it doesn't do ballet exclusively and never did. But since its cachet has worn off, there doesn't seem to be a special reason to go and see the company. True, it hasn't found many good original ballets to do, but it has that failing in common with just about every other repertory company, and in works good, bad, and in-between it can boast a standard of performance that is among the highest in American ballet. Yet "ballet people" aren't among the core supporters of DTH in anything like the numbers they should be. The current engagement at the City Center is being gratifyingly well attended, but the audience seems to be largely new to ballet. *Really* new. It yelps at the cygnets' pas de quatre in *Swan Lake*; it ogles every leap the way matinee audiences used to years ago. Perhaps the biggest element missing from this audience is the *nouveau* ballet public. For that public, ballet doesn't meet a deep need, it's just something to appropriate and feel easy with. I think the reason that DTH hasn't been appropriated is the feeling that it really doesn't belong to anybody. Even responsive and aware people I know seem to consider DTH faintly boring; maybe it's because they don't sense the company's appeal going past them out to some special-interest group like ballet fans or black people, and consequently they don't get the thrill of enjoying something that's really meant for others. And that is the way we enjoy things these days; we participate in other people's pleasures. There's no kick in going to see a G-rated horse movie, no matter how good it is. Whereas there's plenty in going to see a lurid true-confession movie like *All That Jazz* and roasting it afterward. *All That Jazz* is a Bob Fosse true confession; the time has come when a superchoreographer can be the hero of a major motion picture. We peer in on Fosse's specialized world; we revel in all that arcana. The next step is to make a movie about a homosexual superchoreographer. The separate particles are already out there in other shows and movies; you can feel them gravitating toward each other. (Make the guy Jewish and you've got the next Mel Brooks classic.)

So much popular entertainment since the sixties has derived its popularity from being aimed in a certain way at minority audiences (Midler once camped for a gay audience) that a broad base is almost automatically suspect. Ballet is narrow, but for some years now it has eluded categorization as a minority art. As it gains in general acceptance, though, internal categories appear—like "classical" versus "modern" or "neoclassical" or "Romantic" or "traditional." It's as if the great new public had to keep narrowing and specializing its taste in what it was once pleased to accept as just plain ballet. Subdivision is one way of holding on to the exclusivity of an art form, but amateurish distinctions can interest no one for long. In ballet there is a presumption—a fallacy, I believe—that the historical provenance of a work influences or ought to influence the way we experience it. Is this a neoclassical dagger that I see before me? All ballets, whether from the nineteenth or the twentieth century, are danced in the present tense and in the present mood, and *all* dance styles, no matter what their proponents may call them, are some variation on contemporary. This fact alone may be enough to explain why the style of dancing called ballet has caught on; more and more people perceive that it is of and for now. Yet, at the same time, it must contend with the inflamed snobbery that calls for categories, labels, pigeonholes, ways of breaking down and particularizing the experience in advance, ways of confusing the uninitiated. The joke in all this is that the experience of ballet is both more and less complicated than its *nouveau* connoisseurs wish to make it. Dance Theatre of Harlem quite naturally occupies a category of its own; else there would be no reason for it to exist. It descends and departs from the tradition of American ballet in the same way that American ballet forty-five years ago descended and departed from Russo-European ballet. Demonstrably, a Harlem company fills a need for cultural inflection. There is such a thing as black classicism, and it is a phenomenon, not an invention. Paradoxically, the stresses that black dancers lay on classical style end by bleaching it, but it comes out pure rather than white. One arrives at another standard of transparency. If you really watch the company for its dancing, it is not difficult to arrive at this other standard. It may be more difficult to retain your confidence in the process by which you have done so. That is what I meant by the complicated experience of ballet. That black classicists are classicists with a difference is visibly evident, but because the style both isolates and neutralizes their color it's as if they'd shuffled their cards of identity. Either they're not exotic enough for some people or they're too exotic—the difference amounts to inadmissible deviation. Well, classical norms are set by classical dancers, not their critics. The DTH norm is there to be seen. The trouble is, not enough people are going to see it.

The company this season took a calculated risk in putting on Act II of *Swan Lake* and opening it in New York instead of breaking it in on tour. Frederic Franklin staged it; with a few changes in choreography and some adjustments to modern practice (Benno, the Prince's friend, dances a variation but does not assist in the pas de deux), this version stems from the old Ballet Russe *Swan Lake* that Franklin used to dance with Alexandra Danilova. In these first performances, DTH looked much as it did at its inception, a decade ago—as if it were making a conscientious bid for respectability. The principals, Lydia Abarca and Ronald Perry, seemed overawed and overcoached; one could hardly blame them for the unfelt performances they gave. Abarca's soft musculature and infolding line could make her a resourcefully unorthodox Odette, but she was directed into rigidly orthodox positions. In a later performance, Virginia Johnson and Eddie Shellman were conventionally fluent but sound asleep. I wish the company had revived Balanchine's 1951 City Center version. It contained enough of the old choreography to please traditionalists, and it was staged with a musical and theatrical vitality that might still make sense to young dancers. For now, the DTH production justifies itself in the performing of the corps—*Swan Lake* seldom sees ensembles of such refined vigor. Two enormously tall lieutenant swans, Denise Nix and Lorraine Graves, left a vivid impression in waltz choreography that had been raised a few notches in difficulty. The stage picture is satisfying to look at, with its windswept sky and stark branches by Steven Rubin and its sunset lighting by Kevin Tyler. This is a sepia-and-pastel *Swan Lake*: the swans are dressed by Carl Michell in varying shades of pale blue, with Odette in the palest blue. Only the hunters' Aussie hats and the Sorcerer's masquerade-ball outfit are disruptive. While it isn't the best possible *Swan Lake,* it is one worth keeping and getting right, which will mean getting it to happen inside the dancers. The technical challenge is most clear-cut in the adagio, with its extended cantilena; but there is also a symbolic victory that the company wants to attain. White American dancers have managed to make themselves credible in this "Russian" classic; black dancers should have no trouble once the exam jitters are past.

Danilova was on hand this season to stage *Paquita,* a set of Spanish-style dances from the ballet by Petipa to music of Leon Minkus and Ernest Deldevez. The dancers, more at ease with the idiom, responded happily. The ballet's high point is an adagio in which fourteen girls provide a constantly changing frame for the lead couple; it looks like *La Bayadère* superimposed on *Don Quixote.* But those girls also perform without support some of the same figures the ballerina is given to perform with her cavalier—a unique and unforgettable drama. Elena Carter was both robust and delicate as the ballerina; Joseph Wyatt lent stylish assistance in the pas de deux and led a dashing pas de trois. The solo variations, all for women, are elegantly particularized as to accent and shape, but for these dancers they are easy conquests. And for a supposedly unfamiliar ballet they have a familiar look—not only shades of the Shades and of *Don Quixote* appear but also the Lilac Fairy and Aurora. *Paquita* is grand-style Petipa in a gala mood, but this revival finds him a trifle less imaginative than possibly he once was. For a third première, there was Glen Tetley's *Greening,* a ballet done originally for the Stuttgart company in 1975 and typical of the Tetley style, which exercises dancers hectically in short-winded and, so far as I can see, utterly incoherent movement combinations. Whenever the chunky phrase-units become too gaspingly tight, Tetley rushes in a lot of lifts, which have the effect of prolonging the impetus of a movement. It's just a deception, of course, like opening a bricked-up window on an airless room, but Tetley's ballets hardly ever fail to go over with an audience, and *Greening,* which seemed to follow a twisty narrative about the death and renewal of love or friendship or camaraderie in company class, must be counted a hit. If nothing else, it gave the habitually reserved Virginia Johnson some glamorous passages to dance with her hair loose.

The first two weeks of the engagement also brought fervent and scrupulous performances of Balanchine's *Serenade* and *The Four Temperaments,* and some glowing *Corsaires* with Carter and Perry. The interesting thing about this pas de deux, which DTH has always understood, is that both roles are feminine. But the woman is a civilized lady and the man is half savage. From the audience's point of view, there is no question which is sexier. Perry took Nijinsky's Golden Slave as his model; crouching with his eyes rolling in lust, undulating his torso, he was no less innocent than when flaring into a grande pirouette or a sit-spin leap. The company's outstanding classical stylist, Perry is also its most versatile performer; he appears in everything, sometimes so self-effacingly that he is unrecognizable. Like the rest of the company, he is ripe for the appreciation and encouragement of an intelligent ballet audience. But that audience also has its needs. I'm afraid that as long as DTH is unable to provide either the star choreographers or star dancers who could establish a clearer sense of its identity, it isn't going to have, in this country at least, the response it deserves. Abroad, it regularly electrifies the sophisticates. The dancers in the company are its richest resource; nightly they carry the cause of black classicism, and they do it virtually unaided. It may be a comment on our own sophistication that their fine dancing is not enough—that it can be brushed off as something to be expected, like sanitation in a restaurant.

Arthur Mitchell and Karel Shook, the directors of DTH, seem to have used as a guide to policy making W. B. Yeats's phrase "the fascination of what's difficult." The perfect ballet for them right now, setting the seal on their already admirably chosen Balanchine repertory, might be *Apollo*, which has as its theme the human aptitude for art and its growth from awkward instinct to mature expression. The fascination not only of what's difficult but of what's beautiful—and often the two are the same—motivates Apollo's destiny; the choreography does not lack for unpretty but rapturously beautiful images of arduousness and strain. Peter Martins has returned to the role in the New York City Ballet production, which since last year has been a truncated one. In his second performance of the season, Martins restored the solo that begins the second, major scene of the ballet— and so only the prologue, in which Apollo is born, is missing. Martins has the disadvantage of looking like the Apollo Belvedere—not the Apollo Balanchine has in mind—and he has to restrain his characteristic noble style in order to appear credibly immature. It was impressive to see him moving with a looser, less guarded grandeur, and even some primal rough energy, in the solos. Yet in his dances with Terpsichore and the other Muses Martins still makes a paternal Apollo. The opposite impression—of raw youth—was created by Jean-Pierre Frohlich. Perfect as Puck or Pan, Frohlich is simply too lightweight to sustain and develop an image of power, and no one else in the cast—neither Patricia McBride as Terpsichore nor Stephanie Saland and Elyse Borne as Calliope and Polyhymnia—was much good. Martins's Terpsichore was Heather Watts, substituting for Suzanne Farrell and using those misguided Farrellish mannerisms that have occasionally spoiled her dancing in the past. Kyra Nichols and then Merrill Ashley made strong débuts as Polyhymnia. Karin von Aroldingen completed the "tall" cast, dancing without spontaneity or flow. The conducting, by Hugo Fiorato, for the Frohlich cast was unwontedly slow. Robert Irving for the Martins performances set a quicker pace, but the music sounded glazed. and all the good moments in the dancing couldn't keep the ballet from seeming bloodless. Despite Baryshnikov's rousing performances last year, there is a pall over *Apollo*—a consequence, perhaps, of the reverence the dancers feel for the choreography and the solemnity with which they approach every step. When the Muses reach up from the floor to link arms with Apollo, they respond to the rising chords in the music as if they were receiving Holy Communion. What should be a set of simple gestures directly and untendentiously timed to the music becomes a ceremony of exaggerated, scooped-out ports de bras. When Balanchine means to make an exalted image, he makes one—as in the fantail of arabesques that opens in what is now the ballet's final moment. This is choreography that needs no elaboration by its dancers.

Martins's development as a choreographer has been remarkable in the past year. The company has his *Sonate di Scarlatti*, ten dances of vivacity and force, mostly allegro, set to a suite of piano pieces and using themes of courtship and rivalry. Martins creates affectionate, unsentimental dances for women; Lourdes Lopez and Lisa Hess are standouts in the Scarlatti ballet, and for a Public Library benefit concert at Alice Tully Hall he made a fine show out of Stravinsky's *Eight Easy Pieces* for Susan Gluck, Roma Sosenko, and Stacy Caddell. Martins's work is clean, polished, and witty; his construction is sound; his references (to Balanchine in *Eight Easy Pieces*) are distinct from his influences (Balanchine, Robbins, and Bournonville in the Scarlatti). I fear the men's dances in the Scarlatti are too hard for the dancers Martins has chosen to do them, and although they perform well, Bart Cook and Heather Watts don't seem to have the hang of the choreography in the ballet's one slow number. It might be salutary to see Martins himself in the principal male role, with Farrell.   —*January 28, 1980*

Swing Street Revisited

Fancy Free, the Jerome Robbins–Leonard Bernstein ballet about three sailors on shore leave, takes place on a hot summer night in 1944, the year of the ballet's première. The side street in Manhattan and the bar where the sailors drink were designed in Sunday-comics colors by Oliver Smith; their real-life counterparts were probably somewhere along the Hudson River piers, but the setting of the ballet has always seemed to be Fifty-second Street, or "Swing Street," as the block between Fifth and Sixth is now designated—the street of the jazz clubs that, like roistering sailors on shore leave, are with us no more. The ballet begins with a blues record playing in the dark; the song is "Big Stuff," by Leonard Bernstein, and in the American Ballet Theatre production the voice on the record has been Billie Holiday's for thirty-five years. I had never been able to tell what the song was—it was just a snatch of sound that preceded the overture. In the new production that Robbins has just supervised for New York City Ballet, Dee Dee Bridgewater sings in a specially made studio recording, and the record plays on long enough for us to identify the melody as the same one Bernstein uses in the pas de deux. When the curtain rose on the New York City Ballet production, I expected more revelations, and in fact the performance did resemble a newly scrubbed painting. Hard lines and colors appeared in place of soft edges and allusive pastels; vague contours and pliant, careless brushstrokes were erased. But the high definition wasn't a return to the original style; it was totally new, and it did strange things to *Fancy Free*. The central situation—of sailors picking up girls—seemed tense, the humor fell flat, with larky bits of business clinging to the stage like the edges of a damp soufflé. The dancers tried hard—maybe too hard. The breeziness and the innocence of the piece eluded every attempt to nail them to the ground.

A character ballet with musical-comedy overtones, *Fancy Free* is not at all typical of New York City Ballet, but at last year's School of American Ballet benefit performance the three solos were successfully performed by Jean-Pierre Frohlich, Mikhail Baryshnikov, and Peter Martins. At this year's benefit, the whole ballet was given, fully dressed in Smith's décor and Kermit Love's original costumes, and with Bart Cook in Baryshnikov's place and Stephanie Saland and Lourdes Lopez as the pickups. Last week, it went on the NYCB bills, where it joins the largest selection of Robbins ballets in active repertory, including the two that stand beside it as his masterpieces—*Afternoon of a Faun* and *Dances at a Gathering*. I would add *Interplay* to that list but for the fact that, after all these years, the eight dancers—who must be eight *young* dancers to be believable in the juvenile roles Robbins created—are seldom able to rise evenly and with full force to the technical demands of the choreography, which is classical-acrobatic with jazz accents. The current NYCB casts are probably the best classical dancers that *Interplay* has ever had, and their classical correctness has the effect of enclosing their 1945 hepcat roles in amused quotation marks. The dancers, though young, seem discriminating where earlier generations of NYCB dancers just seemed square. But *Interplay* celebrates its antique grooviness a little too thinly for comfort. I believe in the dancers' emphasis on correctness; I think it gives the ballet a clearer and truer sentiment than some of the show-bizzy interpretations we have seen. But that choice is helpless. Unlike the dancers of the forties and fifties, current casts aren't prey to the jive; they aren't familiar with any developed dance vocabulary outside the ballet. They're classical because they know no other technique.

Interplay and now *Fancy Free* point up the coincidences in the dance styles of an era—instances of momentary correspondence that flow across the board from the most academic to the most colloquial dance forms and that may be extended into parallels capable of nourishing the most academic, if not the most colloquial. Classical academic ballet goes on when the Lindy, the Shag, the Twist, and the Boogaloo are gone. But classical style is also mutable from generation to generation. The steps in the syllabus may be the same, but even the mechanics of execution bear the imprint of an era. In old ballet films, that imprint leaps out at you. The ballet dancers of the forties appear to have had more in common with the samba line at the Copacabana than they have with ballet dancers of today. Whatever that common impulse was, it is unrecapturable. The great overlapping wave of popular expression in dance and song came in the first fifty years of our century; we are still drifting in the hollow of that wave. And, in the absence of any comparably strong popular dance tradition, classicism today is impoverished. Our era dotes on the beauty of classical style at its purest and most austere. But it can also be an anemic purity, bled dry of support material, cut off from any enlivening influence of the vernacular. In the NYCB *Fancy Free*, the dancers' idea of a pop style is heavy and swaggering —the opposite of their own classical style and the opposite of the pop style of the forties, which was also lightly objective. They make the same kind of mistake singers make when they try to do the old popular songs; the words are doled out as if they belonged to the singer and not the song. (The arrogant stylizations of the PBS series "Song by Song" are the worst example of what I mean.) Agnes de Mille denounces disco as "autoerotic," but most show dancing is beefed-up narcissism, and both forms of dance, like the music that is written for them, are rhythmically dull. No classical tradition can survive this kind of drain, and choreographers, when they turn to old popular music and old popular dances, are largely unable to provide more than artificial resuscitation. In comparison with their strained efforts, *Fancy Free* was a lucky bum—the right ballet at the right time for American dance.

Different dance forms in the same era are more closely related than the same dance forms in different eras. We can imagine Balanchine's counting on the appeal of his *Serenade* to an audience that had seen Astaire-Rogers and Jessie Matthews movies. But photographs of *Serenade* taken in the thirties are disconcerting. Had the ballet not been kept in repertory, it might have had to be wholly re-created. Changing its shape now subtly, now radically, *Serenade* has over the years maintained its place and its essence: it has always been recognizably *Serenade*. The hope of perpetuation and continuity lies in repertory; so does the expectancy of permissible change. Without a continuous record of performances, even Ballet Theatre might find it difficult to stage an authentic *Fancy Free*. NYCB dancers have no skill in throwaway gesture. When the sailors tease the girl with the red shoulder bag, the action that at Ballet Theatre can look ad lib is so precisely set and executed that it becomes harsh: these boys might be muggers. And Martins and Saland massage the tender little pas de deux into an explosive sexual encounter. Saland in any case is too knowing, too seductive, and Lopez is

too patrician for the streetwise but "nice" girls that the ballet is supposed to
be about. The casting of the men is off, too. As characters, Martins and
Baryshnikov might have been plausible buddies, with Frohlich as a kind of
mascot. Now Martins, especially since he's been given the pas de deux,
looks like the star of the show, with Cook and Frohlich in support. Cook
dances the second, lyrical variation with a great deal of charm and care, but
he has the same misfortune that he has in *Stravinsky Violin Concerto*, of
being unequally cast against Martins. The second cast was better balanced.
Judith Fugate and Delia Peters are both believable white-collar working
girls. Fugate is as knowing as Saland but more vulnerable, and Peters sets
the comic tone the instant we see her long, droll face appearing around a
corner of the set. Douglas Hay, Christopher Fleming, and Joseph Duell,
performing the variations in that order, weren't—except for Duell—as brilliant as the first cast, but their spirits were higher, their control of the
ballet's moods was much more secure, and they looked like high-school–
age sailors. If virtuoso dancing is what *Fancy Free* is really about, Robbins
has been lying to us all these years.

Most of the events of note at City Ballet this season have been recyclings
or restagings. Besides *Fancy Free*, Robbins put on a suite of extracts from
the *Dybbuk* ballet he did several years ago with Bernstein, and Balanchine
has made a new piece of sorts, *Walpurgisnacht Ballet*, based on his dances
for a production of Gounod's *Faust* at the Paris Opéra in 1975. The
Robbins-Bernstein *Dybbuk* was a strangely misty affair, neither following
the famous old Yiddish play nor letting it alone. The ballet hung around
awhile under a new title, *The Dybbuk Variations*, and then it disappeared,
Robbins presumably having given up his idea of a dance commentary that
never disclosed its subject. The themelessness of the ballet and the name-
lessness of its horrors were intended, I think, to magnify the mystery of the
events related in the play. In *Suite of Dances (From "The Dybbuk Variations")* I seem to hear a voice saying, "Well, at least it works as dance."
It's dance insofar as it isn't drama; the eight episodes that Robbins has
excerpted don't really work at all. The steps are a progression of static
changes in body shape which never yield a cumulative image. In place of an
image, there is atmospheric business—stooping, twisting, shielding the eyes.
Bart Cook or Helgi Tomasson heads an ensemble of six men, three of whom
have solo variations. Especially with Cook in the lead, one can't help thinking of *Fancy Free* and the steep drop between it and this latest Robbins-
Bernstein creation. And in Robbins's case I can't help thinking that there
must be a personal dybbuk involved who saps his energy and turns him to
the pursuit of cosmic bellyaches in dance. Just when did Anna Sokolow
creep under Robbins's skin? The looming, empty portentousness of his
Dybbuk choreography has the look of one of her ethnic-expressionistic
sagas. Occasionally, the old Robbins spirit flies upward, as in Victor Castelli's
extraordinary butterfly tours-jetés. This is like a lungful of air, and the

normally limp Castelli seems to increase in strength and size as he flies. (Next to his Candy Cane in *The Nutcracker,* this is his finest moment.) Strange that the airiest of the *Dybbuk* dances should also be the weightiest. It's quite possible that the men were better dancers in 1974 than they are now; it's also possible that gravity in the form in which Robbins seeks it eludes him.

Balanchine this season brought back his *Cortège Hongrois,* which is *Raymonda* recycled, and not for the first time, either. It is rather coarse-grade ballet kitsch for much of the way; then suddenly, with the Grand Waltz, it's superb. In the opening section of this number, Balanchine quotes his *Raymonda Variations* for sixty-four measures, although in that piece he has the steps occurring to different music. But probably the great *Raymonda Variations* contained quotations, too—from previous Balanchine *Raymondas* or from the Maryinsky version whence they sprang. Even more interesting than the recurrence of steps, though, is the fact that they don't— or don't for long—recur in the same sequence. In the *Cortège* waltz, bits are flown in from all parts of the opening *Variations* waltz and are fitted into a new and coherent, completely familiar whole. This has been, in fact, Balanchine's basic approach when reconstructing various "Maryinsky" pieces— not only *Raymonda* but also *Swan Lake* and, for all we know, *Harlequinade.* One feels that in reshuffling the material he penetrates a work's substance, exposing an inner fiber that makes out of an apparently arbitrary fusion of ballet steps an entity we can recognize as "Essence of *Raymonda.*" It's a choreographer's game; Balanchine even jokes about it in *Cortège* when he holds off the ballerina's most famous passage—the plunging relevés-passés—until almost the last minute. The actual last minute, which used to have the whole cast posed and looking at the ballerina as if she were about to retire (the production was a farewell gift to Melissa Hayden), has been changed. The dancers now all face front and hold their tableau as if in tribute to the heritage of *Raymonda.*

I suppose some people will see the *Walpurgisnacht Ballet* as kitsch, too. It's a big, all-girl ballet in the innocent, cheerfully banal Paris Opéra style we know from *La Source* and *Ballo della Regina.* The only connection to *Faust* that I can see is in its visionary use of classic feminine types (maenads, bacchantes—all quite Parisian and proper, of course) and in the central role, which has been largely remade for Suzanne Farrell. The choreography here is diabolical and at the same time angelic; we think of poor Faust offstage, suspended between Heaven and Hell. There is a man's role in the ballet. Adam Lüders appeared as Farrell's partner but did not dance a solo. The single male variation was taken over by Farrell, along with some traditionally masculine steps, and she also danced a waltz variation that began with a series of off-balance grands battements and ended with some utterly novel devil's-trill chaînés that seemed to build on her thrilling multiple soutenu turns in *Chaconne.* Ended with them? Not quite. If memory serves, she froze the chaînés sequence shut, took a lightly careless attitude-front pose, held it, and leapt off. All this was accomplished without a single visible transition. This new or semi-new ballet was unveiled on the gala program with *Fancy Free*. Further performances may be scheduled before the season is over. It is a ballet to be seen many times. The simple patterns of the ensembles and the clear and buoyant solos for Heather Watts and Stephanie Saland scarcely prepare you for the complexity of Farrell's role, which in adagio as well as allegro passages goes beyond *Chaconne*. And that, right now, is about as far as anyone has gone.   —*February 11, 1980*

Present at the Creation

An old theatre program in my files tells me I saw *Rune* in 1960, danced by Merce Cunningham and the company he had then—Carolyn Brown, Viola Farber, Marilyn Wood, Judith Dunn, and Remy Charlip. I remember nothing of the event; it came at the end of a program that consisted of *Summerspace, Changeling* (the solo in which Cunningham, wearing a red bathing cap, seemed to struggle in amniotic fluid), and the satiric vaudeville *Antic Meet*. For someone who had never seen Cunningham's kind of dancing before, this was a lot to take in. Cunningham revived *Rune* a few years ago, and his company has been performing it since. It is still a loaded experience, the more so now that its aesthetic is no longer current either in the company or in the art world at large. *Rune*, which has music by Christian Wolff, scored for six or seven instruments, connects with ideas of indeterminacy, discontinuity, and chance action in the music and painting of the fifties; a note in the 1960 program informs us that "the continuity of this dance is so arranged that it can change from performance to performance." I'm not aware that Cunningham gives *Rune* this way today. The dancers have enough to master in the mechanics of the choreography, which expresses its period even more profoundly than its aleatoric structure does. *Rune*, like *Summerspace*, represents the lyrical Cunningham style at its peak. It passes like a cloudless day amid the tumultuous allegro of the later repertory, and each dancer in it stands in and commands space like a soloist. Today's Cunningham dancers are more of an ensemble, more impersonal in expression, and more regularized as to technique. Technically, their foundation is ballet, whereas in dancers of the fifties and sixties it was more likely to be modern dance of one school or another. But the important distinction between yesterday and today is that Cunningham style was then alive and hot in a way that it is no longer; it was emerging through a process of technical discrimination and was being rationalized in performance. See-

ing *Rune* at the City Center last week, I could feel the heat of that performance I blanked out on twenty years ago—feel it not as full-force revelation
but as a distant flickering glow, a surmise about the past. Yes, this was once
a great piece, and the fifties must have been golden to have produced it.

There is no substitute for seeing a work performed by dancers who were
present at the creation. Cunningham was in those days inventing for himself
as well as training others in his inventions; the style came from inside. When
Catherine Kerr stands alone upstage in *Rune* and turns her head as others
enter, I'm aware only that something wonderful that used to happen is not
happening now. But when she is being partnered by Cunningham in his
newest work, *Duets*, I'm very much aware of Catherine Kerr; she's herself
and not a stand-in for Viola Farber. At the same time, I don't feel Kerr's
presence the way I might have felt Farber's or Brown's. She simply doesn't
weigh as much in the equations that Cunningham currently works with.
Perhaps no one else does, either. The company Cunningham has today is a
remarkably strong and gifted one, of sterling Silver Age caliber. The only
thing that shows it up is a Golden Age revival.

There is a theory that Merce Cunningham is primarily a soloist, only
secondarily a choreographer. And it is true that he has maintained his
status as the greatest American-born inventor of contemporary dance
largely through his perception of the needs and resources of the performer.
He is still showing us his personal magic, as in the solo *Tango*, with its
concise feats of coordination performed mostly in place. But Cunningham
at sixty doesn't create from inside anymore. I think a large share of the gut
feeling that used to go into his choreography now goes into his filmmaking.
The choreography, while brilliant and fascinating as only his can be, looks
more like problem solving. He has always been a believer in restricted
means, in working within confines. God knows what limitations he must
have placed upon the making of the six pas de deux in *Duets*; they look like
the dance equivalent of no-hands juggling on the high wire. Yet *Duets*
comes off the most felicitous of his new pieces. *Roadrunners* and *Locale* are
both successful, but they're measurably successful—the actual deed measured
against a gamut of possibilities. *Duets* runs its gamut so fast you think there
can't be more to come; but there is, and still more. It hides its possibilities
by disclosing them.

Duets features the women of the company almost as if they were ballerinas, and on one level the interest of the piece deepens as we watch
Cunningham ring changes on academic definitions of leverage, balance, and
support. His women grow upright and free—standing about two feet away
from their partners, they seem to challenge them for support—yet they're
capable of winding themselves like vines around a column. And they can
sustain adagio motion with an almost winged attack and follow-through,
even though they're not on point and Cunningham is very sparing, as usual,
of lifts. Here is a link to Old Style that has not been broken. The women of

Rune, too, had to have superb adagio technique. But what I chiefly remember when I think about *Duets* is the suddenness with which each couple appeared and made a clear shape different from and yet consistent with the shape just before. That elastic differentiation was what gave the piece a vividness beyond the scope of academic or anti-academic bravura. *Duets* has the economical abundance of Cunningham's current work at its finest, and it has a truly collaborative score by an Irish father-and-son team of drummers, Peadar and Mel Mercier. The monochromatic pounding, with its varied tattoos, matches both the narrow spectrum and the fertility of the choreography. Like David Tudor's score for *Sounddance,* the sound adds pressure to our concentration on the dancing—but a temperate, not an agitating, pressure. The dancers are, of course, unaffected by it; it is tempting, though, to relate the wild moments when the drumming gets very loud to moments in the dance, such as Karole Armitage's three hair-raising leaps onto her partner's back.

Jon Gibson's score for *Fractions,* originally composed for solo flute, was (like *Rune*) played this season on a piano, so we lost the amplified breath of the flute player which seemed so appropriate to a dance score. Everyone knows that in a Cunningham production the dance, the sound, and the décor are created independently. Points of agreement or disagreement are part of the unpredictable flow of a performance. An unsystematized system has its rewards in scores that are in effect collaborative (*Rune, Duets, Fractions*), coercive (*Sounddance*), evocative (*Inlets*), or neutral (*Fractions* on the piano). Yet there are hazards. I've expressed irritation with some of the scores Cunningham has used lately. Breaking down the causes of irritation, I find that the scores I dislike most are those with sudden loud noises (*Exchange*); those with words (a list lengthened by *Roadrunners* and *Locale*); and non-scores—the kind that are pitched so low or incorporate so much silence that the chief accompaniment becomes the panting of the dancers. Non-scores—*Torse* is an example—may start with a good intention; the composer may just be trying to keep out of the way of the dancing. But there is a line between effacement and dereliction. The panting in *Torse* focusses our attention on the exertions of the dancers instead of on the dance. But then the element of excruciation in *Torse* was very noticeable this season, particularly in Part I. *Torse* is the ultimate classroom ballet and may be the ultimate I Ching ballet, too. The steps are utterly unforeseen permutations of academic combinations, and they come in such thick clusters that the audience is as winded as the dancers. I have enjoyed watching *Torse* in studio presentations, as part of an Event miscellany, even on film. As a twenty- or thirty-minute stage spectacle, and especially as the opening work on a program, it is a killer.

Roadrunners, with its suggestions of Near and Far Eastern temple dance and sculpture, displays Cunningham eccentricity of a more conventional kind. Much of the continuity of the piece is insistently absurdist, a mode I don't find too congenial, but the organic consistency of *Roadrunners* is certainly impressive. I suppose one would have to count as "organic" the accompaniment, by Yasunao Tone, in which ancient Chinese tales about imaginary kingdoms and their inhabitants are read aloud from the pit. As always, though, words spoken while dancing is going on immediately divorce our attention from the dance. In *Roadrunners*, the words were dismembered and their syllables split between two speakers, Takehisa Kosugi and John Cage. This was more intrusive than usual; hearing dissociated syllables does not lessen our interest in the words, it only drives us to listen harder ("Sex-ual or-gans are i-*den*-ti-cal in the male and fe-male"). I don't know which is coyer: the pretense that the words don't apply to the dance or the "coincidence" that they do. Those of us who object to this double-pronged assault are accused of a distaste for ambiguity, for the rich unregulated texture of life. We're wrong for wanting to see a dance performance without being pawed by musicians. Would that great fusionist of the arts Diaghilev really have loved Cunningham (as the company's ads say) with the dance and the music pulling not in the same direction but in opposite ones? Musicians of the Cage school often seem to be as insensitive to verbal meaning as they are to dance meaning: they're like those graphic artists who design the catalogues of their shows in unreadable typefaces. (Cage's writings are often printed in a mixture of typefaces selected by chance.) *Locale*, composed by Kosugi, uses word dissociation in the hope, no doubt, that we will hear sounds, just sounds. A word is repeated several times and, after an interval, another word, and so on. Just as the words begin to make a sentence, the curtain falls. The pain I feel as I report this is nothing compared with the pain of sitting there listening. Oh, those 1947 rebels!

An alternative version of this score is heard in the movie of *Locale*—no words but lots of groans and moans. When I first saw this exuberant new film of Cunningham's, no soundtrack had yet been attached; I reacted to sheerly visual stimulation. Seen on a monitor, the bouncing in the extended panning shots that characterize the picture wasn't anything like the turbulence that was nearly intolerable when projected in 16-mm on the screen at the City Center. The scale was too gigantic to be comfortably read. *Locale* is yet another kind of experience when done live. It is a lot slower, but it's not just the tempo and fluidity of the film that one misses; it's the way things are integrated in space that makes the biggest difference. About all there is to recognize in the stage version is incidents; it has an *incidental* resemblance to the film.

And an incidental revelation of the film is the striking good shape the dancers were in when they made it. *Locale* was shot a year ago, not long after Cunningham had assembled his present company. With only one exception, the same dancers are with him today. All but Armitage and Chris

Komar went through the City Center season looking under par. Even the redoubtable Robert Kovich performed without his customary edge, and many of the younger women had lost the attack and the cohesive style they were beginning to show a year and a half ago. Not until *Duets* did they dance with spirit and sharpness, and the only time the whole company seemed to relax was in *Changing Steps et cetera*, the charming suite of small-scale dances which Cunningham has festooned with excerpts from other pieces. Probably it was performing in flu season that got everybody down. But, flu or no flu, look at that repertory! Of fifteen ballets, there are possibly a dozen that rank among the world's most intricate and strenuous, and eight of these bring on everybody or nearly everybody in the company. To perform this lavish, high-density rep there are exactly fifteen dancers, counting Cunningham. Who can afford to fall sick or sprain a muscle? No wonder the dancers looked ashen and joyless so much of the time. *Torse II* down, *III* coming up. —*March 10, 1980*

Murder, He Said, Said He

As thirty-nine-year-old suicidal Jane in a disaster-prone show called *When We Were Very Young*, Twyla Tharp played a part that fits the way she looks and dances. The hellbent energy, the comic, hard-boiled defensiveness, the quizzical temperament, and the beautiful, sexy legs were accommodated in the role of a furious child-woman whose motor races all the way to destruction. Accommodated but not released. The show, as staged by Tharp herself from a script by Thomas Babe, was so shapeless that although she worked very hard as Jane, she only seemed to be getting started when the curtain came down. Worse, there was no room in the script for dances; Babe's playlet and John Simon's music, both commissioned for this project, were bereft of dance cues. Tharp supplied the dances anyway, and the brusque, driven style she used sat oddly with the vagaries of Babe's text—the dances looked like a series of assaults on meaning. Only one or two of them were set pieces that carried their own life. The result was that a ninety-minute "dansical" choreographed and staged (and christened) by Twyla Tharp for her company's first season on Broadway had less dance interest than one had a right to expect. Except for her own role, which was the only substantial role and which was largely a sketchy, uncoordinated farrago of bits, there was not a thing in the show that needed to be seen by an enthusiast of Twyla Tharp's.

As for having any other kind of interest, the show was thick enough with episodes of clamor and violence to seem a familiar spectacle to a Broadway audience. Toward the end, there was the obligatory reconciliation episode (called "Reconciliation" in the program); we could recognize it by feel, the way we recognize the penultimate moment in a TV drama we're only half watching. The show had these conventional textures, but it also had an unconventional structure, with the action skipping back and forth in time, scrambling the characters' identities or layering fantastic events on top of actual ones, and this may have seemed important, original, even avant-garde. In fact, scene after scene was plunged into confusion, but if that bothered the audience at the Winter Garden, it didn't let on. At both the performances I attended, this audience, which was not a partisan dance audience but a genuine, pleasure-seeking Broadway crowd, behaved as if being up to its eyes in murk were perfectly normal. When the curtain fell (a bit early for a Broadway show, but that may have been an advantage in the transit strike), the theatre was filled with the sound of hearty approval. People who have mistrusted Tharp's success from the beginning are taking this latest hit as evidence of yet another concession to glamour and commerce. The fact that it's a weak show that will probably never be done again apparently makes no difference—it's the judgment of Broadway that matters. But if it had flopped the show would still have been a failure, not least because it tends to confirm the things Tharp's detractors have been saying. Tharp, in this one misadventure, has indeed gone Broadway, and she needn't have.

Tharp's work—I am not familiar with Babe's—has often had a naive look, though it is far from naive in substance. The look came from her use of folk and popular music and dance forms, from her precocity of invention, and from her affection for past eras of popular entertainment. She has had her "Broadway show" in the works for some time; last year excerpts were previewed in her season at the Brooklyn Academy, where they played more excitingly than they do in the actual production. This was long before Babe came into it. One might expect her vision to be the dominant one, but it isn't—her vision isn't even her own. From those previews, there was no way to guess that what was germinating was a musical about parents and children who may unexpectedly take each other's places. If this was Babe's contribution, it is not at all a bad idea for a show that was to be played entirely by dancers. But Tharp seems to have been thinking in Broadway terms from the start, in loud colors, cute bits of business, cheeky attitudes. The naiveté in this case is all in the staging; she simply hasn't known how to put the thing across. And was it worth putting across? We got flashes of something genuine in the discontinuities that at times made Jane the same age as her son. Twyla Tharp belongs in a children's musical; I'd love to see her in some version of *Oz* playing a scowling half-pint combination of Dorothy and the Wicked Witch. *Deuce Coupe*, her ballet about teen-agers in the sixties, and *The Bix Pieces*, her dance "about remembering," are next of kin to *When We Were Very Young*. But there wasn't much of a family resemblance. The staging wasn't in the light, lyrical style of *Deuce Coupe* or *The Bix Pieces*—it was in a broad, tough, clodhopping style. When a moment of direct lyric emotion occurred, it looked satirical. Maybe it was satirical. This is the hard-edged Tharp that many people find unpleasant. She has used the style before (in parts of *Ocean's Motion*, the fifties counterpart of *Deuce Coupe*, and in *The Fugue*, to mention two examples in the Winter Garden repertory), but she's never used it ambiguously. If the movement wasn't self-explanatory, it was explained by the music. Away from her usual mode of concentration on movement or on movement to music, Tharp seems lost. She commits all kinds of boners. Playing children, her dancers stood around like hulks with their toes turned in. She distinguishes between the chorus, in anonymous white leotards, and the characters, in baggy pants and hair curlers, and then blurs the distinction constantly by having the chorus dancers alternate with the character dancers in the four character parts (mother, father, daughter, son). Jane's wardrobe of flower prints, outsize tea gowns, a bathrobe, a raincoat, a baseball cap is in the clunking Lotte Goslar tradition of eccentricity. But what is the meaning, if any, of Jane's *black* leotard? Have alter egos ever worked in dance? Has a narration that has to be shouted over orchestral climaxes ever been heard? And where have we ever seen narrators suspended on platforms high over the stage? (Santo Loquasto's set has ladders, but they're never used.)

Collaborating with Babe, Tharp seems to have taken what she wanted from his text and let him keep the rest. Jane's tragedy is that she's unfit for life as a grownup. We're told that she died in a hospital after a fire, but there are also implications of suicide. Anyway, Jane dies in her fortieth year and goes to Child Heaven, Babe's point being, I suppose, that only children who grow up are really dead. As a father telling the story of Jane, his mother, to his small daughter, Babe narrates the play, filling the air with sentimental ironies and phrases like "the green straight light of the springtime." The script sounds like high-contrast radio dialogue for the Softie and the Shrewdie.

> NARRATOR: *Dead. Deceased. Went away.*
> CHILD: *Grew up, you mean?*

Sitting up in their aerie (which Jennifer Tipton has lit like a radio booth), these two are the ones who dominate the show. The child actress Gayle Meyers, with her impatient attack, her glib way with profanity, and her impeccable mike technique, may be Babe's caricature of Twyla as a moppet. But, unlike the script for *The Bix Pieces*, which turned the performance into something between a lecture-demonstration and a public confession, Babe's text doesn't catalyze the action. And the action only now and then corresponds to the text. Tharp doesn't develop any of the scenic possibilities in the fire or in Child Heaven, but she does use the suicide (a plunge off the stage into the pit), and she loves best of all the travesty on the lines from the A. A. Milne book that gives the show its title. Indeed, by taking

> *James James*
> *Morrison Morrison*
> *Weatherby George Dupree*
> *Took great*
> *Care of his Mother*
> *Though he was only three*

and pretending that the poem is some sort of cryptogram of incest, the show gains the nearest thing it has to a central conceit. The conceit is so unpalatable in its kittenish cynicism that one may miss it simply by refusing to believe that it is there. In fact, I did miss it the first time I saw the show. I went back hoping to get closer to the play's intention, and lo. One of Twyla Tharp's earlier word-and-dance experiments, *The Double Cross*, contained the line "Believing is seeing." I began to see that, on the level on which this show wants to succeed, there was something not only promising but inspiring in

> *James James*
> *Said to his Mother,*
> *"Mother," he said, said he:*
> *"You must never go down to the end of the town,*
> *if you don't go down with me."*

Anyone with half a dirty mind can see the possibilities. And there's that other great line, about Mother having been "mislaid." The incestuous emphasis doesn't turn A. A. Milne's whimsy against itself; it's too awkwardly expressed to do much damage to anything (and it's even more whimsically adorable than A. A. Milne). Tom Rawe plays Dan, Jane's husband; Raymond Kurshals is Jason, her son. (Katie Glasner, as the daughter Megan, has little to do.) There's more role-switching between father and son than there is in the story of Oedipus, but even here Tharp is inconsistent, dancing what the program calls a "Sensuality" pas de deux with neither man. Is her partner, John Carrafa, a double for the father or the son?

About the only sin Tharp doesn't commit is the sin of making her dancers sing and recite dialogue. They do "James James" repeatedly as a choral chant timed to a march step; only Tharp ever speaks more than one line. The score has no songs. John Simon has provided mood music, and his moods come out of a can. His best contribution is a disco dance, but not even the ingenious slow-rolling choreography can turn it into theatre music. *When We Were Very Young* isn't a musical; it isn't a dansical. Like so many shows that are being produced today, it's a booksical. Unlike so many of those, it doesn't have a big costly set. Perhaps thinking to make art of adversity, Tharp commissioned a "poverty" production from Loquasto—motley street clothing, dancewear, a set made of cardboard cartons. I've never seen this normally resourceful, elegant designer at such a loss. Loquasto has not so much designed a production as provided building blocks for one. The point of using cardboard cartons, surely, is to show how economically they do the work of expensive scenery, but there are so many cartons on the stage of the Winter Garden as to make no appreciable difference when they're rearranged from scene to scene. Anyway, isn't it too late to try and make the tacky budget-production idea work? Poverty as a theatrical idea lost its validity the minute the audience started showing up in denim. Cardboard cartons are the equivalent of the police sirens and Klaxons that we hear in Simon's score when the scene changes to a street (and a little flag drops down saying "Street"). Klaxons in 1980!

When We Were Very Young is the clumsiest attempt to do something new and different that a gifted choreographer has made since Jerome Robbins's Watermill. Next to Robbins, Tharp looks like a true kamikaze. His problem was strained seriousness; hers is strained kitsch. When We Were Very Young ran in repertory with a number of her other pieces, all of them superior artistically and vastly more entertaining. Tharp has never had to struggle or dissemble for her work to have popular appeal. She drew full houses every night during the three-week engagement, no small achievement in a theatre the size of the Winter Garden. Brahms' Paganini, the other première of the season, was the only work set to music that wasn't jazz or pop or rock; like all the others, it was cheered to the echo. Tharp has choreographed both books of Brahms's piano variations. The first book, danced nonstop by one male soloist, is a tour de force comparable to the Baryshnikov solo in Push Comes to Shove. In the second half, the spectacle of autonomous virtuosity is replaced by the spectacle of interdependent virtuosity in a group. Two couples run close, fast changes on the theme of body leverage, linkage, manipulation, and displacement in space. It's sudden-death acrobatic partnering—the dance as corrida. Shelley Washington with Kurshals and Shelley Freydont with Carrafa display a brash precision; in the second cast, Christine Uchida with Anthony Ferro and Freydont with John Malashock are only marginally less formidable. A fifth dancer (Jennifer Way) turns occasionally through the scene without joining in, a reminder of the first dancer's autonomy. Brahms' Paganini is an overwhelming confirmation of Tharp's skill at her true craft, choreography. In the solo, danced with tenacity by Richard Colton or with calm assurance by William Whitener, we see her picking up new steps (scratch-spins—from John Curry?), remodelling old ones, and making connections between steps mean something, too. The new virtuosity seeks continuous expression, not intermittent dazzle. In the quartet, the dancers' precision mitigates the presence of danger. So does the style of the choreography, which mingles lucidity with perversity and bravura with burlesque. Depending on your tolerance for what it does to Brahms, it can seem overproduced—like using Seurat's technique to do "L'il Abner." Like Pop Art, which in fact it is.

Astonishing to think that when Tharp made *Deuce Coupe*, seven years ago, she knew almost nothing about partnering. Her company now dances the piece in the Joffrey Ballet version, including the parts that were originally composed for Joffrey dancers. In "Wouldn't It Be Nice," the girls' point technique is still advancing, but this is a company that has extended its range to include classical dancers like Whitener without losing—indeed, while strengthening, authoritatively through Shelley Washington—its "folk" identity. The ballerina role is given full-fledged interpretation by Rose Marie Wright, who looks in her clouds of white tulle like an enormous out-of-scale mother swan. When she leads on the other dancers in "Cuddle Up," she seems to be taking them all under her wing. Wright is a veteran Tharp dancer dancing a Tharp role that happens to be couched in the ballet vocabulary. There's no break in her style between the regulation ballet steps, which she does, and the steps everybody else does. I think this is what Tharp intended all along. Sara Rudner was back to dance her solo better, possibly, than she'd ever danced it before. The only false note in the production was the sixties political slogans painted on the backcloth by "graffiti" artists, which weren't in keeping with the subject of the ballet. The painting itself was fine. Programming *The Fugue* in between *Eight Jelly Rolls* and *Deuce Coupe* took nerve, and, as it turned out, this austere trio performed in silence on a miked stage took a while to seduce the audience. But I thought Tharp minimized its chances by casting three men in roles made for three women. With the men (Rawe, Kurshals, Carrafa) stomping about like disconsolate stagehands, the piece loses all its wildness and incongruity, and nothing takes the place of the tension that comes into it when it is danced, as it was a few seasons ago, by a woman and two men.

Now that Tharp knows partnering, does she know all? Has she taken choreography as far as she can go? *Brahms' Paganini*, for all its brilliance, compounds known strengths. The quartet is more extravagantly wrought but not greater than the duets in *Baker's Dozen*, which was new last year. The solo is way out there, but it is Tharp challenging the dancer, not Tharp challenging herself. I think she may have undertaken the unaccustomed risks of *When We Were Very Young* out of a need to find and develop a fresh area of expertise. She gets nearly everything wrong, and when she's right—for Broadway—she's terrible. Is it merely accidental that this début in Robbins-Fosse territory should have found her technically unready but dead on pitch in less tangible matters of attitude and tone? At first, the surprising thing about her work here is its absence of tone. She misuses tight dance continuity to bind heterogeneous story elements, for example, which produces a tonelessness characteristic of the amateur. But Tharp's work also has the manic-depressive tonelessness, the directionless anger, the mordancy we feel throughout our theatre today. I haven't seen this much bile in Tharp since she first began choreographing. Fifteen or so years ago, she was going in for outrage—invading the audience, throwing props around. A lot of people were doing that then. But Tharp was madder than most. At the same time, she was funnelling her energy into "conceptual" structures that would have totally neutralized emotion if structures were capable of such a thing. As she progressed in technique, her rhetoric became emotionally more permissive. But her own emotion had lightened a good deal by then; she could be neutral even when her work wasn't. *When We Were Very Young* represents a first attempt in an unfamiliar field, a floundering, self-conscious attempt to declare herself a dramatic personality. Technically, she's back in the period when she choreographed her tantrums and smashed chairs on the stage. How, looking at the shambles she has made of this latest upscale venture, can anyone call her work slick? It's as raw as· a new wound. How can anyone, looking at that last big solo she dances, not see the murder in her eye as she launches the manège to a musical pickup that sounds like the start of *Oklahoma!?* No, this isn't the Judson Church, it's the Winter Garden. And this is the Tharp of 1980, swimming with the tide and willing to go under, all over again.

The greatest acrobats I've ever seen were in the Shenyang troupe that came from the People's Republic of China to the City Center for the briefest of stands several years ago, during the Ping-Pong era in American-Chinese relations. The Shanghai Acrobatic Theatre, which has just left the City Center to begin a three-month cross-country tour, is, I understand, no relation to Shenyang. All the more amazing, then, that it should be just as impressive, if not quite as spectacular, and in a wider variety of tumbling, balancing, juggling, and illusionist tricks. The Shanghai acrobats are for the most part very young, with pliant young bones and sinews. The contortionists don't have the forbidding knotty muscularity that usually makes this specialty, to me, so unattractive. All the bodies look smoothly conditioned and show a springy grace. Apparently, there is good gymnastic training to be had in Shanghai and good dance training as well.

Occasionally, the show falls short in suspense. An incessant orchestra gives away the payoff of every stunt. And the young women who spin plates atop handfuls of bamboo sticks and who keep on doing it even while rolling completely over on the floor never let us see, even for an instant, that the plates aren't *fixed* to the sticks—that they *can* stop twirling and even fall. In *Circus Techniques*, by Hovey Burgess, the chapter "Spinning a Plate on a Stick" warns the neophyte, "It is important not to panic just because it is wobbling. A gyroscopic object's tendency to stay in place is incredible." Even so. These cool maidens could be performing in a science fair. The Jolly Cooks used, instead of hand-held sticks, poles, which they stood on end. They'd get the rice bowls going and then forget all about them until one would start to wobble, then another, then another. Somehow, the fact that there were enough cooks to tend the bowls made all the frantic rushing and shrieking funnier than if there'd been only one. The Jolly Cooks did everything at top speed. For a finish, they fired a stream of plates across the stage at one poor cook, who just managed to keep himself from being cut in half by catching them in a stack.

Whether to come within an eyelash of disaster or to remain serenely secure is not always left to the performer. Those acts that involve hurling people through the air onto each other's shoulders need no dramatization. Neither do those in which pagodas of objects are built on noses or foreheads. The man who performs this feat in the Shanghai company makes a fine tall stack of trays of glasses and trays of vases and trays of assorted unidentifiable but obviously breakable objects, and at the end the whole teetering thing lights up like a chandelier. At the *very* end, still balancing, the juggler braces himself between two ladders and climbs them. This man, Zhang Guoliang, must be among the world's most skillful practitioners of object-upon-object balance juggling. But he did not drive from my mind his counterpart in Shenyang, a small woman who looked to be about fifty. (Zhang Guoliang is also of middle years, which suggests either that the art is dying or that it takes that long to master it.) Along with her name, I have forgotten what-all she piled on top of her nose, but it made something altitudinous. I do remember that a tray holding four bowls of water was at the bottom and a tray holding four eggs stood on end was at the top. And what the lady did was take a baton and whap the side of the pagoda once. Whap! and all the intervening objects flew away, leaving the four eggs to plop into the four bowls of water. It is not known for how many minutes they boiled. —*April 21, 1980*

Doing the *Old Low Down*

No Maps on My Taps, which can be seen over PBS stations, is a sweet, reflective, back-alley movie about three aging hoofers in Harlem—how they live and, when they can manage to get a gig, how they work. Chuck Green, Bunny Briggs, and Howard (Sandman) Sims are all former headliners. Chuck Green was the dancing half of Chuck and Chuckles, the appointed heirs to Buck and Bubbles. Bunny Briggs became famous in the twenties as a child star. Sandman Sims began as a boxer, cutting steps in the resin box; he did his sand dance at the Apollo for seventeen years. All three men are fine dancers still. The film shows that, and it depicts them as the last of a great line—artists who would like to pass their tradition along but know there are no takers. Although the tap-dance revival that began in the sixties has lately risen to a peak, its dominant mood is elegiac; it fits in with the recycled old musicals, the fads for forties clothes and hairstyles and furnishings, and the Preservation Society reverence in which we now hold the popular art of the past. Chuck Green and Bunny Briggs and Sandman Sims, along with a dozen other veterans of the swing-bebop era, are being seen and celebrated these days by new audiences. Tap-dance studios are full. But as an art of the people tap barely survives; it is a subcultural expression, like jazz. In *No Maps on My Taps*, Sandman Sims blames rock for the ruin of tap, and he tells the manager of the Apollo, "Rock closed this theatre." The manager quietly replies that rock is what people get on their radios. Times change. "For the three of us, it's probably the last hooray," Sims says. One wishes it weren't true.

One wishes, too, that the last hooray weren't also, for so many in the audience, the first one. Many of the black dancers of Sims's generation have had to wait until now to become known to white audiences. And it is, by and large, the white audience that has rediscovered tap. The performance scenes in the film, at Small's Paradise, were staged by the filmmaker, George T. Nierenberg; it had been years since Small's had booked tap-dancers. On Harlem streets, we are introduced to dancers who have never been seen downtown and probably never will be. But when Sims speaks of the talent walking down the street going to waste, he doesn't mean these obscure older men, some of whom have never had professional careers; he means the young people who aren't plugged in to the tradition. Sims thinks that all you have to do is show them what they've been missing—not an Astaire or Kelly movie but an old-time Apollo show, with a band, a singer, a dancer, and a novelty act. Well, the show might be a hit, but how many new tap-dancers would it produce? White boys didn't need to see and hear white musicians to know they wanted to play jazz; they wanted jazz—it was the air they breathed. A young black today would have to adopt tap as a conscious artistic vocation and practice it in isolation. Some young blacks have done so, but too few to count.

In another new film, *Tapdancin'*, the current tap scene is so exhaustively presented and analyzed that one wonders about the dancers who are left out and the questions that aren't answered. It's sad to hear a great performer like Honi Coles say that he believes he could have done better but for racism; it sounds logical, as when Sandman Sims says of the young, "They never see a black dancer dance where it relates to them." But what are we to think when the camera turns from Coles to pick up some passing teenagers? There go the disinherited? Hollywood couldn't make a star of Paul Draper, and it was probably because Draper (who is one of the dancers *Tapdancin'* omits) had a style that in its own terms was as pure as the style of the blacks. There were other white dancers who came closer to what the blacks actually did. These white men had no impact comparable to Astaire's and Kelly's, because they weren't musical-comedy dancers, and musical comedy was what Broadway and Hollywood produced. A large grudge can be held against commercial theatre and film on racial grounds; the record is bad enough without incriminating the future, too. If kids don't want to tap-dance anymore, there are plenty of reasons, and they're probably the same for whites as for blacks.

The decline of tap is linked to the decline of big-band jazz and jazz-affiliated pop. If music for dancing is being mass-produced today, it isn't the listenable, rhythmically intricate music that tap masters understand. *Tap-dancin'* (a Christian Blackwood film) seeks out some of the new tappers, but only one, Camden Richman, has something to show and something to say. Camden Richman, like nearly all this younger generation, is female and white, and she may be the best technician of the lot. In her film interview, she makes the point that tap technique, following bebop, developed such complexity that by the late forties it wasn't mass-marketable. Richman may be correct on the historical evolution, but I think that the reason for the decline in mass appeal wasn't what came into the music but what went out. Richman's model is Honi Coles (you can hear the resemblance), and it seems that she has also based her performance on her idea of historical jazz dance. She dances with the Jazz Tap Percussion Ensemble, consisting of two other white dancers and an instrumental group, also white; the dancers call themselves "tap percussionists," but though they emulate the Harlem hoofers' technique, what they in fact present is percussive Perrier. The JTPE, which appeared this winter at the American Theatre Laboratory, was formed last year in Los Angeles. It's a cool, laid-back bunch; at its best, the dancing provides a discreetly absorbing panorama of sound. The nuances are a little overstarched, just as the sensibility is a little modern-dance frugal. The musical-comedy approach, which includes sex, glamour, high spirits, is ruled out. Comedy is not done, though one may be witty. Richman, in addition to her technical ease and personal elegance, has a sense of play. But JTPE tends to embody an attitude or a theory rather than a style, and I find the music supercilious. Only in a horizonless environment like L.A. would one try to make art out of watered-down entertainment. The JTPE brings to mind all those theses on the pressure of the big cities and its influence on jazz. Maybe the postwar decline of the cities had something to do with making tap dance obsolete (or driving it underground); we're growing conscious of it again now that we're restoring our cities.

Blacks, of course, could never afford to give up the city. For them, tap is an urban art and an art of urbanity. It started on the levee; today, we think of pavement under tapping feet. In both *No Maps on My Taps* and *Tap-dancin'*, which are complementary in treatment, and even in subject, we are taken from littered, glaring streets into stuffed apartments, bleak rehearsal studios, and dressing rooms so bare it's a wonder that anything can be prepared there. Sandman Sims shows his small son the place in the alley behind the Apollo where the hoofers used to gather for their challenge dances. This is in *No Maps*, which is often shown as a prelude to a live stage production starring the dancers in the film. It may be seen locally in that format this summer. In the meantime, we have had several stupendous evenings of live tap at the Brooklyn Academy of Music, which this month repeated its program called *Steps in Time*, bringing out not only Sims and Green and Briggs and Coles and the tap fraternity known as the Copasetics but also the Nicholas Brothers, who are in a class by themselves. Except for Gregory Hines, the young star of *Eubie!*, it was a grandfatherly assortment. But the Nicholas Brothers couldn't be anybody's grandfathers; they still look like uncorked genies. They came on late, introduced by film clips of some of their greatest numbers. In *Stormy Weather*, they descended a giant staircase in air splits, brother flying over brother and landing on every other stair—no, not landing: *crashing* fully split to the floor and then twist-squeezing himself upright. When they got to the bottom, they squeezed up one last time, did a couple of pirouettes, raced back up the stairs, and slid down two ramps toward the camera, and at that point the real Nicholas Brothers stepped through the screen. (One of the delights of the two new tap movies is their inclusion of old Hollywood footage—Buck and Bubbles in *No Maps on My Taps*, the Four Step Brothers in *Tapdancin'*, Bill Robinson in both.) I had seen the Nicholas Brothers a few years ago, looking like the fatigued and distracted old-timers they had every right to be. In Brooklyn, though, they were really on: whizzing through their pirouettes, flashing the flashiest hands ever. One can't say they actually, miraculously, *danced* those old tap routines, but how they performed! Maybe the electricity of the other dancers got to them: the dry-bone delicacy (never arid) of Honi Coles clicking out light, dense confettilike taps while standing virtually motionless; Coles and Henry (Phace) Roberts donning Bojangles derbies and levitating through "Doin' the New Low Down;" Buster Brown bouncing, careering, mincing, skating, and losing a tap (Coles yelling, "You always wanted to be Peg Leg Bates"); Bubba Gaines tap-jumping rope to "Perdido," then double-timing to "Who?" A tap fest can easily grow tiring, but not when sparks are flying and each performer dances in rapport with all the others. Not when what they do transcends its technical mystery and becomes an evocation of life. *Steps in Time* is biographies, inescapably, of black men. The lives are so intensely lived onstage that after the show we don't speculate about them—whether the dancers drink beer like us and shop at the Safeway. Although we may well wonder how some of them pay the rent.

Steps in Time is not, as some tap evenings have been, an informal, improvised affair; it's a finely tooled, professionally mounted vaudeville-style show, with the excellent Rudy Stevenson band backing up the dancers.

In the finale, which brings on the whole cast in a shim sham, there is a good deal of competitive ad-libbing, and it's then that Harold Nicholas performs two of his signature stunts—sliding across the stage through a tunnel of legs (which he originally did at the suggestion of George Balanchine) and back-flipping into a split. Earlier, Sandman Sims, another dazzler, had shown his enormous range (of which the chugging, scuffing dance in the sand is only a portion), his exhilarating grand-scale dynamics, and his flair for comedy. In *No Maps on My Taps*, Sims is the sparkplug, inciting and sustaining much of the continuity, actively enjoying his newfound celebrity. Briggs is sociable on camera, but he's basically indifferent to its presence, a sealed-off, haunted man. When his mother, who died several years ago, is mentioned, he neither hides nor demonstrates his grief. His dancing in the film is winning, totally committed; on the stage it has those qualities but also an edge of melancholy. In Green's eyes, there is fire and despair. He looks more frail in the film than he does on the stage, and though we linger on him at the fadeout, he's the least communicative of the three. How does he like being put in a Hall of Fame perspective after years of neglect? We never find out.

It was Green and the late Baby Laurence, they say, who fomented the tap revival in Harlem, drawing dancers together who hadn't seen each other in years. Green is now the esteemed elder of the tribe, the one all the others refer to as "a giant" or "a genius," but when he talks long-distance to his mentor, the seventy-eight-year-old John Bubbles, he's the dutiful protégé. "How you doin'?" demands Bubbles. "You creatin' any?" Green's solution to any problem is what one imagines it must have been for fifty years: "More jobs in better places." The title of the movie comes from a song he sings to himself with that half-hallucinated glint in his eye. Like Briggs, he seems unmindful of the camera, but once, when Sims deliberately provokes him and he cries out dramatically, "Don't tetch me!," one isn't sure. Green is so solitary and so resigned in his solitude that under normal everyday provocation he doesn't need to appear hostile. His civility is like Briggs's—part of a performer's code—but it is also the civility of an isolated man, whereas Briggs, in his round-eyed, child-star bewilderment, is withdrawing out of pain. (When he dances, he no longer looks at the audience.) Green, as he grows older, grows stronger and purer, breezier and more precise. Age completes him; he's the King Lear of tap. *No Maps on My Taps* captures the quintessential Green, dancing one of his favorite routines to "Caravan." In Brooklyn a couple of weeks ago, he surpassed this exhibition. In his boxy tuxedo with the vented coattails and the ankle-length pants, in long bump-toed shoes, Green looks twice the eccentric he really is, but his style is sui generis, no doubt about it. The gunboat shoes stay flat-footed through a maze of stiletto taps, and we don't see the heel drops that sound like wash-tub thumps. When Green wants to get visual, he gives us air turns with heel clicks, ungainly hops with cartwheeling arms, ungainlier swooping pivots in a crouch, coattails awhirl. Or he skids back and forth, one foot flat and the other swinging. What Green does can be imitated but it can't be learned. It's soul food for the senses.   —*April 28, 1980*

Inside the Ballets Russes

Richard Buckle's *Diaghilev* (Atheneum) was published last year—one of several conspicuous events that marked the fiftieth anniversary of its subject's death—and Diaghilev consciousness is still rising. The gallery exhibitions, the books, and the television documentaries keep coming, and a movie on Nijinsky's life has just been released, after many years of fruitless negotiation between various picture makers and the dancer's widow. Apart from this general public awareness, there is a new scholarly interest in Russian cultural history and the part played in it by the ballet. The so-called Silver Age of Russian culture—roughly the last decade of the nineteenth century to the end of the First World War—is under renewed critical speculation as Serge Diaghilev's period of emergence. The ballet was in flower: the final masterpieces of Petipa and the first ones of Fokine were being created. But it was Diaghilev, though his connection with ballet had been tentative at best, who took Russian dancers abroad, chose their repertory, and made their name. Because the Ballets Russes remained in exile, the tendency of Western commentators has been to evaluate its achievements in isolation from the country and the epoch that formed them. Richard Buckle isn't unmindful of the historical background, but the new scholarly trends haven't touched him. His early chapters have the thin, "special" credibility of English Chekhov. Besides, it soon becomes evident that Buckle is infatuated at least as much with the celebrity of those he writes about as with their artistry. In an unusually frank preface, he says that he and a colleague cut some seventy thousand words from his original manuscript. Did any of them concern the movements—literary and artistic and, yes, political—that pushed Diaghilev and his circle to a key position among the aesthetes and intellectuals of St. Petersburg? We dimly overhear some large Chekhovian rumblings in the words Buckle quotes from a speech Diaghilev made in 1905:

> *We are witnesses of the greatest moment of summing-up in history, in the name of a new and unknown culture, which will be created by us, and which will also sweep us away. That is why, without fear or misgiving, I raise my glass to the ruined walls of the beautiful palaces, as well as to the new commandments of a new aesthetic. The only wish that I, an incorrigible sensualist, can express, is that the forthcoming struggle should not damage the amenities of life, and that the death should be as beautiful and as illuminating as the resurrection.*

Beyond characterizing it as "most unexpected," Buckle does nothing with this speech but pass it on to us. It's apparently more important to him that Diaghilev knew Chekhov personally and tried to interest him in becoming the editor of *Mir Iskusstva*, the first enterprise in which Diaghilev sought to enlist the leading artists and intellectuals of his day.

Like most Englishmen who just missed being there at the time, Buckle was profoundly influenced by the impact of Diaghilev's London seasons, by the magic of Diaghilev's name and its appetizingly blackish tinge. Buckle's thirst for aesthetic sensation made him for years one of the liveliest of English dance critics, and he is a good art critic. As a biographer, he falls rather too easily and too soon under Diaghilev's personal spell, but he performs impressively as a connoisseur of Russian painting, and he provides detailed descriptions of the hero's early labors: the magazine *Mir Iskusstva* (*The World of Art*), the epochal exhibition of Russian historical portraits in the Tauride Palace, in St. Petersburg, and the exposition of Russian painting in Paris. *Mir Iskusstva* and the three thousand historical portraits, many never seen before publicly, were meant by Diaghilev to reveal Russia to itself; the show in Paris and its sequel—the concerts of Russian music, with Chaliapin singing *Boris Godunov* at the Paris Opéra—revealed Russia to the West. The following year, 1909, brought Nijinsky, Pavlova, and the first of Paris's *Saisons Russes* of ballet. There was no turning back to Russia after that. The sequence of events is dazzling, yet we get no feeling of exhilaration or discovery in Buckle's account of it. And though we have read of it a thousand times—and Buckle covered it himself in *Nijinksy* (Simon & Schuster, 1972)—the magnitude of Diaghilev's success on that opening night in Paris still comes as a surprise. How did Diaghilev get here, anyway? Between *Diaghilev* and *Nijinsky*, Buckle lays out all the stepping stones (there is one appalling reversal when Diaghilev's backer—none other than the Grand Duke Vladimir, the Tsar's uncle—suddenly dies and the money for the ballet season evaporates on the eve of departure), but the events, no matter how fattened by stratagems and intrigues that have lately come to light, are insignificant without some perspective in which to view them. One has no sense from Buckle of the dimensions of Diaghilev's world, so much smaller than our own. Consequently, it is never clear how an upstart from the provinces—Diaghilev was a distiller's grandson from Perm and, as Buckle assures us, "of no consequence in St. Petersburg"—seized the right to export the capital's main cultural resources. In those days, the flow of ideas within and across national boundaries was contained and stimulated by a relatively small intelligentsia, which had its titled members (like Count Harry von Kessler in Berlin) and its untitled ones (like Diaghilev and Savva Mamontov, the railroad magnate who discovered Chaliapin). Patronage of the arts was no longer the prerogative of the aristocracy. A comer like Diaghilev moved along the aristocratic circuit, although he knew that neither he nor it would last. (That, surely, is the meaning of his toast to the "new aesthetic.") The Great War destroyed forever the system of caste and privilege through which people had possessed and sponsored art; those who tried to operate with a facsimile of that system had obligations far in excess of what it could support. Too far, as time would prove. We cannot read of the *Mir Iskusstva* staff meetings—where an enlightened salon atmosphere was mingled with Old Russian courtesy, where unrestrained and often explosive discussions swirled around the silent nanny sitting watch over the samovar—without envying so many privileges enjoyed at once. And we also feel the fragility of the great dispensation this new élite would bring to pass. Out of those St. Petersburg evenings would come the Ballets Russes, the means by which artists would soon control and almost as soon lose the means of production. We speak nothing but good, these days, of the Ballets Russes. However, if it was the first dance company to constitute itself a vehicle for serious art, it was also the first company to surrender seriousness to constantly changing estimates of what an audience would take.

Without Diaghilev, none of it would have happened. Yet fifty-one years after his death we know very little about this pivotal figure in modern art. It isn't just that he belongs to a sunken world and that all but a handful of the ballets he produced are dead. His letters have never been collected; his critical writings, which are ample, have never been translated. There exists an extensive autobiographical memoir translated from Russian into French by Boris Kochno and from French into English by Richard Buckle; it has never been published. We follow Diaghilev's story, more exhaustively recounted in the Buckle book than in any other; we marvel at the man's abilities. As for the man himself, no sooner have we begun to assemble *this* historical portrait than it snaps together by itself with a wink and a tired smile. Can Diaghilev really be nothing more than the sum of his observers' clichés? He was large, at times fat, and with an oversized head, most often caricatured as that of a bull or a bulldog. As a youth travelling in Europe, he let people think he was a Russian nobleman. He had already acquired a reputation for being dictatorial and ruthless. He called himself a dandy; he was openly homosexual. And this theatrical mixture was inflamed by the gift of hubris. The closest he came to the court appointment he coveted was a minor position on the staff of Prince Volkonsky, the director of the Imperial Theatres. From this post, Diaghilev edited the Imperial Theatres yearbook, making a lavish production of it, and he began to push for the authority to mount ballets. When he was rebuffed, he took a stand and got sacked. Those who saw in this disaster Diaghilev's opening to the West are right; it was his only way out. But how to find it?

Now the biographer must beware, as simple ambition diverges into a complex set of maneuvers. Diaghilev was twenty-eight at the time of his dismissal. It took him eight years of hard work to find the escape route, which lay in exporting the ballet—are we to believe that he never regarded it opportunistically? His mission was to serve Russian art, and he must have seen that to serve Russian art he needed to serve himself. Diaghilev's genius was to know how to do that. He began by casting himself not as a creator but as a catalyst. Assessing his qualifications for the role of impresario, he wrote a celebrated letter to his stepmother beginning, "I am first a great charlatan," and ending, "I have all that is necessary save the money—but that will come." Most writers on Diaghilev cite this cold and witty letter; Buckle does not. He leaves out most of the canonical anecdotes and quotations ("*Etonne-moi!*") and still compiles more than six hundred pages of feverish activity. One feels that for Buckle just the record—facts that haven't yet decomposed into legend—is enough. He writes, "I am a great believer in the importance of dates, being sure that an exact chronology of Diaghilev's movements and decisions . . . must precede an analysis of his states of mind." No one could quarrel with that. But Buckle tracks down so many day-by-day minutiae that the movements and decisions become ends in themselves, and he never gets around to states of mind. Imprisoned within a mountainous bubble of memorabilia, Diaghilev seems loftier, more intransigently mysterious, and more remote than ever.

The jottings and cullings hardly ever turn into a line of thought. Buckle has trouble sustaining any single subject for more than a page. Open the book at random and this is what you get:

> *Braque must come at once, half-price, to Monte Carlo. Auric must be stopped from coming, as his ballet could not be rehearsed yet, but he must send the score of* Les Matelots. *(But Auric arrived three days later, all the same.) Idzikovsky wanted to return and would be free from the end of April: Diaghilev would take him back on the same terms as before. Who was to conduct at Barcelona at the end of April? The conditions of Defosse were absurd. Nuvel must enquire about Inghelbrecht and Baton. Was Ansermet free?*

Or this:

> *Diaghilev stayed about ten days in Florence, talking to Sitwell and lunching at Montegufoni. They also lunched once or twice at Fiesole and Sitwell took him to see the gardens of the Villa Gamberaia. Diaghilev, Kochno, Lifar and Berners went out to lunch with Contessa (Mimi) Pecci-Blunt at Marlia near Lucca, where photographs were taken among the statues on the stage of the open-air theatre. Balanchine and Dukelsky arrived together on 14 September.*

This sort of thing makes the book heavy going, even though it is a light read. Big movements and decisions are difficult to distinguish from little ones. When Buckle writes that "the second turning point" is at hand, we can't remember what the first one was, and he doesn't remind us. A text so lacking in synthesis, in interpretation, can still be useful: future biographers will refer to the million and one checkpoints assembled in this source book. Even so, they will have to reckon with numerous small aberrations. Buckle is a name-dropper. The Ballets Russes avalanche of names is not enough; on top of *that* he dribbles names that don't even make news. The Ballets Russes plays Spokane, "where Bing Crosby was growing up." (The company played Boston, too, where Lincoln Kirstein was growing up, but although that fact would have made more of a point Buckle doesn't mention it.) Trying for historical breadth, Buckle can be bewildering. He gives us the bloodlines of the society folk who were Diaghilev's patrons. He interweaves the early part of Diaghilev's story with that of Mathilde Kschessinskaya, the politically powerful assoluta of the Maryinsky, with no apparent objective other than to prove that she wasn't the cause of Diaghilev's dismissal. The climax of one of the last pyramids of trivia is the request (refused) of a Mr. A. Eumorfopoulos that a performance of *Petrushka* be rescheduled so that he might see it on a certain day. We have to assume that this person, not otherwise identified, is nobody, and that Buckle has mentioned him *because* he is nobody; among the glittering names, he's there to amuse us, like the delivery boy who is invited to stay for the party. In 1954, Buckle organized a Diaghilev exhibition that drew 165,000 spectators in Edinburgh and London. He later wrote a good book about his experiences, *In Search of Diaghilev*. When it came to the writing of his two ballet biographies, he seems to have relied on documents and their juxtaposition in much the way he would have in setting up an exhibition. In place of showcases, spotlights, blowups, and other techniques of differentiation and dramatization, he provides the reader with nothing—only the sporadic murmur of the tour guide telling us when to move on.

Until Buckle's *Diaghilev*, the standard biography in English had been *Diaghileff: His Artistic and Private Life*, written by Arnold Haskell in collaboration with Walter Nuvel, a Diaghilev associate. Cyril Beaumont, in a stream of critical articles and reminiscence, has given the most reliable seismographic indications of the impact of the Russian Ballet on the British. Tremors have been registered by the Sitwells. The Bloomsbury crowd, who we know attended the ballet—John Maynard Keynes even married Lydia Lopokova—wrote comparatively little about it, but they seem not to have dissented from the prevailing reaction, which was one of thrilled fascination. The Russian Ballet, it seems, became popular with the general public more quickly in London than in Paris. By 1927, Ralph Vaughan Williams was complaining of "that dreadful pseudo-cultured audience." (Even if the composer was peeved by Diaghilev's rejection of his ballet *Job*, Buckle should not have let the comment pass without investigating its validity.) If the annual volume of memorabilia printed in books or sold at auction is an index, Diaghilev's grip on the British imagination is still powerful. One reason may be that his name is almost an anagram of Svengali. He is seen today much as he was seen in his time—as a manipulator, charming or deceitful, of those under his spell. One has never had to know much about the inner workings of the Ballets Russes to cast Nijinsky as Trilby. And after the break with Diaghilev, it was in London that Nijinsky's first attempts to create for himself failed. Returning to the Ballets Russes, Nijinsky tried again: *Till Eulenspiegel,* with décor by Robert Edmond Jones, was produced in America without Diaghilev; it was a distinguished work, but it was never seen abroad. The rumor grew that Nijinsky was a puppet whose strings had been dropped. In both England and America, the popular view of Diaghilev may have been influenced by John Barrymore as Svengali. By the time Haskell's book came out here, in 1935, Barrymore, then the greatest actor in movies, had also played a Diaghilev-like promoter (in *The Mad Genius*), in the same oily style. Diaghilev's personality as we know it is more Noël Coward suave than John Barrymore unctuous; still, it's unquestionably a star personality and almost fatally subject to lurid definition.

Like all men—producers, publishers—who fulfill themselves through the work of other artists, Diaghilev can never entirely escape suspicion. The most powerful contribution to his villainous reputation was made by the publication in 1933 of Romola Nijinsky's biography of her husband. Romola's death, two years ago, lifted a few veils of discretion from the work of biographers, but Buckle writing about Diaghilev in 1979 is unable to produce many more revelations than Buckle writing about Nijinsky in 1972. The sober historian finds no basis for the charge of the aggrieved wife that Diaghilev exploited Nijinsky and then destroyed him out of homosexual vengefulness. Neither can he prove that Nijinsky, once he left Diaghilev's side for Romola's, was ever less than totally faithful to her. The plain fact of the matter would appear to be that the Diaghilev-Nijinsky affair wasn't that sexually charged to begin with. What, then, did destroy Nijinsky? The temptation to blame Diaghilev has not been entirely avoided by Vera Krasovskaya, Nijinsky's latest biographer. In *Nijinsky* (Schirmer), the malign influence is exercised largely in the creative realm. Krasovskaya writes of Diaghilev:

> It was he who opened up the Elysian fields of artistic creativity to Nijinsky. And it was he who took away Nijinsky's sense of inner freedom, his independence. From the very beginning the relationship was an unequal one; Nijinsky (to quote the proverb) had to eat out of his hands. The more clearly Diaghilev revealed, both for himself and for others, the dancer's precious artistic nature, the more he constrained Nijinsky's human nature, and, involuntarily, stimulated the seeds of a disease that perhaps need not have taken root.

This is a bit fancy. The causes of Nijinsky's schizophrenia can hardly be attributed to the abrasions of a classic master-disciple relationship. We can believe, as Krasovskaya does, that Nijinsky played out some of the humiliation of that relationship in *Petrushka* without having to take offense on his part. But Nijinsky seems to have been strangely susceptible to strong-willed persons who could organize his life. He may never have experienced the inner freedom that Krasovskaya says Diaghilev took away. When, later on, she says that "for all her genuine love of Nijinsky, the solicitous Romola became a hindrance to his art," Krasovskaya makes more sense. Nijinsky's fate seems to have been shaped as much by the passivity of his character as by his illness. Romola replaced Diaghilev as his mentor, but she could not offer him the life as an artist that he had led with Diaghilev, and Krasovskaya believes, as many do, that his breakdown was brought on by separation from his art. First, as an enemy alien he was confined by the war to his wife's country, Hungary. Then, when he returned to the Ballets Russes, he suffered from the back-seat status his marriage consigned him to in Diaghilev's eyes, especially now that there was Léonide Massine to be nurtured into a great artist.

About one thing Romola was right: Diaghilev's sexual jealousy seems really to have been monstrous—both comical and dangerous. (When she sees a homosexual conspiracy in the initial rejection of her husband by Diaghilev's circle, she's right at least about the pervasiveness of the rejection: even Stravinsky, who was not homosexual, fell in with it.) Diaghilev had reason to be jealous of women around his men, and he could be savage when threatened. The story of how he enlisted detectives to tail Massine and Vera Savina during their secret affair, and how, when proof of infidelity was obtained, he had the detectives strip Savina and throw her naked into Massine's room, is told in many versions. In Buckle's version, it is Diaghilev himself who strips Savina, first getting her drunk, and the whole episode is only a bit of hearsay. The story should have been either substantiated or laid to rest; it is the worst incident of Diaghilev's violence I have heard of. (He once threw Bakst bodily out of his apartment.) Too bad that Buckle, who seems to have interviewed every survivor of the Diaghilev era and asked all the embarrassing questions, did not query Massine or Savina, who became Massine's first wife; both were alive at the time the book was written.

Buckle's book is not so much about Diaghilev as about what others have thought of him. In another strange passage, he refutes Misia Sert's allegation of "Bacchanalian orgies" by saying, "She may have implied drink, drugs or boys, but it was against Diaghilev's nature to drink to excess and he was not promiscuous." Which leaves drugs. And on this Buckle is silent. It was part of Diaghilev's function to give scandal, as he was well aware, and he must have tolerated a good amount of evil gossip; it didn't hurt business. In Paris, he gave artistic scandal, saying of the *Sacre du Printemps* riot, "Just what I wanted." Although, as Buckle notes, he immediately became the leader of Paris's gay underworld, that was neither here nor there. For Diaghilev, the homosexual life was, among other things, a way of moving with extra speed within the tight intercontinental world of the prewar years; that is what it may have meant for Nijinsky, too, when he was first taken up by the elegant Prince Lvov and then passed on to Diaghilev. Prince Volkonsky, Count Kessler, Jean Cocteau: consciously or unconsciously, these men and others formed a chain that was to be Diaghilev's route to fame, and Nijinsky's right along with him. In England, too, there were contacts, but English society as a whole was almost too generous, too welcoming. Small wonder: it was paying Diaghilev reparations for its treatment of Oscar Wilde. Of the two capitals that courted the Russian Ballet, London may not have been more vehement than Paris, but it has proved to be far more possessive. As custodians of the Diaghilev image, Paris has only his former lieutenant Boris Kochno, who writes too little, and Serge Lifar, who writes too much. Whatever Diaghilev may have felt privately about his English patrons—he appears to have remained fond of England—it was the Paris audience he worked for right up until the end.

That came suddenly in 1929, of complications following a diabetic attack. He was a worn-out old man of fifty-seven. As his life's work, he had taken upon himself the ordeal of seeing modern ballet through its first twenty years. A virtue of Buckle's crushingly detailed, workaday chronicle is that it cannot help showing us Diaghilev as the vagabond, beggar, and desperate man he must often have been. Krasovskaya's book tries to get at the truth about Nijinsky by going to the opposite extreme. She writes in a romantic, quasi-fictional style, entering people's minds and reporting conversations that neither she nor anyone else can have overheard. Vera Krasovskaya is Russia's most respected ballet historian. This, the first of her books to appear in English and, by all accounts, the least typical, is a monograph disguised as a docudrama. For all the highly colored prose, there is a core of reality which is not found in any other book on Nijinsky's life. Krasovskaya has imagined the whole career as a logical progression of events shaped by creative ambition. She is careful to say when that ambition is Diaghilev's and when it is Nijinsky's. She shows exactly how the Diaghilev repertory grew out of the Maryinsky one. She gives us a concise picture, hitherto unseen by Western eyes, of the great dancer performing for his home audience both before and after the triumph in Paris. She lacks the critical weaponry of a Lincoln Kirstein (whose *Nijinsky Dancing* located the dancer's career among the phenomena of modern art), but then she has written her book as if in defiance of distinctions not only between criticism and biography but between biography and fiction. Some of her conclusions may be overwrought, but they are not foolish; a pity she chose to compromise them by her method. In spite of that choice, though, and in spite of John E. Bowlt's artless translation, her *Nijinsky* is a reliable guide to a life the full truth of which can never be known. The final testimony has already been taken, in the diary that Nijinsky kept after he had gone mad and after he had entered upon the religious passion that replaced dancing in his life. Romola's edition of the diary appeared in 1936; last year, the complete manuscript was sold at auction. If the expurgated portions are ever published, they can only give us more of Vaslav Alyosha Karamazov Nijinsky —more of his tortured spirit. Even the obscenities that they are said to contain are not inconsistent with his view of himself as "the clown of God" or with the priapic images that ran through his choreography, from the Faun to Till, and from the escapades of *Jeux* to the primitive rituals of *Le Sacre du Printemps*.

Although only *L'Après-midi d'un Faune* survives to be seen by audiences today, Nijinsky's reputation as a choreographer stands very high, and his artistic personality is not obscure. It is the nature of that personality, I think, together with the known facts of his life—his affair with Diaghilev, his marriage and its consequences, his mental illness—that arouses unappeasable interest. Because this artistic personality of his is of a piece with his life, it continues to seem sensational to us. Nijinsky made the relation between the dancer's sexuality and the dancer's art absolute. Yet Nijinsky was not Isadora—or, rather, he was Isadora buoyed by the formidable apparatus of the Ballets Russes, its pool of dancers, its collective wisdom. If the trilogy of *Faune*, *Jeux*, and *Sacre* has any biographical meaning at all, it is a biography of the orgasm: at first self-induced, later consciously manipulated through the piquancy and perversity of intimate relations, and finally a vast and sweated communal seizure, with death and life occurring together in a shattering rhythm—what Jacques Rivière called "the terrifying labor of the cells." In all this, Nijinsky may not be reflecting his own sexual progress so much as responding to the pressures of his time. It was an age of revolution, and in his own way he was as much a prophet as Marx or Freud. One may say that the ballets form a parallel to Nijinsky's sexual life (adolescent soloist joins human race, fathers two). In *Sacre*, though, there is also an opening out into the political world. Four years later, the individual destroyed in the name of the race would become the apocalyptic message of the Russian Revolution. Indeed, the première of *Sacre* came on the eve of the greatest blood bath in history, in which that message would be ratified. Stravinsky's music (and, we must suppose, the choreography that went with it) can be interpreted as a sign that the end of civilization was at hand; yet, of course, it is also a purely musical prophecy. It seems that in that moment art was enormous—globally important, visionary—in a way that it has never been since. But if art was enormous, it was surely also true that the world to which its vision referred was not yet our megaworld. Today, all that is forgotten. We see the achievement of Stravinsky and Nijinsky largely as one of redesigning the art of dance; the sense of a new design has stayed with us, whereas the metaphysical impulse for it has not—and could not be recaptured even if, by some miracle, the choreography could be restored.

Nijinsky's diary, which records his obsession with the war, reminds us that if he had enacted fantastic and exotic creatures (the Favorite Slave, the Blue God, the Spirit of the Rose) in many of the ballets that were made for him by Fokine, he himself was a man who had lived and danced in the real world. His next ballet after *Sacre* had been the saga of Till—Petrushka as revolutionist. The notion that a ballet dancer could be part of the intellectual history of his time is starting to seem less absurd to us than it once did, although the current film about Nijinsky is content to give us the standard movie portrait of a tormented and, in this case, homosexual genius. Truffaut once said that intellectuals recognize in movies only their own kind of meaning. The same might be said of intellectuals and ballet. Nijinsky was not an intellectual, therefore he did not *think*, he only suffered. Well, yes, he was not an intellectual. He was an idea.

Nijinsky's appearance offstage was nondescript, and he was a poor conversationalist, so he seems to have had few friends among Diaghilev's brilliant Parisian followers. Misia Sert might have understood him; she, too, was a Russian-born Pole, and she had an uncanny instinctive sympathy with the artists of her time, especially composers, but she considered Nijinsky "an idiot of genius"—not for cultivation. It was another *polonaise*, Marie Rambert (born Miriam Ramberg), who drew close to Nijinsky and helped him in his work. Misia Sert, wealthy, influential, talented, was Diaghilev's handmaiden: she was there when he needed money for his first Paris season; she was there when he received the telegram announcing Nijinsky's marriage; she was there in Venice when he died. Gifted with musical insight (she had been a piano prodigy) and a sense of the moment, Misia was more to Diaghilev than a patron and a confidante; she was one of his closest advisers —the only woman member of his cabinet—and a factor in the creation of some of his most important ballets. Misia Sert would have been a presence if Diaghilev had never invaded Paris. With the Ballets Russes as a focus for her energies, she became a force.

In *Misia* (Knopf), Arthur Gold and Robert Fizdale have composed a full-length biography of a woman who profoundly affected the cultural and social fashions that we have identified with Paris since the century began. The authors do not minimize her centrality and her importance to Diaghilev. At the same time, the light and brittle tone with which they carry off their multiple and often flashy tales of the Belle Epoque makes us slightly uncomfortable in Misia's presence. Instead of the tolerant muse of Upper Bohemia lying back on her cushions as trays of dizzying anecdotes are passed, she begins to seem a bright, tart lady who would bring us to attention with a rap of her fan. That contradiction, to be sure, may be traced to Misia's own character. She was assertive and supine, glamorous and indifferent to glamour, a troublemaker and a diplomat, frivolous and serious, right and wrong.

She was, in short, a woman of passion; there was about her nothing of the spartan conviction that might have been expected to animate a rich woman who pledged herself to art. The picture of her and Diaghilev laughing conspiratorially in a train compartment, which is printed both in *Diaghilev* and in *Misia*, tells us much about the appeal that she held for him. Misia was a hedonist; pleasure was the source of her dedication, as it was of his, and it was what made both of them infallible and vulnerable at the same time.

Misia, born Godebska, the daughter of the sculptor Cyprien Godebski, married and divorced three husbands, which alone would have made her a cynosure. The last of these, the Spanish painter José-Maria Sert, was the one she loved best. When he fell in love with the young woman who would be his next wife, so did she; she could let neither of them go. Just as one longs for Virginia Woolf to have written about the Nijinsky whose mental affliction so closely matched her own, one wants Colette on the private life of her friend Misia. Proust portrayed Misia, in her social role, as Mme Verdurin, the risen bourgeois hostess, and, though not the historical Mme Sert (Proust used Misia also as the basis of Princess Yourbeletieff), it is this Mme Verdurin-Sert whom Gold and Fizdale capture and who turns out to have the most meaning for us. Born in the same month of the same year, Misia and Diaghilev arrived just in time to propel the democratization of art into creative efflorescence, and Misia also assisted at the birth of a new social élite. Perhaps her greatest triumph as a hostess was the introduction into Parisian society of a peasant-born tradeswoman named Chanel. Unlike Diaghilev, Misia lived on into old age, but she was nearly blind when she died, a morphine addict mourning her lost loves. (According to Gold and Fizdale, Diaghilev sniffed cocaine.)

The many glowing full-color plates in *Misia* testify to the productivity of this singular muse. At the end of the book, the woman who sat for Renoir, Toulouse-Lautrec, Vuillard, and Bonnard is photographed: a thin, rather tough-looking old lady in a sailor hat and sling-back pumps. She is standing in the Accademia Museum in Venice; her gaze is bleak. The times she saw, the work she inspired have long since become history. Yet her photograph —it is by Horst and helplessly a fashion photograph—shocks us; for all that we have been told, we cannot take her measure. What is it about Misia, Diaghilev, and their world that inspires intimacy, even vulgarity, in commentators? Because they reduced art to fashion and knowledge to taste, are they never to be taken seriously? Is the history of which they were a part to remain scandalous forever? Gold and Fizdale, the famous duo-pianists, are excellent gossips; probably no one else could have done this very necessary first study of Misia as well as they. But it is getting late. The old woman in the sailor hat has been dead for thirty years. We must stop hoarding and start sifting the ruins. —*May 12, 1980*

"Le Sacre"
Without Ceremony

When Paul Taylor was working on *Scudorama* in 1963, he used a record of *Le Sacre du Printemps* as a rehearsal score; new music was composed in time for the première. A few weeks ago, at the City Center, he presented his production of *Le Sacre* and had the hit of the dance season. Although Taylor is the logical choreographer for this mighty music, he has turned out a completely unpredictable piece of work. Instead of the orchestral version of the score, he has staged the two-piano reduction that Stravinsky made for Nijinsky's use in rehearsing the original choreography. If Taylor's *Sacre*, which he calls *Le Sacre du Printemps (The Rehearsal)*, has any resemblance to *Scudorama*, I missed it. And I wouldn't have looked for derivations from Nijinsky's ballet, but those flattened, two-dimensional body positions, angled limbs, and parallel feet are immediately apparent in Taylor's choreography. Taylor may be commemorating a rehearsal period in the life of two companies—his own and the Ballets Russes. When the curtain rises, to an unfamiliar tinkle of familiar notes, a dance company is onstage warming up. This turns into a formal rehearsal, and then into a frame for the action, which has nothing to do either with Stravinsky's scenario or with any *Sacre* scenario ever devised. Instead of tribal rituals and human sacrifices (which Taylor had given us in *Runes*), we see a farce composed of scenes from crime melodramas of the silent-movie era. The characters include a private dick in Harold Lloyd spectacles, a mother, a kidnapped child, and a slew of Oriental villains. The melodrama may be the ballet the company is rehearsing or it may represent something going on backstage or it may be simple parallel action; the way the scenes are intercut with the rehearsal makes any interpretation possible. Taylor's associative links seem random—*are* random—but he never loses the audience. All the pieces are designed to fit together in a jigsawlike pattern, and the pattern, no matter how tenuously matched, is unbreakable. The jigsaw shapes seem hewn out of the dancers' bodies. There are opaque moments here and there, but even as we flounder we feel the tug of stylistic consistency.

The integrity of this *Sacre* is a Taylor miracle. A past-master at building multilevel allusive structures, Taylor knows that you can swing from branch to branch as long as it is the same tree. In his *Sacre*, the Nijinsky references are reinforced by their implicit Taylorishness; they look so ingrown that we can choose to see them as products of Taylor's long association with the painter Alex Katz. Katz's forays into two-dimensional "depth" have been represented on Taylor's stage in such pieces as *Private Domain* and *Diggity*.

Taylor as a dance-maker shares some of Katz's major concerns; he's very nearly Katz's dance double. But when he's expressing those concerns, as in *Le Sacre* or in another new piece closely related to it, called *Profiles*, Katz is not the designer; there's no need for him. John Rawlings's designs for *Le Sacre* are in a starkly cinematic palette of black, white, and gray with one or two splashes of red. Linear motifs—Art Deco circles and grilles—indicate a bedroom or a bar or a jail. The pulp Expressionism of the costumes and décor, the "screenplay" plot, and the dance style seem to blend in one great crashing image. The blunt, thick bodies cringe and lurch, hurtle and bound, all in one piece, dense with impacted energy. These loaded silhouettes with their pump-handle arms and swivelling heads are, perhaps, Taylor's comment on the "perverse" inventions of Nijinsky; he shows us how vivid a dance shape can be made by reducing the body's options for extension and directing its energy toward rather than away from the core. As with all theories of polar opposition, this anti-classicism makes a classical statement —it gives us the irreducible essence of expression. And to a master of classical style like Taylor (I intend the primary meaning of the term, not the secondary, academic meaning, which refers to ballet) the reductions and simplifications and limitations are so many opportunities for virtuosity.

But Taylor's *Sacre* is also a comedy, and Taylor's comic sense is not really located in his cartoon-classical body shapes. *Profiles* uses the same shapes and many of the same movements that make up *Le Sacre*, but it is a grave, lyrical essay with no plot. What makes *Le Sacre* a comedy is the music. By stripping the score of its orchestration, Stravinsky exposed its pistons and gears, and it's this mechanistic aspect of the music that Taylor responds to. He hears the ticktock ostinato that winds up those massive charging rhythms—hears it as the music of automatons chugging to their doom in a deterministic universe. He can even risk a certain amount of over-determinism: the baby, who is thrown around like the baby in a Punch-and-Judy show, expires along with the rest of the cast, stabbed reflexively by the last man to die in a climactic piling up of corpses. Taylor isn't funny at the music's expense; he works *with* the music and is twice as funny in his straight-faced way as a consciously irreverent parodist would have been. Maybe Taylor himself got wound up in the coils of the music; there's an inevitability, a rightness, about this *Sacre* that seems to issue from a musical mind of the purest sort. By the time we come to the Dance of the Chosen Maiden—the peak moment in the original production—we have so completely forgotten the music's historic connections that we're jolted when Taylor reminds us of them. He has Ruth Andrien launch herself into the dance the minute her baby dies, and it's a real twister, filled with irregular phrases none of which accord with the music's irregularity and all of which must be attacked at the highest energy level. Andrien dances in a delirium of precision—between the bar lines, so to speak—and maintains unwavering rhythmic accuracy: a marvellous performance.

Along with the pleasure of musical transparency that this *Sacre* gives us, there is the pleasure of diagrammatic visualization, which leads the eye through the thickets of the scenario. Some of these visual clues are identifiable Taylor fantasies, but most of them are imponderable in origin. Wherefore these "Chinese" configurations in the choreography, and how could Taylor have known they'd make perfect sense to us? Taylor takes us back beyond the silent films to the primitive superstitious imagery that those films tapped. Along with Warner Oland and Anna May Wong and the tong wars in the streets, he gives us a kind of fiercely grinning terroristic "Orientalism" in the very physique of his dances. Those are jigsaw ideograms that pass before us. The omnipresent impassive rehearsal mistress played by Bettie de Jong in cossack dress is quite obviously a fate figure who fits into the Ballets Russes picture. But she also reminds us of Big Bertha, the malevolent life-size music-box doll Taylor created for De Jong in 1970. *Big Bertha* was revived this season with De Jong as pitilessly terrifying as ever, and with Thomas Evert giving a powerful, harrowing performance in Taylor's old role as her chief victim. One might compile a sizable list of Taylor works under the heading "Motiveless Malignity"; it is one of his favorite themes. *Le Sacre* would be on the list, and not merely on the strength of the De Jong character. (Curiously, De Jong is the only mechanical figure in *Big Bertha* and the only nonmechanical one in *Le Sacre*.) Unlike *Big Bertha* or *Nightshade* or *Dust*, *Le Sacre* is too cheerful, too impersonally efficient to be disturbing. It is a work that sweeps us deep into Taylor's world and honors its preceptors at the same time: Nijinsky, Martha Graham (who once danced the Chosen Maiden in choreography by Massine), and, not least of all, Stravinsky. It is very likely the best *Sacre* we shall ever see, and we can only regret that the composer is not here to see it, too. Of the many fine dancers in the full-company cast, I must mention, besides De Jong and Andrien, Christopher Gillis as the clockwork detective, Elie Chaib as the gangleader, Monica Morris as his moll, and Lila York as a slow-witted gunsel.

In 1959, Martha Graham and George Balanchine joined forces to produce *Episodes*, an hour-long ballet to the complete orchestral works of Anton von Webern. There was no attempt to agree on subject matter or treatment. Working independently and for the most part with their own dancers, each choreographer did something typical: Graham a meditation on Mary, Queen of Scots, and Balanchine a suite of dances barren of dramatic or emotional implication. The Balanchine suite has remained in the repertory of the New York City Ballet with the exception of one of its segments, a solo created for Paul Taylor, then one of Graham's dancers. Graham's contribution, which she also calls *Episodes*, was retired until last year, when, as a gesture to the London audience, it was revived for her company's season at Covent Garden. *Episodes* comes from a period—a year after *Clytemnestra*—when Graham could still work magic as a performer and as a choreographer. She brought her hypnotic presence to the part of Mary, commanding the stage as Mary surrogates filled in the dancing with male figures from Mary's past, the Earl of Bothwell conspicuous among them. The role of Elizabeth, taken by Sallie Wilson, of Balanchine's company, was a distant counterweight to the role of Mary, with moderate amounts of dancing and extended passages of hieratic mime. In her stiff brocade gown, Elizabeth sat or stood, a majestic pawn of the state. The climax of the piece came when Mary and Elizabeth faced each other across the stage in a game of tennis. Each moved but slightly; as stroke followed minimal stroke, the space between the two queens became a battleground where the Four Marys writhed with their partners in the contest for power.

The 1979 staging, which was seen this spring during the Graham company's season at the Met, is a very different affair. The roles of Mary and Elizabeth (now taken by Susan McLain and Peggy Lyman) have been equalized and sentimentalized. Mary is now pathetic rather than tragic, a Catholic martyr toward whom Graham angles the audience's sympathy. (In her own performance, Graham was a complex Mary, indecisive and weak as well as noble and wronged.) Elizabeth has become a straightforward villain, sweeping down from her perch (the set is a replica of David Hays's wooden bridge and pedestals) with huge, voracious strides and taking over the stage in a hammy solo. The part of Bothwell is also less imaginatively written than it was, and the physical differences between Tim Wengerd and the role's originator, Bertram Ross, don't seem to have been adequately allowed for. Wengerd looked lost. (Bothwell's predatoriness and slinkiness appear to have been transferred to Elizabeth.) The Four Marys have merged with a background chorus; the male consorts whom Graham designated as the courtiers Riccio, Darnley, and Chastelard have disappeared. The fateful game of tennis has been moved to an earlier point in the music (Six Pieces, Opus 6), so it no longer takes place to the spaced gong strokes. And it has been vulgarly rechoreographed. The two queens play with a rope between them, and they swing their racquets and stomp their feet like impatient contenders in a Virginia Slims tournament. There is no struggling ensemble in their midst. Later, the rope is used to bind Mary's wrists; Susan McLain, who has a lovely soft presence, makes a fine effect of this. What twenty years before was an ironic and subtle discourse on the structure of power has become a schoolgirl's gloss on that dream queen Mary.

Year by year, the Graham repertory loses veracity, and not all of the loss can be attributed to time's erosion. If Graham were not consciously and willingly working below herself, she'd be as pathetic as Mary. But the company's current revivals and attempts at new works have a solidity of craftsmanship that suggests she knows what she's doing and is doing it from pure practical necessity. Strictly speaking, there are no new works. Everything new is old in spirit and ages old in form. But premières are good for business. The revivals are at the mercy of young uncomprehending dancers (this season's crop is especially green), and the coaching of the Graham staff does not seem to be of the best. It is easy to see why Graham prefers recensions to revivals. If she gives up too much of what makes a work revivable in the first place, the reason may be in the condition of the old works that have been barely, creakingly maintained in repertory. Even the older dancers are unable to give us more than a fleeting impression of the Graham performances that made these works viable. This was, after all, a most personal repertory, and its creator now seems concerned to eliminate from it all traces of her own personal gesture and quality of vision. Playing at the Met puts the company at a further disadvantage; the place has prestige, but it dwarfs the repertory. Graham is not indifferent to the problem. Whenever new works or revivals are produced at the Met, they have been, if nothing else, in proper scale. *Judith*, one of the season's new-old works, remounts Noguchi's scenery in amplified form. Judith and Holofernes move between sculptural islands occupying themselves with costume changes in distractingly elegant fabrics by Halston. The new *Episodes* begins with a formal procession of courtiers to the sound of a bagpipe; it goes on too long, but it fills the stage.

Graham's recension of her past has alienated that portion of her public which is just now preparing her place in history. Dance scholars are refused permission to see her historic rehearsal films; choreographers who wish to stage her work for their own companies are rebuffed. Graham choreography was missing from the historical survey of modern dance which was presented recently by the Utah Repertory Dance Theatre here in New York; not even classroom exercises were permitted. (Ludicrous of the Graham organization, which is booked into the Met, to be taking fright from a tiny university-based company playing at the Theatre of the Riverside Church.) Graham's dance style has been long out of fashion, but now even Graham the institution is out. The younger members of the dance community don't like Halston or Nureyev or Liza Minnelli; they don't accept the new works, and since Graham herself is careless of history, they aren't lured by the publicity's use of the word "legend." Meanwhile, the audience that comes to the Met gives every work careful inspection and decides to believe in what it sees. That the repertory is old-fashioned may be for this audience a virtue. But along with the literary plots and their high moral tone, along with the classiness of the occasion and the big-name supporting cast, this public gets what Graham is still offering as the one sure token of her formerly abundant gifts—her knowledge of theatre and of choreography as a discipline. To those who say that "under the circumstances" they'd rather not go—even for the first time—it might be said that under the circumstances is the way things are done in the theatre. To see the Graham operation today is to see it instructively in extremis. No matter how abortive the project or dismaying the performance, one can sense control and refinement in the sheer process of installation. The new *Episodes*, to my mind gratingly inadequate, is (apart from that bagpipe procession) still what engineers would call a sweet job. Like a wise counsellor, Graham speaks to us through her understanding of craft. No one who claims an interest in dance should miss that.

Balanchine's *Episodes* used to follow immediately after the Graham company had taken its bows. At the New York City Ballet this season, I noticed that the opening dance, with its ensemble of four couples drawn up in a tight formal rank, was a mirror image of the Four Marys and their partners. The courtly "Renaissance" choreography could have been Balanchine establishing conscious links to Graham's theme. Balanchine's own theme, which is the danceability or undanceability of Webern's music, was more distinctly pronounced in its day than it ever has been since. *Episodes* endures rather less as a classic than as a commemoration of a phase in the company's development. At the moment, it is being worthily performed by an almost all-new cast, and the orchestra is playing the microscopic scores with unusual clarity. And Allegra Kent, alone of the original cast, is there to reincarnate the ballet's most persuasive image. —*May 19, 1980*

Ashley, Balanchine, and "Ballade"

George Balanchine's *Ballade* is a small, perfect vanity case of a ballet, the kind of exquisite miniature that Balanchine fashions from time to time when he wants to make a fuss over one of his ballerinas. Generally, for this purpose he turns to French composers—to Delibes for *Sylvia Pas de Deux* and *La Source*, to Chabrier for *Trois Valses Romantiques*, to Ravel for *Sonatine*. The music for *Ballade* is Fauré's Ballade for Piano and Orchestra, Opus 19. It doesn't sound like Balanchine music, but then neither, at first, did the selections from Fauré's *Pelléas et Mélisande* and *Shylock* when he presented them as the score of *Emeralds*. The French wit and sparkle that in Balanchine's view enhance the image of a lovely woman are subdued in Fauré; the ironies are more subtle, more nostalgic. The momentum of *Ballade* isn't urgent, and in the first couple of performances it tended to flag toward the end. By the third performance, the dancers were stepping up their attack, and the whole ballet was enveloped in a satisfying balmy glow. Less satisfying by far were the scenery and costumes, borrowed from the Degas section of a dodo called *Tricolore*, which was supposed to have had choreography by Balanchine but was staged by other hands. Reviving Rouben Ter-Arutunian's décor may be Balanchine's way of making up the loss of *Tricolore,* but the heavy swags with which the stage is hung are no better than they were before at reducing the proportions of the State Theatre's proscenium to a condign intimacy. *Ballade,* a small-scale ballet with a fragile mood, could use a smaller stage. That being out of the question, it could do without these nuisance hangings, which lock Balanchine's choreography into static segments of space. Apparently, we must suffer them now that the trees in *Vienna Waltzes* are disappearing.

Ballade was made for Merrill Ashley, but a different Merrill Ashley from the brilliant and forceful ballerina of *Ballo della Regina. Ballade* slows her down, softens her edges, amplifies her presence, and stretches her range —all through its pursuit of the legato phrase. Balanchine, in that way he has of trying to expand a dancer's range by casting against type, had put Ashley repeatedly into adagio roles. *Emeralds,* the ballet she was least suited to, was the one he insisted on longest. (Now it seems to be *Swan Lake.*) In *Ballade,* he has made an Ashley version of *Emeralds;* not only does he explore the legato phrase, he reconstructs it in terms of Ashley's technique. He will ask her to end a taut string of déboulés by slowly opening through passé into arabesque. And that is only the simplest example I can give of the characteristic lengthy but packed phrase he has invented for her in this ballet. With their built-in elasticity and unforeseen climaxes and connections, the phrases don't stand out as feats; they merge in a continuous rippling flow. The effect of it is like seeing a *Ballo della Regina* marked moderato cantabile, all the brillant steps melting into one prolonged, reposeful lilting phrase. Another effect is to divorce Ashley from her habit of presenting herself as the sum of her technical specialties. The pliant evolutions that offer so charged a view of a "new" Ashley are only one half of the novelty. The other half has less to do with dancing than with the creation of an atmosphere for the dancing to happen in, a task that Balanchine has traditionally taken upon himself. This time, he has left it to the ballerina to decide what emotion—poignant, sentimental, tragic, grandly impersonal—the experience of the ballet will convey to the audience. For though *Ballade* is a gift to Ashley, and a deeply appreciative one, it is also a challenge. Technically, Ashley meets the challenge, dancing with a virtuosity more serene at every performance. But the emotional flavor of *Ballade* is just now a little bland, almost insipid. By calling on Ashley's nondancing resources as a ballerina, Balanchine may have issued her the most critical challenge of her career.

Ashley's partner in this ballet is Ib Andersen, the new soloist from the Royal Danish Ballet, and although he is gracious, sympathetic, and attractive both as a dancer and as a partner, he doesn't leave a vivid impression, largely because Ashley doesn't make much of him. She doesn't use the opportunities Balanchine has given her to react when he appears or when he disappears. He comes on and she freezes, like a deer at bay. When they're dancing together, the harmony between them—which is striking, because the elfin Andersen looks unexpectedly good with Ashley, a Laurie to her

Jo—leads to no development in the mood of the ballet. It adds nothing to Ashley when she dances alone; she doesn't appear to be thinking of him, or even thinking of love. *Ballade* has a passage almost exactly like one in the "Tales from the Vienna Woods" section of *Vienna Waltzes* when, after dancing with her partner, the ballerina dances alone against the female corps. It is Balanchine's way of "eavesdropping" on the woman's feelings. The privacy of the moment is enhanced by the presence of the other women: we feel there are things she might tell them that she would never tell any man. In *Vienna Waltzes*, Karin von Aroldingen dances at this moment with something like blushing abandon; it is then that we know how powerfully the waltz spell and the spell of her young lover grip her. Balanchine's success with Von Aroldingen in this role and his attempt to stage a similar success with Ashley recall to us the fact that the two women were often cast together in *Emeralds*. There, too, each was seen alone and then with a man. It seemed to matter very much to Balanchine that they show the sexual transition between the two situations, and they hardly ever did. Ashley's partner in *Ballade* was to have been Von Aroldingen's waltz partner, Sean Lavery; Andersen stepped in after Lavery had injured himself in rehearsal. But even if we grant that Lavery is more imposing in his bearing than Andersen, he would still have to be acknowledged by the ballerina in order to exist. (By the end of "Tales from the Vienna Woods," Lavery has become so luminous in Von Aroldingen's mind that she appears to abase herself slightly when she curtsies to him.) Balanchine has actually given the male dancer in *Ballade* a solo, but no matter how strongly Andersen dances it, he must dance it in a vacuum until Ashley recognizes him as her lover. Then his solo will not be just a solo, and the little girls behind him will become projections of Ashley or of her desire, not just an ensemble.

Balanchine doesn't always use this power of the ballerina to focus and control the mind of the audience, although with actress-dancers like Melissa Hayden and Violette Verdy he tended to use it more often than not. Like Petipa's, his ballets are more likely to be expressed from the man's point of view, and he has used the unemotional style of American ballerinas as an object, a created effect. American men, too, tend to be unemotional, which transfers as affectlessness to the stage. Balanchine has dramatized this (think of the two great male roles in *The Four Temperaments*), but it doesn't seem to sustain his interest, and that may be why so many of his principal male dancers are not American. I can recall other occasions like *Ballade*, when Balanchine has tried to provoke one of his ballerinas out of her impassivity, but none so pointed in their provocation. As Merrill Ashley is an extreme case, so his tactics must be extreme. Ashley must be the most flatly American, romantically unresonant dancer whom he has ever made a star. She's the modern liberated woman as ballerina—aggressive, workproud, mistrustful of glamour, dependent on no one for her effects. Her independence of her partner is not an illusion but a fact, which she demonstrated on opening night of the season when Robert Weiss became disabled in the middle of *Ballo della Regina* and she finished the performance without him. Ashley respects facts, and it is facts that she delivers when she performs. All her effects come from her dancing, not from her person. Although she has developed a flawlessly gracious performing manner, it's just a manner; Merrill Ashley doesn't seem to believe that she herself is of any interest to us. In her way, she's guided by the same principles as those "post-modern" choreographers who reduce dancing to the laws of mechanics. For her, classical style is not an analysis of personality but an achievement from which personality must be rigorously excluded. She has absorbed Balanchine's ideal of selflessness in dancing and given it back to him in neutered form.

Ballade is evidence that Balanchine is unwilling to let Merrill Ashley carry on as if she were an uninteresting woman. To understand why this is not what it appears—a case of the Master in apostasy—one has only to look at what he does with Ashley's technique in *Ballade*. Ashley usually overwhelms her roles through sheer brilliance. *Ballade* takes the curse off her technique by personalizing it. Balanchine has performed similar wonders for generations of great American dancers: they've been fascinating not just because of what they do but because what they do reflects so clearly who they are. Ashley may have baffled Balanchine initially by refusing to be anybody. She was Miss Allegro, Miss Instrument-of-the-Choreographer, Miss Watch-My-Steps. Pure dancers of this type are usually too self-critical to relax in front of an audience. Maybe when Ashley looks out at us she looks into a mirror and shrinks. Whatever she's doing—and her habit is to do it impeccably—she seems to want to withdraw. *Ballade* reshapes her technique so that the way she dances becomes a legitimization and a rationalization of the way she *looks* when she dances. Psychological as well as physical considerations are involved, and perhaps even dominate. In any case, the choreography not only permits but caters to Ashley's characteristic angularity and to something effaced and averted in her temperament. Steps and positions that are four-square or directly aimed at the audience are for the most part avoided. Flying through space, diving into penchée, trilling along in perfect bourrées, Ashley is no less active than usual, only she always seems to be shooting off at a tangent. Not even *Ballo* comes this close to a true portrait. Curious, though: she dances full out with forthright power, yet the quality of her expression is oblique. The only thing that's missing from the ballet is a motive for this obliquity. Balanchine has understood something important about Ashley; he's let her be as she is wont to be. Yet he wants to see a dramatic justification. He wants, I think, the kind of total involvement she shows in her great performance of *Tchaikovsky Piano Concerto No. 2*—an involvement that is beginning to extend beyond her own role to the entire ballet. All that must happen in *Ballade*, and more, and in a new key. Just as the choreography pulls a new lyricism from her body, so it demands an emotional commitment to its implicit dramatic situation. Ashley hardly ever looks at her partner; she glances, she smiles, but she never really looks at him. Is she running from him? Making him up in her mind? When Ashley decides that the placing and weighing of Andersen's presence in the ballet is her responsibility, she'll have matured as a performer. A prodigious dancer will have become a ballerina.

The word that Balanchine most often uses when speaking about the *Ballade* genre of ballet is "perfume." When Alexandra Danilova teaches the fairy variations from *The Sleeping Beauty*, she will often speak of Petipa and perfume. And when she demonstrates the steps she revels in their femininity. The ballerinas with whom Balanchine has worked extend from Danilova, who embodies the obligation of a woman to be glamorous and seductive on the stage, to Merrill Ashley, who embodies her obligation not to. Suzanne Farrell is almost as far removed from Ashley as she is from Danilova. Coquetry is false to her; when she uses it, she's apt to start bobbing her head like a horse. Yet Farrell is sexually very potent on the stage, and consciously so. Is that the reason that many of the young women of the company appear to have switched from her to Ashley as their model, or are they looking at Ashley's beautiful steps? Farrell's technical execution is less scrupulous these days than has been her custom. Perhaps she'd like to show us that there's more to dancing than steps. Surely, though, there should not be less to the steps. The awesome things I recall her doing in the preview of the new *Walpurgisnacht Ballet* last season were indifferently sketched in at the première, a couple of weeks ago. But her Terpsichore in *Apollo* was the glory I remembered its being, and her performance of the dual role in another Stravinsky piece, *Monumentum/Movements*, was as enlivening as ever.

Walpurgisnacht and *Ballade* are both being widely underestimated as Balanchine compositions. In *Walpurgisnacht*, which originated in a production of *Faust* at the Paris Opéra a few years ago, we have a charming demonstration of Balanchine's ability to do much with little; he uses a handful of steps and only as much technique as the dancers of the Opéra could manage, and he spreads a feast. (Farrell's role was revised for her.) Bounty of this sort may be possible only to the very wise. Daniel Levans's *Concert Waltzes*, now being performed by American Ballet Theatre, at the Met, does not do a great deal with the little it has to work with (originally the very young troupe called U.S. Terpsichore); still, it does a surprising amount. Levans shows signs of having grasped an essential Balanchine secret: it's not how many steps you have, it's how many fit the music. In Levans's ballet, I could have wished for more variety in the situations, more excitement from the two principals (Marianna Tcherkassky and Kevin McKenzie), and maybe occasionally a different port de bras for the corps, but I never lacked a sense that the choreography was filling out the musical phrase. While I regret that Levans wasn't encouraged to develop his ballet for a large stage and for the skills of mature professional dancers, the only criticism I would make is in the area of its greatest strength—rhythm. It's too evenly steady, relying on phrase-by-phrase continuity. There should be a rhythmic perspective, in which the phrases could assume different shapes and colors and still pull the ballet ahead. That, at least, is what I think I see in such "easy" Balanchine pieces as *Walpurgisnacht* and *Ballade*. If young choreographers are seeing something else—well, O.K. One secret at a time.

—*June 2, 1980*

Keeper of the Flame

La Bayadère, which we now have at the Met in three complete acts, by American Ballet Theatre, was the most important ballet produced by Marius Petipa between *The Daughter of the Pharaoh* (1862), which secured his position as ballet master of the Imperial Theatres, and *The Sleeping Beauty* (1890), his masterpiece. Both *The Daughter of the Pharaoh* and *La Bayadère* were revived at the beginning of this century, but only *La Bayadère* entered the modern repertory. The elements it shared with the earlier ballet (vivid spectacle, plenty of exotic fauna, and an opium trance) were considered less interesting than those it shared with the later one—and with *Swan Lake*. In *La Bayadère*, Petipa strove to develop a drama of consequence in the story of Solor, India's noblest warrior, who is torn between the pure love of Nikiya, a bayadère, or temple dancer, and the sensual allure of Gamzatti, the Raja's daughter. Solor's betrayal of Nikiya for Gamzatti is echoed in the story of Siegfried, Odette, and Odile. But the enduring importance of *La Bayadère* lies in Petipa's vision of classical academic dancing, crystallized in a single scene. Solor conjures the dead Nikiya; she appears in the Kingdom of the Shades, refined to essence by her ritual dances and multiplied to infinity by the corps de ballet. Death as a setting for abstraction had appeared in *Giselle* and other ballets of the Romantic era. *La Bayadère* extended the implication: "death" was not just a setting but an image sustained by lyrical and plastic values in a closed system of correspondences. Death's kingdom was the Elysium, the nirvana, of pure dance.

Petipa achieved this transcendent metaphor in 1877—the year *Swan Lake* first appeared, in the inadequate Moscow production. His revisions of *Giselle*, undertaken with Ludwig Minkus, the composer of *La Bayadère*, came a decade later. When he planned the new *Swan Lake*, he entrusted the swan scenes to an assistant, Lev Ivanov. Ivanov composed his dances "symphonically," as was Petipa's custom; by then, if Russian historians are to be believed, the Petipa tradition had been safely launched. Names associated with that tradition crop up continually in the performance history of *La Bayadère*: Solor, a split role in the original production, was mimed by Ivanov and danced by Pavel Gerdt; Gerdt and Ekaterina Vazem, the first Nikiya, had among their pupils Nicolai Legat and Agrippina Vaganova, who in later years made revisions to the ballet which were accepted as authoritative. (Revisions closer to our time, such as those by Vakhtang Chabukiani in 1940, are stylistically disputable.) The last ballerina whom Petipa rehearsed as Nikiya was Anna Pavlova, who performed the role with such precision that she achieved a kind of transubstantiation, according to André Levinson: drama gave way to symbolism in "*la vibration musicale des lignes allongées et pures.*" The ballet remained unknown in the West until the 1960's. Ballet Theatre has had the Shades scene, in Natalia Makarova's staging, since 1974. The production of the complete ballet, which Makarova has also supervised, is the first outside Russia and the first to restore the final act, with the destruction of the temple and the apotheosis of the lovers, since the Russians dropped it during an economy wave in 1919.

As expected, neither of the unfamiliar acts (Makarova's first act encompasses two of Petipa's) contains anything to match the Kingdom of the Shades—or the Tent of Solor, as it is now called. An elaborate classical divertissement in Act I is the only other extended display of dancing, and it's a disappointment. Solor performs his interpolated (by Chabukiani) solo here, and the charming variation for Gamzatti that follows begins like one of the Shades' dances but then develops ideas of its own. The rest of the choreography either lollops along in a Petipa vein from which the ore has already been mined or veers into anachronisms that suggest choreographers of a much later vintage than Petipa or his heirs. The Gamzatti-Solor pas de deux is flanked by two contrapuntal trios, which seems traditional enough. But the structural links in this lavallière of an adagio are repeatedly broken by the unharmonious movements of the two principals. The overhead lifts, which occur throughout the ballet, are especially nonsensical here.

Makarova and her assistant, Elena Tchernichova, appear to have done a good deal of rummaging among the assortment of Petipaisms and post-Petipaisms that make up the traditional Leningrad version of the ballet. The first act squirts samples of exotic or grotesque dancing into the exposition before ladling on the classical treats, yet under the labels it's all the same beef tea. The dances are differentiated as entertainment, not as events in a drama. As dances, they haven't enough internal tension to be looked at closely. Yet if they're formula dances in a formula plot, haven't they been misaligned? Nikiya is a character dancer who dies and goes to classical Heaven, but there's not such a great difference between her heavenly dances and Gamzatti's earthly ones. We never get to see Nikiya lead the temple dancers in a dance; it is Gamzatti who is the ballerina of the divertissement in the betrothal scene even though Petipa and subsequent choreographers specified entrées for the bayadères. Was one of these entrées—possibly the one that resembles a Shades variation—once a dance for Nikiya? Was Gamzatti's dancing role in this scene confined to the betrothal pas de deux? These sound like prescriptive questions. Well, I'd almost rather see the prescriptions filled than get the answers, which must lie somewhere in Russia's Petipa archives.

In contrast to Act I, Makarova's Act III appears to be entirely her invention, without recourse to the Petipa sample case. John Lanchbery underlines the departure with his wholesale rewriting of the Minkus score. (His fancying-up of the Shades' music is less tolerable.) The scene is the wedding in the temple, into which Nikiya intrudes as a ghost, and Makarova builds it into a pas d'action in the true sense of the term—a dance in which something really happens. Nikiya, constantly appearing and disappearing, intervenes in a supported adagio, snatches away flowers intended for the bride, replaces her in the groom's arms. Makarova has imagined the episode as an agitated version of the passage in which the Sylph comes between James and Effie in Filippo Taglioni's *La Sylphide*—which it may have been in the first place. (Petipa was certainly thinking back to Taglioni's *Le Dieu et la Bayadère* when he constructed his own ballet.) The pas d'action has the same kind of mythic force as the astral encounters in Act II. None of the action in Act I has that quality, even for a moment. What it has is hocus-pocus, as in Nikiya's veiled entrance and her ceremonial gestures over the sacred flame. Makarova tries to build mystery with a Nikiya-Solor pas de deux that anticipates their more famous one in the next act; but anticipation weakens what should be a singular moment. Maybe the first pas de deux in the Shades scene—the one in which the bayadère anoints Solor and pledges him to her—should come here. Two duets in succession have never made much sense in the Shades scene. There is another curious doubling of effects in the veil that the High Brahman removes to reveal Nikiya and the veil that the Raja removes to reveal Gamzatti. When Gamzatti then waves around another veil, her meaning is uncertain: is it "my rival" or "my wedding"? In *La Bayadère*, veils are identified with the temple dancer and with the high mystery of her calling; later, they are identified with death. Extending the symbolism to the bridal veil may be irresistible, but better to leave to *Giselle* the things that are *Giselle*'s and to *Bayadère* the things that are *Bayadère*'s. The only outré connection that matters is the one that the audience has always made for itself between bayadère and ballerina (or wili and ballerina). The morbidity and pathos of the white acts in these ballets are essential to the atmosphere of nineteenth-century ballet. A generation after *Giselle*, the ghastly, crazed vocation of the dancer is purified in *La Bayadère*. Temple dancers are holy, elevated by what Martha Graham in our time has called "divine dissatisfaction." And Graham also likes to say, "Where dancers stand, that is hallowed ground."

Nikiya, the keeper of the flame, is one of those archetypal ballet characters who symbolize the life and art of the dancer. Because the libretto of *La Bayadère* doesn't keep the symbolism active, as the libretto of *Giselle* does, Nikiya as a character isn't real to us; we don't know who she is until the Shades scene, and we don't understand her passionate fury when she attacks her rival and when she brings down the temple. She's really a shatterer of worlds—a goddess of holy vengeance who may have her origin in the Upanishads. In terms of *La Bayadère* and Western theatrical practice, she incarnates the hysteria of sacred love. Choreographically, though, her role is divided between two kinds of "sacred" dance—the classicism of the Shades scene and the rather emaciated "Hindu" plastique of Act I. The role seems designed—or redesigned—to show off range rather than to embody a fixed emotion. When we think of dancers who could make the contradictions in the role work as a unified portrait, not many come to mind. Vazem, of the original cast, seems to have been a steely technician who made Petipa's steps in the Shades scene crisply legible. The sacred-profane Christian-pagan stereotypes of Western dance were a venerable tradition that had been defined, seemingly for all time, by the opposite styles of Marie Taglioni and Fanny Elssler. In *La Bayadère*, Eastern dualism seems to have played a part in breaking down the Western either/or stereotype of the ballerina. The role of Nikiya is really more advanced psychologically than the dual role of Odette-Odile. If Petipa found a perfect Nikiya before Pavlova, history does not record it. Certainly, not until Pavlova does the idea of combining two temperaments in one ballerina achieve force. Pavlova was both Taglioni and Elssler, virgin and bacchante. Her position in dance at the gateway to the modern era is obscure only because the gateway has receded into the mist. For the same reason, today's actresses don't know Duse; her repertory is as dead as Pavlova's. I will make a guess that Nikiya's dances in Act I stem from Pavlova's era; they look thin because once they were filled with Pavlova.

This is hard on any dancer of today, to whom Pavlova's modernity is less comprehensible than the proficiency of a Vazem. As Nikiya, Makarova hasn't yet been seen at her best. Taken with leg cramps on opening night, she projected dimly and curtailed some of her choreography in the Shades scene. A week later, a knee injury forced her out of a nationwide television performance after the first act. The ballet stands up without her; the solidity of nineteenth-century construction insures that. I've seen Nikiya done by Jolinda Menendez and, as the television pinch-hitter, Marianna Tcherkassky. Each made an acceptable stage picture—Menendez in the mime and floorwork of Act I and Tcherkassky in Act II. But Makarova must know more about *La Bayadère* than any other ballerina alive. When in *A Dance Autobiography* (Knopf) she describes the "liturgical character" of the first Nikiya-Solor pas de deux in the Shades scene and says that "the opening of the leg à la seconde . . . should be performed like opening a missal," we recognize the analytical powers of an artist trained to see the most delicate emotional distinctions in movement and make us see them, too. It isn't just talk; Makarova really does dance like that. (Her characterization of this pas de deux persuades me that its rightful place is in Act I, in front of the temple.)

When Makarova brings up "coloration" in movement, she is speaking from her strength as a dramatic dancer—a hard strength to transmit to others. She has managed to transmit something to the Shades corps de ballet. But after six years ABT is still putting out Shades soloists who color the movement gray. In the new divertissement, the dancers are able to show vividly only what they have been taught for this production; there's no foundation for it. Everybody mimes at the same speed, forcing the chest forward and the head back. Martine van Hamel, with her grand-scale dancing and her easy flow of postures and gestures, makes a pleasant Gamzatti, but even she is likely to fall into the all-purpose ship's-prow pose at crucial moments (when she sees Solor's portrait; when she sees *him*). Though she has even less of an existence as a character than Nikiya, a strongly acted and danced Gamzatti can make this *Bayadère* a two-ballerina vehicle. (I don't agree that it should be, but apparently the Kirov has cast two principals for years.) Where, ABT, are your ballerinas? Solor was never a great role for Anthony Dowell with the Royal Ballet, but he has acquired just enough flamboyance in recent seasons to bring it off. He is able to mime in period style, carrying the opium hallucinations all the way to derangement à la Edwin Booth in Act III. Patrick Bissell, a dancer of enormous talent who is still unconsummated as an artist, has a tender, serious presence. His Solor is dreamily innocent; when he soars into his variation, his power is so great and so carelessly disposed (I don't mean technically; it is that as well, alas) that he seems beyond good and evil. He's as much a victim as Nikiya. The other characters have walking, running, or crouching roles. The High Brahman, who loves Nikiya, is a real character, but Alexander Minz seems to think he is a plot hinge. At the Maryinsky, roles like this were largely invented by their interpreters, and they must be reinvented in revivals.

I have saved till last the best news about this production, which is that it is a scenic wonder. PierLuigi Samaritani has designed seven painted drops, alluding now to Persian miniatures, now to Mogul painting of the nineteenth century, now to Maryinsky-style architectural décor, now to the untrammelled spaces of antiquity's sacred groves and Elysian Fields. His stylistic derivations are never flighty; his weighted nineteenth-century details are never solemn. With his lighting designer, Toshiro Ogawa, he makes a perfect Mt. St. Helens out of the destruction of the temple. Theoni Aldredge's costumes are keyed to the scenery in a balanced profusion of effects. The ballet—the two outer acts, anyway—needs this kind of support. It is a frail vision of the past that Makarova has given us in her unaccustomed role of choreographer-director, but it is an extremely useful one. Although much is arguable, nothing in her staging is tentative or apologetic. It means to fill a gap in knowledge and does so with consistently engaging grace.

—June 16, 1980

Slowly Then the History of Them Comes Out

First, it was Louis Horst and Martha Graham. Then it was John Cage and Merce Cunningham. Now, it seems, Philip Glass and Robert Wilson, between them, are filling the role of mentor to the choreographers who are shaping the most pervasive new dance aesthetic. Glass, like Horst and Cage, has composed for dancers—notably, for Lucinda Childs and Andrew deGroat, with whom he began to work after collaborating with them and Wilson in 1976, in *Einstein on the Beach*. Wilson, except in the most informal sense, does not choreograph, but as a writer and director of esoteric visionary plays and as a teacher of movement he has been the biggest influence, after Cunningham, on choreographers working today. These young (or young*er*) choreographers—among them Childs and DeGroat and Meredith Monk and Kenneth King—reflect different aspects of Wilson's work, just as Trisha Brown and Steve Paxton and Douglas Dunn reflect different aspects of Cunningham's work. They all belong to the generation commonly referred to as "post-modern," although "post-Cunningham" would be a better term. The various streams of activity which they represent, Wilson's included, are all ultimately traceable to the climate of inspiration which was established by Cage and Cunningham thirty years ago. Even the big idea that seems to divide the mysterians from the mercists—the idea of a return to music— isn't really as sharp a break with the older tradition as it seems. (That secession was actually launched some time ago by Paul Taylor and continued in due course by Twyla Tharp.) Cage and Cunningham taught that a musical accompaniment and a dance have nothing in common but the length of time each takes to happen. Of course, they have much more in common—the theory of aleatoric structure was never denied, either in the dancing or in the music. A dance to a Glass score is also likely to be constructed according to the same laws as the music—laws of "repetitive structure and modular form," to quote a recent program note—but whether it then goes its own way or not is open to question. Besides principles of construction, there is a very heavy beat tying dance and music together, and usually, although not always, there is a cryptic, spectral, incantatory atmosphere. These two elements—the beat and the misterioso atmosphere— aren't much, but they're enough to create a new sensation in dance. And they're beginning to crop up all over the place.

In recent weeks, I have seen a DeGroat work choreographed to Glass music; a new ballet presented by the Alvin Ailey company to a portion of the score of *Einstein on the Beach*; a film about choreographers which incorporated part of Lucinda Childs's *Dance*, with its score by Glass; a "Dance in America" TV show in which this trend was represented by Laura Dean dancing to her own music; and a live concert by Dean, again dancing to her own music. Before she took to composing her own scores, Dean used to collaborate with Steve Reich, the country's other best-known composer of loop music, or music of incessant repetition. Terry Riley and Sergio Cervetti have also worked with dancers in this form. But it is Glass who has come to dominate the dance field. When Laura Dean composes, she sounds not like Reich but like Glass; and Meredith Monk, who has been producing her own sound for a long time, has done several remarkably Glass-like scores. School of Glass tends to feature electronic keyboards, eerie harmonies, pulsing rhythms, and vocalise; it is very loud. Like rock, School of Glass is meant to engulf you. As Andrew Porter wrote in his review of *Einstein on the Beach*, once the listener realizes that the endless repetitions are actually going somewhere, Glass's music is easy to take for quite long spells. Glass habitually works in long forms: a piece called *Music in Twelve Parts* lasts four hours. "The mind may wander now and again," Porter adds, "but it wanders within a new sound world that the composer has created." To be within that world is to experience music as a succession of instants. Glass has asked that his listeners surrender their usual equipment of memory and anticipation; perhaps the reason he is attracted to dance is that dance is a present-tense art form, with no precise way of recalling or predicting itself. Glass's hammering beat seems to drive dancers ever onward into the outer space of unanticipated movement.

This doesn't mean that the movement will be new; it means that the sensation of the movement will be new. In the work of Childs and DeGroat and Dean, the steps are elementary, with no embellishments of technique. The repetition aims at creating a cumulative effect of movement beyond the movements that you see, and the total experience of action and sound can be all-involving. To those who are susceptible to this intangible process, there are degrees of abstraction and purity even within the ultimate high that it provides. Lucinda Childs's choreography is a maze of footpaths laid out with Euclidean austerity. To her followers, she was the first—some say the only—choreographer to elevate the sensations of the form to the level of an aesthetic. They may be right, although in actual fact the aesthetic came first. Childs worked for years cutting her school figures in silence. When she added music, the figures took on a brightly sensuous elegance, a change she acknowledged with a switch in costume: corduroys were discarded for flowing silk and lamé. But basically Childs does what she has always done. The atmosphere of chic that envelops her performances these days can be as irritating to those who know why she does it as to those who, like me, don't. Childs has evolved something that looks like prehistoric ballet. The erect, springy carriage, the walking and skipping and hopping patterns seem to want to accumulate technique. I see nothing in their logic to prevent their turning into actual dance steps. Maybe they will, and we'll see the first SoHo Civic Ballet.

At the moment, Childs's work is closer to that of her fellow-minimalist Trisha Brown than it is to her fellow-cultist Laura Dean. Dean, like De-Groat, like William Dunas, like the intramedia specialists Monk and King, and like numerous other choreographers from unallied schools (Kei Takei, Phoebe Neville, Anthony LaGiglia), is a mysterian. The shadows and strategies of Robert Wilson hang heavy over them all. Brown isn't like that. Her work is sunny and open, with a practical base easy—fatally easy—to penetrate. If she uses music at all, it's usually an afterthought—a bit of country-and-Western sing-along or early rock. Like Steve Paxton's, Brown's concerts resemble workshops in which the audience is taught movement logic. The leap in logic which takes us from the studio into the theatre is never made. (When Brown gets a theatrical idea, it usually pertains to production, not movement. At her most recent concert, her company danced through clouds of steam.) For a while, Brown and Childs and Dean were alike in having intensively systematic methods of producing choreography as an end in itself. Childs and Dean have customarily presented surface as substance. But in Dean's latest work, *Music* (at the Brooklyn Academy), the naive, plainspoken little phrases seemed to dissolve back into a motive for doing them, which was apparently to put the dancers into a trance. I found myself looking not at a dance but at a rite. Perhaps the resemblance to the Gurdjieff dances in the movie *Meetings with Remarkable Men* was intentional; perhaps not. Dean's dances have always had their trancelike sections, their protracted sequences of dervishlike spinning, which put me off; *Music* is the first dance to start building up a trance with the first step. Instead of developing her formal choreographic devices, Dean seems bent on evolving ever more extended exercises in concentration for her dancers. The first forty or so minutes of *Music* (the whole piece lasts seventy-five minutes) were devoted to a slow-motion legato exercise performed by the group of six in unison while an orchestra consisting of piano, violin, and synthesizer sustained an unbroken wave of chords. It looked like T'ai Chi stuck in a groove, and the audience expressed its disgruntlement by walking out in numbers. The choreography turned to individual variations in canon, then to an allegro section, where it settled into the familiar spinning patterns. One couldn't just close one's eyes and spin in a "new sound world"; Dean's music for *Music* is as compulsive and lethargic as her dances. Fellow-worshippers in the audience gave the company an ovation while those of us who'd stuck it out tiptoed up the aisle.

DeGroat began his performance series at the Midtown Y with a film of himself spinning with a rope; the film was projected as DeGroat in person performed the same rope dance in the dark. Then several dancers did some low-grade ballet steps to a tape of Chopin. By the time the ensemble threw itself into a scrimmage of runs and lifts while a voice intoned and spelled out "Brick Brintzonhofe" over and over, we were well versed in DeGroat-style mysterianism. It seems to take something from everybody; the aspect I am most uneasy about is its celebration of the work of Christopher Knowles, but I may be guilty of humanistic overreaction. Knowles is afflicted with brain damage; the things he does with typewriters and tape recorders (for example, the "Brick Brintzonhofe" spiel) also inspire Wilson, who considers him a poet. The way DeGroat dances suggests that he may have adopted Knowles as an alter ego. DeGroat often looks uncoordinated and inarticulate, yet he also has assurance and control. The mixture of rough and smooth in his choreography seems to have been planned by a master. It's apathetic yet alert—heads-up ritualism. *Red Notes*, the work to the Glass score, is an anthology of influences, in which DeGroat in one way or another sums up the whole of the post-modern scene for which Glass and Wilson have acted as co-mentors and throws in a few clues to *their* influences. Not that there are any surprises; instead of a Knowles text, *Red Notes* ("Read Notes") has one by Gertrude Stein, the patron saint of the avant-garde, and it includes the lines from *The Making of Americans* which could be the epigraph of post-modernism: "Slowly everything comes out from each one in the kind of repeating each one does . . . Slowly then the history of them comes out from them." If Stein were talking about dancers and repertory, her meaning could not be clearer. My quarrel with post-modernism is not with repetition—it's with ritualistic repetition. Ritualistic repetition—ritualized ritual, in other words—makes repeating more important than "the history of them." It sentimentalizes the process of repetition by attributing to it more power than it possesses. "Natural movement" is enshrined, yet movements that are paltry and meager cannot make history no matter how many times they are done. When virtuosity is absent, personality counts for more than it perhaps should. The whole post-modern movement, from Yvonne Rainer onward, has been anti-personality, yet at this moment it is teetering on the brink of star worship. Childs and Glass are stars of increasing magnitude; Dean is amassing a cult. DeGroat's work, on the whole, has a force and variety that Dean's doesn't have, but it's also more ambivalent, heading toward, then steering away from a broad-scale popular approach. The grossest appeal that the Glass kind of music can make is to the audience for head music. At its most coyly surrealistic, DeGroat's choreography is head dance. In *Red Notes*, there's the druggy dissociative structure, the bits of sacerdotal imagery, and such light-show whammies as a giant shadow of a hand drawing arrows on a movie screen as the dancers beneath troop back and forth in lines. Above all, there's the pounding beat that binds one thing to another—that makes a monotonous, few-toned, desultory set of dances into a unified work of orgiastic vivacity.

Kathryn Posin's *Later That Day*, done for the Ailey company's spring season at the City Center, is set to Glass music, but because it isn't inside the world of the music, it manages to do more with it than the house choreographers so far have dreamed of doing. Where Childs and DeGroat have used Glass as if his were the only kind of music there is, Posin catches up his peculiarities and accounts for them in her choreography. *Later That Day* doesn't resemble *Einstein on the Beach*; if it resembles anything, it's *Les Noces*. Dancers enter in a long line while a chorus repeatedly intones a five-note phrase. A couple (bride and groom?) crouches to one side on a platform. On the other side, Dudley Williams, in a three-piece suit, sits reading at a lectern or stands and waves his arms like a signalman. Preacher, guests, and bridal couple compose a triad; all are dressed by Christina Giannini in sleek playclothes of the 1920's. The guests pose and move in antiphonal harmony with the couple, like a Greek chorus. The action is entirely static, but at the end some new element has recharged the proportions of the triad. The element is time; Williams stands looking at his watch, amazed. As the response of a more conventional choreographer to the incitements of "new" music, *Later That Day* is highly suggestive. Without condescension or undue simplification, Posin manages to relate Glass to the world outside electronic circuitry and afflatus. She has found ritualistic images that match the sound, but she hasn't followed the sound to a land's-end depletion. And, by the looks of things, she has had an easier time of it than the post-moderns have had with their windy ongoing mystique.

Repetition is the sacred right of performing artists—actors, dancers, musicians. Performance art is a category in which nonperforming arts may be endowed with the repetitive, mutable aspects of music or dance. You have to see a successful performance artist, like David Gordon, to believe that it can work. Gordon's areas are dance, words, and sometimes photographs; that everything comes together on a high level of interest has to do not with the power of one or another medium, or even with their power in combination, but with the personalities of Gordon and his partner, Valda Setterfield. Their most recent concert, held in their loft, was a "performance collage," made up of previous works assembled in a new format and framing sections of new work. With Gordon, the creative process is always retrospective. The evening was a pleasure both in its novelties and in its recapitulations, but I want to bring up instead Gordon's recent movie and television appearances, in which he appears among his colleagues as post-modernism's most articulate spokesman. In both *Beyond the Mainstream* (part of the PBS "Dance in America" series) and *Making Dances*, a documentary on seven post-modern choreographers, by Michael Blackwood, the importance of personality in work of this kind is accidentally stressed. Although plain, small-scale post-modern movement is easier to convey on film than other kinds of dance, the experience of a performance is, if anything, harder; it may take a whole evening to build up. The camera can show neither transitions nor highlights comfortably, but it feeds on interviews. Here, and in the cinéma-vérité–style studio rehearsals, is where we form our impressions of the choreographers. Gordon rises to the top not only because the film medium magnifies his personality but because he is used to having his personality considered a major element in his work. The David Gordon who talks to the camera is the same David Gordon who appears as a character in David Gordon/Pick-Up Company presentations. To be sure, he usually appears at some point in the evening as a talking character, but, curiously, neither *Beyond the Mainstream* nor *Making Dances* captures that aspect of his performance. The chief interest, for me, of both these films was the bafflement they reflected. A lot of post-modernism is baffling to me, and I was looking to them for enlightenment. Instead, the burden of explanation was for the most part on the choreographers and what they could think of to say.

One of Gordon's provocative comments (in *Making Dances*) is an analogy with the movies. While movie-goers of the Joan Crawford generation now enjoy *Coming Home* and *Saturday Night Fever* even though the new movies are written, photographed, and cut in an entirely different fashion, "the way people approach dance is peculiarly conservative," he says. "I love *Sleeping Beauty*, too, but I don't have to see only it for the rest of my life." I see the point, but to me the style of dance that Gordon represents is more like television than like new feature films. Audiences have no trouble accepting new ballets, but not many people are willing to take the prosaic, uncultivated look of post-modern dance seriously. Fewer still are willing to relate the materials of this kind of dance to their sources in classic art. In his piece called *The Matter*, Gordon stages a parody of the Entrance of the Shades in *La Bayadère*." "I like it because it repeats itself many times," he says (in *Beyond the Mainstream*). "One ballerina enters, and then the next one enters, and then the next one enters, and it goes on forever. I mean, that ballet was made a very long time ago. And that audience is willing to sit in an opera house and watch forty-some-odd ballerinas come in one at a time, forever." One reason may be that at the end of forever audiences know they're going to get a ballet. It's not just the glamour or the rhetorical style that accounts for the difference in acceptance. The diminished scale of modern and post-modern choreography—the fact that it can't project over opera-house distances—will always limit its appeal. This is why what Gordon calls "art disco"—amplified, big-beat walking music—is getting popular with dancers. It's fantasy-scale stuff, bigger in terms of time than any music, to compensate for dance that is smaller in terms of space than any dance. It goes on forever, and why not? Monotonous repetition, a feature of the folk art of all nations, has also been a factor in the popularity of art of all kinds, high and low. It's the "infinity factor" that keeps Ravel's *Bolero* on the Hit Parade, along with the Triumphal March from *Aida*, the first movement of the "Moonlight" Sonata (a particular favorite of Robert Wilson's), "Mack the Knife," and the Entrance of the Shades from *La Bayadère*. Mysterianism could produce the next masterpiece in kind.

—*June 30, 1980*

Postscript 1982: This article drew protests from Kenneth King, Meredith Monk, and Yvonne Rainer, all of whom wrote me letters and then published them (without my knowledge) in *Live*, a performance arts journal. It's quite possible that their replies, together with a confused ventilation of "the controversy" that appeared in the *Village Voice*, aroused more arousable people than my article did in the first place. That very real possibility plus the fact that none of my correspondents addressed any of the main points of my piece or showed how these were affected by the alleged factual discrepancies tend to confirm my cynic's theory that performers can tolerate only as much criticism as can be converted to the uses of publicity.

Since King, Monk, and Rainer have put their objections into print, I feel no obligation to summarize them here. The uninitiated may be interested to know that King and Monk were incensed by my use of the words "mentor" and "influence" to describe Robert Wilson's relations with them. King, as is his custom, circulated copies of his letter (the first of several), in which he informed one and all that "Meredith Monk, myself (and I believe Lucinda Childs) were most certainly presenting *and* exploring the kind of work we are now known for—years before Robert Wilson. Really it's the other way around." And he adds, "At this point we are all working on very different things in quite different styles."

I pretend to no great understanding of what King, Monk, Childs, and for that matter Wilson are up to. I don't call them the mysterians for nothing. For me, sitting here in the dark, all cats are gray. Naturally, to themselves the cats are all kinds of colors. King claims to be working on different things in different styles. I wouldn't expect him to claim anything else.*

But just which of King's claims can one believe? Part of my research in preparation for this article consisted of King's own testimony to Wilson's importance. Ironically enough, it was in response to a misguided headline in the New York *Times* over a Don McDonagh review of Wilson's production of *The Life and Times of Sigmund Freud*: "Story of Dr. Freud Depicted in Dance by Meredith Monk." (That headline writer must now be doing publicity for Monk.) The misattribution plus McDonagh's bafflement brought on a six-page King circular dated December 21, 1969, and co-signed by Monk and Wilson. Here Wilson is praised as a colleague in the following words:

> *Bob brings to dance an exciting theatrical aesthetic that amalgamates and absorbs his creative and teaching work with children, adults and the handicapped, as well as incorporates his experience in architecture, sculpture, the voice and body movement. . . . I write hopefully expressing some of the com-*

---

* Since my last review of King's work, his style has indeed changed, becoming more involved with dance, less with words.

mon indignation we all feel and to defend and applaud with genuine apprecia-
tion Robert Wilson's work: it seeks out many new directions, full of rich,
overlapping aesthetic possibilities and, perhaps even more importantly, it opens
new channels for future activity among young people with radically different
skills and talents. That is an accomplishment.

It must have been quite an accomplishment, too, for Wilson to change in King's
eyes from valued colleague to "well-known artistic cleptomaniac." The story of
this change has nowhere been published—naturally not, since Wilson's outsize
success has made him an unperson in post-modern circles—one whose name is
never mentioned, even for the record. Historical revisionism has set in. If Monk
believed then what she apparently believes today—that "it was clear from the
beginning that he [Wilson] was a ruthless, ambitious person with few ideas of
his own, and that his career would be fed with the fuel of other artists' work"—
why did she co-sign King's letter in Wilson's behalf?

Yvonne Rainer's diligence as a record-keeper led her to send me a hand-drawn
genealogical table showing just who among those I categorized as mercists influenced whom. If Rainer had read my piece with the care she devoted to her
chart, perhaps she'd have seen that my purpose was to describe affinities and
consequences as they appeared to me, and that "history" as it is invoked in my
title (derived from Gertrude Stein's line) refers to that self-explanation of persons through movement which so much of post-modern dance appears (*appears*,
I say, always *appears*) to be about. They do it, I watch, I paint what I see. Anna
Halprin, one of Rainer's fountainheads, may have been influential at one time;
I cannot see, now, her presence competing with the still active presences of
Cage and Cunningham to influence what people are doing generally or what
Trisha Brown was doing particularly in *Glacial Decoy* (1979), with its décor by
Rauschenberg.

Of course King, Monk, and some others were working before Wilson came
along; I'm talking about what they produced once he did come along. We have
all been entertained by the imaginary characters whose guises Kenneth King has
assumed onstage and off. It wasn't until 1973 and the following year that King
began presenting historical characters. There were evenings in which he appeared heavily disguised, spouting passages from *Thus Spake Zarathustra*. I
remember these Nietzsche presentations only because of King's accent, which
was more Yiddish than German, and because Wilson had already dealt as in-
comprehensibly with Freud and Stalin. In a 1978 concert (see page 82), King
walked forward and backward on a diagonal, very much like Lucinda Childs in
Einstein on the Beach, giving credence to the rumor that Wilson was going to
star them both in an ambulatory version of *Orlando*. Who can doubt that the
main impact of Wilson in the early days derived from his use of slow motion?
Deafman Glance (1970) was an evening-long epic that moved at the speed of a
glacier. Monk *had* used slow motion in the scattered parts of *Juice* (1969), if
not earlier. This was very different from her Wilsonian use of it for interminable
periods over the course of a single evening (*Education of the Girlchild*, 1973).
It was also about this time that she took to calling her work "opera," as Wilson
did his. But these chronological data are relatively unimportant beside the larger
issue of consequentiality. No matter where he got his ideas, Wilson has been
able to aggrandize them so as to create a permissive climate for all those choosing
to work in a certain mode. Characteristically, my correspondents accuse me of
changing my views of the field. It doesn't occur to them that the field may
have changed.

But is criticism/history really the issue here? Post-moderns, like most dancers,
fear the effect of opinion not on what is understood of their work but on their
ability to attract subsidies. I can analyze to exhaustion, but all it's good for in

the eyes of those analyzed is a yes or no vote in the councils of the National Endowment, say, or the Mellon Foundation. King and Monk are actually upset that I was on the NEA dance panel. Presumably, I performed my acts of sabotage against them while David Gordon, Margaret Jenkins, Sally Banes, David White, Allen Robertson, and David Vaughan all sat there helpless. In statistical fact, more post-moderns were awarded NEA grants when I was on the panel than in any previous period.

In February 1981, the Rockefeller Foundation awarded Wilson and Glass $90,000 each—the largest grants it had ever made to artists. My feeling about this is that the post-moderns have won big. Their feeling, most probably, is that I have.

Heart of Darkness

Chivalrous, embattled, euphoric, distraught: the figure of Robert Schumann comes before us where we might least expect to encounter it—in a Balanchine ballet. Seen for the first time during the closing weeks of the State Theatre season, the ballet is set to *Davidsbündlertänze* ("Dances of David's Band"), eighteen piano pieces in which Schumann's compound personality is characterized in musical dialogues of such quicksilver fascination that it or, rather, they call out to be presented in dance form. That no ballet has been successfully achieved before is probably owing to the problem of constructing a stage world for David's Band. This anti-Philistine league was composed of Schumann's multiple selves, to whom he gave fanciful names; it first appeared in his critical writings, and it turned up as part of the supporting cast in *Carnaval*. But how much easier it must have been for Fokine to imagine dance roles for Florestan, Eusebius, and the other Davidites in his ballet *Carnaval* than for Balanchine to transcribe *Davidsbündlertänze*. In *Carnaval*, Schumann had established a theatrical setting of masks and guises. *Davidsbündlertänze* (a sequel, despite its earlier opus number) is introspective, its drama latent, its personae restricted to the dynamic Florestan and the contemplative Eusebius, who, as always, represent the two sides of the composer's nature. There is a clear musical kinship between *Carnaval* and *Davidsbündlertänze*, but it is not one that a choreographer may easily exploit. To put the difference in Schumannesque terms, *Carnaval* was written by Florestan and *Davidsbündlertänze* by Eusebius.

Of course, in the original manuscript the Davidite dances are ascribed to one or the other, and sometimes to both. In the second edition of the score, Schumann expunged all the bylines, together with most of the stage directions—such as "Here Florestan stopped and his lips trembled sorrowfully," before No. 9—and he even dropped the word "Dances" from the title. Between the first (1838) and the second (1850) edition, the major event that occurred in Schumann's life was his marriage to Clara Wieck. *Davidsbündlertänze* was written to her. Schumann noted in a letter, "My Clara will find out for me what is in the dances; they are more her own than anything else of mine." Clara could and did read Schumann's secret language; once they were married, he seemed content to let the music stand on its own. Balanchine has obviously followed the second, "pure" edition. But he has also treated it as program music of the most personal kind. The ballet has four couples, all of whom portray aspects of Robert and Clara. At the same time, the dances can be seen simply as dances. There is no more mystery for the viewer to solve than there is in the music—music that, as Schumann hinted, even he found enigmatic. To Balanchine, the characters of Florestan and Eusebius are less important than the idea of duality which they represent. The ruling emotions of the ballet are neither-nor: happy-sad, light-dark, hot-cold. This is not unusual for a Balanchine ballet. However, in its quality of expression the ballet *is* unusual. Continually and confoundingly, it is forthright and evasive at the same time. The double or duplicit meanings in the dances aren't in any troublesome or recondite allusions—they spring from the mania of Romanticism to encompass all the feelings of life in one music. Schumann relished his mania. "If ever I was happy at the piano," he said of *Davidsbündlertänze*, "it was when I was composing these." But at the head of the original edition he placed a German proverb on the eternal link between *Lust* and *Leid*—pleasure and sorrow.

What strikes most people about the new ballet (to which no name has been given—it is listed in the program as *Robert Schumann's "Davidsbündlertänze"*) is Balanchine's use of a demonstratively dramatic style of choreography. Rumor had predicted another *Liebeslieder Walzer*, the beloved Brahms ballet that is no longer done in New York, but instead the dances are in a style similar to that of *Meditation* and parts of *Don Quixote*. While the format of the piece follows *Liebeslieder* to a certain extent—the four couples dancing a succession of duets to an onstage piano, the women changing from pumps to toe shoes in the course of the dances—the choreography seems to take Schumann's deletion of the word "Dances" as its cue. There are scarcely any dance steps in the *Liebeslieder* mold, and the choreography makes no distinction, as *Liebeslieder* did, between social dancing and ballet. Compared to almost any other piece of Balanchine choreography, even compared to *Meditation*, the ballet has almost no intricacy or sweep of phrase. Instead, we see dancing used as an extension of a dramatic situation: steps are repeated over and over or protracted into poses or connected not by other steps but by walks, runs, hesitant gestures, glances. The lack of density and the free look of the timing make us feel we're witnessing a series of short, probing conversations. And along about the fifth or sixth dance (when point shoes are adopted), the dancers begin to develop the psychological dimensions of real characters. The four couples are divided into two pairs of "twins." The more prominent pair—Suzanne Farrell and Jacques d'Amboise, Karin von Aroldingen and Adam Lüders —perhaps represents Clara and Robert as they were in art and as they were in life. Farrell is Clara the artist and also Robert's (D'Amboise's) muse; Von Aroldingen is Clara the bride and wife, while Lüders, who has the most colorful male role, is Robert the victim of hallucination and derangement— the mad poet who died young. Heather Watts and Peter Martins are paired with Kay Mazzo and Ib Andersen as identical twins who may possibly be Clara and Robert as lovers; twice all four appear in mirror-image dances. If D'Amboise and Lüders are Florestan and Eusebius as positive and negative forces in Schumann's nature, Martins and Andersen are those forces in balance, symmetrically justified by Schumann's union with the perfect woman.

There are three solos. The first, and most eccentric, is Farrell's, to No. 12. Schumann marked it "mit Humor"—but there are other humorous or good-humored dances in the suite. What distinguish Farrell's are, first, its direct, unclouded emotion—it's the only "warm" dance that doesn't contain some icy portent, some hint of its own undoing, either choreographically or musically—and, second, its connection to one of Schumann's famous musical puzzles. In No. 12, the composer repeats the little theme from *Carnaval* that concealed an anagram of his name in its notes. Schumann called this little tease "Sphinxes." Applying this to Farrell, Balanchine gives us the "explanation" of her character: as a muse, she's truly unknowable. And if we don't get the clue from the music, we get it in the choreography: the dancer ends poised in attitude with one finger pointing ahead—the gesture of Polyhymnia (and Terpsichore touching fingers with Apollo), of Dulcinea, and of the Fairy in *Le Baiser de la Fée*. The solos for Von Aroldingen and Lüders both belong to the "biography" of the historical Schumann. Clara searches and weeps, Robert struggles with his devils and throws himself into the Rhine. In Lüders's solo, No. 15, we are again reminded of *Carnaval*—the "Chopin" episode. Schumann had been ridiculed for his impetuous review introducing Chopin to German music-lovers: "Hats off, gentlemen, a genius!" Against the forces of smug reaction David's Band took up arms. In Balanchine's staging, the Philistines make a brief appearance as static figures in black carrying their giant poison pens. Perhaps this is one Schumannesque figment that we don't need to be shown, but visually the inky silhouettes do suggest something of the fantasy of Schumann's polemical style and the influence upon it and upon his music of such writers as Jean Paul (Richter), E. T. A. Hoffmann, and Heinrich Heine.

Lüders does off-balance wheeling pivots, runs to and fro, and tight turns on a diagonal. It is the bombastic high point of the ballet, and the emotional climax has yet to arrive. But first there is a sudden switch in tone and all four couples are dancing a quadrille. As in an earlier "party" scene (No. 13), only more formally pressed, the suggestion is of a moment of grace outside the tensions of private life. When all partners have been exchanged and returned to their places, a recapitulation begins, and as the music gets slower and grows more hushed, the stage is gradually cleared. During this recapitulation, which signals the start of the ballet's long descent to its pianissimo close, the audience gets restless; there have been too many radical transitions and we still haven't reached the ballet's heart. It is at this moment that Balanchine steers straight for troubled waters—those indecisive harmonies and lingering suspensions in the music. Into the vacancy drops the wandering melody of No. 2—the most haunting melody in the score. Farrell and D'Amboise are alone; her off-center half-turns en promenade recall Lüders's anguished pivots, and as they continue we know we're wandering far off course. Is nothing going to happen? Well, there is an acceleration, a rush, a sudden pause capped by a lovely slow-motion exit, but even as you watch, it seems inconclusive. The last dance is Lüders's farewell to Von Aroldingen on a darkened stage; it's like the end of *Duo Concertant*—as inscrutable as that. The piece is not a hit; it doesn't want to be. It mirrors the passion of Robert Schumann, his intransigent daemon, his lust for the unknown. Like his music, it wears its heart on its sleeve even when there's no arm inside.

The décor is a palpitating set of white silk drapes flanking a vista of the Rhine out of which a ghostly cathedral lifts its spires. Balanchine told Anna Kisselgoff in the New York *Times* that Rouben Ter-Arutunian's inspiration was the paintings of Caspar David Friedrich. Gordon Boelzner plays the score wearing a period costume, and Ter-Arutunian's period-influenced clothes for the dancers are successful in every respect save in the childish cut of the men's jackets.

La Bayadère in its new, three-act version has had a very successful first season at the Met. But the real test will come during American Ballet Theatre's next season and the one after that. Will a full-length production that adds nothing substantial to the celebrated Shades scene continue to draw audiences? There *is* Makarova's staging of the wedding pas d'action in the last act, a resourceful piece of work with some fine special effects that end the evening on a suitably preposterous note. But as with ABT's other Petipa-Minkus revival, *Don Quixote*, the Maryinsky treasure chest has been reopened and found to have nothing of value left inside.

When the great Shades scene was first given in the West by Leningrad's Kirov Ballet, in 1961, it set off a wave of anticipatory excitement: surely there must be more where that came from. Since then, the defections of Nureyev, Makarova, and Baryshnikov have made it possible for us to see the remnants of the Petipa canon more or less as they are performed in Leningrad, and by now it seems safe to say that we've seen pretty nearly everything. Until Makarova's staging for ABT, the full *Bayadère* had been performed only in Russia. If Petipa nuggets were there, why hadn't we known about them from the post-Diaghilev wave of defectors who brought us definitive versions of the other Maryinsky classics? It is hard to imagine Balanchine or Danilova reviving a Minkus ballet at a time when most dance critics in this country were music critics who could not even tolerate Tchaikovsky. But they did revive *Paquita* excerpts, even though *La Bayadère* contains Minkus's best music. *La Bayadère* was not among Nicholas Sergeyev's bequests to British ballet—those sumptuous piles of choreographic notation that enabled Ninette de Valois to found the Royal Ballet on the Maryinsky repertory. For Western consumption, Sergeyev prepared *Le Songe du Rajah,* a shortened and revised version of the Shades scene, but this seems never to have been performed. The answer might be that the choreography was too difficult for Western corps de ballet dancers of that period. As for the rest of the ballet, most of it had probably been forgotten or been superseded by other Petipa ballets. (An example of supersession: Aurora, pricked by a spindle, succumbs while dancing in *The Sleeping Beauty,* just as Nikiya, bitten by a snake, had succumbed in *La Bayadère.*)

In an article written in 1971 for *Dance and Dancers,* the Russian dance historian Natalia Roslavleva relates how Vakhtang Chabukiani expanded the role of Solor by moving the wedding pas d'action from Act IV into Act II and rechoreographing it. This was in 1940, when the fourth act had been defunct for two decades and nothing remained of it but the music. Presumably, it is Chabukiani's choreography that we see in Makarova's Act I, and Minkus's Act IV music that we hear. (For Makarova's last act, which restores the episodes that are no longer performed in Russia, the pas d'action music was rewritten by the conductor John Lanchbery.) Roslavleva tells us that although the Petipa pas d'action contained a dance for Solor and one for his bride, Gamzatti, who up to then had not danced, Chabukiani interpolated both solos. Where the music came from she does not say. Nor does she tell us any more about the Petipa choreography than that Solor's number was done by a dance-in (called Slave in the program) and that the pas d'action was still remembered as late as 1925 and 1926, when the old fourth act was briefly restored for some gala performances. The reason I bring up these details is that they go far toward explaining one of the most puzzling things about the ballet as it stands today, which is that the stylistic contrast between the demi-caractère dances of the heroine, Nikiya, and the classical dances of her rival, Gamzatti, dissolves as soon as Nikiya dies and goes to the Kingdom of the Shades. Her dance style is then indistinguishable from Gamzatti's. The idea of a stylistic polarization was undoubtedly an outgrowth of Chabukiani's decision to introduce dances for himself and Gamzatti in Act II, and it sets the whole drama at cross-purposes. The straight classicism that we loosely identify with Petipa's style turns out in this ballet to have specific connotations that make it inapplicable to Gamzatti. We may never know how Petipa conceived the single dance that he allotted to the mime role of Gamzatti; Roslavleva and her sources, which included the ballet master Fyodor Lopukhov, were hipped on the question of Chabukiani. With good reason: Chabukiani's was the hand that shaped *La Bayadère* for modern audiences.

When Martine van Hamel danced Nikiya this season, she minimized the exoticism of the plastique in the first-act dances, making the role—and the ballet at large—a more roundly classical whole. In this way, she avoided the unseemly parallel with Gamzatti. Van Hamel's interpretation is her own; everyone else I have seen do the part does it Makarova's way, which may be the way it has been done over the years at the Kirov, at least since the days of Anna Pavlova. Although the young Pavlova established her greatness in the Shades scene, she must have been extraordinary as the Hindu temple dancer. Later, we remember, she included dances on Indian themes in her repertory, and even toured with Uday Shankar. It is strange that she seems never to have danced anything from *La Bayadère* in the West. The orchestra parts were in her library. And if she—or Olga Spessivtseva—did dance the piece, why was it unknown until 1961? The questions pile up. Lopukhov died in 1973; Roslavleva died in 1977. With each such death, a link to the past is broken. Diligent research is required among survivors and in archives mostly inaccessible to non-Russian scholars. Add to this the fact that the bulk of Russian studies in dance history remain untranslated and you begin to see that dance is truly the illiterate art. Until translators and new research produce the information we need, we have only productions to go on. But these are invaluable. Makarova's *La Bayadère* sets the past in motion. It testifies to the existence of a *Bayadère* tradition and tells us what things have held over the years in performance.

The Bournonville ballets in the repertory of the Royal Danish Ballet provide the same kind of testimony, but their tradition is more obscure, perhaps because until recently they have not had much exposure outside Denmark. There is now a flourishing Bournonville industry, particularly among American dance historians, and the industry was given a boost with the appearance last month of the entire Danish company in eight performances at the Chicago Civic Opera. The company brought seven of its greatest Bournonvilles; *A Folk Tale* was seen for the first time in America, *Napoli* for the first time since 1956. Peter Martins and Peter Schaufuss, dancers who have done much to popularize Danish classicism internationally, were guest artists with their parent company. Scholars could study the productions for historical veracity, and Chicagoans at large could enjoy a splendid dance festival. The sponsoring organization, which in fact calls itself the International Dance Festival, brought off its greatest success in four years of existence—first, by persuading the Danes to come (the dancers, in a unanimous decision, cast the deciding vote), and then by raising the necessary subsidies. Geraldine Freund, the Festival's founder and director, enlisted Mayor Byrne's support and was able to add a matching grant from the city for $25,000 to a long list of private donations. Chicago received the company in style. A Bournonville exhibit, carefully adapted from the major one held in Copenhagen last winter, was mounted at the Public Library. There was official hospitality and, more surprising, there was good box office. The prolonged standing ovations after *La Sylphide*, *Napoli*, and *A Folk Tale* stunned locals no less than the Danes; Chicago isn't known as a ballet town.

Now let other American cities take note. Chicago, which doesn't even support a resident company, proved that Bournonville ballets don't need the "ballet audience." They constitute a tradition of popular entertainment (I might even call it family entertainment) that is robust yet never cheap—that is in fact enriching and ennobling. *A Folk Tale* is as much a fixture in the Danish repertory as *The Nutcracker* is in ours. The Danish standard of performance in acting as well as in dancing remains enviably high. The Civic Opera, with a stage not a great deal larger than the Royal Theatre's in Copenhagen, was comfortably scaled for the delicate, intricate things that Danish dancers uniquely do. May they come again and shine as brightly.

—July 14, 1980

Postscript 1982: I wrongly attributed the musical base of Farrell's solo to a quotation from *Carnaval*, and had the following letter from David Daniel:

"The Sphinxes don't appear in Farrell's variation to No. 12. (There's a quotation from *Carnaval*'s 'Promenade' in No. 3, but it's music she doesn't dance to.) Had they done so, and had Balanchine used them to illumine Farrell's 'character' as Clara the Muse, the ballet's central metaphor would have been reduced to a thinly stretched conceit, because the sphinxes themselves connect Robert not to Clara but to another woman.

"Balanchine has no choice about how his ballets turn out. Indeed, he has often told us he can only do what the music tells him to, and if he's uncertain he rings up the composer on the Communion of Saints Hotline to make sure. Even so, the narrowed opportunities Schumann affords him in *Davidsbündlertänze* make his former lack of freedom look like a License to Commit Personal Expression. It is Schumann himself who has made Clara's presence actual. More than Romantic brain-vapor, she's musically alive in the person of her own genius, and the synthesis of her genius with Robert's breathes on every page. Therefore if Farrell's dances evoke Clara the Muse, it's because Balanchine has literally realized the drama devolving from Schumann's musical process.

"The opening twelve beats contain Clara, Robert, and Clara and Robert. Clara is manifest in the first six by Robert's verbatim quotation from her Mazurka (the 'Motto von C. W.') in the key of G. In the six that follow, Robert twice repeats her rhythmic pattern in his own harmony, imitates her melodic contour while inverting her two-note downward slur, and lands himself on the chord of B major—making the Muse/Poet metaphor as exact as it is concrete. The coincidence of the note-names of these tonal centers with the choreographer's monogram is mere but nonetheless diabolic. Be that as it may. This is the music that plays while Farrell's Clara the Muse bounds onto the stage followed by D'Amboise's Robert the Poet.

"Schumann invents the rest of *DBT* by extension and development of this material and what he finds implicit in it, insuring that Balanchine will remain the man without a choice. It is only inevitable that the choreographer will cast every girl in the image of Clara and every boy in the image of Robert. Naturally Farrell's dances will evoke Clara, and Clara and Robert; but so will everyone else's. And yet not even Balanchine's choice of the music to propel Farrell's Clara the Muse variation is arbitrary. Schumann has given him music with another, extra dimension of Clara—something beyond what is explicitly and implicitly there in the opening 'motto' and its subsequent permutations.

"Farrell's solo music is in the minor mode of the same key (B) that Schumann arrives at when he extends Clara's motive. Its main theme is a reference to a theme by, well, no one knows for sure who actually wrote it, but all are certain it was either Clara or Robert. Its first published appearance is in Clara's Opus 5, *The Spectres' Ballet*, which is also in B-minor; the next, in Robert's Opus 6, *DBT*. Then it shows up in the Allegro section of Robert's Opus 11 sonata, although he had originally meant to publish it as a separate piece under the title *Fandango*. In fact, he wrote it very close to the time Clara wrote *The Spectres' Ballet*, which she had published before he wrote *DBT*. Some experts believe its presence in *DBT* indicates an inspired Robert recalling Clara's piece. Yet others insist that Robert composed his *Fandango* before Clara wrote *The Spectres' Ballet*. They suggest instead that he, in working out various problems in his *Fandango*, might have given her the theme itself, a portion of it, or a bass progression and asked her to expound on it to see what solutions she might come up with. But little more than the fact that he gave her the theme outright to use as she wished would explain why the phrase in Farrell's *DBT* variation can be read as F(lorestan), E(usebius), C L A R A. Clara is not thought to have used ciphers in her music, but Robert is believed to have used an elaborate system of cryptography that enabled him to spell out anything.

"The delicious mystery of its authorship notwithstanding, the simple fact remains that the theme does appear in the works of both: first in Clara's, then twice in Robert's. And when Schumann subsequently refers to it, it can easily be read as his tribute to Clara's creative genius—even if he actually gave her the very material she was to be creative with. It is a coincidence that the music Balanchine has given Farrell's Clara the Muse is Schumann's musical autograph, in which he notates the two sides of his heart and unites them with the name of Clara. You can judge for yourself whether the coincidence is a mere one or not."

Summer Madness

The Metropolitan Opera, in New York, and the Kennedy Center, in Washington, are presenting the Berlin Ballet this summer. In Germany, the ballet of the Deutsche Oper Berlin ranks below the Stuttgart, which makes it internationally very minor league indeed. But, like most German cultural institutions, it enjoys generous government subsidy, and it can afford to travel. Two summers ago, when it appeared at the State Theatre, in Lincoln Center, it pleased the off-season audience with its well-dressed, expensive productions of familiar ballets and its famous guest artists, who were Valery Panov and his wife, Galina Panova. Of the company's own soloists, Vladimir Gelvan had become known here through spotty appearances with American Ballet Theatre; the principal ballerina, Eva Evdokimova, had yet to establish her local reputation. The Russians carried the season, in their fashion. Evdokimova gave a listless *Giselle*, partnered by Gelvan—a performance in which Panov played Hilarion as if he were Igor in the Frankenstein movies. After seeing what Panov could do as a choreographer with Prokofiev's *Cinderella* and what Panova could do with the leading role, I didn't go to the Berlin Ballet again.

This summer, everything has been a little bigger and more ambitious. Rudolf Nureyev has been added to the roster, which makes three refugees from the Kirov reunited in one engagement. The company played the Met, undertaking expenses that are prohibitive to all but the wealthiest state-supported companies. The major attraction is Panov's latest work—a three-act ballet based on Dostoevski's novel *The Idiot*—and, of course, it has Nureyev as Prince Myshkin, Nureyev being the Met's idea of gilt-edged insurance. (A projected Met season by the Paris Opéra Ballet was cancelled when the dancers objected to the addition of Nureyev and other guest stars.) But one feels that with or without Nureyev this is the Berlin Ballet's bid for major-league standing—at least, for off-season major-league standing. The Met management, which has no interest in cultivating a dance audience, is not averse to booking ballet in the summertime, provided it pays its way. The Stuttgart could be relied upon until the death of its artistic director, John Cranko, cast its policies adrift. Canada and Cuba sent their national ballets. Their main failing wasn't just that they had no stars. (Nureyev used to appear regularly with the Canadians.) They also had no "classic" repertory distinctively different from that of the Met's regular tenant, Ballet Theatre. What is a classic? A classic is something that people have heard of. If it isn't *Swan Lake* or *Giselle*, it is *Romeo and Juliet*, *The Taming of the Shrew*, or *Eugene Onegin*, to name three of the most popular ballet-adaptations in the Stuttgart repertory. John Cranko knew all about instant classics and the ballet audience. Other choreographers, both more and less skilled than he, have tried to latch on to the formula. The latest is Valery Panov. Panov's choreography may not become a standing attraction in New York, as Cranko's did, but he is taking out a long-term policy on classics. His *Hamlet* has been commissioned by the Vienna Opera Ballet. He is already talking about *War and Peace*. That Panov shows no aptitude for making dances is less surprising than that he shows none for storytelling and mime. Even if you have read *The Idiot*, his mise en scène has you puzzling over identities and locations all through the first act and into the second. (The program contains an extensive synopsis—of the novel, not of the ballet.) Panov trowels some kind of movement onto the stage, divides it into scenes, and blows upon it with the hot breath of passion. He doesn't choreograph steps or gestures—he choreographs feelings, which are illegible. The audience of sightseers which drifts through New York's theatres in the summertime doesn't expect to understand anything at the ballet, so it doesn't feel cheated. All it wants to be sure of is that this thing is a classic thing—the sort of cultural entertainment that Lincoln Center is famous for, like Richard Burton in *Camelot*. The Met itself seemed unsure of what to call *The Idiot*; its radio ads promised "all the grandeur of opera." After opening night, the only appropriate term was "hit."

The production, a long and costly one, is in fifteen scenes, with a different setting for nearly every scene. These changes, which involve standing scenery as well as projections, were engineered by Günther Schneider-Siemssen and designed by him in a range of modes, from naturalistic to expressionistic. The costumes, of an equal variety and extravagance, are by Bernd Müller. Panov devised the music by combining sections of two film scores, four ballet suites, seven symphonies, one opera, and some chamber music, all by Shostakovich. With its constantly moving scenery, its furs and velours, and its Shostakovich panorama, the show has a certain scope and tonnage. It also has three moments when it is almost a ballet. The first comes in the middle of the second act, with Rogozhin chasing Myshkin through the streets of St. Petersburg to the music of the Eighth Symphony. All this is is a series of diagonal crosses for two dancers and a small male corps; the choreography is mostly jumps and runs, and it isn't very exciting (Panov and Nureyev, both forty-two years old, are past their athletic prime), but it was during this scene that I felt the audience fall for the show. The beginning of the third act is a divertissement in a park during which the courtly Nureyev partners a small girl. And in the closing scene he swings high above the stage from the clapper of a giant bell.

This last scene, which Nureyev performs virtually nude, is the evening's only instance of emotion objectified—its one *image*—and people are going to remember the whole evening by it. As we know from reading his autobiography, Panov has a daredevil meshuganah streak. It took more than fortitude to defy his persecutors as Panov did for twenty-seven months, exposing himself to harassment and his cause to world attention. As a choreographer, in the innocence and shamelessness of his ideas, he's under the divine protection of bad taste. He doesn't seem to know when he has made an effect; he makes it over and over—sliding across the stage to grip the saintly Myshkin around the knees, groping him or having others grope him, throwing himself in alligatorish lunges to the floor, sprinting into the wings with his head thrown back and his toes turned under. When the four principals come together in the third act, the choreography is stuffed to Trockadero excess with fits and ravings. And need I relate what Panov does with Icons and crucifixes and candles and with the murder of Nastasya Filippovna? (She seems to die of bad partnering.) Even the big moment at the end is compromised by incontinence—Panov apparently couldn't resist having Nureyev swing from a rope earlier, in the chase scene.

Nastasya Filippovna (Evdokimova) and Aglaja (Panova) are supporting roles in this two-man show. Incidentally, Nureyev does not play Myshkin as an epileptic. He twitches a bit at one point, but he could easily be in ecstasy at Nastasya's beauty. After seeing Nureyev, I felt no obligation to go and see Gelvan, who originated the role and is Nureyev's alternate on this tour. Nureyev is no actor, but it has become customary to chastise him because he takes over other people's parts. If you believe that *The Idiot* can be a ballet, you can believe Nureyev as Myshkin. I am told that Gelvan does not play an epileptic, either. It would be technically impossible in terms of the meshuganah style.

Nureyev in the context of the Berlin Ballet looks, if not a great dancer, then an extremely intelligent and authoritative one. Though Evdokimova towers over him, she has so little range and force that she does not diminish him. Panova, hard and muscular, with unstretched knees and feet that are sickled in passé, is stylistically outclassed by him. Nureyev in decline has lows and highs; this season he has been careful not to overtax his powers (unlike Panov, who barrels right ahead with his *Don Quixote* pas de deux). His appearances for some time have belonged to the history of his career rather than to the history of his art. What can one say of his appearance in *The Idiot* but that it belongs to the history of tourism?   —*August 4, 1980*

Guest Star

Except for an unscheduled appearance last May with the New York City Ballet, Mikhail Baryshnikov hasn't danced in New York in over a year, and he has kept his performances elsewhere to a minimum. Besides having to nurse the injuries that forced him to withdraw earlier than expected from Balanchine's company, Baryshnikov seems at the moment to prefer inactivity to dancing familiar roles. He has met every feasible challenge that Western ballet repertory holds and has already been far afield in search of new stimuli. Last summer, he worked with the jazz composer Cecil Taylor. In "Baryshnikov on Broadway," a TV special seen earlier this year, he took on another style that was novel to him, however banal it may have seemed to the rest of us. The dance director, Ron Field, homogenized the choreography of various hit shows, so that Baryshnikov's versatility was reduced to his haircuts and his costumes. In the *Guys and Dolls* segment, he looked appetizingly in character as a fifties sharpie, but there was nothing for him to dance. His merger in the finale with the chorus of *A Chorus Line* symbolized the vapidity of the enterprise. For a Baryshnikov, Broadway isn't a frontier worth conquering—not on these terms.

An invitation from the Royal Ballet put the dancer back in his domain. In July, at Covent Garden, Baryshnikov danced two performances as Romeo, a role in which he had already been seen, and then on August 4 he appeared before the Queen Mother on her eightieth birthday, dancing in the ballet that had been arranged for the occasion by Frederick Ashton to Rachmaninoff's Rhapsody on a Theme of Paganini. This was Ashton's first major work in four years, and his first with Baryshnikov. Wisely, perhaps, Ashton did not experiment; the ballet is his interpretation of Baryshnikov's style as set against elements of his own. It's a host-and-guest ballet. Admirers of both men may wish that Ashton had not been quite so accommodating. The pas de deux has one of those prolonged "blind" lifts from which the ballerina (Lesley Collier) is dropped to the floor in arabesque, and it gave Baryshnikov some trouble in performance. In the main, though, Baryshnikov's role consists of solo entrées in the style of his Soviet bravura phase—the phase in which we first saw him. The passagework at the beginning is reminiscent of the fleeting, darting poses of *Vestris* and even of their mime content: there's a split second of "playing the violin" that impishly brings up Paganini. In other ways, too, Ashton's choreography returns Baryshnikov to his ancestral origins in the court ballet of an eighteenth-century city. I'd guess that Ashton prepared for this first collaboration with Baryshnikov by studying not only *Vestris* (those parts of it which are either on film or microscopically reproduced in the book *Baryshnikov at Work*) but also the videotape of Baryshnikov's performance in *Theme and Variations*, a ballet in which Balanchine extrapolated classical style from an eighteenth-century base, in the manner of *The Sleeping Beauty*. But Ashton doesn't stick to this view of Baryshnikov. He is supposed to have summoned the dancer to their first rehearsal saying "Bring all your steps," and as the ballet goes on we get the impression that not one skid, lunge, kick, or convoluted air turn has been left out. The picture of Baryshnikov that the ballet gives us is an inflated, estranged one; he does too much and does it alone, without blending into an overall conception. Although the expansive material suits the melodramatic Rachmaninoff score, it effectively separates Baryshnikov from the rest of the cast and from the Royal Ballet style. Ashton hasn't set down a theme with variations; he's made a Baryshnikov concerto.

Watching *Rhapsody* is as exhilarating as hanging on to a runaway horse. It gets more and more out of hand, yet it never breaks its stride musically. In the vividness and steadiness of its response to the music, it is moment by moment absolutely satisfying. All through the piece, though, this instantaneous sense of completion fights the gathering sense of disproportion. You have to enjoy the ballet at the expense of sympathizing with it. That's if you see Baryshnikov do it. When, as seems inevitable, a Royal dancer takes over the lead, there may be changes in *Rhapsody* that will put it in balance. Or the changes may only expose what the casting of the demon charger Baryshnikov has so far concealed—the weakness of an ensemble that is appealingly young, carefully chosen, talented, but as yet unready to be looked at too closely. Ashton has invested his most sensitive choreography in these six young women and their partners, and he's made them look not like the disadvantaged kids they often seem to be in other ballets but like the flower of a great company. *Rhapsody* bears a superficial resemblance to that other pièce d'occasion, *Birthday Offering*: it is a double septet (7 f., 7 m.), and it has a platform set, which Ashton himself devised from models of eighteenth-century stage architecture. But, except to Baryshnikov and Lesley Collier, Ashton allots no individual variations such as distinguished *Birthday Offering*. Instead, he distributes little individualizing touches that let us think we've seen more of Genesia Rosato or Karen Paisey or Bryony Brind than we actually have. The men are more uniformly handled; once or twice Baryshnikov streaks through their midst, and they explode into échappés and entrechats like corks bobbing in his wake. His genius isn't contagious—it only seems to be. Ashton has also been protective of his ballerina, even contriving at times to give an air of intrigue to the fact that she doesn't dominate the ballet as a ballerina should. He brings her on late, after the "concerto" structure of the Baryshnikov role has been established, and he presents her in a series of privileged, noncompetitive "ballerina" cameos—swathing her, so to speak, in the differing velvets of one genre image after another. Collier is held high above the men's heads, turned, and lowered (in anticipation of the drop in the pas de deux), after which she dances a swift cadenza on point and offers her hand to Baryshnikov, who sweeps her off. Later, in a "vision" scene, she secludes herself upstage while he conducts a leisurely search among the girls. It's his ballet, the choreography seems to say, but it's *her* repertory. The big pas de deux, to the big tune, is muffled and bland; it's not an evocation—it's just one of those things. If Ashton has a weakness, it is for the potency of cheap music. What other great choreographer has done so much to so little (Auber, Hérold, Meyerbeer, Messager, Liszt, Malcolm Arnold)? He has used the Rachmaninoff melody before, as a setting for Moira Shearer in a movie called *The Story of Three Loves*. That setting is not eclipsed by *Rhapsody*.

As for Baryshnikov's performance, he was so much the visiting superstar that he became, for the first time in my experience, almost unlikable. It wasn't just the way Ashton used him, although in the final moments he was glorified almost to the point of parody. It wasn't just the way he was dressed, with gilded wavy locks and jewelled chokers around his throat and knee. There was no indication of injury or unease in his dancing, but the rest period has put extra weight on him, and he now moves with an unctuous slipperiness. This is one of the negative signs of maturity. Baryshnikov has always been rococo, but now he's becoming gloatingly mellifluous. He performs soothingly, condescendingly, and about as joyously as Liberace. I inquired about his Romeos, which I missed, and was told that glib fancywork had entered those performances, too. "It was Broadway Misha," said a young critic. The complacency of the uncontested champion? Or the desperation of the artist seeking an outlet for the uncontainable forms within him? Perhaps a bit of both. Baryshnikov doesn't look fresh in *Rhapsody*. Ashton has indulged an image of him which he has outgrown, just as in *A Month in the Country* he indulged an image of Anthony Dowell which Dowell had outgrown. But Dowell can still be magnetic in the role through the sheer beauty of his dancing; technically, if not psychologically, the choreography advances him. In *Rhapsody*, Baryshnikov hurtles through his technical catalogue. On the first night, he looked like the most sophisticated dancer on earth and the most bored, much as he might have appeared if he had never left Russia. By the last of four performances, he had modified this drastic impression (as well as the golden hair). But for the old sweetness and modesty to return would be wrong—the ballet couldn't use that Misha. As Ashton builds his climax, Baryshnikov is at stage center, while Collier races here, there—anywhere to keep out of the way. The men lift him high. (But it's *her* repertory.) He lands, spins himself to a stop, and, with the music's closing notes—an ironic wisp of a cadence—gives us the mock-innocent " 'Twas nothing!" shrug that Ashton used for Puck and for the Blue Skater in *Les Patineurs*. It is his repertory after all.

Baryshnikov danced in a gold tunic and mustard tights, which, with the gilt and the glitter, made him look like a little golden god. The other dancers —men as well as women—also wore jewelled bands; their heads were wrapped in gold strips. The only unstrident note was the women's soft dresses, in pink and peach and pale yellow. The costume designer, one of Ashton's oldest collaborators, was William Chappell; he has done some classic décors—the Joffrey has *Les Patineurs*, and Baryshnikov has just acquired *Les Rendezvous* for American Ballet Theatre—but the costumes for *Rhapsody* are one dispensable link to *Birthday Offering*, which still uses André Levasseur's ugly puffy costumes. (They look as if pirouettes could be· done inside them.) The title *Birthday Offering* refers to the company's silver anniversary, in 1956. Next year, the Royal Ballet will be fifty years old. Could *Rhapsody* have been a contemporary counterpart to *Birthday Offering* if the company had been able to marshal a comparable display of strength? Its upper ranks are thin. Although the lower ones, from which the supporting cast of *Rhapsody* is drawn, are full of promise, that promise may not be kept. The past two decades have seen too many examples of careers restrained or aborted, of talent unnurtured. The company has no ballerinas under forty; its titular ballerinas are soloists at best. Collier has a sturdy snub-nosed charm and agile toes, which Ashton exploits in *Rhapsody*. But her long, static torso and her lethargic attack seem to immobilize her even when she's speeding over the ground. Marguerite Porter, popular for her Gainsborough looks, cannot meet the technical requirements of the standard ballerina roles. Jennifer Penney, who closed the season in Kenneth Mac-Millan's *Manon*, has striking individuality and beauty, but failure to project makes her insular and pretty.

On top of all this, the company as a whole is showing too many inflexible backs, too much laxity in stretch and turnout. To look at some of the younger men is to wonder where on earth Dowell came from—or Michael Batchelor, who may be his only successor. The Ashton pas de quatre in *Swan Lake*, another touchstone of company strength, was shakily performed (except by Fiona Chadwick, who was good) by two different casts. The Ashton Act IV, which dates from 1963, the same year as the pas de quatre, has been restored. It has been criticized for cold efficiency and abstraction, and there is a certain amount of meaningless clattering about and forming up at the start of the act. But there are wonderful things that follow, notably the extended slow march (to music borrowed from Act III), in which Odette ushers sections of her flock into the wings, returning each time to embrace the Prince, who kneels alone in the middle of the stage. On her last return, she takes a slow piqué balance and hovers over him; the timing of the gradual ascent to the tread of the music forms as poignant an image as any that may be found in the second act. I saw Porter's Odette and Monica Mason's on the same day. Mason, a senior ballerina and a genuine one, danced with relaxed authority, as if for her own pleasure. The grandeur of her bearing is untypical of Royal ballerinas, and she is an infrequent Odette. But she is a model of clean style and musical incisiveness. On this occasion, she opened her phrase to its utmost transparency and gave us moments of illumination as wide and as blank as fate.

It has been an exciting summer season at Covent Garden. Makarova came to do repertory and also to make her début as Natalia Petrovna in *A Month in the Country*—a warm, dreamy, impulsive creature who is brought to earth with a crash. Gelsey Kirkland's début as Juliet (to Dowell's or Wayne Eagling's Romeo) was, according to all reports, a sensation. But the main, enduring attraction for an American visitor was the company itself. The Royal in recession is still spectacular. The entrance of the swan corps in flying arabesque sautée is still exciting. And when the company has nothing else, it still has English grit—a collective spirit that can rise in the face of audience rejection and turn failure into success. It is hard to imagine an American or Russian company keeping its temper for forty-five minutes, as the Royal does, in *Mam'zelle Angot*, a garrulous Massine farce. Rosalyn Whitten, in the title role, was so lucid and alive that I longed to see her in a classical role—a big one. Perhaps I will; the company dances in New York next June. One applauds for tomorrow, on faith.   —*August 25, 1980*

The Entertainer

Roland Petit may not be the greatest name in ballet, but it is a great name in ballet entertainment—possibly the only name. Most choreographers when they succeed in entertaining us, and even when they don't succeed, are aiming at art. Petit hardly ever aims higher than his audience's comfort level. A little sensuality, a little sentiment, a touch of irony or camp make up an evening's diversion. Pretty costumes and scenery are an absolute necessity; so is the semblance, at least, of a plot. If Petit has ever stumbled into art, as I'm told he did in his first big success, *Les Forains,* he soon atoned for it with *Carmen, La Croqueuse de Diamants, Les Demoiselles de la Nuit,* and *Le Loup.* If he has been pretentious, as in his collaboration with Cocteau *Le Jeune Homme et la Mort,* or in his recent Proust ballet, he has not been dull. One of his movies was called *Black Tights*—a title that seems to stand for his whole career. Petit's tradition is not just that of the academy; it takes in the boulevards and the purlieus of apache Paris; it extends as far back as the can-can dancers of Toulouse-Lautrec and as far forward as the *Can-Can* of Cole Porter, which Petit is scheduled to direct for Broadway revival this winter.

Last month, after more than twenty years, a company headed by Petit opened in New York. The Ballet National de Marseille, which Petit organized and has run since 1972, made its local début at the Uris with three ballets, the first and best of them starring Zizi Jeanmaire, whom we last saw in 1964, singing and dancing in *Zizi.* Jeanmaire, who has been married to Roland Petit for twenty-six years—almost as long as she has been an international musical-comedy star—and who will have the lead in *Can-Can,* may be the only classically trained dancer to become a star in the musical theatre and remain, somehow, a ballerina. Vera Zorina did it once, with the help of George Balanchine. Cyd Charisse stood for ballet, but only in the context of MGM musicals. Neither danced for as long a period as Jeanmaire has or created quite so startling and indelible a personal style. The iconography of Zizi includes stemware of an almost prewar vintage: the pulled-up thighs, the switchblade hips that shoot the legs and lock them in their elegant positions bespeak a thoroughness in Franco-Russian classical schooling that is apparently no longer to be had. With her long legs and long arms, her pliant waist, her smooth little head, and her squared-off, molar-baring grin, Jeanmaire maintains a continually active, changelessly visible profile; you couldn't miss it on a dark night at sea.

The Bat, which opened the Uris engagement, is a good illustration of what Petit and Jeanmaire have done over the years to make their glittering names. It shows, too, why their reputations for high professionalism are deserved. The curtain goes up, and Jeanmaire takes the stage in a curly carrot wig, which, with her round cheeks and lack of neck, makes her look like Claudette Colbert. The story has the heroine adopt a disguise to entrap her errant husband. Jeanmaire strips off her black Hausfrau gown, tears off her wig, and there, with her slick gamine hairdo and icicle legs, stands the definitive Zizi. The performance then builds to monstre-sacré proportions. In the second act, she dances a long pas de deux in a .white leotard, every extension, torsion, and balance as carefully judged as Miss Colbert's camera angles. Since the ideal star vehicle is one that lets you know not once but many times why the star is a star, The Bat may be the best—it is certainly the longest—vehicle that Petit has ever fashioned for his wife. He's made her lack of variety seem adorable constancy, her now flinty footwork look like rapscallion spunk. When stars get old, they may lose presence even as their skill in gripping our attention increases; one feels bewildered—held and not held. In The Bat, Jeanmaire is so perfectly focussed—as a dancer, as a personality—that her distance from her physical prime, her lack of genuine physical animation are almost unnoticeable. It's a performance embedded in amber, with a flattering amber-tinted glow.

The rest of the show is all Petit. The libretto, a fantasy on Fledermaus themes, makes no more sense than Fledermaus does, but Petit keeps things moving to an unusually good arrangement, by Douglas Gamley,. of Strauss's music, and pours out a profusion of dances. Those for the men are especially attractive: they include sharply differentiated solos for the bouncy master of revels (Luigi Bonino) and the romantic wandering husband (Denys Ganio); the waiters' galop at the masked ball is the best such number I have seen, surpassing Massine, surpassing even Gower Champion. Petit's mixed ensembles are less effervescent, and the big one at the start of the second act has a flattening effect. Perhaps the costumes, by Franca Scuarciapino, and the scenery, by Giulio Colltellacci, aren't as effective, in this touring version of the production, as they might be. Whatever the reason, the electric current that keeps the first act cresting smoothly begins to sputter in Act II, and the evening ends by disappointing us. At its best, The Bat has an eccentric beauty like that of Méliès's films, but there are moments that seem almost deliberate misses—that skirt magic for showmanship. One occurs during the masked ball, when dancers dressed as pierrots or harlequins suddenly fall down in a trance and the winged figure of the husband appears to the wife swinging upside down, like a bat. She reaches out to steady him, and we expect the moment to develop fantastically. Perhaps he will partner her from this position or take her up with him. But Petit cuts the moment short and hurries on to the next manifestation of Zizi.

Petit has always been too shallow for the ballet audience but just right for the general public. His production of *Coppélia* was out of touch with both audiences. This was an "innovative" version, placed in a garrison town where the female corps de ballet and the soldiers are billeted together and Coppélius is a silver-haired roué. The action shifted uneasily between *rose* and *noir* effects; each shift was off the music. Worse, Petit's dance invention seemed to have deserted him. He set turned-in steps in between turned-out ones, which is like setting words between notes or belches between words; he had Swanilda and her friends doing so many hip wiggles and shoulder rolls that they appeared to be made of jelly. Petit's own performance as Coppélius is a celebrated one, but he fell ill and had to withdraw from the season. Bonino, an engaging, dapper mime, did what he could to lift the evening; when he had to do it by waltzing with a dummy strapped to his feet, I began to think the thing would never rise, and it didn't. Dominique Khalfouni was a thin and constricted Swanilda. Peter Schaufuss's ballon had acquired a strange, gooey consistency. Fortunately, the production is compressed into two acts, with only a snatch of dancing from Act III. The décor, attributed to Ezio Frigerio, was disturbing. This designer has salvaged more than one ballet with his airy, august conceptions. Here his cheerless gray walls and stiff uniforms might have done for any of the starker productions of *Carmen* one sees nowadays; and for the life-size puppets in Coppélius's workshop he substituted a towering display cabinet with swivelling dummy heads and drawers that kept opening and slamming shut. Enterprising, perhaps, but not wondrous.

Petit's Marseille ballets have a budgeted look that doesn't suit their choreographer. One can't help wondering what Petit could have done with *Les Intermittences du Coeur*—here called *Marcel Proust Remembered*—if he'd had the money that the Berlin Ballet spent on Valery Panov's *The Idiot*. And if, like Panov last July, he'd shown the ballet at the Met. My guess is that he'd have had the hit that Panov had with the Met's culture-conscious dance audience. Instead, *Marcel Proust Remembered* went on for only four performances at the Uris, toward the end of the season. It's not a good piece; it's queasily wrong, doomed in every step and gesture. But it's nowhere near the mess that *The Idiot* was. Dancing is helpless to portray any character but that of the dancer and any time but the present. Characters, moreover, who have been given their life in a literary masterpiece that is also an essay on memory would resist adaptation by the best playwrights and filmmakers, but they'd at least have the words that Proust gave them. Still, you can accept the idea of Mme Verdurin's salon coming alive in a ballet as you can never accept Rogozhin meeting Myshkin on the train and starting to discuss Nastasya Filippovna's past—in mime. Petit hasn't actually tried to stage *A la Recherche du Temps Perdu*; the novel's characters—Verdurin, Swann and Odette, Gilberte, Albertine and her friends, Albertine and Marcel, Charlus and Morel, and Saint-Loup—appear in that order in unconnected dance episodes set to disparate pieces of music. There is nothing "Proustian" about the ballet in the sense that the adjective was commonly applied to *Jardin aux Lilas* and *Dim Lustre*, by Antony Tudor. Only in the Albertine-Marcel pas de deux, danced by Khalfouni and Ganio, does one's mind drift back to Marcel's agony. But one's mind also drifts back to Balanchine's Sleepwalker pas de deux in *La Sonnambula* and to other Petit heroes —Don José, le Loup, Cyrano, Quasimodo—who were humiliated in love. There is some mild porn in the scenes involving Charlus and Morel, and Charlus's tastes are the pretext for an extended and rather ludicrously stylized sadomasochistic sequence in which Charlus (Gérard Taillade) flies here and there, impelled by the rhythmically timed punches of some soldiers. When Petit tries to be serious and deep, he's often off-guardedly amusing; ludicrous stylization usually gets him in the end. The finale of *Marcel Proust Remembered* means to depict the society of Proust's time as mechanical, vapid, unheeding. Petit's method has the dancers jerk woodenly about to the polonaise in Wagner's *Rienzi* Overture. The fatally metric execution of the idea was something Kenneth MacMillan avoided when he made the same point in the same way about a later society in *La Fin du Jour*.

Although it has no young women with Jeanmaire's classical breeding, the Marseille ballet is one of the strongest foreign companies to have played here in quite a while—it's no mere backup to its guest stars. Yet in five weeks at the Uris it never managed to find its audience. It is a mistake to put an unknown ballet company on Broadway. The director and star may have had Broadway successes in the past, but those are faded triumphs, and the audience for popular ballet entertainment these days is accustomed to looking for it uptown, where the big and best-known companies play. A Broadway booking for even so worthy and appropriate an artist as Petit only confuses people. The Uris is a newish Broadway theatre, ugly and lacking in atmosphere. Roland Petit may not always be interested in accredited art, but his audience is. —*September 29, 1980*

Americana

Ballet west of the Mississippi is pretty much the creation of the Christensen brothers—Willam, Harold, and Lew—of Utah. Born to a family of music and dance teachers of Danish descent, the brothers as boys toured in vaudeville; they were hoofers as well as classical dancers and, with the

Littlefields of Philadelphia, they became the most productive native-born founders of American ballet. Willam, the oldest brother, has been the principal pathfinder. Having started the Portland Ballet, Willam in 1938 took over the San Francisco Ballet, then a rib of the Opera, and built it into an independent institution. In the early fifties, Lew, a Balanchine star and an established choreographer, assumed the direction of the company—Harold was already in charge of the affiliated school—while Willam went back to Utah and began what eventually became Ballet West. The San Francisco Ballet and Ballet West, of Salt Lake City, are today generally reckoned to be the third- and fifth-largest companies in the nation (with the Joffrey in between). Both have had important New York seasons; Ballet West's début came last spring at the City Center, and San Francisco had a milestone week at the Brooklyn Academy last month. It may be said that with these two companies the Christensens' lifelong mission is fulfilled. Colonizing the entire Western United States will take another generation; that is the mission of younger men. The question is: Which of the younger men now in charge of the territory will take the lead? There is the San Francisco's co-director Michael Smuin and its team of Christensen-Smuin protégés. Further Christensen influences will probably be felt through Kent Stowell, who runs the burgeoning Pacific Northwest Ballet, in Seattle. But under Bruce Marks, who succeeded Willam Christensen in 1978, Ballet West has made a turn away from the Christensen tradition. John Clifford and the Los Angeles Ballet (which comes to the Brooklyn Academy next) are not firmly enough established on their home base to make much of a difference. The powerfully supported Houston Ballet could make a difference if it wished, but its repertory and artistic direction are largely—and peculiarly—London-Festival-Ballet British.

The eclectic Christensen tradition, a bold yet somehow impeccable combination of classical-academic and popular dance, probably got its impetus during the late thirties, when Lincoln Kirstein, temporarily split from Balanchine, started Ballet Caravan out of a near-chauvinistic urge to foster All-Americanism in ballet. Lew Christensen, Eugene Loring, Michael Kidd, William Dollar, and Erick Hawkins were among the members. Of the works that were produced, Christensen's *Filling Station* and Loring's *Billy the Kid* are still being danced. In these ballets, there's the still hearty flavor of vaudeville and the movies—a bit as if Fred Astaire or James Cagney (both of whom Kirstein has acknowledged as actual inspirations) had suddenly discovered fifth position. Balanchine, of course, has always had the healthiest regard for American pop; during the Ballet Caravan years, he was at work on movies and shows. In later years, many dancers formed by the Christensens would pass into Balanchine's company. One who would not was Michael Smuin; when he went East, it was to perform on Broadway and television and to start a night-club act with his wife, Paula Tracy. Smuin and Tracy then joined American Ballet Theatre.

As a choreographer, Smuin is all the places he's been as a dancer; his strength is to have grasped what was "American" in ballet and what was "classical" in popular dance. Eclecticism flows naturally in his choreography; there are no quotation marks to categorize and stiffen effects as they happen. Smuin, who was born in the year of *Filling Station* and *Billy the Kid,* may be the last American choreographer to deal directly in the vernacular, without the crutch of nostalgia. And he handles the material of great popular myths as if those myths had never died. A *Song for Dead Warriors* is about the oppression of the American Indian; though its story is real enough, its emotions and the specific situations that evoke them are suprareal: we're back in the land of *Billy the Kid*—the boyhood land of legend and mythic terror. Smuin is the show-biz descendant of Christensen and Loring; his texture is coarser (a pool-hall scene, expressionistically staged and lit with a green rectangle thrown on the floor, evokes some of Kidd's numbers in *Guys and Dolls*), but his sentiment is no less sincere. Part of the strength of his Indian ballet comes from our feeling that Smuin is unconscious of any relation to *Billy the Kid* or anything else we may have seen before. He can immerse himself in his material even as he manipulates it with formulas—formula racist villains, formula ethnic rape, formula beatings-up—and we succumb afresh, as he has himself.

Nothing is so powerful in the theatre as belief; shamelessness born of innocence is hard to resist. Smuin may push some of his violent scenes too far, but he does not mistake violence for power, and the single most violent scene in the ballet is also the tersest: a stabbing, a scalping, and then death in a fusillade—all acquitted in about five blinding seconds. This ballet has no use for the stylized combat of *Billy the Kid,* and if the fact were mentioned to Smuin he would probably say, "That was fantasy—this is real." Yet some of the most provocative moments in the ballet are deliberately artificial. When the Indians dance, they do aerial turns and jumps; they're great warriors of the past who appear to the young hero in visions. But in the climactic vision they are doing a stomping tribal dance, and we experience the moment not as "truth" but as an extension into a new key of the former dances. If anything, it's more brilliant and idealized than the ballet-style leaps and turns. Smuin begins and ends the ballet with black-and-white photographs of Indians living in degraded conditions, some of which correspond to images in the ballet and were obviously posed and taken with the ballet in mind. But these fake-real photos reinforce the meaning of the lives the ballet is about—lives of literal nightmare, in which pain has become almost ritualized in its ceaseless repetition and facts are indistinguishable from the mythic echoes they release. Who does not feel both real guilt and artificial piety about the Indians? And why is this commingling of guilt and piety so *enjoyable*? Perhaps because of the way the Indians resonate in the American psyche, touching our earliest and most elemental fears and joys. They're a collective childhood memory we want to celebrate, and yet they are disturbing to think about. Venting our loaded feelings theatrically may not take care of the problem, but there's no question that we need to do it. And Smuin has perceived that we need to do it many different ways—lyrically (through music and dancing), luridly (through melodrama), factually (through photographs), scenically (through projections that range from meditative vistas to menacing shadows). There are even things like headlights from a car that appears to be driven onstage and, when the hero's hallucinations are at a peak, a line of demon buffalos charging head-on, which is *not* a projection. All these effects are balanced with fastidious coordination; here more than in the dance scenes Smuin shows his flair for movement and design. Indeed, his contribution is more than choreography. It's as if, having assigned every expressive theatrical resource a separate task, he had then orchestrated the whole in a seamless spectacle and dominated it with his personal vision. The music (Charles Fox), the projections (Ronald Chase), the lighting (Sara Linnie Slocum), the costumes and décor (an uncommonly restrained Willa Kim), and the performing of a large cast are of remarkable quality, but more remarkable still is the authority that fuses them.

I once called Smuin a Belasco; here he's more a Max Reinhardt, but I wonder if even Reinhardt could have reconciled as many contrasts as Smuin does. The visual style of the production is yet another pair: austere and extravagant. Not that Smuin is a great artist. *A Song for Dead Warriors* isn't a ballet one needs to see again. Once catharsis is over, there's not much more it can make happen. Yet I did want to see Smuin's Mozart ballet again. When the company was here two years ago, they left that one out of the repertory and I was relieved not to see it; it sounded dreadful—a ballet to the C-minor Mass. Now that I have seen it, I still think it's a dreadful *idea*, but the ballet itself is not bad. It's exuberant, so pure in spirit that it's totally inoffensive. Smuin, in a program note, says he wanted to make "a completely uninhibited physical celebration of Mozart's music," and the only thing that inhibits him is his limitations as a choreographer; the naiveté of taste that made him want to set a piece of sacred music, and this piece in particular, doesn't extend to his technique. But the technique is nowhere near big enough. Smuin has aimed the choreography away from religiosity (except for a few token gestures). It follows the Mass's structure without forcing a liturgical parallel. Smuin's mind is clearly on adapting Mozart's musical forms to the requirements of a big, brash, variously accomplished but raring-to-go ballet company. In fact, what he has achieved is a physical celebration *to* Mozart's music. *Mozart's C-minor Mass* comes out looking like the definitive company display piece that the repertory needs right now. Smuin has a sharp musical ear, crack timing, and impressive fluency as a craftsman, if not great eloquence. He also has a fatal attraction to great music and great themes, but his innocence is always there to protect him; one could never accuse him of exploitation. Pragmatist yes, opportunist no.

The younger San Francisco choreographers—Robert Gladstein, Tomm Ruud, John McFall—have no impact comparable to Smuin's, but they are patient and serious workers. Gladstein's setting of Leonard Bernstein's *Chichester Psalms*, involving the inhabitants of an embattled kibbutz, impressed many people with its quiet dignity—a bloodless virtue, to my mind; the dancing was just not very interesting. It occurred to me, though, that pieces like this and like *A Song for Dead Warriors* are hardly ever done back East, and while unfashionable is not the same as original, it still invites risks that, in a conformist art like choreography, can be salutary. Privileged isolation may actually be the largest benefit that the Christensens' decision to stay out West has conferred on their successors, and it may be what enables Lew Christensen to keep turning out his delightful anachronistic ballets. *Scarlatti Portfolio*, a batch of sketches of harlequinade characters, is one of his vaudevilles—light, amiable, with a teasing strain of eccentricity. Had I not known the date of composition to be 1979, I'd have guessed 1950. And instead of 1950 I'd have guessed the date of Willam Christensen's *Nothin' Doin' Bar*, also performed in Brooklyn, to be 1938 (because of its resemblance to *Filling Station*). These ballets aren't uselessly dated; they seem to have been stranded by history, but they continue to tell us something about the popular theatre they came out of and about the tradition of synthesis in which so many saw the future of American ballet.

The company, on the whole, left an even stronger impression than it did two years ago. In dancing as well as in choreography, there seemed to be more individual initiative, less conscientious aping of things done elsewhere; the company style had grown larger—more courageous and concerted. There were dancers as well as ballets that I would like to have seen more of. (The week's run could easily have been extended.) Men, as usual in this company, are more exciting than women, but in two duets by Smuin, a new ballerina, Evelyn Cisneros, exemplified the bold new spirit that seems to be sweeping the company. Cisneros has exceptional aplomb along with exceptional softness and refinement—she's not at all brash. Though her technical command is considerable, a lot of her power is still in bud. The San Francisco, with its choreographers and its tradition of male dancing, already has more vitality than most companies across the continent can claim. To have a rising ballerina, too, is a piece of luck.

Another American ballet from that consciously American year of 1938 is *Frankie and Johnny*, by Ruth Page and Bentley Stone. Unlike the Christensen and Loring works, though, it's almost undigested burlesque, with nothing much going on under the surface. At least, that is how it was done by the Cincinnati Ballet in the Brooklyn Center for the Performing Arts series at Brooklyn College. Frederic Franklin staged the ballet, probably from his memory of the 1945 Ballet Russe de Monte Carlo revival; the Cincinnati dancers play it not for any historical values (assuming that these could be recaptured) but for whatever laughs are left in it. In this way, they are sometimes able to revitalize the wheezy old routines. When Frankie discovers Johnny's infidelity and goes into disjointed spasms, Cynthia Ann Roses doesn't suggest that parody of *Giselle* that may have been the original point; she suggests a dancing Gilda Radner, and she's really funny. Like *Filling Station*, *Frankie and Johnny* is the type of street-scene ballet, filled with various and colorful lowlifers, that was once so common. Besides the streetwalkers Frankie and Nellie Bly and the pimp Johnny, there's a fat barkeep, some athletic cops and servicemen, three Salvation Army sisters, and the usual quota of uppity characters. More or less the same cast kept turning up as late as Antony Tudor's *Undertow*, so you can see how absorbing a stereotype it was.

I had not seen the Cincinnati Ballet before and was pleasantly surprised to find it a refreshing, sensibly disciplined, poetically expressive company of dancers who swept through Daniel Levans's *Concert Waltzes* (to Glazunov) and Todd Bolender's *The Still Point* (Debussy) with the kind of ease that one doesn't often encounter, even in high-powered troupes. Someone—most likely David McLain, their artistic director—has taught these dancers to phrase sequences to music so that they look impelled by its pulse, not by mechanical standards of efficiency. This is the beginning of true virtuosity; the Cincinnati dancers are on the right track. Mikhail Messerer, who was presented as a guest star, dancing the *Sleeping Beauty* pas de deux with one of the Cincinnati ballerinas, is on the wrong track—he's on a rusty spur heading back into the past. Messerer, the most recent Bolshoi defector, is thirty-one, yet stylistically he looks older than Maris Liepa, the senior danseur of the Bolshoi. His variation (to the Golden Fairy music) had old Bolshoi virtues of placement and ballon but also the relaxed knees, curled wrists, and dainty manner that even old Bolshoi virtuosos don't give us anymore. The style is not only out of date (like some Christensen ballets); it's out of context, too. If Messerer means to have a place in American ballet, he is in for a period of decalcification that may be more painful than the one Alexander Godunov is undergoing now. He could find few better places to begin than the Cincinnati Ballet.

Brooklyn College and the Brooklyn Academy are running concurrent seasons of out-of-town ballet companies. The week before the Cincinnati Ballet performances, Brooklyn College opened its season with its resident company, the Joffrey II Dancers. The junior company of the Joffrey Ballet always has fresh talent, and it's always fascinating to see the forms that talent can take before it is overhauled by the rigors of the big time. On this occasion, Ron Reagan was making his début among the other young dancers, and the company chose to publicize this with clips—shown on the Cronkite show and most of the other New York news shows—of the worst-choreographed and worst-costumed ballet on the bill. *Court Dances*, however, was a world première. The media view of Reagan's début was of a skinny Martian executing incomprehensible movements in something that looked like death to watch. It *was* death to watch—almost. David Anderson, the choreographer, seemed to have no idea what to do with Gerald Busby's original score or how to present the dancers. Why couldn't the publicity have centered on Reagan's second appearance of the evening, which was in a much livelier and more broadly congenial piece, to big-band music? Reagan not only looked better—pleasantly Bolgerish in a sweater and pleated trousers—he looked like a real dancer. *Threads from a String of Swing* (choreographer: Daryl Gray) is unfocussed and too literal in its treatment of forties hepcats, but it's in a style Americans know about, and Americans who don't know about professional dancing or why the son of a Presidential candidate wants to do it would have understood. Maybe they'd have enjoyed as much as we did at Whitman Hall seeing the son in dances that go back to the father's Hollywood period. The directors of Joffrey II missed their chance to do right not only by Ron Reagan but by the company, by American ballet, and by the history of us all.

—*November 3, 1980*

Makarova on Broadway

Makarova and Company, the latest ballet-on-Broadway experiment, was produced by James M. Nederlander in a four-week run at the Uris and publicized as the début of a new ballet company, but it had all the earmarks of a popular showcase. Stars drawn from the international circuit rotated in the kinds of roles that stars do everywhere. Besides Natalia Makarova, the ballerinas were the Italian Elisabetta Terabust and the Canadian Karen Kain. There were appearances by Fernando Bujones, Peter Schaufuss, and Denys Ganio, the French soloist. Anthony Dowell supported Makarova throughout the run; Cynthia Gregory was given a ballet of her own. To the public, they looked like ballet celebrities in another of those roundups that Nederlander puts on from time to time in his largest and least inviting New York theatre. (At the Uris, a schlockier midtown version of the State Theatre, live music always sounds as if it were on tape. Ballets take place on a stage that can be dominated only by the most belligerent musicals.) But, unlike Nureyev and Friends, Makarova and Company was equipped with a corps de ballet, newly commissioned works, and specially designed sets and costumes, by Rouben Ter-Arutunian. Impractically, it attempted repertory in a showcase format.

Paquita, Act II is an excerpt from the Kirov's Petipa repertory which Makarova was staging in this country for the first time. Obviously intended as a company vehicle, it contains a pas de deux, an interpolated complete pas de trois, and a string of five solo variations. The ballet no sooner got on than it succumbed to the normal allotment of injuries and replacements. The same thing happened to *Pas de Dix*, Balanchine's condensation of the Hungarian divertissement in *Raymonda*. When Makarova, who recently underwent a knee operation, failed to appear one evening, a number of people demanded their money back and were entitled to it; the ads had assured them that she would dance at every performance. The critics began to growl that ballet companies are not born on Broadway. The public, which could make no sense of the cast changes, deletions, and other eruptions in programming (a solo by Dowell came and went with mysterious irregularity), was further put off by the long intermissions and the insubstantial look of the ballets. The two Makarova-Dowell numbers—a Béjart pas de deux set to a Bach sonata (the one that was first danced here a decade ago by Suzanne Farrell and Jorge Donn), and *Ondine*, a new duet by the Australian choreographer Barry Moreland—exhibited at a naked extreme the capacity of these two dancers for making something out of nothing. The fancy-dress number, Lorca Massine's *Vendetta*, was about gypsy love, gypsy backbends, flared nostrils, bangles, gold teeth; Makarova swooned and fought off Ganio, Bujones, and Dowell in turn. The audience took it for comedy. And the audience took for inadequacy the eager, unseasoned trouping of the young corps de ballet. Makarova's recruits were mostly from the School of American Ballet. Many of these students were getting their first major professional experience; some got to dance big Petipa variations. But this gesture of Makarova's, so misunderstood yet so reasonable (what corps of professionals outside New York City Ballet could have shown as high a level of training and style?), was doomed by conflicts that were not foreseen.

The *Paquita* excerpt was, from a dance lover's point of view, the highlight of the season—especially when Nancy Raffa, a sixteen-year-old soloist, took over the leading role from the limited Terabust. Then there were all those American girls in their supremely difficult variations. Makarova often speaks of nurturing American dancers in the style that nurtured her. Perhaps it is pointless to repeat that one cannot carry out pilot projects in crossbreeding in the glare of a Broadway engagement. The revelation of Makarova and Company, though, is that the project itself may be misguided. In *Pas de Dix*, the dancers had the Balanchine choreography right under their skin. But *Paquita* was a frail-fairy pageant, filled with perverse hope: no matter how well the dancers did, in the end it was struggle rather than triumph that one applauded. Not long ago, the Dance Theatre of Harlem gave us a *Paquita* divertissement that *was* a triumph. But Alexandra Danilova's staging is so different from Makarova's as to amount to a different work. Two Russian ballerinas from the same school forty years apart teach two different *Paquitas*. The conflict isn't between student and professional levels of performance; it's between Petrograd and Leningrad. The way American dancers understand Russian classicism—"Petipa" for short —is the way the St. Petersburg-Petrograd generation of émigré Russians has taught it to them. With these Russians, it has always been the rule that the teachings of the academy are shaped by the findings of choreography. Of all the numberless differences between our local accent in Petipa and the current native one, I should say the greatest derives from the Russian academy's loss of its choreographers—first Fokine, then Balanchine—to the West. When the choreographer succession was weakened, the academy fell under the rule of pedagogues. The most immediately striking discrepancy between the post-Imperial–style *Paquita* set by Danilova and the latter-day, Kirov-style one set by Makarova is that Makarova's has a great many more complicated and difficult steps (further complicated by difficult tempos). Danilova's version has dance architecture; Makarova's has none. Danilova's has buoyancy; Makarova's has drive. Danilova's looks choreographically bald; in Makarova's, the dancers split hairs. Danilova, who left Russia in 1924, wouldn't know about the task-masterish accretions that became canonical Petipa; she gives us the dances of her girlhood. The dances Makarova gives us are in a kind of dotage; they're graded-exam dances, exercises from Natalia Dudinskaya's Class of Perfection (which was part of Makarova's girlhood), and the coaching of the great Dudinskaya was inspired not by choreographic precepts but by the teaching of a still greater coach, Agrippina Vaganova. So it goes, back to that moment in history when the classical tradition in Russian dancing lost its creative impetus and turned scientific. The Kirov style in Petipa, for all its slow beauty and fascination, is analytical, overscrutinized. It's a pedant's dream ballet. I couldn't help noticing, too, that Danilova's *Paquita* has a robust ballerina role, while Makarova's has a strangely reduced one. Makarova did not appear in it. And the moment in the Danilova when the swelling grand adagio is made grander still by the corps de ballet's unsupported imitations of the ballerina's supported poses isn't there in the Makarova version; the imitations come at the end and aren't sustained with emphasis. This curious non-understanding of the Petipa ballerina and the centrality of her image occurs also where one might least expect it—in the Kirov's Shades scene of *La Bayadère*. Do these recensions go back to Vaganova or were they committed by a male dancer trying to make room for himself in another of these damnable historic all-girl ballets? Vakhtang Chabukiani, who was Dudinskaya's partner, altered the choreography of *La Bayadère* and may well have revised *Paquita*, too.

As a Petipa ballerina, Makarova is romantic, lyrical, and exotic. She can be Nikiya, Odette, or Odile, but not easily is she Aurora. Her gift is the drama of character and situation; her plasticity is physical histrionics. I rushed to see her in the Hungarian dances in *Raymonda*. In fact, I could already see her doing the solo: snapping the audience to attention with a handclap and a haughty stork step forward, then drifting on her points with one arm cocked behind her head. But Makarova didn't make a tickling little story out of it. She was a limply decorative Hungarian. And in the coda she omitted the flashing coupés–jetés en tournant. This jumper! Knee trouble may still be affecting her performance. In better form, one day she may try again. This role apart, she picked herself a dreary repertory. Would it not have been possible to prepare a production of Ashton's *The Dream*? (Makarova has performed the pas de deux but not the full ballet.) Any of the Ashton pas de deux that Dowell used to dance with Antoinette Sibley would have been preferable to the wispy Béjart or the dull, overextended *Ondine*. For a dramatic vehicle, why not Todd Bolender's *The Still Point*? Why not a new Bolender ballet? A new Ashton, for that matter? I would even have preferred *Aleko*, by Lorca Massine's father, to *Vendetta*. How nice, at least, to have seen the Chagall décor again instead of the Ter-Arutunian.

The ballet that was given to Cynthia Gregory and an ensemble of six women was a heavy, mournful affair set to the most funereal Chopin. The women, in cerements, kept taking hobbled, painful-looking steps on point; they always had one foot in the grave. At the end, Gregory repeated her opening heavy-limbed dance, then straightened up into the light. She also did a whirling dance closer to the style for which she is celebrated. *Studies*, never before performed outside the Soviet Union, is the work of an Estonian choreographer, Maya Murdma. Makarova staged it, leaving evident traces of that distracted, penitential mood she sometimes falls into in *Giselle*. Gregory was as severe as the edge of a knife. When the ballet was over, she'd carved a monument to her technique in blubber. It was a little like what Fernando Bujones does nowadays almost every time he performs. The subject of the performance is execution. Step by step, he overwhelms you, but nothing is connected—there's no plastic energy to define a step series as a phrase. Bujones holds himself in constant tension, as if he meant the look of him to overwhelm us, too. His entrance in *Paquita*, walking slowly downstage with the entire cast turned diagonally to face him, is already overbearing, without the swollen, rigid figure he makes as he walks. As Danilova stages it, the man enters downstage and walks with his back to us; that and the matadorlike arch to his back are enough to establish a formidable glamour. Does Bujones think inhumanly unnatural behavior is appropriate to classical roles? When he has some acting to do—as Basil in *Don Quixote*, for example—he's more relaxed. But the artificial carrying-on seems to be an extension of the boringly immaculate execution. Peter Schaufuss, who partnered Makarova in *Pas de Dix*, is all execution these days, too. His variation was stuffed to the point of suffocation with fancy steps. Superdancers who are so far into technique that they are beyond dancing are like very mannnered actors: they leave the impression that what they do must be art, because it's so unlike life.

Superdancing is encouraged by fame. Dancers get the idea that, like singers, they can make independent careers for themselves by appearing as guest artists with all sorts of companies around the world. But an international ballet repertory comparable to an international operatic repertory does not exist. A dancer who leaves his place in a ballet company soon finds that as an individual marketable skill classical dancing doesn't go very far; it quickly converts into a specialty act. In these circumstances, the limited dancers like Terabust and Kain and Ganio can't develop; the distinguished ones like Gregory and Bujones and Schaufuss can deteriorate. Only a few years ago, as a member of New York City Ballet, Schaufuss was wonderful dancing his *Pas de Dix* role (in the version called *Cortège Hongrois*). As another excuse for stars to parade their specialties, Makarova and Company is hardly needed. As a Nederlander attraction, it doesn't compete with its follow-up—Rudolf Nureyev and the Boston Ballet. Mr. Nureyev dances at every performance. It's his specialty.   —*November 17, 1980*

Footsteps in the Fog

Peter Martins's rise as a choreographer is not only gratifying in its own right; it gives us a chance to see what one of New York City Ballet's most gifted dancers has learned from his study of Balanchine's choreography. Martins is certainly not the first of Balanchine's dancers to turn to choreography, but he is the first in a long time to show enough aptitude and concentration for a career. Though his work has character—hints of irony and hardheadedness glint beneath a placid surface—as yet it doesn't have much originality, and his latest piece, *Lille Suite*, is idiomatically as well as technically very close to Balanchine. But as a conscientious apprentice Martins is more interesting than many "innovative" young choreographers. He understands dance energy—its release, modulation, and momentum—as a function of construction and doesn't rely on the dancers to provide it. He builds logical, distinct sequences without trying for novel or catchy steps. He can create for women on point—a rare talent among the new generation of ballet choreographers. And he may be the most musical of the lot.

His progress has been rapid. In his first half-dozen ballets, all done since 1977, we see him striking out in a bold mood (*Calcium Light Night*), getting in over his head (the Basque section of *Tricolore*), becoming engrossed in small-scale studies (*Rossini Pas de Deux, Sonate di Scarlatti, Eight Easy Pieces*), and, finally, in *Lille Suite*, launching out once again, this time in confident control of large forces and a bold theme. From the first, he grasped an essential lesson from Balanchine: each ballet is a specific world shaped from its music. And somewhere along the line he learned that musical transparency alone is not enough; there must be an independent vision of the dance, which, though it is ordered by the music, does not derive all of its meaning from it. *Lille Suite* is much less exclusively about its music than was *Sonate di Scarlatti*. But it is not entirely a free vision.

The music is Carl Nielsen's Little Suite for Strings, Opus 1, written in 1888—ardent, brooding music from the composer's youth. Martins has set it for a ballerina (Heather Watts), a danseur (Ib Andersen), and a female corps of fourteen led by two demisoloists (Stacy Caddell and Roma Sosenko). Watts and Andersen are nineteenth-century counterparts of the disturbed lovers we first saw in *Calcium Light Night,* and their confrontations and partings are orchestrated and complemented by the female ensemble in the style of the Romantic ballet. Both in its conception—the man as visionary poet, the woman as his ideal and his nemesis, the corps as the maze of time and circumstance they travel through—and in its hard-edged, unsentimental execution, the piece resembles Balanchine's *Divertimento from "Le Baiser de la Fée."* And there's what might be called a climatic resemblance, too: the Nielsen suite, the Stravinsky ballet drawn from a Hans Christian Andersen story, and all Balanchine's Tchaikovsky ballets (of which, courtesy of Stravinsky's subject, *Baiser* is one) come from the same Northern latitudes. Martins has seen that, but maybe he hasn't seen the danger in using *Divertimento from "Le Baiser"* as a model. For, like Balanchine's ballet, Martins's is neither a diversion nor a drama but a bit of both. As a suite from a ballet score, Stravinsky's *Divertimento* carries something of the emotional charge of the full ballet. But Nielsen's suite is more emotionally heterogeneous. In fifteen minutes, it changes its mood so many times that Martins's attempt to pull a consistent dramatic thread through all four of its sections is repeatedly cut short. The ballet ends without having resolved its lovers' crisis and without having explained—found a dramatic use for—the several entrées for Caddell and Sosenko separate from the corps. The first flaw is actually not a flaw; Martins's finesse has made the lovers' condition seem inexplicable and eternal. But not integrating the two demis is a real detriment. Having invoked Balanchine's universe, Martins must obey its laws, and one of these is: No dangling demis. In *Ballet Imperial,* the two demis enter with the second female soloist as little friends and then attach themselves to the principal man as consoling angels. Caddell and Sosenko could be Heather Watts's friends or they could belong to Ib Andersen—as sisters, former lovers, angels as in *Ballet Imperial,* or as seeresses leading him to his fate, à la *Serenade.* The audience will decide for itself who they are, but it must be provoked, it can't just be left with two coryphées in an abstract-ballet background. Apart from this structural weakness, which more than the music's vagaries causes the ballet to seem truncated, there is one awkward transition—when, at the end of the waltz, four girls downstage are stranded just a beat or two short of their exit. I believe both problems can be easily solved. I understand, too, that the ballet, which is being done without scenery, will have some in January, and that this will be coordinated with the rather tropical-looking color-splotched costumes, by Ben Benson, that just now are so puzzling.

Lille Suite comes out of Balanchine in more explicit ways than art usually comes out of art. One could get the idea that the subject of the ballet is really the company, and that Martins is drawing more from artifacts than he is from life. But the vitality of Martins's dances isn't secondhand. Watching *Lille Suite*, I was interested in the dancing for its own sake—interested in the way it kept on getting more expansive until the curtain had to fall and cut it off. Watching the new Jerome Robbins ballet *Rondo*, which was given right after Martins's ballet on opening night, I could only wonder what Robbins was referring to. *Rondo* gives the same impression as *Lille Suite* of being fashioned after a studio-posed object, but it's dry and dusty. Robbins even has a "studio" setting, with one soloist watching informally while the onstage pianist plays for the other and then joining in. He hasn't actually used the idea as often as it seems; I think I resent the cliché less than I do the low energy of the dancing, which the informal, low-key setting seems designed to excuse. *Rondo*, named for the Mozart Rondo in A Minor, played by Gordon Boelzner on the concert grand, has only the two soloists, Kyra Nichols and Stephanie Saland, in practice clothes. You think that some interest might develop from the casting of two women—*these* two women, anyway, who are physically and temperamentally so different—and none ever does. Nichols, moreover, is a stronger dancer than Saland, and Saland, who has a dark, warm, sensuous beauty, makes Nichols look plain —which she isn't. But nothing is done with that, either. The two women are used as twins, to anticipate, echo, or duplicate each other's movements— not to build a dance between them. Robbins could be referring to *Kammermusik No. 2*, in which Balanchine took two similarly ill-matched women, Colleen Neary and Karin von Aroldingen, and carried out a similarly inscrutable experiment in twinship. The difference is that in *Kammermusik* the choreography would have had consequence without the doubling— which added a veneer of virtuosity—while in *Rondo* the choreography is inconsequential and the bifocal effects do not make it less so. There is an inherent logic of forms in classical dancing which Robbins seems intent on explaining to us, not only here but in all the dryly academic pieces he has done, from *Goldberg Variations* onward. This logic is completely available to the soloist. Adding another soloist does not add to the logic; splitting a soloist in half—even if the intent is to expose the strength of the logic by repiecing it—means that neither half is doing the dance. I was unable to follow the pattern of *Rondo* or relate it to the music.

Is *Rondo* called *Rondo* for the same reason that *Lille Suite* is not called *Little Suite* or anything else that might indicate a ballet and not a piece of music? It has become company style and a form of company hype to name ballets after their scores. Balanchine began the practice years ago as a means of dissuading audiences from seeing meanings of a kind that did not exist in his ballets. He was right to change the title of *Le Palais de Cristal* to *Symphony in C*. Because of his doctrinal emphasis on musical values, extra-musical ones are often overlooked, and these certainly exist, although they don't usually take the form of characters and stories and ready-to-hand metaphors. In recent years, there has been a certain defensiveness where extra-musical meanings may be concerned, and the company's programs have taken on the rigid cast of dogma. *Robert Schumann's "Davidsbündlertänze"* is not a good thing to call a ballet that even Balanchine admits is about Schumann's life. *Ballet Imperial* is still imperial—still a meditation on the ballet of Tchaikovsky and Petipa—in its latter-day guise as *Tchaikovsky Piano Concerto No. 2*. And to call a ballet by a number—a "No. 2" or a "No. 3" or a "No. 15," when the repertory does not contain a No. 1 or a No. 14—makes no sense. Lately, there has been a trend to original-language titles. Is the ballet sung in Danish? In German? The day is coming—most probably in the Tchaikovsky Festival of 1981—when *Swan Lake* will appear on the bills as Лебединое озеро *Suite*.

Although it wasn't until 1940 that Balanchine started making his all-dance ballets in pure classical style, he is generally credited with fathering the dominant modern movement in choreography. The so-called abstract ballet had in fact been established by Massine and Nijinska, but *Les Présages*, *Choreartium*, *Rouge et Noir*, and *Chopin Concerto* haven't survived, and for all practical purposes it is to Balanchine that we look to make and break the rules of the genre. Most choreographers under Balanchine's influence—which is now global—don't respond to music sensitively enough to make absolute lyrical expression a real possibility for twenty or thirty minutes at a stretch. And this, as I suggested at the beginning of this review, is only the first requirement. Robert Joffrey is musically very delicate—considerate rather than sensitive. As far as his ballets go, they're often quite pleasant. But they have no point of view either toward the music or toward the world. Joffrey's choice of Satie for his latest piece, *Postcards*, and his use of a Joe Brainard frontcloth covered with Satie memorabilia force an attitude that he seems reluctant to adopt. There's some period flavor in the genteel, florid choreography to the café songs and the concert rags and waltzes, but not enough to complete a picture of Satie's world. One of the group numbers is unthinkably far from that world—closer to the "Sunday in Klamath Falls" number from some folksy fifties musical. With no particular line of attack, the ballet grows repetitious and emptily virtuosic, and, as usual, the Joffrey dancers push everything too hard. Ballet may not be the right medium for these artless trifles of Satie's. In any case, I didn't miss the dances that had to be omitted because of an injury to Luis Fuente. His place in the remaining portions of the ballet was agreeably filled by a dancer new to me, Carl Corry.

Choo San Goh is the prolific young maestro of a sub-Balanchine type of plotless ballet; he's so prolific that his influence is rapidly getting to be global, too. But if Choo San Goh's product resembles Balanchine's it is only in negative particulars: no story, no props, no scenery, neutral costumes. Goh's titles usually refer to the music or to some aspect of Goh's methodology or technique: *Casella 1, 3, 4, Double Contrasts, Fives, Momentum.* As it happens, his latest piece, for the Joffrey, is called *Helena;* of course, there is no Helena in the ballet. I took this to be a flippant comment on ballets named *Paquita* or *Sylvia* in which no Paquita or Sylvia appears, modern audiences having long since lost the taste for the narratives that held up those nineteenth-century shows of dancing. But stripping away excess does not guarantee purity. After seeing six or eight of Goh's works in various repertories—works that would be impossible for me to tell apart, so facelessly efficient are they—I'm persuaded that Goh hears music not as an aural landscape but as a permissive soundtrack with cues for changes in the action. He responds not to shape, structure, or sound but to volume, texture, and mood, and he doesn't make dynamic qualitative changes in the action, he simply switches gears. Goh appears to have thought out his ballets beforehand and to be using the music only to tell him when to go with this or that effect and when to stop. If a score's divisions don't accommodate his plan, he overrides them. In *Double Contrasts,* which has Poulenc's Double Piano Concerto playing in the background, the choreography several times ignored the play between the orchestra and the solo instruments. And Goh's choreography frequently ignores things like climaxes and diminuendos; it has its own highs and lows. Yet it's so exactly fitted to the bar lengths that it *seems* musical. And because it's independently driven it seems to be making a poetic statement—to be fulfilling the second of the requirements for absolute lyrical expression, Balanchine style. On looking back over my experiences of Goh's work, I find that the most impressive of them had the best music—Stravinsky's *Ebony Concerto* for *Introducing . . .* (which I saw done by Dance Theatre of Harlem) and Prokofiev's First Piano Concerto for *Momentum,* the other of the Joffrey's Goh ballets. Is it coincidental that these two composers have also written the best ballet scores of the century? In Goh's pieces, their musical ideas seem to fit themselves to a dance landscape in a kind of backward accommodation. The musical motor is so powerful that, with dancers rushing around in precisely timed fits and starts, it's as if a ballet were being performed.

Goh keeps dancers working hard, and he wastes not a drop of energy. The taut, seamless look of the movement and the high tension that is invariably brought to a pulsating climax at or near the end of the music are sure to win applause. Good moody lighting, such as Jennifer Tipton provides for *Helena,* helps a lot, too. Like automatic writing or video tennis, a Goh ballet seems programmed by some mysterious set of controls, yet it lets the audience do its part. It doesn't presume as much as an Arpino or a Tetley ballet does; it presses us to respond to the same phenomenal urgings that created it. "Well!" it cries out, a little short of breath. "Isn't *that* curious! What do *you* make of *that!*" Goh was born in Singapore and had his dance training in Europe. As assistant artistic director of the Washington Ballet, in Washington, D.C., he has since 1978 become the hottest young choreographer on the American scene. The Washington Ballet played Brooklyn College recently, bringing three of his works. The dancers were not very strong technically. But Goh's choreography made them look strong, sleek, capable. Their movements were programmed for instantaneous effectiveness. With dancers happy, audiences thrilled, and managers satisfied, why should anyone care that none of it has a thing to do with dancing? We've reached a new point in the history of modern abstract ballet—a point of near-computerization, where coded options make choreography. Next to Goh's smooth calibrations, ordinary bad choreography looks paleolithic. Bad choreography usually has some personality. Goh's has none. What it does have is cachet—the equivalent of a designer label.

There was a spate of new ballets at the Joffrey. Laura Dean did *Night* for eight of the younger dancers. She used their extensive training, including their pointwork, to expound in heightened form the style that she has been developing in her own group, but without changing the elementary concepts basic to the style. *Night* is a good piece to see if you've never seen her work—it's maximal minimal Dean. Although she's certainly not a ballet choreographer, Dean isn't as far from mainstream trends as she seems to be at first. Her scores, which she composes, consist of metric configurations laid over chord changes. This kind of music supports dance structures that are as autonomous and insular as if they had *no* musical underpinning. In a primitive way, Dean is as mechanized as Choo San Goh.

In another somewhat dubious gesture toward Satie, the Joffrey revived *Relâche*. This ballet belongs to the history of avant-garde scandal, and it scarcely lends itself to renewal. The revival was as close to the 1924 production by the Ballets Suédois as could be imagined; everything from Francis Picabia's backdrop of row upon row of headlights to his curtain call riding a tricycle was reproduced. The flapper heroine was Starr Danias (acting like a pettish starlet); Gregory Huffman was the dashing boulevardier created by Jean Börlin. Börlin's role as choreographer (and Picabia's place in the curtain call) was taken by Moses Pendleton, one of the founding fathers of Pilobolus. He supplied some fine stuntwork for the male chorus and might have invented further craziness, but he was boxed in by Picabia's scenario and by the music, which was written to its specifications. *Relâche* glorified speed, sensation, hedonism, frivolity, Dada. Much of its mood and many of its personages are captured in the film that was commissioned from René Clair as an entr'acte. The film, seventeen and a half minutes long, was shown in the Joffrey production and drew boos. It has grown slow and stale, like the ballet as a whole. *Relâche* is a relic, not a classic. There is something fundamentally bourgeois in its outlook. It celebrates art from the consumer's point of view. *Parade*, for all that it, too, defies revival (it also has been attempted by the Joffrey), is still recognizably the testament of artists to the strange new world of the twentieth century. And Satie's music for it is superior to *Relâche*.

—December 1, 1980

Mythology

The revised, enlarged edition of *Orpheus* at the New York City Ballet works surprisingly well. There have been no extensive changes in choreography—only the Furies scene is new—but the piece looks different from the revival that was mounted two years ago for Baryshnikov. It looks different from the way *Orpheus* has ever looked. Peter Martins is Orpheus, and, with a commensurately tall and blond Karin von Aroldingen and Adam Lüders as Eurydice and the Angel of Death, the ballet is persuasive in a whole new set of terms. The enlarging process began with Isamu Noguchi's scenery in 1972, when the ballet was restaged for the Stravinsky Festival. The new dimensions and the use of coarser materials thickened the atmosphere. The current Viking cast breathes this air comfortably. Even the Bacchantes seem to be Valkyries who have stormed down the Thracian peninsula from the Rhine. Balanchine has prolonged the life of a ballet once presumed lost by giving a new life to its characters. In the old, small-scale *Orpheus*, first produced in 1948 at the City Center, Nicholas Magallanes was the poet, frail and limp, with a muscular, barrel-chested Angel (Francisco Moncion) to support and guide him on his way to the Underworld. Martins is a physically powerful Orpheus whose passive grieving is all the more moving because it seems unnatural to him. And his Angel, Lüders, is a spidery androgynous intellectual.

Lüders's vigilance and delicacy are different from Moncion's massive calm; the quality of tenderness in the Angel's support of Orpheus is different, too. Moncion's quality was animal warmth; Lüders's is pure intelligence —it doesn't get mixed up with sympathy. Lüders is extraterrestrial austere. The "Greek" austerity, the Mediterranean tinge of religious ritual, is missing from this revival, and it's largely because of the way he looks and moves. In addition to the thick ropes wound around his limbs and torso (which Orpheus now also wears—formerly, he wore a few flat strips), the Angel has on a black skintight helmet with an elephant trunk hanging down the middle of his face. The design is an extension of the black rope that bisects him from cranium to crotch when he first appears. Orpheus' mask reminded Stravinsky of a baseball catcher's. Lüders's headgear makes us think of a spaceman, a scuba diver, or an anesthetist, and it keeps his bisected or dual nature constantly before us. When he lunges close to the ground or braces the body of Orpheus, his long legs are like grappling hooks; the men are two mountain climbers yoked together, first with that black rope or air hose, then with Orpheus' lyre, slung between them.

Martins has never been as quiet and slack and listless as he is in the first half of *Orpheus*, yet he's rhythmically charged. The nondance character of the role is not a negation of his dance energy; neither was the nondance role of Junker Ove in *A Folk Tale*, which Martins performed recently with the Royal Danish Ballet. His Orpheus, like Baryshnikov's (once he got the hang of the part), comes out of the operatic-mime tradition. The role as originally conceived seems to have come more from the modern dance. Balanchine and Lincoln Kirstein had the year before sponsored the première of Merce Cunningham's *The Seasons*, which had décor by Noguchi. Not that there's necessarily a connection; however, the larval passivity of Orpheus is unlike anything a ballet dancer is trained to express. The reconstituted "classical" Orpheus has been achieved without changing a step. The Furies, though, have always had weak choreography. Noguchi designed them as hellhounds sprouting quills all over, like porcupines. Stravinsky set them quivering in perpetual agitato. Balanchine arranged a disconcerting rhythm chorus of high kicks in relevé and pumping elbows. If Noguchi had not done the décor, the only conceivable visual style would have been seventeenth-century Renaissance, in keeping with the Monteverdian roots of Stravinsky's score. Shallow grotesquerie would have been appropriate if Hades had been a Renaissance court; demons in doublets and allegorical masks were a constant feature of the seventeenth-century *ballet à grand spectacle*. Balanchine's Hades is Halloween. The new staging, by Peter Martins, eliminates a lot of the jollity, expands the corps of Furies, and puts it more aggressively to work on the Lost Souls, who cower beneath their rocks or out in the open, making little mounds to be jumped over. The head Fury, with his egregious split jumps, has been deleted. Now it is Pluto who joins the hands of Orpheus and Eurydice. But the Pas des Furies is still a lightweight affair, irretrievably athletic. It's a great relief when the scampering feet are stilled and Pluto, affected by Orpheus' song, wheels slowly to reveal the captive Eurydice pinned to his back.

Eurydice's solo, with its leggy contrapposto, its hesitations, its anguish, its fleeting Arcadian moods, is one of the sweetest Balanchine has made; it ranks with—and gesturally resembles—Calliope's solo in *Apollo*. Karin von Aroldingen dances it about as well as she dances Calliope badly. Eurydice's earthiness and womanliness bring out her best qualities. Von Aroldingen is wrong for the sprite Calliope; her forte is gravity, and in recent seasons she has come to symbolize a kind of humanity I don't recall seeing in any other

Balanchine ballerina. Von Aroldingen isn't tantalizing anymore in the first movement of *Tchaikovsky Suite No. 3*. The mystery has worn thin. As she plods toward and away from the dreaming young man, all she has is a kind of steadfast patience. It's the quality that Balanchine exploits so beautifully in *Vienna Waltzes*. Von Aroldingen's triumph as Eurydice came just before her Clara Schumann in *Davidsbündlertänze*. She is Clara the faithful, Clara the wife. Like Eurydice, she is at the center of her husband's affections, but is she at the center of his art—his obsessed mind? That is the question. It is the answer to this question which, in Balanchine's interpretation of the Orpheus myth, brings on the poet's tragedy. In Von Aroldingen's interpretation, it's the mere wifeliness of her presence. Von Aroldingen isn't imperious or devouring, as other Eurydices have been; she's so modest that her demands on Orpheus as they journey home come to seem something he can easily satisfy without tempting fate. After all, she only wants him to recognize her, his wife—how can he deny her this? Her sensuality has about it a submissiveness so trusting that we feel Orpheus is driven to rip off his mask as much by pity as by physical craving. She doesn't ask much, yet the little she does ask kills her. The death shroud swallows her up.

The Orpheus-Eurydice pas de deux before the shimmering silk curtain is justly celebrated. She follows in his footsteps (his arabesque, then hers, a beat behind), coils herself about him, whispers seductively in his ear, recalling their past life. With his eyes averted, they dance one of their little dances—a 1948-style Lindy. (In *L'Après-midi d'un Faune*, the Faun and the Nymph do a 1912-style tango.) She dies as in the myth, before the upper world is reached. Orpheus wanders in Limbo. He's lost his lyre—lost all his secrets. The sky turns red, foretelling his own bloody death. The Bacchantes appear: one, then several; then he's surrounded. Hanging on to his mask for protection, he tries to evade the swarm. The scene must be carefully done to avoid seeming like touch football. This season, it looked reblocked. The Bacchantes, led by Florence Fitzgerald, killed with stiletto precision, like Dorothy Sayers murderesses. (Robbins's harpies in *The Cage* are out of Mickey Spillane.) The blondly radiant Sean Lavery or the darkly soulful Victor Castelli made a good Apollo, though the Apotheosis has lost a lot of its sacred meaning.

For Ib Andersen's début with the company last spring, Balanchine rechoreographed sections of the male soloist role in the first movement of *Symphony in C*. It has become a minor tradition for Balanchine to do this when new dancers take the role, and he also revises the third movement from time to time. But Balanchine has stopped freezing the revisions. The first movement is now done in two versions—"Andersen" and "Lüders." I've lost count of the options open to the male soloist of the third movement. *Symphony in C* is the best refutation there is of the theory that Balanchine's art lies in his steps. It's like saying that a great writer's art lies in his diction. Balanchine can devise many combinations of perfect steps to the same music. It is true that some steps are preferable to others; Balanchine's first thoughts are often his best. But he has proved too many times that "definitive" choreography is mostly the choreography we're used to seeing. There are textual differences in the way *Theme and Variations* is performed by New York City Ballet and by American Ballet Theatre; there are even textual differences in the way NYCB performs it from one season to the next. A few weeks ago, both of the principals, running out to take their places in the finale, entered downstage, in front of instead of behind the corps. A mistake, I hope, and not a change. One can list many "mistakes" that have become changes. The critic Robert Greskovic recently noticed the simplification of a passage in *Allegro Brillante* where the men repeat arabesque à terre four times instead of stating four different arabesques. I suppose that if you don't know the more interesting version you won't miss it, but if you remember it chances are it's because the music has cemented it in your mind.

Steps are not sacrosanct, as Balanchine shows; yet our nostalgia may have been conditioned by the exactness of his musical response. In the male solo of *Divertimento No. 15*, my mind's eye persists in seeing a double tour en l'air that was deleted years ago—the music keeps forcing it into view. But it doesn't seem to matter musically whether the *Theme and Variations* ballerina does gargouillades in her first variation or simple pas de chat. The point is that she do well whatever she does. Gargouillades, which were inserted for Gelsey Kirkland's début in the role, don't happen to suit Kyra Nichols or Heather Watts, both of whom took the ballerina role this season, and problems arose from other personalized accretions. One passage in the pas de deux which Merrill Ashley makes excitingly distinctive is the series of little tendu swings of the foot this way and that as she prepares for the giant swing into arabesque. It's as if she can't for a second decide where to aim the arabesque. Dancers who don't have Ashley's ability to flick her weight in different directions can't help making the passage fuzzy. Neither Nichols nor Watts was miscast, though. Watts was the better prepared. She's not as well equipped as Nichols and not perfectly suited to the style of the choreography, but she had the edge in nerve and stamina. Nichols rushed her big effects in the pas de deux—hitting an arabesque pose several counts ahead of time, holding, then letting go, again too soon. It was Watts who had the fuller phrase, the more restful attack. Nichols, though, has a fine record in Tchaikovsky ballets. Maybe the Ashley roles she's been getting are making her abrupt; she's now done *Ballo della Regina* as well as *Square Dance*. These may have been Balanchine's antidote for the slight lethargy that used to mar her dancing. If so, haven't they more than done their work?

Nichols, who has been poised on the brink of stardom for some time and had been held back by injury, could make it this season. She's beautiful, strong, and scrupulous. Just now in *The Nutcracker* she's the company's most dazzling Sugar Plum. But she's not always fully present. In the first movement of *Symphony in C*, she has everything she needs to light up the stage except—one can't help thinking—the hunger to be there. Young Darci Kistler in the second movement has that hunger and all the other stuff, too: an astonishing début. From the ground up—her feet and legs are prodigiously long and strong—Kistler has a fledgling power mightier than many dancers have in their maturity. She's not one of the sleeping beauties, either; she beams out, a child diva. It's a pleasure to see her next to Suzanne Farrell, who is riding a crest this season. Casting linked them: in the same ballet (*Walpurgisnacht*), in the same role (second movement, *Symphony in C*), in similar roles (Scherzo, *Suite No. 3*; Scherzo, *Diamonds*). It may have been in the two Tchaikovsky scherzos that the generational connection was most obvious. Tchaikovsky seems to be recalling the enchanted wood of Mendelssohn's *A Midsummer Night's Dream*; musically and choreographically, the subject is Titania, an archetype to whom Balanchine has returned again and again.

Dancers don't have to incarnate myths to become Balanchine ballerinas, however. The evidence suggests that all they need is a two-syllable first name. It should be a trochee and, if possible, the second name should be a trochee, too. In former days, the thing was to have an amphibrach for a first name, ending in "a." (This rule, like the current one, applies to American-born dancers. The foreign-born must seek other formulas.) The amphibrachic (Maria, Diana, Melissa, Patricia, Allegra, Jillana) gave way to the trochaic with the advent of Suzanne Farrell. Suzanne is iambic; Farrell is trochaic. At first, studying the pattern, I thought this must be the great exception—the Great Iamb. It didn't even bother to crack the mold. Then I discovered Farrell's real name: Roberta.   —*December 15, 1980*

Split Week

American Ballet Theatre, Kennedy Center, Washington, D.C. The repertory for this first season under the artistic direction of Mikhail Baryshnikov seems designed according to the old Ballet Theatre principles of selection, which Lucius Beebe defined in the souvenir program of the inaugural season, in 1940: "The best that is traditional, the best that is contemporary and, inevitably, the best that is controversial." The opening week's bills include an unusual proportion of modern classics; then come *Giselle*, *Bayadère*, and *Nutcracker*. Baryshnikov had staged an abbreviated *Raymonda*, scheduled for the second night. But his hand is evident from the start.

Opening night, December 10. None of the ballets on the program would be there without Baryshnikov. Ashton's *Les Rendezvous* and Balanchine's *The Prodigal Son* are his acquisitions, as is the fragment of Kirov Petipa called *Pas d'Esclave*. Twyla Tharp's *Push Comes to Shove* was created for him five years ago; it's the only piece he dances in tonight. The evening was to have featured Gelsey Kirkland's return to the company after a year's leave. But a correction slip in the program informs the audience that Kirkland and Patrick Bissell, who was to have been her partner in the *Pas d'Esclave*, will not appear. They were in fact fired the day before by Herman Krawitz, executive director of the Ballet Theatre Foundation, for being "chronically late and chronically absent" from rehearsals.

There is no question that the dismissals cast a pall. Marianna Tcherkassky dances competently, if colorlessly, in *Les Rendezvous*. The role, made for Alicia Markova, seems especially well suited to Kirkland's fine-lined lyricism and brio. Nevertheless, the ballet is a success in this, its first American production. *Les Rendezvous* is one of four Ashton works that survive from the thirties. Its form—a suite of lighthearted classical dances—puts it closer to *Les Patineurs* than to *Façade* or *A Wedding Bouquet*, but it has in common with the last piece an ineffable English aura. Ashton's stylish young people meeting and cavorting in a park and William Chappell's set of green lawn and white grillwork are perfectly united; together they retain the peculiar "Regency" flavor of English town fashions in the twenties and early thirties. *Les Rendezvous* is an urban frolic. The women, in their frothy beribboned party dresses and long white gloves, look like English debs; with their escorts they seem at times to be engaging in an obscure social ritual. The manners of the piece, whether formal or colloquial, are thick with intrigue. (I imagine that Balanchine's *Cotillon*, made the previous year, was like this, too.) When the men do a Spanish dance all by themselves, or when they pair off to lift the women prone and rock them, the social texture of the piece is at its thickest. Four younger girls go about in a group, more sedate relatives of the Mayfair sillies in *Façade*. In classical terms, they're "attendants to the scene"; at the end, when everyone leaves through the high gate, they stay behind to give us Ashton's signature finis—the antic flip of the palms that says, "So goes the world." No doubt Ashton and Chappell intended nothing more than a classical ballet in Balletland, but as a memento of the "white" thirties the piece seems not only specifically English but fateful as well—a literal evocation of Cyril Connolly's condemned playground.

The American cast does no more to capture meanings of this sort than the dancers of the Sadler's Wells Royal Ballet whom I saw do the piece a year ago; any cast has all it can handle in the execution of the dances. In the ballerina's principal variation, Ashton seems to define his personal vision of feminine classical style. The choreography is full of unexpected and contradictory details. She pirouettes to a stop, then immediately whirls to a different stop. As in Royal Ballet dancing to this day, we notice crisp épaulé address, elaborately shaped arms, flourishing wrists and hands. The mid-body is vigorous but quiet. In the lower body, the emphasis on elegant extremities recurs: the instep is quicker than the thigh. For all the dancers, Ashton has devised a *Rendezvous* walk on toe with the torso twisting from side to side and the hands crossed high above the head. And in a pas de trois for a girl and two boys he invents the ultimate instep dance; its leit-motiv is pas de cheval done around and around the stage, alternating with hops in arabesque and small beaten steps. It is all set in a single rapid tempo, and it must be the most difficult-to-sustain number in the ballet. Rebecca Wright, Warren Conover, and Peter Fonseca are a capable trio. I disagree with the casting of Danilo Radojevic in the leading male role. Stanislas Idzikowski, who originated it, was a demi-caractère stylist. The tendency today in demi-caractère roles is to cast the less polished classical dancers. This defeats the expressive purpose of the category. The colors in demi-caractère dancing come about through emphasis on the part of the dancer, not through slurred and incorrect form. The Sadler's Wells cast David Ashmole, whose dancing was clean but not very strong. Radojevic is strong but coarse. The compromise, if there must be one, is in the wrong direction.

By coincidence, the music for *Les Rendezvous* is the ballet music from an opera by Auber—*L'Enfant Prodigue*. The ABT *Prodigal Son* is a replica of New York City Ballet's current production except that rescaled backcloths have been substituted for NYCB's small (and shabby) ones and the dance of the two Servants has been restored. *The Prodigal Son* has always been a great piece, but it needs a dancer who can act. Dancers as powerful as Edward Villella and Baryshnikov have needed to be extra-powerful actors in order to hold their spell during the long mime scenes. Even so, a portion of the audience was always audibly disappointed when the Son wasn't danc-ing. Tonight, young Robert La Fosse, making his début, does well as a dancer. He has the natural elevation for the two high leaps in the first scene. In the seduction scene, he projects a calflike innocence. But when it comes to the Son's degradation and return home he can't act at all. Everything he does looks memorized. I think young dancers have a problem understanding what the Son is guilty of and why he must suffer; he seems overpunished for a little mild rebellion. And if the Siren also humiliates him—well, isn't it all a bit masochistic? Cynthia Gregory, tonight's Siren, is about as stony and venomous a torturess as the ballet can ever have seen. Her slow, insulting way of positioning her thighs in ballonné, her condescending pinpoint bal-ances make the heart quail. The male corps of dithering goons is very good, too. (Was it Balanchine's comment on the homoeroticism of the Diaghilev company?) Derogatoriness, obscenity of every description, is one of the two great driving forces behind the ballet; the other is the belief in forgiveness and salvation. They are tandem forces, each indispensable to the other. In spite of La Fosse's blankness, the orgy and the despoilment are effective. But the rest of the ballet is glazed over. Two glazed sisters greet the Prodigal's return; a glazed Father receives him. Prokofiev's great score must carry the final scenes alone.

Pas d'Esclave, a harem-trouser number from the first act of the Kirov's *Corsaire*, contains nothing we haven't seen before in this line, and it is attached to harrowingly stilted music by one Prince Oldenburg. (The dance was originally a novelty interpolated by Petipa into the first Russian production of Mazilier's ballet, in 1858.) Hearty performing is needed to save it. Alexander Godunov is still wandering in his wilderness. He is appreciably a better dancer than he was a year ago, but he still looks as if he might give it all up to play the guitar. Susan Jaffe, a new corps de ballet dancer from Bethesda, Maryland, has the long, finely tempered body and easy extension that this kind of Soviet ballet exotica seems intended for, but she does not, in this hastily scheduled début, project much more than a wooden bravura. The dance concerns Gulnare, a slave sold at auction. She dances the whole entrée with her head and shoulders swathed in a veil. Russians do love their veil dances. Whether they have loved steps well enough to preserve them for over a hundred years seems doubtful.

In *Push Comes to Shove* ("the best that is controversial"), I cannot take my eyes off Baryshnikov. He's thinner than when I last saw him, and has renewed himself. He keeps you from seeing what he is going to do next, and when he does it he is completely satisfying. The ballet's last movement has been revised to include more business with the derby hats, and Baryshnikov's role has been retimed to look even wilder and more ad lib than it used to. The changes were supervised by Twyla Tharp. They are not departures but intensifiers—like the repainting of Bakst's *Schéhérazade* in exaggerated colors which was said to have been necessary to match the public's memory of it. After Baryshnikov, the funniest performer on the stage is Kristine Elliott, normally a stolid, even an opaque dancer. Here she dances stolidly on purpose and becomes a deadpan comedienne.

December 11. Another insert in the program, this time to announce the dedication of the evening's performance to John Lennon, "whose music will always be a part of our lives."

Les Sylphides has Elliott in the Waltz, Cynthia Harvey in the Prelude, and Cheryl Yeager in the Mazurka. Harvey does the pas de deux with Baryshnikov, who is dancing this role for the first time in the West. Except for him, it's Ballet Theatre's usual sleepy *Sylphides*. Although the dancers have been recoached in their parts, they haven't been weaned from their underenergized style; because of Baryshnikov's superb energy, it looks more intractable than ever. ABT's *Sylphides* has been a tradition for forty years; it can only change gradually, as a result of stylistic changes in the company at large.

Rodeo comes on strong. The blood-red corral is an eyesore, the cowboy hats and splotched jeans look seedy (and too much like life), and the jokes weigh a ton. The ballet is so good-natured and clever it deserves freshening up, but it's hardly the national treasure that it was claimed to be a generation ago. *Rodeo* is folk art of a modest stripe. People still speculate on how much of it may have come out of *Billy the Kid*; does anyone speculate on how much of *Annie Get Your Gun* may have come out of *Rodeo*? De Mille's expert storytelling has one flaw—the lack of a climax that would show the heroine's inner conversion from tomboy to sweetheart. All we get is the outer one. And as soon as we get it the focus switches away from her to the Champion Roper and his sexy tap-dancing. For all her heavy clowning, Jolinda Menendez is a likably kinetic Cowgirl. When her bronco bucks, she gets her knees and elbows flapping like loose hinges. Kevin McKenzie makes a lanky and charming Champion Roper, and his tap technique is more than passable. The Saturday night social dances in *Rodeo* place it in the ragtime era. This is the civilized Old West of living memory; civilization is, in fact, the ballet's subject. Copland's score is a bit overconfident, so it's surprising how many times it dissolves into pure emotion or into pure pit-piano exuberance. There's a minute or two when the orchestra plays a rag at top speed under its breath while Saturday Night vignettes unfold on the stage. Copland and De Mille collaborate marvellously in these intimate moments, and in other ways as well. When De Mille attempts something different—a hollering and stomping square dance that is "outside time"—Copland is silent, and the episode expands into an epic moment.

Raymonda is feasible only in suite form. Petipa complained privately of Glazunov's "phlegmatic talent," and he never again collaborated with the composer on a full-length ballet. Baryshnikov's suite is a loose-leaf collection of dances, some from Act II, most from Act III. Santo Loquasto's court scene is backed by a Moorish grille and lit by suspended candelabra; against this décor his three different sets of sparkling white costumes precisely suggest the ballet's atmosphere, its mixture of sugary fantasy and gloom. The dancing begins moodily, with the Act II pas de deux, and goes straight on to the third-act wedding dances. The choreography is Kirov-inspired. The folk dances are vodka, but too much ice water has got into the adagios. In addition to her third-act "balalaika" solo, the ballerina has one of the second-act variations; of the less familiar numbers in this assortment, it has the best steps. Martine van Hamel was the company's grandest Raymonda a few years ago, when Nureyev's production of the full ballet was being performed, and she is grand again but slightly overanimated at times, as if to make up for the vacuity of the choreography. As Jean de Brienne, Godunov wears a minuscule bandeau with his back hair hanging stiff as a snood—stiffer, since it doesn't move even when he turns.

December 12, matinee. Baryshnikov's Prodigal Son, as anyone who saw his television performance will remember, is one of his finest creations. Today, he overplays a little the Son's suffering and homecoming, as if demonstrating point by point the content of these scenes. And his matted wet hair and dirt-smeared body suggest that he has crawled through slime to reach his father's gate. Van Hamel is a predictably voluptuous Siren; what wasn't so predictable, perhaps, is the wit with which she informs every gesture. She's as lacquered as Gregory but not as cold. When she winds her velvet train around her thighs and through her crotch, then flips the rest over one arm and poses like a Chanel model, one wants to laugh. Everything the Siren does is absurd on a level so high it becomes awesome, and she switches from one thing to another in a flash. After the mannequin strut, she drops to her knees and beats her chest, her back, her chest; the anguish of centuries wails through her. In the mutually manipulative erotic pas de deux with the Prodigal, she turns herself several times into objects. And, of course, she's the figurehead in the ingenious "boat" scene. Through all this, Van Hamel is vividly alive and female; when she folds her leg around the Prodigal's waist she's as happy as a pythoness with a lion cub. And Baryshnikov gazes up at her, happy and dazed. He thinks she's the most beautiful thing on earth.

Interplay. Neither a fresh-looking production nor an especially keen performance. Yet Robbins's sense of form is so exposed that the ballet carries anyway. Baryshnikov is right to keep it in.

Rodeo with Ruth Mayer as a much too sophisticated Cowgirl. Mayer gives the impression that she's wearing Calvin Klein jeans. With La Fosse as a young and simple Champion Roper she doesn't appear to have a thing in common. This is a dude-ranch *Rodeo*.

December 12, evening. La Fosse in *Prodigal* is better, more attentive to his musical cues in the mime episodes. Crawling away from the scene of his downfall, he pauses and stares out at us like Michelangelo's Damned Soul. Gregory is unwaveringly even, and Joseph Carman and Charles Maple are impeccably salacious as the Servants.

I get through to the second layer of *Les Rendezvous*, watching it more as pure dance, less as a reflection of its time and place. On this plane, it isn't as absorbing as the later *Les Patineurs*; its formal structure isn't as sound, or continually evolving. The choreography for the ballerina (Tcherkassky) includes two series of inside pirouettes opening to arabesque—the step that Merrill Ashley does as doubles in *Ballo della Regina*. Leslie Browne, Gregory Osborne, and Ronald Perry are a sharp pleasure cantering through the park in their pas de trois.

The Moor's Pavane. Godunov with his hair sprayed dark, McKenzie as the Friend, Van Hamel as his wife, and Gregory as Desdemona. All for naught. My eye keeps drawing small boxes around the quartet, trying to place it in its rightful space. The stages at Connecticut College, Jacob's Pillow, Hunter College, and the 92nd Street Y (all stages on which I can recall seeing this work in years past) more accurately represent that space than the opera-house stages where it is usually seen nowadays, or thought to be seen. All one *sees* is big costumes changing places, with now and then a leg sticking out.

A big event in tonight's *Raymonda*: Magali Messac, who led the Grand Pas Hongrois in the first performance, makes her début as the ballerina. Messac is a French dancer who a few years ago left the Hamburg State Opera for the Pennsylvania Ballet, where Baryshnikov saw her. This is her first season with Ballet Theatre and her first big ABT part. I hope to see her often. Messac's style revives the lost art of the great European ballerinas of twenty and thirty years ago. It's prudent and subtle and has a completely individual transparency and glow. The years at the Pennsylvania Ballet have made her technically more expansive; she dances in the right scale for the ABT dancers around her and in a complementary style, and her Raymonda takes on an enchanting Old World lustre. Her partner is Ross Stretton, replacing Victor Barbee at short notice. Stretton is the tall, thin young man who just a few weeks ago was all over the Joffrey repertory, trying to find himself. At Ballet Theatre, he'll presumably dance the classical roles he seems more suited to. Tonight, he functions mostly as Messac's partner; lack of rehearsal time has forced him to leave out his variation.

New York City Ballet, Lincoln Center. *The Nutcracker*, December 13. The biggest dance moments are the Waltz of the Snowflakes at the end of Act I and the Waltz of the Flowers and the pas de deux, which form the climax of Act II. Balanchine's production was first staged in 1954, and his style in the Snowflakes waltz was classic Maryinsky. One sees steps that he doesn't use much anymore, such as those romping sautés that go one way with third-arabesque arms that go another. The Waltz of the Flowers is also filled with 1890's-style conceits; the odd thing is that it doesn't also look 1954—it looks utterly contemporary. Maybe the changes in company style over the years have been more easy to incorporate in its spaciousness and sweep than in the more compacted figures of Snowflakes. (That Flowers is a transcendent masterpiece of composition may also have something to do with it.)

Darci Kistler may be the youngest Dewdrop to lead Flowers. Tonight, she shoots through the line of girls like a hare. Her lean legs and brittle assurance bring flashes of the role's originator, Tanaquil LeClercq. Heather Watts, one of our better Dewdrops, makes her début as the Sugar Plum Fairy—not a very auspicious one. The solo is neat but flat, and, in spite of Peter Martins as the cavalier, the adagio lacks drama. But most of the company's ballerinas give offish performances as Sugar Plum. This role, like Snowflakes, bears the imprint of the fifties. More specifically, it bears the imprint of Maria Tallchief. Kyra Nichols is the first in a very long series to recapture fully the wide dynamics, chiselled épaulement, steady aplomb, and delicate musical accents that characterize the role. She even looks a little like Tallchief.

December 14, matinee. It's Kistler's turn as Sugar Plum. She gives the steps of the variation an unusual clarity but doesn't quite absorb their eccentricity. Ib Andersen is her partner, and the adagio goes smoothly except for one of the shoulder lifts. Then the balances crumble. Kistler recovers admirably, winningly. But the final plunges are a shade too perilous. Nichols as a crystalline Dewdrop dominates the performance. Here she looks like no one but herself. She has a special way of giving multiple pirouettes a slight renversé finish, so that the spiral peaks, then curls.

December 14, evening. Suzanne Farrell, who could not be less suited to the syntax of the Sugar Plum's choreography, nevertheless surmounts it by reason of her superb timing, her personal grandeur, and her instinctive reliance on a great partner, Peter Martins. Watts is a buoyant Dewdrop. I must mention also Maria Calegari's fine dancing in this role last week and lay plans to catch her Sugar Plum before the calendar turns.

—*December 29, 1980*

Harlem's Fokine, Koner's Humphrey

Fokine's *Schéhérazade* is not about the sultan's faithless wife who told stories for a thousand and one nights to stave off a death sentence. It isn't about one of her stories. Nor has it anything to do with the titles for the parts of Rimsky-Korsakov's tone poem—"Sinbad's Ship," "Festival in Baghdad," etc.—that provide the score. The faithless sultana in the ballet, Zobeide, wriggles impatiently while her husband prepares to go hunting; the minute he's out of sight, Zobeide and the rest of the harem ladies bribe the Chief Eunuch to release the slaves. A door opens and out slithers a flock of glistening young men in harem pants and jewelled shackles. Another door opens: more slitherers. A third door opens and out pops Nijinsky. What happens next brought on fevers in Parisian audiences seventy years ago—so all the books say. In no time the Shah returns, scimitars flash, and the orgy becomes a massacre out of Delacroix. Zobeide's favorite slave, cut down in midair, falls headlong and thrashes the floor, Cocteau wrote, "like a fish on the bottom of a boat." (His leap, equally spectacular and very dangerous, from a platform ten feet high, is something of which history has not told.) This convulsive molto agitato death is followed by a droopy legato one: Zobeide, resisting the Shah's henchmen, plunges a dagger between her breasts as the curtain falls.

The books don't say when the thrill of *Schéhérazade* stopped rolling through audiences. By the middle of the thirties, the ballet had become an object of parody (by Balanchine, in the musical *On Your Toes*). But the Ballet Russe de Monte Carlo touring production of the forties was popular with American audiences. Frederic Franklin, who was the Golden Slave to Danilova's Zobeide in those days, has now revived the ballet for Dance Theatre of Harlem on the very stage, at the City Center, where the Monte Carlo used to dance it. A theory worth testing holds that no ballet revival goes back more than forty years in authenticity. Visually, this seems to be true of the new production. The Bakst scenery that stunned Paris looks all too Maria Montez. It was re-created by Geoffrey Guy (who performed the same service for the London Festival Ballet revival seen here a few years ago), and lit by Nicholas Cernovitch. The colors seem to have burned out—the fabled greens and blues have an ashy tone. The dancers have been fitted with a new set of sherbet-colored costumes, designed by Carl Michell. Their freshness is preferable to 1981 Bakst knockdowns, but a better option still would have been the commissioning of an original production from that wizard designer Geoffrey Holder, retaining only the Fokine choreography, which turns out to be much stronger than its reputation would allow.

A program note by Karel Shook, co-director of DTH, rejects the idea of new choreography that "might possibly appeal more to the tastes and sensibilities of the current public than the original"—rejects it on the ground that "only a master of master choreographers could accomplish anything which would come close to Fokine." He's right. The movement design is part of the music and part of the style of its era, which Shook identifies as Art Nouveau. And it is deliberately designed movement, not the programmed spontaneity that one reads of. The annals of *Schéhérazade* ripple with wavelets of the ballet's own abandon and give the impression that much of it was formless pantomime, and much of *that* improvised. But the fleshy exuberance has a solid core. As a piece of dance construction, the orgy scene keeps itself well hidden in layers of cushions, platters of fruit, voluptuous writhing, and other circumstantial nonsense. The way it breaks out, drowses, revives and recapitulates, and stops dead on the peak of a crescendo when the Shah's men return is theatrical strategy in the grand manner. The dead stop freezes the stage picture as Rimsky's sea music goes on heaving. Then the picture cracks, and the climax passes over into the slaughter. The ensembles could be diagrammed with absolute mathematical precision. The Golden Slave leaps over and over on one spot in one wide rhythm while the company whirls around him in another. The orgy duets wend their way on a downstage diagonal; when the slaughter commences, everyone rushes in waves on an upstage one—rushes out, then back in, falling down and getting up, flooding the stage and damming it. The stylized sexiness of the dancing is of course ludicrous—the skipping in crouches, the continuously weaving backbends. And there are sets of people, as in *Firebird,* who do one little step—like prancing with stiff vertical arms and horizontal palms. One hardly knows which is more amusing, the decorousness or the commotion. But though the style of the choreography tends more toward perfected show dancing than toward classicism, one knows its maker for the polyrhythmic, architectonic Fokine of *Les Sylphides*.

The most one asks of a revival, especially one coming seventy years after a sensational première, is that it not embarrass history too much and that it furnish a few particulars of the sort that eyewitnesses always seem to leave out of account. Even Fokine, in *Memoirs of a Ballet Master*, when he describes Ida Rubinstein's Zobeide as she stood waiting for her lover's entrance, says only that "she waits for him with her entire body." Virginia Johnson, the DTH Zobeide, gives us the exact stance: legs braced in deep fondu, body arched backward in a swoon of anticipation. The moment doesn't slip by. We see what Fokine meant, even though the psychology of 1910 doesn't permit us to feel it. Although he's more Douglas Fairbanks than Nijinsky, Eddie Shellman's Golden Slave also satisfies our expectations. But any revival, no matter how bad, would give us enough information to color the blanks in our mental picture of the ballet. The value of the DTH *Schéhérazade* to me is that it colors blanks I didn't know were there. I don't see a company straining to interpret ancient psychology and dead aesthetics; I do see dancers performing with unaffected good sense and making the most of Fokine's gift whenever it accords with their own. The dance core of *Schéhérazade* is a discovery few companies could make. One can imagine a Joffrey revival restoring Bakst to glory, but Fokine? Conversational pantomime, sweeping or intimate, is not a Harlem specialty—no American company does it well. But seeing Fokine in the abstract (so to speak) does no harm to his genius and even rehabilitates an aspect of it in our eyes.

Mikhail Fokine was born in 1880. This *Schéhérazade* is the only centenary salute a ranking American company has been able to muster. Worthy though it is, is it the best we could have done? *Schéhérazade*, after all, was once a titillating dance drama; can these bones live? (Touring the United States in the forties, it must surely have titillated as a drama of what was then called "miscegenation." A black cast removes that angle and rights the ethnic balance—for the first time in history.) As a Fokine ballet of the Diaghilev era, *Le Pavillon d'Armide* would seem to be far more appropriate to the talents of contemporary dancers and the tastes of contemporary audiences. The first of his works to conquer Europe, it was the soonest eclipsed, and it has been revived only in fragments. Next to *Les Sylphides*, it represents the fullest exposure of Fokine's classical style. That's what the books say, anyway.

It is better to get one's history in the theatre, if one can, than out of books. Dances are perishable goods, and one must try to distinguish history from the wistful preservation of a legend. Still, one has at least a chance of forming an impression of a bygone figure like José Limón if one sees (starting next week at the City Center) the company that persists in his name. I went to the Theatre of the Riverside Church to see a program of two long works by Pauline Koner, one of them her celebrated 1962 solo *The Farewell*, in homage to Doris Humphrey. Koner no longer dances; the separate parts of the solo were done on this occasion by members of the Pauline Koner Dance Consort. Before they came on, Koner, who is as long of wind as Schéhérazade, gave a talk analyzing the choreography, describing the conditions of its creation, demonstrating its leading motifs, explaining her attitude toward her work, and—most provocative of all—telling us, in terms both general and specific, what it means. Pauline Koner studied with Fokine, but there's not much evidence of it in her work, and she barely mentioned his name. The great influence was Humphrey, and Koner tells us what she learned from her both as a pupil and as a dancer who performed with the Humphrey-Limón concert group for fifteen years. If Koner is representing her teacher correctly, she must have been one of the great naifs of modern times—one who went about categorizing movement and devising dances in a total vacuum. I believe Humphrey did try, somewhat fecklessly, to rationalize much that was inchoate in dance as she knew it (which was Denishawn dance), but as Koner portrays her she is a color-blind maker of patchwork quilts. Quilts are done with mottoes: "Death separates us from our loved ones, but Life goes on"; "In Solitude is Strength." Expression is homiletic and abstract at the same time. One arrives at a "statement" by twisting natural movement out of its sockets and concealing its origins as simple mime. Koner's type of movement is insistently gestural, diminutive, pale, and static. "Development" is repetition or moving the gesture around the stage or softening it or turning it upside down. There doesn't seem to be anything in her work—except, perhaps, length—that she can't demonstrate, even now. When the Koner Consort dancers came on, finally, to give us the full-scale paintings from their leader's sketches, they just gave us longer sketches.

Pauline Koner has been a popular teacher for many years; her Humphrey-derived catalogue of methods easily lends itself to a syllabus and to show-and-tell lectures before the public. Many young dancers consider her outmoded, although what she teaches is not an outmoded aesthetic of dance—it's an aesthetic of feeling. Emotion is what it's all about. She demonstrates one of her entrances in *The Farewell*, pauses, and says, "I always know I've done it right if I get cold chills at that point." What about cold chills for the audience? Feelings that are for the performer alone betray the professed concern of the Koner generation with form, substance, communication. A later generation, rebelling against this pretense, tossed out "made" movement and emotional subject matter. But the rebellion didn't go far enough.

An unofficial credo of modern dance has always been "What's right for me is right for you," and it's not Koner's fault if there are dancers—young ones—who live by it to this day.

The other work on the program was *Solitary Songs*, the second half of which is group choreography. Although there was little formal difference, the effect of more people on the stage was refreshing. One didn't feel trapped by the Grand Solipsism. *—January 26, 1981*

Camping in Cleveland

Wagner called Beethoven's Seventh Symphony "the Apotheosis of the Dance," misleading Isadora Duncan into using it as a dance score; it was one of the messianic Isadora's greatest follies. Léonide Massine also used the music, during his symphonic period; in his case, "folly" is perhaps not quite the word—"boner" is more like it. By this declension, Dennis Nahat's *Celebrations*, the latest assault on the Seventh, should be a howler—and it is, it is. Nahat has trodden the primrose path with a bravado that might be touching if it weren't so blind. Not only doesn't he know what history and his own ear could have told him—that the Seventh is undanceable dance music—he doesn't seem to understand that such a category exists. Nahat, the resident choreographer of the Cleveland Ballet, was responsible for four of the six ballets the company presented in its début season at the Brooklyn Academy. (He was listed as co-choreographer of the fifth ballet, and in the sixth he danced the leading role. An evening with the Cleveland Ballet tended to be a Nahat evening.) Nahat is not a tyro; he did ballets for American Ballet Theatre before moving to Cleveland, with another ABT dancer, Ian Horvath, and founding a company there. I never liked the ABT work, but I wasn't prepared for the reckless things Nahat is doing now. What Edwin Denby said of Massine's experiment with the Seventh—"He is using famous names to advertise his wares"—could be said of Nahat's *Celebrations*, and also of his *Things Our Fathers Loved*, which appropriates no fewer than nineteen of Charles Ives's songs. His *songs*. I wonder if Nahat thinks choreography can be set to just any kind of music. Dumbfoundingly, Nahat is a musician who plays the piano and that testiest of stringed instruments the viola and who encourages conscientious musical direction in the Cleveland organization. The Ives songs were sung and played from the pit by three good artists: Wayne Turnage, Grayson Hirst, and Gladys Celeste Mercader. The company came to Brooklyn with its own orchestra—a high-caliber ensemble led by Dwight Oltman or Stanley Sussman. Nahat's recklessness is perhaps not as unassuming as it seems. Maybe he doesn't think that ballets can be made to any music; maybe he thinks that *his* ballets can.

As a choreographer, Nahat doesn't proceed the way you might think a musician would. He's unable to pull off credible ballets to relatively unresisting scores, like Mendelssohn's First Piano Concerto and Brahms's Viola Quintet in G Major, and part of the reason for the failure is that the dancing doesn't make musical sense. A music critic, Alan Rich, has written of Nahat's *Brahms Quintet,* calling it "one of the most beautiful ballets I have ever seen" and saying that the music ("horribly strained, pseudo-solemn, grossly overwritten") was hardly suited to choreography but that Nahat circumvented this by choreographing its "mood" rather than its "movement." If I understand Rich correctly—and I'm not sure I do—he's saying that a choreographer can actually triumph over a bad piece of music by ignoring the way it is written. But dance impetus that comes from nothing more than mood isn't interesting enough to sustain a whole ballet; it doesn't, to my mind, sustain *Brahms Quintet.* In the Beethoven, Nahat inevitably gets caught trying to separate his soundtrack from the formal progression of the music. His efforts to avoid a schematic visualization look arbitrary and willful, yet an instant of direct connection turns the ballet into a Silly Symphony. It's a crushingly uneven contest. In the last movement, the dancers are tossed like minnows in a whale's spout. *Brahms Quintet,* done originally for ABT, is a searching and delicate affair compared with the ballets that have been done for Cleveland. Not that Nahat has given up searching; there's evidence throughout the current work that he hopes to invent new ways of dealing with the abstract ballet. The trouble, though, is that it's always new ways of choreographing mood rather than movement; his response to a piece of music is to the most obvious thing about it. This makes him a popular choreographer. He keeps up an appeal to what one hears in music when one doesn't listen; he stays within the music's broad rhythmic boundaries and structural divisions, changes the picture on cue, and gives audiences a foolish and happy sense of correspondence. But there's more to it. Nahat drains music of its content and refills it with something of his own that people call personality. In *Quicksilver,* the Mendelssohn concerto succumbs, bit by bit, to Nahatization. Nahat himself, in the principal role, makes this process easier to see, but since he's the kind of choreographer who turns other dancers into replicas of himself he really doesn't have to be onstage.

You could scarcely ask for an odder duck to set a norm by. Tall, thin, and slinky, with a beaky nose, huge hungry eyes, and a ruff of curly black hair, Nahat makes a naturally compelling commedia dell'arte figure, and at ABT he was cast almost exclusively in character-comic roles: Third Sailor in *Fancy Free,* Devil in *Three Virgins and a Devil,* Dance Master in *Gaîté Parisienne.* The role that defined him best was not his best role; as end man in the male kick line fashioned by Alvin Ailey in *The River,* Nahat carried on in the best drag-show tradition. The role seems to have set his style: as a performer, he became a camp. As a choreographer, he appeared to have serious aspirations. But now his choreography is unserious and unreal; he's a camp in everything he does. *Quicksilver* is Nahat camp inflated to full-company scale. Everybody has a shoulder squirm, a high kick, a head lolling in languor, a droopy wrist, a leering eye. Nahat's command of classical technique, always less than full, has also been transferred to his dancers. They've got what you might call a style laid over an unsound technical base. The style in all its shaky coherence makes the Cleveland Ballet a show with Nahat as its star. He's at the center of *Things Our Fathers Loved,* posturing extensively in a downlight as vignettes of the past drift by. As Nahat performs this supposedly sober role, his meditating and soliloquizing appear to be all about himself, in ways that have nothing to do with the past. He's as unconnected to the ballet as the ballet is to the Ives songs. He's even wearing his *River* non-costume—tights and bare torso.

The Cleveland Ballet may not be quite as much a personal showcase as it looked in Brooklyn. Ian Horvath, who was out sick, did not perform any of his roles. As artistic director, he's had some influence; there are several chunky young Horvaths in the company. But the Horvath I recall as technically an accomplished dancer hasn't been able to spread his example wide enough to compete with the Nahat norm. Although both men teach, it is clear that their dancers are being bred mainly from Nahat's choreography. In the one non-Nahat piece, *The Green Table,* they were too soft and mushy. Nahat, as Death, had to force an impersonation of a physique and strength of movement he doesn't possess; he'd have been better off as the oily Profiteer. *US,* the piece credited to him and Horvath, was so much like the other Nahat pieces that it might as well have been one. It was surprising only in its sameness. *US* is one of those cavalcades of popular dance which are now obligatory in ballet repertory. One might have expected the breeziness of the material to set off some kind of spark in Nahat, but there's no more life in his Irving Berlin and Jelly Roll Morton than there is in his Mendelssohn and Brahms. The Turkey Trot, the Lindy, and the Frug all have the same shape and tension, and the ballet ends in another campy kick line, to "This Land Is Your Land."

A couple of weeks ago, I wrote about solipsism in the modern dance. The ballet counterpart of that is the company formed in the image of the choreographer, who is usually a soloist self-drafted to train dancers and build a repertory. Such "choreographers" are not likely to have the objectivity it takes to analyze other dancers' abilities or the energy to create for them; their own careers as soloists will have inhibited the development of that kind of interest. When they get to a position of control over a company, they unthinkingly perpetuate themselves. Bruce Marks, at Ballet West, in

Salt Lake City, has created two or three Bruce Markses, and his ballets, as seen in New York last spring, reflected the limitations of the dancer that Bruce Marks was—a modern dancer who became a ballet soloist in mid-career. Marks isn't as ambitious a choreographer as Nahat. He seems to do different kinds of pieces in order to fill out a repertory, not to explore the art of choreography. John Clifford, the director of the Los Angeles Ballet, probably should be exploring the art of choreography; instead, he's depleting himself trying to work in several hand-me-down styles at once and educate dancers and the public, too. Last November, his company played the Brooklyn Academy—much too soon for it to be showing itself in New York. Except for Laura Flagg, the dancers looked raw or underrehearsed, or both. Clifford, when choreographing in the Balanchine style, fell back on prefabricated Balanchine combinations—something he wouldn't have done when he was working for New York City Ballet. Clifford doesn't turn dancers into versions of himself, and one or two of his dances for the winsome Flagg were reminiscent of the fine work he once did for Gelsey Kirkland. But he has labored in Los Angeles since 1973 with nothing much in the way of local support, and the repertory he's building shows signs of desperation. He's using all kinds of strategies to win an audience except patient, imaginative seduction.

A company's fortunes can depend less on artistic direction than on a city's structure, its living and working patterns, and its communal spirit. Just as there is no discernible city called Los Angeles, there is no discernible aesthetic for the Los Angeles Ballet. Chicago, with its amorphous structure, has yet to raise and sustain a ranking company. In Cleveland, the Nahat-Horvath enterprise is supported with a zeal that belies the various fiscal panics the city is said to suffer from. Dayton, Akron, and Cincinnati have reputable companies, but though in-state competition may have set Cleveland off, Nahat and Horvath are now driving toward national eminence, with the full encouragement of their backers. When the Los Angeles company played here, I didn't write about it, because I felt the Brooklyn venture had been a mistake. But the Cleveland Ballet, too, is in its infancy—it's in the vanity stage of its founders' aspirations. Clifford started out the same kind of strident performer as Nahat. His taste as a choreographer is about the same grade of coarse, but he's stronger in technique, stronger in discipline. Nahat has flair and a gift for self-aggrandizement. Clifford is squandering real talent. Does it come to the same thing in the end? Is the only difference between the Los Angeles Ballet and the Cleveland a board of directors?   —February 9, 1981

Uptown, Downtown, and Out on the Island

Our contemporary theatrical dance was defined about the middle of the century by a shift from fiction to fact. A contemporary dance is about *this* dancer doing *these* steps in *this* time, and it differs from the modernism of the years before, which was essentially concerned with impersonation, or else needed impersonation as a pretext, so that dancers could be thought of as representing characters and emotions not their own. A decisive emphasis in an art form is never more persuasive than when it is being called into question. In our time, excitement over a new choreographer or a new movement in choreography has often been provoked by the philosophical edge of the novelty—the edge that cuts two ways at once, past and future. We take for granted the formal emphasis of our own day—so much so that the differences between a première in a SoHo loft and one at Lincoln Center will seem irreconcilable. But these dances are likely to be philosophically allied in their confirmation of fact as form. In ballet, expectations have been so altered in the past thirty years that even audiences who still care more for stars than they do for choreography care for them as dancers doing steps, not as gods of health, sex, or fashion, although once dancers enter the tournament of celebrities they're as subject to misinterpretation as anyone else. At New York City Ballet, audiences are told that ballets are about music; that doesn't make them any less about dancers. In Peter Martins's new ballet, it's the dancers and what Martins has done for them that give the piece substance; it's not the music. And for the ballet to have been about the music would have been pointless, since it is only the concert suite from *Histoire du Soldat* which Martins has used, and not (mercy!) the full score, with its boring story about the Soldier and the Devil. Using program music nonprogrammatically, though, is hazardous, and Martins hasn't entirely escaped the net of implications that cling to the music. Still, a generation ago he wouldn't have attempted to escape, and his dancers would have been invisible without their masks of character and plot.

The Eglevsky Ballet, Long Island's only classical company, has always been a plucky band. Having a local audience to serve but no local pool of dancers, it draws on the same Manhattan schools that feed the big New York companies. This disadvantage was to some extent offset by the name and reputation of its founder, André Eglevsky. Moreover, until his death, in

1977, Eglevsky maintained close ties with New York City Ballet, and his use of the Balanchine repertory and Balanchine's dancers as guest artists brought Long Island communities some of the blessings of proximity. The blessings continued with the appointment, a couple of years ago, of Edward Villella as artistic coordinator. Villella is not just another big name. He has helped the company attract and retain better dancers, raise its overall technical level, and acquire live musical accompaniment. And he has begun to turn out choreography that looks, for the first time in his career, as if he were putting his whole mind to it.

A recent performance at Hofstra University, in Hempstead, showed the kinds of progress that have been made in the past year. The program, which opened with a brightened-up *Concerto Barocco*, included a group of stylized "tea dances" arranged to Noël Coward tunes by the company ballet master, Michael Vernon, and closed with Villella's latest pieces—one of them set to a Tchaikovsky adagio and the other an explosive jazz workout to Leonard Bernstein's *Prelude, Fugue, and Riffs*. Without live music, a company looks bush-league. And the music must be played as written; piano reductions, such as the company was still using last spring for *Donizetti Variations*, won't do. The Bach concerto is now played by an orchestra (at a driving pace); so were the Coward songs, although, apart from "Some Day I'll Find You," they weren't very interesting. The dancing was not notably subtle, but it was completely serious classical dancing, neither mechanical nor sentimental. The dancers seemed to respond best to the Villella ballets, which are designed to keep everybody keenly concentrating.

In Vernon's *Recollections*, the idea of using terse little mime scenes and blackouts more for their decorative value than as narrative links between dances needed to be more forcefully presented. The Cowardish Art Deco attitudes hadn't enough style to be a comment on style. The Villella pieces, with their steadily involving all-dance action and high morale, were popular with the audience. The vitality is real; Villella can sustain pressure without resorting to acts of aggression. He's not tricksily inventive, although he can get a bit busy at times. Sections of *Adagio Cantabile* (from Tchaikovsky's *Souvenir de Florence*), overpacked with steps and movement, tended to flail. The ballet's brightest patch was an engagingly asymmetrical solo performed by Mitchell Flanders. *Prelude, Fugue, and Riffs* put three couples onstage for eight minutes and kept them as ecstatically absorbed as kittens with a skein of yarn. Villella's resources as a choreographer go beyond his personal style as a performer. He's taking a fresh look at movement without bothering to give it a brand name. However, the intensity as well as the humility of the effort is entirely characteristic.

It's interesting to think what Villella might do with dancers of the caliber of New York City Ballet's Darci Kistler, Ib Andersen, Helene Alexopoulos, Maria Calegari, Jean-Pierre Frohlich, Kyra Nichols, Heather Watts, Victor Castelli, Bart Cook, and Daniel Duell. All ten of them are in the new

Martins ballet, looking good and knowing it. If Villella's dancers are kittens, these are circus cats; Martins alternately strokes and whips them into line. The piece, which divides the musical selections into four dance episodes, has all of his by now customary tact and good carpentry. There's only one passage that settles oddly into the joins—the slow walks to place and the long, portentous wait in the chorale that comes just before the coda. Ronald Bates bathes this section in a golden glow; it's the oddest of all the monochromatic panels of light he's chosen to use. The moment doesn't fit in with the rest of the ballet, yet it doesn't upset anything, because it's there under the same compulsion as everything else: it comes when it comes and then it's over. Martins's ballets so far have built logically one on another. The new ballet is a follow-up to *Eight Easy Pieces,* also to music by Stravinsky. It may be just too logical a sequel. Martins responds to the various aspects of the score; its qualities of scale, density, metrical irregularity, even its pungency of mood, are all faithfully registered. But it's as if the choreography were taking a series of tests. Its answers are all correct, its test score is perfect, and yet the ballet is hollow, a shining example of craft without passion. Stravinsky, a household god at New York City Ballet, is not always benevolent. In *Histoire du Soldat,* as in certain works by Picasso, inspiration has been drained of its savor by rampant imitation. The jazz-expressionist idiom, taken up by Kurt Weill and others, is a young man's music that has grown old.

I can sympathize with Martins's passionless response. But I think the work also shows disengagement of another, more dubious kind—the kind that may signal a retreat from commitment because commitment is not clever. Martins is good enough at suave surfaces to compose whole ballets out of them for quite some time. However, he is also too valuable an artist to give himself up to a facile sophistication. The choreography for the Tango-Waltz-Ragtime section is a remarkable mixture of assurance and caution, as if Martins were conscious of a descent to stale cabaret yet wanted to tough it out. A strange, smooth, ambivalent work. Can we not have, next time around, Martins minus smarts?

And can we have Gelsey Kirkland back? Kirkland and Patrick Bissell were guests of the Eglevsky Ballet—their first appearance since their dismissal by American Ballet Theatre. A large New York contingent turned out to see the outcasts and to cheer them, ABT fashion. They danced the *Don Quixote* pas de deux, and my misgivings about their physical condition —they'd both gained weight, and Kirkland is now decidedly plump all over—were heightened by their performances. Kirkland rushed through hers on one prolonged note of forced vivacity, from the first flick of her fan to the last bouquet-laden curtsy. She and Bissell didn't even wait for the applause to build or the flowers to start falling; they went straight into their footlights routine as if it were part of the dance. And though Kirkland has gained strength along with her weight, she was using it to slam out the sort of crude bravura spins and balances one might expect of a Bolshoi second-rater. It was the saddest exhibition I've seen given by a dancer whose artistry is increasingly placed at the service of a gift for mimicry. She's dancing the public's idea of Gelsey Kirkland as a star.   —*February 23, 1981*

Think Punk

It is seldom that a young choreographer makes a début doing a new thing that is exactly the right thing. Karole Armitage's début, two years ago, was so startlingly new and so right—for her, for her dancers, for dance—that one drew back cautiously, wondering whether one had seen a real début or a fluke. Armitage has gone on working, giving concerts in the usual downtown places (the Grey Art Gallery, The Kitchen, the American Theatre Laboratory) as well as in the less usual ones, and though some of her experiments have been inscrutable, all of them have been marked by an underlying consistency, a clear sense of pattern and direction, and a flair for discovery. These are qualities that were embryonically present in her first piece. What that event is remembered for, though, is its audacity in bringing concert dance together with punk-rock music. It took place in a high-school gym on West Sixteenth Street—an enormous, brightly lit space with a platform at one end, where the band (called the The) was stationed. The gym stayed brightly lit from start to finish of the performance; apart from some neon tubes strewn around the place, which gave an effect of light on light, no attempt was made at stage lighting or décor. The dancers came through a door at the far end of the gym and gradually made their way toward the audience, which was grouped at the other end. Their movements were almost all violent, flung-out, harsh; and all were done on the largest possible scale—that is, on the borderline of distortion. The figures didn't appear swollen with excess and the movement wasn't hysterically jammed; it was limpid even at flailing speeds and with magnum-force attack. With minor diversions, the choreography kept to its main path across the floor, and the steady oncoming diagonal course toward the audience was like a slow crescendo. As they came toward you, the dancers—there were only three of them, including Armitage—seemed to accumulate the power of a mass image, almost a monstrous one. The band, firing intermittent blasts without warning, acted as an additional magnifier. Some punk rock, I take it, does cross the border into distortion; at the volume the The played, sounds appeared within sound, echoing the light-on-light of the neon tubes. And, to round out the reverberant picture, the dancers were dressed in some sort of punk-chic scroungewear made of pilled-out synthetic fur in Day-Glo colors. How it ended I don't recall; I think the dancers just found another door close by. I do remember that at the end of the concert the band played encores for anyone who cared to get up and dance. Most of the audience had just enough inner-ear coordination left to get home.

Karole Armitage is one of Merce Cunningham's dancers, and one of the best he has ever had. Before joining the Cunningham company, she danced in Europe with the Grand Théâtre de Genève, which has a Balanchine repertory. She seems to me just now the only dancer besides Balanchine's own Suzanne Farrell who is capable of prodigious bodily feats of scale and balance, although even in these admirable extremes she doesn't resemble Farrell so much as she resembles a former Cunningham dancer, Viola Farber. As choreographers, Armitage and Farber are alike also in their fascination with violence, but Armitage isn't uncontrollably fascinated, as Farber sometimes has been. Armitage's control of her theme, like her personal control of her technique, has the power of drawing audiences in. I care for nothing I know about punk rock and its world, yet I'm absorbed and persuaded by an Armitage concert; I find reality in the ugliness and the terrorism, and beauty in their conversion to raw expression. The need of dancers of Armitage's generation to be raw in just this way is a subject that can be debated. Armitage has never struck me as a dilettante. To me, she's applying Cunningham's aesthetic to conditions as she finds them, making a connection to the outside world, making order out of chaos.

Armitage may also be the only one of the latest post-Cunningham generation of choreographers who's as self-aware as Cunningham is. Not only self-aware as a soloist, with certain specialties, but also self-aware as a classicist with a commitment to classicism's physical integrity of expression. Armitage keeps testing that integrity by mocking it—reducing its means, abrading its textures, pitting it against grinding distractions, placing it in faddish, conceivably unwholesome contexts. Her most recent evening, held at the American Theatre Laboratory, was called *Drastic Classicism*. It was every bit of that: classicism in hellish straits, handed over to the dark powers. Yet—"strait is the gate which leadeth unto life"—it transcended its own wildness to become a vindication of formal values in dancing. And it did so not eventually, as the evening ripened, but immediately, the minute Armitage and Chris Komar along with four other Cunningham-descended dancers swung into action in a room pulsing with the roar of four guitars and a set of drums. The key to Armitage's success is surely her understanding of her own power as a dancer and her ability to use other dancers with the same understanding. Komar, a brilliant dancer who normally looks pent up even in Cunningham pieces, was released here. Michael Bloom, who has performed here and there but is scarcely a professional dancer (in Armitage pieces he always keeps his glasses on), also gave a perfect performance in his own range. The two parts of the evening, divided by an intermission, were basically the same set of intensive inventions for dancers, with a volatile scenario allowing for costume and makeup changes, exits and entrances. At one point in the second part, children entered and took flash pictures of the dancing. Armitage began the evening in white tights with a sawed-off black tank top and ended it in a blue tulle tutu over baggy pants, looking like two Toulouse-Lautrec clowns put together. The dancewear of the studio and the punk-style street costumes were jaggedly intercut, as if both styles were masquerades and one could plausibly begin where the other left off. Dancing and punk behavior collaborated; dancers and musicians intermingled, sharing the stage, everybody dressing up funny, with painted faces. Dancers braced themselves against guitarists for their high battements or picked up guitars themselves. Where there was proper choreography, it looked like stringent classwork, taking up one obsession after another: staccato phrases, legato phrases, staccato/legato attacks on no phrase whatsoever. All this to a perfectly vicious din. (NO PHRASE, I wrote in my notebook as the walls shook.)

In its overall effect, *Drastic Classicism* was an extension and a refinement of the gym event of 1979, a retrieval of classical dance values from their irrelevant mold of decorum. Decorous music, decorous costumes, decorous body positions and steps were thrown out, together with the notion that all these should be decorously related. Relations were expressed (as in the best of Cunningham) but not decorously. Each separate element—the visual design (by Charles Atlas), the music (lead guitar: Rhys Chatham), and the choreography—advanced similar notions at different times or different notions at the same time of what the other elements were up to; one felt the force of a controlling idea without being able to say precisely what it was. And beyond this Cunningham-style presentation lay something that we could identify as Armitage's own discovery—the annihilative fury of rock music as a scourge analogous to the flaying of the systematic and the habitual in the dance. The horrific sound of the electric band was void of musical content; no melody, no apparent harmony (though the guitars were carefully tuned), not even, at times, a beat—just amplified chordal strumming. Just as sound opened within sound and tones braided with overtones, the dancing risked organic destruction to promote organic regrowth; it had its own qualities of fission and density. And play. I don't for a minute believe in the punk image of Karole Armitage; I do believe in her appropriation of it as a guise of virtuosity and an occasion of fun, much as I believe in Balanchine's appropriation of "gypsy" character work for Farrell. Armitage's punkness is a sophisticated ploy. I guess as long as she goes on working with punk material she'll appear a little bit precious, but she'll probably never get as precious as Jim Self, because there's so much more she can do as a dancer. Self, a former Cunningham colleague of Armitage's, now presents himself very wittily in his own concerts. I like Self and I see his work with interest, but the punk dandyism that in Armitage is a means of expression is in Self the end of it, at least for now. Other choreographers

—Douglas Dunn, for one—use punk chic mostly for their costumes; they haven't moved into the punk aesthetic. Armitage's position at the moment is between the fashionable involvement of Self and the noninvolvement of Robert Kovich, another Cunningham alumnus, who in turning to choreography seems reluctant to say clearly why he has done so. A fine dancer, Kovich gave a first concert some weeks ago that was a display of fine dancing; he didn't administer any tests, either of himself or of his material.

It must be difficult for dancers based in Cunningham to go out on their own without repeating the master's work or rejecting it. It must be twice as difficult to get any vitality out of the older expressionistic modern-dance forms that Cunningham himself repudiated long ago. Kathryn Posin is a modern-dance traditionalist who is most exciting when she operates against her tradition—when she brings classical ballet bodies into play to break up the moldy rhetoric, say, or when she makes one of her street-people pieces that really smell of the streets and not the studio. A few days after seeing the Armitage concert, I saw Posin's company on the other side of town, at the Emanu-El Midtown YMHA, in a neighborhood where people with pink hair are a fairly common sight. The concert began with *By the Light of the Memory Bank*, a vividly dreamlike transposition of big-city squalor. Parts of . it were prosaic and unnecessary—the parts that showed a lab-coated technician at a computer console, bearing out some indefinite allegory hinted at in the title. Posin is most obscure when she's attempting to explain. The reality of the piece lay in what it was able to express in nonliteral dance terms of the ritual behavior of city-dwellers, some of it degraded, most of it just numb. The taped music was the mostly hard rock of Brian Eno or the B-52's; the dancers moved to it or through it in a trance of timelessness. It was Fourteenth Street superrealism.

Posin's street scene was very different from Armitage's punk masquerade, and if it had less impact, owing to more conventional expression, it was still a lively and original work. Posin is a better choreographer than nine-tenths of the anticonventional formalists who have drawn most of the critical attention in the last decade. She has a romantic's love of sleaze; she's observant and poetic. She has no appetite for decadence in her art; she can't show you ronds de jambe shattering and deteriorating in six different ways as Armitage can, and she takes an expressionistic view of contemporary pure-process music. *Galena Summit* is set to a Steve Reich score. It's not as good as the Philip Glass ballet that Posin did for the Ailey company, or as good as her *Waves*, which tactically it resembles. In the Glass piece, the choreography complements the music by way of contrast; its imagery and structure are its own. In *Waves*, a resilient phrase sustained impetus on a broad scale. In the Reich, the basic phrase unit seems to be doing what the music is doing without getting any momentum from it, and the image it finds to express the ongoing wavelike pulse—mountain climbing—seems to me entirely too fatalistic. *Dust*, the third work on the program, by the company co-director J. Michael Kane, showed the same kind of thoughtful wrong-headedness and went on too long. Still, it was a good evening. Kane, whom I had never before seen, is a powerful, smooth, and versatile dancer, and the company as a whole—seven strong, including Posin—dances with marvellous elasticity and accuracy. Posin herself performs more as a member of an ensemble than as a star. Her tough, bouncy, feline energy isn't featured in relation to the other women, all of whom have exceptional abilities. Posin has always shown good taste in dancers. This is the best company she has put together in her nine years as artistic director, and it is one of the three or four best modern-dance companies in the country.   —*March 9, 1981*

So Rare

The curtain went up on New York City Ballet's last performances of *La Source* this season, and instead of the big bare stage that always looked so bleak in this ballet there was a set. It was not a new set; the painted columns and garlands came from Jerome Robbins's Verdi ballet, *The Four Seasons*, and were intended by the designer, Santo Loquasto, to evoke the ballet of the Paris Opéra during the Second Empire. The setting is appropriate to Delibes's *La Source*—or, rather, the musical excerpts on which Balanchine has based his divertissement-style ballet. Loquasto's colonnade could also be used for *Ballo della Regina* and *Walpurgisnacht Ballet*, two Balanchine pieces similarly constructed and recalling the same period and genre. But for some reason these "opera" ballets of Balanchine's to music from *Don Carlos* and *Faust* hold the stage without scenery, whereas his "Opéra" ballet celebrating Delibes's first dance score doesn't. Not that there's magic in opera ballets; *Donizetti Variations* (to dances from the opera *Don Sebastian*) needs a set almost as badly as *La Source*. But *Donizetti Variations* gets its semi-parodic point over, and until the entrance of the corps, halfway through, *La Source* isn't even a semi-parody; its freshness and purity of fancy is one of the remarkable things about it.

La Source is temperamentally French as *Donizetti Variations* is temperamentally Italian. The ballet is about the national character, its vigor and refinement, its love of lucid expression. But *Donizetti Variations* is also about the national theatre, and *La Source* is like it only in part. The little corps of Opéra girls interrupts a subtle and tender pas de deux and transforms it into a vehicle for *gaieté lyrique*. It is not unusual for Balanchine to give us two sides of the pas de deux in the same ballet. He does it again in *Chaconne*, which is about the Opéra of an earlier epoch. But in *La Source* the intimacy is peculiarly fragile and protracted, and it is dispelled by the virtuosity of the later sections (as it isn't in *Chaconne*). In fact, the concluding section of *La Source*, set to the "Naïla" waltz, originally belonged to an earlier Balanchine-Delibes ballet. Whatever Balanchine intended the *La Source* pas de deux to be (it was created in 1968 for Violette Verdy, partnered by John Prinz), it no longer is. But in its present-day form, and especially in its present-day set, it is an enchanting, if slightly schizoid, ballet.

The pas de deux section of the ballet has two adagios, the first sighingly romantic, the second more open and theatrically demonstrative. When the ballerina (in these performances, Merrill Ashley) goes into her climactic slow promenades à la seconde, we can feel the impending transition to an explicit theatrical mood become almost a necessity. The female ensemble that leaps on out of nowhere, though, is very strange at first. I think these coryphées in their petal-pink tutus become intelligible in the "intermezzo" portion of the music, when they back slowly, slowly toward the audience with their arms making pretentious traceries in the air. Here are Opéra artistes for sure. The affectation at once familiarizes them to us, and the ballet goes good-naturedly on to fill a high place among Balanchine ballets of a certain type—ballets that tell us something about the past history of the art. The Division of Commentary and Pastiche contains many exhibits (*Scotch Symphony, Allegro Brillante, Swan Lake, Raymonda Variations, Cortège Hongrois*—the list is long), none more appealing than the Second Empire trio: *La Source* and *Ballo della Regina* and *Walpurgisnacht*. These all have an intensely feminine energy appropriate to a period when even male roles were done by women. And they are all Balanchine ballets; their period is something we see through his sense of stylistic inflection. Balanchine does not always observe documentary truth. The two variations for the male dancer in *La Source* are historically anomalous. There are no male solos in *Coppélia*, the Second Empire's own masterpiece. For his revival, Balanchine interpolated two. The second of these, from the score of *Sylvia*, stands with the mazurka in *La Source* among the finest male variations in the repertory. Strange that this defiance of history should not have continued in *Ballo della Regina*, where the lone male's solos are separate from but not equal to the women's. In *Walpurgisnacht*, Adam Lüders gets a single parenthetical entrée—not even a full variation. (Is there nowhere in all of Gounod a scrap of music that could serve?)

Next to the high color of *Walpurgisnacht* and *Ballo della Regina*, *La Source* appears pale and silvery. It has no diablerie, no fioritura dancing, but its momentum is irresistible. Near the end, the ballerina, lifted by that momentum, leaps into her partner's arms across a sudden void of silence. The leap is unaware of its own wit—it comes up as naturally as froth on a wave. And even though by this time we're deep inside the ballet's image of Parisian theatrical style, we don't feel in the humorous twinge of this moment anything so antic as parody. Instead, I think, we realize how we've coasted straight into it on a current of pure sensation, and, thinking about it later, we may also realize that this current, despite its change of direction, had been running clean since the start of the ballet. *La Source* may be a mixed package, but the exhilaration it imparts is unalloyed. It's as if Balanchine and Delibes had conspired across the distance of a century in qualities of rhythmic tension and release which we recognize as witty—ironically witty, wit achieved through purely lyrical means. The rarest kind.

La Source at the Opéra in 1866, and again in the 1872 revival for which Delibes altered his score, was in four scenes. The plot, vaguely Oriental in derivation, dealt with a nature spirit named Naïla, whose power is linked to a mountain spring—*la source*. Delibes was responsible only for the middle two scenes; Minkus wrote the rest. The so-called "Naïla" waltz, however, was originally a separate composition, part of a divertissement written by Delibes to build up an 1867 Paris revival of Adam's *Le Corsaire*. That it eventually became involved with the score of *La Source* seems evident, but scholars are uncertain how this amalgamation came about. The current issue of *Dance Chronicle* contains an article by Thomas D. Dunn tracing the evolution of *La Source*. And in *Salmagundi*, Robert Garis discusses Balanchine ballets of "the middle range"—the non-masterpieces (like *La Source*) that are crucial to the repertory and make it "a true repertory." Garis also writes in a fresh vein about Balanchine as a collaborator and about the poverty of costumes and décor at New York City Ballet, which leads me back to the subject of the décor in *La Source*. It isn't ideal; it evokes only in the most general terms the atmosphere of the ballet. But at least it establishes some basis for speculation on that atmosphere. Garis calls his article "Balanchine Institutionalized." One might privately call the "new" *La Source* "*La Source* Institutionalized." Usually, the company's practice of cannibalizing sets and costumes weakens their effect in the original ballet without lending the recipient ballet anything more than a decent cover for its nudity. (The use of a *Harlequinade* drop in *Union Jack* is an example.) This time, the effect is a strengthening of identity. In the Tchaikovsky Festival in June, the company is to experiment with a standing pluralistically adaptable set, by Philip Johnson. It will be interesting to see how this works.

There was a new backcloth in the second act of *A Midsummer Night's Dream*—a really new one, by David Hays, depicting a pavilion of salmon-pink swags held up on stilts. I thought it had a sour look, but both acts of the ballet were in such good shape that I didn't mind. The new scenery permits *A Midsummer Night's Dream* to be done in repertory (like *Coppélia*) rather than as a separate attraction for which the stage must be specially hung (like *The Nutcracker*). Rehearsal and performance on a regular and frequent basis would be welcome. When this lavish, complex, and beautiful ballet was last given a mini-season, two years ago, it looked sluggish and tacky, and was badly cast. In this winter's run, the only major miscasting was Karin von Aroldingen and Nina Fedorova, who were both ponderous Titanias. *A Midsummer Night's Dream*, to Mendelssohn's music, is a full-evening ballet that demands almost as much intent looking and listening as we give to Balanchine's more concentrated essays in choreography. Does that make it a masterpiece or a piece in which, as in one of Garis's middle-range ballets, one recognizes the hand of a master? Most people find all the formal dancing in the second act disappointing after the consummate blend of dancing and acting in Act I. The dances are not in divertissement style, they're in Balanchine's extended symphonic style. (In addition to the incidental music, he uses the Symphony No. 9 for Strings and the *Son and Stranger* Overture.) In the perspective of his work as a whole, their originality doesn't stand out the way everything in Act I does.

Like the Handel spectacle *The Figure in the Carpet* (1960), *A Midsummer Night's Dream* (1962) may have been designed to appeal to people who found *The Nutcracker* too simple. Moods and textures shift rapidly in the dances in Theseus' pavilion. A stately courtiers' procession (the Wedding March) gives way to a royal entertainment—a light and graceful ballet danced by seven couples. Then the whole court masses behind the three bridal couples—Theseus and Hippolyta, Hermia and Lysander, Helena and Demetrius. Each time I see this profuse and streaming "symphonic" number, it seems as if the middle couple, Theseus and Hippolyta, would dominate. But they never do; Balanchine's tact keeps the climaxes exploding in triplicate. The stars of the second act are the lead couple in the pas de quatorze. Is there another adagio outside of *Divertimento No. 15* as involved, as involving, in the forms of sensuous complicity? And where else but in that great Mozart ballet are there allegro dances as airily Mozartian as the group dances that frame the pas de deux? In olden days, there was an astonishing intervention in this pas de deux by the six men of the group, who performed very slow and even développés in arabesque and lunges in arabesque fondue. Ever since Balanchine trimmed the dances to pacify restless *Nutcracker*-prone audiences, the act has seemed too short. So much of the choreography is a condensation to begin with; in condensed and abstracted form, it continues the first act's story of love and folly. A sophisticated audience is given the drama's meaning in the form of transparent dance metaphors. After the night's cycle of confusion, the current of young emotion is replenished and redeemed, there at the source of lyrical expression. The mountain spring.

As for Act I, it presents Balanchine's synoptic vision functioning as a continuous narrative. The prologue stands complete in itself, holding the action of the ballet as a ball hanging from a Christmas tree reflects the whole tree. The fairy royalty, the mixed-up pairs of lovers, and the mechanicals are all introduced and the story is under way before the overture is finished. We begin with entrances for the littlest fairies, frail and quick as water beetles; then come their bigger butterfly sisters, and Puck, their leader, who arrives just in time to form with three butterflies the tetrachord played by the reeds in the orchestra. The first human being we see is Helena, weeping, so distracted on her diagonal journey across the stage that she doesn't notice—or can't see—that the leaf she plucks to dry her tears is held out to her by Puck. Nor does she know that the breeze cooling her cheeks is fanned by clusters of small fairy hands. Oberon and Titania enter from opposite sides of the stage and meet in the center, each with an entourage: Oberon and his little band of elves and butterflies, Titania and her corps de ballet of tall and leggy neo-Botticellian nymphs. Oberon, the elf king, is small; he wears a gold tunic, white tights, a crown of gilt bay leaves. The statuesque Titania, in one of her pink negligees, is attended by a cavalier in blue who holds a floral canopy over her head. Both monarchs wear, as long and glittery trains, shower curtains of the best quality, and Oberon swishes his impatiently as he gesticulates, claiming the tiny page at Titania's side— the Indian changeling—for his own. Titania, who doesn't move an inch during Oberon's speech, rejects the claim angrily, and the two confront each other nose to nose as the scene shifts by means of a blackout to another part of the forest. As Mendelssohn alternates his *ff*s and *pp*s, the pace of the crosscutting starts to quicken. We swing from high spirits to serenity to perturbation, from upset in the fairy kingdom to turmoil among the lovers. When the lights come up again on Oberon and Titania, their quarrel is an exact repeat of the first one but faster, more urgent. The two adamant profiles coming together, apart, together are an uncanny transcription of the lines from the play "And now they never meet in grove, or green . . . But they do square." The action completes its rounds of introduction, and we come back to Helena, the emotional center of the play. Like a slow-fading spotlight, she lingers, an unresolved image left over from the giddy cyclical pattern Balanchine has established. The overture winds down, ending the way it began, with the faint moto perpetuo of the fairies diminishing into a silence broken only by the four chords on the pipes of Pan. We are ready to begin.

And when we are ready to end, Balanchine creates another of these crystalline montages, embracing lost lovers, Hippolyta's hunt, Puck's wiles, and Titania's contagious fogs in a scene of mounting excitement. The music is not part of Mendelssohn's score for the play. Nor, incredibly, is the music to which Balanchine sets the most complicated part of the story, covering the successive phases of the lovers' predicament and Puck's attempted resolution.

The dance highlight of the first act is Oberon's scherzo. Ib Andersen was fluent but lacked force—the quality that has eluded just about everyone who has attempted the role except its originator, Edward Villella. Andersen, after a season of tryouts in every type of role, hit his stride at the very end. The limpid accuracy he brought to *La Source* wasn't unexpected, but the sharp attack—the element missing from his Oberon—was.   —*March 23, 1981*

Masterpiece Theatre

The Boston Ballet's new *Swan Lake* is a civic monument reared to culture. It's not *Swan Lake* for *Swan Lake*'s sake; it's *Swan Lake* as a symbol —another sign of progress in a city that already has much to show in its new government buildings and commercial centers, its rehabilitated waterfront, and its communications industry. The Boston Ballet is not on a par with the Boston Symphony or Sarah Caldwell's Opera Company of Boston, and normally there'd be no point in going there just to see *Swan Lake*. But I wanted to see the renovated Music Hall, now called the Metropolitan Center, where the ballet was being given, and where the Royal Ballet will play this summer. And to see what so world-famous a designer as Julia Trevelyan Oman had wrought. As things turned out, there was more to discover than a new theatre and a new décor. The production is staged in depth—it's swift, lively, and full. There are twenty-two swans in the lakeside scenes, and no obvious ringers at court. (In American Ballet Theatre's version, we can spot the supers the minute the curtain goes up.) No great departures either in concept or in choreography occur; this is one of those tame *Swan Lakes* where everything is just a little different—exactly the sort of production for a metropolis wishing to possess a classic in a version distinctive yet discreet. The second act, which was staged by James Capp, the company ballet master, is in the standard version by Petipa and Ivanov, while Acts I and III are by Bruce Wells, and Act IV is by Violette Verdy. Wells's arrangements are most intrusive in Act III, where their underlying principle —that more ballet is better ballet—violates the dichotomy between classical and character dance. Wells isn't the first choreographer to give us a Spanish Dance on point, or the first to think that by doubling the amount of fancywork in each set piece he heightens our pleasure in it. But I was moved to accept his terms, because of his rhythmic precision and because of the stylistic limitations of the Boston company. Character dance, after all, is a specialty that takes time to build up. (The Russians use specially trained dancers to this day.) It could be argued that learning to do a really good czardas (and the Petipa czardas in *Swan Lake* is first-rate) does more for a dancer than mastering the trickier ballet enchaînements that Wells has composed here. But dancers with no character-folk tradition may be uneasy performers. Certainly Wells got zesty performing out of his "character" ensembles—if not always the best dancing. Violette Verdy's contribution is weightier, both in dance values and in dramatic values. And one must suppose that, as co-director of the company, she supervised more than the fourth act. (The Valse Bluette, in the second act, blocked out à la Balanchine, is her interpolation.) But her presence is overshadowed by Julia Trevelyan Oman's. It is Oman's scenery that provides the production with its indispensable unifying element, and it is Oman's costumes that almost break it to pieces. I say almost; Oman keeps the suspense up until the very end, when the proportion of distinction to discretion, which has been in doubt all evening, suddenly comes right. Discretion rules. Beauty is achieved. But it's the balancing act of the year.

Oman is indisputably the star of this show, and she seems to have been given carte blanche. The traditional setting of *Swan Lake* is medieval-fabulous. Oman's is the seventies and eighties of the last century—the period of the music. The fabulous dimension that is so clearly requested by the music is replaced by an unseemly gentility. The palace and its grounds suggest any old stately mansion one might buy a ticket to tour, and one would have to be awfully starry-eyed to see magic in women in bustles being escorted by men in gold braid. Oman's flair for middle and late Victoriana is known to us through her two Ashton ballets, *Enigma Variations* and *A Month in the Country*, her *Fledermaus* for Covent Garden, which has been seen here on satellite relay, and her art direction for the movie *The Charge of the Light Brigade*. Her historical sense is always, in anything she dresses, independently impressive, though her sense of place seems to be unveeringly British. *A Month in the Country*, adapted from Turgenev's play, is as pretty as an English breakfast, and she clothes her dancers in *Swan Lake* as if she thought Tchaikovsky were Tennyson, or maybe Arthur Conan Doyle. Her hunting party sets out in tweeds and deerstalker caps and confronts the swans with rifles. Historical-geographical sense is really not that important in ballet anyway; what matters is a sense of fantasy or of fantastic reality. Oman uses a decorative swan motif for the proscenium borders and for the panels and niches inside the palace. This is an old designers' device in *Swan Lake*; while Oman doesn't overdo it, or, worse, attach any psychological significance to it, it struck me the way it always does—as doodling. More pertinent to the mood—to the *mind*—of *Swan Lake* was her palace interior, with its painted backdrop showing two double colonnades extended to infinity. The lake scenes are sepia glens with vistas of Rhineland peaks and crags framed by thin autumn foliage in Act II and bare winter branches in Act IV. The sets get progressively better until with the Act IV drop, its stark branches traced in snow, we really are half in one world, half in another. Without a constant tension between the natural and the supernatural, *Swan Lake* doesn't work. It was a conscious attempt by its makers to recapture the dualism of the Romantic ballet at its peak. Oman doesn't succeed with her costumes, as she eventually does with her sets, in creating two planes of meaning. She's distressingly, even ludicrously literal. In the white acts, Von Rothbart is a giant befeathered owl, with a huge round head, staring glass eyes, and a beak. In the ballroom scene, he's a deranged-looking bald-headed diplomat out of *The Green Table*. The worst costume of all is Prince Siegfried's in Act I: an Eton collar, a vest with a red ribbon across it, and a pair of white tights. Compared with this getup, the "swan" tutus, with their suggestion of plumage, hardly register. Siegfried is a more betwixt-and-between creature than Odette, but somehow it's not the same.

Some years ago, a *Sleeping Beauty* designed by Desmond Heeley for the Stuttgart Ballet placed the third act in the court of Tsar Alexander III— another attempt to glorify the composer's own epoch at the expense of the one he envisioned in his score. Egon Madsen, as the Prince, appeared at court in his underwear. Then, there was Nicholas Georgiadis's *Beauty* for the National Ballet of Canada, in which Nureyev entered wearing boots like the other men and took up a conspicuous amount of time removing them in order to be able to dance. More recently, we had Roland Petit's *Coppélia*, in which Frantz was the only male dressed as a dancer. There's something wrong with a production that makes the male lead look as if he'd left off his pants, and usually what's wrong is the attempt to dress the ballet in a new period. Do these inventive designers never ponder the fact that every ballet that has come down to us from the nineteenth century is one in which the setting allows men to wear tights plausibly? If it's not the Middle Ages, it's the seventeenth or the eighteenth century. Knee breeches easily become a dancer's costume. *La Fille Mal Gardée* and *Coppélia*, with their rebellious bumpkins, are sans-culotte ballets. (*Fille* actually had its première in the year of the French Revolution.) *La Sylphide* is, of course, in kilts, and the other Bournonville ballets are dressed in a variety of national costumes and uniforms, none of a period later than the early nineteenth century. Siegfried and Von Rothbart in *Swan Lake* are knights. Their landscape is the legendary Rhineland of *Lohengrin* and of *Undine*, the opera that Tchaikovsky discarded unfinished, retaining only a duet that he then rewrote as the second-act adagio in *Swan Lake*. Oman could have transferred Tchaikovsky's ballet to Arthurian England; it would have been a clean substitution. What she's actually done is *Idylls of the King* in knickers.

The Prince's birthday party in Act I includes no female guests of his rank. Though his male friends consort with the peasant girls, he never does, and when the Princess Mother suggests that he marry, the thought seems to cross his mind for the first time. By placing what we know as the Black Swan music in Act I, Tchaikovsky may have intended a Rosaline for this Romeo. Without that music—which, as John Warrack points out in his *Tchaikovsky Ballet Music* (University of Washington Press), is related to the big waltz in Act I—or a reasonable substitute, the staging must contrive to suggest what the Prince's experiences with women have been up to now, and from that we can infer what's on his mind when he broods. Bruce Wells's staging places the Prince in an unusually warm filial relationship to Wolfgang, his tutor, but we've no idea what his thoughts are when he "confesses" in his solo, and his isolation has no bearing on the events of the next act. We don't even think of Odette until the end of Act I, when the swans are sighted. A virgin prince is not the best company in the love scenes of Act II. And from the way Wells stages and Donn Edwards behaves in the Black Swan episode in Act III (the music and most of the steps are traditional), I got the impression that Siegfried knew that Odile was not Odette and decided to pledge himself to her anyway. Wells brings the pleading vision of Odette far downstage, as if to show us that it's a different girl—which makes nonsense of the fact that Odette in Act II and Odile in Act III are danced by the same ballerina (in the performances I saw, Elaine Bauer).

In the fourth act, Verdy manages to avoid the melodramatic frenzy of Siegfried's traditional entrance to that gusher of a crescendo. She does it by having the swans toss en masse from side to side of the stage, then freeze as he enters in ronds de jambe renversés. We see him projected against a commotion that answers the music—quite a different effect from seeing him rush headlong into a vacuum. The music that follows this—that must always follow this, even though Tchaikovsky placed it in Act III—is that strange andante con moto that builds in another crescendo, this one with the tread of Fate in it. Odette comes to the Prince, who supports her in a penchée embrace. There is no hint of hope or aspiration in their brief adagio; at the end she shakes her head "no." The pas d'action is tastefully done: no comic-book struggle with the Sorcerer, no thrashings as he dies— the flock surrounds him and he's crushed unseen. In the Apotheosis, the lovers, who have rushed off together, presumably to commit suicide, appear in their boat irradiated. At the last moment—the seconds tick away in the music—the staging and the setting collaborate in an image of real power: the swans fold themselves down to sleep, and, as the boat passes on, snow starts to fall. Michel Sasson's conducting was at its firmest in building and sustaining the long numbers that characterize this act—numbers that, Warrack says, have "a close thematic argument and a symphonic development unprecedented in ballet music." In other parts of the score, Sasson's tempos were inclined to slacken or speed up arbitrarily. A dragging beat made a moment like Benno's passing down the line of swans look more important than it is.

The music sounded bright and clear in the Metropolitan Center, a palatial old theatre with an auditorium something like the Mark Hellinger's but more than twice as big, and with several banks' worth of marble in its lobby and foyers. This Swan Lake was two years in the works, and it is one of a series of multi-act grand-scale productions planned by the Boston Ballet with the Metropolitan Center in mind; Cinderella is next; then maybe Giselle; and then and then. The Boston Ballet is thinking big these days, and perhaps that's necessary to build community support and to attract funding. As artistic policy, though, it is defensible only so long as big does not mean big and hollow. The dazzling façade provided by Julia Trevelyan Oman did not quite conceal the fact that the company wasn't putting on much of a *dance* show. Only Nicolas Pacana, in the Polish mazurka, seemed to dance as well as he performed. The danger in mounting the big box-office classics is that dancers won't be challenged to improve; they can hide behind a couple of stars, wear costumes, walk around, act a bit, dance now and then—nothing too strenuous. Technical standards in modern ballet have advanced to a point where "the classics" may actually retard a company's development—unless, of course, they're done with discipline and style. (The Bruce Wells solution—make the steps more difficult—is really an evasion of the problem of style.) It is dispiriting to think what Boston's *Swan Lake* would have been like without the cohesive force of Oman's ideas, batty though some of them are. Not until the fourth act, with Tchaikovsky looking forward to modern ballet, with Verdy's logical and fluid groupings and unequivocal sense of tragic gesture, with Sasson's conducting, did the Boston dancers rise to the challenge of dance drama. It was also Oman's finest moment. Audiences filing out between the marble walls could carry home with them a glimpse of the ballet they hadn't seen.   —*April 6, 1981*

Additions and Subtractions

Viola Farber was a great soloist when she turned to choreography, and for years she remained a great soloist; her choreography was never more than functional, an apparatus for performance. That is no longer true. A Farber evening is less performance-centered than it used to be; it sustains a more sheerly choreographic interest. And whether it is solo or ensemble choreography seems not to matter so much as the type of musical accompaniment Farber chooses. Farber hasn't only redesigned her priorities, she's also switched to music after years of moving mostly to silence or to electronically processed scores. All the pieces on her program at the City Center had music played live on conventional instruments, and all seemed to represent precisely calibrated reactions by Farber to her music. Music, in fact, seems to be her main area of experimentation these days, and while it's good to see an artist of her generation unsettling herself and taking risks, the results show a fair amount of confusion over what risk to take, so even her successes are clouded with uncertainty.

In *Solo*, to a percussion score, Farber as the soloist was overwhelmed by the strategies of the percussionist, Jean-Pierre Drouet. The big crescendo at the end even made me *look* at Drouet. But then another percussion score by Drouet proved not enough of a support for a weakly prolix group number called *Ledge.* In *Bequest,* the choreography ran neck and neck with a Mendelssohn trio. On and on it ran, through binary and ternary melodies, through expositions and developments and recapitulations. It was "musical" choreography with a vengeance. One could say that in selecting her accompaniment for these pieces Farber made the wrong choices—differently wrong choices—but it is hard to know whether to attribute her successes to right choices or to some other factor. Both of the successful pieces—one was a group composition, one was a duet—happened to have piano scores. My guess is not that Farber has an affinity with the piano but, rather, that she hasn't as yet found complete energy as a musical choreographer—that she's still sketching, and fine-tuning her sketches. The City Center concert had in common with the last Farber concert I can recall seeing the fact that the first pieces on the program were the best, or seemed to be. No matter how good or how individually interesting subsequent pieces may have been, their qualities didn't show up. The effect was one of repetition. A current Farber evening is likely to be a study in dissipation. For the audience, it's an exercise in concentration, and usually it's an exhausting one. At the City Center, by the time the Mendelssohn came around (it was last on the program), I found I couldn't get through it. Choreographically, nothing seemed to take effect once we'd seen *Bright Stream,* to Alan Evans's piano score, and *Tea for Three,* to selections from Bizet's piano suite *Jeux d'Enfants.* It was as if Farber had laid out her terms and then had to spend the rest of the evening defending them.

Since the relation of movement to music is inherently an unequal one, intelligent choreography seeks the illusion of an equation, not the fact of one. The choreography can start from inside the music and grow organically in a parallel structure, as in *Bright Stream.* Or it can stay wholly outside the music and rub up against it. Farber uses this option in the Bizet and gets satire from the friction. The choreography is designed for Farber herself and Sarah Stackhouse, a guest artist formerly with the Limón company; the two women dance simultaneous solos in their personal and quite unrelated styles, and the effect of distraction and doggedness is good enough to last, both as musical commentary and as comedy, for the duration of the piece, if not beyond. The title of this duet is *Tea for Three* because it was meant to be a trio; injury prevented the participation of the ballet dancer Sallie Wilson. But the third party could also be Bizet, whose music is left to go its own way while the dancers go theirs. Stackhouse is full-bodied, roundly proficient, and romantic, while Farber uses her waywardness and disjointedness with the most subtle discrimination she will show all evening. As a choreographer, Farber understands the limitations of dance in relation to music and how to capitalize on them, and I think she understands these things instinctively. In the Mendelssohn, I felt intellectual force taking the place of instinct; it's what makes the energy of the piece seem shadowy, tenacious yet unreal. Although, who knows? It might be quite real in another place, on another program.

While the Farber company performed downstairs in The Space at City Center, the Lar Lubovitch company was upstairs in the main theatre. Lubovitch's choreography is undeceptively simple. It never transcends procedural mechanics, and it always seems to begin and end on the same spot without having gone anywhere in between. Cocteau said that the opium trance makes one and one equal not two but eleven. Good choreography makes music plus dance add up to dreamlike quantities. Lubovitch's choreography is obstinately one on one with the music, and now that he's using scores by Steve Reich and Philip Glass—transparent music that exposes its processes—his own process has come to seem even more shallow. In *Marimba* and *Cavalcade* one hears Reich's music steadily evolving through repetition, but one watches choreography that merely repeats itself in a frozen manner without ever finding a thread through the repetitions or an equivalent to the catalyzing harmonic changes in the music which turn simple addition into advanced calculus.

Lubovitch's choreography never did have any catalytic force, but I believe it once had more nerve than it has now. (I'm thinking of his Ives pieces.) For nerve, Lubovitch has substituted twerpiness, as in *Exsultate Jubilate,* in which he *dares* to set Mozart's vocal score while at the same time signalling to us that it can't be done. People patter about barefoot, wave their arms importantly, or, as the voice (Judith Raskin's) soars to heaven in a cadenza, stand wriggling and twitching, as if undecided just how to fill in *that* blank. The presumption is that they'd filled in the others. Lubovitch makes a joke of his incapacity, but it reminded me of the time a certain tenor, playing a singer whose voice was breaking down, chose "Il mio tesoro" to break down in; one knew he couldn't have sung it straight. In *Beau Danube,* the orchestra (on tape, like all Lubovitch's orchestras) plays the waltz while four physical culturists in old-fashioned bathing suits exercise in a different rhythm. There is a palace in the background, and it is snowing. Haven't we seen this droll Dada anti-waltz before? The obvious intention is frictional satire (as in *Tea for Three*), but the result is so synthetic that it might itself be the subject of satire. Like *Exsultate Jubilate, Beau Danube* is a form of banter that Lubovitch hasn't earned the right to toss around. Where's the wit in using "See Spot run" choreography when it's all you've got?

A surprising number of people who attended the Merce Cunningham season that preceded Lubovitch's at the City Center walked out in a huff at intermissions. If they knew Cunningham's name well enough to buy tickets in the first place, you'd think they'd know what it stood for. Cunningham has adapted himself over the years to changing conditions, but he's never really changed the way he works. Among those who walked out could have been the sons and daughters of people who'd walked out on *Rune* or *Aeon* or *Crises*.

Within the methods and procedures that remain basic to Cunningham's work, a creative pattern has been evolving in the past few years. It can generally be expected that two or three group works a year will be produced, and that at least one of them will employ the full company of fourteen dancers and will have been composed first for film and video, then adapted to the stage. Last year's bimedia presentation was *Locale*; along with it we had the powerful and virtuosic *Duets* and a lighter and jokier piece, *Roadrunners*. This season, we saw the new *Channels/Inserts* in its stage version only; the film-video version has yet to be edited. The choreography seemed more intensively yet more freely developed than in the two other new pieces; as in *Locale*, as in *Fractions*, the camera has stimulated Cunningham's imagination as well as his ingenuity. The things that seem chiefly to distinguish *Fielding Sixes* and *10's with Shoes* in Cunningham's mind—the phrase counts referred to in the titles—were not that apparent to me. In *10's with Shoes*, the emphatic, almost military cut of the steps, which could have been inspired by the jazz shoes the dancers wore, gave the piece a prevailingly comic tone. But except for this topographical feature there was nothing to keep one from seeing *10's with Shoes*, along with the other new works of the season, as forming one gigantic ongoing work—a kind of cumulative Cunningham extravaganza. The idea that the choreography possesses a logic that can flow from one piece to another is the principle behind the Event, a concert-style presentation that Cunningham devises by splicing parts of different works together to make a new whole. During a recent period when large, well-equipped theatres were hard to come by, Cunningham programmed nothing but Events, and they became quite popular—a new way of seeing Cunningham, and a better way, it was suggested, since the designers who could have collaborated in discrete works for the theatre were mostly not very good. But when Cunningham did get back into the theatre the quality of the visual design proved to be remarkable. The company owes much of its impact since then to the contributions of two artists, Mark Lancaster and Charles Atlas.

What had in fact deteriorated was not visual design but sound accompaniment. The Events hadn't spared us the experience of that deterioration, but simply because of their informality we could forgive and forget what we heard during Events. At the City Center this season, the exodus up the aisles must have included some people who just couldn't face another onslaught by John Cage's musicians. More than half the repertory was blighted by abrasive, exasperating, or ridiculous intrusions from the pit. For *Fielding Sixes*, Cage superimposed or otherwise distorted a bunch of Irish jigs, recording them with their rhythms all out of kilter. One of my favorite dances, *Signals*, suffered from the repeated intrusion of garish end-title music from old Hollywood movies. Sitting here and there among those who didn't walk out were people in headsets, with Sony Walkman cassette-players on their laps. What, I wonder, were they tuned in to while the rest of us were enduring the house din? Some of the better scores, perhaps, of John Cage? —*April 20, 1981*

Old School Ties

With a single exception (the excellent flamenco troupe of Maria Benitez), the Dance Umbrella series that has occupied the City Center basement all month has presented companies with links to the modern-dance establishment as it could have been defined in the sixties, before the rebels of that era declared it dead. After twenty years, many of those links are nominal; this time, we really do seem to be seeing the last of modern dance. For a while, the rebels offered an alternative, but the aesthetic of postmodernism (as it came to be christened just the other week) finally foundered on its proclaimed indifference to technique. It was not, on the whole, something dancers could study. The constructed physique, in all its jealously enforced variations, was a legacy of the old guard which had become a plague, but it did, after all, allow something to happen in a dance besides choreography.

It's that something else that is still missing, only now the loss is retroactive. Nearly every post–post-modern choreographer is conscious of bringing back things the post-moderns wanted to leave out—drama (or emotion), narrative, music, "danciness"—but the approach to a negotiable dance technique has been cautious in the extreme. Indifference to technique has played a part, along with the tremendous rise in popularity of ballet, in stamping out those technical and stylistic distinctions among companies which used to be the glory of American modern dance. Paradoxically, as more careers in dance open up, dancers are narrowing their technical base. To be a Cunningham dancer, a Farber dancer, a Tharp dancer no longer means that one's primary technical equipment is perfected in company class. Twyla Tharp's dancers study with the ballet teacher Maggie Black; company class emphasizes straight ballet. But Tharp's emergence, in the sixties, coincided with the breakdown of the old systems. In the companies that adhere to the older traditions, one sees either a modified style or a mottled one, with stylistic assertion, counterassertion, and patches of deadness all contending. And the overall emphasis falls on choreography, rather than on choreography plus dance technique. What the dancers do seems more dictated and their way of doing it more neutral than in former days.

The only company on the Dance Umbrella programs with a collective signature was Margaret Jenkins's company, from San Francisco. And it writes an old-fashioned script, stretched but not sleek, large but not opened-up in the ballet sense, relaxed and natural but not frumpy. Jenkins may be the last of the old-school modern dancers who can keep up a connection with the past. Like the San Francisco Ballet, the Jenkins company seems to thrive far from the conformist pressures of New York. The old ideal of ensemble polish that doesn't rub out individual differences, that leaves a dancer his natural dignity and grace—one rarely sees it here anymore. The unsleek, undriven look of Jenkins dancers is presented as a united front. When my eye demanded a perfectly balanced line, they didn't always provide it, but they did show plastic energy—plenty of it, on a great big scale. The surge through the lower body, so clearly motivated and directed, so ample, is one of the beauties of Jenkins-trained dancers. It gives them a pelvic command of space; they don't need to lift their arms to exist in three dimensions.

Jenkins's choreography doesn't push this distinctiveness as hard as it might. The invention tends to proliferate without expanding or concentrating an inner logic, and even in a short piece like the new *Harp* there are too many things going on at once: movement ideas coming from multiple sources, intricate timing, unpredictable staging, country music with an overlay of drumming (to which the dancers respond with a tap dance). It gets a little hazy. Another new work, *Versions by Turns*, seems to rely on a spoken script, composed by Michael Palmer, to hold it together. I left the performance, though, thinking not of choreography but of a company and its tradition. Jenkins's range as a teacher-choreographer reflects the breadth of her own training, which extended from Merce Cunningham to José Limón. She has settled by choice in the Cunningham camp: her pupils feed Cunningham's company; she has taught at his school. It may be that some of those earlier Cunningham works which have recently been revived and judged inappropriate to his present company could find a new life in San Francisco.

When people speak of Paul Taylor's company as the last of the great modern-dance companies, I think they're referring to the marvellous cohesiveness and conviction with which the company performs and the almost primitive energy of the dances; the whole spectacle is unlike anything else that one can see today. But Taylor was also a prophet of post-modernism. His first works predicted (and his *Esplanade* summed up) the era of the deconstructed dancer. Taylor, a major establishment figure with a style as individual as a thumbprint, has no school and does not teach a technique. Cunningham (to name the greatest choreographer who directly precedes Taylor in the descent from Denishawn)—Cunningham, who has a school and does teach a technique, also has a company that has changed quite a lot stylistically in the past decade. Taylor's has changed hardly at all. Another curious fact is that Taylor, whose style might be thought hopelessly idiosyncratic, has worked with ballet dancers and, with equal success, has staged his dances for ballet companies. The latest of these is *Airs*, to a suite of dances by Handel, which was introduced by the Taylor company in 1978. Taylor had previously set the choreography, at the behest of American Ballet Theatre, on dancers of that company; feeling dissatisfied with the results, he withdrew the piece. This season, ABT gave its première of *Airs*, incorporating changes that Taylor had made for his own production. Not unexpectedly, since it had looked rather "ballet" on Taylor's company, the choreography looked charming on the ABT cast, most of which was chosen from the corps. Taylor hadn't bent his style too far. Falling casually into those characteristic bowed and turned-in positions isn't easy for ballet dancers, but if most of them were winded before the performance was half over it was because they were seriously trying to embrace the style, and not just doing the steps. *Airs* is a major ABT acquisition—as pleasurable a challenge for the audience as it is, very evidently, for the dancers.

When you compare *Airs* at the Met with *Airs* at the City Center, where Taylor is having his own season, or, even more instructively, when you compare either version with *Arden Court*, the newest piece danced by the Taylor company, you begin to see the reason that Taylor is able to remain consistent and adaptable at the same time. If "the Taylor technique" does not exist as a course of study, it is likely that Taylor does not seriously recognize the existence of other techniques, either. In some profound sense, he is technically incurious. Coming along at a time when Graham and Cunningham, among others, were already operating productive modern-dance academies, Taylor may have felt that he had no contribution to make, or that any contribution he was capable of would be released in the act of choreography. He imparts a Taylor rhythm to his dancers, even a Taylor musculature, yet one feels that he is not concerned to explore movement beyond an immediate expressive need. Ever since he formed his mature style, it has been clear that Taylor's expressive needs are not created by him. They arise in answer to an outside demand (he told the New York *Times*, speaking of *Arden Court*, "The motivation was the dear dancers"), and then take their definitive shape from a piece of music. Since inspiration comes from sources outside his control—or as far outside his control as dancers and music can be once he has selected them—he can count on meeting each need freshly as it comes along; nothing in him will have anticipated it. I was in a record store recently and noticed an L.P. that had Martinů's Double Concerto on one side and Poulenc's Concert Champêtre on the other. The possibility that Taylor had made Part Two of *American Genesis* to the Martinů and then, a few years later, flipped the record over and made *Dust* did not seem at all unlikely. "Divine arbitrariness" fairly describes Taylor's temperament as an artist. (It is the theme of one of his self-portraits in a now abandoned work, *Orbs*.)

Of course, Taylor's musical acuteness allows him a fecundity of response that is not given to everyone. This season, he revived *Public Domain*, which makes a little too extended a joke of his ability to meet any musical situation. But this musical sense is the most golden of his gifts. It's what gives momentum and bounce to his plastic sense. Taylor found his lyrical style in 1962, with his first Handel ballet, *Aureole*. Everything that style was then it is now, only more so. For his new piece, Taylor has once again envisioned a world of baroque forms, using not Handel this time but William Boyce— the symphonies as arranged by Constant Lambert for the Vic-Wells Ballet. (Ninette de Valois set her "Rowlandson" piece, *The Prospect Before Us*, to this music.) But *Arden Court* recalls *Aureole*, much as *Airs* does, and it recalls its manner of construction, as *Airs* does not. That is, it doesn't just build complex structures in place of the simple ones in *Aureole*; it builds complexity within a limited range—it's *Aureole* exploding from inside, like a crystal. In *Aureole*, which will be given by the company this week, the invention keeps nakedly materializing out of two or three steps. *Arden Court* is far more profuse, but it doesn't spread out in range. Taylor is less persuasive widening his rhetoric than he is deepening it. The material of *Airs* contains accretions that he might not have considered for his own dancers and that don't suit them particularly. *Arden Court*, though, takes a few basic shapes and plunders them for cognates. The final movement, with its progression of X-shaped lifts, jumps, and cartwheels, is Taylor at his most fastidious and profligate.

The company has acquired the largest and most talented male ensemble in its history, which is saying a lot; even without Taylor to personify it, the masculine strain in the company style has always been dominant. *Arden Court* is built primarily on variations for its male sextet. Yet the three women in the cast don't seem slighted. Taylor will, by reversing role stereotypes in his pas de deux, recharge the vitality of the form, and he does it here as a deliberate way of weighting the women's roles. Both men's and women's roles follow a process of permutation—the process that lies at the heart of baroque expression. *Arden Court* forms a baroque trilogy with *Aureole* and *Airs*. Unlike its predecessors, it seems destined to remain the exclusive property of the Taylor dancers. What they do cannot be distinguished from the way they do it. *Arden Court* is the trilogy's monument to modern dance.

Historic modern dance was the subject of "The Early Years," four days' worth of lectures, conferences, and performances held at the State University of New York at Purchase. Clans gathered; primogenitors were celebrated. The attempts to revive the old dances, though, were no more gratifying than other attempts have been. It isn't just a question of performance. All the Denishawn scarf and spear dances were authoritatively performed and they still invited our condescension. The movement studies, on the other hand, were examples of condescension on the part of their makers. Whether given an abstract motive, as in Doris Humphrey's *Two Ecstatic Themes*, or a dramatic one, as in Charles Weidman's *Lynchtown*, the movement was spelled out with eye-glazing insistence. "Variations and Conclusion" from Humphrey's *New Dance* is not as stuffy or slow-witted, yet its thinness has always puzzled me. Though it uses a more refined accent, the choreography has about as much to say as "The Continental" in *The Gay Divorcee*, which was created at approximately the same time. "Variations and Conclusion" is known for its use of stairlike boxes on and around which the dancers move—a treatment of the stage area which seems to me to declare rather than defeat the problem of organizing a dance in space. Despite their disappointing quality, there is some value in preserving these pieces; they should be seen—once—by everyone interested in dance history. I disagree on the need to preserve Helen Tamiris's *Negro Spirituals*, which takes schoolmarmish condescension to the borders of racial insult.

Isadora Duncan lived and danced in a world apart, if we can judge from Annabelle Gamson's representation of her solos. Gamson's program at Purchase included her Scriabin studies from Duncan's Soviet period, along with what is now Gamson's masterpiece of Duncanism, *The Blue Danube*. Clad in a white tent and with her white hair flowing, Gamson suggests not so much a portrait of the mature Isadora as a cameo of her, and her dancing is in a similarly impressionistic vein. In *The Blue Danube*, the inflections of her line through a series of rhapsodic poses, her gradations of attack and recoveries of impetus, were the best dancing of the evening. And though Gamson is more calculating in her effects than I have been led to think Isadora was, there are moments that seem quite uncalculated when her resemblance to a Genthe photograph or a Walkowitz drawing is absolute. —*May 4, 1981*

A New Old "Giselle"

Somebody else's version of an old folk tale is never as magical as the one we grew up with. Though the meaning is the same, the details are different, and it's the details that capture the imagination and bring the meaning alive. One of Mikhail Baryshnikov's first acts on taking over the direction of American Ballet Theatre was to throw out the company's production of *Giselle* and substitute a close approximation of the version he used to perform in Russia with the Kirov Ballet. For Baryshnikov's staging, which we saw this season at the Metropolitan, Oliver Smith modified his first-act setting and painted a new backcloth, new musical insertions were orchestrated by Ivana Themmen, and new ankle-length costumes for the Wilis were ordered. But, unlike the production that it replaces, this isn't *Giselle* restudied—it's a simple exchange of one set of details for another. The Kirov's *Giselle* traces itself back to Petipa, and Baryshnikov believes devoutly in its authenticity, but it turns out to have less edge to it than ABT's late-1960's model; it looks scrappy, capricious, reduced. Because no great amount of thought lies behind it—nothing much lies behind it but taste—there's not a great deal one can argue with. It's a case of My *Giselle* against Yours.

ABT's 1968 production, by David Blair, introduced a sympathetic Hilarion, brought on the Peasant Pas de Deux (then a novelty for ABT) at an opportune moment, and in other ways extended and sharpened the dramatic logic of the first act. All this took time, and much of it was waste motion. The libretto of *Giselle*, a heady mixture of fantasy and superstition, is not so much a folk tale as it is an old wives' tale. Attempts to impose logic and plausibility only expose the frail premise on which the dance spectacle of the second act is built. Although some of Blair's innovations were eventually dropped, the company still did not revert to the practice of putting on *Giselle* with another ballet. Baryshnikov has managed to do this, largely by cutting the Peasant Pas de Deux and shortening Hilarion's scenes. (The character created by Blair must now be created in each performance by the dancer who plays the role.) The Peasant Pas de Deux, an interpolation in the original production and an intrusion in every production since, is the sort of thing you have to invent reasons to enjoy. In ABT's version, dancing had to suffice; the Royal Ballet, at least, has some good choreography, by Frederick Ashton. Along with these cuts, there have also been some additions: the speech of Giselle's mother, which explains the legend of the Wilis, and an unaccountably extended Pas des Vendanges, in which the villagers bang noiseless tambourines out of synchrony with the tambourines in the pit. But, by and large, Baryshnikov has made a fast first act.

It should be fast. The whole purpose of Act I, as its authors realized, is to set up Act II. Baryshnikov's speed, though, is the speed of impatience, not of economy. To say that Act I sets up Act II is not to say that the plot doesn't bear telling. In Baryshnikov's treatment, the ballet opens in the manner of the Kirov and the Bolshoi productions: Albrecht and Wilfrid run on and hide, followed by Hilarion, who runs on and hides. In the first minute, three men have entered who look alike and act alike. In a play, this would be excusable; in a ballet, it's a minute wasted. There are absurdities in the staging. Hilarion should not have to enter Albrecht's cottage by the window when the door is unlocked. Immediately after Bathilde and Courland go into Giselle's cottage to get some rest, the villagers, with their wine festival, set up a racket right outside the door. This is probably un-avoidable; it happens in every *Giselle* I have ever seen. We accept it, just as we accept the improbability of a royal hunting party putting up in a hut. Opera-goers know these conventions well, and *Giselle* comes to us from a period that saw close affinities between opera and ballet. (Carlotta Grisi, the first Giselle, was also a singer, though not as famous a singer as her cousin Giulia.) Blair saved the convention of the wine festival from complete sterility by restoring the focus to Giselle as quickly as possible. But instead of his little scene showing her being crowned queen of the festival (which also appeared in the original production) we now see some anonymous Bacchus being carried through on a barrel. The Mad Scene is an extended absurdity that an incurable, cultish sentimentality has elected to the status of a touchstone. Unlike the operatic Mad Scenes on which it is modelled, it is a descent into naturalistic bathos. (No one would think of performing it out of context.) Yet it has no psychological depth. The ballerina is con-fronted with a stark contrivance, and we watch to see how she will bring it off. Théophile Gautier conceived the ballet *Giselle* after reading about the Wilis in Heine's *De l'Allemagne,* but he left the writing of Act I to a skilled librettist, Vernoy de Saint-Georges, whom he afterward commended for bringing about "the pretty death we needed." Dying prettily yet persuasively exercises a ballerina's tact rather than her art. The Blair staging brought on the whole company to witness the scene, while Baryshnikov, following Kirov custom, has only the villagers, and Albrecht and Wilfrid, who leave at the end of the scene. Baryshnikov, whose own interpretation of Albrecht's role used to differ at this point, yields to tradition.

Baryshnikov prefers the Russian staging of the scene where Albrecht first sees the specter of Giselle, then kneels and prays for it to return. I like it, too—much better than the flitty comings and goings of the previous setting (and Albrecht's "tawt I taw a putty tat" reactions). The atmo-spherics, though, are really shabby: for *feux follets,* two stagehands shake clusters of lights from the wings. Although there weren't enough Wilis on the stage (there never have been, at ABT), they danced better than I had ever seen them dance. This is a Baryshnikov triumph not to be underestimated. But he has chosen to incorporate it in this home-style production, which does little to advance our understanding of the ballet, and in some respects even retards it. Is Baryshnikov getting ready for a new look at *Giselle*—a possible break with tradition? He gives no hint of an original perspective here. And when we look up his thoughts in his book *Baryshnikov at Work,* we find such discouraging assertions as "The dramatic material of *Giselle,* Act II, is not rich in substance, but with careful preparation and thought it can be meaningful." This is certainly in line with Baryshnikov's own per-formance in this act, which is unsurpassed but is overwhelmingly a dance performance; one would call it rich in passion but not in drama. He sees the second-act drama in simplistic terms: "Albrecht fights to hold on to Giselle and fights to live." It is the Russian view, the view that has prevailed in the West ever since the initial tours of the Kirov and the Bolshoi showed us their monumentally pure second acts, heavily contrasted with the verismo of Act I. With Rudolf Nureyev's performances and then with Natalia Makarova's, the dramatic web of the second act was reduced to a single thread—the bond of love between Giselle and Albrecht—and the only suspense lay in whether the Wilis would get Albrecht before four o'clock. That's the way it is in Baryshnikov's current production; the bond between the lovers is even stronger, because there's less of Myrtha to make demands upon it.

The deterioration of *Giselle* as a dance drama is reflected in the demotion of Myrtha from a ballerina's role to a soloist's. It has been a gradual process, down and down over the years. Now Baryshnikov excludes her from the Wilis' adagio. Her entrance is limited to a single diagonal of bourrées to a downstage exit, after which she reappears almost immediately from the same downstage wing and begins the solo with the myrtle scepters. Myrtha's stage-skimming crosses, her re-entries at unexpected points, the weighty incantation of her dance along the ground were all intended to describe her authority in that space, on that spot of earth, and under it. These are graves on which she dances, and they are, as we see in a moment, the graves of dancers. Myrtha prepares the drama. Anyone who has not experienced the thoroughness of her preparation has not felt the icy breath of *Giselle*. None of the three Myrthas I saw this season did more than warm up the house for the stars. None gave clear directions to the lovers beyond a peremptory "Dance!" or "Continue!" Without Myrtha's influence on the course of action, the action doesn't make sense. Who would know, from watching the ballet, that Giselle's dances as Albrecht stands by the crucifix are dances of seduction—that as an instrument of the queen's will she's trying to lure him out of his sanctuary? Who would even guess there could be a motive behind the solo adagio with which she opens her dance? Much less the duplicitous motive we find in Gautier's description of how, as Giselle "commenced her dance with slow and languid steps, eagerly watching the first streaks of light in the horizon," she "sought to disguise her powers of attraction, and merely made a faint and languid pretense of dancing, fearful of beguiling her lover from his post." And so, as the situation develops, we go from adagio to allegro:

> The inexorable Myrtha compelled the shrinking Giselle to dance with greater energy and animation; and, obeying the mandate, she gave herself up to the full delight of the moment,—flying, bounding, floating, as it were, upon mid air; while her lover, forgetting the certain destruction that awaited him, flew to her side, took part in her dances, her attitudes, deeming himself but too happy to die for one so dear.

Gautier's account, one of the essays in *Les Beautés de l'Opéra*, was written after the ballet had become a hit. (I quote from the London edition of

1845, available in an excellent facsimile reprint from Da Capo Press.) If it sounds like the fond author supplying ingenious motives after the fact, how much closer we come, through Gautier's words, to the intention of the ballet d'action than we ever do in a performance. Surely, if the role of Giselle is what its devotees claim—the supreme test of the actress-dancer—that test comes in the second act, when the ballerina must act *through* her dancing. And which would we rather see her aim for—the outer limits of virtuosity, as defined by Gautier, or the undemanding generalizations of Ballet Theatre's synopsis: "Giselle resolves to protect him. She dances with him until the clock strikes four, at which hour the Wilis lose their power"? We don't see much more than this in what happens on the stage. We even see contradictions. When he walks her lightly over the ground in a series of supported temps levés en arabesque, it isn't clear that she's covering for his exhaustion; it looks more the other way around. The conception of *Giselle* as a dance drama is badly served by presenting the eventful second act as a ballet blanc surrounded by a plot. The Wilis, deprived of their bridal wreaths and veils, wearing their new long bell-shaped gowns, could be the corps de ballet of *Serenade*. Isn't it a bit late in the day to be streamlining the classics? The old Kirov prejudices that this production reflects are as insupportable as the underlying assumption of the Blair version that Act I is fascinating.

Inspired Giselles are possible even within the vaporish terms of the role. I saw none this time. Cynthia Gregory contributed an effectively wrought Mad Scene, and she has at last stopped trying to look petite and fey. But though she danced up to scale, she still kept the dynamic range short; an impression of bubble-lightness set in and never varied. Magali Messac has inherited Gregory's tall-girl jitters. She shrank her dancing, erased the bracing line of her shoulders, and out of numerous droopy arabesques extended doggy paws of devotion. Her hairdo and makeup were not becoming. I left thinking Giselle just wasn't her role (whereas, with decent choreography, she'd be a marvellous Myrtha). But Messac is an uncommonly fine dancer and an intelligent actress, and I've loved her in all her roles this season, even *Theme and Variations*, to which she really is physically unsuited. She ought to be encouraged to try Giselle again, without corrupting her style. Dancers often confuse correct style with conformity to a physical type. A film of Spessivtseva (whose type is closer to Messac's than, say, Makarova's is) shows her to have been a forthright Giselle, with big legs and a fat braid hanging down her back. Gelsey Kirkland, though heavy and off form, is still the perfect waiflike Giselle, still capable of giving a transporting performance. On this occasion, she performed better than she danced, and she trouped better than she performed, and at every stage Baryshnikov was there to match her. When, toward the end of the second act, her strength began to give out, he doubled his; he flew, he bounded, he soared through

Gautier's catalogue, and the roles of the two principals were for once consciously reversed.

Kevin McKenzie's minimal acting and lanky, diffident presence in Act I didn't prepare me for his formidable dancing in Act II. He gave only half a performance (and Messac, his Giselle, could have used a wholehearted partner), but it had style. Alexander Godunov has style, too—old-Bolshoi style. With his carefully sculpted pageboy, his low necklines, and his massive, girlish legs, Godunov is like one of those oddly virile pantywaists in Russian ballet films of the thirties and forties—the ones who wore heeled shoes and bloomers. Godunov isn't narcissistic; he's a big, blond anachronism, and he has, as Albrecht, none of the dramatic power I would have expected after seeing him in the Bolshoi repertory. He danced well. He partnered Gregory with consideration. His footwork is much sharper, his phrasing smoother, than it was a year ago. Yet when he's in the air all you see is that hair standing on end like a tongue of flame, and when he's on the ground, walking and miming, he's in his own far-off world. One can only reckon with him as one of this ballet's more inscrutable absurdities.

There's no accounting for regional tastes. The Houston Ballet brought a repertory to the Brooklyn Academy last month that could have come and, in part, did come straight from London. Ben Stevenson, formerly of the London Festival and Royal ballets, showed his *Four Last Songs*; Glen Tetley, who has long been London's idea of a serious American ballet choreographer, was represented by *Praeludium*. The two ballets, solemn and tedious affairs, were followed by *The Lady and the Fool*, a revival of a Sadler's Wells piece by John Cranko, who here attempted lightness and wit, but with an imprecision that suggested that his mind was elsewhere at the time. Stevenson, the artistic director, has turned Houston into a reactionary outpost of British ballet. The company style is not what you'd expect of Texans; the dancers are evenly trained and theatrically aware, but they look like British dancers of twenty years ago. The main draw was *Papillon*, by a Royal Ballet colleague of Stevenson's, Ronald Hynd. *Le Papillon*, a "ballet-pantomime," was originally produced at the Paris Opéra in 1860, with music by Offenbach, a libretto by Marie Taglioni and Vernoy de Saint-Georges (the same who wrote *Giselle*), and with choreography credited to Mme Taglioni. Hynd's ballet is a pastiche of a pastiche. *Le Papillon* tried to revive the Golden Age of Romantic ballet on the talents of Emma Livry, who was Taglioni's protégée; Offenbach's score suggests that the attempt contained an element of spoof. John Lanchbery's orchestration for Houston makes Offenbach rambunctious rather than vivacious, and Hynd's ballet is crassly conceived. Mime is confused with broad acting. The role of the witch who turns the heroine into a butterfly was taken in travesty by Richard Munro, whose top-banana antics were abetted by William Pizzuto as the chief lepidopterist. Characterless character-acting does not sustain comedy in ballet unless you think ballet itself is a joke. Houston surely wants more of its company than this?

The lightning visit of the Atlanta Ballet to Brooklyn College was a contrast in nearly every way. Here was serious and charming dancing in a recognizably American style. Robert Barnett's school was New York City Ballet, and it shows in the company he directs. But his dancers also have a good, strong local accent. They were, as an ensemble, most admirable in *Raymonda Variations*, and would obviously have been even better with live accompaniment. An impressive season, all too short.   —*May 18, 1981*

ᴅ*Dear Little Girl and* ᴅ*Boy Land*

The annual workshop performances of the School of American Ballet were a little different this year. The young dancers, who customarily appear in repertory pieces chosen and reconstructed by their teachers, were seen instead in ballets specially prepared for the occasion by Peter Martins and Jacques d'Amboise and Joseph Duell and Adam Lüders, who are all, of course, members of New York City Ballet. The one exception to this novel programming was a reduced version of Balanchine's *La Source* staged by Suki Schorer, a former member of New York City Ballet who has been for some years one of the school's most respected instructors. The Schorer revivals of Balanchine are always a big item on the workshop programs, an important bridge between school practice and company style. The Bournonville revival, in past years the province of Stanley Williams, was undertaken this year by Lüders. It, too, is a big item, celebrating the old French school and its contribution to the Franco-Russian Imperial tradition nurtured by Petipa and inherited by Balanchine. *Pas de Trois and Gallopade*, from *The Childhood of Erik Menved*, was arranged by Lüders from a Bournonville manuscript in the Royal Library of Copenhagen. Assisted by the scholar Knud A. Jürgensen, Lüders worked, as Williams had when reviving *La Vestale* in 1977, with steps he had never seen in performance, *Pas de Trois and Gallopade* having passed out of the repertory in Bournonville's own day. The result was choreography that mixed the familiar and the farfetched in proportions characteristic of Bournonville but also, and perhaps more so, of Lüders's Bournonville. Although *The Childhood of Erik Menved* dates from 1843, the year after *Napoli*, parts of the male solo—a form in which Bournonville excelled—look unlike the solos in

Napoli or any others in the master's canon. However you took it, the piece was another sign of involvement by the company in the school's affairs and an impressive exhibit in a program that turned out to be as much a choreographers' as a dancers' showcase.

As it happened, the major attraction was a revival of a piece that was first performed in 1893. This was, though, an original, starting-from-scratch work by Peter Martins, who composed the choreography to Riccardo Drigo's *The Magic Flute* with no aid other than a piano reduction of the score. Incomplete orchestral parts arrived late from Russia and were filled out hastily by local hands. The music, whether Drigo meant it to or not, sounds like his *Harlequinade*, only weaker. Even without the striking rhythmic correspondences between the two scores (which have at times a tracing-paper symmetry), there are plot resemblances that almost seem to be forcing Martins's hand. The farmer's daughter, Lise, pledged by her parents to a doddering marquis but loving the young peasant Luke, is eventually won by Luke when a passing god hands him power over his enemies. Not only *Harlequinade* is evoked, not only *La Fille Mal Gardée*: the magic flute that makes people dance against their will equals the magic violin in Bournonville's *Kermesse in Bruges* (1851), a ballet that Martins has known from youth. (There is no plot relation to Mozart's *The Magic Flute*.) Martins doesn't try to avoid these parallels; he underlines them. The benevolent god, here a goddess, is none other than La Bonne Fée of *Harlequinade*. When Lise is obliged to dance with the old marquis, her lover intervenes in the pas de deux the way Colas does in *La Fille Mal Gardée*. Lise has four friends who do a perky variation, like the gavotte of the four ladies of Harlequin's entourage. And the finale, with the whole cast twitching and galumphing around the stage to the tweedly flute tune, is a reprise of the climax of *Kermesse*, just as it must have been in 1893. *The Magic Flute* was originally produced, with choreography by Lev Ivanov, for the students of the Imperial Ballet School of St. Petersburg; Luke was the thirteen-year-old Mikhail Fokine. Later, when the ballet entered the Maryinsky repertory, Pavlova danced Lise—one of her first comedy roles. It is a children's piece, with the conventional plot mechanics and dance forms miniaturized in forty minutes. The temptation for sophisticated New York children is to play down to it. But Martins took his dancers through the thickets of a primeval genre without scraping their sensibilities and without exposing too painfully the standing American deficiency in the art of mime. He let his cast be klutzy Americans as long as they were rhythmically punctual and didn't mug too much. Their eighteenth-century French pastoral style seemed to have come by way of Cole Porter and Bert Lahr. Only James Sewell, playing the bandy-legged lecherous marquis, brought a character to life. It's hard to make an original dent in archaic formula farce, and Martins didn't take the occasion as a test of his originality. Yet I laughed outright only once, and it was at a conceit of his, when the goddess approached disguised as a hooded hermit, inching along a parapet and playing the flute theme—on a trumpet.

Martins recognizes the farcical characters and situations for as much sense as is in them and not an ounce more. And he counts on our recognizing them, too, from our knowledge of stock material. This is an important lesson, and one that I want to return to in a moment. It has a special kind of importance in relation to the young cast of *The Magic Flute*, because if Martins has been forbearing in his direction of the farce element in the piece, he's been unusually strict and demanding in his choreography of the dances. It's as if he'd said to the students, "Maybe you can't act, but you can dance. Show me something extra." The kids make up for their acting by exceeding themselves as dancers; I don't believe I've ever seen a school piece, apart from one of Balanchine's, that asked as much. Luke's solo variation begins with a huge rond de jambe sweep into a triple turn in attitude. Lise has one solo with a fan and another, long and taxing, to pizzicato music; neither dance would do dishonor to a ballerina. The dances for the ensemble as well as those for the principals are inventively accented and rhymed; they capture the period flavor—amorous and slightly sticky—of the music. Drigo seems to have been a salon composer conscripted into the theatre. Except for the waltz finale, which can stand with the score of *Harlequinade*, he is not at his best in *The Magic Flute*. Undaunted, Martins has heard and envisioned a world of old-fashioned "young" emotion. It's impossible to believe that Ivanov's original choreography could have been half as good. We'd be dancing it now.

Martins also contributed a curtain-raiser, to Tchaikovsky's *Capriccio Italien*, that odd piece which begins with Alpine bugle calls and then gives way to schizophrenia—half Slavic pomp and half Italian–street-song exuberance. Martins has done a parody in the form of an autobiographical sketch: his choreography is half *Diamonds* and half *Napoli*—equal halves Balanchine and Bournonville. If *The Magic Flute* shows Martins's humor, *Capriccio Italien* shows his wit. It's not the refined, tense wit of *Suite from Histoire du Soldat*; it's the free, jovial, slightly vulgar wit that we see in some of Martins's own comic performances, and it's a great deal of fun. Joseph Duell's *La Création du Monde* also drew on his ballet—heritage, I suppose the word is, in view of the solemnity of Duell's choreography. The 1923 jazz-influenced score by Darius Milhaud has been rendered in hard-edged academic patterns, all very precise, all very fluent, with none of the life and breath of jazz in them. Milhaud's jazz, to be sure, has its ersatz side, but for last year's workshop Duell performed the same kind of meticulous taxidermy on Gottschalk—it was *Cakewalk* without the cake. To Duell, who is twenty-five years old, there may be no other dance tradition to call upon than ballet. Milhaud's jazz and Gottschalk's ragtime have gone the way of the dances that inspired them; only classicism endures. A wiggle of the hips, a snap of the fingers are atavistic reminders of the way we *used* to dance. In ballet—specifically, in the Balanchine repertory (*La Création du Monde* has the look of the Stravinsky Balanchine)—Duell seems to find all the fire and sex and bluesiness he needs without simulating a feeling for jazz. And this is odd; Duell is the keenest of the New York City Ballet sailors in Jerome Robbins's *Fancy Free*. As a choreographer, he has come along at a time when the popular dancing that fed Balanchine's inspiration has disappeared into the forms in which Balanchine expressed it. And so Duell's inspiration is fed secondhand. Perhaps, one day, Balanchine's ballets will have the kind of currency that makes generical reference to them as easy to recognize as the references to *Harlequinade* and *Fille* and *Kermesse* in *The Magic Flute*. Young Joe Duell seems to think that day has already come. And he is not the only budding choreographer who thinks so. (I was reminded of the remark of a choreographer-teacher who recently visited New York to teach classes in a great modern-dance studio: "Nobody knows anything anymore but ballet.")

There was remarkable dancing to be seen in every one of these pieces. The school pours out its exquisite female creatures at a steady rate and is beginning to match them with good boys. Lisa Jackson and Afshin Mofid in *Capriccio Italien*, Mofid again in *La Source*, Marisa Cerveris or Deborah Wingert in the same ballet, and the two different trios who danced *Pas de Trois and Gallopade* (in one of which James Sewell proved that he dances as well as he mimes)—all were excellent. So was the cast of *La Création du Monde*; it struck me while watching this that very few professional ballet companies in the land can do this sort of thing better, and many are applauded for a lot worse. Shawn Stevens, a lithe, Brooke Shields type of beauty, had the lead, and she was also one of Martins's Lises. The other, Katrina Killian, had more ability. Just now Stevens is a hot performer who needs to develop technique. The Lukes, Sean Savoye and Jock Soto, were also oppositely tuned. Savoye was a charmer, like Stevens (though too young-looking for her), but Soto could match Killian technically. Joseph Malbrough was equally convincing as the Adam of *La Création* and as a docile retainer of the marquis in *The Magic Flute*. That work, incidentally, is said to be bound for the New York City Ballet repertory. *Capriccio Italien* will be seen as part of the company's Tchaikovsky Festival this month.

I haven't mentioned Jacques d'Amboise's *My Father* because nothing much happened in it. The tinies of the school were brought on to stand, bow, and pose while we heard a tape of Judy Collins singing. Her song seemed to matter more to D'Amboise than their dancing.

The idea that a farce cannot be made to yield meanings that exceed its capacities holds true of any genre. Limitations are imposed in the very notion of farce, of melodrama, or of musical comedy, and, while genres may be mixed, they may not be mixed arbitrarily, just to see the colors run. Peter

Anastos's new ballet, *Domino*, makes that fatal mistake. It starts by invoking the pinkly sweet operetta world of Victor Herbert, some of whose best tunes have been arranged by Peter Nocella to form a score, and it works up such a comic head of steam, what with its smoldering gypsy abductors and its dithering abductee who is right where she wants to be, that the *noir* ending is simply unbelievable. I'm not even sure I saw it happen. Anastos, a former director and star of the drag company Les Ballets Trockadero de Monte Carlo, learned about comedy and genre from having to develop a parody repertory. There's probably no other young ballet choreographer who is as good as Anastos is at getting laughs or who can build up so many sly allusions without being cornered by them. Perhaps because it was steeped in the ambiguity of a drag performance, Anastos's material was unusually clear and definite. His Trockadero masterpiece, *Yes, Virginia, Another Piano Ballet*, was performed with mixed casts by the Pennsylvania Ballet this season at the Brooklyn Academy. Although it didn't transcend its origins, it still got all its laughs. Naturally, now that he's working for regular ballet companies—*Domino*, also seen in Brooklyn, is an original work for the Pennsylvania Ballet—Anastos is eager to extend and deepen his range. But he seems to live and think in genre attitudes, and the main difficulty with the sudden turn that *Domino* takes is that it doesn't twist the material in an unforeseen direction—it abandons one *kind* of material for another. The ending is as gratuitous and unsatisfying as if the projectionist had put the last reel of a horror movie onto a Lubitsch comedy.

Even as a drag comedian, Anastos had a light touch. The opening scene of *Domino*, with M'lady in her boudoir, has this tickling, frivolous eroticism. M'lady, who appears to be modelled on Jeanette MacDonald, is in her lingerie, and a sextet of fluffy maids (called Powderpuffs) trips in to get her ready for a big date at a masked ball. The minute she's alone, gypsies come right into the bedroom and get her, and except for the fact that she drops her domino, which her boyfriend finds, we'd think it was a fantasy. In the gypsy camp, there's a big ballet number, surprisingly dense. Ensembles, pas de deux, solos tumble through the forest, wild and free. The gypsy chief (Jeffrey Gribler) bounds like Mikhail Mordkin, with a bow and arrow; M'lady nearly dies from the garlic on his breath. La Gitana—how well we know her!—shows off her rather more classy repertory of pouts and pointwork. (This is a delicious performance by Victoria Lyras, equalled by Sari Braff as M'lady. Anastos also gets headlong cooperation from the women in the "feminine" roles in *Another Piano Ballet*.) Now the captive is about to get it, but the Mounties are coming to the rescue, so everyone dons cloaks and dominoes and creeps about in the dark. The Mounties never do come on. Who comes on is the boyfriend (Paul Vitali). Everything becomes twice as murky, and under the strains of "Sweethearts" and "Toyland" we hear intimations of *La Valse*. What happens to the heroine is not quite what happens in *La Valse*, though, and I'm not the only one who missed it. Don

McDonagh in the New York *Post*: "Her young man . . . violently snatches her from a fate worse than death." Nancy Goldner in the *Soho Weekly News*: "The heroine is waltzed to death by her boyfriend." In fact, as I later found out, he strangles her. The End. If this can happen in Victor Herbert's world, then Anastos and his co-scenarist, Don Daniels, know something that Herbert didn't know, and it cheapens their use of his music. As for Ravel and Balanchine and their elegant *ballet noir*: waltz fever and dances of death haunted the European lyrical imagination throughout the nineteenth century. When the heroine dies in *La Valse*, the shock has been rolling toward us for a hundred and fifty years. *Domino* leapfrogs over *La Valse* to its horrific conclusion as if *La Valse* were itself an authenticating genre reference, like the images of Romanticism it is full of. Anastos, in one way, and Joseph Duell, in another, are using Balanchine ballets as summary material, not recapitulating or re-creating the process by which the ballets work but only pointing out that they exist.   —*June 1, 1981*

Grand Pas Petipa

To judge from the classical revivals at American Ballet Theatre this season, there must have been many men called Marius Petipa active in Russian ballet during the latter half of the nineteenth century. There was Petipa the conserver, who reset *La Fille Mal Gardée*, and many ballets by other choreographers, for the Russian repertory. There was Petipa the purveyor of national and character dances, who filled whole acts of *Don Quixote* and *La Bayadère* and *Raymonda* and *Swan Lake* with his exotic specialties. There was the classical Petipa, who made symmetrical dances for legions of young women in a spirit of tender innocence, and there was the jaded Petipa, who shuffled the same tired steps from variation to variation and from ballet to ballet. Then, there was the Petipa from whom most of the blessings at ABT flow. This Petipa, who lived well into the twentieth century and made his home at the Kirov Ballet, was the arbiter of the entire canon. What he chose to preserve, what he chose to subject to shall we say progressive renewal was indeed arbitrary; one never knows what to expect from this fellow, and his latter-day accomplishments tend to becloud his past ones.

The jaded repetitions may, in fact, be the work of this new-day maestro in a nonideological mood, or they may represent a diminished legacy passed on from prerevolutionary days, when by a variety of factions the canon was held in low esteem. In either case, many of the dances we know from Kirov-derived productions of *La Bayadère* and *Don Quixote* and

Paquita and *Le Corsaire* are interchangeable, and have been interchanged over the years. During a live all-Petipa broadcast from the Met on PBS, Mikhail Baryshnikov spoke of Petipa's habit of switching variations "for some lady to some other lady." But interpolations aren't the whole problem in identifying the provenance of the dances. Formula choreography—steps for some music fitted to some other music—turns up often, especially in the Minkus ballets. Since Minkus was Petipa's most frequent collaborator, a large portion of the Petipa canon is without discussable content. One is not surprised that the same steps recur in ballet after ballet—steps are, after all, the material of creation, and not creation itself. But to see steps recur unsupported by the change in context, uncharged by a new musical or dramatic atmosphere, is to wonder not only how creation could have come about in the first place but also how it serves the art to reintroduce such undifferentiated material. Taking the material on faith as the surviving work of a genius involves the acceptance of a stunning hypothesis. How could *this* Petipa have developed the grand style and stayed its undisputed master until, in the last decade of his career, Tchaikovsky came along to vindicate him?

It's a relief to get away from the Petipa-Minkus quandary and into the latest batch of Petipa acquisitions, which, for the most part, are not repetitions of things we have seen before. Petipa revived *La Fille Mal Gardée* in 1885, to the excruciating music of Hertel. (Yes, worse than Minkus!) The ABT reconstruction of the Act I pas de deux, staged by Diana Joffe, has a persuasive low-key sparkle, especially in the woman's role, danced by Marianna Tcherkassky. The style is unlike any we might recognize as Petipa's; it's closer to Bournonville's. Although Tcherkassky is on point, her dances are not really point dances, and the supported adagio is a prefiguration of the grand style rather than the real, full-blown thing. The man's role, in a more familiar key, was delivered with sledgehammer force by Fernando Bujones. For *Jardin Animé*, an excerpt from *Le Corsaire*, Petipa had besides Minkus some infectious music by Delibes, which we know as the "Naïla" waltz from *La Source*. It would be interesting if the performance of the waltz, its choreography, and the variations for two soloists had been of the quality of the *Fille* fragment, but in fact it was not so. The music had been muddily orchestrated for ABT by Hershy Kay. The steps were executed as in any old Minkus ballet. Ballet Theatre's dancers are performing their Petipa these days strictly step by step and beat by beat. There's method and utility in what they do, and sometimes a fine expository clarity, but they're not bringing much to the party. The company's conductors seem to have no idea when to abet this strictness and when to ease up on it. Only Paul Connelly, the assistant conductor, understands how to bring elasticity and tension to a dance score, and he was not the conductor of *Jardin Animé*. Too bad, because the four-square, squat and chunky performance is a misreading of what ought to be (and, as given by the Kirov, probably is) a rapturous lyrical experience.

Balanchine's *La Source* could be a useful stylistic guide. If Joffe had been sent to see it, she might not have committed an error in the one passage that Balanchine has obviously remembered from Petipa—when the girls (in *Jardin Animé*) place their floral hoops on the floor, making a path for the soloist to prance through. The prance is in the music, and both Petipa and Balanchine end it with a leap into arabesque fondue. At ABT, the leap has no punch. The way Balanchine times it, it lands, unexpectedly, on a silent downbeat. One must believe that if he quoted Petipa this was the reason.*

Baryshnikov was careful to make the point, in that same intermission interview, that his Petipa presentations were "the original, as far as we know. I wouldn't put my head on it." There is regulation Petipa; there is revisionist Petipa. But the new third act of *The Sleeping Beauty*, done in Oliver Messel's set and with some trashy substitutes for his costumes, cannot be taken seriously from any point of view. A Bluebird adagio that looks like a crib from *La Bayadère*, a male Bluebird variation that omits most of the characteristic Bluebird steps, hard and heavy Jewel fairies, a charmless Puss in Boots, and a belabored Red Riding Hood lead up to a grand pas de deux that the stars apparently choreograph themselves. Baryshnikov has been at great pains this season to strengthen technical execution at the corps level and among the demisoloists, and to a noticeable extent he has succeeded. The School of Petipa has been basic to this effort. But what Baryshnikov and his staff call Petipa is not an integrated or a consistent regimen. Within the regimen, there is room for differentiation, stylistic versatility, and contrast. But there is no room for contradiction. The brave new pas de trois in Act I of *Swan Lake* hardly agrees with the inertia that, despite changes in choreography, continues to undermine the whole production. In the long run, consistency is going to count for more than authenticity.

I get lost in the imagery of Crowsnest, sometimes pleasurably, sometimes blankly. Crowsnest, which consists of Martha Clarke, Felix Blaska, and Robby Barnett, has been in existence for two years, but it just made its début in New York. I got seated late at the Public Theatre, and the show began before I'd had a chance to look at the program. It didn't matter; in a few seconds I recognized the place, and I was held by it for some time before the drifting and dreaming set in and the spell broke. The three were onstage when the curtain went up. Some jazz started playing, and they began walking fast in circles, first alone, then together, then alone again. Clarke wore a short black velvet dress with her hair frizzed, Barnett was in tails, and Blaska, with a goatee, had on a black raincoat. They wore blue

* *Postscript 1982:* According to Bronislava Nijinska's recently published *Early Memoirs* (Holt, Rinehart & Winston), St. Petersburg's *La Source* was "remounted in 1902 by Achille Coppini in an attempt to produce a ballet that was different from the style of early Petipa."

shoes and walked against a painted backcloth by Robert Andrew Parker—a composition in misty blue and gray blocks that suggested a city. It was a rich, full illusion: New York or Paris on a sodden spring night, back streets filling with the smoky sound of the old Duke Ellington band and with the scent of danger. (The piece is called *Don't Mean a Thing*, after the Ellington tune.) There's a certain inevitability in what happens: Clarke seems to be a prostitute, and she has some rough encounters with the two men; Blaska is a flasher. But one is absorbed by the larger spectacle of people living intensely in their own worlds. Barnett, who is elegantly drunk, contrives to suggest that he has slept in his suit of tails but not rented it. Crowsnest is the offspring of Pilobolus Dance Theatre; although there's less emphasis on acrobatics, the mime is still dazzlingly, physically brazen and almost completely abstract. The sense of persons and places comes about through vibration, through resonant gesture. When a concrete idea arises— from, say, Clarke's getting too roughly handled and landing on the floor like a rag doll with her legs spread—I could wish it were less banal. Then, too, the physicality limits expression. It can be a happy limitation, as when Barnett and Blaska go careering around the stage joined side by side as if Blaska were riding in Barnett's sidecar. But there is also a tendency to trust blindly in the truth of appearances, to go on joining bodies, to mistake friction for vibration.

Crowsnest is not your average mime troupe. Clarke and Barnett, along with the rest of Pilobolus, practically invented free-association abstract mime, and they're aware of the dangers of going too far or of just going on, which is the greatest temptation of all. After about ten minutes, *Don't Mean a Thing* dissolved into scattershot effects (though Barnett on his motorcycle brought it briefly back). *Haiku*, composed of many short movement sketches separated by blackouts, was formally far more of a success. It was neat and clean; it avoided diddling in the materiality of the form. But for Crowsnest it felt like a concession. The great Japanese mimes Eiko and Koma achieve their supreme epiphanies through the intensification of a single effect. Crowsnest aims for constancy rather than unity, and its habit is to proceed from one effect to another in a more or less continuous line. The line cut short is not a real method; like Pilobolus's *Monkshood's Farewell*, it's a dead end.

The first group piece that Crowsnest made, *The Garden of Villandry*, was presented last, as if in the hope that we might see it as an extended haiku. The cast is in turn-of-the-century summer whites. The men walk very slowly on a tilt with their hands in their pockets; they hold the woman's body canted into space; they turn and glance; they hold modest arabesques. In the film *Martha Clarke Light & Dark*, also shown at the Public, we see this piece in preparation, and it works better in closeup than it does on the stage. Like the other Crowsnest scores, the slow movement of Schubert's Piano Trio in B Flat is used for pace and atmosphere but not for structure; lack of structural definition makes the piece seem vagrant from the start. By this time, too, the triangularity of Crowsnest's group compositions has become oppressive. Why always one woman and two men? That casting is practically a haiku in itself. There's not much leeway dramatically. No matter how neutral the terms are in partnering, there's always an odd man out, and the sexual dynamics within the group cannot go far beyond the variations presented in this program. Another problem is that Clarke and Barnett are much stronger performers than Blaska and are constantly trying to dispel that inequality by merging with the group. Barnett does it naturally and gracefully. With one of the most riveting presences in all theatre, he rivets when he wants to. He seems to love fading out of himself, escaping in full view, and he's as content on the sidelines as he is in the spotlight.

When Clarke fades into the group, she looks happier there, and is it a coincidence that in both of her solos her face is masked? Clarke shares Barnett's virtuosity. She contains the same range of contradictions: heavy-light, monstrous-fey, ugly-glamorous. She has the same kind of sensitive, slightly battered clown face. The two of them—in Pilobolus they were often teamed—appear to have been born for theatre in the same minute. But Clarke seems uneasy about being the apex of the triangle. Maybe she rejects the easy domination her position gives her; maybe there's a group ethos lingering from Pilobolus days. But Crowsnest isn't really a group; it has no identity as such, and that's largely because Clarke is unwilling to state her presence unequivocally. In Nocturne, she performs barebreasted, wearing a bulky tulle skirt and toe shoes, and with her head wrapped in gauze. The costume is adapted from De Meyer's enigmatic photograph "Woman with a Mask," and Clarke seems to want to tell the story behind the photograph. I'm not sure I understand her story. Once her terms are grasped—and they're fairly obvious (she has made the woman a decrepit ballerina)—one is left to ponder their meaning; no further light is shed on the subject. Nocturne is one of a series of melancholy "women in theatre" studies, and as a ready-made pictorial image it's also a companion piece to Fallen Angel, in which Clarke is a birdwoman out of Max Ernst's book of collages Une Semaine de Bonté. (Both solos are shown being rehearsed in the film.) Clarke, completely hidden in a blue silk gown and a beaked head, gives us another baffler. The costume tells all. The costume tells nothing. The movement inside the dress serves only to restate the dress. Who are these headless women? Is there a thing going on about heads? Recently, Clarke directed the actress Linda Hunt as Elizabeth I in Elizabeth Dead, by George Trow. A lot of Elizabeth's monologue was quite graphically concerned with the beheading of Mary, Queen of Scots, and Clarke's staging was in the clinical-grotesque style that she is increasingly favoring for her own solos. One wouldn't know from an evening with Crowsnest how glowingly expressive her face is, and the solos aren't anatomically expressive. Martha Clarke is as complete a theatrical artist as any woman performing today, but in

Crowsnest, which was her idea, she leaves a meager impression. (You'd never guess, either, that she's one of the funniest women alive.) No doubt she intends to disturb, but I wonder if she meant to be so personal about it. For one who can suggest so much to cut herself so far back is a waste, painful to witness. The final image is one of self-mutilation. —*June 15, 1981*

Tchaikovsky

The New York City Ballet's Tchaikovsky Festival began with Suzanne Farrell, in a formal tutu of solemn black, floating downstage on her long, sensitive points, her hands joined in prayer. And it ended pianissimo, with an image of a giant's heart beating its last under a black shroud, followed by the blowing out of a single candle on a darkened stage. It was as if Balanchine, in bracketing the whole festival with memento mori, were deliberately overturning the moral of the Stravinsky Festival, held a year after the composer's death, at the end of which Balanchine came onstage and drank a jaunty vodka toast, in the Russian fashion, "to the health of the guy that died." Farrell's Prayer, set to the Preghiera from the fourth orchestral suite (*Mozartiana*), was preceded by a short concert, conducted by Robert Irving, of dramatic compositions on themes of love and death: the *Romeo and Juliet* Overture-Fantasy, with its closing cantilena that slowly withdraws in lingering contemplation of Juliet's bier; Lisa's aria from *Pique Dame*, sung as she waits by the canal in which she will drown herself; Lensky's aria before the duel in *Eugene Onegin*; the love duet for tenor and soprano from the abandoned opera *Undine*, which lent its music to the second act of *Swan Lake* and its dramatic situation to the fourth act. On the final program of the festival, the Elégie from *Suite No. 3* and the Andante Elegiaco (pas de deux) from *Diamonds* paved the way for a presentation of three movements from the "Pathétique" Symphony, in which Tchaikovsky is thought to have meditated on his own death. The Allegro con Grazia, with its mysterious five-beat waltz, was set by Jerome Robbins as a pas de deux for Patricia McBride and Helgi Tomasson with an ensemble of ten girls. Irving then led the orchestra in a brisk, unpompous rendition of the March. The Adagio Lamentoso, which ends the symphony, was done by Balanchine in the Gothic-horror style in which he treated Schumann's misery and attempted suicide in his version, last year, of *Davidsbündlertänze*. (Tchaikovsky, like Schumann, tried to drown himself, and eventually he did commit suicide. The facts of the case have been recently recounted in David Brown's article in *The New Grove*.) The hooded processions in *Adagio Lamentoso* also recall the death of Don Quixote, until now Balanchine's most opulent staging of the artist's martyrdom. Tchaikovsky, who really was sacrificed on the altar of social hypocrisy, is seen as another of Balanchine's victim-heroes. All this didn't make the Tchaikovsky Festival itself a lugubrious affair. *Mozartiana*, Balanchine's fourth production of Tchaikovsky's homage to Mozart, began this time with the Preghiera, but after this ceremonial moment had passed, the ballet evolved into the spiciest that Balanchine has done in some time. His other festival pieces were the Garland Dance from *The Sleeping Beauty* and *Hungarian Gypsy Airs*, a setting of the folk ballads that Tchaikovsky orchestrated in the last year of his life. Robbins, also in sprightly form, produced a pas de deux for Darci Kistler and Ib Andersen to the middle movement of the First Piano Concerto. His major work for the festival and its biggest hit was *Piano Pieces*, for which he returned to the most appealing vein of *Dances at a Gathering*. John Taras, Peter Martins, Joseph Duell, and Jacques d'Amboise fulfilled their festival assignments, for the most part, by celebrating the music and exercising institutional aesthetics. In all, fourteen ballets were introduced in ten days and shown alongside the company's regular Tchaikovsky repertory, which is the world's strongest. If most of the premières were not even potential contributions to this repertory, it was still a Tchaikovsky Festival—business as usual, in other words, at New York City Ballet. The only difference was that Day One and Day Ten were hung with crêpe.

In the marvellous ballets of the Balanchine-Tchaikovsky repertory—*Diamonds* and *Piano Concerto No. 2* and *Serenade* and *Allegro Brillante* and *Suite No. 3* (including *Theme and Variations*) and the single-act version of *Swan Lake*, and even *Waltz of the Flowers*, which was the festival's sole excerpt from *The Nutcracker*—Tchaikovsky's melancholy is always accounted for, not only as the pervasive mood of his Andantes and Elegies but as a persistent aura edging even his brightest moments. In *Waltz of the Flowers*, the appearance of the third melody, in B minor, has an effect of sudden estrangement—an effect that is answered in the choreography by the soloist's isolated entrance against the corps. It's such a wonderful, surging moment that it doesn't feel strange—it feels like a pang of elation. This complex, elating melancholy in Tchaikovsky is something no other choreographer has captured, just as no other choreographer has demonstrated more clearly the difference between exalted emotion and obsessive brooding in the adagio sequences. By custom, Balanchine has stayed away from the heavier symphonies, the more overwrought symphonic poems and overtures. For the purposes of choreography, the rhythmic propulsion and transparent orchestral textures of Tchaikovsky are best without the introspective thickening to which he was sometimes prone. Constant Lambert, in a brilliant essay on Tchaikovsky, compared the second theme of the slow movement of the Fifth Symphony with the cello melody of the Adagio in *The Sleeping Beauty*, when Aurora appears to the Prince in a vision. "The purely physical similarity between the two tunes is astonishing, but they inhabit entirely different psychological worlds. In one, Tchaikovsky is cry-ing for the moon; in the other, he is content to gaze at its beauty."

When Balanchine has yielded to Tchaikovskian introspection, it has usu-ally been to stage vision scenes of a more problematic nature than the one in *The Sleeping Beauty*. Yet compare the Andante of *Piano Concerto No. 2* with *Meditation*. In the former ballet (christened *Ballet Imperial*), he took an unwieldly nondance composition—the first movement is inordinately long, broad, and melodramatic—and made a great ballet out of it. The key to his success may possibly be the fact that nowhere in the concerto does Tchaikovsky look inward and shed tears. There is a certain sweetness-of-pain in the Andante, but the overriding emotion is one of dignified resigna-tion. Sweetness-of-pain comes back in *Meditation*, together with nostalgia, regret, and some central enigma one would have thought impossible to depict in dance. With Farrell's help, though, Balanchine did it. The "story" in *Meditation*, a pas de deux with D'Amboise created in 1963, is of lovers who are completely involved with one another yet never meet—never be-come one. The music is dedicated to Nadezhda von Meck, the great benefactor of Tchaikovsky whom he never met; possibly Farrell in the ballet is an echo of Von Meck, and her relation with D'Amboise may be, in part, an evocation of the patron's relation with the composer—benevolent, loving, all-comprehending, dependent, yet distant. In *Meditation*, Farrell wears a draped costume and loose hair. In Balanchine iconography, flowing hair and dress have come to signify the muse of the Romantic poet: see *La Sonnam-bula*, the Elegy of *Serenade*, the first part of *Chaconne*, which deals with the Orpheus myth, and the finale of *Walpurgisnacht Ballet*, which is populated with the dream women of Gounod's Faust. In *Suite No. 3*, the stage teems with girls in long hair and streaming chiffon, and the atmosphere is so thick that, under the influence of festival Tchaikovskiana, it was impossible not to see these portions of the *Suite* as a more meretricious sequel to *Meditation* —as a parade of the women in Tchaikovsky's life. In the Elégie, the glam-orous, inscrutable creature who steps out of the crowd and then back into it, leaving the hero in despair, could be the ideal woman whom Tchaikovsky worshipped but never found. She could be Désirée Artôt, the soprano with whom he was briefly in love; she could also be his mother, who died when he was a boy. In the Valse Mélancolique, the ballerina is like a siren or a witch holding the man under a spell. Antonina Milyukova, the woman who pursued Tchaikovsky until, disastrously, he married her, was probably men-tally unbalanced, but in Tchaikovsky's all too suggestible mind she seems to have been mixed up with Tatiana in *Eugene Onegin*, and that may be why her reflection in the ballet is not an altogether sinister one. In the Scherzo, the two principals dance freely, side by side. Is the girl Tchaikovsky's sister, whom he adored, and for whose children he wrote some of his most famous compositions? The weakness of *Suite No. 3*, apart from its involvement of Balanchine with the more subjective Tchaikovsky, is that there's no connection between the scheme of the first three movements and the classical ballet (composed twenty-two years earlier) that follows, to the Tema con Variazioni. The classical ballerina is, like all such Balanchine creations, a character in her own right. Since she is based on Aurora in *The Sleeping Beauty*, it is tempting to interpret the progress of *Suite No. 3* as a mirror of the process of sublimation by which life is transformed into art. In this interpretation, Tchaikovsky lived a life of Romantic chaos, which he distilled into Classical art.

In two ballets made for the festival by Joseph Duell and Peter Martins, this view of Tchaikovsky is upheld. Duell's *Introduction and Fugue* (the opening movement of the Suite No. 1) is a condensation of the action of *Suite No. 3*. The composer (Adam Lüders) is visited by amorphous forms that coalesce in the shape of a cathedral arch. The divine calling of the artist then gives way to his creation, which is a large and formal classical ballet, much like *Theme and Variations*. It hardly matters whether Lüders's artist-alchemist-priest is Tchaikovsky or Balanchine (Lüders was also Schumann in *Davidsbündlertänze*), or that the idea behind the ballet is imitative and naive. Duell has worked it out gracefully without imposing on the music more pressure, second by second, than it can accept. I don't believe his Romantic-Classical, Life-Art antinomies (I don't believe them in *Suite No. 3*, either, if indeed they are there), but I think he was right to try for some kind of extramusical dramatic continuity. His mistake was in trying to make this extramusical continuity the story of the music. The ballet doubles back on itself in an extremely dubious way. In Martins's ballet, arranged to the First Symphony (minus the first movement), the notional content is secreted in continuity that is stiffly formal and, when we get to the "ballet" part of the ballet (Martins, like Duell, has had to set a fugue), is even more so. The choreography, beguilingly well knit, is modestly presented; it calls our attention to the music, to the ballerina (Kistler), to the costumes ("Romantic" tutus, switching to "Classical" ones for the fugue), even to the set—never to itself. In its reticence, its calm good nature and workmanship, *Symphony No. 1* is Martins's most "Danish" ballet. (The waltz in the third movement even sounds like a waltz in the Danish ballet classic *A Folk Tale*.) In the finale, the stage empties while blue and white lights play for a full minute on the extraordinary transparent-plastic set designed for the festival by Philip Johnson and John Burgee. The effect doesn't quite come off; there aren't enough colors to make this aurora borealis the climax that the "Winter Dreams" Symphony demands. Or did Martins edit out the reds and yellows as being not in good taste? One could believe it; a fancier light show would need a more aggressive ballet.

Johnson and Burgee's Crystal Cathedral, in Garden Grove, California, was the inspiration for their "ice palace" Tchaikovsky set, designed at Balanchine's request. The architects have done what no modern stage designer I know of has yet accomplished—enclosed and defined stage space with a neutral décor capable of assuming as much or as little presence as may be demanded by individual ballets. Its ice-white color and striated forms were put through nearly two dozen variations in the course of the festival, and can be put through many more—indeed, must be, since festival programs are to alternate with repertory for the rest of the season, and the set cannot be flown in and out. Like any theme-and-variations scheme, the set is a systemic thing, and one would not like to see it overused. It places everything in a fantastic and geometric universe, where not every ballet—not even every Tchaikovsky ballet—belongs. *Serenade,* to me, needs the pristine, unbounded territory of a bare stage, and festival performances of *Divertimento from "Le Baiser de la Fée"* only served to italicize its mixed nature—part divertissement, part drama—and its need of a fluid background in which an unreal "ice" décor could be contrasted with a snug domestic one. (Alexandre Benois, who originally proposed and designed Stravinsky's Tchaikovsky ballet, surely derived his Alpine setting from *Manfred.*)

The company also made a special effort in the matter of costumes. Every ballet was dressed, and only the *Garland Dance* was noticeably in hand-me-downs. Leotards and T-shirts never made an appearance. What the festival seemed to be saying visually bore out one of the problems of festival choreography: that Tchaikovsky cannot be expressed in absolutist, abstract terms. Balanchine has known this all along, but the House of Balanchine, which is run on doctrinaire formalist principles, was thrown into insoluble dilemmas by the moods and dramas in Tchaikovsky's music. John Taras, a house choreographer of long standing, elected the either/or treatment: stretches of pure dancing interrupted by mime scenes. The treatment worked, or might be made to work, in the waltz from *Eugene Onegin,* which concluded the program called *Tempo di Valse.* The company's apprentices, for whom Taras staged the number, had no idea how to move when they weren't dancing full tilt, but that didn't impede the waltz, which went with a fine sweep. Taras has a touch with ensemble set pieces; last year he staged some sparkling dances from Glinka's *A Life for the Tsar* for the School of American Ballet. His big festival ballet, *Souvenir de Florence,* was placid as dance and inscrutable as drama. The large cast, in all-white Russian native dress by Ter-Arutunian, seemed to be acting out a story by Erich Maria Remarque about a field hospital in the Crimea. Jacques d'Amboise's *Concert Fantasy* involved some cadets at a prom where the Three Fates were keeping a vigil. By the second performance, this jumble had been cut in half. D'Amboise did two other numbers. In *Scherzo Opus 42,* a heavily impudent vaudeville skit for McBride and a group of men, one barely recognized New York City Ballet, but *Valse-Scherzo* touched on a continuing NYCB puzzle: Who are Kyra Nichols and Daniel Duell, and why are they so often paired? The two are husband and wife, but neither temperamentally nor physically are they a stage couple. And despite Duell's slight stature and his skill in low leaps with quicksilver retiré changes, he's not really a jester type. Robbins choreographs for him as if he were; D'Amboise does, too. Nichols, of course, is one of the strongest bravura ballerinas in the company, but the feats she performed in *Valse-Scherzo* barely registered, and I didn't think she functioned as well in Robbins's *Piano Pieces* as the two other principal women, Heather Watts and Maria Calegari. Give Nichols a Balanchine role, though, and the uncompromising terms in which she dances are lucid and complete. In a Balanchine-Tchaikovsky ballet like *Piano Concerto No. 2* or *Theme and Variations*, she springs to life. The festival was lucky to have her.

It didn't have Farrell, and, but for a few token appearances, it didn't have Merrill Ashley, whose recovery from a hip injury last year is still incomplete. In the première performance of *Mozartiana*, Farrell hurt her foot, and though she finished the evening, neither she nor the ballet has been seen since. *Meditation* also had to be withdrawn. (The *Diamonds* pas de deux as done by Ashley was a curiosity—as remote from Ashley's style as *Ballo della Regina* would have been from Farrell's.) Another ballet that came and went was *Hungarian Gypsy Airs*, for Karin von Aroldingen, with Lüders and a mixed ensemble. This, until *Adagio Lamentoso*, was the strangest event of the festival. Patterned after the *Tzigane* done for Farrell and Martins in the Ravel Festival (1975), it could hardly fail to arouse invidious comparisons. That it did not also defeat them seems untypical of Balanchine; one left thinking that he *must* have some tricks up his sleeve which a single performance failed to reveal. Since Von Aroldingen was also dancing her première with an injury, it was hard to tell what he intended. The rest of the choreography, for Lüders and the corps, appeared, like the music, none too distinguished.

Balanchine's *Garland Dance*, clearly a pièce d'occasion, may also disappear—unless, of course, he decides to surround it with *The Sleeping Beauty*. Its borrowed finery notwithstanding, the dance is a living rebuke to the Royal Ballet version and to the Petipa exhibits at American Ballet Theatre—especially *Jardin Animé*, with its stolid rhythm and its miles of nonfunctioning garlands. Balanchine weaves the floral arches into the dance, and he uses them as colonnades for the entrance of the children's corps, just as Petipa must have done. (The Bolshoi's "Petipa" production of *The Sleeping Beauty* has this same entrance.) When the children have been put through their paces with the adult corps, and when it seems that every permutation of garland and dancer, grownup and child has been run through once, Balanchine brings on nine more girls with nine rope garlands, and you know what a full stage really is, and what world enough and time are in choreography. The *Garland Dance* is essentially a background, scene-setting configuration, not a showpiece. It's a ponderous carrousel; the point of it is to display the tiered society of a fairy-tale kingdom that might have been designed by Watteau. The formations are all circles and grids—no dramatic diagonals or wedges, as in *Waltz of the Flowers*—and there are only about three steps, all obligatory. My favorite waltz step is the Duncanish scuff-kick into attitude front; the children do it deliciously, and toward the end they break formation and rush dizzyingly to place from opposite sides of the stage. The stage picture blurs, re-forms, and freezes, a human pyramid yoked with flowers. Balanchine is not in the picture—Petipa is.

Or so we think. Yet, just as *Mozartiana* is Mozart for ears that have heard Tchaikovsky, so this *Garland Dance* is Petipa for eyes that have seen Balanchine. It was so, too, with Stravinsky on Tchaikovsky in *Le Baiser de la Fée*. Following the *Divertimento*, we were given Tchaikovsky songs by the festival soprano, Karen Hunt, among them "None but the Lonely Heart," from which Stravinsky fashioned the climax of his ballet. This was a festival in which precedents were exposed and honored. The last and grandest of the selections in *Mozartiana* is the ten variations on a theme that Mozart took from Gluck. Balanchine follows suit, setting a string of alternating solos for the ballerina and the danseur, as he did in the gavotte of *Chaconne*. Ib Andersen danced opposite Farrell. The variations are about male and female strengths polarized in allegro rhythms, and they devastate certain hallmarks of Balanchine style, especially Balanchine style for Farrell. Her step sequences and timings are irregular and unforeseen, yet not uncharacteristic; she looks like a tape of herself run backward. Andersen beats and flies in the bonny manner that Robbins exploits so well in *Piano Pieces*, but with an effect of greater science and power.

In *Mozartiana*, Balanchine is that heartless and enchanting virtuoso suprême whom we identify with Mozart or with the Tchaikovsky of *Theme and Variations*, *The Nutcracker*, and *The Sleeping Beauty*. In *Adagio Lamentoso*, whole choirs of muses weep, and the *Nutcracker* angels come to the funeral with wings five feet high, holding lilies instead of Christmas trees. It's Balanchine crying for the moon.   —*June 29, 1981*

Love's Body

The subjects that dance cannot touch on, such as war, disease, poverty, and death (as a fact, not as a symbol), are the subjects that fascinate Kenneth MacMillan, or seem to. Add to this list a pervasive concern with sex in its physical aspect, and there is every reason to suspect him of vainglorious ambition, at the most, or opportunism, at the least. MacMillan also likes to adapt popular plays, operas, and movies, and he's invariably to be found right in the thick of the latest international trend in choreography.

His two newest works, performed by the Royal Ballet at the Met, are *Gloria* and *Isadora*. *Gloria*, set to a Poulenc Mass, is a liturgical ballet of the type associated nowadays with the Czech choreographer Jiří Kylián. MacMillan hots up the genre with references to the dead of the First World War; his inspiration was Vera Brittain's 1933 autobiography, *Testament of Youth*, which became a best-seller all over again in England when the BBC dramatized it last year. As for *Isadora*, its multimedia precedents include a fair number of ballets so bad one wonders why MacMillan wasn't dissuaded from launching his own. *Isadora* contains twice as many erotic pas de deux as the last MacMillan full-evening ballet, *Mayerling*. It deals in the touchiest of all the subjects on the untouchable list—dance itself. And it complicates things still further by adopting two narrative devices that have never worked properly in dance—past-tense reflection and double casting. Isadora Duncan is played by an actress, Mary Miller, and also by a dancer, Merle Park (alternating with Sandra Conley). The familiarity—the tackiness—of these devices (not even Martha Graham ever fully got away with them) does not ease our understanding of whatever it was that MacMillan wished to say about the life and work of Isadora. So now he caps his sins of volition with the sin of poor craftsmanship.

But all that, as Sam Spade says in *The Maltese Falcon*, is on one side. It is easy to compile a case against MacMillan; on the other side stands the fact of his talent. MacMillan's work, even when it is shoddy, is so much stronger and more stageworthy than the hackwork it resembles that charges of blind ambition and bad taste are irrelevant. The worst thing about *Isadora* is that it's not really MacMillan's show; it's Gillian Freeman's. Miss Freeman is the scenarist of *Isadora*, as she was of *Mayerling*; her specialty seems to be reducing movies to scenic occasions for MacMillan's choreography, only here she has the upper hand. If *Mayerling* resembled a silent movie arranged for the stage, *Isadora* is like an illustrated lecture. But MacMillan, who was imaginatively caught up in the death-degradation-disease themes of *Mayerling*, seems uninvolved and uninterested in any aspect of *Isadora* save the love scenes. With so much use of speech (the script quotes *My Life* extensively as well as six other Duncan books), with the most calamitous scenes in Isadora's life punctuated by outcries of pain (both actress and dancer yell lustily), the dancing was bound to take a subservient role. And, the way the climaxes are handled, the re-creations of Duncan's dances really have no place. Her bereavement, for instance, is staged three different ways. The lifeless bodies of the children are brought in, heralded by Paris Singer, who, aghast, stumbles and falls again and again, and rises as Isadora falls, and falls again as she rises, and when the rising and falling and rolling and tangling cease Merle Park opens her mouth in a silent scream and Mary Miller wails from across the stage. That's one treatment. Next, a lengthy, hushed scene of spectators in the rain witnessing the cortège. Umbrellas fold one after another as the two small coffins pass, followed by Miller as Isadora, a grand figure in a long purple mantle and train. A woman starts to address her in a broken voice: "Isadora—!" She passes on. Next, Park as Isadora dances her bereavement, only she doesn't. We've already seen enough, and the pastiche of Duncan dance which MacMillan has contrived for this moment is too frail to support such a statement. It's too frail throughout the ballet. MacMillan can't make Duncan dancing as vivid as its biographical context, and he's fearful of condescending to it, so he concentrates not on the dancer but on her intimate life and colorful times. He satirizes the fossilized ballet of Duncan's period (the Alhambra, not the Maryinsky) with a vengeance that Duncan herself might well have thought excessive, and he has his merry way with a tribe of vaudeville flamenco dancers, with all social dances from the tango to the Charleston, and with Loie Fuller. Fuller, who was celebrated by the poets and artists of her day, presented abstract spectacles of light on waving silk. She doesn't come off well in the films that were made of her, but that is no reason to take her any less seriously than Edward Gordon Craig, who also experimented with abstract design in the theatre, and whom Freeman and MacMillan take very seriously indeed. Fuller's act as staged by MacMillan looks like her filmed *Fire Dance* with a Charlie Chaplin ending. But while Fuller's historical importance is ground to rubble, the episode of the Fuller dancer who accosted Isadora is inflated into a full-blown lesbian pas de deux, with poor Monica Mason suppliant in a union suit of gold lamé. (Duncan's problem with Nursey, as she relates in *My Life*, was not lesbianism but homicidal mania. And in Duncan's version the whole episode is comically dismissed.)

The Nursey incident is the first of many in which Isadora is treated by MacMillan as a sex object. And treated none too kindly or gently. Isadora's men, from the Hungarian actor Oskar Beregi (Derek Deane) to Craig (Julian Hosking) to Singer (Derek Rencher) and Sergei Esenin (Stephen Jefferies), are all depicted in the quality of their sexual passion for her. Beregi, the "Romeo" to whom she so famously lost her virginity, is affectionate but callous; the rest are brutal, overmastering men. Not even the anonymous gigolo (Ashley Page) or the Man on the Beach (Ross MacGibbon), who fathered her third child, handles her tenderly. There are so many floor-slamming, whizbang adagios, with so many acrobatic crotch-held lifts, that they cancel each other out; the heaving and flailing limbs, the convolutions that turn Merle Park's body into Silly Putty cease to have impact. The only one of these panting pas de deux that carries any expressive charge after the first big one (with Craig) is the one with Esenin, in which Isadora really is pulped, and her desperation and exhaustion ought to be moving. But by the time Esenin appears, in Act II, the audience is punch-drunk. And we're also confused: is MacMillan showing us a series of sadomasochistic relationships or is the violence inherent in his idea of heterosexual passion? The only other key MacMillan composes in—rapture—is the same as violence, but with heads thrown back in ecstasy. Thus it is that Isadora, radiant, ravenous, succumbs to Craig, and thus it was for most of the way in *Manon*. In *Mayerling* (a ballet that has never been shown in New York; *Manon* was last seen here five years ago), MacMillan for the first time used the pas de deux not merely to indicate at-it-again sex but to define specific erotic atmospheres crucial to his theme. Rudolf, the syphilitic prince who carried out a suicide pact with his mistress, was in history's view politically frustrated, but in MacMillan's view he was also a prisoner of sex, and each pas de deux was a dramatic fulcrum. MacMillan had found the perfect dynamic metaphor for his drama of venery. In *Isadora*, nothing thematic hinges on those pas de deux. Whether Isadora was a masochist, whether she was sexually insatiable are questions that lie apart from and are pathetically diminished by the blows dealt her by fate. MacMillan can only depict the blows as they occurred; no strategy works to pull them into complicity with a psychosexual analysis of Isadora's character. Yet MacMillan's insistence on the sex life—far too heavily and artfully worked to be mere titillation—suggests that he does think there's some fateful complicity somewhere. The first half of the evening ends with Isadora howling in childbirth; the second half ends with her lying dead in the Bugatti as her last words are intoned: "*Adieu, mes amis. Je vais à la gloire.*" Does MacMillan think God punished her for a whore?

I'd suspect *Gloria* of attempting psychosexual analysis of the Lost Generation, right there on the battlefield, if it didn't seem more likely that MacMillan is failing here the same way he failed in *Isadora*—with significant form. (Or, to move from one of Clive Bell's terms to one of T. S. Eliot's, his objective correlative has got out of hand.) The metaphors in MacMillan's work are not all sexual. Still, sex is the ruling metaphor; it's what lends urgency and fluency to his dance language. Amid so much that is misguided and misapplied in *Gloria*—starting with the sung Latin Mass as accompaniment for a ballet—it may be trivial to cite MacMillan's metaphors; after all, any ballet put where God can see it would look trivial. But MacMillan's offense is not only the one against taste—it's also an offense against meaning. He brings on tin-helmeted soldiers, covered with the dust of the trenches, and also a whole slew of wispy girls in gray. Ghosts or memories of wives and lovers, angels of mercy or of death—we're never sure who they're supposed to be. MacMillan's acrobatic-expressionistic dance language is similarly ambivalent. In its continual self-investigation, its kneading and twisting and joining of body shapes and body parts, it reaches a kind of creative delirium—a mystique of physique. A language so powerfully organic forces into being a connective logic almost as a natural consequence of its growth, and a choreographer may take these dumb intuitive connections for signs of ideas. I think that in *Gloria* MacMillan uses this tumescent language for a comparatively modest purpose—to show how it was between men and women in the war—and the language inflates and perverts his meaning unconscionably. In the Agnus Dei section, he takes the basic Kylián unit of two men and one woman and manipulates it to its nearest correlative in life (that is to say, in sex), and he doesn't stop until he has got an image of the woman pronged between the two men. It's like that so much of the time in *Gloria* that we have to decide on a theme. The title *Gloria* means what Isadora's *"la gloire"* meant—death. But the death that hangs over the boys and girls of the ballet has nothing to do with the war. So *Gloria* isn't about war—it's about choreography trying to be ideas. If death is present at all, it's in the orgasmic extinction of a metaphor.

MacMillan's ideas don't inevitably turn into porn—only his big ideas do, the ideas that are needed for the big subjects. You could say that *La Fin du Jour* is about culture and style at the dawn of the technological age, but MacMillan hasn't approached it that way. I think he began by moving his dancers around like robots, and the "meanings" took off from there, just as they do when he's manipulating gross anatomy. What saves *La Fin du Jour* from grandiosity is that it *starts* with a metaphor not of its own making ("like robots") and builds up novelty as it goes along. It's a superficial ballet, but then it has superficiality as a subject. I wish MacMillan could have shown more ballets like it this season. (Or just more ballets; as the Royal's principal choreographer, he was surely entitled to more than three ballets in three weeks.) But I can see the mishap of *Isadora* as a logical outcome of *Mayerling* and *Gloria*. It's the ultimate trap for self-reflexive choreography—a ballet about a dancer. MacMillan gets caught the minute he tries to make a dramatically expressive solo for Isadora in a style other than Duncan pastiche. The moment occurs during one of Isadora's visits to Russia, when she sees, or thinks she sees, children's coffins. The solo, which is made up of floorwork unmistakably in the Graham style, is highly ambiguous in every other respect. It might be MacMillan's homage to Graham as a Duncan descendant, but surely it isn't: Martha Graham is a descendant of Ruth St. Denis. It might be Isadora expressing her grief over the casualties of tsarist persecution. It might be Isadora telling Craig (who is present) that she is pregnant. The one thing it can't be is Isadora showing him a new dance, although the Russian dance school that she was not to start until the next decade comes into being on the spot. *Isadora* as a dance drama is undone by scenes like this. Perhaps MacMillan and Freeman should have produced *Marilyn*. Think of that death scene! Think of all the pas de deux!

The dance-sex-death nexus of *Mayerling* would be possible in *Isadora* only if it weren't a ballet—if, that is, Gillian Freeman's ideas dominated the stage completely. But then that nexus, faint and furtive though it may be, is the only thing that keeps this *Isadora* from being a stage version of the Vanessa Redgrave film of 1968, and it's MacMillan's contribution. The ballet leaves out the unconsummated loves, such as Heinrich Thode, Gabriele D'Annunzio, and, most conspicuously, Konstantin Stanislavski, whose effect on Isadora drove her to hot and cold Russian baths. These men weren't in the movie, either, though they might well have been. The ballet keeps having to fight off comparisons not only with that movie but with any movie. Compared with what goes on nowadays in X-rated films, Mac-Millan's sex scenes are nothing. I'm not even sure they are pornographic. Dancers' bodies as we see them on the stage are stripped of those sexual attributes which might get in the way of the dance. Can there be porn without flesh? MacMillan is the only choreographer in the world who could have posed the question.

Because it's not really a ballet, *Isadora* is not the kind of work in which casting matters a great deal. It's no secret that the leading role was intended for the former Royal ballerina Lynn Seymour, who a few years ago danced a memorable Isadora in a ballet by Frederick Ashton, and who, years before that, was a MacMillan discovery—his Juliet and his Anastasia. The dancer on whom the role was actually constructed, Merle Park, is a little thin and sallow for Isadora but is a keenly intelligent performer nonetheless. Though Sandra Conley, with her bigger legs, long arms, and full-toned port de bras, looks more like the pictures of Isadora that obviously inspired MacMillan, she's less dramatically incisive, and her size makes her harder for the men to throw around. Mary Miller, a tall, full-figured woman, does the speaking role with a flawless American accent. Her young Isadora is a vim-and-vigor Californian, a bit too games-mistressy for the poet-philosopher that Isadora was even then. In later scenes, wearing a kimono and a magenta wig, she's a portly trollop. She attempts one dance solo, *La Marseillaise*, and comes off quite a bit worse than Redgrave did. Do the British, who have no tradition of modern dance, really believe that a fair account of Isadora's performing can be given by an amateur? (When Isadora bares her breast to the Boston audience, though, it has to be the actress who does it, not the dancer.) *Isadora* has an original score, by Richard Rodney Bennett, that supports it at every turn without claiming any distinction for itself. It includes discreet imitations of the Brahms, Liszt, and Chopin piano music to which Isadora performed. The designer is the resourceful Barry Kay. By means of a curtain hung from a steel ring, a few screens and projections, and some atmospheric bric-a-brac, he follows Isadora from London to Berlin, from Boston to Nice, and his St. Petersburg railway station may be the only justification for that ambiguous dance scene. Almost as good is his bright-blue Bugatti, enshrined center stage like a mummy's tomb before it is driven a few feet down a ramp, with Isadora inside.

MacMillan's three ballets may be seen as three ballets in a series. The machine age that is prefigured at the end of *Gloria*, when the women's bodies turn into airplanes, and that is elaborately depicted in those same terms in *La Fin du Jour* may well have links to that Bugatti. (Isadora, having seen the Diaghilev ballet "hopping madly about in Picasso pictures," writes to Craig, "If that is Art I prefer Aviation.") *La Fin du Jour* gives us the Riviera world of mechanized sensation which Isadora knew in her last days, where modes of travel and leisure, sex and fashion—where human beings themselves—seem to have rolled off the same assembly line. MacMillan's meaning, enhanced by Ian Spurling's designs, is in the movement. In *Gloria*, Andy Klunder's designs and the quotation from Vera Brittain which is inscribed in the program notes lend the ballet a meaning that the choreography doesn't project. A few years ago, MacMillan did *Requiem*, another liturgical ballet, for the Stuttgart Ballet; it was a major contribution to the solemn new expressionism being promoted then at the Stuttgart and since then throughout Europe. The ballet, a memorial to John Cranko, was revoltingly sanctimonious. It had a tricky décor, by Yolanda Sonnabend, which contributed nothing to it. MacMillan did it in Stuttgart because Covent Garden's board of directors had raised objections to his chosen music, Fauré's Requiem. (*Song of the Earth* had initially been resisted for the same reason.) What caused the board's change of heart over *Gloria* I have no idea. But I think *Requiem* may be the ballet that Covent Garden believes it has now in *Gloria*. Apart from the inevitable crucifixion imagery, *Gloria* isn't pious, and it certainly isn't patriotic. It's only the ballet that at that moment MacMillan wanted or was driven to make.   —*July 13, 1981*

The Royal at Fifty

Ars longa, vita brevis. In ballet, that dictum could be reversed. Dancers outlive their creations. At the Paris Opéra, a special box is reserved for *"anciennes étoiles,"* from which, presumably, they gaze in wonder and dismay at the transfigured glories of their youth. The perpetuation of a dance tradition is no simple task of preservation but, rather, a constant effort of modification and renewal guided by the estimation and re-estimation of constituent strengths in the flux of time. The passion for the exotic was a constituent of the classical tradition into the twentieth century, but it was no longer a strength, and so, once the New World had contributed its cowboy and jazz ballets, it was discarded. Guardians of tradition are vigilant lest some real strength be surrendered before its time. Once a central feature has been eliminated, it is very hard to get it back. It is especially damaging to eliminate features of style, since the way a company dances is the result of conditioning both conscious and unconscious. At peak expression, the conscious elements of style are absorbed by the unconscious; this has an almost moral force of persuasion in performance. It is, in fact, the only kind of style to have, because the collective force of it is always greater than the cumulative details of a regimen or the sum of individual talents or the scope of choreography. Looking at the Bolshoi, one sees certain traits of style that we in the West reject; one sees, in fact, a whole different gamut of stylistic permissiveness. Yet these traits aren't lazily selected, and the Bolshoi's style exists above and beyond the terrible ballets it dances; it's a unanimous expressive urge that is there to respond to, whether you like the ballets or not, or even whether you like the technique or not.

If a company has the grand style, has this collective moral elegance, chances are you don't think about the technique, so unconscious and unwilled is it. Watching the Royal Ballet do the great classical ballets it brought to New York this season, my eye was repeatedly drawn to the dancers' technique, because it was always just beginning to disappear into style. And though some dancers, like Merle Park and Lesley Collier, could force it out of sight, they gained no conviction from having done so. The technique simply wasn't doing what the dancers needed it for. Like dancers everywhere, they tried to make up for it with extroverted performing; the result was that they were both vivacious and dim.

In a fiftieth-anniversary year—the company was founded in 1931—one doesn't want to have to talk technique about the Royal Ballet. Technique— the means by which dancers gain their effects—is the quantitative, style the qualitative source of the impression a company makes. Each company sets its own standards of technique and style, though for companies that play in opera houses the technique as a general rule conforms to opera-house scale. I don't think—near-capacity audiences obviously disagreed with me—that the Netherlands Dance Theatre has enough technique to play the Metropolitan Opera House; its means are insignificant on the great stage. And though there were full houses for the Royal Ballet, which preceded the Netherlands company at the Met, I didn't think the Royal made the total impression it should have; it couldn't control and harmonize its means in the service of its style. It was sad to see how far the company had wandered from its sense of the grand style in the classical tradition. In that style, formed by Frederick Ashton out of Petipa and brought to a pitch of perfection in the sixties, the company used to dance *The Sleeping Beauty* and *Swan Lake*. In these same pieces this season, the corps was still a model of uniformity but no longer a model of strict discipline. It wasn't the corps that had danced *La Bayadère*. And how many of the soloists struggling to come to terms with Aurora or Odette or Florestan or the Bluebird could have been mustered for a performance of *Monotones* as crystalline as the ones we used to see? Even without the two great signature pieces of the sixties, the repertory chosen for New York was a constant reminder of the grandeur that was. Former dancers were missed, but the collective authority with which they danced was missed even more. Memories of Margot Fonteyn were inescapable in *Daphnis and*

Chloë; otherwise, the ghost has been laid. But the loss to a great company of its stylistic sense is a loss of—not identity, precisely, but something critical to it. The Royal, in the last ten years, has lost its superego.

Ashton and Ninette de Valois were present for the season. The third of the trio of founders, Constant Lambert, died in 1951, leaving a vacancy as musical director that has never been adequately filled. (His protégé, Robert Irving, went to New York City Ballet.) But now, with both Ashton and De Valois in retirement for more than a decade, the artistic policy of the Royal Ballet shows signs of revolution. The directors of the seventies—first Kenneth MacMillan and now Norman Morrice, with MacMillan as principal choreographer—have turned English ballet away from its native classicism and toward the turgid expressionism in force on the European continent from Stuttgart to Amsterdam, from Paris to Hamburg. In her foreword to a commemorative volume, *The Royal Ballet: The First Fifty Years*, by Alexander Bland (Doubleday), De Valois writes of the need for periodic change, and recommends that change be carried out "with a detachment producing a calm contemplation of any temporary moments of stagnation." Is this her attitude as she sits nightly in her box watching the institution she created drift into the Stuttgart whirlpool? Is detachment what Ashton feels as he contemplates the stagnation—temporary?—of the style he forged? It may be that expressionistic tendencies were always implicit in English ballet. They were there in some of MacMillan's early work with Lynn Seymour. John Cranko, who mobilized the Stuttgart Ballet, was a Royal alumnus. Morrice is a product of Ballet Rambert. Marie Rambert, who in the sixties turned her company into a workshop for the Continentals and their followers, had sponsored the first efforts of Frederick Ashton and Antony Tudor, the two choreographers whose work may be taken to symbolize the historic directions in English ballet. It was Ashton who proved to be the more fertile of the two, and it was his pearly classicism, descended from Franco-Russian models, that shaped the Royal Ballet. Ashton has often spoken of the effort he felt he had to make, in *Symphonic Variations*, to get the ballet back to classical principles after the war. One of the wartime hits, Robert Helpmann's *Hamlet*, was revived this season. Perhaps it stands as an example of the kind of thing Ashton was getting away from, but its compressed pantomime is so futile and at the same time so juicy that it appears quite harmless. At any rate, English ballet is not now being threatened, as it may have been then, by actors rampant in tights. The danger is from this new religiose preoccupation with the human body and its contortions which I wrote about in relation to MacMillan's ballets a couple of weeks ago. Although MacMillan has shown his winged abilities as a classicist in traditional academic terms, he seems to have abandoned that whole side of his career. As the leading artistic influence on the Royal Ballet, he could not have made a more drastic decision. It wasn't supposed to, but the Royal season showed the effects of that decision.

What might be called the Tudor strain—thick, dark, Teutonic, quasi-dramatic—is now in the ascendant in MacMillan's work, and it has claimed the Royal dancers and their technique. Ashton was represented by five ballets, ranging from *Symphonic Variations* to his newest piece, *Rhapsody*. His fourth act of *Swan Lake* was also shown, along with his interpolations in that ballet and some of his choreography for *The Sleeping Beauty*. The company danced it all with a shaky gentility, whereas the performances of MacMillan's three ballets seemed to come from a core of strength. The Ashton retrospective was lavish but badly timed, a case of too much too late. *Daphnis* and *Symphonic Variations* had deteriorated even under Ashton's own regime (and had been superseded by *The Two Pigeons* and *Monotones*). *Scènes de Ballet*, a 1948 piece to the Stravinsky score, seemed not to have deteriorated but to have ossified. The terse phrases, the veneer of chic, the enigmatic wit of the groupings, with dancers facing in different directions—all this was fascinating high-style, if not grand-style, invention. But it looked unlived-in, a chunk of the past without organic connection to the present. (There is a strong resemblance to sections of *Cinderella*, Ashton's other 1948 ballet that is still being danced at Covent Garden.) *Scènes de Ballet*, which hadn't been seen here since 1955, was given a wary two performances. The dancers made a special effort, but their blank, soldierly correctness didn't tell me much. In *Rhapsody*, the corps work was more relaxed, more confident, but no more polished than it was in the première performances I saw in London last fall. And Anthony Dowell was uncomfortable and artificial in the role created for Mikhail Baryshnikov. Dowell alternated with Stephen Beagley, on whom part of the role had originally been worked out. It seemed unfair to both dancers that none of the virtuosic bits had been adjusted to their abilities. *A Month in the Country* depends a good deal less on virtuosity, but it, too, was compromised by casting. Ashton, it appears, has become a guest choreographer of marginal utility. A *Rhapsody* that really belonged to the Royal Ballet would have shown a resplendent Dowell (or a rising Beagley) leading his company to the summit. But Ashton's strategy—guarded exposure for Collier and the corps; spectacular, custom-tailored choreography for Baryshnikov—does not convert to the purpose of a company showcase. Ashton's triumph was the fourth act of *Swan Lake*; the choral spread of it looked beautiful on the Met stage. Earlier, though, we'd seen his Pas de Quatre, and even his Tarantella, vanquished by inadequate performance. The Pas de Quatre comes from the high sixties, but the decay of the Tarantella—one of those perennial Royal highlights—was quite unexpected. (A comparable shock in *The Sleeping Beauty* is the Puss-in-Boots episode: the sweetness is gone. The divertissement is now a series of painful descents—Florestan pas de trois, Bluebirds, cats.)

Why should the Royal be failing in the standard items of its classical repertory? To an American observer with three weeks of ill-served Petipa and ill-chosen Ashton to guess from, the answer must be that it is no longer a classical company. No group of dancers in the world, no matter how strong their tradition has been, can remain strong unless the tradition is forwarded and renewed by their artistic direction. The MacMillan ballets, with their gymnastic contortions, their squirmy plastique, are actively hostile to the maintenance of sound classical technique. Royal technique used to be faulted for its rule-book moderation and lack of scale. Although it hasn't changed a lot, it's not so much small as it is incomplete. One sees partial turnout, lazy thighs, unstretched knees, sketchy footwork. The lower body is underworked while the upper body is exaggeratedly braced in épaulé. The "Petipa" ideal of épaulement was to oppose head to shoulder and shoulder to spine with the continuous tension of a garland wound around a turning column. The Royal produces a wide chandelierlike yoke hung with bunchy ornamentation, all twisting fervently around a vertical axis of tallow. The eel plastique of the MacMillan ballets influences "classical" épaulement in alarming ways. One Florestan trio yanked itself about so wildly that it swam out of focus.

There have always been certain features of Royal ballerina style that I've found unappealing, like the excitability in allegro. It's fine for fairies and coquettes but not for serious women, unless, as in *A Month in the Country*, it has a dramatic motive. And with the loss of firmness and fullness in the technique a kind of blowsiness has crept in. Genesia Rosato and Rosalyn Whitten managed to make this quality attractive in the small parts that they were given, but, again, it isn't serious. The beauties of the English style are almost all in adagio. The lift up and out of développé in Odette's variation, especially when it unfolds into arabesque, has always made a heroic image when the English do it. But the marvellous poetic understanding that Fonteyn brought to the Rose Adagio hasn't been passed on to the current generation. And the current production of *The Sleeping Beauty* is a heart-twisting disappointment. It has been revised a couple of times since the première, in 1977. Act II is now decently concluded to the music that Tchaikovsky wrote, the egregious "Awakening" pas de deux has been dropped, and there is only a brief pause before the house curtain reopens on Catalabutte posed in silhouette in the throne room. Is it madness to go on insisting on an *onstage* transition when the sequence following the Panorama, which involves several onstage transitions, is still a dismal failure? In the old days, it was seen as if from the Prince's point of view. Now it's from the point of view of a stage manager with a stopwatch in his hand. Considering how little importance is attached to the Prince, the Sarabande he does in the second act seems a conspicuous waste of time. The intrada to the bridal pas de deux, which involved a unison mime speech by the courtiers, ought not to have been omitted. The lesser of Ashton's two Garland Dances is still the one being used.

Shall I go on with this? It's like straightening the pictures in a room that has been bombed. When you've seen all the Auroras and they're either sturdily dull or helplessly weak, when the best performance in the Prologue is given not by the dancing fairies but by Monica Mason's Carabosse (her stentorian presence was fine, too, as Gertrude in *Hamlet*), when the first thing you see in Act III—Leslie Edwards's Catalabutte—is also the last thing that will remind you of third acts gone by, why suppose that *The Sleeping Beauty* is anymore the symbol of Royal Ballet excellence? I find myself newly curious about the production I never saw—the 1973 Mac-Millan one. It was so disdained that it was withdrawn after two years. Could it have been MacMillan's attempt to possess the company's classical style by way of modification and renewal of its chief masterpiece? Nothing now remains of MacMillan's dances; even his vestigial Tom Thumb has been deleted from the current production. Staged by De Valois and revised by her in what seem to have been ever more wishful attempts to recapture a lost vitality, this *Beauty* starts gloriously, but the evening goes on and the vision keeps receding. It's a mirage. We never do reach the castle.

Jiří Kylián, who went from the Royal Ballet School to the Stuttgart Ballet to the Netherlands Dance Theatre, has acknowledged a debt to MacMillan, but though his *Soldiers' Mass* came three months after *Gloria*, I don't think there's a direct connection between the two pieces. The only way in which they're alike is that they both ask you to believe in what you read in the program rather than in what you see on the stage. Expressionism in dance has traditionally been movement that has emotion built into it. The Mac-Millan-Kylián school is not concerned with drama or psychology; it is non-situational and ritualistic. The relation between the movement and its emotional source is highly cryptic; one must be a believer. Kylián's dance ideas are extremely limited. In just two New York seasons, he has exposed them all and pushed some to the point of mannerisms. In his new pieces, especially in *Overgrown Path*, he now and then breaks clear of formula calisthenics, but soon he's back to some well-worn device. Kylián satisfies the public's love of stunt work and its craving for significance. It may be part of the ritual to keep on doing it in the same old way.   —*July 27, 1981*

Bounty

With its première, last June, clouded by injury and recasting, and all subsequent performances at the State Theatre cancelled, *Mozartiana* naturally became an irresistible magnet when the New York City Ballet announced it for the summer season in Saratoga. I saw it, at last, at a matinee.

The amphitheatre of the Saratoga Performing Arts Center was flooded with daylight, the stage was noisy, and the orchestra, under Hugo Fiorato, played bumpily. The children in the cast were local recruits, who seemed younger and less well prepared than their School of American Ballet predecessors. Ib Andersen, who dances the lead opposite Suzanne Farrell, had not yet pulled his performance together. In general, the ballet's health is still fragile, but what a ballet. Set to Tchaikovsky's orchestrations of four compositions by Mozart, it is one of Balanchine's most bountiful creations, and he has achieved it with uncommonly narrow means. *Mozartiana* is the world in a bubble. As the opening event of the Tchaikovsky Festival a couple of months ago, it seemed to set the keynote, but to anyone who had never heard of Tchaikovsky or Mozart or Balanchine, or of Farrell or any of the other dancers, it would explain everything.

The cast is small and oddly chosen. Farrell and Andersen don't appear mated, the way Farrell and Peter Martins do, or Farrell and Jacques d'Amboise. Andersen has a stripling, asexual quality; he doesn't mate easily with anybody. Even the very young Darci Kistler looks better with Sean Lavery or Christopher d'Amboise than she does with Andersen. In *Apollo*, Andersen looks fine as the boy-god, but later, when he comes into his maturity and has to dominate the Muses, he's unconvincing, especially with Farrell as Terpsichore. Balanchine in *Mozartiana* uses Andersen's slightness in relation to Farrell as part of a scheme. It is, first, a way of accentuating the mild force of the music and its spiritual temper. Tchaikovsky, we may remember, revered Mozart as "the musical Christ" (compared with the Jehovah of Beethoven). The ballerina's dances in *Mozartiana* are lighter, airier, more restricted in their sensuous range than they are in *Chaconne*, which Farrell performs opposite Martins or Adam Lüders. She hurls no thunderbolts here; instead, one sees a fiery glow of pinpoints clustered in the sky. And then the feathery fall through space. Andersen's dances are also concentrated and aerial, but if he's light, she's lighter. Balanchine in his casting and use of Andersen has removed much of the gravity from the male end of the male-female partnership, but he hasn't upset the balance. The result lifts the whole ballet into an upper atmosphere; we breathe new air—the ether of *Mozartiana*.

The ballerina and her partner are, of course, a unit, but the ballet is structurally diffuse for most of its length. Andersen doesn't even enter until the final section—the Theme and Variations, which he dances with Farrell. The rest of the dancers—a male soloist, four women, and four little girls—aren't defined in their relations to each other until the finale. The little girls flank Farrell in the opening number, then disappear. The four women, who might be their grown-up counterparts, aren't identified with either of the men. Balanchine has avoided setting up the obvious correspondences and turnabouts. Although we sense the connection between the big and the small girls and between them and Farrell (for one thing, they're all dressed alike), it's an elusive and mysterious connection. And who is the second man? You might think that Balanchine would cast this lone male dancer in contrast to Andersen, but in fact it's Victor Castelli, another lightweight. Balanchine has used mirror symmetry before, but *Mozartiana* is a broken mirror; its parts don't come together until the end, and when they cohere it's not so much through the mutual gravitation of structural components as through the cumulative sense of the dancing. *Mozartiana* is transcendentally coherent. Castelli, in the finale, finds his place among the women, the little girls are relinked (literally) with Farrell, and Farrell is bonded to Andersen, but it goes beyond that. The ending of *Mozartiana* is more than a vision of ballet's great chain of being; the dancers are bound together by invisible skeins of movement. It happens because Balanchine, instead of just giving us his decisions about who belongs where, shows us how he arrived at them. In the working out of the dances, the casting proves itself. When the dancers stop and pose and the curtain starts to come down, they seem united in the totality called *Mozartiana*. In the Farrell-Andersen section, the sympathetic reverberations in the movement—he finishes a double pirouette as she begins a triple—create a kind of spiritual fusion. Balanchine's attack on *Mozartiana* is so unconcerted on the surface that the ballet seems to be going nowhere special. But the total effect is of an achieved process. I don't know if it's a great ballet—only that the quality it has is the quality of Balanchine's greatest.

This *Mozartiana* is the fourth version of Balanchine's ballet. The first was produced in Paris and London by Les Ballets 1933. The following year, a revised and simplified *Mozartiana* was included in the repertory of the fledgling American Ballet alongside a new work to another Tchaikovsky score, *Serenade*. The revival a decade later by the Ballet Russe de Monte Carlo was apparently closer to the initial version; Christian Bérard reworked his original costumes and décor. (In the fifties, a touring group led by the Monte Carlo's ballerina, Alexandra Danilova, performed the ballet in a reduction for four soloists.) The current production is not a revival but a new ballet. Although *Mozartiana* has never been a big ballet, it has had a more active ensemble, whose members took part in the variations of the closing section. In the Monte Carlo version, the ballerina and the danseur had two pas de deux but only one solo apiece. The Preghiera, which is now a straightforward point number danced by the ballerina, was then performed by a soloist, who, veiled in black, was suspended between two shrouded figures. (She hung not from a pole, as is often written, but from the arms of one bearer, braced against the shoulders of the other.) This curious passage, with its funereal overtones, has no counterpart in the new ballet, which modulates between temperate and winsome moods. Rouben Ter-Arutunian's stiff black Maryinsky-style tutus (with white underskirts for Farrell) appear to be derived from his *Harlequinade*; Castelli wears the black satin Scaramouche costume from that ballet. These "Molière"outfits are similar to some that were worn in the original *Mozartiana*, and in Andersen's two-tone vest is an explicit reminder of Bérard.

Farrell's Preghiera, which is set at the beginning of the ballet, is an invocation rather than a dirge, but with no more liturgical suggestion than the Prayer in *Coppélia*. The choreography here and elsewhere magnificently exploits Farrell's long, slender points—their eager nibbling of the floor in bourrée, their slow or sudden flexions in relevé, their stalky elegance in parades and poses. In the Preghiera, she several times stands motionless on one foot, lifting a monumental thigh in second-position passé. Later, she walks or strides or hops on point, or beats, or draws her knees up in high, rich pas de chat, or she swivels into a blur of inside pirouettes still holding the knee in perfect second-position passé. There is more rapid small needle-work in Farrell's variations than is customary in Balanchine's choreography for her, and the stitchery is invisible—you don't see the minute prepara-tions. This is a Farrell specialty from early days, and it grows out of an emphasis in Balanchine's training. Besides that, Farrell seems to have mas-tered on her own another secret of control, which has to do with music and momentum. With her—and with almost no one else—a dance phrase is not a simple in-through-and-out but a complex set of subdivisions inferred from the music. Other dancers are more or less broad in their relation to music; Farrell is more or less subtle. The reason more people can't follow her is that they can't hear what she hears—they're unprepared for dancing that points out the broad musical sense of a passage only to dive inside the elastic mesh of its infrastructure. The way Farrell's transitions and recov-eries are carried out, she's never not dancing. Yet she's not overactive—on the contrary. Because her dance impetus in its smallest and most gradual discriminations may make her appear almost stationary at times, one can't enjoy Farrell just by looking; one must look and listen. The supported adagio in *Mozartiana* may be the most finely worked one that Balanchine has yet made for her. Set to an extended violin cadenza, it's about the flowering of form within form. It isn't preciously delicate, and the scale it reaches is enormous; however, a descent from point to flat foot, a quarter-turn shift of weight, a change of direction are events of the greatest signifi-cance. It's this quality of expansion within restricted limits that Balanchine seems to be concentrating on just now in Farrell. He's made it the subject of *Mozartiana*, and his musical justification is the extraordinary Theme and Variations, in which the same melody is rendered over and over, with ever more inspiriting nonmelodic or submelodic invention. The musical process is very much like the one we hear in the Theme and Variations of *Diverti-mento No. 15* or of *Suite No. 3*, but the dance process in those ballets is not nearly so close a parallel to the music.

Ib Andersen has been handed a smashing role. He doesn't have to domi-nate or lead Farrell in this ballet, and his solos, which in their density might be described as Bournonville-baroque, represent a new peak in Balanchine's invention for male allegro technique. Not since he made Edward Villella's choreography to the Glinka "Divertimento Brillante" have we seen anything like them. Andersen's trouble is partly lack of preparation. As a newcomer, he's been put through the usual bewildering assortment of roles; in the Tchaikovsky Festival, he appeared in more new ballets than any other male dancer. But Andersen also suffers from a kind of overconditioning common among technicians of his grade; he can be blandly perfect. He looks "Mozartian," but he doesn't seem to be very responsive musically; he danced the principal role in *Divertimento No. 15* in a monotone. In *Mozartiana*, Balanchine lights a few small fires under Andersen. You can see moments of ignition, but I'm not persuaded that stamina and confidence are all this dancer needs to make a blaze. Castelli's performance, which I was seeing in Saratoga for the first time, is more unruly than Andersen's, yet it's exciting in a way that Andersen's is not. (If Castelli had Andersen's discipline, and Andersen had Castelli's dance sense . . .) In the Gigue, Castelli twists and leaps close to the ground. The style of the choreography, its swift jokes and deferential manner, suggests a comedian entertaining at court. Though all his dancing has been strikingly energized of late, Castelli has unusual intensity in this part. A lot of his steps are à terre, and the deep-black jagged ink line in which they are traced does provide a contrast to Andersen. It could be pushed even harder—Castelli's infernal gaiety against Andersen's "angelic" buoyancy.

But it will always be Suzanne Farrell's ballet. The four women who appear toward the end of the Gigue and remain to dance the Minuet are all projections of Farrell; the resemblance, unmistakable, is what gives the ballet its mysterious amplitude. When Farrell arrives in the Theme, strolling arm in arm with Andersen, she walks in air perfumed by now invisible permutations of herself, and she dances four variations, one for each member of the shadow quartet. As she returns, strolling, at the end of the ballet, the cast assembles for the first time, its tiny ranks expanding with cosmic implication. Thus does the master choreographer aggrandize the gifts and presence of a ballerina. Thus does he reveal her, sovereign in her kingdom of ballet—the one among the many who are one.

In Jerome Robbins's *Piano Pieces* you see the dancers' individual qualities and sense Robbins's delight in them. The ballet is a pleasant, uncomplicated experience, with no pretensions. Its "Russians" are Ludwig Bemelmans peasants; they appear in the opening and closing sections of the ballet dancing their happy faux-naif dances, and one of them, a kind of Ivan the Fool, has solos sprinkled all through the piece. (Ib Andersen's relief at having such a simple part is palpable.) One whole dance, a chorale, is done clustered on one spot, with sinkings and risings in plié timed against "from the heart" salutes extended slowly to the earth, slowly to the sky. The choreography in the middle section is in a nonidiomatic, lyrical vein. It is danced by three couples, and reaches its high point in the pas de deux for Maria Calegari and Joseph Duell. Calegari has the ballerina's big secret. She can compel your attention by the shape she gives to a phrase, and she can extend her control of phrasing over hypnotically long sequences. Calegari, always a talented dancer, had a phase, a few years ago, when she would go ropy in her line and look mentally dizzed-out. Now she's a collected, closely knit, but still pliant young ballerina-on-the-rise, with a genuinely glamorous presence. In *Piano Pieces*, she pedals her long legs with a languorous strength and puts the audience under a spell.

Piano Pieces was the hit of the Tchaikovsky Festival in New York; it was in Saratoga, too. The company repeated most of its festival pieces in Saratoga with the famous plastic setting reduced to one back wall. The amphitheatre stage, though, was equipped with a handsome new curtain, by Yasuhide Kobashi. Actually, there are two curtains: a solid panel, painted with pale iridescent colors, is decorated with swirling nebulae and perforated with small, twinkling portholes. It rises to reveal luxurious drapes of pewter lamé. There was no need for it or any other curtain to rise again on *Hungarian Gypsy Airs*, in which Balanchine says nothing he has not said better before. Peter Martins's *Capriccio Italien* and John Taras's *Eugene Onegin* waltz were efficiently performed by company regulars, but the original student casts had more charm. Neither ballet is a repertory piece. One had to be in a very indulgent festival mood for a program that consisted of *Capriccio Italien*, J. d'Amboise's *Scherzo Opus 42*, *Hungarian Gypsy Airs*, and Martins's *Symphony No. 1*. The next day, *Mozartiana*, *Piano Pieces*, and *Tempo di Valse*, with Balanchine's wonderful new Garland Dance from *The Sleeping Beauty*, restored the balance. The Saratoga casts, which brought out a great number of local children, emphasized the extent to which Balanchine is using very young dancers these days. He had never before put children into *Mozartiana*. However, the first ballerina in that ballet, and one of the stars of Les Ballets 1933, was Tamara Toumanova, fourteen years old at the time.   —*August 10, 1981*

Index

A Note on the Type

This book is set in Electra, a Linotype face
designed by W. A. Dwiggins (1880–1956), who was responsible
for so much that is good in contemporary book design.
Although a great deal of his early work was in advertising
and he was the author of the standard volume Layout in Advertising,
Mr. Dwiggins later devoted his prolific talents to book typography
and type design and worked with great distinction in both fields.
In addition to his designs for Electra, he created the Metro,
Caledonia, and Eldorado series of type faces, as well as a number
of experimental cuttings that have never been issued commercially.

Electra cannot be classified as either modern or old-style.
It is not based on any historical model, nor does it echo
a particular period or style. It avoids the extreme contrast
between thick and thin elements that marks most modern faces
and attempts to give a feeling of fluidity, power, and speed.

This book was composed
by Maryland Linotype, Inc.,
Baltimore, Maryland.
It was printed and bound by
Maple Press, York, Pennsylvania.